THE PORTABLE THOREAU

THE PORTABLE

Thoreau

EDITED, AND WITH AN INTRODUCTION, BY
Carl Bode

THE VIKING PRESS
NEW YORK

First published in the United States of America
by The Viking Press 1947
Paperbound edition published 1957
Reprinted 1959, 1960 (twice), 1961, 1962, 1963
Revised edition published 1964
Reprinted 1964 (twice), 1965, 1966 (twice), 1967, 1968 (twice),
1969 (three times), 1970 (twice), 1971 (twice),
1972 (twice), 1974 (twice)

Reissued in a new format in 1980 by The Viking Press
625 Madison Avenue, New York, N.Y. 10022

Library of Congress catalog number: 47-1945
ISBN 0-670-70417-2 (clothbound)
ISBN 0 14 015.031 5 (paperbound)

Printed in the United States of America
by Kingsport Press, Inc., Kingsport, Tennessee
Set in Linotype Caledonia

The passages from Thoreau's *Journal* are published
through the courtesy of Houghton Mifflin Co.

The poems printed in this volume come from the
Collected Poems of Henry Thoreau, copyrighted by Carl Bode.
The editor's Epilogue first appeared in *The Massachusetts Review.*

Contents

INTRODUCTION BY THE EDITOR   1

CHRONOLOGY   28

NATURAL HISTORY OF MASSACHUSETTS, 1842   31

A WINTER WALK, 1843   57

THE MAINE WOODS, 1848
    The Wilds of the Penobscot   76
    Life in the Wilderness   88

CIVIL DISOBEDIENCE, 1849   109

A WEEK ON THE CONCORD AND MERRIMACK
RIVERS, 1849   139

POEMS
    I Am a Parcel of Vain Strivings Tied   228
    In the Busy Streets, Domains of Trade   230
    I Knew a Man by Sight   230
    Lately, Alas, I Knew a Gentle Boy   231
    Each More Melodious Note I Hear   233
    Independence   233
    Not Unconcerned Wachusett Rears His Head   234
    My Friends, Why Should We Live   234
    Low in the Eastern Sky   235
    Great Friend   236
    Fog   237
    Brother Where Dost Thou Dwell   238
    This Is My Carnac, Whose Unmeasured Dome   239
    Love Equals Swift and Slow   240
    Though All the Fates Should Prove Unkind   240
    Manhood   241
    Between the Traveler and the Setting Sun   241
    Nature   242

A YANKEE IN CANADA, 1853
 Concord to Montreal   243

WALDEN, 1854
 Economy   258
 Where I Lived, and What I Lived For   334
 Reading   351
 Sounds   363
 Solitude   383
 Visitors   390
 The Bean Field   404
 The Village   416
 The Ponds   422
 Baker Farm   448
 Higher Laws   456
 Brute Neighbors   469
 Housewarming   482
 Former Inhabitants; and Winter Visitors 499
 Winter Animals   513
 The Pond in Winter   524
 Spring   539
 Conclusion   559

JOURNAL, 1858   573

WALKING, 1862   592

LIFE WITHOUT PRINCIPLE, 1863   631

CAPE COD, 1864
 The Wellfleet Oysterman   656

THE LAST DAYS OF JOHN BROWN, 1860 676

EPILOGUE BY THE EDITOR   683

BIBLIOGRAPHY   697

Introduction by the Editor

As I see it there are three lives of Henry Thoreau. The first is the conventional one. It inhabits the encyclopedias, the polite biographies, and the world of American literary folklore. The second is marked by some dispute and doubt; its two great areas of argument concern Thoreau and Emerson's wife and the timing of Thoreau's growth and decline as a literary artist. The third is so controversial that it has only been hinted at in print; it is Thoreau's unconscious life. Of course these lives mingle and at times merge. I should like to say something about each of them, and not least about the life beneath the surface. That life I shall, in fact, consider separately in the Epilogue.

IT WAS a fine fall day. The river turned a singular blue when the wind ruffled it, and contrasted brightly with the tawny fields. Thoreau stopped to watch and then continued his walk. On his way he made it his business to count the rings in some oak-tree stumps. Fifty-three or fifty-four was the average. When he returned home, his sister Sophia brought him a drawer of her acorns to examine. He looked closely at the half-full drawer. Here were the seeds for many an oak. Yet as he studied the acorns more attentively he noticed that almost half had grubs in them already and would never grow. The crop of oak trees would be lean. But he labored no moral.

1

Sometime before the end of this fourth day of November, 1860, he sat down to write a letter. How much of it occupied his mind while he counted oak-tree rings or looked at red-oak acorns no one can say. The letter, however, developed into one of the most significant he ever sent. It emerged as a manifesto.

It went to Daniel Ricketson, New Bedford Quaker and one of Thoreau's greatest admirers. The year *Walden* came out Ricketson had written Thoreau a long epistle of praise for the book. He had added a pen picture of himself, a description of his shanty that likened it to the hut at Walden Pond, and an invitation for Thoreau to visit him. Thoreau had answered, although a little tardily, and so a correspondence had ensued. At first Ricketson had made the mistake of addressing Thoreau as "Dear Walden" and one can imagine Thoreau's look on reading that sentimental salutation. Notwithstanding, visits were exchanged and in spite of clear conflicts of temperament in the two writers, a friendship developed that showed itself for four and a half years. ("We have got along pretty well together in several directions," Thoreau was to say, "though we are such strangers in others.") Then so far as Thoreau was concerned the friendship stopped. Or that at least was what Daniel Ricketson thought.

He continued to write Thoreau and he filled his letters with invitations and reproaches. Ricketson's hurt feelings showed themselves increasingly. He complained about Thoreau's neglect. Why didn't Thoreau write? Or visit New Bedford again? Thoreau, he mourned, must be cold and anti-social, indifferent to his obligations toward fellow men. Finally, after Ricketson had besieged him with prose—and verse—for a year and a half, the Concord man replied. He turned on Ricketson with a hard explicitness. The disciple deserved some sort of an answer and Thoreau gave it to him. In doing so he also provided us with one of the clearest statements we have about his fundamental view of life.

This then was the manifesto of November 4, 1860; this was the letter launched at Ricketson. It begins politely enough, with Thoreau's thanks for the laudatory verses Ricketson sent. But after that Thoreau breaks out: "Why will you waste so many regards on me, and not know what to think of my silence? Infer from it what you might from the silence of a dense pine wood. . . . My silence is just as inhuman as that, and no more. You know that I never promised to correspond with you, and so, when I do, I do more than I promised." Such are his pursuits and habits, Thoreau continues, that he rarely goes abroad. He has enjoyed his visits with Ricketson and regrets that he cannot enjoy them more often. But after this concession he repels Ricketson again and says flatly: "Life is short, and there are other things also to be done. I admit that you are more social than I am, and far more attentive to 'the common courtesies of life' but this is partly for the reason that you have fewer or less exacting private pursuits." Thoreau has his own private life to live, his own aims to pursue.

The mere fact that his aims were far from the average ones, Thoreau might have explained, forced him to be all the more strenuous in pursuing them. Walking in the woods, and alone—living as a poet—was his business. Too many neighbors had made it painfully clear to him that it was not the business of anyone else in Concord, not even the most shiftless of the Irish, certainly not the business of a Harvard graduate.

Thoreau goes on with his answer to Ricketson, asserting that he hardly knows what to say; indeed he repudiates Ricketson's letter entirely. "I do not feel addressed by this letter of yours. It suggests only misunderstanding. Intercourse may be good, but of what use are complaints and apologies? Any complaint *I* have to make is too serious to be uttered, for the evil cannot be mended." That is the heart of Thoreau's indictment. By now he notices that he is nearing the bottom of the third page, so he concludes half-contemptuously, "Turn over a new leaf." The rest—one page remains—is a polite commonplace. It can afford to be; Thoreau has made his point. He ends with a few details about Concord apples and acorns, and a wish to be remembered to Ricketson's family.

Such was Henry Thoreau's last notable battle in the major war of his life, the war to repel any and all invasions of his vitally essential privacy. He needed privacy to walk, to think, and to write. He had found that out long ago. Thoreau was a solitary, as his original biographers pointed out. Later writers, wishing to present a more balanced picture of him, have sometimes stressed his social nature instead. Their case has its merits. Yet in broadest, most basic terms Thoreau was still, I think, a man alone.

From the beginning he seems to have liked being by himself. He was not apparently a very typical boy. Henry Seidel Canby, Thoreau's most perceptive biographer, notes that he was "a dreamy child, who 'hated games, street parades and shows' and 'company in the house.' " Even then he appears to have "loved nature more than man." In fact Thoreau himself speaks out later more than once. Writing in his Journal of August, 1845, for example, he recalls fondly that it was twenty-three years since he had been brought from Boston to see Walden Pond for the first time. Then he was only five years old, but he confesses in the Journal that "That woodland vision for a long time made the drapery of my dreams." Nature always was to make its claims on him, and one of its strongest appeals was precisely that it presented a sympathetic setting for his thoughts, a drapery, as he said, for his dreams. There was no human element to intrude. No other pair of human eyes tried to look at his and thus challenge him. What he saw in Walden was, he goes on significantly, that "sweet solitude my spirit seemed so early to require" to invite his noblest thoughts. No plainer admission is needed. And Thoreau ends this passage from the Journal with a paragraph of singular satisfaction. "Well, now," he remarks, "tonight my flute awakes the echoes over this very water. . . . Even I have at length helped to clothe that fabulous landscape of my imagination."

Thoreau was twenty by the time he finished Harvard, and there, if anywhere, he might have been expected to be comradely. One or two firm friendships did emerge. He learned to like his classmate Henry Vose so well that he paid Vose the compliment of asking him favors, and his esteem for Stearns Wheeler is touchingly recorded. But intrinsically Thoreau stayed the same. A few years after graduation he could sit alone in his hut at Walden and remember dryly that at "Cambridge College" he had been forced to pay thirty dollars each year for a room only a little larger than his hut—and that at college "the occupant suffers the inconvenience of many and noisy neighbors."

Upon leaving Harvard in 1837 Thoreau started to keep a journal. Ultimately it had thousands of entries, but the second entry—as early as that—is entitled "Solitude" and in it Thoreau confesses that he seeks a garret. It is true that he had his reasons. Surrounded as he was now in his mother's house by female relatives and paying guests, he must at times have longed even for the noisy neighbors of Hollis Hall. After all, they could be shut out and they would not require the starchy politeness one should use with maiden aunts. This crowding was to last for years. The family house was always too small for the solitary Thoreau, and that is certainly one reason he built a cabin for himself at Walden.

Yet Thoreau depended on his immediate family and never lost touch with them. Even when he was living at Walden, he often came home. And when he was away anywhere else he sent his family letters that show an ample affection. To his mother he wrote of worn-out clothes and other mundane matters. His sisters got letters from him with touches of humor and a bit of learning. The letters to his brother John indicate that Henry's love for him was profound. When John died after what began as a trivial accident, it was a long time before Henry recovered from the effect of the loss. It was a close-knit if undemonstrative family.

Since much evidence shows that the Thoreaus trusted and enjoyed one another, there were very probably few obvious tensions of the kind that arose whenever Henry went outside of the family circle. Toward the other relatives and the paying guests, furthermore, he could, after a time, adopt an attitude of impersonality based on commonplace daily contact. But when he left the house and an outsider confronted him, I believe that Thoreau felt an intense need for mutual sincerity. He felt barriers existing between himself and the persons he met, and was compelled to break down the barriers and to break the tension. He tried to cut through to essentials—"Man's noblest gift to man is his sincerity" —but as a result the tension was as often as not increased instead of eliminated. Outsiders were baffled by Thoreau's forced directness. They saw a man who was apt to take literally even a casual "How's everything?" and try to give it an exact and globe-girdling reply; for Thoreau in 1838 is telling himself, "If thy neighbor hail thee to inquire how goes the world, feel thyself put to thy trumps to return a true and explicit answer."

So a chance meeting could turn into an ordeal. Eyes would seldom meet directly, and that was well; their force was much too strong. Nevertheless, a challenge lay in every encounter. It would seem that in his relations with others Henry Thoreau was, by and large, afraid, and yet that fear made him all the braver. He was afraid of others with all the aversion of a shy childhood and a reserved adolescence. But the fact that he knew, sincerely, that he had so much to give—and that in almost every encounter he had the sounder, truer things to say—must have afforded him some incentive to break down human barriers. It is a rare thinker who does not wish to communicate his thoughts, and Thoreau was no exception. Consequently, he was more than forthright in his social relationships; he was brusque. The outcome was that in the long run, since people could not easily see the shyness, they remembered only the abrupt challenge Thoreau made to them. That was the impression which survived. Even Ralph Waldo Emerson in his famous eulogy on Thoreau, the "Biographical Sketch," had to say: "There was somewhat military in his nature not to be subdued, always manly and able, but rarely tender, as if he did not feel himself except in opposition. He . . . required a little sense of victory." "Hence," added Emerson, "no equal companion stood in affectionate relations with one so pure and guileless."

A quarter of a century earlier, when the famous acquaintanceship between Emerson and Thoreau was first beginning, he had been able to write of "My Henry

Thoreau" in a tone full of affection and respect. Yet their relationship, typically, turned out to be a difficult one. It can be argued that by reason of Emerson's prominence the connection between the two men was not representative, that it could not serve as a test case; but on the other hand Emerson brought with him far more than normal perceptiveness and sympathy to offset the fact of his fame. The dominant theme on Thoreau's side, it must be said, was protestant independence. His letters show occasional flashes of gratitude toward Emerson (not that Emerson was aiming at that, of course) but they are overbalanced by the hard words Thoreau much more often uses. A passage that Thoreau wrote in his Journal shows, better than Thoreau knew, how perverse his attitude could be: "Talked, or tried to talk, with R.W.E. Lost my time—nay, almost my identity. He, assuming a false opposition where there was no difference of opinion, talked to the wind —told me what I knew—and I lost my time trying to imagine myself somebody else to oppose him." Thoreau could seldom agree with his peers.

Emerson, Nathaniel Hawthorne, Margaret Fuller, and the few others of nearly equal stature all admitted Thoreau's intellectual powers and his integrity. Notwithstanding, none felt warm friendship toward him for any length of time. For them the challenge was always there.

Only when Thoreau reached middle age and happened to cross the trail of a trapper or some elderly ne'er-do-well did the challenge disappear. Then he was apt to relax and talk of fishing or muskrats or the last big snow. Since there was plainly no chance of mental competition, since Thoreau saw before him no peer, he spoke more affably. With Concord characters like George Melvin the muskrat trapper or George Minott the old farmer, he learned to be at home. He liked the "simple, reserved countrymen, my neighbors." "I am grateful for Minott . . . and Melvin," he says. He liked them, though, because they made no more demands on him than nature did. In other words, they minded their own business and gave him only as much company as he asked. Back in 1841 he had announced his aim: "I would be in society as in the landscape; in the presence of nature there is no reserve, nor effrontery." He could stand at ease with a trapper, but an Emerson would not fade into the landscape; he had to be taken on his own subtle terms.

Yet during his young manhood especially, Henry Thoreau often longed for the "Great Friend," the one true enough to transcend even nature. He erected his ideal into, practically, a religion: true friendship "is a pure divine affinity." Sincerity and reserve will be its keynotes. The reserve will be so great, the regard will be so high and hidden, as to be almost unearthly. But it will not be a barrier. In one of his best poems, about a young visitor to his home, Edmund Sewall, Thoreau says:

> If I but love that virtue which he is,
>   Though it be scented in the morning air,
> Still shall we be truest acquaintances,
>   Nor mortals know a sympathy more rare.

Friendship on such terms, though, could easily become inhuman. Moreover, in line with Thoreau's utter sincerity, if he saw any weakness in a friend he must let him know; and Thoreau admits this in another poem to someone else:

> Surely, surely, thou wilt trust me
> When I say thou dost disgust me. . . .
> It were treason to our love,
> And a sin to God above,

One iota to abate
Of a pure impartial hate.

So Thoreau will be bound to tell his friend exactly what he feels; but there happens to be no answering poem in which he invites the friend to do the same thing to him. Small wonder Emerson said Thoreau had no friends. A few acquaintances only, a hunter or an old farmer with whom he could ease his mind by trading data about the snows.

There was, however, a difference between Thoreau as a friend and Thoreau as a lover. For Henry Thoreau did fall in love, and probably twice. He was two years out of college when Ellen Sewall, sister of the Edmund to whom Thoreau addressed the quatrain just quoted, arrived in Concord for a visit. It was summertime and vacation. Henry was free from his teaching duties; so was his brother John. Between them and with the aid of a chaperone—named Prudence—they managed to show Ellen the attractions of Concord in the summer. Both young Thoreaus fell in love with Ellen. Neither, ultimately, won her. Henry wrote her letters and composed poems, with no word in them about anyone's disgusting anyone else. The brusqueness of his theory of friendship is gone. In its place, though, there is a truly quixotic substitute: a theory of love so rarefied as to be, again, nearly impossible to translate into normal human terms. He does more than set Ellen on a pedestal; he nearly deifies her.

But he needed to do more than that to marry her. Her father opposed the match and Ellen herself must have realized that her feelings were closer to sympathy than to love. She gave in to her father's wishes and sent Henry her refusal. In her correspondence with Prudence Ward, the former chaperone, Ellen speaks of it: "I wrote to H.T. . . . I never felt so badly at sending a letter in my life." Thereafter, Thoreau wrote much in his Journal, humanly enough, about unrequited love.

He recovered at length, we can judge further from the Journal and his other papers, if not without scars. Six months after Ellen rejected him Thoreau was invited to live in the Ralph Waldo Emerson household, and there he found a chance for a fuller emotional life. He unbent somewhat as time familiarized him with the Emersons although he could never enter that feminine domain the kitchen without blushing. And then through inevitable daily contact he learned to know Emerson's wife, the mistress of the household, and she came to play a large part in his thoughts. Whether she interested Henry on the rebound after his rejection by Ellen, or whether this was simply another case of a young man attracted to a quiet and understanding older woman, or whether the emotion was far stronger still, it is hard to be sure. At any rate, here, close by, was Lidian Emerson, dark and with a sort of plain, severe beauty. Henry Thoreau focused his attention on her.

The growth of Thoreau's feeling for Lidian has been sensitively deduced by Canby from letters and the Journal. Less is known about Lidian's own attitude but we can guess that she was not profoundly moved. Irrespective of how much Lidian felt, or allowed herself to feel, Henry's regard for her developed in depth and strength. He wanted, he wrote at one point in their relationship, a "love of woman quite transcending marriage." The woman, though, frightened perhaps by his emotion, became distant and reserved. The months passed and Thoreau had to admit, at length, that "his sister," as he referred to her, "whom I love I almost have no more to do with." Finally he recognized that everything was over: "And now another friendship is ended. . . . I am perfectly sad at parting from you.

. . . Morning, noon, and night, I suffer a physical pain, an aching of the breast which unfits me for my tasks. It is perhaps most intense at evening."

For Thoreau no woman ever replaced Lidian, and the suffering he felt is reflected periodically in his most private writings. However, as time went on, his inner life grew calmer once again—and more prosaic. His outer life continued to be filled with as much activity as he would allow. He always cherished a "broad margin of leisure" wherever he went. With due allowance for that margin, he slipped into something like a routine as he approached middle age. He settled down. The routine included occasional strolls with his erratic neighbor Ellery Channing, talks with Emerson himself or Bronson Alcott, visits to the Ricketsons at New Bedford, a few longer trips elsewhere; mainly, however, excursions alone—careful daily journeys through the Concord woods and meadows. Then at the end of the day, journalizing, "High in my chamber in the frosty nights," he suggests in one of his poems. He began to fill his notebooks almost entirely with observations instead of ideas. Gradually the Journal entries grew and accumulated. Thoreau scrawled records of rains and woodland particulars on page after swiftly written page. The philosophy disappeared, drowned in a flood of natural description. He lost some of his tenseness in human relationships; and correspondingly his first hard sincerity, although not lost, was dispersed. The search for the "Great Friend" was neglected in the business of surveying. Now Thoreau earned money from time to time by measuring the Concord fields that he had before only wandered over. The saunterer became the surveyor, and Apollo, as Thoreau sometimes said, went to work for King Admetus.

There was a tragedy in the career of Henry Thoreau. Certainly it did not lie in his refusal by Ellen Sewall, who later smiled on hearing of his eccentricities. Nor did it lie in his failure to find the "Great Friend" he earnestly sought. Nor even in Lidian Emerson's turning away from him, although that played its part by chilling his emotional life. It was something deeper. The tragedy lay, I think, in the slow crumbling of Thoreau's own conception of his life work.

Without a doubt economic factors played an important part, although they too were not entirely responsible for converting a major American writer into merely an amateur botanizer. Yet it is true that the problem of making a living, the right living, harried Thoreau from the start. It was important from the day he left college. When Thoreau received his diploma from Harvard, class of 1837, he had a future to face that was much more circumscribed than the one which confronts the graduate of today. Certain things were expected, a century ago, of a Harvard man. Because he was—relatively at least—of the intellectual elite, people presumed that he would make the most of his training and abilities. He would not waste them; he would not fritter them away.

Three fields only were open to him. He could go into the ministry; many of the graduates did, and that was earlier considered their most suitable place. Or he could go into a secular profession—teaching particularly or law or even medicine. These professions were second in esteem but nevertheless highly respectable. Or, lastly, he could go into trade. That might be all right, especially when sanctioned by the promise of success. There were advantages to becoming a Boston merchant. But there the list ended. Moreover, two of the three possibilities were clearly unacceptable to Thoreau. His

contempt for the Boston businessman and all he stood
for was born early, so trade was out of the question.
And his distrust for the church as an institution almost equaled his contempt for trade. No one ever
pointed out Thoreau as a church-goer; on Sunday morning when almost all Concord heeded the church bell,
Henry Thoreau went for a walk by Walden Pond. Law,
furthermore, held no appeal for him nor did its cus-
tomary partner, politics. Both entailed service to the
state and Thoreau would have none of that. Nor would
medicine do as a career. That left teaching.

It was not much of a choice. Nevertheless, Thoreau
began to gather his letters of recommendation, among
them one from Emerson. It turned out that Thoreau did
not have to look around very far. A vacancy developed
in Concord itself, so the September after commence-
ment he became the teacher of Concord's town school.
He applied himself to his job but the real Thoreau
emerged soon in spite of everything. Before the first
month was finished he had resigned over a question
of discipline—he was against flogging and the school
committee was for it. That left him without work, and
in the next year and a half he cast about for openings
as far away as Louisville, Kentucky. Thereafter, joining
forces with his more adaptable brother John, he once
again decided to try at home. Accordingly, the two
young men established their own Concord Academy.
Henry taught Greek, Latin, and mathematics, as well
as nature study. His program of classes was not heavy
yet it is still remarkable that he lasted as long as he
did. By March of 1841, however, the Thoreaus had
abandoned the academy despite a waiting list of pupils;
and Henry, done with school teaching, thought himself ready to launch out on his own.

In spite of his optimism, he had to live. So the next

month found him writing in his Journal, "Great thoughts hallow any labor. Today I earned seventy-five cents heaving manure out of a pen, and made a good bargain of it." But then for four years, until he went to Walden, a struggle took place. The bargains were sometimes good but more often bad. At various times during this period he was employed as, among other things, laborer, handyman at the Emersons', tutor for Emerson's nephew, editor, lecturer, and pencil-maker. He came to understand, however, with increasing certainty what he wanted to do and what he wanted to be. Later on, his idea of what his job should be would deteriorate but that would not occur until almost ten years after Walden. Now, at any rate, he felt he had, first of all, a life to live for its own sake; and secondly he had a message to give. Not a message in the old theological sense of the word but a message nevertheless. He wanted to be a "quill-driving" minister at large, a preacher without a pulpit. He believed that his job was to become a writer but a writer in a noble Transcendental way—a poet first in what he did and next in what he wrote.

In his desire to unify his life and work, he had Emerson's fine precedent. Emerson had left his pulpit in Boston because he could no longer reconcile the church's ideas with his own, and then he had carved out a unique and much more fitting career for himself. Emerson furnished his young neighbor with an example to imitate and a precept to follow as well. The precept was Emerson's challenging essay of 1836, "Nature," which became the bible of New England Transcendentalism. Thoreau read it, and it must certainly have opened up and strengthened his ideas. Out of it his own Transcendentalism emerged. This single essay, we can see now, contained nearly all the ideas that later characterized the whole Transcendentalist movement. The affirmation of a knowledge beyond that gained through the five senses; the belief in the supremacy of spirit over matter (even to the extent of a "noble doubt" as to whether nature itself existed); the reverence for, and enjoyment of, nature in spite of any doubts as to its final reality; the declaration of a high, unselfish standard of personal conduct, and with it a caustic criticism of the shoddy way in which the business of the world was conducted—all these are to be found in "Nature," and Thoreau was ready for them.

The path for Thoreau's Transcendentalism had been prepared not only by his personal inclinations but also by his college training. Too often the tendency has been to go far afield in searching for the sources of Transcendentalism. Yet here at Harvard Thoreau, like Emerson before him, studied a school of philosophy which denied that knowledge came merely through the senses and which affirmed a knowledge through a "common sense" that was superior to it. Everyone had this sense, said the Scottish "common sense" philosophers Thoreau read as an antidote to John Locke, but it was innate; it came from within a person and surpassed anything he would acquire from outside. In other words, intuition "transcended" tuition just as spirit "transcended" matter.

Through the required reading in his Harvard classes, as well as his browsing in the Harvard Library, Thoreau was consequently predisposed toward the sermon of Emerson's "Nature." This reading, added to his previous bent, was enough to promise a philosophy with remarkable similarities to Emerson's. The story is that some of the ideas in his Journal turned out later to be so like Emerson's that a mutual friend recognized the similarities and brought Thoreau and Emerson together as disciple and master. As would be expected, however, the disciple's doctrine proved to be different in several respects from his master's. Thoreau could not even then believe as much as did Emerson in a knowledge beyond that gained by the senses, and Thoreau's ideas about reality always stressed a cautious balance between matter and spirit. However, he followed Emerson in his bold allegiance to the individual instead of to the group and in his emphasis on respecting one's inner bent. In fact he taught the master the full meaning of "self-reliance." And he surpassed Emerson in his Transcendental enthusiasm for nature in any guise. It is true that nature itself later became to Thoreau less of a deity and more of a collection of detail; but even nature just as scenery afforded, he always thought, the ideal setting for bringing out the best in man.

Nature could, Thoreau realized with especial keenness in those varied years between college and Walden, bring out the best in him and help him to be a poet. But he still wondered how much of a compromise he would have to make in order to live as a poet, and how he could support himself while living that way. He wondered whether he could not make enough money as a writer to take care of his modest needs. At the beginning of Thoreau's literary career this must have looked like a fairly feasible answer to his problem. He had no way of knowing that the total amount of money he would earn by his pen throughout his whole life would be minute. As it turned out, even in the final months of his life Thoreau had to chaffer with publishers; and the very last letter he wrote stoically undervalues his literary work. It was plain to him even at the start, however, that it would be easier to break into print if he first made a name for himself elsewhere.

The "lecture field" looked wide open and seemed to offer a suitable opportunity, so Thoreau tried to enter it.

The lyceum was a major channel for adult education a hundred years ago. Almost every town had its winter course of lectures and its wooden platform that was mounted from week to week by the great or near-great—and usually at what seems today a modest fee. Still, a man like Emerson supported himself by his lyceum appearances and traveled all over the country. It took Thoreau, on the other hand, a long while to become known; and he never made a very imposing figure before his audience anyway—short, awkward-seeming as he was, with cold blue eyes and an indifferent delivery. Yet toward the end he was receiving inquiries about his lectures from places as remote from Concord in those days as Ohio and upstate New York. He left us evidence of that when he thriftily kept many of the inquiries and used their backs for nature notes.

Thoreau's lyceum engagements had, in the long run, an important effect on his general method of writing. Most of the essays he managed to publish later on began as platform lectures, and that accounts for their tone of direct address to the reader. They exhort and they inform. They face the reader much more squarely than did Thoreau himself when he stood on the platform. They read simply and clearly—just as Thoreau might have liked to speak. Moreover, they look effortless although they are not. Thoreau's manuscripts are filled with words and paragraphs that have been crossed out, rewritten, and rewritten again. His method of writing, as he himself described it, included the preparation of at least three versions of a work. Thoreau said he would start out by jotting his ideas down in the Journal, next he would consolidate them into a lecture, and finally he would revise the lecture into an essay. The group of essays, for instance, that the *Atlantic Monthly* was to buy during the last year of Thoreau's life grew out of lectures he had given earlier. But that was twenty years after Thoreau first looked to lecturing as a way to help make a living. It did not solve the financial problem of the years just before Walden.

Thoreau could not copy the pleasant power of Emerson's address, and he would not copy any of the large group of successful nonentities who made their living by amusing the public on the pretext of instructing it. So, as it happened, Thoreau went to work for Emerson himself, and not exactly as a lecturer. Emerson wanted him to act as a handyman and helper and to take charge of things generally while he was gone. Thoreau, being Thoreau, did this in a matter-of-fact American way, with no sacrifice of his independence.

Occasionally, at the same time, Thoreau did odd jobs for other persons too. In some cases he probably had to remind himself that "Great thoughts hallow any labor"; in others he did not. At any rate, he lived at Emerson's house for two years starting in 1841, acted at times there as philosopher as well as gardener, and probably soon began to fall in love with Lidian Emerson. In 1843 he left and went to Staten Island to tutor Emerson's nephew—and to try the New York literary market. Between times he wrote for and helped to edit a unique "little magazine," the Transcendentalist *Dial*. Limited in circulation, uneven in quality, esoteric in appeal, it nevertheless developed a considerable influence on contemporary literature and ideas. *The Dial* printed the first item Thoreau ever published and a number of good later ones. It helped to make him known but like Thoreau's lecturing such writing was never something a person could live on. In fact it paid him nothing at all.

Meanwhile, even members of Thoreau's family wondered at times what sort of career he was after. So did some of his other relatives, as well as an occasional busybody among his family's paying guests. More than once, no doubt, someone in the group made it clear that he (or probably she) would like to know when Henry was going to start making a respectable living. How soon was he going to straighten out? Just what was he planning to do? These were questions many a Concord neighbor also asked and kept on asking until the end of Thoreau's life. The questions were put with a sidelong glance at his old clothes and muddy shoes— no garb for a Harvard graduate.

His answer, as Thoreau wrote firmly in his Journal, was that he intended to be a poet.

By which he meant, needless to say, no languid and perfumed esthete. The poet to him was the highest representative of modern mankind; he was close kin to the ancient seer and prophet. He was nobler than the scientist, superior to the philosopher. Thoreau stated the requirements for the ideal poet early: "The collector of facts must possess a perfect physical organization; the philosopher, a perfect intellectual organization. But in the true poet they are so fairly but mysteriously balanced, that we can see the results of both, and generalize even the widest deductions of philosophy." So he collects facts, and they are the facts of wood and field because there nature—best of all influences on the poet—has her dominion. In doing this he is a scientist. Also he makes deductions from facts and in addition seeks to establish theories. In doing that he is a philosopher. But in their very own provinces he transcends both the scientist and the philosopher, and thus emerges as the true poet.

The poet's noblest work, Thoreau added as a corollary, was his life; and his poetry would grow out of his life. But the poetry would never be as important as the life—"Is not eternity a lease for better deeds than verse?" Nevertheless, it must be a true account, completely honest and absolutely sincere. The poetry could be couched in either prose or rhyme. The form was not important. Thoreau wrote both and could consider both as being poetry because of the fact that a poem is by definition any organic product of a genuine poet. So the book *Walden,* for example, and Thoreau's noted Grecian lyric "Smoke" could each be termed poems. What counted was that they were the work of a poet.

Thoreau's is without doubt one of the most ambitious conceptions of the role of poet that American literature has seen. It is the idea of a great man; yet of a man who, like everyone else, had to support himself and fulfill his physical needs. And, despite the hallowing effect of fine thoughts, pitching manure out of a pen was no answer to his economic problem. Nor apparently were his other expedients, even lecturing. The problem remained: How was he to live strictly as a poet and still support himself? Perhaps, Thoreau decided now, Thomas Carlyle had the right idea: lessen your denominator. Reduce your wants and live a simple life. It was well worth considering. The time was ripe for the cabin at Walden. The site was ready; Emerson owned some land that lay next to Walden Pond, only a mile or so from Concord, and he was willing to let Thoreau use it. So in the spring of 1845 Thoreau put up a sturdy little building there. It had but one room, and no lock to the door and no curtain to the window; but it was enough.

July 4, 1845, was the day he chose to move his few belongings to the Pond. In that era the Fourth of July was a much more important folk festival than it is now. But Thoreau showed for its traditional fanfare the same Olympian indifference he extended to Christmas. It was just another day except as judged by his own standards. July 4 fell on a Friday, and by Saturday Thoreau has established himself. Friday he was too busy moving, apparently, to write in his Journal; but he makes up for it the next day when he begins his Journal entry at Walden by writing with quiet triumph, "Yesterday I came here to live."

The day after that he answers the question as to why he came. Later, the answer was to be expanded into a famous and frequently quoted passage in *Walden* but the original sentence is also worth remembering. "I wish to meet the facts of life," he writes, "—the vital facts, which are the phenomena or actuality the gods meant to show us—face to face, and so I came down here." It was as simple, and as complex, as that.

So he came. He hoed beans, he entertained visitors, he sat by himself and pondered; and he wrote. Before coming to Walden he had published only a scattering of essays and a few good poems. Now he wrote out the full draft of *A Week on the Concord and Merrimack Rivers,* drawing from the two river journeys that he and his brother John had made. It became a book of days, filled with so much scholarly allusion and Transcendental philosophy that they obscured the clean line of the voyage and caused the book to be a failure at the press. Yet it was a unique American achievement. It was a vigorous work if uneven and Thoreau at Walden had no notion that the public was going to ignore it.

At the Pond too he scrawled out the first version of his most famous book, which was to be translated into a dozen different languages. *Walden* itself is the expanded record of Henry Thoreau's determination to meet the basic facts of life, to reduce life to its lowest terms, and to find its essence. "Life! who knows what it is, what it does?" he had asked himself the Sunday after he moved in. The book is the answer and it is the answer that Thoreau was looking for. The lesson is deceptively liberal but its application is a hard one. Nevertheless, if anyone should want to be a poet and philosopher in America, there is a way. Though the mass of men lead lives of quiet desperation a true poet need not. He must follow his inner bent relentlessly, however. Having faced life and reduced it to the essentials, he will thereafter be able to set his own standards and hold to them. "The greater part of what my neighbors call good," Thoreau says, "I believe in my soul to be bad, and if I repent of anything, it is very likely to be my good behavior. What demon possessed me that I behaved so well? You may say the wisest thing you can, old man—you who have lived seventy years, not without honor of a kind—I hear an irresistible voice which invites me away from all that. One generation abandons the enterprises of another like stranded vessels." Go on your own voyages and go alone.

Such was Thoreau's prime cockcrow to the world, with more than the average amount of brag to it, as he himself observed. Yet he had good reason. By going off to Walden Pond he was able to formulate two of the notable books of his century, along with a number of significant essays. All this in the space of two years and two months. By the middle of 1846 the *Week* was ready for publication and *Walden, or Life in the Woods* was well forward in its writing. By the end of '46 the critical essay on Thomas Carlyle was finished, among others, and sent to his admirer Horace Greeley. So, when Thoreau quit Walden Pond on a dull summer afternoon in 1847 and returned to live in Concord, he could well afford to. He had lived and written as a poet. He had faced life, and he had demonstrated how it could be overmatched. Now he thought he had other things to do, so he left his cabin never to come back.

The rest of his life as a writer, though he did not know it, was to be an anticlimax.

Thoreau produced one more outstandingly provocative work, the essay on "Civil Disobedience," printed in 1849. He generated much of the power for it by spending the night in jail. He had "signed off" from an unjust state and church—he would have no part of them nor would he pay a cent of taxes to support them. As a result he was forced to pass a night locked up. Later he tried to write urbanely about "My prisons" but the words smolder nevertheless. He remembered the curious eyes that looked past him the next day when he was let out. And he remembered, and would continue to remember, the basic principle for which he went to jail: that if a man knows in his heart that a social institution is doing wrong, he must fight the institution—not with "rifle and knife" but with conscientious civil disobedience. It was a principle Gandhi would study in South Africa after the turn of the century, and with substantial results.

Yet only a year or two after the publication of "Civil Disobedience" Thoreau proved that he could be active as well as passive in fighting the tyranny of the state. He was drawn into the struggle against Negro slavery, and the fact that many of his own neighbors were pro-slavery at the time let him see all the more clearly that he had to take sides. His family had early been abolitionists and had helped to lay the groundwork for Henry's participation. However, in the beginning he had felt that there were more immediate forms of slavery to fight first. He saw that people in Concord and everywhere else were enslaved by hunger, by property, and by social conformity—chained down so thoroughly that most men did lead lives of quiet desperation but would do nothing about it. So Thoreau had originally turned on the abolitionists and the rest, and told them, "Ye are all slaves." In fact one of his poems mocks the abolitionists' vehemence:

> Make haste & set the captive free!—
> Are ye so free that cry?
> The lowest depths of slavery
> Leave freedom for a sigh.

Free yourself first, was his perception then. But when Massachusetts, in compliance with the Fugitive Slave Law, began to send the escaped slaves within its borders back to the South, that brought the issue home to Thoreau.

From 1851 on, consequently, he gave the abolitionists more and more support. He lectured and wrote for the cause, basing his attack not upon hatred for the South but upon fundamental ethical principles. If he needed any incentive beyond the fact of Negro slavery in Massachusetts, it was furnished by his meeting John Brown of Kansas. Thoreau had never been a hero-worshiper, yet something in the bearded, violent old man impressed him deeply. Brown was a fanatic but in a noble cause. The more Thoreau considered him, the more impressive he became. When Brown led the raid at Harper's Ferry, most Northern newspapers and Northern conservatives reviled him. Thoreau sprang to his defense, and his essays on Brown represent the most impassioned writing he ever achieved.

But this was the last outburst of Thoreau's creative energy. His fight against Negro slavery was the only prominent event in his last years. It was important, nevertheless, it did not bulk large in comparison with the quiet day-by-day pattern of Thoreau's later life. The months and seasons passed; Thoreau kept on writing. His Journal was deluged with the natural detail already mentioned. Correspondingly, the Transcendentalism that had started out as a strong affirmation of spirit and intuitive knowledge became a more nearly ordinary philosophy. Even the stress on the special value of the individual lessened somewhat. Nature, though, whatever its form, remained important and alive to Thoreau throughout his whole career. Only a great cause like abolition and a great man like John Brown could draw Thoreau's attention away from some aspect of nature for even a short time. All other things combined to maintain it as his ideal and his best resource—not the least among those things being human indifference to Thoreau's work as a poet or writer. The fact that men failed to appreciate Thoreau's writing inevitably pulled him farther away from them and closer to nature.

Indeed, general recognition of Thoreau as a writer came with disheartening slowness. The *Week* stayed a publisher's failure till after his death, while even *Walden* attracted only a small body of readers. Thoreau could write gravely to Daniel Ricketson, in answer to Ricketson's first letter, "I was gratified by your prompt and hearty acceptance of my book. Yours is the only word of greeting I am likely to receive from a dweller in the woods like myself." Only in the final two years of his life did he need to spend much time in preparing articles for the press. By then he was so ill with tuberculosis that his sister Sophia had to write out his letters for him. She also helped him to see the last group of essays to the printer. The *Atlantic Monthly* was glad to get them although it haggled about details. But Thoreau never lived to see the essays appear. He was dead by May 1862, at the age of forty-four.

So the saunterer and the surveyor were gone; the poet, it may be, had died ten years before. Still, the poet had struggled hard to live, and most of Thoreau's young manhood had been spent in trying to find out how a poet could support himself and yet remain a true poet. His retreat, or advance rather, to Walden Pond had turned out to be his happiest solution, for by going there he proved himself and his philosophy. But after that he conformed gradually to something resembling the Concord mold. Not of course out of respect for Concord but because his own ideal of life became more prosaic. His enthusiasm for the individual against the group diminished somewhat at the end, though love for the freedom of the individual itself remained. And underneath, I think, he kept some of his peculiar philosophic atomism.

From the shores of Walden Pond Thoreau looked at man, and nature and society as well, and estimated what he saw. In his prime he saw only values but that was enough. His best writing is the expression of a mind that weighed those values with relentless care, weighed them to a fineness that almost everyone else tries uncomfortably to avoid. With the same determination, furthermore, that he evaluated the principles of other men, he evaluated his own. The ultimate in his evaluations is compressed into a couplet he scribbled down in the Journal and then revised for publication in the *Week*; and it is conclusive:

> My life has been the poem I would have writ,
> But I could not both live and utter it.

CARL BODE

Chronology

1837: Henry Thoreau graduates from Harvard at twenty, comes home to Concord, and looks for a career. At Ralph Waldo Emerson's suggestion probably, also begins a Journal.

1838: Gives his first lecture before the Concord Lyceum, thus initiating a practice that was to have an important effect on his writing. Becomes an intimate of Emerson.

1839: With his brother John, embarks on a "fluvial excursion" along the Concord and Merrimack, and gathers material for the *Week*. Falls in love with Ellen Sewall.

1840: Makes his bow as a poet: the Transcendentalist *Dial* prints his lyric about Edmund Sewall, brother of Ellen. In November Ellen Sewall finally rejects Thoreau.

1841: As handyman and friend, takes up residence with the Emersons. Is attracted to Lidian Emerson.

1842: Publishes in the *Dial*, which carries nine of his best poems and his essay "Natural History of Massachusetts." His beloved brother John Thoreau dies.

1843: Leaves Emerson's home to act as tutor to Emerson's nephew at Staten Island and to try his luck with the New York literary market. Publishes a few more essays and poems.

1845: Goes to live in a hut beside Walden Pond. Commences his period of greatest literary productivity.

1846: Travels to Maine; gathers some of the material later to go into *The Maine Woods*.

1847: Ends Walden experiment; resumes residence at the Emerson home.

1848: Sartain's *Union Magazine* prints "Ktaadn and the Maine Woods."

1849: Thoreau's first book, the *Week*, and most influential essay, "Civil Disobedience," published.

1851: Thoreau aligns himself with the abolitionists.

1853: Busy as surveyor in Concord; sees publication of opening portions of *A Yankee in Canada;* visits Maine woods for the second time.

1854: *Walden; or, Life in the Woods* published.

1855: First episodes of *Cape Cod* appear in *Putnam's Monthly Magazine;* the rest are withdrawn when the editor tries to censor Thoreau.

1856: Thoreau surveys and lectures; stays briefly at Horace Greeley's farm. Is introduced to Walt Whitman in New York.

1857: Fight over slavery intensifies; Thoreau meets John Brown and is deeply impressed by him.

1860: More essays, including two on Brown, are printed; Thoreau goes on last camping excursion: climbs Monadnock in company with Ellery Channing. At end of year becomes ill.

1861: In search of good health, travels to Minnesota. Works up final group of essays for *The Atlantic Monthly,* including "Walking" and "Life without Principle."

1862: Dies of tuberculosis in spring.

A Natural History of Massachusetts[1]

This is much more than Massachusetts. It started out as a book review, unsigned, in R. W. Emerson's Dial for July, 1842. But it gives the subject, Reports—on the Fishes, Reptiles, and Birds; the Herbaceous Plants and Quadrupeds; the Insects Injurious to Vegetation; and the Invertebrate Animals of Massachusetts, little more than a bow at the beginning and a hasty good-by at the end. In between, Thoreau has put some of the most genial observation of nature he ever achieved. Later on he became a more exact observer but he never became a happier one. The outline of the Report can be discerned but it serves only as a suggestion for his own fresh thoughts, only as a point of departure. Into the context of his essay he has woven a number of his poems as well as two smooth Anacreontics that he has translated from the Greek. It is some distance from the Greek poet's "Return of Spring" to "Insects Injurious to Vegetation," and Thoreau's heart is purely with the former. The Massachusetts legislature which authorized the original Report would have had good cause to be surprised at what it started.

C. B.

BOOKS of natural history make the most cheerful winter reading. I read in Audubon with a thrill of delight, when the snow covers the ground, of the magnolia, and the Florida keys, and their warm sea-breezes; of the fence-rail, and the cotton-tree, and the migrations of the rice-bird; of the breaking up of winter in Labra-

---

[1] Reports—on the Fishes, Reptiles, and Birds; the Herbaceous Plants and Quadrupeds; the Insects Injurious to Vegetation; and the Invertebrate Animals of Massachusetts. Published agreeably to an Order of the Legislature, by the Commissioners on the Zoölogical and Botanical Survey of the State.

dor, and the melting of the snow on the forks of the
Missouri; and owe an accession of health to these reminiscences of luxuriant nature.

> Within the circuit of this plodding life,
> There enter moments of an azure hue,
> Untarnished fair as is the violet
> Or anemone, when the spring strews them
> By some meandering rivulet, which make
> The best philosophy untrue that aims
> But to console man for his grievances.
> I have remembered, when the winter came,
> High in my chamber in the frosty nights,
> When in the still light of the cheerful moon,
> On every twig and rail and jutting spout,
> The icy spears were adding to their length
> Against the arrows of the coming sun,
> How in the shimmering moon of summer past
> Some unrecorded beam slanted across
> The upland pastures where the Johnswort grew;
> Or heard, amid the verdure of my mind,
> The bee's long smothered hum, on the blue flag
> Loitering amidst the mead; or busy rill,
> Which now through all its course stands still and dumb,
> Its own memorial—purling at its play
> Along the slopes, and through the meadows next,
> Until its youthful sound was hushed at last
> In the staid current of the lowland stream;
> Or seen the furrows shine but late upturned,
> And where the fieldfare followed in the rear,
> When all the fields around lay bound and hoar
> Beneath a thick integument of snow.
> So by God's cheap economy made rich
> To go upon my winter's task again.

I am singularly refreshed in winter when I hear of
service-berries, poke-weed, juniper. Is not heaven made
up of these cheap summer glories? There is a singular
health in those words, Labrador and East Main, which
no desponding creed recognizes. How much more than
Federal are these States! If there were no other vicis-

situdes than the seasons, our interest would never tire. Much more is a-doing than Congress wots of. What journal do the persimmon and the buckeye keep, and the sharp-shinned hawk? What is transpiring from summer to winter in the Carolinas, and the Great Pine Forest, and the Valley of the Mohawk? The merely political aspect of the land is never very cheering; men are degraded when considered as the members of a political organization. On this side all lands present only the symptoms of decay. I see but Bunker Hill and Sing-Sing, the District of Columbia and Sullivan's Island, with a few avenues connecting them. But paltry are they all beside one blast of the east or the south wind which blows over them.

In society you will not find health, but in nature. Unless our feet at least stood in the midst of nature, all our faces would be pale and livid. Society is always diseased, and the best is the most so. There is no scent in it so wholesome as that of the pines, nor any fragrance so penetrating and restorative as the life-everlasting in high pastures. I would keep some book of natural history always by me as a sort of elixir, the reading of which should restore the tone of the system. To the sick, indeed, nature is sick, but to the well, a fountain of health. To him who contemplates a trait of natural beauty no harm nor disappointment can come. The doctrines of despair, of spiritual or political tyranny or servitude, were never taught by such as shared the serenity of nature. Surely good courage will not flag here on the Atlantic border, as long as we are flanked by the Fur Countries. There is enough in that sound to cheer one under any circumstances. The spruce, the hemlock, and the pine will not countenance despair. Methinks some creeds in vestries and churches do forget the hunter wrapped in furs by the Great Slave Lake, and that the

Esquimaux sledges are drawn by dogs, and in the twilight of the northern night the hunter does not give over to follow the seal and walrus on the ice. They are of sick and diseased imaginations who would toll the world's knell so soon. Cannot these sedentary sects do better than prepare the shrouds and write the epitaphs of those other busy living men? The practical faith of all men belies the preacher's consolation. What is any man's discourse to me, if I am not sensible of something in it as steady and cheery as the creak of crickets? In it the woods must be relieved against the sky. Men tire me when I am not constantly greeted and refreshed as by the flux of sparkling streams. Surely joy is the condition of life. Think of the young fry that leap in ponds, the myriads of insects ushered into being on a summer evening, the incessant note of the hyla with which the woods ring in the spring, the nonchalance of the butterfly carrying accident and change painted in a thousand hues upon its wings, or the brook minnow stoutly stemming the current, the luster of whose scales, worn bright by the attrition, is reflected upon the bank!

We fancy that this din of religion, literature, and philosophy, which is heard in pulpits, lyceums, and parlors, vibrates through the universe, and is as catholic a sound as the creaking of the earth's axle; but if a man sleep soundly, he will forget it all between sunset and dawn. It is the three-inch swing of a pendulum in a cupboard, which the great pulse of nature vibrates by and through each instant. When we lift our eyelids and open our ears, it disappears with smoke and rattle like the cars on a railroad. When I detect a beauty in any of the recesses of nature, I am reminded, by the serene and retired spirit in which it requires to be contemplated, of the inexpressible privacy of a life—how silent and unambitious it is. The beauty there is in mosses must be considered from the holiest, quietest nook. What an admirable training is science for the more active warfare of life! Indeed, the unchallenged bravery which these studies imply, is far more impressive than the trumpeted valor of the warrior. I am pleased to learn that Thales was up and stirring by night not unfrequently, as his astronomical discoveries prove. Linnaeus, setting out for Lapland, surveys his "comb" and "spare shirt," "leathern breeches" and "gauze cap to keep off gnats," with as much complacency as Bonaparte a park of artillery for the Russian campaign. The quiet bravery of the man is admirable. His eye is to take in fish, flower, and bird, quadruped and biped. Science is always brave; for to know is to know good; doubt and danger quail before her eye. What the coward overlooks in his hurry, she calmly scrutinizes, breaking ground like a pioneer for the array of arts that follow in her train. But cowardice is unscientific; for there cannot be a science of ignorance. There may be a science of bravery, for that advances; but a retreat is rarely well conducted; if it is, then is it an orderly advance in the face of circumstances.

But to draw a little nearer to our promised topics. Entomology extends the limits of being in a new direction, so that I walk in nature with a sense of greater space and freedom. It suggests besides, that the universe is not rough-hewn, but perfect in its details. Nature will bear the closest inspection; she invites us to lay our eye level with the smallest leaf, and take an insect view of its plain. She has no interstices; every part is full of life. I explore, too, with pleasure, the sources of the myriad sounds which crowd the summer moon, and which seem the very grain and stuff of which eternity is made. Who does not remember the shrill roll-call of the harvest-fly? There were ears for these sounds in Greece long ago, as Anacreon's ode will show.

"We pronounce thee happy, Cicada,
For on the tops of the trees,
Drinking a little dew,
Like any king thou singest,
For thine are they all,
Whatever thou seest in the fields,
And whatever the woods bear.
Thou art the friend of the husbandmen,
In no respect injuring anyone;
And thou art honored among men,
Sweet prophet of summer.
The Muses love thee,
And Phoebus himself loves thee,
And has given thee a shrill song;
Age does not wrack thee,
Thou skillful, earthborn, song-loving,
Unsuffering, bloodless one;
Almost thou art like the gods."

In the autumn days, the creaking of crickets is heard at noon over all the land, and as in summer they are heard chiefly at nightfall, so then by their incessant chirp they usher in the evening of the year. Nor can all the vanities that vex the world alter one whit the measure that night has chosen. Every pulse-beat is in exact time with the cricket's chant and the tickings of the death-watch in the wall. Alternate with these if you can.

About two hundred and eighty birds either reside permanently in the State, or spend the summer only, or make us a passing visit. Those which spend the winter with·us have obtained our warmest sympathy. The nuthatch and chickadee flitting in company through the dells of the wood, the one harshly scolding at the intruder, the other with a faint lisping note enticing him on; the jay screaming in the orchard; the crow cawing in unison with the storm; the partridge, like a russet link extended over from autumn to spring, preserving unbroken the chain of summers; the hawk with warrior-

like firmness abiding the blasts of winter; the robin[1] and
lark lurking by warm springs in the woods; the familiar
snowbird culling a few seeds in the garden or a few
crumbs in the yard; and occasionally the shrike, with
heedless and unfrozen melody bringing back summer
again:

> His steady sails he never furls
> At any time o' year,
> And perching now on Winter's curls,
> He whistles in his ear.

As the spring advances, and the ice is melting in the
river, our earliest and straggling visitors make their appearance. Again does the old Teian poet sing as well for
New England as for Greece, in the

RETURN OF SPRING

> Behold, how, Spring appearing,
> The Graces send forth roses;
> Behold, how the wave of the sea
> Is made smooth by the calm;
> Behold, how the duck dives;
> Behold, how the crane travels;
> And Titan shines constantly bright.
> The shadows of the clouds are moving;
> The works of man shine;
> The earth puts forth fruits;
> The fruit of the olive puts forth.
> The cup of Bacchus is crowned,
> Along the leaves, along the branches,
> The fruit, bending them down, flourishes.

---

[1] *A white robin and a white quail have occasionally been seen. It
is mentioned in Audubon as remarkable that the nest of a robin
should be found on the ground; but this bird seems to be less particular than most in the choice of a building-spot. I have seen its
nest placed under the thatched roof of a deserted barn, and in one
instance, where the adjacent country was nearly destitute of trees,
together with two of the phoebe, upon the end of a board in the loft
of a sawmill, but a few feet from the saw, which vibrated several
inches with the motion of the machinery.*

The ducks alight at this season in the still water, in company with the gulls, which do not fail to improve an east wind to visit our meadows, and swim about by twos and threes, pluming themselves, and diving to peck at the root of the lily, and the cranberries which the frost has not loosened. The first flock of geese is seen beating to north, in long harrows and waving lines; the jingle of the song sparrow salutes us from the shrubs and fences; the plaintive note of the lark comes clear and sweet from the meadow; and the bluebird, like an azure ray, glances past us in our walk. The fish hawk, too, is occasionally seen at this season sailing majestically over the water, and he who has once observed it will not soon forget the majesty of its flight. It sails the air like a ship of the line, worthy to struggle with the elements, falling back from time to time like a ship on its beam ends, and holding its talons up as if ready for the arrows, in the attitude of the national bird. It is a great presence, as of the master of river and forest. Its eye would not quail before the owner of the soil, but make him feel like an intruder on its domains. And then its retreat, sailing so steadily away, is a kind of advance. I have by me one of a pair of ospreys, which have for some years fished in this vicinity, shot by a neighboring pond, measuring more than two feet in length, and six in the stretch of its wings. Nuttall mentions that "the ancients, particularly Aristotle, pretended that the ospreys taught their young to gaze at the sun, and those who were unable to do so were destroyed. Linnaeus even believed, on ancient authority, that one of the feet of this bird had all the toes divided, while the other was partly webbed, so that it could swim with one foot, and grasp a fish with the other." But that educated eye is now dim, and those talons are nerveless. Its shrill scream seems yet to linger in its throat, and the roar of the sea in its wings. There is the tyranny of Jove in its claws, and his wrath in the erectile feathers of the head and neck. It reminds me of the Argonautic expedition, and would inspire the dullest to take flight over Parnassus.

The booming of the bittern, described by Goldsmith and Nuttall, is frequently heard in our fens, in the morning and evening, sounding like a pump, or the chopping of wood in a frosty morning in some distant farm-yard. The manner in which this sound is produced I have not seen anywhere described. On one occasion, the bird has been seen by one of my neighbors to thrust its bill into the water, and suck up as much as it could hold, then, raising its head, it pumped it out again with four or five heaves of the neck, throwing it two or three feet, and making the sound each time.

At length the summer's eternity is ushered in by the cackle of the flicker among the oaks on the hillside, and a new dynasty begins with calm security.

In May and June the woodland quire is in full tune, and, given the immense spaces of hollow air, and this curious human ear, one does not see how the void could be better filled.

> Each summer sound
> Is a summer round.

As the season advances, and those birds which make us but a passing visit depart, the woods become silent again, and but few feathers ruffle the drowsy air. But the solitary rambler may still find a response and expression for every mood in the depths of the wood.

> Sometimes I hear the veery's[1] clarion,
> Or brazen trump of the impatient jay,
> And in secluded woods the chickadee

---

[1] *This bird, which is so well described by Nuttall, but is apparently unknown by the author of the Report, is one of the most common in the woods in this vicinity, and in Cambridge I have heard the col-*

> Doles out her scanty notes, which sing the praise
> Of heroes, and set forth the loveliness
> Of virtue evermore.

The phoebe still sings in harmony with the sultry
weather by the brink of the pond, nor are the desultory
hours of noon in the midst of the village without their
minstrel.

> Upon the lofty elm-tree sprays
> The vireo rings the changes sweet,
> During the trivial summer days,
> Striving to lift our thoughts above the street.

With the autumn begins in some measure a new
spring. The plover is heard whistling high in the air over
the dry pastures, the finches flit from tree to tree, the
bobolinks and flickers fly in flocks, and the goldfinch
rides on the earliest blast, like a winged hyla peeping
amid the rustle of the leaves. The crows, too, begin now
to congregate; you may stand and count them as they
fly low and straggling over the landscape, singly or by
two and threes, at intervals of half a mile, until a hundred have passed.

I have seen it suggested somewhere that the crow was
brought to this country by the white man; but I shall
as soon believe that the white man planted these pines
and hemlocks. He is no spaniel to follow our steps; but
rather flits about the clearings like the dusky spirit of the
Indian, reminding me oftener of Philip and Powhatan
than of Winthrop and Smith. He is a relic of the dark
ages. By just so slight, by just so lasting a tenure does
superstition hold the world ever; there is the rook in
England, and the crow in New England.

---

lege yard ring with its trill. The boys call it "yorrick," from the
sound of its querulous and chiding note, as it flits near the traveler
through the underwood. The cowbird's egg is occasionally found in
its nest, as mentioned by Audubon.

> Thou dusky spirit of the wood,
> Bird of an ancient brood,
> Flitting thy lonely way,
> A meteor in the summer's day,
> From wood to wood, from hill to hill,
> Low over forest, field, and rill,
> What wouldst thou say?
> Why shouldst thou haunt the day?
> What makes thy melancholy float?
> What bravery inspires thy throat,
> And bears thee up above the clouds,
> Over desponding human crowds,
> Which far below
> Lay thy haunts low?

The late walker or sailor, in the October evenings, may hear the murmurings of the snipe, circling over the meadows, the most spirit-like sound in nature; and still later in the autumn, when the frosts have tinged the leaves, a solitary loon pays a visit to our retired ponds, where he may lurk undisturbed till the season of moulting is passed, making the woods ring with his wild laughter. This bird, the Great Northern Diver, well deserves its name; for when pursued with a boat, it will dive, and swim like a fish under water, for sixty rods or more, as fast as a boat can be paddled, and its pursuer, if he would discover his game again, must put his ear to the surface to hear where it comes up. When it comes to the surface, it throws the water off with one shake of its wings, and calmly swims about until again disturbed.

These are the sights and sounds which reach our senses oftenest during the year. But sometimes one hears a quite new note, which has for background other Carolinas and Mexicos than the books describe, and learns that his ornithology has done him no service.

It appears from the Report that there are about forty quadrupeds belonging to the State, and among these

one is glad to hear of a few bears, wolves, lynxes, and
wildcats.

When our river overflows its banks in the spring,
the wind from the meadows is laden with a strong scent
of musk, and by its freshness advertises me of an unexplored wildness. Those backwoods are not far off then.
I am affected by the sight of the cabins of the muskrat,
made of mud and grass, and raised three or four feet
along the river, as when I read of the barrows of Asia.
The muskrat is the beaver of the settled States. Their
number has even increased within a few years in this
vicinity. Among the rivers which empty into the Merrimack, the Concord is known to the boatmen as a dead
stream. The Indians are said to have called it Musketaquid, or Prairie River. Its current being much more
sluggish and its water more muddy than the rest, it
abounds more in fish and game of every kind. According to the History of the town, "The fur-trade was here
once very important. As early as 1641, a company was
formed in the colony, of which Major Willard of Concord was superintendent, and had the exclusive right to
trade with the Indians in furs and other articles; and
for this right they were obliged to pay into the public
treasury one twentieth of all the furs they obtained."
There are trappers in our midst still, as well as on the
streams of the far West, who night and morning go
the round of their traps, without fear of the Indian. One
of these takes from one hundred and fifty to two hundred muskrats in a year, and even thirty-six have been
shot by one man in a day. Their fur, which is not nearly
as valuable as formerly, is in good condition in the winter and spring only; and upon the breaking up of the ice,
when they are driven out of their holes by the water, the
greatest number is shot from boats, either swimming or
resting on their stools, or slight supports of grass and

reeds, by the side of the stream. Though they exhibit considerable cunning at other times, they are easily taken in a trap, which has only to be placed in their holes, or wherever they frequent, without any bait being used, though it is sometimes rubbed with their musk. In the winter the hunter cuts holes in the ice, and shoots them when they come to the surface. Their burrows are usually in the high banks of the river, with the entrance under water, and rising within to above the level of high water. Sometimes their nests, composed of dried meadow-grass and flags, may be discovered where the bank is low and spongy, by the yielding of the ground under the feet. They have from three to seven or eight young in the spring.

Frequently, in the morning or evening, a long ripple is seen in the still water, where a muskrat is crossing the stream, with only its nose above the surface, and sometimes a green bough in its mouth to build its house with. When it finds itself observed, it will dive and swim five or six rods under water, and at length conceal itself in its hole, or the weeds. It will remain under water for ten minutes at a time, and on one occasion has been seen, when undisturbed, to form an air-bubble under the ice, which contracted and expanded as it breathed at leisure. When it suspects danger on shore, it will stand erect like a squirrel, and survey its neighborhood for several minutes, without moving.

In the fall, if a meadow intervene between their burrows and the stream, they erect cabins of mud and grass, three or four feet high, near its edge. These are not their breeding-places, though young are sometimes found in them in late freshets, but rather their hunting-lodges, to which they resort in the winter with their food, and for shelter. Their food consists chiefly of flags and fresh-water mussels, the shells of the latter being left in large quantities around their lodges in the spring.

The Penobscot Indian wears the entire skin of a musk-rat, with the legs and tail dangling, and the head caught under his girdle, for a pouch, into which he puts his fishing-tackle, and essences to scent his traps with.

The bear, wolf, lynx, wildcat, deer, beaver, and marten have disappeared; the otter is rarely if ever seen here at present; and the mink is less common than formerly.

Perhaps of all our untamed quadrupeds, the fox has obtained the widest and most familiar reputation, from the time of Pilpay and Aesop to the present day. His recent tracks still give variety to a winter's walk. I tread in the steps of the fox that has gone before me by some hours, or which perhaps I have started, with such a tip-toe of expectation as if I were on the trail of the Spirit itself which resides in the wood, and expected soon to catch it in its lair. I am curious to know what has determined its graceful curvatures, and how surely they were coincident with the fluctuations of some mind. I know which way a mind wended, what horizon it faced, by the setting of these tracks, and whether it moved slowly or rapidly, by their greater or less intervals and distinctness; for the swiftest step leaves yet a lasting trace. Sometimes you will see the trails of many together, and where they have gamboled and gone through a hundred evolutions, which testify to a singular listlessness and leisure in nature.

When I see a fox run across the pond on the snow, with the carelessness of freedom, or at intervals trace his course in the sunshine along the ridge of a hill, I give up to him sun and earth as to their true proprietor. He does not go in the sun, but it seems to follow him, and there is a visible sympathy between him and it. Sometimes, when the snow lies light and but five or six inches deep, you may give chase and come up with one on foot. In such a case he will show a remarkable presence of mind, choosing only the safest direction, though he may lose ground by it. Notwithstanding his fright, he will take no step which is not beautiful. His pace is a sort of leopard canter, as if he were in no wise impeded by the snow, but were husbanding his strength all the while. When the ground is uneven, the course is a series of graceful curves, conforming to the shape of the surface. He runs as though there were not a bone in his back. Occasionally dropping his muzzle to the ground for a rod or two, and then tossing his head aloft, when satisfied of his course. When he comes to a declivity, he will put his fore feet together, and slide swiftly down it, shoving the snow before him. He treads so softly that you would hardly hear it from any nearness, and yet with such expression that it would not be quite inaudible at any distance.

Of fishes, seventy-five genera and one hundred and seven species are described in the Report. The fisherman will be startled to learn that there are but about a dozen kinds in the ponds and streams of any inland town; and almost nothing is known of their habits. Only their names and residence make one love fishes. I would know even the number of their fin-rays, and how many scales compose the lateral line. I am the wiser in respect to all knowledges, and the better qualified for all fortunes, for knowing that there is a minnow in the brook. Methinks I have need even of his sympathy, and to be his fellow in a degree.

I have experienced such simple delight in the trivial matters of fishing and sporting, formerly, as might have inspired the muse of Homer or Shakespeare; and now, when I turn the pages and ponder the plates of the Angler's Souvenir, I am fain to exclaim,

> "Can such things be,
> And overcome us like a summer's cloud?"

Next to nature, it seems as if man's actions were the most natural, they so gently accord with her. The small seines of flax stretched across the shallow and transparent parts of our river are no more intrusion than the cobweb in the sun. I stay my boat in mid-current, and look down in the sunny water to see the civil meshes of his nets, and wonder how the blustering people of the town could have done this elvish work. The twine looks like a new river-weed, and is to the river as a beautiful memento of man's presence in nature, discovered as silently and delicately as a footprint in the sand.

When the ice is covered with snow, I do not suspect the wealth under my feet; that there is as good as a mine under me wherever I go. How many pickerel are poised on easy fin fathoms below the loaded wain! The revolution of the seasons must be a curious phenomenon to them. At length the sun and wind brush aside their curtain, and they see the heavens again.

Early in the spring, after the ice has melted, is the time for spearing fish. Suddenly the wind shifts from northeast and east to west and south, and every icicle, which has tinkled on the meadow grass so long, trickles down its stem, and seeks its level unerringly with a million comrades. The steam curls up from every roof and fence.

> I see the civil sun drying earth's tears,
> Her tears of joy, which only faster flow.

In the brooks is heard the slight grating sound of small cakes of ice, floating with various speed, full of content and promise, and where the water gurgles under a natural bridge, you may hear these hasty rafts hold conversation in an undertone. Every rill is a channel for the juices of the meadow. In the ponds the ice cracks with a merry and inspiriting din, and down the larger streams is whirled grating hoarsely, and crashing its way along, which was so lately a highway for the woodman's team and the fox, sometimes with the tracks of the skaters still fresh upon it, and the holes cut for pickerel. Town committees anxiously inspect the bridges and causeways, as if by mere eye-force to intercede with the ice and save the treasury.

> The river swelleth more and more,
> Like some sweet influence stealing o'er
> The passive town; and for a while
> Each tussock makes a tiny isle,
> Where, on some friendly Ararat,
> Resteth the weary water-rat.
>
> No ripple shows Musketaquid,
> Her very current e'en is hid,
> As deepest souls do calmest rest
> When thoughts are swelling in the breast,
> And she that in the summer's drought
> Doth make a rippling and a rout,
> Sleeps from Nahshawtuck to the Cliff,
> Unruffled by a single skiff.
> But by a thousand distant hills
> The louder roar a thousand rills,
> And many a spring which now is dumb,
> And many a stream with smothered hum,
> Doth swifter well and faster glide,
> Though buried deep beneath the tide.
> Our village shows a rural Venice,
> Its broad lagoons where yonder fen is;
> As lovely as the Bay of Naples
> Yon placid cove amid the maples;
> And in my neighbor's field of corn
> I recognize the Golden Horn.
>
> Here Nature taught from year to year,
> When only red men came to hear—
> Methinks 't was in this school of art
> Venice and Naples learned their part;
> But still their mistress, to my mind,
> Her young disciples leaves behind.

The fisherman now repairs and launches his boat. The best time for spearing is at this season, before the weeds have begun to grow, and while the fishes lie in the shallow water, for in summer they prefer the cool depths, and in the autumn they are still more or less concealed by the grass. The first requisite is fuel for your crate; and for this purpose the roots of the pitch pine are commonely used, found under decayed stumps, where the trees have been felled eight or ten years.

With a crate, or jack, made of iron hoops, to contain your fire, and attached to the bow of your boat about three feet from the water, a fish-spear with seven tines and fourteen feet long, a large basket or barrow to carry your fuel and bring back your fish, and a thick outer garment, you are equipped for a cruise. It should be a warm and still evening; and then, with a fire crackling merrily at the prow, you may launch forth like a cucullo into the night. The dullest soul cannot go upon such an expedition without some of the spirit of adventure; as if he had stolen the boat of Charon and gone down the Styx on a midnight expedition into the realms of Pluto. And much speculation does this wandering star afford to the musing night-walker, leading him on and on, jack-o'-lantern-like, over the meadows; or, if he is wiser, he amuses himself with imagining what of human life, far in the silent night, is flitting mothlike round its candle. The silent navigator shoves his craft gently over the water, with a smothered pride and sense of benefaction, as if he were the phosphor, or light-bringer, to these dusky realms, or some sister moon, blessing the spaces with her light. The waters, for a rod or two on either hand and several feet in depth, are lit up with more than noonday distinctness, and he enjoys the opportunity which so many have desired, for the roofs of a city are indeed raised, and he surveys the midnight economy of the fishes. There they lie in every variety of posture; some on their backs, with their white bellies uppermost, some suspended in mid-water, some sculling gently along with a dreamy motion of the fins, and others quite active and wide awake—a scene not unlike what the human city would present. Occasionally he will encounter a turtle selecting the choicest morsels, or a muskrat resting on a tussock. He may exercise his dexterity, if he sees fit, on the more distant and active fish, or fork the nearer into his boat, as potatoes out of a pot, or even take the sound sleepers with his hands. But these last accomplishments he will soon learn to dispense with, distinguishing the real object of his pursuit, and find compensation in the beauty and never-ending novelty of his position. The pines growing down to the water's edge will show newly as in the glare of a conflagration; and as he floats under the willows with his light, the song sparrow will often wake on her perch, and sing that strain at midnight which she had meditated for the morning. And when he has done, he may have to steer his way home through the dark by the north star, and he will feel himself some degrees nearer to it for having lost his way on the earth.

The fishes commonly taken in this way are pickerel, suckers, perch, eels, pouts, breams, and shiners—from thirty to sixty weight in a night. Some are hard to be recognized in the unnatural light, especially the perch, which, his dark bands being exaggerated, acquires a ferocious aspect. The number of these transverse bands, which the Report states to be seven, is, however, very variable, for in some of our ponds they have nine and ten even.

It appears that we have eight kinds of tortoises, twelve snakes—but one of which is venomous—nine frogs and toads, nine salamanders, and one lizard, for our neighbors.

I am particularly attracted by the motions of the serpent tribe. They make our hands and feet, the wings of the bird, and the fins of the fish seem very superfluous, as if Nature had only indulged her fancy in making them. The black snake will dart into a bush when pursued, and circle round and round with an easy and graceful motion, amid the thin and bare twigs, five or six feet from the ground, as a bird flits from bough to bough, or hang in festoons between the forks. Elasticity and flexibleness in the simpler forms of animal life are equivalent to a complex system of limbs in the higher; and we have only to be as wise and wily as the serpent, to perform as difficult feats without the vulgar assistance of hands and feet.

In May, the snapping turtle (*Emysaurus serpentina*) is frequently taken on the meadows and in the river. The fisherman, taking sight over the calm surface, discovers its snout projecting above the water, at the distance of many rods, and easily secures his prey through its unwillingness to disturb the water by swimming hastily away, for, gradually drawing its head under, it remains resting on some limb or clump of grass. Its eggs, which are buried at a distance from the water, in some soft place, as a pigeon-bed, are frequently devoured by the skunk. It will catch fish by daylight, as a toad catches flies, and is said to emit a transparent fluid from its mouth to attract them.

Nature has taken more care than the fondest parent for the education and refinement of her children. Consider the silent influence which flowers exert, no less upon the ditcher in the meadow than the lady in the bower. When I walk in the woods, I am reminded that a wise purveyor has been there before me; my most delicate experience is typified there. I am struck with the pleasing friendships and unanimities of nature, as when the lichen on the trees takes the form of their leaves. In the most stupendous scenes you will see delicate and fragile features, as slight wreaths of vapor, dew-lines, feathery sprays, which suggest a high refinement, a noble blood and breeding, as it were. It is not hard to account for elves and fairies; they represent this light grace, this ethereal gentility. Bring a spray from the wood, or a crystal from the brook, and place it on your mantel, and your household ornaments will seem plebeian beside its nobler fashion and bearing. It will wave superior there, as if used to a more refined and polished circle. It has a salute and a response to all your enthusiasm and heroism.

In the winter, I stop short in the path to admire how the trees grow up without forethought, regardless of the time and circumstances. They do not wait as man does, but now is the golden age of the sapling. Earth, air, sun, and rain are occasion enough; they were no better in primeval centuries. The "winter of *their* discontent" never comes. Witness the buds of the native poplar standing gayly out to the frost on the sides of its bare switches. They express a naked confidence. With cheerful heart one could be a sojourner in the wilderness, if he were sure to find there the catkins of the willow or the alder. When I read of them in the accounts of northern adventurers, by Baffin's Bay or Mackenzie's River, I see how even there, too, I could dwell. They are our little vegetable redeemers. Methinks our virtue will hold out till they come again. They are worthy to have had a greater than Minerva or Ceres for their inventor. Who was the benignant goddess that bestowed them on mankind?

Nature is mythical and mystical always, and works with the license and extravagance of genius. She has her luxurious and florid style as well as art. Having a pilgrim's cup to make, she gives to the whole—stem, bowl,

handle, and nose—some fantastic shape, as if it were to
be the car of some fabulous marine deity, a Nereus or
Triton.

In the winter, the botanist need not confine himself
to his books and herbarium, and give over his outdoor
pursuits, but may study a new department of vegetable
physiology, what may be called crystalline botany, then.
The winter of 1837 was unusually favorable for this.
In December of that year, the Genius of vegetation
seemed to hover by night over its summer haunts with
unusual persistency. Such a hoar-frost as is very uncommon here or anywhere, and whose full effects can never
be witnessed after sunrise, occurred several times. As I
went forth early on a still and frosty morning, the trees
looked like airy creatures of darkness caught napping;
on this side huddled together, with their gray hairs
streaming, in a secluded valley which the sun had not
penetrated; on that, hurrying off in Indian file along
some watercourse, while the shrubs and grasses, like
elves and fairies of the night, sought to hide their diminished heads in the snow. The river, viewed from the
high bank, appeared of a yellowish-green color, though
all the landscape was white. Every tree, shrub, and spire
of grass, that could raise its head above the snow, was
covered with a dense ice-foliage, answering, as it were,
leaf for leaf to its summer dress. Even the fences had
put forth leaves in the night. The center, diverging, and
more minute fibers were perfectly distinct, and the edges
regularly indented. These leaves were on the side of the
twig or stubble opposite to the sun, meeting it for the
most part at right angles, and there were others standing
out at all possible angles upon these and upon one another, with no twig or stubble supporting them. When
the first rays of the sun slanted over the scene, the
grasses seemed hung with innumerable jewels, which

jingled merrily as they were brushed by the foot of the
traveler, and reflected all the hues of the rainbow, as he
moved from side to side. It struck me that these ghost
leaves, and the green ones whose forms they assume,
were the creatures of but one law; that in obedience to
the same law the vegetable juices swell gradually into
the perfect leaf, on the one hand, and the crystalline
particles troop to their standard in the same order, on
the other. As if the material were indifferent, but the
law one and invariable, and every plant in the spring
but pushed up into and filled a permanent and eternal
mould, which, summer and winter forever, is waiting to
be filled.

This foliate structure is common to the coral and the
plumage of birds, and to how large a part of animate
and inanimate nature. The same independence of law
on matter is observable in many other instances, as in
the natural rhymes, when some animal form, color, or
odor has its counterpart in some vegetable. As, indeed,
all rhymes imply an eternal melody, independent of any
particular sense.

As confirmation of the fact that vegetation is but a
kind of crystallization, every one may observe how,
upon the edge of the melting frost on the window, the
needle-shaped particles are bundled together so as to
resemble fields waving with grain, or shocks rising here
and there from the stubble; on one side the vegetation
of the torrid zone, high-towering palms and wide-spread
banyans, such as are seen in pictures of oriental scenery;
on the other, arctic pines stiff frozen, with downcast
branches.

Vegetation has been made the type of all growth; but
as in crystals the law is more obvious, their material
being more simple, and for the most part more transient
and fleeting, would it not be as philosophical as con-

venient to consider all growth, all filling up within the limits of nature, but a crystallization more or less rapid?

On this occasion, in the side of the high bank of the river, wherever the water or other cause had formed a cavity, its throat and outer edge, like the entrance to a citadel, bristled with a glistening ice-armor. In one place you might see minute ostrich-feathers, which seemed the waving plumes of the warriors filing into the fortress; in another, the glancing, fan-shaped banners of the Lilliputian host; and in another, the needle-shaped particles collected into bundles, resembling the plumes of the pine, might pass for a phalanx of spears. From the under side of the ice in the brooks, where there was a thicker ice below, depended a mass of crystallization, four or five inches deep, in the form of prisms, with their lower ends open, which, when the ice was laid on its smooth side, resembled the roofs and steeples of a Gothic city, or the vessels of a crowded haven under a press of canvas. The very mud in the road, where the ice had melted, was crystallized with deep rectilinear fissures, and the crystalline masses in the sides of the ruts resembled exactly asbestos in the disposition of their needles. Around the roots of the stubble and flowerstalks, the frost was gathered into the form of irregular conical shells, or fairy rings. In some places the icecrystals were lying upon granite rocks, directly over crystals of quartz, the frostwork of a longer night, crystals of a longer period, but, to some eye unprejudiced by the short term of human life, melting as fast as the former.

In the Report on the Invertebrate Animals, this singular fact is recorded, which teaches us to put a new value on time and space: "The distribution of the marine shells is well worthy of notice as a geological fact. Cape Cod, the right arm of the Commonwealth, reaches out into the ocean, some fifty or sixty miles. It is nowhere

many miles wide; but this narrow point of land has
hitherto proved a barrier to the migrations of many species of Mollusca. Several genera and numerous species,
which are separated by the intervention of only a few
miles of land, are effectually prevented from mingling
by the Cape, and do not pass from one side to the other.
. . . Of the one hundred and ninety-seven marine species, eighty-three do not pass to the south shore, and
fifty are not found on the north shore of the Cape."

That common mussel, the *Unio complanatus,* or more
properly *fluviatilis,* left in the spring by the muskrat
upon rocks and stumps, appears to have been an important article of food with the Indians. In one place, where
they are said to have feasted, they are found in large
quantities, at an elevation of thirty feet above the river,
filling the soil to the depth of a foot, and mingled with
ashes and Indian remains.

The works we have placed at the head of our chapter,
with as much license as the preacher selects his text, are
such as imply more labor than enthusiasm. The State
wanted complete catalogues of its natural riches, with
such additional facts merely as would be directly useful.

The reports on Fishes, Reptiles, Insects, and Invertebrate Animals, however, indicate labor and research, and
have a value independent of the object of the legislature.

Those on Herbaceous Plants and Birds cannot be of
much value, as long as Bigelow and Nuttall are accessible. They serve but to indicate, with more or less
exactness, what species are found in the State. We detect several errors ourselves, and a more practiced eye
would no doubt expand the list.

The Quadrupeds deserved a more final and instruc-
tive report than they have obtained.

These volumes deal much in measurements and minute descriptions, not interesting to the general reader,

with only here and there a colored sentence to allure him, like those plants growing in dark forests, which bear only leaves without blossoms. But the ground was comparatively unbroken, and we will not complain of the pioneer, if he raises no flowers with his first crop. Let us not underrate the value of a fact; it will one day flower in a truth. It is astonishing how few facts of importance are added in a century to the natural history of any animal. The natural history of man himself is still being gradually written. Men are knowing enough after their fashion. Every countryman and dairy-maid knows that the coats of the fourth stomach of the calf will curdle milk, and what particular mushroom is a safe and nutritious diet. You cannot go into any field or wood, but it will seem as if every stone had been turned, and the bark on every tree ripped up. But, after all, it is much easier to discover than to see when the cover is off. It has been well said that "the attitude of inspection is prone." Wisdom does not inspect, but behold. We must look a long time before we can see. Slow are the beginnings of philosophy. He has something demoniacal in him, who can discern a law or couple two facts. We can imagine a time when "Water runs down hill" may have been taught in the schools. The true man of science will know nature better by his finer organization; he will smell, taste, see, hear, feel, better than other men. His will be a deeper and finer experience. We do not learn by inference and deduction and the application of mathematics to philosophy, but by direct intercourse and sympathy. It is with science as with ethics—we cannot know truth by contrivance and method; the Baconian is as false as any other, and with all the helps of machinery and the arts, the most scientific will still be the healthiest and friendliest man, and possess a more perfect Indian wisdom.

A Winter Walk

*Emerson, when he sent this essay to the printer for pub-
lication in his* Dial, *wrote Thoreau that he liked "its faithful
observation and its fine sketches of the pickerel-fisher and the
woodchopper." There were some other things he did not like
as well, so he took an editor's privilege and cut them out. But
he left the pleasant, even writing and the warm, still un-
technical appreciation of nature.*

C. B.

THE wind has gently murmured through the blinds,
or puffed with feathery softness against the windows, and occasionally sighed like a summer zephyr lifting the leaves along, the livelong night. The meadow
mouse has slept in his snug gallery in the sod, the owl
has sat in a hollow tree in the depth of the swamp, the
rabbit, the squirrel, and the fox have all been housed.
The watch-dog has lain quiet on the hearth, and the
cattle have stood silent in their stalls. The earth itself has
slept, as it were its first, not its last sleep, save when
some street sign or woodhouse door has faintly creaked
upon its hinge, cheering forlorn nature at her midnight
work—the only sound awake 'twixt Venus and Mars—
advertising us of a remote inward warmth, a divine
cheer and fellowship, where gods are met together, but
where it is very bleak for men to stand. But while the
earth has slumbered, all the air has been alive with
feathery flakes descending, as if some northern Ceres
reigned, showering her silvery grain over all the fields.

We sleep, and at length awake to the still reality of a
winter morning. The snow lies warm as cotton or down

upon the window sill; the broadened sash and frosted panes admit a dim and private light, which enhances the snug cheer within. The stillness of the morning is impressive. The floor creaks under our feet as we move toward the window to look abroad through some clear space over the fields. We see the roofs stand under their snow burden. From the eaves and fences hang stalactites of snow, and in the yard stand stalagmites covering some concealed core. The trees and shrubs rear white arms to the sky on every side; and where were walls and fences, we see fantastic forms stretching in frolic gambols across the dusky landscape, as if Nature had strewn her fresh designs over the fields by night as models for man's art.

Silently we unlatch the door, letting the drift fall in, and step abroad to face the cutting air. Already the stars have lost some of their sparkle, and a dull, leaden mist skirts the horizon. A lurid brazen light in the east proclaims the approach of day, while the western landscape is dim and spectral still, and clothed in a somber Tartarean light, like the shadowy realms. They are Infernal sounds only that you hear—the crowing of cocks, the barking of dogs, the chopping of wood, the lowing of kine, all seem to come from Pluto's barnyard and beyond the Styx—not for any melancholy they suggest, but their twilight bustle is too solemn and mysterious for earth. The recent tracks of the fox or otter, in the yard, remind us that each hour of the night is crowded with events, and the primeval nature is still working and making tracks in the snow. Opening the gate, we tread briskly along the lone country road, crunching the dry and crisped snow under our feet, or aroused by the sharp, clear creak of the wood sled, just starting for the distant market, from the early farmer's door, where it has lain the summer long, dreaming amid the chips and stubble; while far through the drifts and powdered windows we see the farmer's early candle, like a paled star, emitting a lonely beam, as if some severe virtue were at its matins there. And one by one the smokes begin to ascend from the chimneys amid the trees and snows.

The sluggish smoke curls up from some deep dell,
The stiffened air exploring in the dawn,
And making slow acquaintance with the day
Delaying now upon its heavenward course,
In wreathèd loiterings dallying with itself,
With as uncertain purpose and slow deed
As its half-awakened master by the hearth,
Whose mind still slumbering and sluggish thoughts
Have not yet swept into the onward current
Of the new day—and now it streams afar,
The while the chopper goes with step direct,
And mind intent to swing the early axe.
First in the dusky dawn he sends abroad
His early scout, his emissary, smoke,
The earliest, latest pilgrim from the roof,
To feel the frosty air, inform the day;
And while he crouches still beside the hearth,
Nor musters courage to unbar the door,
It has gone down the glen with the light wind,
And o'er the plain unfurled its venturous wreath,
Draped the treetops, loitered upon the hill,
And warmed the pinions of the early bird;
And now, perchance, high in the crispy air,
Has caught sight of the day o'er the earth's edge,
And greets its master's eye at his low door,
As some refulgent cloud in the upper sky.

We hear the sound of woodchopping at the farmers' doors, far over the frozen earth, the baying of the housedog, and the distant clarion of the cock—though the thin and frosty air conveys only the finer particles of sound to our ears, with short and sweet vibrations, as the waves subside soonest on the purest and lightest liquids, in which gross substances sink to the bottom. They come clear and bell-like, and from a greater distance in the horizon, as if there were fewer impediments than in summer to make them faint and ragged. The ground is sonorous, like seasoned wood, and even the ordinary rural sounds are melodious, and the jingling of the ice on the trees is sweet and liquid. There is the least possible moisture in the atmosphere, all being dried up or congealed, and it is of such extreme tenuity and elasticity that it becomes a source of delight. The withdrawn and tense sky seems groined like the aisles of a cathedral, and the polished air sparkles as if there were crystals of ice floating in it. As they who have resided in Greenland tell us that when it freezes "the sea smokes like burning turf-land, and a fog or mist arises, called frost-smoke," which "cutting smoke frequently raises blisters on the face and hands, and is very pernicious to the health." But this pure, stinging cold is an elixir to the lungs, and not so much a frozen mist as a crystallized midsummer haze, refined and purified by cold.

The sun at length rises through the distant woods, as if with the faint clashing, swinging sound of cymbals, melting the air with his beams, and with such rapid steps the morning travels, that already his rays are gilding the distant western mountains. Meanwhile we step hastily along through the powdery snow, warmed by an inward heat, enjoying an Indian summer still, in the increased glow of thought and feeling. Probably if our lives were more conformed to nature, we should not need to defend ourselves against her heats and colds, but find her our constant nurse and friend, as do plants and quadrupeds. If our bodies were fed with pure and simple elements, and not with a stimulating and heating diet, they would afford no more pasture for cold than a leafless twig, but thrive like the trees, which find even winter genial to their expansion.

The wonderful purity of nature at this season is a most pleasing fact. Every decayed stump and moss-grown stone and rail, and the dead leaves of autumn, are concealed by a clean napkin of snow. In the bare fields and tinkling woods, see what virtue survives. In the coldest and bleakest places, the warmest charities still maintain a foothold. A cold and searching wind drives away all contagion, and nothing can withstand it but what has a virtue in it, and accordingly, whatever we meet with in cold and bleak places, as the tops of mountains, we respect for a sort of sturdy innocence, a Puritan toughness. All things beside seem to be called in for shelter, and what stays out must be part of the original frame of the universe, and of such valor as God himself. It is invigorating to breathe the cleansed air. Its greater fineness and purity are visible to the eye, and we would fain stay out long and late, that the gales may sigh through us, too, as through the leafless trees, and fit us for the winter—as if we hoped so to borrow some pure and steadfast virtue, which will stead us in all seasons.

There is a slumbering subterranean fire in nature which never goes out, and which no cold can chill. It finally melts the great snow, and in January or July is only buried under a thicker or thinner covering. In the coldest day it flows somewhere, and the snow melts around every tree. This field of winter rye, which sprouted late in the fall, and now speedily dissolves the snow, is where the fire is very thinly covered. We feel warmed by it. In the winter, warmth stands for all virtue, and we resort in thought to a trickling rill, with its bare stones shining in the sun, and to warm springs in the woods, with as much eagerness as rabbits and robins. The steam which rises from swamps and pools is as dear and domestic as that of our own kettle. What fire could ever equal the sunshine of a winter's day, when the meadow mice come out by the wall-sides, and the chickadee lisps in the defiles of the wood? The warmth comes directly from the sun, and is not radiated from the earth, as in summer; and when we feel his beams on our backs as we are treading some snowy dell, we are grateful as for a special kindness, and bless the sun which has followed us into that by-place.

This subterranean fire has its altar in each man's breast; for in the coldest day, and on the bleakest hill, the traveler cherishes a warmer fire within the folds of his cloak than is kindled on any hearth. A healthy man, indeed, is the complement of the seasons, and in winter, summer is in his heart. There is the south. Thither have all birds and insects migrated, and around the warm springs in his breast are gathered the robin and the lark.

At length, having reached the edge of the woods, and shut out the gadding town, we enter within their covert as we go under the roof of a cottage, and cross its threshold, all ceiled and banked up with snow. They are glad and warm still, and as genial and cheery in winter as in summer. As we stand in the midst of the pines in the flickering and checkered light which straggles but little way into their maze, we wonder if the towns have ever heard their simple story. It seems to us that no traveler has ever explored them, and notwithstanding the wonders which science is elsewhere revealing every day, who would not like to hear their annals? Our humble villages in the plain are their contribution. We borrow from the forest the boards which shelter and the sticks which warm us. How important is their evergreen to the winter, that portion of the summer which does not fade, the permanent year, the unwithered grass! Thus simply, and with little expense of altitude, is the surface of the earth diversified. What would human life be without forests, those natural cities? From the tops of mountains they appear like smooth-shaven lawns, yet whither shall we walk but in this taller grass?

In this glade covered with bushes of a year's growth, see how the silvery dust lies on every seared leaf and twig, deposited in such infinite and luxurious forms as by their very variety atone for the absence of color. Observe the tiny tracks of mice around every stem, and the triangular tracks of the rabbit. A pure elastic heaven hangs over all, as if the impurities of the summer sky, refined and shrunk by the chaste winter's cold, had been winnowed from the heavens upon the earth.

Nature confounds her summer distinctions at this season. The heavens seem to be nearer the earth. The elements are less reserved and distinct. Water turns to ice, rain to snow. The day is but a Scandinavian night. The winter is an arctic summer.

How much more living is the life that is in nature, the furred life which still survives the stinging nights, and, from amidst fields and woods covered with frost and snow, sees the sun rise!

> "The foodless wilds
> Pour forth their brown inhabitants."

The gray squirrel and rabbit are brisk and playful in the remote glens, even on the morning of the cold Friday. Here is our Lapland and Labrador, and for our Esquimaux and Knistenaux, Dog-ribbed Indians, Novazemblaites, and Spitzbergeners, are there not the ice-cutter and woodchopper, the fox, muskrat, and mink?

Still, in the midst of the arctic day, we may trace the summer to its retreats, and sympathize with some contemporary life. Stretched over the brooks, in the midst of the frost-bound meadows, we may observe the submarine cottages of the caddis-worms, the larvae of the

Plicipennes; their small cylindrical cases built around themselves, composed of flags, sticks, grass, and withered leaves, shells, and pebbles, in form and color like the wrecks which strew the bottom,—now drifting along over the pebbly bottom, now whirling in tiny eddies and dashing down steep falls, or sweeping rapidly along with the current, or else swaying to and fro at the end of some grass-blade or root. Anon they will leave their sunken habitations, and, crawling up the stems of plants, or to the surface, like gnats, as perfect insects henceforth, flutter over the surface of the water, or sacrifice their short lives in the flame of our candles at evening. Down yonder little glen the shrubs are drooping under their burden, and the red alderberries contrast with the white ground. Here are the marks of a myriad feet which have already been abroad. The sun rises as proudly over such a glen as over the valley of the Seine or the Tiber, and it seems the residence of a pure and self-subsistent valor, such as they never witnessed—which never knew defeat nor fear. Here reign the simplicity and purity of a primitive age, and a health and hope far remote from towns and cities. Standing quite alone, far in the forest, while the wind is shaking down snow from the trees, and leaving the only human tracks behind us, we find our reflections of a richer variety than the life of cities. The chickadee and nuthatch are more inspiring society than statesmen and philosophers, and we shall return to these last as to more vulgar companions. In this lonely glen, with its brook draining the slopes, its creased ice and crystals of all hues, where the spruces and hemlocks stand up on either side, and the rush and sere wild oats in the rivulet itself, our lives are more serene and worthy to contemplate.

As the day advances, the heat of the sun is reflected

by the hillsides, and we hear a faint but sweet music, where flows the rill released from its fetters, and the icicles are melting on the trees; and the nuthatch and partridge are heard and seen. The south wind melts the snow at noon, and the bare ground appears with its withered grass and leaves, and we are invigorated by the perfume which exhales from it, as by the scent of strong meats.

Let us go into this deserted woodman's hut, and see how he has passed the long winter nights and the short and stormy days. For here man has lived under this south hillside, and it seems a civilized and public spot. We have such associations as when the traveler stands by the ruins of Palmyra or Hecatompolis. Singing birds and flowers perchance have begun to appear here, for flowers as well as weeds follow in the footsteps of man. These hemlocks whispered over his head, these hickory logs were his fuel, and these pitch pine roots kindled his fire; yonder fuming rill in the hollow, whose thin and airy vapor still ascends as busily as ever, though he is far off now, was his well. These hemlock boughs, and the straw upon this raised platform, were his bed, and this broken dish held his drink. But he has not been here this season, for the phoebes built their nest upon this shelf last summer. I find some embers left as if he had but just gone out, where he baked his pot of beans; and while at evening he smoked his pipe, whose stemless bowl lies in the ashes, chatted with his only companion, if perchance he had any, about the depth of the snow on the morrow, already falling fast and thick without, or disputed whether the last sound was the screech of an owl, or the creak of a bough, or imagination only; and through his broad chimney-throat, in the late winter evening, ere he stretched himself upon the straw, he looked up to learn the progress of the storm, and, seeing the bright stars of Cassiopeia's Chair shining brightly down upon him, fell contentedly asleep.

See how many traces from which we may learn the chopper's history! From this stump we may guess the sharpness of his axe, and from the slope of the stroke, on which side he stood, and whether he cut down the tree without going round it or changing hands; and, from the flexure of the splinters, we may know which way it fell. This one chip contains inscribed on it the whole history of the woodchopper and of the world. On this scrap of paper, which held his sugar or salt, perchance, or was the wadding of his gun, sitting on a log in the forest, with what interest we read the tattle of cities, of those larger huts, empty and to let, like this, in High Streets and Broadways. The eaves are dripping on the south side of this simple roof, while the titmouse lisps in the pine and the genial warmth of the sun around the door is somewhat kind and human.

After two seasons, this rude dwelling does not deform the scene. Already the birds resort to it, to build their nests, and you may track to its door the feet of many quadrupeds. Thus, for a long time, nature overlooks the encroachment and profanity of man. The wood still cheerfully and unsuspiciously echoes the strokes of the axe that fells it, and while they are few and seldom, they enhance its wildness, and all the elements strive to naturalize the sound.

Now our path begins to ascend gradually to the top of this high hill, from whose precipitous south side we can look over the broad country of forest and field and river, to the distant snowy mountains. See yonder thin column of smoke curling up through the woods from some invisible farmhouse, the standard raised over some rural homestead. There must be a warmer and more genial spot there below, as where we detect the vapor

from a spring forming a cloud above the trees. What
fine relations are established between the traveler who
discovers this airy column from some eminence in the
forest and him who sits below! Up goes the smoke as
silently and naturally as the vapor exhales from the
leaves, and as busy disposing itself in wreaths as the
housewife on the hearth below. It is a hieroglyphic of
man's life, and suggests more intimate and important
things than the boiling of a pot. Where its fine column
rises above the forest, like an ensign, some human life
has planted itself—and such is the beginning of Rome,
the establishment of the arts, and the foundation of empires, whether on the prairies of America or the steppes
of Asia.

And now we descend again, to the brink of this woodland lake, which lies in a hollow of the hills, as if it were
their expressed juice, and that of the leaves which are
annually steeped in it. Without outlet or inlet to the eye,
it has still its history, in the lapse of its waves, in the
rounded pebbles on its shore, and in the pines which
grow down to its brink. It has not been idle, though
sedentary, but, like Abu Musa, teaches that "sitting still
at home is the heavenly way; the going out is the way
of the world." Yet in its evaporation it travels as far as
any. In summer it is the earth's liquid eye, a mirror in
the breast of nature. The sins of the wood are washed
out in it. See how the woods form an amphitheater
about it, and it is an arena for all the genialness of nature. All trees direct the traveler to its brink, all paths
seek it out, birds fly to it, quadrupeds flee to it, and the
very ground inclines toward it. It is nature's saloon,
where she has sat down to her toilet. Consider her silent
economy and tidiness; how the sun comes with his
evaporation to sweep the dust from its surface each
morning, and a fresh surface is constantly welling up;

and annually, after whatever impurities have accumulated herein, its liquid transparency appears again in the spring. In summer a hushed music seems to sweep across its surface. But now a plain sheet of snow conceals it from our eyes, except where the wind has swept the ice bare, and the sere leaves are gliding from side to side, tacking and veering on their tiny voyages. Here is one just keeled up against a pebble on shore, a dry beech leaf, rocking still, as if it would start again. A skillful engineer, methinks, might project its course since it fell from the parent stem. Here are all the elements for such a calculation. Its present position, the direction of the wind, the level of the pond, and how much more is given. In its scarred edges and veins is its log rolled up.

We fancy ourselves in the interior of a larger house. The surface of the pond is our deal table or sanded floor, and the woods rise abruptly from its edge, like the walls of a cottage. The lines set to catch pickerel through the ice look like a larger culinary preparation, and the men stand about on the white ground like pieces of forest furniture. The actions of these men, at the distance of half a mile over the ice and snow, impress us as when we read the exploits of Alexander in history. They seem not unworthy of the scenery, and as momentous as the conquest of kingdoms.

Again we have wandered through the arches of the wood, until from its skirts we hear the distant booming of ice from yonder bay of the river, as if it were moved by some other and subtler tide than oceans know. To me it has a strange sound of home, thrilling as the voice of one's distant and noble kindred. A mild summer sun shines over forest and lake, and though there is but one green leaf for many rods, yet nature enjoys a serene health. Every sound is fraught with the same mysteri-

ous assurance of health, as well now the creaking of the
boughs in January, as the soft sough of the wind in July.

When Winter fringes every bough
  With his fantastic wreath,
And puts the seal of silence now
  Upon the leaves beneath;

When every stream in its penthouse
  Goes gurgling on its way,
And in his gallery the mouse
  Nibbleth the meadow hay;

Methinks the summer still is nigh,
  And lurketh underneath,
At that same meadow mouse doth lie
  Snug in that last year's heath.

And if perchance the chickadee
  Lisp a faint note anon,
The snow is summer's canopy,
  Which she herself put on.

Fair blossoms deck the cheerful trees,
  And dazzling fruits depend;
The north wind sighs a summer breeze,
  The nipping frosts to fend,

Bringing glad tidings unto me,
  The while I stand all ear,
Of a serene eternity,
  Which need not winter fear.

Out on the silent pond straightway
  The restless ice doth crack,
And pond sprites merry gambols play
  Amid the deafening rack.

Eager I hasten to the vale,
  As if I heard brave news,
How nature held high festival,
  Which it were hard to lose.

I gambol with my neighbor ice,
　And sympathizing quake,
As each new crack darts in a trice
　Across the gladsome lake.

One with the cricket in the ground,
　And fagot on the hearth,
Resounds the rare domestic sound
　Along the forest path.

Before night we will take a journey on skates along
the course of this meandering river, as full of novelty
to one who sits by the cottage fire all the winter's day,
as if it were over the polar ice, with Captain Parry or
Franklin; following the winding of the stream, now
flowing amid hills, now spreading out into fair meadows, and forming a myriad coves and bays where the
pine and hemlock overarch. The river flows in the rear
of the towns, and we see all things from a new and
wilder side. The fields and gardens come down to it
with a frankness, and freedom from pretension, which
they do not wear on the highway. It is the outside and
edge of the earth. Our eyes are not offended by violent
contrasts. The last rail of the farmer's fence is some
swaying willow bough, which still preserves its freshness, and here at length all fences stop, and we no
longer cross any road. We may go far up within the
country now by the most retired and level road, never
climbing a hill, but by broad levels ascending to the
upland meadows. It is a beautiful illustration of the
law of obedience, the flow of a river; the path for a sick
man, a highway down which an acorn cup may float
secure with its freight. Its slight occasional falls, whose
precipices would not diversify the landscape, are celebrated by mist and spray, and attract the traveler from
far and near. From the remote interior, its current con-
ducts him by broad and easy steps, or by one gentler

inclined plane, to the sea. Thus by an early and constant yielding to the inequalities of the ground it secures itself the easiest passage.

No domain of nature is quite closed to man at all times, and now we draw near to the empire of the fishes. Our feet glide swiftly over unfathomed depths, where in summer our line tempted the pout and perch, and where the stately pickerel lurked in the long corridors formed by the bulrushes. The deep, impenetrable marsh, where the heron waded and bittern squatted, is made pervious to our swift shoes, as if a thousand railroads had been made into it. With one impulse we are carried to the cabin of the muskrat, that earliest settler, and see him dart away under the transparent ice, like a furred fish, to his hole in the bank; and we glide rapidly over meadows where lately "the mower whet his scythe," through beds of frozen cranberries mixed with meadow-grass. We skate near to where the blackbird, the pewee, and the kingbird hung their nests over the water, and the hornets builded from the maple in the swamp. How many gay warblers, following the sun, have radiated from this nest of silver birch and thistledown! On the swamp's outer edge was hung the supermarine village, where no foot penetrated. In this hollow tree the wood duck reared her brood, and slid away each day to forage in yonder fen.

In winter, nature is a cabinet of curiosities, full of dried specimens, in their natural order and position. The meadows and forests are a *hortus siccus*. The leaves and grasses stand perfectly pressed by the air without screw or gum, and the birds' nests are not hung on an artificial twig, but where they builded them. We go about dryshod to inspect the summer's work in the rank swamp, and see what a growth have got the alders, the willows, and the maples; testifying to how many warm suns, and fertilizing dews and showers. See what strides their boughs took in the luxuriant summer—and anon these dormant buds will carry them onward and upward another span into the heavens.

Occasionally we wade through fields of snow, under whose depths the river is lost for many rods, to appear again to the right or left, where we least expected; still holding on its way underneath, with a faint, stertorous, rumbling sound, as if, like the bear and marmot, it too had hibernated, and we had followed its faint summer trail to where it earthed itself in snow and ice. At first we should have thought that rivers would be empty and dry in midwinter, or else frozen solid till the spring thawed them; but their volume is not diminished even, for only a superficial cold bridges their surfaces. The thousand springs which feed the lakes and streams are flowing still. The issues of a few surface springs only are closed, and they go to swell the deep reservoirs. Nature's wells are below the frost. The summer brooks are not filled with snow-water, nor does the mower quench his thirst with that alone. The streams are swollen when the snow melts in the spring, because nature's work has been delayed, the water being turned into ice and snow, whose particles are less smooth and round, and do not find their level so soon.

Far over the ice, between the hemlock woods and snow-clad hills, stands the pickerel-fisher, his lines set in some retired cove, like a Finlander, with his arms thrust into the pouches of his dreadnaught; with dull, snowy, fishy thoughts, himself a finless fish, separated a few inches from his race; dumb, erect, and made to be enveloped in clouds and snows, like the pines on shore. In these wild scenes, men stand about in the scenery, or move deliberately and heavily, having sacrificed the sprightliness and vivacity of towns to the dumb sobriety of nature. He does not make the scenery less wild, more than the jays and muskrats, but stands there as a part of it, as the natives are represented in the voyages of early navigators, at Nootka Sound, and on the Northwest coast, with their furs about them, before they were tempted to loquacity by a scrap of iron. He belongs to the natural family of man, and is planted deeper in nature and has more root than the inhabitants of towns. Go to him, ask what luck, and you will learn that he too is a worshiper of the unseen. Hear with what sincere deference and waving gesture in his tone he speaks of the lake pickerel, which he has never seen, his primitive and ideal race of pickerel. He is connected with the shore still, as by a fishline, and yet remembers the season when he took fish through the ice on the pond, while the peas were up in his garden at home.

But now, while we have loitered, the clouds have gathered again, and a few straggling snowflakes are beginning to descend. Faster and faster they fall, shutting out the distant objects from sight. The snow falls on every wood and field, and no crevice is forgotten; by the river and the pond, on the hill and in the valley. Quadrupeds are confined to their coverts and the birds sit upon their perches this peaceful hour. There is not so much sound as in fair weather, but silently and gradually every slope, and the gray walls and fences, and the polished ice, and the sere leaves, which were not buried before, are concealed, and the tracks of men and beasts are lost. With so little effort does nature reassert her rule and blot out the traces of men. Hear how Homer has described the same: "The snowflakes fall thick and fast on a winter's day. The winds are lulled, and the snow falls incessant, covering the tops of the mountains, and the hills, and the plains where the lotus tree grows, and the cultivated fields, and they are falling by the inlets and shores of the foaming sea, but are silently dissolved by the waves." The snow levels all things, and infolds them deeper in the bosom of nature, as, in the slow summer, vegetation creeps up to the entablature of the temple, and the turrets of the castle, and helps her to prevail over art.

The surly night wind rustles through the wood, and warns us to retrace our steps, while the sun goes down behind the thickening storm, and birds seek their roosts, and cattle their stalls.

> "Drooping the lab'rer ox
> Stands covered o'er with snow, and *now* demands
> The fruit of all his toil."

Though winter is represented in the almanac as an old man, facing the wind and sleet, and drawing his cloak about him, we rather think of him as a merry woodchopper, and warm-blooded youth, as blithe as summer. The unexplored grandeur of the storm keeps up the spirits of the traveler. It does not trifle with us, but has a sweet earnestness. In winter we lead a more inward life. Our hearts are warm and cheery, like cottages under drifts, whose windows and doors are half concealed, but from whose chimneys the smoke cheerfully ascends. The imprisoning drifts increase the sense of comfort which the house affords, and in the coldest days we are content to sit over the hearth and see the sky through the chimmey-top, enjoying the quiet and serene life that may be had in a warm corner by the chimney-side, or feeling our pulse by listening to the low of cattle in the street, or the sound of the flail in distant barns all the long afternoon. No doubt a skillful physician could determine our health by observing how these simple and natural sounds affected us. We enjoy now, not an Oriental, but a Boreal leisure, around warm stoves and fireplaces, and watch the shadow of motes in the sunbeams.

Sometimes our fate grows too homely and familiarly serious ever to be cruel. Consider how for three months the human destiny is wrapped in furs. The good Hebrew Revelation takes no cognizance of all this cheerful snow. Is there no religion for the temperate and frigid zones? We know of no scripture which records the pure benignity of the gods on a New England winter night Their praises have never been sung, only their wrath deprecated. The best scripture, after all, records but a meager faith. Its saints live reserved and austere. Let a brave, devout man spend the year in the woods of Maine or Labrador, and see if the Hebrew Scriptures speak adequately to his condition and experience, from the setting in of winter to the breaking up of the ice.

Now commences the long winter evening around the farmer's hearth, when the thoughts of the indwellers travel far abroad, and men are by nature and necessity charitable and liberal to all creatures. Now is the happy resistance to cold, when the farmer reaps his reward, and thinks of his preparedness for winter, and, through the glittering panes, sees with equanimity "the mansion of the northern bear," for now the storm is over,

"The full ethereal round,
Infinite worlds disclosing to the view,
Shines out intensely keen; and all one cope
Of starry glitter glows from pole to pole."

The Maine Woods

A year after Thoreau retired to Walden Pond he felt, it may be, a strong surge of wanderlust, so he headed for the backwoods of Maine. There he showed himself a genuine woodsman. When he wrote up his "Ktaadn" travelogue he sent it on to his friend Horace Greeley, who did his best to place it. Greeley finally succeeded although Thoreau never received much more than $50 or $75 for his work. John Sartain's Union Magazine bought the manuscript and presented it to its readers in five installments (of which the first two are given here) during 1848. The readers got their money's worth.

C. B.

THE WILDS OF THE PENOBSCOT

ON THE 31st of August, 1846, I left Concord in Massachusetts for Bangor and the backwoods of Maine, by way of the railroad and steamboat, intending to accompany a relative of mine, engaged in the lumber trade in Bangor, as far as a dam on the West Branch of the Penobscot, in which property he was interested. From this place, which is about one hundred miles by the river above Bangor, thirty miles from the Houlton military road, and five miles beyond the last log hut, I proposed to make excursions to Mount Ktaadn, the second highest mountain in New England, about thirty miles distant, and to some of the lakes of the Penobscot, either alone or with such company as I might pick up there. It is unusual to find a camp so far in the woods at that season, when lumbering operations have ceased, and I was glad to avail myself of the circumstance of a gang of men being employed there at that time in repairing the injuries caused by the great freshet in the spring. The mountain may be approached more easily and directly on horseback and on foot from the northeast side, by the Aroostook road, and the Wassataquoik River; but in that case you see much less of the wilderness, none of the glorious river and lake scenery, and have no experience of the batteau and the boatman's life. I was fortunate also in the season of the year, for in the summer myriads of black flies, mosquitoes, and midges, or, as the Indians call them, "no-see-ems," make traveling in the woods almost impossible; but now their reign was nearly over. Ktaadn, whose name is an Indian word signifying highest land, was first ascended by white men in 1804. It was visited by Professor J. W. Bailey of West Point in 1836; by Dr. Charles T. Jackson, the State Geologist, in 1837; and by two young men from Boston in 1845. All these have given accounts of their expeditions. Since I was there, two or three other parties have made the excursion, and told their stories. Besides these, very few, even among backwoodsmen and hunters, have ever climbed it, and it will be a long time before the tide of fashionable travel sets that way. The mountainous region of the State of Maine stretches from near the White Mountains, northeasterly one hundred and sixty miles, to the head of the Aroostook River, and is about sixty miles wide. The wild or unsettled portion is far more extensive. So that some hours only of travel in this direction will carry the curious to the verge of a primitive forest, more interesting, perhaps, on all accounts, than they would reach by going a thousand miles westward.

The next forenoon, Tuesday, September 1, I started with my companion in a buggy from Bangor for "up river," expecting to be overtaken the next day night at Mattawamkeag Point, some sixty miles off, by two more

Bangoreans, who had decided to join us in a trip to the mountain. We had each a knapsack or bag filled with such clothing and articles as were indispensable, and my companion carried his gun.

Within a dozen miles of Bangor we passed through the villages of Stillwater and Oldtown, built at the falls of the Penobscot, which furnish the principal power by which the Maine woods are converted into lumber. The mills are built directly over and across the river. Here is a close jam, a hard rub, at all seasons; and then the once green tree, long since white, I need not say as the driven snow, but as a driven log, becomes lumber merely. Here your inch, your two and your three inch stuff begin to be, and Mr. Sawyer marks off those spaces which decide the destiny of so many prostrate forests. Through this steel riddle, more or less coarse, is the arrowy Maine forest, from Ktaadn and Chesuncook, and the headwaters of the St. John, relentlessly sifted, till it comes out boards, clapboards, laths, and shingles such as the wind can take, still, perchance, to be slit and slit again, till men get a size that will suit. Think how stood the white pine tree on the shore of Chesuncook, its branches soughing with the four winds, and every individual needle trembling in the sunlight—think how it stands with it now—sold, perchance, to the New England Friction-Match Company! There were in 1837, as I read, two hundred and fifty sawmills on the Penobscot and its tributaries above Bangor, the greater part of them in this immediate neighborhood, and they sawed two hundred millions of feet of boards annually. To this is to be added the lumber of the Kennebec, Androscoggin, Saco, Passamaquoddy, and other streams. No wonder that we hear so often of vessels which are becalmed off our coast being surrounded a week at a time by floating lumber from the Maine woods. The mission of men there seems to be, like so many busy demons, to drive the forest all out of the country, from every solitary beaver swamp and mountainside, as soon as possible.

At Oldtown, we walked into a batteau-manufactory. The making of batteaux is quite a business here for the supply of the Penobscot River. We examined some on the stocks. They are light and shapely vessels, calculated for rapid and rocky streams, and to be carried over long portages on men's shoulders, from twenty to thirty feet long, and only four or four and a half wide, sharp at both ends like a canoe, though broadest forward on the bottom, and reaching seven or eight feet over the water, in order that they may slip over rocks as gently as possible. They are made very slight, only two boards to a side, commonly secured to a few light maple or other hardwood knees, but inward are of the clearest and widest white pine stuff, of which there is a great waste on account of their form, for the bottom is left perfectly flat, not only from side to side, but from end to end. Sometimes they become "hogging" even, after long use, and the boatmen then turn them over and straighten them by a weight at each end. They told us that one wore out in two years, or often in a single trip, on the rocks, and sold for from fourteen to sixteen dollars. There was something refreshing and wildly musical to my ears in the very name of the white man's canoe, reminding me of Charlevoix and Canadian Voyageurs. The batteau is a sort of mongrel between the canoe and the boat, a fur-trader's boat.

The ferry here took us past the Indian island. As we left the shore, I observed a short, shabby, washerwoman-looking Indian—they commonly have the woebegone look of the girl that cried for spilt milk—just from "up river," land on the Oldtown side near a grocery, and, drawing up his canoe, take out a bundle of skins in one hand, and an empty keg or half-barrel in the other, and scramble up the bank with them. This picture will do to put before the Indian's history, that is, the history of his extinction. In 1837 there were three hundred and sixty-two souls left of this tribe. The island seemed deserted today, yet I observed some new houses among the weather-stained ones, as if the tribe had still a design upon life; but generally they have a very shabby, forlorn, and cheerless look, being all back side and woodshed, not homesteads, even Indian homesteads, but instead of home or abroad-steads, for their life is *domi aut militiae,* at home or at war, or now rather *venatus,* that is, a hunting, and most of the latter. The church is the only trim-looking building, but that is not Abenaki, that was Rome's doings. Good Canadian it may be, but it is poor Indian. These were once a powerful tribe. Politics are all the rage with them now. I even thought that a row of wigwams, with a dance of powwows, and a prisoner tortured at the stake, would be more respectable than this.

We landed in Milford, and rode along on the east side of the Penobscot, having a more or less constant view of the river, and the Indian islands in it, for they retain all the islands as far up as Nicketow, at the mouth of the East Branch. They are generally well-timbered, and are said to be better soil than the neighboring shores. The river seemed shallow and rocky, and interrupted by rapids, rippling and gleaming in the sun. We paused a moment to see a fish hawk dive for a fish down straight as an arrow, from a great height, but he missed his prey this time. It was the Houlton road on which we were now traveling, over which some troops were marched once towards Mars' Hill, though not to Mars' *field,* as it proved. It is the main, almost the only, road in these parts, as straight and well made, and kept in as good repair as almost any you will find anywhere. Everywhere we saw signs of the great freshet—this house standing awry, and that where it was not founded, but where it was found, at any rate, the next day; and that other with a waterlogged look, as if it were still airing and drying its basement, and logs with everybody's marks upon them, and sometimes the marks of their having served as bridges, strewn along the road. We crossed the Sunkhaze, a summery Indian name, the Olemmon, Passadumkeag, and other streams, which make a greater show on the map than they now did on the road. At Passadumkeag we found anything but what the name implies—earnest politicians, to wit—white ones, I mean—on the alert to know how the election was likely to go; men who talked rapidly, with subdued voice, and a sort of factitious earnestness you could not help believing, hardly waiting for an introduction, one on each side of your buggy, endeavoring to say much in little, for they see you hold the whip impatiently, but always saying little in much. Caucuses they have had, it seems, and caucuses they are to have again—victory and defeat. Somebody may be elected, somebody may not. One man, a total stranger, who stood by our carriage in the dusk, actually frightened the horse with his asseverations, growing more solemnly positive as there was less in him to be positive about. So Passadumkeag did not look on the map. At sundown, leaving the river road awhile for shortness, we went by way of Enfield, where we stopped for the night. This, like most of the localities bearing names on this road, was a place to name which, in the midst of the unnamed and unincorporated wilderness, was to make a distinction without a difference, it seemed to me. Here, however, I noticed quite an orchard of healthy and well-grown apple trees, in a bearing state, it being the oldest settler's house in this region, but all natural fruit and comparatively worthless for want of a grafter. And so it is generally, lower down the river. It would be a good speculation, as well as a favor conferred on the settlers, for a Massachusetts boy to go down there with a trunk full of choice scions, and his grafting apparatus, in the spring.

The next morning we drove along through a high and hilly country, in view of Cold-Stream Pond, a beautiful lake four or five miles long, and came into the Houlton road again, here called the military road, at Lincoln, forty-five miles from Bangor, where there is quite a village for this country—the principal one above Oldtown. Learning that there were several wigwams here, on one of the Indian islands, we left our horse and wagon and walked through the forest half a mile to the river, to procure a guide to the mountain. It was not till after considerable search that we discovered their habitations —small huts, in a retired place, where the scenery was unusually soft and beautiful, and the shore skirted with pleasant meadows and graceful elms. We paddled ourselves across to the island side in a canoe, which we found on the shore. Near where we landed sat an Indian girl, ten or twelve years old, on a rock in the water, in the sun, washing, and humming or moaning a song meanwhile. It was an aboriginal strain. A salmon-spear, made wholly of wood, lay on the shore, such as they might have used before white men came. It had an elastic piece of wood fastened to one side of its point, which slipped over and closed upon the fish, somewhat like the contrivance for holding a bucket at the end of a well-pole. As we walked up to the nearest house, we were met by a sally of a dozen wolfish-looking dogs, which may have been lineal descendants from the ancient Indian dogs, which the first voyageurs describe as "their wolves." I suppose they were. The occupant soon appeared, with a long pole in his hand, with which he beat off the dogs, while he parleyed with us—a stalwart, but dull and greasy-looking fellow, who told us, in his sluggish way, in answer to our questions, as if it were the first serious business he had to do that day, that there *were* Indians going "up river"—he and one other —today, before noon. And who was the other? Louis Neptune, who lives in the next house. Well, let us go over and see Louis together. The same doggish reception, and Louis Neptune makes his appearance—a small, wiry man, with puckered and wrinkled face, yet he seemed the chief man of the two; the same, as I remembered, who had accompanied Jackson to the mountain in '37. The same questions were put to Louis, and the same information obtained, while the other Indian stood by. It appeared that they were going to start by noon, with two canoes, to go up to Chesuncook to hunt moose—to be gone a month. "Well, Louis, suppose you get to the Point (to the Five Islands, just below Mattawamkeag) to camp, we walk on up the West Branch tomorrow—four of us—and wait for you at the dam, or this side. You overtake us tomorrow or next day, and take us into your canoes. We stop for you, you stop for us. We pay you for your trouble." "Ye'," replied Louis, "may be you carry some provision for all—some pork— some bread—and so pay." He said, "Me sure get some moose"; and when I asked if he thought Pomola would let us go up, he answered that we must plant one bottle of rum on the top; he had planted good many; and when he looked again, the rum was all gone. He had been up two or three times; he had planted letter—English, German, French, etc. These men were slightly clad in shirt and pantaloons, like laborers with us in warm weather. They did not invite us into their houses, but met us outside. So we left the Indians, thinking ourselves lucky to have secured such guides and companions.

There were very few houses along the road, yet they did not altogether fail, as if the law by which men are dispersed over the globe were a very stringent one, and not to be resisted with impunity or for slight reasons. There were even the germs of one or two villages just beginning to expand. The beauty of the road itself was remarkable. The various evergreens, many of which are rare with us—delicate and beautiful specimens of the larch, arbor vitae, ball spruce, and balsam fir, from a few inches to many feet in height—lined its sides, in some places like a long front yard, springing up from the smooth grass plots which uninterruptedly border it, and are made fertile by its wash; while it was but a step on either hand to the grim, untrodden wilderness, whose tangled labyrinth of living, fallen, and decaying trees only the deer and moose, the bear and wolf can easily penetrate. More perfect specimens than any front-yard plot can show grew there to grace the passage of the Houlton teams.

About noon we reached the Mattawamkeag, fifty-six miles from Bangor by the way we had come, and put up at a frequented house still on the Houlton road, where the Houlton stage stops. Here was a substantial covered bridge over the Mattawamkeag, built, I think they said, some seventeen years before. We had dinner—where, by the way, and even at breakfast, as well as supper, at the public-houses on this road, the front rank is composed of various kinds of "sweet cakes," in a continuous line from one end of the table to the other. I think I may safely say that there was a row of ten or a dozen plates of this kind set before us two here. To account for which, they say that, when the lumberers

come out of the woods, they have a craving for cakes
and pies, and such sweet things, which there are almost
unknown, and this is the *supply* to satisfy that *demand*.
The supply is always equal to the demand, and these
hungry men think a good deal of getting their money's
worth. No doubt the balance of victuals is restored by
the time they reach Bangor—Mattawamkeag takes off
the raw edge. Well, over this front rank, I say, you, coming from the "sweet cake" side, with a cheap philosophic indifference though it may be, have to assault
what there is behind, which I do not by any means mean
to insinuate is insufficient in quantity or quality to supply that other demand, of men, not from the woods but
from the towns, for venison and strong country fare.
After dinner we strolled down to the "Point," formed by
the junction of the two rivers, which is said to be the
scene of an ancient battle between the Eastern Indians
and the Mohawks, and searched there carefully for relics, though the men of the barroom had never heard
of such things; but we found only some flakes of arrowhead stone, some points of arrowheads, one small leaden
bullet, and some colored beads, the last to be referred,
perhaps, to early fur-trader days. The Mattawamkeag,
though wide, was a mere river's bed, full of rocks and
shallows at this time, so that you could cross it almost
dry-shod in boots; and I could hardly believe my companion, when he told me that he had been fifty or sixty
miles up it in a batteau, through distant and still uncut
forests. A batteau could hardly find a harbor now at its
mouth. Deer and caribou, or reindeer, are taken here
in the winter, in sight of the house.

Before our companions arrived, we rode on up the
Houlton road seven miles to Molunkus, where the Aroostook road comes into it, and where there is a spacious
public house in the woods, called the "Molunkus House,"

kept by one Libbey, which looked as if it had its hall for
dancing and for military drills. There was no other evidence of man but this huge shingle palace in this part
of the world; but sometimes even this is filled with travelers. I looked off the piazza round the corner of the
house up the Aroostook road, on which there was no
clearing in sight. There was a man just adventuring
upon it this evening in a rude, original, what you may
call Aroostook wagon—a mere seat, with a wagon
swung under it, a few bags on it, and a dog asleep to
watch them. He offered to carry a message for us to
anybody in that country, cheerfully. I suspect that, if
you should go to the end of the world, you would find
somebody there going farther, as if just starting for
home at sundown, and having a last word before he
drove off. Here, too, *was* a small trader, whom I did not
see at first, who kept a store—but no great store, certainly—in a small box over the way, behind the Molunkus signpost. It looked like the balance-box of a patent
hay-scales. As for his house, we could only conjecture
where that was; he may have been a boarder in the
Molunkus House. I saw him standing in his shop door
—his shop was so small, that, if a traveler should make
demonstrations of entering in, *he* would have to go out
by the back way, and confer with his customer through
a window, about his goods in the cellar, or, more probably, bespoken, and yet on the way. I should have gone
in, for I felt a real impulse to trade, if I had not stopped
to consider what would become of him. The day before,
we had walked into a shop, over against an inn where
we stopped, the puny beginning of trade, which would
grow at last into a firm copartnership in the future town
or city—indeed, it was already "Somebody & Co.," I
forget who. The woman came forward from the pene-
tralia of the attached house, for "Somebody & Co." was

in the burning, and she sold us percussion-caps, canalés and smooth, and knew their prices and qualities, and which the hunters preferred. Here was a little of everything in a small compass to satisfy the wants and the ambition of the woods—a stock selected with what pains and care, and brought home in the wagon-box, or a corner of the Houlton team; but there seemed to me, as usual, a preponderance of children's toys—dogs to bark, and cats to mew, and trumpets to blow, where natives there hardly are yet. As if a child born into the Maine woods, among the pine cones and cedar berries, could not do without such a sugar-man or skipping-jack as the young Rothschild has.

I think that there was not more than one house on the road to Molunkus, or for seven miles. At that place we got over the fence into a new field, planted with potatoes, where the logs were still burning between the hills; and, pulling up the vines, found good-sized potatoes, nearly ripe, growing like weeds, and turnips mixed with them. The mode of clearing and planting is to fell the trees, and burn once what will burn, then cut them up into suitable lengths, roll into heaps, and burn again; then, with a hoe, plant potatoes where you can come at the ground between the stumps and charred logs; for a first crop the ashes sufficing for manure, and no hoeing being necessary the first year. In the fall, cut, roll, and burn again, and so on, till the land is cleared; and soon it is ready for grain, and to be laid down. Let those talk of poverty and hard times who will in the towns and cities; cannot the emigrant who can pay his fare to New York or Boston pay five dollars more to get here— I paid three, all told, for my passage from Boston to Bangor, two hundred and fifty miles—and be as rich as he pleases, where land virtually costs nothing, and houses only the labor of building, and he may begin life as Adam did? If he will still remember the distinction of poor and rich, let him bespeak him a narrower house forthwith.

LIFE IN THE WILDERNESS

When we returned to the Mattawamkeag, the Houlton stage had already put up there; and a Province man was betraying his greenness to the Yankees by his questions. Why Province money won't pass here at par, when States' money is good at Fredericton—though this, perhaps, was sensible enough. From what I saw then, it appears that the Province man was now the only real Jonathan, or raw country bumpkin, left so far behind by his enterprising neighbors that he didn't know enough to put a question to them. No people can long continue provincial in character who have the propensity for politics and whittling, and rapid traveling, which the Yankees have, and who are leaving the mother country behind in the variety of their notions and inventions. The possession and exercise of practical talent merely are a sure and rapid means of intellectual culture and independence.

The last edition of Greenleaf's Map of Maine hung on the wall here, and, as we had no pocket-map, we resolved to trace a map of the lake country. So, dipping a wad of tow into the lamp, we oiled a sheet of paper on the oiled tablecloth, and, in good faith, traced what we afterwards ascertained to be a labyrinth of errors, carefully following the outlines of the imaginary lakes which the map contains. The Map of the Public Lands of Maine and Massachusetts is the only one I have seen that at all deserves the name. It was while we were engaged in this operation that our companions arrived.

They had seen the Indians' fire on the Five Islands, and so we concluded that all was right.

Early the next morning we had mounted our packs, and prepared for a tramp up the West Branch, my companion having turned his horse out to pasture for a week or ten days, thinking that a bite of fresh grass and a taste of running water would do him as much good as backwoods fare and new country influences his master. Leaping over a fence, we began to follow an obscure trail up the northern bank of the Penobscot. There was now no road further, the river being the only highway, and but half a dozen log huts, confined to its banks, to be met with for thirty miles. On either hand, and beyond, was a wholly uninhabited wilderness, stretching to Canada. Neither horse nor cow, nor vehicle of any kind, had ever passed over this ground; the cattle, and the few bulky articles which the loggers use, being got up in the winter on the ice, and down again before it breaks up. The evergreen woods had a decidedly sweet and bracing fragrance; the air was a sort of diet-drink, and we walked on buoyantly in Indian file, stretching our legs. Occasionally there was a small opening on the bank, made for the purpose of log-rolling, where we got a sight of the river—always a rocky and rippling stream. The roar of the rapids, the note of a whistler duck on the river, of the jay and chickadee around us, and of the pigeon woodpecker in the openings, were the sounds that we heard. This was what you might call a brand-new country; the only roads were of Nature's making, and the few houses were camps. Here, then, one could no longer accuse institutions and society, but must front the true source of evil.

There are three classes of inhabitants who either frequent or inhabit the country which we had now entered:

first, the loggers, who, for a part of the year, the winter
and spring, are far the most numerous, but in the summer, except a few explorers for timber, completely desert it; second, the few settlers I have named, the only
permanent inhabitants, who live on the verge of it, and
help raise supplies for the former; third, the hunters,
mostly Indians, who range over it in their season.

At the end of three miles we came to the Mattaseunk
stream and mill, where there was even a rude wooden
railroad running down to the Penobscot, the last railroad we were to see. We crossed one tract, on the bank
of the river, of more than a hundred acres of heavy timber, which had just been felled and burnt over, and was
still smoking. Our trail lay through the midst of it, and
was well-nigh blotted out. The trees lay at full length,
four or five feet deep, and crossing each other in all
directions, all black as charcoal, but perfectly sound
within, still good for fuel or for timber; soon they would
be cut into lengths and burnt again. Here were thousands of cords, enough to keep the poor of Boston and
New York amply warm for a winter, which only cum-
bered the ground and were in the settler's way. And
the whole of that solid and interminable forest is doomed
to be gradually devoured thus by fire, like shavings, and
no man be warmed by it. At Chocker's log hut, at the
mouth of Salmon River, seven miles from the Point,
one of the party commenced distributing a store of
small, cent picture-books among the children, to teach
them to read, and also newspapers, more or less recent,
among the parents, than which nothing can be more
acceptable to a backwoods people. It was really an important item in our outfit, and, at times, the only currency that would circulate. I walked through Salmon
River with my shoes on, it being low water, but not
without wetting my feet. A few miles farther we came

to "Marm Howard's," at the end of an extensive clearing, where there were two or three log huts in sight at once, one on the opposite side of the river, and a few graves even, surrounded by a wooden paling, where already the rude forefathers of *a* hamlet lie, and a thousand years hence, perchance, some poet will write his "Elegy in a Country Churchyard." The "Village Hampdens," the "mute, inglorious Miltons," and Cromwells, "guiltless of" their "country's blood," were yet unborn.

> "Perchance in this *wild* spot *there will be* laid
>   Some heart once pregnant with celestial fire;
> Hands that the rod of empire might have swayed,
>   Or waked to ecstasy the living lyre."

The next house was Fisk's, ten miles from the Point at the mouth of the East Branch, opposite to the island Nicketow, or the Forks, the last of the Indian islands. I am particular to give the names of the settlers and the distances, since every log hut in these woods is a public house, and such information is of no little consequence to those who may have occasion to travel this way. Our course here crossed the Penobscot, and followed the southern bank. One of the party, who entered the house in search of someone to set us over, reported a very neat dwelling, with plenty of books, and a new wife, just imported from Boston, wholly new to the woods. We found the East Branch a large and rapid stream at its mouth and much deeper than it appeared. Having with some difficulty discovered the trail again, we kept up the south side of the West Branch, or main river, passing by some rapids called Rock-Ebeeme, the roar of which we heard through the woods, and, shortly after, in the thickest of the wood, some empty loggers' camps, still new, which were occupied the previous winter. Though we saw a few more afterwards, I will make one account serve for all. These were such houses as the lumberers of Maine spend the winter in, in the wilderness. There were the camps and the hovels for the cattle, hardly distinguishable, except that the latter had no chimney. These camps were about twenty feet long by fifteen wide, built of logs—hemlock, cedar, spruce, or yellow birch—one kind alone, or all together, with the bark on; two or three large ones first, one directly above another, and notched together at the ends, to the height of three or four feet, then of smaller logs resting upon transverse ones at the ends, each of the last successively shorter than the other, to form the roof. The chimney was an oblong square hole in the middle, three or four feet in diameter, with a fence of logs as high as the ridge. The interstices were filled with moss, and the roof was shingled with long and handsome splints of cedar, or spruce, or pine, rifted with a sledge and cleaver. The fireplace, the most important place of all, was in shape and size like the chimney, and directly under it, defined by a log fence or fender on the ground, and a heap of ashes, a foot or two deep within, with solid benches of split logs running round it. Here the fire usually melts the snow, and dries the rain before it can descend to quench it. The faded beds of arbor vitae leaves extended under the eaves on either hand. There was the place for the water pail, pork barrel, and wash basin, and generally a dingy pack of cards left on a log. Usually a good deal of whittling was expended on the latch, which was made of wood, in the form of an iron one. These houses are made comfortable by the huge fires, which can be afforded night and day. Usually the scenery about them is drear and savage enough; and the logger's camp is as completely in the woods as a fungus at the foot of a pine in a swamp; no outlook but to the sky overhead; no more clearing than is made by cutting down the trees of which it is built, and those which are necessary for fuel. If only it be well sheltered and convenient to his work, and near a spring, he wastes no thought on the prospect. They are very proper forest houses, the stems of the trees collected together and piled up around a man to keep out wind and rain— made of living green logs, hanging with moss and lichen, and with the curls and fringes of the yellow birch bark, and dripping with resin, fresh and moist, and redolent of swampy odors, with that sort of vigor and perennialness even about them that toadstools suggest.[1] The logger's fare consists of tea, molasses, flour, pork (sometimes beef), and beans. A great proportion of the beans raised in Massachusetts find their market here. On expeditions it is only hard bread and pork, often raw, slice upon slice, with tea or water, as the case may be.

The primitive wood is always and everywhere damp and mossy, so that I traveled constantly with the impression that I was in a swamp; and only when it was remarked that this or that tract, judging from the quality of the timber on it, would make a profitable clearing, was I reminded, that if the sun were let in it would make a dry field, like the few I had seen, at once. The best shod for the most part travel with wet feet. If the ground was so wet and spongy at this, the dryest part of a dry season, what must it be in the spring? The woods hereabouts abounded in beech and yellow birch, of which last there were some very large specimens; also

---

[1] Springer, in his Forest Life (1851), says that they first remove the leaves and turf from the spot where they intend to build a camp, for fear of fire; also, that "the spruce-tree is generally selected for camp-building, it being light, straight, and quite free from sap"; that "the roof is finally covered with the boughs of the fir, spruce, and hemlock, so that when the snow falls upon the whole, the warmth of the camp is preserved in the coldest weather"; and that they make the log seat before the fire, called the "Deacon's Seat," of a spruce or fir split in halves, with three or four stout limbs left on one side for legs, which are not likely to get loose.

spruce, cedar, fir, and hemlock; but we saw only the stumps of the white pine here, some of them of great size, these having been already culled out, being the only tree much sought after, even as low down as this. Only a little spruce and hemlock beside had been logged here. The Eastern wood which is sold for fuel in Massachusetts all comes from below Bangor. It was the pine alone, chiefly the white pine, that had tempted any but the hunter to precede us on this route.

Waite's farm, thirteen miles from the Point, is an extensive and elevated clearing, from which we got a fine view of the river, rippling and gleaming far beneath us. My companions had formerly had a good view of Ktaadn and the other mountains here, but today it was so smoky that we could see nothing of them. We could overlook an immense country of uninterrupted forest, stretching away up the East Branch toward Canada on the north and northwest, and toward the Aroostook valley on the northeast; and imagine what wild life was stirring in its midst. Here was quite a field of corn for this region, whose peculiar dry scent we perceived a third of a mile off, before we saw it.

Eighteen miles from the Point brought us in sight of McCauslin's, or "Uncle George's," as he was familiarly called by my companions, to whom he was well known, where we intended to break our long fast. His house was in the midst of an extensive clearing or intervale, at the mouth of the Little Schoodic River, on the opposite or north bank of the Penobscot. So we collected on a point of the shore, that we might be seen, and fired our gun as a signal, which brought out his dogs forthwith, and thereafter their master, who in due time took us across in his batteau. This clearing was bounded abruptly, on all sides but the river, by the naked stems of the forest, as if you were to cut only a few feet square in the midst of a thousand acres of mowing, and set down a thimble therein. He had a whole heaven and horizon to himself, and the sun seemed to be journeying over his clearing only the livelong day. Here we concluded to spend the night, and wait for the Indians, as there was no stopping-place so convenient above. He had seen no Indians pass, and this did not often happen without his knowledge. He thought that his dogs sometimes gave notice of the approach of Indians half an hour before they arrived.

McCauslin was a Kennebec man, of Scotch descent, who had been a waterman twenty-two years, and had driven on the lakes and headwaters of the Penobscot five or six springs in succession, but was now settled here to raise supplies for the lumberers and for himself. He entertained us a day or two with true Scotch hospitality, and would accept no recompense for it. A man of a dry wit and shrewdness, and a general intelligence which I had not looked for in the back woods. In fact, the deeper you penetrate into the woods, the more intelligent, and, in one sense, less countrified do you find the inhabitants; for always the pioneer has been a traveler, and, to some extent, a man of the world; and, as the distances with which he is familiar are greater, so is his information more general and far reaching than the villager's. If I were to look for a narrow, uninformed, and countrified mind, as opposed to the intelligence and refinement which are thought to emanate from cities, it would be among the rusty inhabitants of an old-settled country, on farms all run out and gone to seed with life-everlasting, in the towns about Boston, even on the highroad in Concord, and not in the back woods of Maine.

Supper was got before our eyes in the ample kitchen, by a fire which would have roasted an ox; many whole logs, four feet long, were consumed to boil our tea-kettle—birch, or beech, or maple, the same summer and winter; and the dishes were soon smoking on the table, late the armchair, against the wall, from which one of the party was expelled. The arms of the chair formed the frame on which the table rested; and, when the round top was turned up against the wall, it formed the back of the chair, and was no more in the way than the wall itself. This, we noticed, was the prevailing fashion in these log houses, in order to economize in room. There were piping-hot wheaten cakes, the flour having been brought up the river in batteaux—no Indian bread, for the upper part of Maine, it will be remembered, is a wheat country—and ham, eggs, and potatoes, and milk and cheese, the produce of the farm; and also shad and salmon, tea sweetened with molasses, and sweet cakes, in contradistinction to the hot cakes not sweetened, the one white, the other yellow, to wind up with. Such we found was the prevailing fare, ordinary and extraordinary, along this river. Mountain cranberries (*Vaccinium Vitis-Idaea*), stewed and sweetened, were the common dessert. Everything here was in profusion, and the best of its kind. Butter was in such plenty that it was commonly used, before it was salted, to grease boots with.

In the night we were entertained by the sound of raindrops on the cedar splints which covered the roof, and awaked the next morning with a drop or two in our eyes. It had set in for a storm, and we made up our minds not to forsake such comfortable quarters with this prospect, but wait for Indians and fair weather. It rained and drizzled and gleamed by turns, the livelong day. What we did there, how we killed the time would perhaps be idle to tell; how many times we buttered our boots, and how often a drowsy one was seen to sidle off to the bedroom. When it held up, I strolled up and down the bank, and gathered the harebell and cedar berries, which grew there; or else we tried by turns the long-handled axe on the logs before the door. The axe-helves here were made to chop standing on the log—a primitive log of course—and were, therefore, nearly a foot longer than with us. One while we walked over the farm and visited his well-filled barns with McCauslin. There were one other man and two women only here. He kept horses, cows, oxen, and sheep. I think he said that he was the first to bring a plow and a cow so far; and he might have added the last, with only two exceptions. The potato-rot had found him out here, too, the previous year, and got half or two thirds of his crop, though the seed was of his own raising. Oats, grass, and potatoes were his staples; but he raised, also, a few carrots and turnips, and "a little corn for the hens," for this was all that he dared risk, for fear that it would not ripen. Melons, squashes, sweet corn, beans, tomatoes, and many other vegetables, could not be ripened there.

The very few settlers along this stream were obviously tempted by the cheapness of the land mainly. When I asked McCauslin why more settlers did not come in, he answered, that one reason was, they could not buy the land, it belonged to individuals or companies who were afraid that their wild lands would be settled, and so incorporated into towns, and they be taxed for them; but to settling on the State's land there was no such hindrance. For his own part, he wanted no neighbors—he didn't wish to see any road by his house. Neighbors, even the best, were a trouble and expense, especially on the score of cattle and fences. They might live across the river, perhaps, but not on the same side.

The chickens here were protected by the dogs. As McCauslin said, "The old one took it up first, and she taught the pup, and now they had got it into their heads that it wouldn't do to have anything of the bird kind on the premises." A hawk hovering over was not allowed to alight, but barked off by the dogs circling underneath; and a pigeon, or a "yellow-hammer," as they called the pigeon woodpecker, on a dead limb or stump, was instantly expelled. It was the main business of their day, and kept them constantly coming and going. One would rush out of the house on the least alarm given by the other.

When it rained hardest, we returned to the house, and took down a tract from the shelf. There was the "Wandering Jew," cheap edition, and fine print, the "Criminal Calendar," and "Parish's Geography," and flash novels two or three. Under the pressure of circumstances, we read a little in these. With such aid, the press is not so feeble an engine, after all. This house, which was a fair specimen of those on this river, was built of huge logs, which peeped out everywhere, and were chinked with clay and moss. It contained four or five rooms. There were no sawed boards, or shingles, or clapboards, about it; and scarcely any tool but the axe had been used in its construction. The partitions were made of long clapboard-like splints, of spruce or cedar, turned to a delicate salmon-color by the smoke. The roof and sides were covered with the same, instead of shingles and clapboards, and some of a much thicker and larger size were used for the floor. These were all so straight and smooth, that they answered the purpose admirably, and a careless observer would not have suspected that they were not sawed and planed. The chimney and hearth were of vast size, and made of stone. The broom was a few twigs of arbor vitae tied to a stick; and a pole was suspended over the hearth, close to the ceiling, to dry stockings and clothes on. I noticed that the floor was full of small, dingy holes, as if made with a gimlet, but which were, in fact, made by the spikes, nearly an inch long, which the lumberers wear in their boots to prevent their slipping on wet logs. Just above McCauslin's, there is a rocky rapid, where logs jam in the spring; and many "drivers" are there collected, who frequent his house for supplies; these were their tracks which I saw.

At sundown McCauslin pointed away over the forest, across the river, to signs of fair weather amid the clouds —some evening redness there. For even there the points of compass held; and there was a quarter of the heavens appropriated to sunrise and another to sunset.

The next morning, the weather proving fair enough for our purpose, we prepared to start, and, the Indians having failed us, persuaded McCauslin, who was not unwilling to revisit the scenes of his driving, to accompany us in their stead, intending to engage one other boatman on the way. A strip of cotton cloth for a tent, a couple of blankets, which would suffice for the whole party, fifteen pounds of hard bread, ten pounds of "clear" pork, and a little tea, made up "Uncle George's" pack. The last three articles were calculated to be provision enough for six men for a week, with what we might pick up. A tea-kettle, a frying-pan, and an axe, to be obtained at the last house, would complete our outfit.

We were soon out of McCauslin's clearing, and in the evergreen woods again. The obscure trail made by the two settlers above, which even the woodman is sometimes puzzled to discern, ere long crossed a narrow, open strip in the woods overrun with weeds, called the Burnt Land, where a fire had raged formerly, stretching northward nine or ten miles, to Millinocket Lake. At the end of three miles, we reached Shad Pond, or

Noliseemack, an expansion of the river. Hodge, the Assistant State Geologist, who passed through this on the 25th of June, 1837, says, "We pushed our boat through an acre or more of buck-beans, which had taken root at the bottom, and bloomed above the surface in the greatest profusion and beauty." Thomas Fowler's house is four miles from McCauslin's, on the shore of the pond, at the mouth of the Millinocket River, and eight miles from the lake of the same name, on the latter stream. This lake affords a more direct course to Ktaadn, but we preferred to follow the Penobscot and the Pamadumcook lakes. Fowler was just completing a new log hut, and was sawing out a window through the logs, nearly two feet thick, when he arrived. He had begun to paper his house with spruce bark, turned inside out, which had a good effect, and was in keeping with the circumstances. Instead of water we got here a draught of beer, which, it was allowed, would be better; clear and thin, but strong and stringent as the cedar sap. It was as if we sucked at the very teats of Nature's pine-clad bosom in these parts—the sap of all Millinocket botany commingled—the topmost, most fantastic, and spiciest sprays of the primitive wood, and whatever invigorating and stringent gum or essence it afforded steeped and dissolved in it—a lumberer's drink, which would acclimate and naturalize a man at once—which would make him see green, and, if he slept, dream that he heard the wind sough among the pines. Here was a fife, praying to be played on, through which we breathed a few tuneful strains—brought hither to tame wild beasts. As we stood upon the pile of chips by the door, fish hawks were sailing overhead; and here, over Shad Pond, might daily be witnessed the tyranny of the bald eagle over that bird. Tom pointed away over the lake to a bald eagle's nest, which was plainly visible more than a mile off, on a pine, high above the surrounding forest, and was frequented from year to year by the same pair, and held sacred by him. There were these two houses only there, his low hut and the eagles' airy carload of fagots. Thomas Fowler, too, was persuaded to join us, for two men were necessary to manage the batteau, which was soon to be our carriage, and these men needed to be cool and skillful for the navigation of the Penobscot. Thom's pack was soon made, for he had not far to look for his waterman's boots, and a red flannel shirt. This is the favorite color with lumbermen; and red flannel is reputed to possess some mysterious virtues, to be most healthful and convenient in respect to perspiration. In every gang there will be a large proportion of red birds. We took here a poor and leaky batteau, and began to pole up the Millinocket two miles, to the elder Fowler's, in order to avoid the Grand Falls of the Penobscot, intending to exchange our batteau there for a better. The Millinocket is a small, shallow, and sandy stream, full of what I took to be lamprey-eels' or suckers' nests, and lined with musquash-cabins, but free from rapids, according to Fowler, excepting at its outlet from the lake. He was at this time engaged in cutting the native grass—rush-grass and meadow-clover, as he called it—on the meadows and small, low islands of this stream. We noticed flattened places in the grass on either side, where, he said, a moose had laid down the night before, adding, that there were thousands in these meadows.

Old Fowler's, on the Millinocket, six miles from McCauslin's, and twenty-four from the Point, is the last house. Gibson's, on the Sowadnehunk, is the only clearing above, but that had proved a failure, and was long since deserted. Fowler is the oldest inhabitant of these woods. He formerly lived a few miles from here, on the south side of the West Branch, where he built his house sixteen years ago, the first house built above the Five Islands. Here our new batteau was to be carried over the first portage of two miles, round the Grand Falls of the Penobscot, on a horse-sled made of saplings, to jump the numerous rocks in the way; but we had to wait a couple of hours for them to catch the horses, which were pastured at a distance, amid the stumps, and had wandered still farther off. The last of the salmon for this season had just been caught, and were still fresh in pickle, from which enough was extracted to fill our empty kettle, and so graduate our introduction to simpler forest fare. The week before they had lost nine sheep here out of their first flock, by the wolves. The surviving sheep came round the house, and seemed frightened, which induced them to go and look for the rest, when they found seven dead and lacerated, and two still alive. These last they carried to the house, and, as Mrs. Fowler said, they were merely scratched in the throat, and had no more visible wound than would be produced by the prick of a pin. She sheared off the wool from their throats, and washed them, and put on some salve, and turned them out, but in a few moments they were missing, and had not been found since. In fact, they were all poisoned, and those that were found swelled up at once, so that they saved neither skin nor wool. This realized the old fables of the wolves and the sheep, and convinced me that that ancient hostility still existed. Verily, the shepherd-boy did not need to sound a false alarm this time. There were steel traps by the door, of various sizes, for wolves, otter, and bears, with large claws instead of teeth, to catch in their sinews. Wolves are frequently killed with poisoned bait.

At length, after we had dined here on the usual backwoods fare, the horses arrived, and we hauled our bat-

teau out of the water, and lashed it to its wicker carriage, and, throwing in our packs, walked on before,
leaving the boatmen and driver, who was Tom's brother,
to manage the concern. The route, which led through
the wild pasture where the sheep were killed, was in
some places the roughest ever traveled by horses, over
rocky hills, where the sled bounced and slid along, like
a vessel pitching in a storm; and one man was as necessary to stand at the stern, to prevent the boat from being
wrecked, as a helmsman in the roughest sea. The philosophy of our progress was something like this: when
the runners struck a rock three or four feet high, the sled
bounced back and upwards at the same time; but, as the
horses never ceased pulling, it came down on the top of
the rock, and so we got over. This portage probably followed the trail of an ancient Indian carry round these
falls. By two o'clock we, who had walked on before,
reached the river above the falls, not far from the outlet
of Quakish Lake, and waited for the batteau to come
up. We had been here but a short time, when a thunder-
shower was seen coming up from the west, over the still
invisible lakes, and that pleasant wilderness which we
were so eager to become acquainted with; and soon the
heavy drops began to patter on the leaves around us. I
had just selected the prostrate trunk of a huge pine, five
or six feet in diameter, and was crawling under it, when,
luckily, the boat arrived. It would have amused a sheltered man to witness the manner in which it was un-
lashed, and whirled over, while the first water-spout
burst upon us. It was no sooner in the hands of the eager
company than it was abandoned to the first revolutionary impulse, and to gravity, to adjust it; and they might
have been seen all stooping to its shelter, and wriggling
under like so many eels, before it was fairly deposited
on the ground. When all were under, we propped up

the lee side, and busied ourselves there whittling thole-
pins for rowing, when we should reach the lakes; and
made the woods ring, between the claps of thunder,
with such boat-songs as we could remember. The horses
stood sleek and shining with the rain, all drooping and
crestfallen, while deluge after deluge washed over us;
but the bottom of a boat may be relied on for a tight
roof. At length, after two hours' delay at this place,
a streak of fair weather appeared in the northwest,
whither our course now lay, promising a serene evening
for our voyage; and the driver returned with his horses,
while we made haste to launch our boat, and commence
our voyage in good earnest.

There were six of us, including the two boatmen.
With our packs heaped up near the bows, and ourselves
disposed as baggage to trim the boat, with instructions
not to move in case we should strike a rock, more than
so many barrels of pork, we pushed out into the first
rapid, a slight specimen of the stream we had to navi-
gate. With Uncle George in the stern, and Tom in the
bows, each using a spruce pole about twelve feet long,
pointed with iron,[1] and poling on the same side, we
shot up the rapids like a salmon, the water rushing and
roaring around, so that only a practiced eye could distinguish a safe course, or tell what was deep water and
what rocks, frequently grazing the latter on one or both
sides, with a hundred as narrow escapes as ever the Argo
had in passing through the Symplegades. I, who had
had some experience in boating, had never experienced
any half so exhilarating before. We were lucky to have
exchanged our Indians, whom we did not know, for these
men, who, together with Tom's brother, were reputed
the best boatmen on the river, and were at once indispensable pilots and pleasant companions. The canoe

---

[1] *The Canadians call it* picquer de fond.

is smaller, more easily upset, and sooner worn out; and the Indian is said not to be so skillful in the management of the batteau. He is, for the most part, less to be relied on, and more disposed to sulks and whims. The utmost familiarity with dead streams, or with the ocean, would not prepare a man for this peculiar navigation; and the most skillful boatman anywhere else would here be obliged to take out his boat and carry round a hundred times, still with great risk, as well as delay, where the practiced batteau-man poles up with comparative ease and safety. The hardy "voyageur" pushes with incredible perserverance and success quite up to the foot of the falls, and then only carries round some perpendicular ledge, and launches again in

"The torrent's smoothness, ere it dash below,"

to struggle with the boiling rapids above. The Indians say that the river once ran both ways, one half up and the other down, but that, since the white man came, it all runs down, and now they must laboriously pole their canoes against the stream, and carry them over numerous portages. In the summer, all stores—the grindstone and the plow of the pioneer, flour, pork, and utensils for the explorer—must be conveyed up the river in batteaux; and many a cargo and many a boatman is lost in these waters. In the winter, however, which is very equable and long, the ice is the great highway, and the loggers' team penetrates to Chesuncook Lake, and still higher up, even two hundred miles above Bangor. Imagine the solitary sled-track running far up into the snowy and evergreen wilderness, hemmed in closely for a hundred miles by the forest, and again stretching straight across the broad surfaces of concealed lakes!

We were soon in the smooth water of the Quakish

Lake, and took our turns at rowing and paddling across it. It is a small, irregular, but handsome lake, shut in on all sides by the forest, and showing no traces of man but some low boom in a distant cove, reserved for spring use. The spruce and cedar on its shores, hung with gray lichens, looked at a distance like the ghosts of trees. Ducks were sailing here and there on its surface, and a solitary loon, like a more living wave—a vital spot on the lake's surface—laughed and frolicked, and showed its straight leg, for our amusement. Joe Merry Mountain appeared in the northwest, as if it were looking down on this lake especially; and we had our first, but a partial view of Ktaadn, its summit veiled in clouds, like a dark isthmus in that quarter, connecting the heavens with the earth. After two miles of smooth rowing across this lake, we found ourselves in the river again, which was a continuous rapid for one mile, to the dam, requiring all the strength and skill of our boatmen to pole up it.

This dam is a quite important and expensive work for this country, whither cattle and horses cannot penetrate in the summer, raising the whole river ten feet, and flooding, as they said, some sixty square miles by means of the innumerable lakes with which the river connects. It is a lofty and solid structure, with sloping piers, some distance above, made of frames of logs filled with stones, to break the ice.[1] Here every log pays toll as it passes through the sluices.

We filed into the rude loggers' camp at this place, such as I have described, without ceremony, and the cook, at that moment the sole occupant, at once set

---

[1] Even the Jesuit missionaries, accustomed to the St. Lawrence and other rivers of Canada, in their first expeditions to the Abenaquinois, speak of rivers ferrées de rochers, shod with rocks. See also No. 10 Relations, for 1647, p. 185.

about preparing tea for his visitors. His fireplace, which the rain had converted into a mud-puddle, was soon blazing again, and we sat down on the log benches around it to dry us. On the well-flattened and somewhat faded beds of arbor vitae leaves, which stretched on either hand under the eaves behind us, lay an odd leaf of the Bible, some genealogical chapter out of the Old Testament; and, half buried by the leaves, we found Emerson's Address on West India Emancipation, which had been left here formerly by one of our company, and *had made two converts to the Liberty party here,* as I was told; also, an odd number of the *Westminster Review,* for 1834, and a pamphlet entitled "History of the Erection of the Monument on the Grave of Myron Holly." This was the readable or reading matter in a lumberer's camp in the Maine woods, thirty miles from a road, which would be given up to the bears in a fortnight. These things were well thumbed and soiled. This gang was headed by one John Morrison, a good specimen of a Yankee; and was necessarily composed of men not bred to the business of dam-building, but who were jacks-at-all-trades, handy with the axe, and other simple implements, and well skilled in wood and water craft. We had hot cakes for our supper even here, white as snowballs, but without butter, and the never-failing sweet cakes, with which we filled our pockets, foreseeing that we should not soon meet with the like again. Such delicate puffballs seemed a singular diet for backwoodsmen. There was also tea without milk, sweetened with molasses. And so, exchanging a word with John Morrison and his gang when we had returned to the shore, and also exchanging our batteau for a better still, we made haste to improve the little daylight that remained. This camp, exactly twenty-nine miles from Mattawamkeag Point by the way we had come, and about one hundred from Bangor by the river, was the last human habitation of any kind in this direction. Beyond, there was no trail, and the river and lakes, by batteaux and canoes, was considered the only practicable route. We were about thirty miles by the river from the summit of Ktaadn, which was in sight, though not more than twenty, perhaps, in a straight line.

Civil Disobedience

It is one of the brighter ironies of literature that this, the most electric of Thoreau's essays, should have been first published in a polite miscellany entitled Æsthetic Papers and edited by the Bostonian sister-in-law of Nathaniel Hawthorne. It came out just a year after the Communist Manifesto, in 1849. The comfort it has for adherents of Karl Marx is scant but it is not quite the source of strength to today's conservatives either that its opening sentence would seem to imply. The iron rigor of Thoreau's philosophic anarchy is uncomfortable to both sides. But Gandhi, struggling in South Africa, knew it to be just what he wanted ("It left a deep impression upon me," he later admitted); and across the oceans its results are still being read.

C. B.

I HEARTILY accept the motto, "That government is best which governs least"; and I should like to see it acted up to more rapidly and systematically. Carried out, it finally amounts to this, which also I believe —"That government is best which governs not at all"; and when men are prepared for it, that will be the kind of government which they will have. Government is at best but an expedient; but most governments are usually, and all governments are sometimes, inexpedient. The objections which have been brought against a standing army, and they are many and weighty, and deserve to prevail, may also at last be brought against a standing government. The standing army is only an arm of the standing government. The government itself, which is only the mode which the people have chosen to execute their will, is equally liable to be abused and perverted before the people can act through it. Witness the present Mexican war, the work of comparatively a few individuals using the standing government as their tool; for, in the outset, the people would not have consented to this measure.

This American government—what is it but a tradition, though a recent one, endeavoring to transmit itself unimpaired to posterity, but each instant losing some of its integrity? It has not the vitality and force of a single living man; for a single man can bend it to his will. It is a sort of wooden gun to the people themselves. But it is not the less necessary for this; for the people must have some complicated machinery or other, and hear its din, to satisfy that idea of government which they have. Governments show thus how successfully men can be imposed on, even impose on themselves, for their own advantage. It is excellent, we must all allow. Yet this government never of itself furthered any enterprise, but by the alacrity with which it got out of its way. *It* does not keep the country free. *It* does not settle the West. *It* does not educate. The character inherent in the American people has done all that has been accomplished; and it would have done somewhat more, if the government had not sometimes got in its way. For government is an expedient by which men would fain succeed in letting one another alone; and, as has been said, when it is most expedient, the governed are most let alone by it. Trade and commerce, if they were not made of india-rubber, would never manage to bounce over the obstacles which legislators are continually putting in their way; and, if one were to judge these men wholly by the effects of their actions and not partly by their intentions, they would deserve to be classed and punished with those mischievous persons who put obstructions on the railroads.

But, to speak practically and as a citizen, unlike those who call themselves no-government men, I ask for, not at once no government, but *at once* a better government. Let every man make known what kind of government would command his respect, and that will be one step toward obtaining it.

After all, the practical reason why, when the power is once in the hands of the people, a majority are permitted, and for a long period continue, to rule is not because they are most likely to be in the right, nor because this seems fairest to the minority, but because they are physically the strongest. But a government in which the majority rule in all cases cannot be based on justice, even as far as men understand it. Can there not be a government in which majorities do not virtually decide right and wrong, but conscience?—in which majorities decide only those questions to which the rule of expediency is applicable? Must the citizen ever for a moment, or in the least degree, resign his conscience to the legislator? Why has every man a conscience, then? I think that we should be men first, and subjects afterward. It is not desirable to cultivate a respect for the law, so much as for the right. The only obligation which I have a right to assume is to do at any time what I think right. It is truly enough said that a corporation has no conscience; but a corporation of conscientious men is a corporation *with* a conscience. Law never made men a whit more just; and, by means of their respect for it, even the well-disposed are daily made the agents of injustice. A common and natural result of an undue respect for law is, that you may see a file of soldiers, colonel, captain, corporal, privates, powder-monkeys, and all, marching in admirable order over hill and dale to the wars, against their wills, ay, against their common sense and consciences, which makes it very steep marching indeed, and produces a palpitation of the heart. They have no doubt that it is a damnable business in which they are concerned; they are all peaceably inclined. Now, what are they? Men at all? or small movable forts and magazines, at the service of some unscrupulous man in power? Visit the Navy Yard, and behold a marine, such a man as an American government can make, or such as it can make a man with its black arts—a mere shadow and reminiscence of humanity, a man laid out alive and standing, and already, as one may say, buried under arms with funeral accompaniments, though it may be,

> "Not a drum was heard, not a funeral note,
>   As his corse to the rampart we hurried;
> Not a soldier discharged his farewell shot
>   O'er the grave where our hero we buried."

The mass of men serve the state thus, not as men mainly, but as machines, with their bodies. They are the standing army, and the militia, jailers, constables, *posse comitatus,* etc. In most cases there is no free exercise whatever of the judgment or of the moral sense; but they put themselves on a level with wood and earth and stones; and wooden men can perhaps be manufactured that will serve the purpose as well. Such command no more respect than men of straw or a lump of dirt. They have the same sort of worth only as horses and dogs. Yet such as these even are commonly esteemed good citizens. Others—as most legislators, politicians, lawyers, ministers, and office-holders—serve the state chiefly with their heads; and, as they rarely make any moral distinctions, they are as likely to serve the devil, without *intending* it, as God. A very few—as heroes, patriots, martyrs, reformers in the great sense, and *men* —serve the state with their consciences also, and so necessarily resist it for the most part; and they are commonly treated as enemies by it. A wise man will only be useful as a man, and will not submit to be "clay," and "stop a hole to keep the wind away," but leave that office to his dust at least:

> "I am too high-born to be propertied,
>   To be a secondary at control,
>   Or useful serving-man and instrument
>   To any sovereign state throughout the world."

He who gives himself entirely to his fellow men appears to them useless and selfish; but he who gives himself partially to them is pronounced a benefactor and philanthropist.

How does it become a man to behave toward this American government today? I answer, that he cannot without disgrace be associated with it. I cannot for an instant recognize that political organization as *my* government which is the *slave's* government also.

All men recognize the right of revolution; that is, the right to refuse allegiance to, and to resist, the government, when its tyranny or its inefficiency are great and unendurable. But almost all say that such is not the case now. But such was the case, they think, in the Revolution of '75. If one were to tell me that this was a bad government because it taxed certain foreign commodities brought to its ports, it is most probable that I should not make an ado about it, for I can do without them. All machines have their friction; and possibly this does enough good to counterbalance the evil. At any rate, it is a great evil to make a stir about it. But when the friction comes to have its machine, and oppression and robbery are organized, I say, let us not have such a machine any longer. In other words, when a sixth of the population of a nation which has undertaken to be the refuge of liberty are slaves, and a whole country is unjustly overrun and conquered by a foreign army, and subjected to military law, I think that it is not too soon for honest men to rebel and revolutionize. What makes this duty the more urgent is the fact that the country so overrun is not our own, but ours is the invading army.

Paley, a common authority with many on moral questions, in his chapter on the "Duty of Submission to Civil Government," resolves all civil obligation into expediency; and he proceeds to say that "so long as the interest of the whole society requires it, that is, so long as the established government cannot be resisted or changed without public inconveniency, it is the will of God . . . that the established government be obeyed—and no longer. This principle being admitted, the justice of every particular case of resistance is reduced to a computation of the quantity of the danger and grievance on the one side, and of the probability and expense of redressing it on the other." Of this, he says, every man shall judge for himself. But Paley appears never to have contemplated those cases to which the rule of expediency does not apply, in which a people, as well as an individual, must do justice, cost what it may. If I have unjustly wrested a plank from a drowning man, I must restore it to him though I drown myself. This, according to Paley, would be inconvenient. But he that would save his life, in such a case, shall lose it. This people must cease to hold slaves, and to make war on Mexico, though it cost them their existence as a people.

In their practice, nations agree with Paley; but does anyone think that Massachusetts does exactly what is right at the present crisis?

"A drab of state, a cloth-o'-silver slut,
  To have her train borne up, and her soul trail in the dirt."

Practically speaking, the opponents to a reform in Massachusetts are not a hundred thousand politicians at the

South, but a hundred thousand merchants and farmers here, who are more interested in commerce and agriculture than they are in humanity, and are not prepared to do justice to the slave and to Mexico, *cost what it may*. I quarrel not with far-off foes, but with those who, near at home, co-operate with, and do the bidding of, those far away, and without whom the latter would be harmless. We are accustomed to say, that the mass of men are unprepared; but improvement is slow, because the few are not materially wiser or better than the many. It is not so important that many should be as good as you, as that there be some absolute goodness somewhere; for that will leaven the whole lump. There are thousands who are *in opinion* opposed to slavery and to the war, who yet in effect do nothing to put an end to them; who, esteeming themselves children of Washington and Franklin, sit down with their hands in their pockets, and say that they know not what to do, and do nothing; who even postpone the question of freedom to the question of free trade, and quietly read the prices-current along with the latest advices from Mexico, after dinner, and, it may be, fall asleep over them both. What is the price-current of an honest man and patriot today? They hesitate, and they regret, and sometimes they petition; but they do nothing in earnest and with effect. They will wait, well disposed, for others to remedy the evil, that they may no longer have it to regret. At most, they give only a cheap vote, and a feeble countenance and Godspeed, to the right, as it goes by them. There are nine hundred and ninety-nine patrons of virtue to one virtuous man. But it is easier to deal with the real possessor of a thing than with the temporary guardian of it.

All voting is a sort of gaming, like checkers or backgammon, with a slight moral tinge to it, a playing with right and wrong, with moral questions; and betting naturally accompanies it. The character of the voters is not staked. I cast my vote, perchance, as I think right; but I am not vitally concerned that that right should prevail. I am willing to leave it to the majority. Its obligation, therefore, never exceeds that of expediency. Even voting *for the right* is *doing* nothing for it. It is only expressing to men feebly your desire that it should prevail. A wise man will not leave the right to the mercy of chance, nor wish it to prevail through the power of the majority. There is but little virtue in the action of masses of men. When the majority shall at length vote for the abolition of slavery, it will be because they are indifferent to slavery, or because there is but little slavery left to be abolished by their vote. *They* will then be the only slaves. Only *his* vote can hasten the abolition of slavery who asserts his own freedom by his vote.

I hear of a convention to be held at Baltimore, or elsewhere, for the selection of a candidate for the Presidency, made up chiefly of editors, and men who are politicians by profession; but I think, what is it to any independent, intelligent, and respectable man what decision they may come to? Shall we not have the advantage of his wisdom and honesty, nevertheless? Can we not count upon some independent votes? Are there not many individuals in the country who do not attend conventions? But no: I find that the respectable man, so called, has immediately drifted from his position, and despairs of his country, when his country has more reason to despair of him. He forthwith adopts one of the candidates thus selected as the only *available* one, thus proving that he is himself *available* for any purposes of the demagogue. His vote is of no more worth than that of any unprincipled foreigner or hireling native, who may have been bought. O for a man who is a *man*, and, as my neighbor says, has a bone in his back which you cannot pass your hand through! Our statistics are at fault: the population has been returned too large. How many *men* are there to a square thousand miles in this country? Hardly one. Does not America offer any inducement for men to settle here? The American has dwindled into an Odd Fellow—one who may be known by the development of his organ of gregariousness, and a manifest lack of intellect and cheerful self-reliance; whose first and chief concern, on coming into the world, is to see that the almshouses are in good repair; and, before yet he has lawfully donned the virile garb, to collect a fund for the support of the widows and orphans that may be; who, in short, ventures to live only by the aid of the Mutual Insurance company, which has promised to bury him decently.

It is not a man's duty, as a matter of course, to devote himself to the eradication of any, even the most enormous, wrong; he may still properly have other concerns to engage him; but it is his duty, at least, to wash his hands of it, and, if he gives it no thought longer, not to give it practically his support. If I devote myself to other pursuits and contemplations, I must first see, at least, that I do not pursue them sitting upon another man's shoulders. I must get off him first, that he may pursue his contemplations too. See what gross inconsistency is tolerated. I have heard some of my townsmen say, "I should like to have them order me out to help put down an insurrection of the slaves, or to march to Mexico— see if I would go"; and yet these very men have each, directly by their allegiance, and so indirectly, at least, by their money, furnished a substitute. The soldier is applauded who refuses to serve in an unjust war by those who do not refuse to sustain the unjust government which makes the war; is applauded by those whose own act and authority he disregards and sets at naught; as if the state were penitent to that degree that it hired one to scourge it while it sinned, but not to that degree that it left off sinning for a moment. Thus, under the name of Order and Civil Government, we are all made at last to pay homage to and support our own meanness. After the first blush of sin comes its indifference; and from immoral it becomes, as it were, *un*moral, and not quite unnecessary to that life which we have made.

The broadest and most prevalent error requires the most disinterested virtue to sustain it. The slight reproach to which the virtue of patriotism is commonly liable, the noble are most likely to incur. Those who, while they disapprove of the character and measures of a government, yield to it their allegiance and support are undoubtedly its most conscientious supporters, and so frequently the most serious obstacles to reform. Some are petitioning the State to dissolve the Union, to disregard the requisitions of the President. Why do they not dissolve it themselves—the union between themselves and the State—and refuse to pay their quota into its treasury? Do not they stand in the same relation to the State that the State does to the Union? And have not the same reasons prevented the State from resisting the Union which have prevented them from resisting the State?

How can a man be satisfied to entertain an opinion merely, and enjoy *it?* Is there any enjoyment in it, if his opinion is that he is aggrieved? If you are cheated out of a single dollar by your neighbor, you do not rest satisfied with knowing that you are cheated, or with saying that you are cheated, or even with petitioning him to pay you your due; but you take effectual steps at once to obtain the full amount, and see that you are never cheated again. Action from principle, the perception and the performance of right, changes things and relations; it is essentially revolutionary, and does not consist wholly with anything which was. It not only divides States and churches, it divides families; ay, it divides the *individual*, separating the diabolical in him from the divine.

Unjust laws exist: shall we be content to obey them, or shall we endeavor to amend them, and obey them until we have succeeded, or shall we transgress them at once? Men generally, under such a government as this, think that they ought to wait until they have persuaded the majority to alter them. They think that, if they should resist, the remedy would be worse than the evil. But it is the fault of the government itself that the remedy *is* worse than the evil. *It* makes it worse. Why is it not more apt to anticipate and provide for reform? Why does it not cherish its wise minority? Why does it cry and resist before it is hurt? Why does it not encourage its citizens to be on the alert to point out its faults, and *do* better than it would have them? Why does it always crucify Christ, and excommunicate Copernicus and Luther, and pronounce Washington and Franklin rebels?

One would think, that a deliberate and practical denial of its authority was the only offence never contemplated by government; else, why has it not assigned its definite, its suitable and proportionate, penalty? If a man who has no property refuses but once to earn nine shillings for the State, he is put in prison for a period unlimited by any law that I know, and determined only by the discretion of those who placed him there; but if he should steal ninety times nine shillings from the State, he is soon permitted to go at large again.

If the injustice is part of the necessary friction of the

machine of government, let it go, let it go: perchance it will wear smooth—certainly the machine will wear out. If the injustice has a spring, or a pulley, or a rope, or a crank, exclusively for itself, then perhaps you may consider whether the remedy will not be worse than the evil; but if it is of such a nature that it requires you to be the agent of injustice to another, then, I say, break the law. Let your life be a counter-friction to stop the machine. What I have to do is to see, at any rate, that I do not lend myself to the wrong which I condemn.

As for adopting the ways which the State has provided for remedying the evil, I know not of such ways. They take too much time, and a man's life will be gone. I have other affairs to attend to. I came into this world, not chiefly to make this a good place to live in, but to live in it, be it good or bad. A man has not everything to do, but something; and because he cannot do *everything*, it is not necessary that he should do *something* wrong. It is not my business to be petitioning the Governor or the Legislature any more than it is theirs to petition me; and if they should not hear my petition, what should I do then? But in this case the State has provided no way: its very Constitution is the evil. This may seem to be harsh and stubborn and unconciliatory; but it is to treat with the utmost kindness and consideration the only spirit that can appreciate or deserves it. So is all change for the better, like birth and death, which convulse the body.

I do not hesitate to say, that those who call themselves Abolitionists should at once effectually withdraw their support, both in person and property, from the government of Massachusetts, and not wait till they constitute a majority of one, before they suffer the right to prevail through them. I think that it is enough if they have God on their side, without waiting for that other one. Moreover, any man more right than his neighbors constitutes a majority of one already.

I meet this American government, or its representative, the State government, directly, and face to face, once a year—no more—in the person of its tax-gatherer; this is the only mode in which a man situated as I am necessarily meets it; and it then says distinctly, Recognize me; and the simplest, the most effectual, and, in the present posture of affairs, the indispensablest mode of treating with it on this head, of expressing your little satisfaction with and love for it, is to deny it then. My civil neighbor, the tax-gatherer, is the very man I have to deal with—for it is, after all, with men and not with parchment that I quarrel—and he has voluntarily chosen to be an agent of the government. How shall he ever know well what he is and does as an officer of the government, or as a man, until he is obliged to consider whether he shall treat me, his neighbor, for whom he has respect, as a neighbor and well-disposed man, or as a maniac and disturber of the peace, and see if he can get over this obstruction to his neighborliness without a ruder and more impetuous thought or speech corresponding with his action. I know this well, that if one thousand, if one hundred, if ten men whom I could name—if ten *honest* men only—ay, if *one* HONEST man, in this State of Massachusetts, *ceasing to hold slaves,* were actually to withdraw from this copartnership, and be locked up in the county jail therefor, it would be the abolition of slavery in America. For it matters not how small the beginning may seem to be: what is once well done is done forever. But we love better to talk about it: that we say is our mission. Reform keeps many scores of newspapers in its service, but not one man. If my esteemed neighbor, the State's ambassador, who will devote his days to the settlement of the question of human rights in the Council Chamber, instead of being threatened with the prisons of Carolina, were to sit down the prisoner of Massachusetts, that State which is so anxious to foist the sin of slavery upon her sister— though at present she can discover only an act of in-hospitality to be the ground of a quarrel with her—the Legislature would not wholly waive the subject the following winter.

Under a government which imprisons any unjustly, the true place for a just man is also a prison. The proper place today, the only place which Massachusetts has provided for her freer and less desponding spirits, is in her prisons, to be put out and locked out of the State by her own act, as they have already put themselves out by their principles. It is there that the fugitive slave, and the Mexican prisoner on parole, and the Indian come to plead the wrongs of his race should find them; on that separate, but more free and honorable, ground, where the State places those who are not *with* her, but *against* her—the only house in a slave State in which a free man can abide with honor. If any think that their influence would be lost there, and their voices no longer afflict the ear of the State, that they would not be as an enemy within its walls, they do not know by how much truth is stronger than error, nor how much more elo-quently and effectively he can combat injustice who has experienced a little in his own person. Cast your whole vote, not a strip of paper merely, but your whole in-fluence. A minority is powerless while it conforms to the majority; it is not even a minority then; but it is irre-sistible when it clogs by its whole weight. If the alterna-tive is to keep all just men in prison, or give up war and slavery, the State will not hesitate which to choose. If a thousand men were not to pay their tax-bills this year, that would not be a violent and bloody measure, as it would be to pay them, and enable the State to commit violence and shed innocent blood. This is, in fact, the definition of a peaceable revolution, if any such is possible. If the tax-gatherer, or any other public officer, asks me, as one has done, "But what shall I do?" my answer is, "If you really wish to do anything, resign your office." When the subject has refused allegiance, and the officer has resigned his office, then the revolution is accomplished. But even suppose blood should flow. Is there not a sort of blood shed when the conscience is wounded? Through this wound a man's real manhood and immortality flow out, and he bleeds to an everlasting death. I see this blood flowing now.

I have contemplated the imprisonment of the offender, rather than the seizure of his goods—though both will serve the same purpose—because they who assert the purest right, and consequently are most dangerous to a corrupt State, commonly have not spent much time in accumulating property. To such the State renders comparatively small service, and a slight tax is wont to appear exorbitant, particularly if they are obliged to earn it by special labor with their hands. If there were one who lived wholly without the use of money, the State itself would hesitate to demand it of him. But the rich man—not to make any invidious comparison—is always sold to the institution which makes him rich. Absolutely speaking, the more money, the less virtue; for money comes between a man and his objects, and obtains them for him; and it was certainly no great virtue to obtain it. It puts to rest many questions which he would otherwise be taxed to answer; while the only new question which it puts is the hard but superfluous one, how to spend it. Thus his moral ground is taken from under his feet. The opportunities of living are diminished in proportion as what are called the "means" are increased. The best thing a man can do for his culture when he is rich is to endeavor to carry out those schemes which he entertained when he was poor. Christ answered the Herodians according to their condition. "Show me the tribute-money," said he—and one took a penny out of his pocket—if you use money which has the image of Caesar on it, and which he has made current and valuable, that is, *if you are men of the State,* and gladly enjoy the advantages of Caesar's government, then pay him back some of his own when he demands it. "Render therefore to Caesar that which is Caesar's, and to God those things which are God's"—leaving them no wiser than before as to which was which; for they did not wish to know.

When I converse with the freest of my neighbors, I perceive that, whatever they may say about the magnitude and seriousness of the question, and their regard for the public tranquillity, the long and the short of the matter is, that they cannot spare the protection of the existing government, and they dread the consequences to their property and families of disobedience to it. For my own part, I should not like to think that I ever rely on the protection of the State. But, if I deny the authority of the State when it presents its tax bill, it will soon take and waste all my property, and so harass me and my children without end. This is hard. This makes it impossible for a man to live honestly, and at the same time comfortably, in outward respects. It will not be worth the while to accumulate property; that would be sure to go again. You must hire or squat somewhere, and raise but a small crop, and eat that soon. You must live within yourself, and depend upon yourself always tucked up and ready for a start, and not have many affairs. A man may grow rich in Turkey even, if he will be in all respects a good subject of the Turkish government. Confucius said: "If a state is governed by the principles of reason, poverty and misery are subjects of shame; if a state is not governed by the principles of reason, riches and honors are the subjects of shame." No: until I want the protection of Massachusetts to be extended to me in some distant Southern port, where my liberty is endangered, or until I am bent solely on building up an estate at home by peaceful enterprise, I can afford to refuse allegiance to Massachusetts, and her right to my property and life. It costs me less in every sense to incur the penalty of disobedience to the State than it would to obey. I should feel as if I were worth less in that case.

Some years ago, the State met me in behalf of the Church, and commanded me to pay a certain sum toward the support of a clergyman whose preaching my father attended, but never I myself. "Pay," it said, "or be locked up in the jail." I declined to pay. But, unfortunately, another man saw fit to pay it. I did not see why the schoolmaster should be taxed to support the priest, and not the priest the schoolmaster; for I was not the State's schoolmaster, but I supported myself by voluntary subscription. I did not see why the lyceum should not present its tax bill, and have the State to back its demand, as well as the Church. However, at the request of the selectmen, I condescended to make some such statement as this in writing: "Know all men by these presents, that I, Henry Thoreau, do not wish to be regarded as a member of any incorporated society which I have not joined." This I gave to the town clerk; and he has it. The State, having thus learned that I did not wish to be regarded as a member of that church, has never made a like demand on me since; though it said that it must adhere to its original presumption that time. If I had known how to name them, I should then have signed off in detail from all the societies which I never signed on to; but I did not know where to find a complete list.

I have paid no poll-tax for six years. I was put into a jail once on this account, for one night; and, as I stood considering the walls of solid stone, two or three feet thick, the door of wood and iron, a foot thick, and the iron grating which strained the light, I could not help being struck with the foolishness of that institution which treated me as if I were mere flesh and blood and bones, to be locked up. I wondered that it should have concluded at length that this was the best use it could put me to, and had never thought to avail itself of my services in some way. I saw that, if there was a wall of stone between me and my townsmen, there was a still more difficult one to climb or break through before they could get to be as free as I was. I did not for a moment feel confined, and the walls seemed a great waste of stone and mortar. I felt as if I alone of all my townsmen had paid my tax. They plainly did not know how to treat me, but behaved like persons who are underbred. In every threat and in every compliment there was a blunder; for they thought that my chief desire was to stand the other side of that stone wall. I could not but smile to see how industriously they locked the door on my meditations, which followed them out again without let or hindrance, and *they* were really all that was dangerous. As they could not reach me, they had resolved to punish my body; just as boys, if they cannot come at some person against whom they have a spite, will abuse his dog. I saw that the State was half-witted, that it was timid as a lone woman with her silver spoons, and that it did not know its friends from its foes, and I lost all my remaining respect for it, and pitied it.

Thus the State never intentionally confronts a man's

sense, intellectual or moral, but only his body, his senses. It is not armed with superior wit or honesty, but with superior physical strength. I was not born to be forced. I will breathe after my own fashion. Let us see who is the strongest. What force has a multitude? They only can force me who obey a higher law than I. They force me to become like themselves. I do not hear of *men* being *forced* to live this way or that by masses of men. What sort of life were that to live? When I meet a government which says to me, "Your money or your life," why should I be in haste to give it my money? It may be in a great strait, and not know what to do: I cannot help that. It must help itself; do as I do. It is not worth the while to snivel about it. I am not responsible for the successful working of the machinery of society. I am not the son of the engineer. I perceive that, when an acorn and a chestnut fall side by side, the one does not remain inert to make way for the other, but both obey their own laws, and spring and grow and flourish as best they can, till one, perchance, overshadows and destroys the other. If a plant cannot live according to its nature, it dies; and so a man.

The night in prison was novel and interesting enough. The prisoners in their shirtsleeves were enjoying a chat and the evening air in the doorway, when I entered. But the jailer said, "Come, boys, it is time to lock up"; and so they dispersed, and I heard the sound of their steps returning into the hollow apartments. My room-mate was introduced to me by the jailer as "a first-rate fellow and a clever man." When the door was locked, he showed me where to hang my hat, and how he managed matters there. The rooms were whitewashed once a month; and this one, at least, was the whitest, most simply furnished, and probably the neatest apartment in the town. He naturally wanted to know where I came from, and what brought me there; and, when I had told him, I asked him in my turn how he came there, presuming him to be an honest man, of course; and, as the world goes, I believe he was. "Why," said he, "they accuse me of burning a barn; but I never did it." As near as I could discover, he had probably gone to bed in a barn when drunk, and smoked his pipe there; and so a barn was burnt. He had the reputation of being a clever man, had been there some three months waiting for his trial to come on, and would have to wait as much longer; but he was quite domesticated and contented, since he got his board for nothing, and thought that he was well treated.

He occupied one window, and I the other; and I saw that if one stayed there long, his principal business would be to look out the window. I had soon read all the tracts that were left there, and examined where former prisoners had broken out, and where a grate had been sawed off, and heard the history of the various occupants of that room; for I found that even here there was a history and a gossip which never circulated beyond the walls of the jail. Probably this is the only house in the town where verses are composed, which are afterward printed in a circular form, but not published. I was shown quite a long list of verses which were composed by some young men who had been detected in an attempt to escape, who avenged themselves by singing them.

I pumped my fellow-prisoner as dry as I could, for fear I should never see him again; but at length he showed me which was my bed, and left me to blow out the lamp.

It was like traveling into a far country, such as I had never expected to behold, to lie there for one night. It seemed to me that I never had heard the town clock strike before, nor the evening sounds of the village; for we slept with the windows open, which were inside the grating. It was to see my native village in the light of the Middle Ages, and our Concord was turned into a Rhine stream, and visions of knights and castles passed before me. They were the voices of old burghers that I heard in the streets. I was an involuntary spectator and auditor of whatever was done and said in the kitchen of the adjacent village inn—a wholly new and rare experience to me. It was a closer view of my native town. I was fairly inside of it. I never had seen its institutions before. This is one of its peculiar institutions; for it is a shire town. I began to comprehend what its inhabitants were about.

In the morning, our breakfasts were put through the hole in the door, in small oblong-square tin pans, made to fit, and holding a pint of chocolate, with brown bread, and an iron spoon. When they called for the vessels again, I was green enough to return what bread I had left; but my comrade seized it, and said that I should lay that up for lunch or dinner. Soon after he was let out to work at haying in a neighboring field, whither he went every day, and would not be back till noon; so he bade me good-day, saying that he doubted if he should see me again.

When I came out of prison—for some one interfered, and paid that tax—I did not perceive that great changes had taken place on the common, such as he observed who went in a youth and emerged a tottering and gray-headed man; and yet a change had to my eyes come over the scene—the town, and State, and country— greater than any that mere time could effect. I saw yet more distinctly the State in which I lived. I saw to what extent the people among whom I lived could be trusted as good neighbors and friends; that their friendship was for summer weather only; that they did not greatly propose to do right; that they were a distinct race from me by their prejudices and superstitions, as the Chinamen and Malays are; that in their sacrifices to humanity they ran no risks, not even to their property; that after all they were not so noble but they treated the thief as he had treated them, and hoped, by a certain outward observance and a few prayers, and by walking in a particular straight though useless path from time to time, to save their souls. This may be to judge my neighbors harshly; for I believe that many of them are not aware that they have such an institution as the jail in their village.

It was formerly the custom in our village, when a poor debtor came out of jail, for his acquaintances to salute him, looking through their fingers, which were crossed to represent the grating of a jail window, "How do ye do?" My neighbors did not thus salute me, but first looked at me, and then at one another, as if I had returned from a long journey. I was put into jail as I was going to the shoemaker's to get a shoe which was mended. When I was let out the next morning, I proceeded to finish my errand, and, having put on my mended shoe, joined a huckleberry party, who were impatient to put themselves under my conduct; and in half an hour—for the horse was soon tackled—was in the midst of a huckleberry field, on one of our highest hills, two miles off, and then the State was nowhere to be seen.

This is the whole history of "My Prisons."

I have never declined paying the highway tax, because I am as desirous of being a good neighbor as I am of being a bad subject; and as for supporting schools, I am doing my part to educate my fellow-countrymen now. It is for no particular item in the tax bill that I refuse to pay it. I simply wish to refuse allegiance to the State, to withdraw and stand aloof from it effectually. I do not care to trace the course of my dollar, if I could, till it buys a man or a musket to shoot one with—the dollar is innocent—but I am concerned to trace the effects of my allegiance. In fact, I quietly declare war with the State, after my fashion, though I will still make what use and get what advantage of her I can, as is usual in such cases.

If others pay the tax which is demanded of me, from a sympathy with the State, they do but what they have already done in their own case, or rather they abet injustice to a greater extent than the State requires. If they pay the tax from a mistaken interest in the individual taxed, to save his property, or prevent his going to jail, it is because they have not considered wisely how far they let their private feelings interfere with the public good.

This, then, is my position at present. But one cannot be too much on his guard in such a case, lest his action be biased by obstinacy or an undue regard for the opinions of men. Let him see that he does only what belongs to himself and to the hour.

I think sometimes, Why, this people mean well, they are only ignorant; they would do better if they knew how: why give your neighbors this pain to treat you as they are not inclined to? But I think again, This is no reason why I should do as they do, or permit others to suffer much greater pain of a different kind. Again, I sometimes say to myself, When many millions of men, without heat, without ill will, without personal feeling of any kind, demand of you a few shillings only, without the possibility, such is their constitution, of retracting or altering their present demand, and without the possibility, on your side, of appeal to any other millions, why expose yourself to this overwhelming brute force? You do not resist cold and hunger, the winds and the waves, thus obstinately; you quietly submit to a thousand similar necessities. You do not put your head into the fire. But just in proportion as I regard this as not wholly a brute force, but partly a human force, and consider that I have relations to those millions as to so many millions of men, and not of mere brute or inanimate things, I see that appeal is possible, first and instantaneously, from them to the Maker of them, and, secondly, from them to themselves. But if I put my head deliberately into the fire, there is no appeal to fire or to the Maker of fire, and I have only myself to blame. If I could convince myself that I have any right to be satisfied with men as they are, and to treat them accordingly, and not according, in some respects, to my requisitions and expectations of what they and I ought to be, then, like a good Mussulman and fatalist, I should endeavor to be satisfied with things as they are, and say it is the will of God. And, above all, there is this difference between resisting this and a purely brute or natural force, that I can resist this with some effect; but I cannot expect, like Orpheus, to change the nature of the rocks and trees and beasts.

I do not wish to quarrel with any man or nation. I do not wish to split hairs, to make fine distinctions, or set myself up as better than my neighbors. I seek rather, I may say, even an excuse for conforming to the laws of the land. I am but too ready to conform to them. Indeed, I have reason to suspect myself on this head; and each year, as the tax-gatherer comes round, I find myself disposed to review the acts and position of the general and State governments, and the spirit of the people, to discover a pretext for conformity.

"We must affect our country as our parents,
And if at any time we alienate
Our love or industry from doing it honor,
We must respect effects and teach the soul
Matter of conscience and religion,
And not desire of rule or benefit."

I believe that the State will soon be able to take all my work of this sort out of my hands, and then I shall be no better a patriot than my fellow-countrymen. Seen from a lower point of view, the Constitution, with all its faults, is very good; the law and the courts are very respectable; even this State and this American government are, in many respects, very admirable, and rare things, to be thankful for, such as a great many have described them; but seen from a point of view a little higher, they are what I have described them; seen from a higher still, and the highest, who shall say what they are, or that they are worth looking at or thinking of at all?

However, the government does not concern me much, and I shall bestow the fewest possible thoughts on it. It is not many moments that I live under a government, even in this world. If a man is thought-free, fancy-free, imagination-free, that which *is not* never for a long time appearing *to be* to him, unwise rulers or reformers cannot fatally interrupt him.

I know that most men think differently from myself; but those whose lives are by profession devoted to the study of these or kindred subjects content me as little as any. Statesmen and legislators, standing so completely within the institution, never distinctly and nakedly behold it. They speak of moving society, but have no resting-place without it. They may be men of a certain experience and discrimination, and have no doubt invented ingenious and even useful systems, for which we sincerely thank them; but all their wit and usefulness lie within certain not very wide limits. They are wont to forget that the world is not governed by policy and expediency. Webster never goes behind government, and so cannot speak with authority about it. His words are wisdom to those legislators who contemplate no essential reform in the existing government; but for thinkers, and those who legislate for all time, he never once glances at the subject. I know of those whose serene and wise speculations on this theme would soon reveal the limits of his mind's range and hospitality. Yet, compared with the cheap professions of most reformers, and the still cheaper wisdom and eloquence of politicians in general, his are almost the only sensible and valuable words, and we thank Heaven for him. Comparatively, he is always strong, original, and, above all, practical. Still, his quality is not wisdom, but prudence. The lawyer's truth is not Truth, but consistency or a consistent expediency. Truth is always in harmony with herself, and is not concerned chiefly to reveal the justice that may consist with wrong-doing. He well deserves to be called, as he has been called, the Defender of the Constitution. There are really no blows to be given by him but defensive ones. He is not a leader, but a follower. His leaders are the men of '87. "I have never made an effort," he says, "and never propose to make an effort; I have never countenanced an effort, and never mean to countenance an effort, to disturb the arrangement as originally made, by which the various States came into the Union." Still thinking of the sanction which the Constitution gives to slavery, he says, "Because it was a part of the original compact—let it stand." Notwithstanding his special acuteness and ability, he is unable to take a fact out of its merely political relations, and behold it as it lies absolutely to be disposed of by the intellect—what, for instance, it behooves a man to do here in America today with regard to slavery—but ventures, or is driven, to make some such desperate answer as the following, while professing to speak absolutely, and as a private man—from which what new and singular code of social duties might be inferred? "The manner," says he, "in which the governments of those States where slavery exists are to regulate it is for their own consideration, under their responsibility to their constituents, to the general laws of propriety, humanity, and justice, and to God. Associations formed elsewhere, springing from a feeling of humanity, or any other cause, have nothing whatever to do with it. They have never received any encouragement from me, and they never will." [1]

They who know of no purer sources of truth, who have traced up its stream no higher, stand, and wisely stand, by the Bible and the Constitution, and drink at it there with reverence and humility; but they who behold where it comes trickling into this lake or that pool, gird up their loins once more, and continue their pilgrimage toward its fountainhead.

No man with a genius for legislation has appeared in America. They are rare in the history of the world. There are orators, politicians, and eloquent men, by the thousand; but the speaker has not yet opened his mouth to speak who is capable of settling the much-vexed questions of the day. We love eloquence for its own sake, and not for any truth which it may utter, or any heroism it may inspire. Our legislators have not yet learned the comparative value of free trade and of freedom, of union, and of rectitude, to a nation. They have no genius or talent for comparatively humble questions of taxation and finance, commerce and manufactures

---

[1] These extracts have been inserted since the lecture was read.

and agriculture. If we were left solely to the wordy wit of legislators in Congress for our guidance, uncorrected by the seasonable experience and the effectual complaints of the people, America would not long retain her rank among the nations. For eighteen hundred years, though perchance I have no right to say it, the New Testament has been written; yet where is the legislator who has wisdom and practical talent enough to avail himself of the light which it sheds on the science of legislation?

The authority of government, even such as I am willing to submit to—for I will cheerfully obey those who know and can do better than I, and in many things even those who neither know nor can do so well—is still an impure one: to be strictly just, it must have the sanction and consent of the governed. It can have no pure right over my person and property but what I concede to it. The progress from an absolute to a limited monarchy, from a limited monarchy to a democracy, is a progress toward a true respect for the individual. Even the Chinese philosopher was wise enough to regard the individual as the basis of the empire. Is a democracy, such as we know it, the last improvement possible in government? Is it not possible to take a step further towards recognizing and organizing the rights of man? There will never be a really free and enlightened State until the State comes to recognize the individual as a higher and independent power, from which all its own power and authority are derived, and treats him accordingly. I please myself with imagining a State at last which can afford to be just to all men, and to treat the individual with respect as a neighbor; which even would not think it inconsistent with its own repose if a few were to live aloof from it, not meddling with it, nor embraced by it, who fulfilled all the duties of neighbors and fellow men. A State which bore this kind of fruit, and suffered it to drop off as fast as it ripened, would prepare the way for a still more perfect and glorious State, which also I have imagined, but not yet anywhere seen.

A Week on the
Concord and Merrimack Rivers

Thoreau's American book of days was printed only because he himself footed the bill. It was luxury publishing and he was often to remember the fact. The book is supposedly the record of Henry and John Thoreau's water journeys, their "fluvial excursions." Actually the travel account is mere framework. The scholar is much more apparent than the traveler, for the original narrative has been weighted down with learned allusions and quotations. Thoreau sees a certain stretch of the river, for example, and describes it; but he is also apt to remind the reader of its history, of the settlers who suffered on its banks, and of the classical parallels to their misadventures. It is true that Thoreau's allusive, ornamented style is at times the sign of the thinker, seeking the universals behind the particulars. But at other times the thrifty journalizer is also apparent, utilizing his old essays and random pieces by stuffing them into the story. The result is a rambling and not always happy one; consequently, some parts of the chapters to follow have been cut as have three of the chapters themselves. Thoreau himself slightly revised the Week after it came out in 1849, and this is his later text.

C. B.

CONCORD RIVER

Beneath low hills, in the broad interval
Through which at will our Indian rivulet
Winds mindful still of sannup and of squaw,
Whose pipe and arrow oft the plough unburies,
Here in pine houses built of new-fallen trees,
Supplanters of the tribe, the farmers dwell.

EMERSON.

THE Musketaquid, or Grass-ground River, though probably as old as the Nile or Euphrates, did not begin to have a place in civilized history until the fame of its grassy meadows and its fish attracted settlers out of England in 1635, when it received the other but kindred name of Concord from the first plantation on its banks, which appears to have been commenced in a spirit of peace and harmony. It will be Grass-ground River as long as grass grows and water runs here; it will be Concord River only while men lead peaceable lives on its banks. To an extinct race it was grass-ground, where they hunted and fished; and it is still perennial grass-ground to Concord farmers, who own the Great Meadows, and get the hay from year to year. "One branch of it," according to the historian of Concord, for I love to quote so good authority, "rises in the south part of Hopkinton, and another from a pond and a large cedar-swamp in Westborough," and flowing between Hopkinton and Southborough, through Framingham, and between Sudbury and Wayland, where it is sometimes called Sudbury River, it enters Concord at the south part of the town, and after receiving the North or Assabet River, which has its source a little farther to the north and west, goes out at the northeast angle, and, flowing between Bedford and Carlisle, and through Billerica, empties into the Merrimack at Lowell. In Concord, it is in summer from four to fifteen feet deep, and from one hundred to three hundred feet wide, but in the spring freshets, when it overflows its banks, it is in some places nearly a mile wide. Between Sudbury and Wayland the meadows acquire their greatest breadth, and when covered with water, they form a handsome chain of shallow vernal lakes, resorted to by numerous gulls and ducks. Just above Sherman's Bridge, between these towns, is the largest expanse; and when the wind blows freshly in a raw March day, heaving up the surface into dark and sober billows or regular swells, skirted as it is in the distance with alder swamps and smoke-like maples, it looks like a smaller Lake Huron, and is very pleasant and exciting for a landsman to row or sail over. The farmhouses along the Sudbury shore, which rises gently to a considerable height, command fine water prospects at this season. The shore is more flat on the Wayland side, and this town is the greatest loser by the flood. Its farmers tell me that thousands of acres are flooded now, since the dams have been erected, where they remember to have seen the white honey-suckle or clover growing once, and they could go dry with shoes only in summer. Now there is nothing but blue-joint and sedge and cut-grass there, standing in water all the year round. For a long time, they made the most of the driest season to get their hay, working some-times till nine o'clock at night, sedulously paring with their scythes in the twilight round the hummocks left by the ice; but now it is not worth the getting when they can come at it, and they look sadly round to their wood-lots and upland as a last resource.

It is worth the while to make a voyage up this stream, if you go no farther than Sudbury, only to see how much country there is in the rear of us: great hills, and a hundred brooks, and farmhouses, and barns, and hay-

stacks, you never saw before, and men everywhere; Sudbury, that is *Southborough* men, and Wayland, and
Nine-Acre-Corner men, and Bound Rock, where four
towns bound on a rock in the river, Lincoln, Wayland,
Sudbury, Concord. Many waves are there agitated by
the wind, keeping nature fresh, the spray blowing in
your face, reeds and rushes waving; ducks by the hundred, all uneasy in the surf, in the raw wind, just ready
to rise, and now going off with a clatter and a whistling
like riggers straight for Labrador, flying against the stiff
gale with reefed wings, or else circling round first, with
all their paddles briskly moving, just over the surf, to
reconnoiter you before they leave these parts; gulls
wheeling overhead, muskrats swimming for dear life,
wet and cold, with no fire to warm them by that you
know of, their labored homes rising here and there like
haystacks; and countless mice and moles and winged
titmice along the sunny, windy shore; cranberries tossed
on the waves and heaving up on the beach, their little
red skiffs beating about among the alders; such healthy
natural tumult as proves the last day is not yet at hand.
And there stand all around the alders, and birches, and
oaks, and maples, full of glee and sap, holding in their
buds until the waters subside. You shall perhaps run
aground on Cranberry Island, only some spires of last
year's pipe-grass above water to show where the danger
is, and get as good a freezing there as anywhere on the
Northwest Coast. I never voyaged so far in all my life.
You shall see men you never heard of before, whose
names you don't know, going away down through the
meadows with long ducking guns, with water-tight boots
wading through the fowl-meadow grass, on bleak, wintry, distant shores, with guns at half-cock; and they shall
see teal—blue-winged, green-winged—sheldrakes, whis-
tlers, black ducks, ospreys, and many other wild and

noble sights before night, such as they who sit in parlors
never dream of. You shall see rude and sturdy, experienced and wise men, keeping their castles, or teaming
up their summer's wood, or chopping alone in the woods;
men fuller of talk and rare adventure in the sun and
wind and rain, than a chestnut is of meat, who were out
not only in '75 and 1812, but have been out every day
of their lives; greater men than Homer, or Chaucer, or
Shakespeare, only they never got time to say so; they
never took to the way of writing. Look at their fields,
and imagine what they might write, if ever they should
put pen to paper. Or what have they not written on the
face of the earth already, clearing, and burning, and
scratching, and harrowing, and plowing, and subsoiling,
in and in, and out and out, and over and over, again
and again, erasing what they had already written for
want of parchment.

As yesterday and the historical ages are past, as the
work of today is present, so some flitting perspectives
and demi-experiences of the life that is in nature are in
time veritably future, or rather outside to time, perennial, young, divine, in the wind and rain which never
die.

> The respectable folks,
> Where dwell they?
> They whisper in the oaks,
> And they sigh in the hay;
> Summer and winter, night and day,
> Out on the meadow, there dwell they.
> They never die,
> Nor snivel nor cry,
> Nor ask our pity
> With a wet eye.
> A sound estate they ever mend,
> To every asker readily lend;
> To the ocean wealth,
> To the meadow health,

To Time his length,
To the rocks strength,
To the stars light,
To the weary night,
To the busy day,
To the idle play;
And so their good cheer never ends,
For all are their debtors, and all their friends.

Concord River is remarkable for the gentleness of its current, which is scarcely perceptible, and some have referred to its influence the proverbial moderation of the inhabitants of Concord, as exhibited in the Revolution, and on later occasions. It has been proposed that the town should adopt for its coat of arms a field verdant, with the Concord circling nine times round. I have read that a descent of an eighth of an inch in a mile is sufficient to produce a flow. Our river has, probably, very near the smallest allowance. The story is current, at any rate, though I believe that strict history will not bear it out, that the only bridge ever carried away on the main branch, within the limits of the town, was driven up-stream by the wind. But wherever it makes a sudden bend it is shallower and swifter, and asserts its title to be called a river. Compared with the other tributaries of the Merrimack, it appears to have been properly named Musketaquid, or Meadow River, by the Indians. For the most part, it creeps through broad meadows, adorned with scattered oaks, where the cranberry is found in abundance, covering the ground like a moss-bed. A row of sunken dwarf willows borders the stream on one or both sides, while at a greater distance the meadow is skirted with maples, alders, and other fluviatile trees, overrun with the grape-vine, which bears fruit in its season, purple, red, white, and other grapes. Still farther from the stream, on the edge of the firm land, are seen the gray and white dwellings of the inhabitants. According to the valuation of 1831, there were in Concord two thousand one hundred and eleven acres, or about one seventh of the whole territory, in meadow; this standing next in the list after pasturage and unimproved lands; and, judging from the returns of previous years, the meadow is not reclaimed so fast as the woods are cleared. . . .

The sluggish artery of the Concord meadows steals thus unobserved through the town, without a murmur or a pulse-beat, its general course from southwest to northeast, and its length about fifty miles; a huge volume of matter, ceaselessly rolling through the plains and valleys of the substantial earth with the moccasined tread of an Indian warrior, making haste from the high places of the earth to its ancient reservoir. . . .

The Mississippi, the Ganges, and the Nile, those journeying atoms from the Rocky Mountains, the Himmaleh, and Mountains of the Moon, have a kind of personal importance in the annals of the world. The heavens are not yet drained over their sources, but the Mountains of the Moon still send their annual tribute to the Pasha without fail, as they did to the Pharaohs, though he must collect the rest of his revenue at the point of the sword. Rivers must have been the guides which conducted the footsteps of the first travelers. They are the constant lure, when they flow by our doors, to distant enterprise and adventure; and, by a natural impulse, the dwellers on their banks will at length accompany their currents to the lowlands of the globe, or explore at their invitation the interior of continents. They are the natural highways of all nations, not only leveling the ground and removing obstacles from the path of the traveler, quenching his thirst and bearing him on their bosoms, but conducting him through the most interesting scenery, the most populous portions of the globe, and where the animal and vegetable kingdoms attain their greatest perfection.

I had often stood on the banks of the Concord, watching the lapse of the current, an emblem of all progress, following the same law with the system, with time, and all that is made; the weeds at the bottom gently bending down the stream, shaken by the watery wind, still planted where their seeds had sunk, but ere long to die and go down likewise; the shining pebbles, not yet anxious to better their condition, the chips and weeds, and occasional logs and stems of trees that floated past, fulfilling their fate, were objects of singular interest to me, and at last I resolved to launch myself on its bosom and float whither it would bear me.

SATURDAY

Come, come, my lovely fair, and let us try
Those rural delicacies.
QUARLES, *Christ's Invitation to the Soul.*

At length, on Saturday, the last day of August, 1839, we two, brothers, and natives of Concord, weighed anchor in this river port; for Concord, too, lies under the sun, a port of entry and departure for the bodies as well as the souls of men; one shore at least exempted from all duties but such as an honest man will gladly discharge. A warm, drizzling rain had obscured the morning, and threatened to delay our voyage, but at length the leaves and grass were dried, and it came out a mild afternoon, as serene and fresh as if Nature were maturing some greater scheme of her own. After this long dripping and oozing from every pore, she began to respire again more healthily than ever. So with a vigorous shove we launched our boat from the bank, while the flags and bulrushes courtesied a Godspeed, and dropped silently down the stream.

Our boat, which had cost us a week's labor in the spring, was in form like a fisherman's dory, fifteen feet long by three and a half in breadth at the widest part, painted green below, with a border of blue, with reference to the two elements in which it was to spend its existence. It had been loaded the evening before at our door, half a mile from the river, with potatoes and melons, from a patch which we had cultivated, and a few utensils; and was provided with wheels in order to be rolled around falls, as well as with two sets of oars, and several slender poles for shoving in shallow places, and also two masts, one of which served for a tent-pole at night; for a buffalo-skin was to be our bed, and a tent of cotton cloth our roof. It was strongly built, but heavy, and hardly of better model than usual. If rightly made, a boat would be a sort of amphibious animal, a creature of two elements, related by one half its structure to some swift and shapely fish, and by the other to some strong-winged and graceful bird. The fish shows where there should be the greatest breadth of beam and depth in the hold; its fins direct where to set the oars, and the tail gives some hint for the form and position of the rudder. The bird shows how to rig and trim the sails, and what form to give to the prow, that it may balance the boat and divide the air and water best. These hints we had but partially obeyed. But the eyes, though they are no sailors, will never be satisfied with any model, however fashionable, which does not answer all the requisitions of art. However, as art is all of a ship but the wood, and yet the wood alone will rudely serve the purpose of a ship, so our boat, being of wood, gladly availed itself of the old law that the heavier shall float the lighter, and though a dull waterfowl, proved a sufficient buoy for our purpose.

> "Were it the will of Heaven, an osier bough
> Were vessel safe enough the seas to plough."

Some village friends stood upon a promontory lower down the stream to wave us a last farewell; but we, having already performed these shore rites, with excusable reserve, as befits those who are embarked on unusual enterprises, who behold but speak not, silently glided past the firm lands of Concord, both peopled cape and lonely summer meadow, with steady sweeps. And yet we did unbend so far as to let our guns speak for us, when at length we had swept out of sight, and thus left the woods to ring again with their echoes; and it may be many russet-clad children, lurking in those broad meadows, with the bittern and the woodcock and the rail, though wholly concealed by brakes and hardhack and meadow-sweet, heard our salute that afternoon.

We were soon floating past the first regular battle-ground of the Revolution, resting on our oars between the still visible abutments of that "North Bridge" over which in April, 1775, rolled the first faint tide of that war which ceased not till, as we read on the stone on our right, it "gave peace to these United States." . . .

That slight shaft had now sunk behind the hills, and we had floated round the neighboring bend, and under the new North Bridge between Ponkawtasset and the Poplar Hill, into the Great Meadows, which, like a broad moccasin-print, have leveled a fertile and juicy place in nature. . . .

Gradually the village murmur subsided, and we seemed to be embarked on the placid current of our dreams, floating from past to future as silently as one awakes to fresh morning or evening thoughts. We glided noiselessly down the stream, occasionally driving a pickerel or a bream from the covert of the pads, and the smaller bittern now and then sailed away on sluggish wings from some recess in the shore, or the larger lifted itself out of the long grass at our approach, and carried its precious legs away to deposit them in a place of safety. The tortoises also rapidly dropped into the water, as our boat ruffled the surface amid the willows, breaking the reflections of the trees. The banks had passed the height of their beauty, and some of the brighter flowers showed by their faded tints that the season was verging towards the afternoon of the year; but this somber tinge enhanced their sincerity, and in the still unabated heats they seemed like the mossy brink of some cool well. The narrow-leaved willow (*Salix Purshiana*) lay along the surface of the water in masses of light green foliage, interspersed with the large balls of the button-bush. The small rose-colored polygonum raised its head proudly above the water on either hand, and flowering at this season and in these localities, in front of dense fields of the white species which skirted the sides of the stream, its little streak of red looked very rare and precious. The pure white blossoms of the arrowhead stood in the shallower parts, and a few cardinals on the margin still proudly surveyed themselves reflected in the water, though the latter, as well as the pickerel-weed, was now nearly out of blossom. The snake-head (*Chelone glabra*) grew close to the shore, while a kind of coreopsis, turning its brazen face to the sun, full and rank, and a tall dull-red flower (*Eupatorium purpureum,* or trumpet-weed) formed the rear rank of the fluvial array. The bright-blue flowers of the soapwort gentian were sprinkled here and there in the adjacent meadows, like flowers which Proserpine had dropped, and still farther in the fields or higher on the bank were seen the purple gerardia, the Virginian rhexia, and drooping neottia or ladies'-tresses; while from the more distant waysides which we occasionally passed, and banks where the sun had lodged, was reflected still a dull-yellow beam from the ranks of tansy, now past its prime. In short, Nature seemed to have adorned herself for our departure with a profusion of fringes and curls, mingled with the bright tints of flowers, reflected in the water. But we missed the white water-lily, which is the queen of river flowers, its reign being over for this season. He makes his voyage too late, perhaps, by a true water clock who delays so long. Many of this species inhabit our Concord water. I have passed down the river before sunrise on a summer morning, between fields of lilies still shut in sleep; and when, at length, the flakes of sunlight from over the bank fell on the surface of the water, whole fields of white blossoms seemed to flash open before me, as I floated along, like the unfolding of a banner, so sensible is this flower to the influence of the sun's rays.

As we were floating through the last of these familiar meadows, we observed the large and conspicuous flowers of the hibiscus, covering the dwarf willows and mingled with the leaves of the grape, and wished that we could inform one of our friends behind of the locality of this somewhat rare and inaccessible flower before it was too late to pluck it; but we were just gliding out of sight of the village spire before it occurred to us that the farmer in the adjacent meadow would go to church on the morrow, and would carry this news for us; and so by the Monday, while we should be floating on the Merrimack, our friend would be reaching to pluck this blossom on the bank of the Concord.

After a pause at Ball's Hill, the St. Anne's of Concord

voyageurs, not to say any prayer for the success of our voyage, but to gather the few berries which were still left on the hills, hanging by very slender threads, we weighed anchor again, and were soon out of sight of our native village. The land seemed to grow fairer as we withdrew from it. Far away to the southwest lay the quiet village, left alone under its elms and buttonwoods in mid-afternoon; and the hills, notwithstanding their blue, ethereal faces, seemed to cast a saddened eye on their old playfellows; but, turning short to the north, we bade adieu to their familiar outlines, and addressed ourselves to new scenes and adventures. Naught was familiar but the heavens, from under whose roof the voyageur never passes; but with their countenance, and the acquaintance we had with river and wood, we trusted to fare well under any circumstances.

From this point the river runs perfectly straight for a mile or more to Carlisle Bridge, which consists of twenty wooden piers, and when we looked back over it, its surface was reduced to a line's breadth, and appeared like a cobweb gleaming in the sun. Here and there might be seen a pole sticking up, to mark the place where some fisherman had enjoyed unusual luck, and in return had consecrated his rod to the deities who preside over these shallows. It was full twice as broad as before, deep and tranquil, with a muddy bottom, and bordered with willows, beyond which spread broad lagoons covered with pads, bulrushes, and flags.

Late in the afternoon we passed a man on the shore fishing with a long birch pole, its silvery bark left on, and a dog at his side, rowing so near as to agitate his cork with our oars, and drive away luck for a season; and when we had rowed a mile as straight as an arrow, with our faces turned towards him, and the bubbles in our wake still visible on the tranquil surface, there stood the fisher still with his dog, like statues under the other side of the heavens, the only objects to relieve the eye in the extended meadow; and there would he stand abiding his luck, till he took his way home through the fields at evening with his fish. Thus, by one bait or another, Nature allures inhabitants into all her recesses. This man was the last of our townsmen whom we saw, and we silently through him bade adieu to our friends.

The characteristics and pursuits of various ages and races of men are always existing in epitome in every neighborhood. The pleasures of my earliest youth have become the inheritance of other men. This man is still a fisher, and belongs to an era in which I myself have lived. Perchance he is not confounded by many knowledges, and has not sought out many inventions; but how to take many fishes before the sun sets, with his slender birchen pole and flaxen line, that is invention enough for him. It is good even to be a fisherman in summer and in winter. Some men are judges, these August days, sitting on benches, even till the court rises; they sit judging there honorably, between the seasons and between meals, leading a civil, politic life, arbitrating in the case of Spaulding *versus* Cummings, it may be, from highest noon till the red vesper sinks into the west. The fisherman, meanwhile, stands in three feet of water, under the same summer's sun, arbitrating in other cases between muckworm and shiner, amid the fragrance of water-lilies, mint, and pontederia, leading his life many rods from the dry land, within a pole's length of where the larger fishes swim. Human life is to him very much like a river,

"renning aie downward to the sea."

This was his observation. His honor made a great discovery in bailments.

I can just remember an old brown-coated man who was the Walton of this stream, who had come over from Newcastle, England, with his son—the latter a stout and hearty man who had lifted an anchor in his day. A straight old man he was, who took his way in silence through the meadows, having passed the period of communication with his fellows; his old experienced coat, hanging long and straight and brown as the yellow pine bark, glittering with so much smothered sunlight, if you stood near enough, no work of art but naturalized at length. I often discovered him unexpectedly amid the pads and the gray willows when he moved, fishing in some old country method—for youth and age then went a-fishing together—full of incommunicable thoughts, perchance about his own Tyne and Northumberland. He was always to be seen in serene afternoon haunting the river, and almost rustling with the sedge; so many sunny hours in an old man's life, entrapping silly fish; almost grown to be the sun's familiar; what need had he of hat or raiment any, having served out his time, and seen through such thin disguises? I have seen how his coeval fates rewarded him with the yellow perch, and yet I thought his luck was not in proportion to his years; and I have seen when, with slow steps and weighed down with aged thoughts, he disappeared with his fish under his low-roofed house on the skirts of the village. I think nobody else saw him; nobody else remembers him now, for he soon after died, and migrated to new Tyne streams. His fishing was not a sport, nor solely a means of subsistence, but a sort of solemn sacrament and withdrawal from the world, just as the aged read their Bibles.

Whether we live by the seaside, or by the lakes and rivers, or on the prairie, it concerns us to attend to the nature of fishes, since they are not phenomena confined to certain localities only, but forms and phases of the life in nature universally dispersed. The countless shoals which annually coast the shores of Europe and America are not so interesting to the student of nature as the more fertile law itself, which deposits their spawn on the tops of mountains and on the interior plains; the fish principle in nature, from which it results that they may be found in water in so many places, in greater or less numbers. The natural historian is not a fisherman who prays for cloudy days and good luck merely; but as fishing has been styled "a contemplative man's recreation," introducing him profitably to woods and water, so the fruit of the naturalist's observations is not in new genera or species, but in new contemplations still, and science is only a more contemplative man's recreation. The seeds of the life of fishes are everywhere disseminated, whether the winds waft them, or the waters float them, or the deep earth holds them; wherever a pond is dug, straightway it is stocked with this vivacious race. They have a lease of nature, and it is not yet out. The Chinese are bribed to carry their ova from province to province in jars or in hollow reeds, or the water-birds to transport them to the mountain tarns and interior lakes. There are fishes wherever there is a fluid medium, and even in clouds and in melted metals we detect their semblance. Think how in winter you can sink a line down straight in a pasture through snow and through ice, and pull up a bright, slippery, dumb, subterranean silver or golden fish! It is curious, also, to reflect how they make one family, from the largest to the smallest. The least minnow that lies on the ice as bait for pickerel looks like a huge sea-fish cast up on the shore. In the waters of this town there are about a dozen distinct species, though the inexperienced would expect many more.

It enhances our sense of the grand security and serenity of nature to observe the still undisturbed economy and content of the fishes of this century, their happiness a regular fruit of the summer. The fresh-water sunfish, bream, or ruff (*Pomotis vulgaris*), as it were without ancestry, without posterity, still represents the fresh-water sunfish in nature. It is the most common of all, and seen on every urchin's string; a simple and inoffensive fish, whose nests are visible all along the shore, hollowed in the sand, over which it is steadily poised through the summer hours on waving fin. Sometimes there are twenty or thirty nests in the space of a few rods, two feet wide by half a foot in depth, and made with no little labor, the weeds being removed, and the sand shoved up on the sides, like a bowl. Here it may be seen early in summer assiduously brooding, and driving away minnows and larger fishes, even its own species, which would disturb its ova, pursuing them a few feet, and circling round swiftly to its nest again; the minnows, like young sharks, instantly entering the empty nests, meanwhile, and swallowing the spawn, which is attached to the weeds and to the bottom, on the sunny side. The spawn is exposed to so many dangers that a very small proportion can ever become fishes, for beside being the constant prey of birds and fishes, a great many nests are made so near the shore, in shallow water, that they are left dry in a few days, as the river goes down. These and the lamprey's are the only fishes' nests that I have observed, though the ova of some species may be seen floating on the surface. The breams are so careful of their charge that you may stand close by in the water and examine them at your leisure. I have thus stood over them half an hour at a time, and stroked them familiarly without frightening them, suffering them to nibble my fingers harmlessly, and seen them erect

their dorsal fins in anger when my hand approached
their ova, and have even taken them gently out of the
water with my hand; though this cannot be accomplished by a sudden movement, however dexterous, for
instant warning is conveyed to them through their denser
element, but only by letting the fingers gradually close
about them as they are poised over the palm, and with
the utmost gentleness raising them slowly to the surface.
Though stationary, they kept up a constant sculling
or waving motion with their fins, which is exceedingly
graceful, and expressive of their humble happiness; for
unlike ours, the element in which they live is a stream
which must be constantly resisted. From time to time
they nibble the weeds at the bottom or overhanging
their nests, or dart after a fly or a worm. The dorsal fin,
besides answering the purpose of a keel, with the anal,
serves to keep the fish upright, for in shallow water,
where this is not covered, they fall on their sides. As
you stand thus stooping over the bream in its nest, the
edges of the dorsal and caudal fins have a singular dusty
golden reflection, and its eyes, which stand out from the
head, are transparent and colorless. Seen in its native
element, it is a very beautiful and compact fish, perfect
in all its parts, and looks like a brilliant coin fresh from
the mint. It is a perfect jewel of the river, the green, red,
coppery, and golden reflections of its mottled sides being
the concentration of such rays as struggle through the
floating pads and flowers to the sandy bottom, and in
harmony with the sunlit brown and yellow pebbles. Behind its watery shield it dwells far from many accidents
inevitable to human life. . . .

Salmon, shad, and alewives were formerly abundant
here, and taken in weirs by the Indians, who taught
this method to the whites, by whom they were used as
food and as manure, until the dam and afterward the

canal at Billerica, and the factories at Lowell, put an end to their migrations hitherward; though it is thought that a few more enterprising shad may still occasionally be seen in this part of the river. It is said, to account for the destruction of the fishery, that those who at that time represented the interests of the fishermen and the fishes, remembering between what dates they were accustomed to take the grown shad, stipulated that the dams should be left open for that season only, and the fry, which go down a month later, were consequently stopped and destroyed by myriads. Others say that the fish-ways were not properly constructed. Perchance, after a few thousands of years, if the fishes will be patient, and pass their summers elsewhere meanwhile, nature will have leveled the Billerica dam, and the Lowell factories, and the Grass-ground River run clear again, to be explored by new migratory shoals, even as far as the Hopkinton pond and Westborough swamp.

One would like to know more of that race, now extinct, whose seines lie rotting in the garrets of their children, who openly professed the trade of fishermen, and even fed their townsmen creditably, not skulking through the meadows to a rainy afternoon sport. Dim visions we still get of miraculous draughts of fishes, and heaps uncountable by the riverside, from the tales of our seniors sent on horseback in their childhood from the neighboring towns, perched on saddle-bags, with instructions to get the one bag filled with shad, the other with alewives. At least one memento of those days may still exist in the memory of this generation, in the familiar appellation of a celebrated train-band of this town, whose untrained ancestors stood creditably at Concord North Bridge. Their captain, a man of piscatory tastes, having duly warned his company to turn out on a certain day, they, like obedient soldiers, appeared promptly on parade at the appointed time, but, unfortunately, they went undrilled, except in the manoeuvres of a soldier's wit and unlicensed jesting, that May day; for their captain, forgetting his own appointment, and warned only by the favorable aspect of the heavens, as he had often done before, went a-fishing that afternoon, and his company thenceforth was known to old and young, grave and gay, as "The Shad," and by the youths of this vicinity this was long regarded as the proper name of all the irregular militia in Christendom. But, alas! no record of these fishers' lives remains that we know, unless it be one brief page of hard but unquestionable history, which occurs in Day Book No. 4, of an old trader of this town, long since dead, which shows pretty plainly what constituted a fisherman's stock in trade in those days. It purports to be a Fisherman's Account Current, probably for the fishing season of the year 1805, during which months he purchased daily rum and sugar, sugar and rum, N. E. and W. I., "one cod line," "one brown mug," and "a line for the seine"; rum and sugar, sugar and rum, "good loaf sugar," and "good brown," W. I. and N. E., in short and uniform entries to the bottom of the page, all carried out in pounds, shillings, and pence, from March 25 to June 5, and promptly settled by receiving "cash in full" at the last date. But perhaps not so settled altogether. These were the necessaries of life in those days; with salmon, shad, and alewives, fresh and pickled, he was thereafter independent on the groceries. Rather a preponderance of the fluid elements; but such is the fisherman's nature. I can faintly remember to have seen this same fisher in my earliest youth, still as near the river as he could get, with uncertain, undulatory step, after so many things had gone down-stream, swinging a scythe in the meadow, his bottle like a serpent hid in the grass; himself as yet not cut down by the Great Mower.

Surely the fates are forever kind, though Nature's laws are more immutable than any despot's, yet to man's daily life they rarely seem rigid, but permit him to relax with license in summer weather. He is not harshly reminded of the things he may not do. She is very kind and liberal to all men of vicious habits, and certainly does not deny them quarter; they do not die without priest. Still they maintain life along the way, keeping this side the Styx, still hearty, still resolute, "never better in their lives"; and again, after a dozen years have elapsed, they start up from behind a hedge, asking for work and wages for able-bodied men. Who has not met such

> "a beggar on the way,
> Who sturdily could gang? . . .
> Who cared neither for wind nor wet,
> In lands where'er he past?"

> "That bold adopts each house he views, his own;
> Makes every purse his checquer, and, at pleasure,
> Walks forth, and taxes all the world, like Caesar";

as if consistency were the secret of health, while the poor inconsistent aspirant man, seeking to live a pure life, feeding on air, divided against himself, cannot stand, but pines and dies after a life of sickness, on beds of down.

The unwise are accustomed to speak as if some were not sick; but methinks the difference between men in respect to health is not great enough to lay much stress upon. Some are reputed sick and some are not. It often happens that the sicker man is the nurse to the sounder.

Shad are still taken in the basin of Concord River, at Lowell, where they are said to be a month earlier than the Merrimack shad, on account of the warmth of the water. Still patiently, almost pathetically, with instinct not to be discouraged, not to be *reasoned* with, revisiting their old haunts, as if their stern fates would relent, and still met by the Corporation with its dam. Poor shad! where is thy redress? When Nature gave thee instinct, gave she thee the heart to bear thy fate? Still wandering the sea in thy scaly armor to inquire humbly at the mouths of rivers if man has perchance left them free for thee to enter. By countless shoals loitering uncertain meanwhile, merely stemming the tide there, in danger from sea foes in spite of thy bright armor, awaiting new instructions, until the sands, until the water itself, tell thee if it be so or not. Thus by whole migrating nations, full of instinct, which is thy faith, in this backward spring, turned adrift, and perchance knowest not where men do *not* dwell, where there are *not* factories, in these days. Armed with no sword, no electric shock, but mere shad, armed only with innocence and a just cause, with tender dumb mouth only forward, and scales easy to be detached. I for one am with thee, and who knows what may avail a crowbar against that Billerica dam?—Not despairing when whole myriads have gone to feed those sea monsters during thy suspense, but still brave, indifferent, on easy fin there, like shad reserved for higher destinies. Willing to be decimated for man's behoof after the spawning season. Away with the superficial and selfish phil-*anthropy* of men—who knows what admirable virtue of fishes may be below low-water-mark, bearing up against a hard destiny, not admired by that fellow creature who alone can appreciate it! Who hears the fishes when they cry? It will not be forgotten by some memory that we were contemporaries. Thou shalt ere long have thy way up the rivers, up all the rivers of the globe, if I am not mistaken. Yea, even thy dull watery dream shall be more than realized. If it were not so, but thou wert to be overlooked at first and at last, then would not I take their heaven. Yes, I say so, who think I know better than thou canst. Keep a stiff fin, then, and stem all the tides thou mayst meet.

At length it would seem that the interests, not of the fishes only, but of the men of Wayland, of Sudbury, of Concord, demand the leveling of that dam. Innumerable acres of meadow are waiting to be made dry land, wild native grass to give place to English. The farmers stand with scythes whet, waiting the subsiding of the waters, by gravitation, by evaporation, or otherwise, but sometimes their eyes do not rest, their wheels do not roll, on the quaking meadow ground during the haying season at all. So many sources of wealth inaccessible. They rate the loss hereby incurred in the single town of Wayland alone as equal to the expense of keeping a hundred yoke of oxen the year round. One year, as I learn, not long ago, the farmers standing ready to drive their teams afield as usual, the water gave no signs of falling; without new attraction in the heavens, without freshet or visible cause, still standing stagnant at an unprecedented height. All hydrometers were at fault; some trembled for their English, even. But speedy emissaries revealed the unnatural secret, in the new floatboard, wholly a foot.in width, added to their already too high privileges by the dam proprietors. The hundred yoke of oxen, meanwhile, standing patient, gazing wishfully meadowward, at that inaccessible waving native grass, uncut but by the great mower Time, who cuts so broad a swath, without so much as a wisp to wind about their horns.

That was a long pull from Ball's Hill to Carlisle Bridge, sitting with our faces to the south, a slight breeze rising from the north; but nevertheless water still runs and grass grows, for now, having passed the bridge between Carlisle and Bedford, we see men haying far off in the meadow, their heads waving like the grass which they cut. In the distance the wind seemed to bend all alike. As the night stole over, such a freshness was wafted across the meadow that every blade of cut grass seemed to teem with life. Faint purple clouds began to be reflected in the water, and the cow-bells tinkled louder along the banks, while, like sly water-rats, we stole along nearer the shore, looking for a place to pitch our camp.

At length, when we had made about seven miles, as far as Billerica, we moored our boat on the west side of a little rising ground which in the spring forms an island in the river. Here we found huckleberries still hanging upon the bushes, where they seemed to have slowly ripened for our especial use. Bread and sugar, and cocoa boiled in river water, made our repast, and as we had drank in the fluvial prospect all day, so now we took a draft of the water with our evening meal to propitiate the river gods, and whet our vision for the sights it was to behold. The sun was setting on the one hand, while our eminence was contributing its shadow to the night on the other. It seemed insensibly to grow lighter as the night shut in, and a distant and solitary farmhouse was revealed, which before lurked in the shadows of the noon. There was no other house in sight, nor any cultivated field. To the right and left, as far as the horizon, were straggling pine woods with their plumes against the sky, and across the river were rugged hills, covered with shrub oaks, tangled with grape-vines and ivy, with here and there a gray rock jutting out from the maze. The sides of these cliffs, though a quarter of a mile distant, were almost heard to rustle while we looked at them, it was such a leafy wilderness; a place for fauns and satyrs, and where bats hung all day to the rocks, and at evening flitted over the water, and fireflies husbanded their light under the grass and leaves against the night. When we had pitched our tent on the hillside, a few rods from the shore, we sat looking through its triangular door in the twilight at our lonely mast on the shore just seen above the alders, and hardly yet come to a standstill from the swaying of the stream; the first encroachment of commerce on this land. There was our port, our Ostia. That straight, geometrical line against the water and the sky stood for the last refinements of civilized life, and what of sublimity there is in history was there symbolized.

For the most part, there was no recognition of human life in the night; no human breathing was heard, only the breathing of the wind. As we sat up, kept awake by the novelty of our situation, we heard at intervals foxes stepping about over the dead leaves, and brushing the dewy grass close to our tent, and once a musquash fumbling among the potatoes and melons in our boat; but when we hastened to the shore we could detect only a ripple in the water ruffling the disk of a star. At intervals we were serenaded by the song of a dreaming sparrow or the throttled cry of an owl; but after each sound which near at hand broke the stillness of the night, each crackling of the twigs, or rustling among the leaves, there was a sudden pause, and deeper and more conscious silence, as if the intruder were aware that no life was rightfully abroad at that hour. There was a fire in Lowell, as we judged, this night, and we saw the horizon blazing, and heard the distant alarm-bells, as it were a faint tinkling music borne to these woods. But the most constant and memorable sound of a summer's night, which we did not fail to hear every night afterward, though at no time so incessantly and so favorably as now, was the barking of the house-dogs, from the loudest and hoarsest bark to the faintest aerial palpitation under the eaves of heaven, from the patient but anxious mastiff to the timid and wakeful terrier, at first loud and rapid, then faint and slow, to be imitated only in a whisper; wow-wow-wow-wow—wo—wo—w—w. Even in a retired and uninhabited district like this, it was a sufficiency of sound for the ear of night, and more impressive than any music. I have heard the voice of a hound, just before daylight, while the stars were shining, from over the woods and river, far in the horizon, when it sounded as sweet and melodious as an instrument. The hounding of a dog pursuing a fox or other animal in the horizon may have first suggested the notes of the hunting-horn to alternate with and relieve the lungs of the dog. This natural bugle long resounded in the woods of the ancient world before the horn was invented. The very dogs that sullenly bay the moon from farmyards in these nights excite more heroism in our breasts than all the civil exhortations or war sermons of the age. "I would rather be a dog, and bay the moon," than many a Roman that I know. The night is equally indebted to the clarion of the cock, with wakeful hope, from the very setting of the sun, prematurely ushering in the dawn. All these sounds, the crowing of cocks, the baying of dogs, and the hum of insects at noon, are the evidence of nature's health or *sound* state. Such is the never-failing beauty and accuracy of language, the most perfect art in the world; the chisel of a thousand years retouches it.

At length the antepenultimate and drowsy hours drew on, and all sounds were denied entrance to our ears.

> Who sleeps by day and walks by night,
> Will meet no spirit, but some sprite.

TUESDAY

On either side the river lie
Long fields of barley and of rye,
That clothe the wold and meet the sky;
And through the fields the road runs by
    To many-towered Camelot.
                              TENNYSON.

Long before daylight we ranged abroad, hatchet in
hand, in search of fuel, and made the yet slumbering
and dreaming wood resound with our blows. Then with
our fire we burned up a portion of the loitering night,
while the kettle sang its homely strain to the morning
star. We tramped about the shore, walked all the muskrats, and scared up the bittern and birds that were
asleep upon their roosts; we hauled up and upset our
boat, and washed it and rinsed out the clay, talking aloud
as if it were broad day, until at length, by three o'clock,
we had completed our preparations and were ready to
pursue our voyage as usual; so, shaking the clay from
out feet, we pushed into the fog.

Though we were enveloped in mist as usual, we
trusted that there was a bright day behind it.

        Ply the oars! away! away!
    In each dewdrop of the morning
        Lies the promise of a day.

    Rivers from the sunrise flow,
        Springing with the dewy morn;
    Voyageurs 'gainst time do row,
    Idle noon nor sunset know,
        Ever even with the dawn.

Belknap, the historian of this State, says that "in the
neighborhood of fresh rivers and ponds, a whitish fog
in the morning lying over the water is a sure indication

of fair weather for that day; and when no fog is seen, rain is expected before night." That which seemed to us to invest the world was only a narrow and shallow wreath of vapor stretched over the channel of the Merrimack from the seaboard to the mountains. More extensive fogs, however, have their own limits. . . .

But now we must make haste back before the fog disperses to the blithe Merrimack water.

> Since that first "Away! away!"
>   Many a lengthy reach we've rowed,
> Still the sparrow on the spray
> Hastes to usher in the day
>   With her simple stanza'd ode.

We passed a canal-boat before sunrise, groping its way to the seaboard, and, though we could not see it on account of the fog, the few dull, thumping, stertorous sounds which we heard impressed us with a sense of weight and irresistible motion. One little rill of commerce already awake on this distant New Hampshire river. The fog, as it required more skill in the steering, enhanced the interest of our early voyage, and made the river seem indefinitely broad. A slight mist, through which objects are faintly visible, has the effect of expanding even ordinary streams, by a singular mirage, into arms of the sea or inland lakes. In the present instance, it was even fragrant and invigorating, and we enjoyed it as a sort of earlier sunshine, or dewy and embryo light.

> Low-anchored cloud,
> Newfoundland air,
> Fountain-head and source of rivers,
> Dew-cloth, dream drapery,
> And napkin spread by fays;
> Drifting meadow of the air,

Where bloom the daisied banks and violets,
And in whose fenny labyrinth
The bittern booms and heron wades;
Spirit of lakes and seas and rivers,
Bear only perfumes and the scent
Of healing herbs to just men's fields!

The same pleasant and observant historian whom we quoted above says that "In the mountainous parts of the country, the ascent of vapors, and their formation into clouds, is a curious and entertaining object. The vapors are seen rising in small columns like smoke from many chimneys. When risen to a certain height, they spread, meet, condense, and are attracted to the mountains, where they either distill in gentle dews, and replenish the springs, or descend in showers, accompanied with thunder. After short intermissions, the process is repeated many times in the course of a summer day, affording to travelers a lively illustration of that is observed in the Book of Job, 'They are wet with the showers of the mountains.'"

Fogs and clouds which conceal the overshadowing mountains lend the breadth of the plains to mountain vales. Even a small-featured country acquires some grandeur in stormy weather when clouds are seen drifting between the beholder and the neighboring hills. When, in traveling toward Haverhill through Hampstead in this State, on the height of land between the Merrimack and the Piscataqua or the sea, you commence the descent eastward, the view toward the coast is so distant and unexpected, though the sea is invisible, that you at first suppose the unobstructed atmosphere to be a fog in the lowlands concealing hills of corresponding elevation to that you are upon; but it is the mist of prejudice alone, which the winds will not disperse. The most stupendous scenery ceases to be sublime when it becomes distinct, or in other words limited, and the imagination is no longer encouraged to exaggerate it. The actual height and breadth of a mountain or a water-fall are always ridiculously small; they are the imagined only that content us. Nature is not made after such a fashion as we would have her. We piously exaggerate her wonders, as the scenery around our home.

Such was the heaviness of the dews along this river that we were generally obliged to leave our tent spread over the bows of the boat till the sun had dried it, to avoid mildew. We passed the mouth of Penichook Brook, a wild salmon stream, in the fog, without seeing it. At length the sun's rays struggled through the mist and showed us the pines on shore dripping with dew, and springs trickling from the moist banks,

> "And now the taller sons, whom Titan warms,
> Of unshorn mountains blown with easy winds,
> Dandle the morning's childhood in their arms,
> And, if they chanced to slip the prouder pines,
> The under corylets did catch their shines,
> To gild their leaves."

We rowed for some hours between glistening banks before the sun had dried the grass and leaves, or the day had established its character. Its serenity at last seemed the more profound and secure for the denseness of the morning's fog. The river became swifter, and the scen-ery more pleasing than before. The banks were steep and clayey for the most part, and trickling with water, and where a spring oozed out a few feet above the river the boatmen had cut a trough out of a slab with their axes, and placed it so as to receive the water and fill their jugs conveniently. Sometimes this purer and cooler water, bursting out from under a pine or a rock, was collected into a basin close to the edge of and level with the river, a fountain-head of the Merrimack. So near

along life's stream are the fountains of innocence and
youth making fertile its sandy margin; and the voyageur
will do well to replenish his vessels often at the uncon-
taminated sources. Some youthful spring, perchance,
still empties with tinkling music into the oldest river,
even when it is falling into the sea, and we imagine that
its music is distinguished by the river-gods from the
general lapse of the stream, and falls sweeter on their
ears in proportion as it is nearer to the ocean. As the
evaporations of the river feed thus these unsuspected
springs which filter through its banks, so, perchance,
our aspirations fall back again in springs on the margin
of life's stream to refresh and purify it. The yellow and
tepid river may float his scow, and cheer his eye with its
reflections and its ripples, but the boatman quenches
his thirst at this small rill alone. It is this purer and
cooler element that chiefly sustains his life. The race
will long survive that is thus discreet.

Our course this morning lay between the territories of
Merrimack, on the west, and Litchfield, once called
Brenton's Farm, on the east, which townships were
anciently the Indian Naticook. Brenton was a fur-trader
among the Indians, and these lands were granted to him
in 1656. The latter township contains about five hundred inhabitants, of whom, however, we saw none, and
but few of their dwellings. Being on the river, whose
banks are always high and generally concealed the few
houses, the country appeared much more wild and primitive than to the traveler on the neighboring roads. The
river is by far the most attractive highway, and those
boatmen who have spent twenty or twenty-five years on
it must have had a much fairer, more wild and memorable experience than the dusty and jarring one of the
teamster who has driven, during the same time, on the
roads which run parallel with the stream. As one ascends

the Merrimack he rarely sees a village, but for the most
part alternate wood and pasture lands, and sometimes a
field of corn or potatoes, of rye or oats or English grass,
with a few straggling apple trees, and, at still longer intervals, a farmer's house. The soil, excepting the best of
the interval, is commonly as light and sandy as a patriot
could desire. Sometimes this forenoon the country appeared in its primitive state, and as if the Indian still inhabited it, and, again, as if many free, new settlers
occupied it, their slight fences straggling down to the
water's edge; and the barking of dogs, and even the
prattle of children, were heard, and smoke was seen
to go up from some hearthstone, and the banks were
divided into patches of pasture, mowing, tillage, and
woodland. But when the river spread out broader, with
an uninhabited islet, or a long, low, sandy shore which
ran on single and devious, not answering to its opposite,
but far off as if it were seashore or single coast, and the
land no longer nursed the river in its bosom, but they
conversed as equals, the rustling leaves with rippling
leaves, and few fences were seen, but high oak woods on
one side, and large herds of cattle, and all tracks seemed
to point to one center behind some statelier grove, we
imagined that the river flowed through an extensive
manor, and that the few inhabitants were retainers to a
lord, and a feudal state of things prevailed. . . .

Here, too, was another extensive desert by the side of
the road in Litchfield, visible from the bank of the river.
The sand was blown off in some places to the depth of
ten or twelve feet, leaving small grotesque hillocks of
that height, where there was a clump of bushes firmly
rooted. Thirty or forty years ago, as we were told, it was
a sheep-pasture, but the sheep, being worried by the
fleas, began to paw the ground, till they broke the sod,

and so the sand began to blow, till now it had extended over forty or fifty acres. This evil might easily have been remedied, at first, by spreading birches with their leaves on over the sand, and fastening them down with stakes, to break the wind. The fleas bit the sheep, and the sheep bit the ground, and the sore had spread to this extent. It is astonishing what a great sore a little scratch breedeth. Who knows but Sahara, where caravans and cities are buried, began with the bite of an African flea? This poor globe, how it must itch in many places! Will no god be kind enough to spread a salve of birches over its sores? Here, too, we noticed where the Indians had gathered a heap of stones, perhaps for their council-fire, which, by their weight having prevented the sand under them from blowing away, were left on the summit of a mound. They told us that arrowheads, and also bullets of lead and iron, had been found here. We noticed several other sandy tracts in our voyage; and the course of the Merrimack can be traced from the nearest mountain by its yellow sandbanks, though the river itself is for the most part invisible. Lawsuits, as we hear, have in some cases grown out of these causes. Railroads have been made through certain irritable districts, breaking their sod, and so have set the sand to blowing, till it has converted fertile farms into deserts, and the company has had to pay the damages.

This sand seemed to us the connecting link between land and water. It was a kind of water on which you could walk, and you could see the ripple-marks on its surface, produced by the winds, precisely like those at the bottom of a brook or lake. We had read that Mussulmans are permitted by the Koran to perform their ablutions in sand when they cannot get water, a necessary indulgence in Arabia, and we now understood the propriety of this provision. . . .

There were several canalboats at Cromwell's Falls passing through the locks, for which we waited. In the forward part of one stood a brawny New Hampshire man, leaning on his pole, bareheaded and in shirt and trousers only, a rude Apollo of a man, coming down from "that vast uplandish country" to the main; of nameless age, with flaxen hair and vigorous, weather-bleached countenance, in whose wrinkles the sun still lodged, as little touched by the heats and frosts and withering cares of life as a maple of the mountain; an undressed, unkempt, uncivil man, with whom we parleyed awhile, and parted not without a sincere interest in one another. His humanity was genuine and instinctive, and his rudeness only a manner. He inquired, just as we were passing out of earshot, if we had killed anything, and we shouted after him that we had shot a *buoy*, and could see him for a long while scratching his head in vain to know if he had heard aright.

There is reason in the distinction of civil and uncivil. The manners are sometimes so rough a rind that we doubt whether they cover any core or sapwood at all. We sometimes meet uncivil men, children of Amazons, who dwell by mountain paths, and are said to be inhospitable to strangers; whose salutation is as rude as the grasp of their browny hands, and who deal with men as unceremoniously as they are wont to deal with the elements. They need only to extend their clearings, and let in more sunlight, to seek out the southern slopes of the hills, from which they may look down on the civil plain or ocean, and temper their diet duly with the cereal fruits, consuming less wild meat and acorns, to become like the inhabitants of cities. A true politeness does not result from any hasty and artificial polishing, it is true, but grows naturally in characters of the right grain and quality, through a long fronting of men and events, and rubbing on good and bad fortune. Perhaps I can tell a tale to the purpose while the lock is filling—for our voyage this forenoon furnishes but few incidents of importance. . . .

Being now fairly in the stream of this week's commerce, we began to meet with boats more frequently, and hailed them from time to time with the freedom of sailors. The boatmen appeared to lead an easy and contented life, and we thought that we should prefer their employment ourselves to many professions which are much more sought after. They suggested how few circumstances are necessary to the well-being and serenity of man, how indifferent all employments are, and that any may seem noble and poetic to the eyes of men, if pursued with sufficient buoyancy and freedom. With liberty and pleasant weather, the simplest occupation, any unquestioned country mode of life which detains us in the open air, is alluring. The man who picks peas steadily for a living is more than respectable, he is even envied by his shopworn neighbors. We are as happy as the birds when our Good Genius permits us to pursue any outdoor work, without a sense of dissipation. Our penknife glitters in the sun; our voice is echoed by yonder wood; if an oar drops, we are fain to let it drop again.

The canalboat is of very simple construction, requiring but little ship-timber, and, as we were told, costs about two hundred dollars. They are managed by two men. In ascending the stream they use poles fourteen or fifteen feet long, pointed with iron, walking about one third the length of the boat from the forward end. Going down, they commonly keep in the middle of the stream, using an oar at each end; or if the wind is favorable they raise their broad sail, and have only to steer. They

commonly carry down wood or bricks—fifteen or sixteen
cords of wood, and as many thousand bricks, at a time
—and bring back stores for the country, consuming two
or three days each way between Concord and Charlestown. They sometimes pile the wood so as to leave a
shelter in one part where they may retire from the rain.
One can hardly imagine a more healthful employment,
or one more favorable to contemplation and the observation of nature. Unlike the mariner, they have the constantly varying panorama of the shore to relieve the
monotony of their labor, and it seemed to us that as they
thus glided noiselessly from town to town, with all their
furniture about them, for their very homestead is a movable, they could comment on the character of the inhabitants with greater advantage and security to themselves than the traveler in a coach, who would be unable
to indulge in such broadsides of wit and humor in so
small a vessel for fear of the recoil. They are not subject
to great exposure, like the lumberers of Maine, in any
weather, but inhale the healthfulest breezes, being
slightly incumbered with clothing, frequently with the
head and feet bare. When we met them at noon, as they
were leisurely descending the stream, their busy commerce did not look like toil, but rather like some ancient
Oriental game still played on a large scale, as the game
of chess, for instance, handed down to this generation.
From morning till night, unless the wind is so fair that
his single sail will suffice without other labor than steering, the boatman walks backwards and forwards on the
side of his boat, now stooping with his shoulder to the
pole, then drawing it back slowly to set it again, meanwhile moving steadily forward through an endless valley
and an ever-changing scenery, now distinguishing his
course for a mile or two, and now shut in by a sudden
turn of the river in a small woodland lake. All the phe-

nomena which surround him are simple and grand, and there is something impressive, even majestic, in the very motion he causes, which will naturally be communicated to his own cháracter, and he feels the slow, irresistible movement under him with pride, as if it were his own energy.

The news spread like wildfire among us youths, when formerly, once in a year or two, one of these boats came up the Concord River, and was seen stealing mysteriously through the meadows and past the village. It came and departed as silently as a cloud, without noise or dust, and was witnessed by few. One summer day this huge traveler might be seen moored at some meadow's wharf, and another summer day it was not there. Where precisely it came from, or who these men were who knew the rocks and soundings better than we who bathed there, we could never tell. We knew some river's bay only, but they took rivers from end to end. They were a sort of fabulous rivermen to us. It was inconceivable by what sort of mediation any mere landsman could hold communication with them. Would they heave to, to gratify his wishes? No, it was favor enough to know faintly of their destination, or the time of their possible return. I have seen them in the summer, when the stream ran low, mowing the weeds in mid-channel, and with hayers' jests cutting broad swaths in three feet of water, that they might make a passage for their scow, while the grass in long windrows was carried down the stream, undried by the rarest hay weather. We admired unweariedly how their vessel would float, like a huge chip, sustaining so many casks of lime, and thousands of bricks, and such heaps of iron ore, with wheelbarrows aboard, and that, when we stepped on it, it did not yield to the pressure of our feet. It gave us confidence in the prevalence of the law of buoyancy, and we imagined

to what infinite uses it might be put. The men appeared
to lead a kind of life on it, and it was whispered that
they slept aboard. Some affirmed that it carried sail, and
that such winds blew here as filled the sails of vessels on
the ocean; which again others much doubted. They had
been seen to sail across our Fair Haven Bay by lucky
fishers who were out, but unfortunately others were not
there to see. We might then say that our river was navi-
gable—why not? In after years I read in print, with no
little satisfaction, that it was thought by some that, with
a little expense in removing rocks and deepening the
channel, "there might be a profitable inland navigation." *I* then lived somewhere to tell of.

Such is Commerce, which shakes the coconut and
breadfruit tree in the remotest isle, and sooner or later
dawns on the duskiest and most simple-minded savage.
If we may be pardoned the digression, who can help
being affected at the thought of the very fine and slight,
but positive relation, in which the savage inhabitants
of some remote isle stand to the mysterious white mariner, the child of the sun?—as if *we* were to have dealings with an animal higher in the scale of being than
ourselves. It is a barely recognized fact to the natives
that he exists, and has his home far away somewhere,
and is glad to buy their fresh fruits with his superfluous
commodities. Under the same catholic sun glances his
white ship over Pacific waves into their smooth bays,
and the poor savage's paddle gleams in the air.

> Man's little acts are grand,
> Beheld from land to land,
> There as they lie in time,
> Within their native clime.
>> Ships with the noontide weigh,
>> And glide before its ray
>> To some retired bay,
>> Their haunt,

> Whence, under tropic sun,
> Again they run,
> Bearing gum Senegal and Tragicant.
> For this was ocean meant,
> For this the sun was sent,
> And moon was lent,
> And winds in distant caverns pent.

Since our voyage the railroad on the bank has been extended, and there is now but little boating on the Merrimack. All kinds of produce and stores were formerly conveyed by water, but now nothing is carried up the stream, and almost wood and bricks alone are carried down, and these are also carried on the railroad. The locks are fast wearing out, and will soon be impassable, since the tolls will not pay the expense of repairing them, and so in a few years there will be an end of boating on this river. The boating at present is principally between Merrimack and Lowell, or Hooksett and Manchester. They make two or three trips in a week, according to wind and weather, from Merrimack to Lowell and back, about twenty-five miles each way. The boatman comes singing in to shore late at night, and moors his empty boat, and gets his supper and lodging in some house near at hand, and again early in the morning, by starlight perhaps, he pushes away upstream, and, by a shout, or the fragment of a song, gives notice of his approach to the lock-man, with whom he is to take his breakfast. If he gets up to his woodpile before noon he proceeds to load his boat, with the help of his single "hand," and is on his way down again before night. When he gets to Lowell he unloads his boat, and gets his receipt for his cargo, and, having heard the news at the public house at Middlesex or elsewhere, goes back with his empty boat and his receipt in his pocket to the owner, and to get a new load. We were frequently advertised of their approach by some faint sound behind us, and looking round saw them a mile off, creeping stealthily up the side of the stream like alligators. It was pleasant to hail these sailors of the Merrimack from time to time, and learn the news which circulated with them. We imagined that the sun shining on their bare heads had stamped a liberal and public character on their most private thoughts.

The open and sunny interval still stretched away from the river sometimes by two or more terraces, to the distant hill-country, and when we climbed the bank, we commonly found an irregular copse-wood skirting the river, the primitive having floated downstream long ago to ——, the "King's navy." Sometimes we saw the river road a quarter or half a mile distant, and the particolored Concord stage, with its cloud of dust, its van of earnest traveling faces, and its rear of dusty trunks, reminding us that the country had its places of rendezvous for restless Yankee men. There dwelt along at considerable distances on this interval a quiet agricultural and pastoral people, with every house its well, as we sometimes proved, and every household, though never so still and remote it appeared in the noontide, its dinner about these times. There they lived on, those New England people, farmer lives, father and grandfather and great-grandfather, on and on without noise, keeping up tradition, and expecting, beside fair weather and abundant harvests, we did not learn what. They were contented to live, since it was so contrived for them, and where their lines had fallen.

> Our uninquiring corpses lie more low
> Than our life's curiosity doth go.

Yet these men had no need to travel to be as wise as Solomon in all his glory, so similar are the lives of men in all countries, and fraught with the same homely ex-

periences. One half the world *knows* how the other half
lives.

About noon we passed a small village in Merrimack
at Thornton's Ferry, and tasted of the waters of Naticook Brook on the same side, where French and his
companions, whose grave we saw in Dunstable, were
ambuscaded by the Indians. The humble village of
Litchfield, with its steepleless meetinghouse, stood on
the opposite or east bank, near where a dense grove of
willows backd by maples skirted the shore. There also
we noticed some shagbark trees, which, as they do not
grow in Concord, were as strange a sight to us as the
palm would be, whose fruit only we have seen. Our
course now curved gracefully to the north, leaving a
low, flat shore on the Merrimack side, which forms a
sort of harbor for canalboats. We observed some fair
elms and particularly large and handsome white maples
standing conspicuously on this interval; and the opposite shore, a quarter of a mile below, was covered with
young elms and maples six inches high, which had
probably sprung from the seeds which had been washed
across.

Some carpenters were at work here mending a scow
on the green and sloping bank. The strokes of their mal-
lets echoed from shore to shore, and up and down the
river, and their tools gleamed in the sun a quarter of a
mile from us, and we realized that boat-building was as
ancient and honorable an art as agriculture, and that
there might be a naval as well as a pastoral life. The
whole history of commerce was made manifest in that
scow turned bottom upward on the shore. Thus did men
begin to go down upon the sea in ships; *quaeque diu
steterant in montibus altis, Fluctibus ignotis insultavêre
carinae;* "and keels which had long stood on high moun-

tains careered insultingly (*insultavêre*) over unknown waves."[1] . . .

During the heat of the day, we rested on a large island a mile above the mouth of this river, pastured by a herd of cattle, with steep banks and scattered elms and oaks, and a sufficient channel for canalboats on each side. When we made a fire to boil some rice for our dinner, the flames spreading amid the dry grass, and the smoke curling silently upward and casting grotesque shadows on the ground, seemed phenomena of the noon, and we fancied that we progressed up the stream without effort, and as naturally as the wind and tide went down, not outraging the calm days by unworthy bustle or impatience. The woods on the neighboring shore were alive with pigeons, which were moving south, looking for mast, but now, like ouselves, spending their noon in the shade. We could hear the slight, wiry, winnowing sound of their wings as they changed their roosts from time to time, and their gentle and tremulous cooing. They sojourned with us during the noontide, greater travelers far than we. You may frequently discover a single pair sitting upon the lower branches of the white pine in the depths of the wood, at this hour of the day, so silent and solitary, and with such a hermitlike appearance, as if they had never strayed beyond its skirts, while the acorn which was gathered in the forests of Maine is still undigested in their crops. We obtained one of these handsome birds, which lingered too long upon its perch, and plucked and broiled it here with some other game, to be carried along for our supper; for, beside the provisions which we carried with us, we depended mainly on the river and forest for our supply. It is true, it did not seem to be putting this bird to its right use to pluck off its

---

[1] *Ovid*, Met. *I. 133.*

feathers, and extract its entrails, and broil its carcass on the coals; but we heroically persevered, nevertheless, waiting for further information. The same regard for Nature which excited our sympathy for her creatures nerved our hands to carry through what we had begun. For we would be honorable to the party we deserted; we would fulfill fate, and so at length, perhaps, detect the secret innocence of these incessant tragedies which Heaven allows.

> "Too quick resolves do resolution wrong.
> What, part so soon to be divorced so long?
> Things to be done art long to be debated;
> Heaven is not day'd, Repentance is not dated."

We are double-edged blades, and every time we whet our virtue the return stroke straps our vice. Where is the skillful swordsman who can give clean wounds, and not rip up his work with the other edge?

Nature herself has not provided the most graceful end for her creatures. What becomes of all these birds that people the air and forest for our solacement? The sparrows seem always *chipper*, never infirm. We do not see their bodies lie about. Yet there is a tragedy at the end of each one of their lives. They must perish miserably; not one of them is translated. True, "not a sparrow falleth to the ground without our Heavenly Father's knowledge," but they do fall, nevertheless.

The carcasses of some poor squirrels, however, the same that frisked so merrily in the morning, which we had skinned and emboweled for our dinner, we abandoned in disgust, with tardy humanity, as too wretched a resource for any but starving men. It was to perpetuate the practice of a barbarous era. If they had been larger, our crime had been less. Their small red bodies, little bundles of red tissue, mere gobbets of venison, would not have "fattened fire." With a sudden impulse we threw them away, and washed our hands, and boiled some rice for our dinner. "Behold the difference between the one who eateth flesh, and him to whom it belonged! The first hath a momentary enjoyment, whilst the latter is deprived of existence!" "Who would commit so great a crime against a poor animal, who is fed only by the herbs which grow wild in the woods, and whose belly is burnt up with hunger?" We remembered a picture of mankind in the hunter age, chasing hares down the mountains; O me miserable! Yet sheep and oxen are but larger squirrels, whose hides are saved and meat is salted, whose souls perchance are not so large in proportion to their bodies.

There should always be some flowering and maturing of the fruits of nature in the cooking process. Some simple dishes recommend themselves to our imaginations as well as palates. In parched corn, for instance, there is a manifest sympathy between the bursting seed and the more perfect developments of vegetable life. It is a perfect flower with its petals, like the houstonia or anemone. On my warm hearth these cerealian blossoms expanded; here is the bank whereon they grew. Perhaps some such visible blessing would always attend the simple and wholesome repast. . . .

Late in the afternoon, for we had lingered long on the island, we raised our sail for the first time, and for a short hour the southwest wind was our ally; but it did not please Heaven to abet us long. With one sail raised we swept slowly up the eastern side of the stream, steering clear of the rocks, while, from the top of a hill which formed the opposite bank, some lumberers were rolling down timber to be rafted down the stream. We could see their axes and levers gleaming in the sun, and the logs came down with a dust and a rumbling sound, which was reverberated through the woods beyond us on our side, like the roar of artillery. But Zephyr soon took us out of sight and hearing of this commerce. Having passed Read's Ferry, and another island called McGaw's Island, we reached some rapids called Moore's Falls, and entered on "that section of the river, nine miles in extent, converted, by law, into the Union Canal, comprehending in that space six distinct falls; at each of which, and at several intermediate places, work has been done." After passing Moore's Falls by means of locks, we again had recourse to our oars, and went merrily on our way, driving the small sandpiper from rock to rock before us, and sometimes rowing near enough to a cottage on the bank, though they were few and far between, to see the sunflowers, and the seed-vessels of the poppy, like small goblets filled with the water of Lethe, before the door, but without disturbing the sluggish household behind. Thus we held on, sailing or dipping our way along with the paddle up this broad river, smooth and placid, flowing over concealed rocks, where we could see the pickerel lying low in the transparent water, eager to double some distant cape, to make some great bend as in the life of man, and see what new perspective would open; looking far into a new country, broad and serene, the cottages of settlers seen afar for the first time, yet with the moss of a century on their roofs, and the third or fourth generation in their shadows. Strange was it to consider how the sun and the summer, the buds of spring and the seared leaves of autumn, were related to these cabins along the shore; how all the rays which paint the landscape radiate from them, and the flight of the crow and the gyrations of the hawk have reference to their roofs. Still the ever rich and fertile shores accompanied us, fringed with vines and alive with small birds and frisking squirrels, the edge of some farmer's field or widow's woodlot, or wilder, perchance, where the muskrat, the little medicine of the river, drags itself along stealthily over the alder leaves and mussel shells, and man and the memory of man are banished far.

At length the unwearied, never-sinking shore, still holding on without break, with its cool copses and serene pasture-grounds, tempted us to disembark; and we adventurously landed on this remote coast, to survey it, without the knowledge of any human inhabitant probably to this day. But we still remember the gnarled and hospitable oaks which grew even there for our entertainment, and were no strangers to us, the lonely horse in his pasture, and the patient cows, whose path to the river, so judiciously chosen to overcome the difficulties of the way, we followed, and disturbed their ruminations in the shade; and, above all, the cool, free aspect of the wild apple trees, generously proffering their fruit to us, though still green and crude—the hard, round, glossy fruit, which, if not ripe, still was not poison, but New English too, brought hither, its ancestors, by ours once. These gentler trees imparted a half-civilized and twilight aspect to the otherwise barbarian land. Still farther on we scrambled up the rocky channel of a brook, which had long served nature for a sluice there, leaping like it from rock to rock, through tangled woods, at the bottom of a ravine, which grew darker and darker, and more and more hoarse the murmurs of the stream, until we reached the ruins of a mill, where now the ivy grew, and the trout glanced through the crumbling flume; and there we imagined what had been the dreams and speculations of some early settler. But the waning day compelled us to embark once more, and redeem this wasted time with long and vigorous sweeps over the rippling stream.

It was still wild and solitary, except that at intervals

of a mile or two the roof of a cottage might be seen over
the bank. The region, as we read, was once famous for
the manufacture of straw bonnets of the Leghorn kind,
of which it claims the invention in these parts; and
occasionally some industrious damsel tripped down to
the water's edge, to put her straw a-soak, as it appeared,
and stood awhile to watch the retreating voyageurs,
and catch the fragment of a boat-song which we had
made, wafted over the water.

> Thus, perchance, the Indian hunter,
>   Many a lagging year agone,
> Gliding o'er thy rippling waters,
>   Lowly hummed a natural song.
>
> Now the sun's behind the willows,
>   Now he gleams along the waves;
> Faintly o'er the wearied billows
>   Come the spirits of the braves.

Just before sundown we reached some more falls in
the town of Bedford, where some stone-masons were
employed repairing the locks in a solitary part of the
river. They were interested in our adventure, especially
one young man of our own age, who inquired at first if
we were bound up to " 'Skeag;" and when he had heard
our story, and examined our outfit, asked us other questions, but temperately still, and always turning to his
work again, though as if it were become his duty. It was
plain that he would like to go with us, and, as he looked
up the river, many a distant cape and wooded shore
were reflected in his eye, as well as in his thoughts.
When we were ready he left his work, and helped us
through the locks with a sort of quiet enthusiasm, telling
us that we were at Coos Falls, and we could still distinguish the strokes of his chisel for many sweeps after we
had left him.

We wished to camp this night on a large rock in the

middle of the stream, just above these falls, but the want of fuel, and the difficulty of fixing our tent firmly, prevented us; so we made our bed on the mainland opposite, on the west bank, in the town of Bedford, in a retired place, as we supposed, there being no house in sight.

THURSDAY

He trode the unplanted forest floor, whereon
The all-seeing sun for ages hath not shone;
Where feeds the moose, and walks the surly bear,
And up the tall mast runs the woodpecker.

. . . .

Where darkness found him he lay glad at night;
There the red morning touched him with its light.

. . . .

Go where he will, the wise man is at home,
His hearth the earth,—his hall the azure dome;
Where his clear spirit leads him, there's his road,
By God's own light illumined and foreshowed.

                                                                EMERSON.

When we awoke this morning, we heard the faint, deliberate, and ominous sound of raindrops on our cotton roof. The rain had patted all night, and now the whole country wept, the drops falling in the river, and on the alders, and in the pastures, and instead of any bow in the heavens, there was the trill of the hair-bird all the morning. The cheery faith of this little bird atoned for the silence of the whole woodland choir beside. When we first stepped abroad, a flock of sheep, led by their rams, came rushing down a ravine in our rear, with heedless haste and unreserved frisking, as if unobserved by man, from some higher pasture where they had spent the night, to taste the herbage by the riverside; but when their leaders caught sight of our white tent through the mist, struck with sudden astonishment, with their fóre feet braced, they sustained the rushing torrent in their rear, and the whole flock stood stock-still, endeavoring to solve the mystery in their sheepish brains. At length, concluding that it boded no mischief to them, they spread themselves out quietly over the field. We learned afterward that we had pitched our tent on the very spot which a few summers before had been occupied by a party of Penobscots. We could see rising before us through the mist a dark conical eminence called Hooksett Pinnacle, a landmark to boatmen, and also Uncannunuc Mountain, broad off on the west side of the river.

This was the limit of our voyage, for a few hours more in the rain would have taken us to the last of the locks, and our boat was too heavy to be dragged around the long and numerous rapids which would occur. On foot, however, we continued up along the bank, feeling our way with a stick through the showery and foggy day, and climbing over the slippery logs in our path with as much pleasure and buoyancy as in brightest sunshine; scenting the fragrance of the pines and the wet clay under our feet, and cheered by the tones of invisible waterfalls; with visions of toadstools, and wandering frogs, and festoons of moss hanging from the spruce trees, and thrushes flitting silent under the leaves; our road still holding together through that wettest of weather, like faith, while we confidently followed its lead. We managed to keep our thoughts dry, however, and only our clothes were wet. It was altogether a cloudy and drizzling day, with occasional brightenings in the mist, when the trill of the tree sparrow seemed to be ushering in sunny hours.

"Nothing that naturally happens to man can *hurt* him, earthquakes and thunderstorms not excepted," said a man of genius, who at this time lived a few miles farther on our road. When compelled by a shower to take shelter under a tree, we may improve that opportunity for a more minute inspection of some of Nature's works. I have stood under a tree in the woods half a day at a time, during a heavy rain in the summer, and yet employed myself happily and profitably there prying with microscopic eye into the crevices of the bark or the leaves of the fungi at my feet. "Riches are the attendants of the miser; and the heavens rain plenteously upon the mountains." I can fancy that it would be a luxury to stand up to one's chin in some retired swamp a whole summer day, scenting the wild honeysuckle and bilberry blows, and lulled by the minstrelsy of gnats and mosquitoes! A day passed in the society of those Greek sages, such as described in the Banquet of Xenophon, would not be comparable with the dry wit of decayed cranberry vines, and the fresh Attic salt of the moss-beds. Say twelve hours of genial and familiar converse with the leopard frog; the sun to rise behind alder and dogwood, and climb buoyantly to his meridian of two hands' breadth, and finally sink to rest behind some bold western hummock. To hear the evening chant of the mosquito from a thousand green chapels, and the bittern begin to boom from some concealed fort like a sunset gun! Surely one may as profitably be soaked in the juices of a swamp for one day as pick his way dry-shod over sand. Cold and damp—are they not as rich experience as warmth and dryness?

At present, the drops come trickling down the stubble while we lie drenched on a bed of withered wild oats, by the side of a bushy hill; and the gathering in of the clouds, with the last rush and dying breath of the wind, and then the regular dripping of twigs and leaves the country over, enhance the sense of inward comfort and sociableness. The birds draw closer and are more familiar under the thick foliage, seemingly composing new strains upon their roots against the sunshine. What were the amusements of the drawing-room and the library in comparison, if we had them here? . . .

We now no longer sailed or floated on the river, but trod the unyielding land like pilgrims. Sadi tells who may travel; among others, "A common mechanic, who can earn a subsistence by the industry of his hand, and shall not have to stake his reputation for every morsel of bread, as philosophers have said." He may travel who can subsist on the wild fruits and game of the most cultivated country. A man may travel fast enough and earn his living on the road. I have at times been applied to, to do work when on a journey; to do tinkering and repair clocks, when I had a knapsack on my back. A man once applied to me to go into a factory, stating conditions and wages, observing that I succeeded in shutting the window of a railroad car in which we were traveling, when the other passengers had failed. "Hast thou not heard of a Sufi, who was hammering some nails into the sole of his sandal; an officer of cavalry took him by the sleeve, saying, Come along and shoe my horse." Farmers have asked me to assist them in haying when I was passing their fields. A man once applied to me to mend his umbrella, taking me for an umbrella-mender, because, being on a journey, I carried an umbrella in my hand while the sun shone. Another wished to buy a tin cup of me, observing that I had one strapped to my belt, and a sauce-pan on my back. The cheapest way to travel, and the way to travel the farthest in the shortest distance, is to go afoot, carrying a dipper, a spoon, and a fish line, some Indian meal, some salt, and some sugar. When you come to a brook or a pond, you can catch fish and cook them; or you can boil a hasty-pudding; or you can buy a loaf of bread at a farmer's house for four-pence, moisten it in the next brook that crosses the road, and dip it into your sugar—this alone will last you a whole day—or, if you are accustomed to heartier living, you can buy a quart of milk for two cents, crumb your bread or cold pudding into it, and eat it with your own spoon out of your own dish. Any one of these things I mean, not all together. I have traveled thus some hundreds of miles without taking any meal in a house, sleeping on the ground when convenient, and found it cheaper, and in many respects more profitable, than staying at home. So that some have inquired why it would not be best to travel always. But I never thought of traveling simply as a means of getting a livelihood. A simple woman down in Tyngsborough, at whose house I once stopped to get a draught of water, when I said, recognizing the bucket, that I had stopped there nine years before for the same purpose, asked if I was not a traveler, supposing I had been traveling ever since, and had now come round again; that traveling was one of the professions, more or less productive, which her husband did not follow. But continued traveling is far from productive. It begins with wearing away the soles of the shoes, and making the feet sore, and ere long it will wear a man clean up, after making his heart sore into the bargain. I have observed that the after life of those who have traveled much is very pathetic. True and sincere traveling is no pastime, but it is as serious as the grave, or any part of the human journey, and it requires a long probation to be broken into it. I do not speak of those that travel sitting, the sedentary travelers whose legs hang dangling the while, mere idle symbols of the fact, any more than when we speak of sitting hens we mean those that sit standing, but I mean those to whom traveling is life for the legs, and death too, at last. The traveler must be born again on the road, and earn a passport from the elements, the principal powers that be for him. He shall experience at last that old threat of his mother fulfilled, that he shall be skinned alive. His sores shall gradually deepen themselves that they may heal inwardly, while he gives no rest to the sole of his foot, and at night weariness must be his pillow, that so he may acquire experience against his rainy days. So was it with us.

Sometimes we lodged at an inn in the woods, where trout-fishers from distant cities had arrived before us, and where, to our astonishment, the settlers dropped in at nightfall to have a chat and hear the news, though there was but one road, and no other house was visible —as if they had come out of the earth. There we sometimes read old newspapers, who never before read new ones, and in the rustle of their leaves heard the dashing of the surf along the Atlantic shore, instead of the sough of the wind among the pines. But then walking had given us an appetite even for the least palatable and nutritious food. . . .

Suns rose and set and found us still on the dank forest path which meanders up the Pemigewasset, now more like an otter's or a marten's trail, or where a beaver had dragged his trap, than where the wheels of travel raise a dust; where towns begin to serve as gores, only to hold the earth together. The wild pigeon sat secure above our heads, high on the dead limbs of naval pines, reduced to a robin's size. The very yards of our hostelries inclined upon the skirts of mountains, and, as we passed, we looked up at a steep angle at the stems of maples waving in the clouds.

Far up in the country—for we would be faithful to our experience—in Thornton, perhaps, we met a soldier lad in the woods, going to muster in full regimentals, and holding the middle of the road; deep in the forest, with shouldered musket and military step, and thoughts of war and glory all to himself. It was a sore trial to the youth, tougher than many a battle, to get by us creditably and with soldier-like bearing. Poor man! He actually shivered like a reed in his thin military pants, and by the time we had got up with him, all the sternness that becomes the soldier had forsaken his face, and he skulked past as if he were driving his father's sheep under a swordproof helmet. It was too much for him to carry any extra armor then, who could not easily dispose of his natural arms. And for his legs, they were like heavy artillery in boggy places; better to cut the traces and forsake them. His greaves chafed and wrestled one with another for want of other foes. But he did get by and get off with all his munitions, and lived to fight another day; and I do not record this as casting any suspicion on his honor and real bravery in the field.

Wandering on through notches which the streams had made, by the side and over the brows of hoar hills and mountains, across the stumpy, rocky, forested, and bepastured country, we at length crossed on prostrate trees over the Amonoosuck, and breathed the free air of Unappropriated Land. Thus, in fair days as well as foul, we had traced up the river to which our native stream is a tributary, until from Merrimack it became the Pemigewasset that leaped by our side, and when we had passed its fountainhead, the Wild Amonoosuck, whose puny channel was crossed at a stride, guiding us toward its distant source among the mountains, at length, without its guidance, we were enabled to reach the summit Agiocochook.

Sweet day, so cool, so calm, so bright,
The bridal of the earth and sky,
The dew shall weep thy fall tonight,
For thou must die.

HERBERT.

When we returned to Hooksett, a week afterward, the melon man, in whose corn-barn we had hung our tent and buffaloes and other things to dry, was already picking his hops, with many women and children to help him. We bought one watermelon, the largest in his patch, to carry with us for ballast. It was Nathan's, which he might sell if he wished, having been conveyed to him in the green state, and owned daily by his eyes. After due consultation with "Father," the bargain was concluded—we to buy it at a venture on the vine, green or ripe, our risk, and pay "what the gentleman pleased." It proved to be ripe; for we had had honest experience in selecting this fruit.

Finding our boat safe in its harbor, under Uncannunuc Mountain, with a fair wind and the current in our favor, we commenced our return voyage at noon, sitting at our ease and conversing, or in silence watching for the last trace of each reach in the river as a bend concealed it from our view. As the season was further advanced, the wind now blew steadily from the north, and with our sail set we could occasionally lie on our oars without loss of time. The lumbermen throwing down wood from the top of the high bank, thirty or forty feet above the water, that it might be sent downstream, paused in their work to watch our retreating sail. By this time, indeed, we were well known to the boatmen, and were hailed as the Revenue Cutter of the stream. As we sailed rapidly down the river, shut in between two mounds of earth, the sounds of this timber rolled down the bank enhanced the silence and vastness

of the noon, and we fancied that only the primeval
echoes were awakened. The vision of a distant scow just
heaving in sight round a headland also increased by contrast the solitude.

Through the din and desultoriness of noon, even in
the most Oriental city, is seen the fresh and primitive
and savage nature, in which Scythians and Ethiopians
and Indians dwell. What is echo, what are light and
shade, day and night, ocean and stars, earthquake and
eclipse, there? The works of man are everywhere swallowed up in the immensity of nature. The Aegean Sea
is but Lake Huron still to the Indian. Also there is all the
refinement of civilized life in the woods under a sylvan
garb. The wildest scenes have an air of domesticity and
homeliness even to the citizen, and when the flicker's
cackle is heard in the clearing, he is reminded that civilization has wrought but little change there. Science is
welcome to the deepest recesses of the forest, for there
too nature obeys the same old civil laws. The little red
bug on the stump of a pine—for it the wind shifts and
the sun breaks through the clouds. In the wildest nature,
there is not only the material of the most cultivated life,
and a sort of anticipation of the last result, but a greater
refinement already than is ever attained by man. There
is papyrus by the riverside, and rushes for light, and the
goose only flies overhead, ages before the studious are
born or letters invented, and that literature which the
former suggest, and even from the first have rudely
served, it may be man does not yet use them to express.
Nature is prepared to welcome into her scenery the
finest work of human art, for she is herself an art so
cunning that the artist never appears in his work.

Art is not tame, and Nature is not wild, in the ordinary sense. A perfect work of man's art would also be
wild or natural in a good sense. Man tames Nature only

that he may at last make her more free even than he found her, though he may never yet have succeeded.

With this propitious breeze, and the help of our oars, we soon reached the Falls of Amoskeag, and the mouth of the Piscataquoag, and recognized, as we swept rapidly by, many a fair bank and islet on which our eyes had rested in the upward passage. Our boat was like that which Chaucer describes in his Dream, in which the knight took his departure from the island,—

> "To journey for his marriage,
> And returne with such an host,
> That wedded might be least and most. . . .
> Which barge was as a man's thought,
> After his pleasure to him brought,
> The queene herselfe accustomed aye
> In the same barge to play,
> It needeth neither mast ne rother,
> I have not heard of such another,
> No maister for the governaunce,
> Hie sayled by thought and pleasaunce,
> Without labour, east and west,
> Alle was one, calme or tempest."

So we sailed this afternoon, thinking of the saying of Pythagoras, though we had no peculiar right to remember it, "It is beautiful when prosperity is present with intellect, and when sailing as it were with a prosperous wind, actions are performed looking to virtue; just as a pilot looks to the motions of the stars." All the world reposes in beauty to him who preserves equipoise in his life, and moves serenely on his path without secret violence; as he who sails down a stream, he has only to steer, keeping his bark in the middle, and carry it round the falls. The ripples curled away in our wake, like ringlets from the head of a child, while we steadily held on our course, and under the bows we watched

"The swaying soft,
Made by the delicate wave parted in front,
As through the gentle element we move
Like shadows gliding through untroubled realms."

The forms of beauty fall naturally around the path of
him who is in the performance of his proper work; as
the curled shavings drop from the plane, and borings
cluster around the auger. Undulation is the gentlest and
most ideal of motions, produced by one fluid falling on
another. Rippling is a more graceful flight. From a hilltop you may detect in it the wings of birds endlessly
repeated. The two waving lines which represent the
flight of birds appear to have been copied from the
ripple.

The trees made an admirable fence to the landscape,
skirting the horizon on every side. The single trees and
the groves left standing on the interval appeared naturally disposed, though the farmer had consulted only his
convenience, for he too falls into the scheme of Nature.
Art can never match the luxury and superfluity of Nature. In the former all is seen; it cannot afford concealed
wealth, and is niggardly in comparison; but Nature,
even when she is scant and thin outwardly, satisfies us
still by the assurance of a certain generosity at the roots.
In swamps, where there is only here and there an evergreen tree amid the quaking moss and cranberry beds,
the bareness does not suggest poverty. The single spruce,
which I had hardly noticed in gardens, attracts me in
such places, and now first I understand why men try to
make them grow about their houses. But though there
may be very perfect specimens in front-yard plots, their
beauty is for the most part ineffectual there, for there is
no such assurance of kindred wealth beneath and around
them, to make them show to advantage. As we have
said, Nature is a greater and more perfect art, the art of

God; though, referred to herself, she is genius; and there is a similarity between her operations and man's art even in the details and trifles. When the overhanging pine drops into the water, by the sun and water, and the wind rubbing it against the shore, its boughs are worn into fantastic shapes, and white and smooth, as if turned in a lathe. Man's art has wisely imitated those forms into which all matter is most inclined to run, as foliage and fruit. A hammock swung in a grove assumes the exact form of a canoe, broader or narrower, and higher or lower at the ends, as more or fewer persons are in it, and it rolls in the air with the motion of the body, like a canoe in the water. Our art leaves its shavings and its dust about; her art exhibits itself even in the shavings and the dust which we make. She has perfected herself by an eternity of practice. The world is well kept; no rubbish accumulates; the morning air is clear even at this day, and no dust has settled on the grass. Behold how the evening now steals over the fields, the shadows of the trees creeping farther and farther into the meadow, and ere long the stars will come to bathe in these retired waters. Her undertakings are secure and never fail. If I were awakened from a deep sleep, I should know which side of the meridian the sun might be by the aspect of nature, and by the chirp of the crickets, and yet no painter can paint this difference. The landscape contains a thousand dials which indicate the natural divisions of time, the shadows of a thousand styles point to the hour.

> "Not only o'er the dial's face
>   This silent phantom day by day,
> With slow, unseen, unceasing pace
>   Steals moments, months, and years away;
> From hoary rock and aged tree,
>   From proud Palmyra's mouldering walls,

From Teneriffe, towering o'er the sea,
  From every blade of grass it falls."

It is almost the only game which the trees play at, this
tit-for-tat, now this side in the sun, now that, the drama
of the day. In deep ravines under the eastern sides of
cliffs, Night forwardly plants her foot even at noonday,
and as Day retreats she steps into his trenches, skulking
from tree to tree, from fence to fence, until at last she
sits in her citadel and draws out her forces into the
plain. It may be that the forenoon is brighter than the
afternoon, not only because of the greater transparency
of its atmosphere, but because we naturally look most
into the west, as forward into the day, and so in the forenoon see the sunny side of things, but in the afternoon
the shadow of every tree.

The afternoon is now far advanced, and a fresh and
leisurely wind is blowing over the river, making long
reaches of bright ripples. The river has done its stint,
and appears not to flow, but lie at its length reflecting
the light, and the haze over the woods is like the inaudible panting, or rather the gentle perspiration of resting nature, rising from a myriad of pores into the attenu-
ated atmosphere.

On the thirty-first day of March, one hundred and
forty-two years before this, probably about this time in
the afternoon, there were hurriedly paddling down this
part of the river, between the pine woods which then
fringed these banks, two white women and a boy, who
had left an island at the mouth of the Contoocook before daybreak. They were slightly clad for the season,
in the English fashion, and handled their paddles un-
skillfully, but with nervous energy and determination,
and at the bottom of their canoe lay the still bleeding
scalps of ten of the aborigines. They were Hannah

Dustan, and her nurse, Mary Neff, both of Haverhill, eighteen miles from the mouth of this river, and an English boy, named Samuel Lennardson, escaping from captivity among the Indians. On the 15th of March previous, Hannah Dustan had been compelled to rise from childbed, and half dressed, with one foot bare, accompanied by her nurse, commence an uncertain march, in still inclement weather, through the snow and the wilderness. She had seen her seven elder children flee with their father, but knew not of their fate. She had seen her infant's brains dashed out against an apple tree, and had left her own and her neighbors' dwellings in ashes. When she reached the wigwam of her captor, situated on an island in the Merrimack, more than twenty miles above where we now are, she had been told that she and her nurse were soon to be taken to a distant Indian settlement, and there made to run the gauntlet naked. The family of this Indian consisted of two men, three women, and seven children, besides an English boy, whom she found a prisoner among them. Having determined to attempt her escape, she instructed the boy to inquire of one of the men, how he should dispatch an enemy in the quickest manner, and take his scalp. "Strike 'em there," said he, placing his finger on his temple, and he also showed him how to take off the scalp. On the morning of the 31st she arose before daybreak, and awoke her nurse and the boy, and taking the Indians' tomahawks, they killed them all in their sleep, excepting one favorite boy, and one squaw who fled wounded with him to the woods. The English boy struck the Indian who had given him the information, on the temple, as he had been directed. They then collected all the provision they could find, and took their master's tomahawk and gun, and scuttling all the canoes but one, commenced their flight to Haverhill, distant about sixty miles by the river. But after having proceeded a short distance, fearing that her story would not be believed if she should escape to tell it, they returned to the silent wigwam, and taking off the scalps of the dead, put them into a bag as proofs of what they had done, and then, retracing their steps to the shore in the twilight, recommenced their voyage.

Early this morning this deed was performed, and now, perchance, these tired women and this boy, their clothes stained with blood, and their minds racked with alternate resolution and fear, are making a hasty meal of parched corn and moose-meat, while their canoe glides under these pine roots whose stumps are still standing on the bank. They are thinking of the dead whom they have left behind on that solitary isle far up the stream, and of the relentless living warriors who are in pursuit. Every withered leaf which the winter has left seems to know their story, and in its rustling to repeat it and betray them. An Indian lurks behind every rock and pine, and their nerves cannot bear the tapping of a woodpecker. Or they forget their own dangers and their deeds in conjecturing the fate of their kindred, and whether, if they escape the Indians, they shall find the former still alive. They do not stop to cook their meals upon the bank, nor land, except to carry their canoe about the falls. The stolen birch forgets its master and does them good service, and the swollen current bears them swiftly along with little need of the paddle, except to steer and keep them warm by exercise. For ice is floating in the river; the spring is opening; the muskrat and the beaver are driven out of their holes by the flood; deer gaze at them from the bank; a few faint-singing forest birds, perchance, fly across the river to the northernmost shore; the fishhawk sails and screams overhead, and geese fly over with a startling clangor; but they do not observe these things, or they speedily forget them. They do not smile or chat all day. Sometimes they pass an Indian grave surrounded by its paling on the bank, or the frame of a wigwam, with a few coals left behind, or the withered stalks still rustling in the Indian's solitary corn field on the interval. The birch stripped of its bark, or the charred stump where a tree has been burned down to be made into a canoe—these are the only traces of man, a fabulous wild man to us. On either side, the primeval forest stretches away uninterrupted to Canada, or to the "South Sea"; to the white man a drear and howling wilderness, but to the Indian a home, adapted to his nature, and cheerful as the smile of the Great Spirit.

While we loiter here this autumn evening, looking for a spot retired enough, where we shall quietly rest tonight, they thus, in that chilly March evening, one hundred and forty-two years before us, with wind and current favoring, have already glided out of sight, not to camp, as we shall, at night, but while two sleep, one will manage the canoe, and the swift stream bear them onward to the settlements, it may be, even to old John Lovewell's house on Salmon Brook tonight.

According to the historian, they escaped as by a miracle all roving bands of Indians, and reached their homes in safety, with their trophies, for which the General Court paid them fifty pounds. The family of Hannah Dustan all assembled alive once more, except the infant whose brains were dashed out against the apple tree, and there have been many who in later time have lived to say that they have eaten of the fruit of that apple tree. . . .

Thus we "sayled by thought and pleasaunce," as Chaucer says, and all things seemed with us to flow; the shore itself and the distant cliffs were dissolved by the undiluted air. The hardest material seemed to obey the same law with the most fluid, and so indeed in the long run it does. Trees were but rivers of sap and woody fiber, flowing from the atmosphere, and emptying into the earth by their trunks, as their roots flowed upward to the surface. And in the heavens there were rivers of stars, and milky ways, already beginning to gleam and ripple over our heads. There were rivers of rock on the surface of the earth, and rivers of ore in its bowels, and our thoughts flowed and circulated, and this portion of time was but the current hour. Let us wander where we will, the universe is built round about us, and we are central still. If we look into the heavens they are concave, and if we were to look into a gulf as bottomless, it would be concave also. The sky is curved downward to the earth in the horizon, because we stand on the plain. I draw down its skirts. The stars so low there seem loath to depart, but by a circuitous path to be remembering me, and returning on their steps.

We had already passed by broad daylight the scene of our encampment at Coos Falls, and at length we pitched our camp on the west bank, in the northern part of Merrimack, nearly opposite to the large island on which we had spent the noon in our way up the river.

There we went to bed that summer evening, on a sloping shelf in the bank, a couple of rods from our boat, which was drawn up on the sand, and just behind a thin fringe of oaks which bordered the river; without having disturbed any inhabitants but the spiders in the grass, which came out by the light of our lamp, and crawled over our buffaloes. When we looked out from under the tent, the trees were seen dimly through the mist, and a cool dew hung upon the grass, which seemed to rejoice in the night, and with the damp air we inhaled a solid fragrance. Having eaten our supper of hot cocoa and bread and watermelon, we soon grew weary of conversing, and writing in our journals, and putting out the lantern which hung from the tentpole, fell asleep.

Unfortunately, many things have been omitted which should have been recorded in our journal; for though we made it a rule to set down all our experiences therein, yet such a resolution is very hard to keep, for the important experience rarely allows us to remember such obligations, and so indifferent things get recorded, while that is frequently neglected. It is not easy to write in a journal what interests us at any time, because to write it is not what interests us.

Whenever we awoke in the night, still eking out our dreams with half-awakened thoughts, it was not till after an interval, when the wind breathed harder than usual, flapping the curtains of the tent, and causing its cords to vibrate, that we remembered that we lay on the bank of the Merrimack, and not in our chamber at home. With our heads so low in the grass, we heard the river whirling and sucking, and lapsing downward, kissing the shore as it went, sometimes rippling louder than usual, and again its mighty current making only a slight limpid, trickling sound, as if our water-pail had sprung a leak, and the water were flowing into the grass by our side. The wind, rustling the oaks and hazels, impressed us like a wakeful and inconsiderate person up at midnight, moving about, and putting things to rights, occasionally stirring up whole drawers full of leaves at a puff. There seemed to be a great haste and preparation throughout Nature, as for a distinguished visitor; all her aisles had to be swept in the night by a thousand handmaidens, and a thousand pots to be boiled for the next day's feasting—such a whispering bustle, as if ten thousand fairies made their fingers fly, silently sewing at the new carpet with which the earth was to be clothed, and the new drapery which was to adorn the trees. And then the wind would lull and die away, and we like it fell asleep again.

FRIDAY

> The Boteman strayt
> Held on his course with stayed stedfastnesse,
> Ne ever shroncke, ne ever sought to bayt
> His tryed armes for toylesome wearinesse;
> But with his oares did sweepe the watry wildernesse.
> SPENSER.

> Summer's robe grows
> Dusky, and like an oft-dyed garment shows.
> DONNE.

As we lay awake long before daybreak, listening to the rippling of the river and the rustling of the leaves, in suspense whether the wind blew up or down the stream, was favorable or unfavorable to our voyage, we already suspected that there was a change in the weather, from a freshness as of autumn in these sounds. The wind in the woods sounded like an incessant waterfall dashing and roaring amid rocks, and we even felt encouraged by the unusual activity of the element. He who hears the rippling of rivers in these degenerate days will not utterly despair. That night was the turning-point in the season. We had gone to bed in summer, and we awoke in autumn; for summer passes into autumn in some unimaginable point of time, like the turning of a leaf.

We found our boat in the dawn just as we had left it, and as if waiting for us, there on the shore, in autumn, all cool and dripping with dew, and our tracks still fresh in the wet sand around it, the fairies all gone or concealed. Before five o'clock we pushed it into the fog, and, leaping in, at one shove were out of sight of the shores, and began to sweep downward with the rushing river, keeping a sharp lookout for rocks. We could see only the yellow gurgling water, and a solid bank of fog on every side, forming a small yard around us. We soon passed the mouth of the Souhegan, and the village of Merrimack, and as the mist gradually rolled away, and we were relieved from the trouble of watching for rocks, we saw by the flitting clouds, by the first russet tinge on the hills, by the rushing river, the cottages on shore, and the shore itself, so coolly fresh and shining with dew, and later in the day, by the hue of the grapevine, the goldfinch on the willow, the flickers flying in flocks, and when we passed near enough to the shore, as we fancied, by the faces of men, that the fall had commenced. The cottages looked more snug and comfortable, and their inhabitants were seen only for a moment, and then went quietly in and shut the door, retreating inward to the haunts of summer.

> "And now the cold autumnal dews are seen
>   To cobweb ev'ry green;
> And by the low-shorn rowens doth appear
>   The fast-declining year."

We heard the sigh of the first autumnal wind, and even the water had acquired a grayer hue. The sumach, grape, and maple were already changed, and the milk-weed had turned to a deep, rich yellow. In all woods the leaves were fast ripening for their fall; for their full veins and lively gloss mark the ripe leaf and not the sered one of the poets; and we knew that the maples, stripped of their leaves among the earliest, would soon stand like a wreath of smoke along the edge of the meadow. Already the cattle were heard to low wildly in the pastures and along the highways, restlessly running to and fro, as if in apprehension of the withering of the grass and of the approach of winter. Our thoughts, too, began to rustle.

As I pass along the streets of our village of Concord on the day of our annual Cattle Show, when it usually happens that the leaves of the elms and buttonwoods begin first to strew the ground under the breath of the October wind, the lively spirits in their sap seem to mount as high as any plowboy's let loose that day; and they lead my thoughts away to the rustling woods, where the trees are preparing for their winter campaign. This autumnal festival, when men are gathered in crowds in the streets as regularly and by as natural a law as the leaves cluster and rustle by the wayside, is naturally associated in my mind with the fall of the year. The low of cattle in the streets sounds like a hoarse symphony or running bass to the rustling of the leaves. The wind goes hurrying down the country, gleaning every loose straw that is left in the fields, while every farmer lad too appears to scud before it—having donned his best peajacket and pepper-and-salt waistcoat, his unbent trousers, outstanding rigging of duck or kerseymere or corduroy, and his furry hat withal—to country fairs and cattle shows, to that Rome among the villages where the treasures of the year are gathered. All the land over they go leaping the fences with their tough, idle palms, which have never learned to hang by their sides, amid the low of calves and the bleating of sheep—Amos, Abner, Elnathan, Elbridge—

"From steep pine-bearing mountains to the plain."

I love these sons of earth, every mother's son of them, with their great hearty hearts rushing tumultuously in herds from spectacle to spectacle, as if fearful lest there should not be time between sun and sun to see them all, and the sun does not wait more than in haying-time.

> "Wise Nature's darlings, they live in the world
> Perplexing not themselves how it is hurled."

Running hither and thither with appetite for the coarse pastimes of the day, now with boisterous speed at the heels of the inspired Negro from whose larynx the melodies of all Congo and Guinea Coast have broke loose into our streets; now to see the procession of a hundred yoke of oxen, all as august and grave as Osiris, or the droves of neat cattle and milch cows as unspotted as Isis or Io. Such as had no love for Nature

> "at all,
> Came lovers home from this great festival."

They may bring their fattest cattle and richest fruits to the fair, but they are all eclipsed by the show of men. These are stirring autumn days, when men sweep by in crowds, amid the rustle of leaves like migrating finches; this is the true harvest of the year, when the air is but the breath of men, and the rustling of leaves is as the trampling of the crowd. We read nowadays of the ancient festivals, games, and processions of the Greeks and Etruscans with a little incredulity, or at least with little sympathy; but how natural and irrepressible in every people is some hearty and palpable greeting of Nature! The Corybantes, the Bacchantes, the rude primitive tragedians with their procession and goat-song, and the whole paraphernalia of the Panathenaea, which appear so antiquated and peculiar, have their parallel now. The husbandman is always a better Greek than the scholar is prepared to appreciate, and the old custom still survives, while antiquarians and scholars grow gray in commemorating it. The farmers crowd to the fair today in obedience to the same ancient law, which Solon or Lycurgus did not enact, as naturally as bees swarm and follow their queen.

It is worth the while to see the country's people, how they pour into the town, the sober farmer folk, now all agog, their very shirt and coat collars pointing forward —collars so broad as if they had put their shirts on wrong end upward, for the fashions always tend to superfluity—and with an unusual springiness in their gait, jabbering earnestly to one another. The more supple vagabond, too, is sure to appear on the least rumor of such a gathering, and the next day to disappear, and go into his hole like the seventeen-year locust, in an ever-shabby coat, though finer than the farmer's best, yet never dressed; come to see the sport, and have a hand in what is going—to know "what's the row," if there is any; to be where some men are drunk, some horses race, some cockerels fight; anxious to be shaking props under a table and above all to see the "striped pig." He especially is the creature of the occasion. He empties both his pockets and his character into the stream, and swims in such a day. He dearly loves the social slush. There is no reserve of soberness in him.

I love to see the herd of men feeding heartily on coarse and succulent pleasures, as cattle on the husks and stalks of vegetables. Though there are many crooked and crabbed specimens of humanity among them, run all to thorn and rind, and crowded out of shape by adverse circumstances, like the third chestnut in the bur, so that you wonder to see some heads wear a whole hat, yet fear not that the race will fail or waver in them; like the crabs which grow in hedges, they furnish the stocks of sweet and thrifty fruits still. Thus is nature recruited from age to age, while the fair and palatable varieties die out, and have their period. This is that mankind.

How cheap must be the material of which so many men are made!

The wind blew steadily down the stream, so that we kept our sails set, and lost not a moment of the forenoon by delays, but from early morning until noon were continually dropping downward. With our hands on the steering-paddle, which was thrust deep into the river, or bending to the oar, which indeed we rarely relinquished, we felt each palpitation in the veins of our steed, and each impulse of the wings which drew us above. The current of our thoughts made as sudden bends as the river, which was continually opening new prospects to the east or south, but we are aware that rivers flow most rapidly and shallowest at these points. The steadfast shores never once turned aside for us, but still trended as they were made; why then should we always turn aside for them? . . .

While we sailed fleetly before the wind, with the river gurgling under our stern, the thoughts of autumn coursed as steadily through our minds, and we observed less what was passing on the shore than the dateless associations and impressions which the season awakened, anticipating in some measure the progress of the year.

> I hearing get, who had but ears,
>   And sight, who had but eyes before,
> I moments live, who lived but years,
>   And truth discern, who knew but learning's lore.

Sitting with our faces now up-stream, we studied the landscape by degrees, as one unrolls a map—rock, tree, house, hill, and meadow assuming new and varying positions as wind and water shifted the scene, and there was variety enough for our entertainment in the meta-

morphoses of the simplest objects. Viewed from this side
the scenery appeared new to us.

The most familiar sheet of water, viewed from a new
hilltop, yields a novel and unexpected pleasure. When
we have traveled a few miles, we do not recognize the
profiles even of the hills which overlook our native village, and perhaps no man is quite familiar with the horizon as seen from the hill nearest to his house, and can
recall its outline distinctly when in the valley. We do not
commonly know, beyond a short distance, which way
the hills range which take in our houses and farms in
their sweep. As if our birth had at first sundered things,
and we had been thrust up through into nature like a
wedge, and not till the wound heals and the scar disappears do we begin to discover where we are, and that
nature is one and continuous everywhere. It is an important epoch when a man who has always lived on the
east side of a mountain, and seen it in the west, travels
round and sees it in the east. Yet the universe is a sphere
whose center is wherever there is intelligence. The sun
is not so central as a man. Upon an isolated hilltop, in an
open country, we seem to ourselves to be standing on
the boss of an immense shield, the immediate landscape
being apparently depressed below the more remote, and
rising gradually to the horizon, which is the rim of the
shield—villas, steeples, forests, mountains, one above
another, till they are swallowed up in the heavens. The
most distant mountains in the horizon appear to rise directly from the shore of that lake in the woods by which
we chance to be standing, while from the mountain-top,
not only this, but a thousand nearer and larger lakes are
equally unobserved.

Seen through this clear atmosphere, the works of the
farmer, his plowing and reaping, had a beauty to our

eyes which he never saw. How fortunate were we who did not own an acre of these shores, who had not renounced our title to the whole! One who knew how to appropriate the true value of this world would be the poorest man in it. The poor rich man! all he has is what he has bought. What I see is mine. I am a large owner in the Merrimack intervals.

> Men dig and dive but cannot my wealth spend,
>   Who yet no partial store appropriate,
> Who no armed ship into the Indies send,
>   To rob me of my orient estate.

He is the rich man, and enjoys the fruits of riches, who summer and winter forever can find delight in his own thoughts. Buy a farm! What have I to pay for a farm which a farmer will take?

When I visit again some haunt of my youth, I am glad to find that nature wears so well. The landscape is indeed something real, and solid, and sincere, and I have not put my foot through it yet. There is a pleasant tract on the bank of the Concord, called Conantum, which I have in my mind—the old deserted farmhouse, the desolate pasture with its bleak cliff, the open wood, the river-reach, the green meadow in the midst, and the moss-grown wild-apple orchard—places where one may have many thoughts and not decide anything. It is a scene which I can not only remember, as I might a vision, but when I will can bodily revisit, and find it even so, unaccountable, yet unpretending in its pleasant dreariness. When my thoughts are sensible of change, I love to see and sit on rocks which I *have* known, and pry into their moss, and see unchangeableness so established. I not yet gray on rocks forever gray, I no longer green under the evergreens. There is something even in the lapse of time by which time recovers itself.

As we have said, it proved a cool as well as breezy

day, and by the time we reached Penichook Brook we were obliged to sit muffled in our cloaks, while the wind and current carried us along. We bounded swiftly over the rippling surface, far by many cultivated lands and the ends of fences which divided innumerable farms, with hardly a thought for the various lives which they separated; now by long rows of alders or groves of pines or oaks, and now by some homestead where the women and children stood outside to gaze at us, till we had swept out of their sight, and beyond the limit of their longest Saturday ramble. We glided past the mouth of the Nashua, and not long after, of Salmon Brook, without more pause than the wind.

> Salmon Brook,
> Penichook,
> Ye sweet waters of my brain,
> When shall I look,
> Or cast the hook,
> In your waves again?
>
> Silver eels,
> Wooden creels,
> These the baits that still allure,
> And dragon-fly
> That floated by,
> May they still endure?

The shadows chased one another swiftly over wood and meadow, and their alternation harmonized with our mood. We could distinguish the clouds which cast each one, though never so high in the heavens. When a shadow flits across the landscape of the soul where is the substance? Probably, if we were wise enough, we should see to what virtue we are indebted for any happier moment we enjoy. No doubt we have earned it at some time, for the gifts of Heaven are never quite gratuitous. The constant abrasion and decay of our lives makes the soil of our future growth. The wood which we now mature, when it becomes virgin mould, determines the character of our second growth, whether that be oaks or pines. Every man casts a shadow; not his body only, but his imperfectly mingled spirit. This is his grief. Let him turn which way he will, it falls opposite to the sun; short at noon, long at eve. Did you never see it? But, referred to the sun, it is widest at its base, which is no greater than his own capacity. The divine light is diffused almost entirely around us, and by means of the refraction of light, or else by a certain self-luminousness, or, as some will have it, transparency, if we preserve ourselves untarnished, we are able to enlighten our shaded side. At any rate, our darkest grief has that bronze color of the moon eclipsed. There is no ill which may not be dissipated, like the dark, if you let in a stronger light upon it. Shadows, referred to the source of light, are pyramids whose bases are never greater than those of the substances which cast them, but light is a spherical congeries of pyramids, whose very apexes are the sun itself, and hence the system shines with uninterrupted light. But if the light we use is but a paltry and narrow taper, most objects will cast a shadow wider than themselves.

The places where we had stopped or spent the night in our way up the river had already acquired a slight historical interest for us; for many upward days' voyaging were unraveled in this rapid downward passage. When one landed to stretch his limbs by walking, he soon found himself falling behind his companion, and was obliged to take advantage of the curves, and ford the brooks and ravines in haste, to recover his ground. Already the banks and the distant meadows wore a sober and deepened tinge, for the September air had shorn them of their summer's pride.

"And what's a life? The flourishing array
Of the proud summer meadow, which today
Wears her green plush, and is tomorrow hay."

The air was really the "fine element" which the poets
describe. It had a finer and sharper grain, seen against
the russet pastures and meadows, than before, as if
cleansed of the summer's impurities.

Having passed the New Hampshire line and reached
the Horseshoe Interval in Tyngsborough, where there is
a high and regular second bank, we climbed up this
in haste to get a nearer sight of the autumnal flowers,
asters, goldenrod, and yarrow, and blue-curls (*Tricho-
stema dichotomum*), humble roadside blossoms, and,
lingering still, the harebell and the *Rhexia Virginica*.
The last, growing in patches of lively pink flowers on
the edge of the meadows, had almost too gay an appearance for the rest of the landscape, like a pink ribbon on the bonnet of a Puritan woman. Asters and
goldenrods were the livery which nature wore at present. The latter alone expressed all the ripeness of the
season, and shed their mellow lustre over the fields, as
if the now declining summer's sun had bequeathed its
hues to them. It is the floral solstice a little after midsummer, when the particles of golden light, the sun-
dust, have, as it were, fallen like seeds on the earth,
and produced these blossoms. On every hillside, and in
every valley, stood countless asters, coreopses, tansies,
goldenrods, and the whole race of yellow flowers, like
Brahminical devotees, turning steadily with their lumi-
nary from morning till night. . . .

There is a peculiar interest belonging to the still later
flowers, which abide with us the approach of winter.
There is something witchlike in the appearance of the
witch-hazel, which blossoms late in October and in November, with its irregular and angular spray and petals

like furies' hair, or small ribbon streamers. Its blossoming, too, at this irregular period, when other shrubs have lost their leaves, as well as blossoms, looks like witches' craft. Certainly it blooms in no garden of man's. There is a whole fairyland on the hillside where it grows.

Some have thought that the gales do not at present waft to the voyager the natural and original fragrance of the land, such as the early navigators described, and that the loss of many odoriferous native plants, sweet-scented grasses and medicinal herbs, which formerly sweetened the atmosphere, and rendered it salubrious— by the grazing of cattle and the rooting of swine—is the source of many diseases which now prevail; the earth, say they, having been long subjected to extremely artificial and luxurious modes of cultivation, to gratify the appetite, converted into a sty and hotbed, where men for profit increase the ordinary decay of nature.

According to the record of an old inhabitant of Tyngsborough, now dead, whose farm we were now gliding past, one of the greatest freshets on this river took place in October, 1785, and its height was marked by a nail driven into an apple tree behind his house. One of his descendants has shown this to me, and I judged it to be at least seventeen or eighteen feet above the level of the river at the time. According to Barber, the river rose twenty-one feet above the common high-water mark at Bradford in the year 1818. Before the Lowell and Nashua railroad was built, the engineer made inquiries of the inhabitants along the banks as to how high they had known the river to rise. When he came to this house he was conducted to the apple tree, and as the nail was not then visible, the lady of the house placed her hand on the trunk where she said that she remembered the nail to have been from her child-

hood. In the meanwhile the old man put his arm inside
the tree, which was hollow, and felt the point of the
nail sticking through, and it was exactly opposite to her
hand. The spot is now plainly marked by a notch in the
bark. But as no one else remembered the river to have
risen so high as this, the engineer disregarded this statement, and I learn that there has since been a freshet
which rose within nine inches of the rails at Biscuit
Brook, and such a freshet as that of 1785 would have
covered the railroad two feet deep.

The revolutions of nature tell as fine tales, and make
as interesting revelations, on this river's banks, as on
the Euphrates or the Nile. This apple tree, which stands
within a few rods of the river, is called "Elisha's apple
tree," from a friendly Indian who was anciently in the
service of Jonathan Tyng, and, with one other man, was
killed here by his own race in one of the Indian wars—
the particulars of which affair were told us on the spot.
He was buried close by, no one knew exactly where,
but in the flood of 1785, so great a weight of water
standing over the grave caused the earth to settle where
it had once been disturbed, and when the flood went
down, a sunken spot, exactly of the form and size of the
grave, revealed its locality; but this was now lost again,
and no future flood can detect it; yet, no doubt, nature
will know how to point it out in due time, if it be necessary, by methods yet more searching and unexpected.
Thus there is not only the crisis when the spirit ceases
to inspire and expand the body, marked by a fresh
mound in the churchyard, but there is also a crisis when
the body ceases to take up room as such in nature,
marked by a fainter depression in the earth.

We sat awhile to rest us here upon the brink of the
western bank, surrounded by the glossy leaves of the
red variety of the mountain laurel, just above the head

of Wicasuck Island, where we could observe some scows which were loading with clay from the opposite shore, and also overlook the grounds of the farmer, of whom I have spoken, who once hospitably entertained us for a night. He had on his pleasant farm, besides an abundance of the beach plum, or *Prunus littoralis,* which grew wild, the Canada plum under cultivation, fine Porter apples, some peaches and large patches of musk- and watermelons, which he cultivated for the Lowell market. Elisha's apple tree, too, bore a native fruit, which was prized by the family; he raised the blood peach, which, as he showed us with satisfaction, was more like the oak in the color of its bark and in the setting of its branches, and was less liable to break down under the weight of the fruit, or the snow, than other varieties. It was of slower growth, and its branches strong and tough. There, also, was his nursery of native apple trees, thickly set upon the bank, which cost but little care, and which he sold to the neighboring farmers when they were five or six years old. To see a single peach upon its stem makes an impression of paradisaical fertility and luxury. This reminded us even of an old Roman farm, as described by Varro: "Caesar Vopiscus Aedilicius, when he pleaded before the Censors, said that the grounds of Rosea were the garden (*sumen,* the tidbit) of Italy, in which a pole being left would not be visible the day after, on account of the growth of the herbage." This soil may not have been remarkably fertile, yet at this distance we thought that this anecdote might be told of the Tyngsborough farm.

When we passed Wicasuck Island, there was a pleasure boat containing a youth and a maiden on the island brook, which we were pleased to see, since it proved that there were some hereabouts to whom our excursion would not be wholly strange. Before this, a canal-boatman, of whom we made some inquiries respecting Wi-casuck Island, and who told us that it was disputed property, suspected that we had a claim upon it, and though we assured him that all this was news to us, and explained, as well as we could, why we had come to see it, he believed not a word of it, and seriously offered us one hundred dollars for our title. The only other small boats which we met with were used to pick up driftwood. Some of the poorer class along the stream collect, in this way, all the fuel which they require. While one of us landed not far from this island to forage for provisions among the farmhouses whose roofs we saw—for our supply was now exhausted—the other, sitting in the boat, which was moored to the shore, was left alone to his reflections.

If there is nothing new on the earth, still the traveler always has a resource in the skies. They are constantly turning a new page to view. The wind sets the types on this blue ground, and the inquiring may always read a new truth there. There are things there written with such fine and subtle tinctures, paler than the juice of limes, that to the diurnal eye they leave no trace, and only the chemistry of night reveals them. Every man's daylight firmament answers in his mind to the brightness of the vision in his starriest hour.

These continents and hemispheres are soon run over, but an always unexplored and infinite region makes off on every side from the mind, further than to sunset, and we can make no highway or beaten track into it, but the grass immediately springs up in the path, for we travel there chiefly with our wings.

Sometimes we see objects as through a thin haze, in their eternal relations, and they stand like Palenque and the Pyramids, and we wonder who set them up, and for what purpose. If we see the reality in things, of what moment is the superficial and apparent longer? What are the earth and all its interests beside the deep surmise which pierces and scatters them? While I sit here listening to the waves which ripple and break on this shore, I am absolved from all obligation to the past, and the council of nations may reconsider its votes. The grating of a pebble annuls them. Still occasionally in my dreams I remember that rippling water.

> Oft as I turn me on my pillow o'er
> I hear the lapse of waves upon the shore,
> Distinct as if it were at broad noonday,
> And I were drifting down from Nashua.

With a bending sail we glided rapidly by Tyngsborough and Chelmsford, each holding in one hand half of a tart country apple pie which we had purchased to celebrate our return, and in the other a fragment of the newspaper in which it was wrapped, devouring these with divided relish, and learning the news which had transpired since we sailed. The river here opened into a broad and straight reach of great length, which we bounded merrily over before a smacking breeze, with a devil-may-care look in our faces, and our boat a white bone in its mouth, and a speed which greatly astonished some scow boatmen whom we met. The wind in the horizon rolled like a flood over valley and plain, and every tree bent to the blast, and the mountains like schoolboys turned their cheeks to it. They were great and current motions, the flowing sail, the running stream, the waving tree, the roving wind. The north wind stepped readily into the harness which we had provided, and pulled us along with good will. Sometimes we sailed as gently and steadily as the clouds overhead, watching the receding shores and the motions of our sail; the play of its pulse so like our own lives, so thin and yet so full of life, so noiseless when it labored hardest, so noisy and impatient when least effective; now bending to some generous impulse of the breeze, and then fluttering and flapping with a kind of human suspense. It was the scale on which the varying temperature of distant atmospheres was graduated, and it was some attraction for us that the breeze it played with had been out of doors so long. Thus we sailed, not being able to fly, but as next best, making a long furrow in the fields of the Merrimack toward our home, with our wings spread, but never lifting our heel from the watery trench; gracefully plowing homeward with our brisk and willing team, wind and stream, pulling together, the former yet a wild steer, yoked to his more sedate fellow. It was very near flying, as when the duck rushes through the water with an impulse of her wings, throwing the spray about her before she can rise. How we had stuck fast if drawn up but a few feet on the shore!

When we reached the great bend just above Middlesex, where the river runs east thirty-five miles to the sea, we at length lost the aid of this propitious wind, though we contrived to make one long and judicious tack carry us nearly to the locks of the canal. We were here locked through at noon by our old friend, the lover of the higher mathematics, who seemed glad to see us safe back again through so many locks; but we did not stop to consider any of his problems, though we could cheerfully have spent a whole autumn in this way another time, and never have asked what his religion was. It is so rare to meet with a man outdoors who cherishes a worthy thought in his mind, which is independent of the labor of his hands. Behind every man's busy-ness there should be a level of undisturbed serenity and industry, as within the reef encircling a coral isle there is always an expanse of still water, where the depositions are going on which will finally raise it above the surface. . . .

We endeavored in vain to persuade the wind to blow through the long corridor of the canal, which is here cut straight through the woods, and were obliged to resort to our old expedient of drawing by a cord. When we reached the Concord, we were forced to row once more in good earnest, with neither wind nor current in our favor, but by this time the rawness of the day had disappeared, and we experienced the warmth of a summer afternoon. This change in the weather was favorable to our contemplative mood, and disposed us to dream yet deeper at our oars, while we floated in imagination farther down the stream of time, as we had floated down the stream of the Merrimack, to poets of a milder period than had engaged us in the morning. Chelmsford and Billerica appeared like old English towns, compared with Merrimack and Nashua, and many generations of civil poets might have lived and sung here.

What a contrast between the stern and desolate poetry of Ossian, and that of Chaucer, and even of Shakespeare and Milton, much more of Dryden, and Pope, and Gray! Our summer of English poetry, like the Greek and Latin before it, seems well advanced towards its fall, and laden with the fruit and foliage of the season, with bright autumnal tints, but soon the winter will scatter its myriad clustering and shading leaves, and leave only a few desolate and fibrous boughs to sustain the snow and rime, and creak in the blasts of age. We cannot escape the impression that the Muse has stooped a little in her flight, when we come to the literature of civilized eras. Now first we hear of various ages and styles of poetry; it is pastoral, and lyric, and narrative, and didactic; but the poetry of runic monuments is of one style, and for every age. The bard has in a great measure lost the dignity and sacredness of his office. Formerly he was called a seer, but now it is thought that one man sees as much as another. He has no longer the bardic rage, and only conceives the deed, which he formerly stood ready to perform. Hosts of warriors earnest for battle could not mistake nor dispense with the ancient bard. His lays were heard in the pauses of the fight. There was no danger of his being overlooked by his contemporaries. But now the hero and the bard are of different professions. When we come to the pleasant English verse, the storms have all cleared away, and it will never thunder and lighten more. The poet has come within doors, and exchanged the forest and crag for the fireside, the hut of the Gael, and Stonehenge, with its circles of stones, for the house of the Englishman. No hero stands at the door prepared to break forth into song or heroic action, but a homely Englishman, who cultivates the art of poetry. We see the comfortable fireside, and hear the crackling fagots, in all the verse. . . .

But here on the stream of the Concord, where we have all the while been bodily, Nature, who is superior to all styles and ages, is now, with pensive face, composing her poem Autumn, with which no work of man will bear to be compared.

In summer we live out of doors, and have only impulses and feelings, which are all for action, and must wait commonly for the stillness and longer nights of autumn and winter before any thought will subside; we are sensible that behind the rustling leaves, and the stacks of grain, and the bare clusters of the grape, there is the field of a wholly new life, which no man has lived; that even this earth was made for more mysterious and nobler inhabitants than men and women. In the hues of

October sunsets, we see the portals to other mansions than those which we occupy, not far off geographically,

> "There is a place beyond that flaming hill,
>   From whence the stars their thin appearance shed,
> A place beyond all place, where never ill,
>   Nor impure thought was ever harbored."

Sometimes a mortal feels in himself Nature—not his Father but his Mother stirs within him, and he becomes immortal with her immortality. From time to time she claims kindredship with us, and some globule from her veins steals up into our own.

> I am the autumnal sun,
> With autumn gales my race is run;
> When will the hazel put forth its flowers,
> Or the grape ripen under my bowers?
> When will the harvest or the hunter's moon
> Turn my midnight into mid-noon?
>   I am all sere and yellow,
>   And to my core mellow.
> The mast is dropping within my woods,
> The winter is lurking within my moods,
> And the rustling of the withered leaf
> Is the constant music of my grief. . . .

It is easier to discover another such a new world as Columbus did, than to go within one fold of this which we appear to know so well; the land is lost sight of, the compass varies, and mankind mutiny; and still history accumulates like rubbish before the portals of nature. But there is only necessary a moment's sanity and sound senses, to teach us that there is a nature behind the ordinary, in which we have only some vague pre-emption right and western reserve as yet. We live on the outskirts of that region. Carved wood, and floating boughs, and sunset skies are all that we know of it. We are not to be imposed on by the longest spell of weather. Let us not, my friends, be wheedled and cheated into good behavior to earn the salt of our eternal porridge, whoever they are that attempt it. Let us wait a little, and not purchase any clearing here, trusting that richer bottoms will soon be put up. It is but thin soil where we stand; I have felt my roots in a richer ere this. I have seen a bunch of violets in a glass vase, tied loosely with a straw, which reminded me of myself. . . .

Thus thoughtfully we were rowing homeward to find some autumnal work to do, and help on the revolution of the seasons. Perhaps Nature would condescend to make use of us even without our knowledge, as when we help to scatter her seeds in our walks, and carry burs and cockles on our clothes from field to field.

> All things are current found
> On earthly ground,
> Spirits and elements
> Have their descents.
>
> Night and day, year on year,
> High and low, far and near,
> These are our own aspects,
> These are our own regrets.
>
> Ye gods of the shore,
> Who abide evermore,
> I see your far headland,
> Stretching on either hand;
>
> I hear the sweet evening sounds
> From your undecaying grounds;
> Cheat me no more with time,
> Take me to your clime.

As it grew later in the afternoon, and we rowed leisurely up the gentle stream, shut in between fragrant and blooming banks, where we had first pitched our tent, and drew nearer to the fields where our lives had passed, we seemed to detect the hues of our native sky in the southwest horizon. The sun was just setting behind the edge of a wooded hill, so rich a sunset as would never have ended but for some reason unknown to men, and to be marked with brighter colors than ordinary in the scroll of time. Though the shadows of the hills were beginning to steal over the stream, the whole river valley undulated with mild light, purer and more memorable than the noon. For so day bids farewell even to solitary vales uninhabited by man. Two herons (*Ardea herodias*), with their long and slender limbs relieved against the sky, were seen traveling high over our heads —their lofty and silent flight, as they were wending their way at evening, surely not to alight in any marsh on the earth's surface, but, perchance, on the other side of our atmosphere, a symbol for the ages to study, whether impressed upon the sky or sculptured amid the hieroglyphics of Egypt. Bound to some northern meadow, they held on their stately, stationary flight, like the storks in the picture, and disappeared at length behind the clouds. Dense flocks of blackbirds were winging their way along the river's course, as if on a short evening pilgrimage to some shrine of theirs, or to celebrate so fair a sunset.

> "Therefore, as doth the pilgrim, whom the night
>   Hastes darkly to imprison on his way,
> Think on thy home, my soul, and think aright
> Of what's yet left thee of life's wasting day:
>   Thy sun posts westward, passed is thy morn,
>   And twice it is not given thee to be born."

The sun-setting presumed all men at leisure, and in a contemplative mood; but the farmer's boy only whistled the more thoughtfully as he drove his cows home from pasture, and the teamster refrained from cracking his whip, and guided his team with a subdued voice. The last vestiges of daylight at length disappeared, and as we rowed silently along with our backs toward home through the darkness, only a few stars being visible, we had little to say, but sat absorbed in thought, or in silence listened to the monotonous sound of our oars, a sort of rudimental music, suitable for the ear of Night and the acoustics of her dimly lighted halls;

"Pulsae referunt ad sidera valles,"

and the valleys echoed the sound to the stars.

As we looked up in silence to those distant lights, we were reminded that it was a rare imagination which first taught that the stars are worlds, and had conferred a great benefit on mankind. It is recorded in the Chronicle of Bernaldez that in Columbus's first voyage the natives "pointed towards the heavens, making signs that they believed that there was all power and holiness." We have reason to be grateful for celestial phenomena, for they chiefly answer to the ideal in man. The stars are distant and unobtrusive, but bright and enduring as our fairest and most memorable experiences. "Let the immortal depth of your soul lead you, but earnestly extend your eyes upwards."

As the truest society approaches always nearer to solitude, so the most excellent speech finally falls into Silence. Silence is audible to all men, at all times, and in all places. She is when we hear inwardly, sound when we hear outwardly. Creation has not displaced her, but is her visible framework and foil. All sounds are her servants, and purveyors, proclaiming not only that their mistress is, but is a rare mistress, and earnestly to be sought after. They are so far akin to Silence that they are but bubbles on her surface, which straightway burst, an evidence of the strength and prolificness of the undercurrent; a faint utterance of Silence, and then only agreeable to our auditory nerves when they contrast themselves with and relieve the former. In proportion as they do this, and are heighteners and intensifiers of the Silence, they are harmony and purest melody.

Silence is the universal refuge, the sequel to all dull discourses and all foolish acts, a balm to our every chagrin, as welcome after satiety as after disappointment; that background which the painter may not daub, be he master or bungler, and which, however awkward a figure we may have made in the foreground, remains ever our inviolable asylum, where no indignity can assail, no personality disturb us.

The orator puts off his individuality, and is then most eloquent when most silent. He listens while he speaks, and is a hearer along with his audience. Who has not hearkened to her infinite din? She is Truth's speaking-trumpet, the sole oracle, the true Delphi and Dodona, which kings and courtiers would do well to consult, nor will they be balked by an ambiguous answer. For through her all revelations have been made, and just in proportion as men have consulted her oracle within, they have obtained a clear insight, and their age has been marked as an enlightened one. But as often as they have gone gadding abroad to a strange Delphi and her mad priestess, their age has been dark and leaden. Such were garrulous and noisy eras, which no longer yield any sound, but the Grecian or silent and melodious era is ever sounding and resounding in the ears of men.

A good book is the plectrum with which our else silent lyres are struck. We not unfrequently refer the interest which belongs to our own unwritten sequel to the written and comparatively lifeless body of the work. Of all books this sequel is the most indispensable part. It should be the author's aim to say once and emphatically, "He said," ἔφη. This is the most the bookmaker can attain to. If he make his volume a mole whereon the waves of Silence may break, it is well.

It were vain for me to endeavor to interpret the Silence. She cannot be done into English. For six thousand years men have translated her with what fidelity belonged to each, and still she is little better than a sealed book. A man may run on confidently for a time, thinking he has her under his thumb, and shall one day exhaust her, but he too must at last be silent, and men remark only how brave a beginning he made; for when he at length dives into her, so vast is the disproportion of the told to the untold that the former will seem but the bubble on the surface where he disappeared. Nevertheless, we will go on, like those Chinese cliff swallows, feathering our nests with the froth which may one day be bread of life to such as dwell by the seashore.

We had made about fifty miles this day with sail and oar, and now, far in the evening, our boat was grating against the bulrushes of its native port, and its keel recognized the Concord mud, where some semblance of its outline was still preserved in the flattened flags which had scarce yet erected themselves since our departure; and we leaped gladly on shore, drawing it up and fastening it to the wild apple tree, whose stem still bore the mark which its chain had worn in the chafing of the spring freshets.

Poems

His deepest personal longings Thoreau either concealed in his Journal or turned into poems. His most fruitful poetic period dated from the time he began writing the Week to shortly before the publication of Walden. His poems are significant utterances, both because of their intrinsic merit and because of his high conception of the role of poet. True, some of the later verses are hasty and prosaic, while some of the early ones imitate Herbert and other metaphysicals. But in between lie a considerable number which contain the essence of Thoreau's Transcendentalism, sensitive, natural, and independent.

C. B.

I AM A PARCEL OF VAIN STRIVINGS TIED

I am a parcel of vain strivings tied
 By a chance bond together,
  Dangling this way and that, their links
  Were made so loose and wide,
   Methinks,
  For milder weather.

A bunch of violets without their roots,
 And sorrel intermixed,
  Encircled by a wisp of straw
  Once coiled about their shoots,
   The law
  By which I'm fixed.

A nosegay which Time clutched from out
 Those fair Elysian fields,

With weeds and broken stems, in haste,
  Doth make the rabble rout
    That waste
  The day he yields.

And here I bloom for a short hour unseen,
  Drinking my juices up,
With no root in the land
  To keep my branches green,
      But stand
  In a bare cup.

Some tender buds were left upon my stem
  In mimicry of life,
But ah! the children will not know,
  Till time has withered them,
      The woe
  With which they're rife.

But now I see I was not plucked for naught,
  And after in life's vase
Of glass set while I might survive,
  But by a kind hand brought
      Alive
  To a strange place.

That stock thus thinned will soon redeem its hours,
  And by another year,
Such as God knows, with freer air,
  More fruits and fairer flowers
      Will bear,
  While I droop here.

IN THE BUSY STREETS, DOMAINS OF TRADE

In the busy streets, domains of trade,
Man is a surly porter, or a vain and hectoring bully,
Who can claim no nearer kindredship with me
Than brotherhood by law.

I KNEW A MAN BY SIGHT

I knew a man by sight,
　　A blameless wight,
Who, for a year or more,
　　Had daily passed my door,
Yet converse none had had with him.

I met him in a lane,
　　Him and his cane,
About three miles from home,
　　Where I had chanced to roam,
And volumes stared at him, and he at me.

In a more distant place
　　I glimpsed his face,
And bowed instinctively;
　　Starting he bowed to me,
Bowed simultaneously, and passed along.

Next, in a foreign land
　　I grasped his hand,
And had a social chat,
　　About this thing and that,
As I had known him well a thousand years.

Late in a wildnerness
　　I shared his mess,

For he had hardships seen,
And I a wanderer been;
He was my bosom friend, and I was his.
And as, methinks, shall all,
Both great and small,
That ever lived on earth,
Early or late their birth,
Stranger and foe, one day each other know

LATELY, ALAS, I KNEW A GENTLE BOY

Lately, alas, I knew a gentle boy,
  Whose features all were cast in Virtue's mould,
As one she had designed for Beauty's toy,
  But after manned him for her own stronghold.

On every side he open was as day,
  That you might see no lack of strength within,
For walls and ports do only serve alway
  For a pretense to feebleness and sin.

Say not that Caesar was victorious,
  With toil and strife who stormed the House of Fame,
In other sense this youth was glorious,
  Himself a kingdom wheresoe'er he came.

No strength went out to get him victory,
  When all was income of its own accord;
For where he went none other was to see,
  But all were parcel of their noble lord.

He forayed like the subtile haze of summer,
  That stilly shows fresh landscapes to our eyes,
And revolutions works without a murmur,
  Or rustling of a leaf beneath the skies.

So was I taken unawares by this,
   I quite forgot my homage to confess;
Yet now am forced to know, though hard it is,
   I might have loved him had I loved him less.

Each moment as we nearer drew to each,
   A stern respect withheld us farther yet,
So that we seemed beyond each other's reach,
   And less acquainted than when first we met.

We two were one while we did sympathize,
   So could we not the simplest bargain drive;
And what avails it now that we are wise,
   If absence doth this doubleness contrive?

Eternity may not the chance repeat,
   But I must tread my single way alone,
In sad remembrance that we once did meet,
   And know that bliss irrevocably gone.

The spheres henceforth my elegy shall sing,
   For elegy has other subject none;
Each strain of music in my ears shall ring
   Knell of departure from that other one.

Make haste and celebrate my tragedy;
   With fitting strain resound ye woods and fields;
Sorrow is dearer in such case to me
   Than all the joys other occasion yields.

———

Is't then too late the damage to repair?
   Distance, forsooth, from my weak grasp hath reft
The empty husk, and clutched the useless tare,
   But in my hands the wheat and kernel left.

If I but love that virtue which he is,
    Though it be scented in the morning air,
Still shall we be truest acquaintances,
    Nor mortals know a sympathy more rare.

EACH MORE MELODIOUS NOTE I HEAR

Each more melodious note I hear
Brings this reproach to me,
That I alone afford the ear,
Who would the music be.

INDEPENDENCE

My life more civil is and free
Than any civil polity.

Ye princes keep your realms
And circumscribed power,
Not wide as are my dreams,
Nor rich as is this hour.

What can ye give which I have not?
What can ye take which I have got?
Can ye defend the dangerless?
Can ye inherit nakedness?

To all true wants time's ear is deaf,
Penurious states lend no relief
Out of their pelf—
But a free soul—thank God—
Can help itself.

Be sure your fate
Doth keep apart its state—

Not linked with any band—
Even the nobles of the land

In tented fields with cloth of gold—
No place doth hold
But is more chivalrous than they are.
And sigheth for a nobler war.
A finer strain its trumpet rings—
A brighter gleam its armor flings.

The life that I aspire to live
No man proposeth me—
No trade upon the street
Wears its emblazonry.

NOT UNCONCERNED WACHUSETT REARS HIS HEAD

Not unconcerned Wachusett rears his head
    Above the field, so late from nature won,
With patient brow reserved, as one who read
    New annals in the history of man.

MY FRIENDS, WHY SHOULD WE LIVE

My friends, why should we live?
Life is an idle war, a toilsome peace;
    Today I would not give
One small consent for its securest ease.

    Shall we out-wear the year
In our pavilions on its dusty plain
    And yet no signal hear
To strike our tents and take the road again?

Or else drag up the slope
The heavy ordnance of nature's train?
Useless but in the hope,
Some far remote and heavenward hill to gain.

LOW IN THE EASTERN SKY

Low in the eastern sky
Is set thy glancing eye;
And though its gracious light
Ne'er riseth to my sight,
Yet every star that climbs
Above the gnarled limbs
Of yonder hill,
Conveys thy gentle will.

Believe I knew thy thought,
And that the zephyrs brought
Thy kindest wishes through,
As mine they bear to you,
That some attentive cloud
Did pause amid the crowd
Over my head,
While gentle things were said.

Believe the thrushes sung,
And that the flower-bells rung,
That herbs exhaled their scent,
And beasts knew what was meant,
The trees a welcome waved,
And lakes their margins laved,
When thy free mind
To my retreat did wind.

It was a summer eve,
The air did gently heave
While yet a low-hung cloud
Thy eastern skies did shroud;
The lightning's silent gleam,
Startling my drowsy dream,
   Seemed like the flash
Under thy dark eyelash.

Still will I strive to be
As if thou wert with me;
Whatever path I take,
It shall be for thy sake,
Of gentle slope and wide,
As thou wert by my side,
   Without a root
To trip thy gentle foot.

I'll walk with gentle pace,
And choose the smoothest place,
And careful dip the oar,
And shun the winding shore,
And gently steer my boat
Where water-lilies float,
   And cardinal flowers
Stand in their sylvan bowers.

GREAT FRIEND

I walk in nature still alone
   And know no one
Discern no lineament nor feature
   Of any creature.

Though all the firmament
  Is o'er me bent,
Yet still I miss the grace
  Of an intelligent and kindred face.

I still must seek the friend
Who does with nature blend,
Who is the person in her mask,
He is the man I ask.

Who is the expression of her meaning,
Who is the uprightness of her leaning,
Who is the grown child of her weaning

The center of this world,
The face of nature,
The site of human life,
Some sure foundation
And nucleus of a nation—
At least a private station.

We twain would walk together
Through every weather,
And see this aged nature,
Go with a bending stature.

FOG

Dull water spirit—and Protean god
Descended cloud fast anchored to the earth
That drawest too much air for shallow coasts
Thou ocean branch that flowest to the sun
Incense of earth, perfumed with flowers—
Spirit of lakes and rivers, seas and rills
Come to revisit now thy native scenes

Night thoughts of earth—dream drapery
Dew cloth and fairy napkin
Thou wind-blown meadow of the air.

BROTHER WHERE DOST THOU DWELL

Brother where dost thou dwell?
  What sun shines for thee now?
Dost thou indeed farewell?
  As we wished here below.

What season didst thou find?
  'Twas winter here.
Are not the fates more kind
  Than they appear?

Is thy brow clear again
  As in thy youthful years?
And was that ugly pain
  The summit of thy fears?

Yet thou wast cheery still,
  They could not quench thy fire,
Thou dids't abide their will,
  And then retire.

Where chiefly shall I look
  To feel thy presence near?
Along the neighboring brook
  May I thy voice still hear?

Dost thou still haunt the brink
  Of yonder river's tide?
And may I ever think
  That thou art at my side?

What bird wilt thou employ
  To bring me word of thee?
For it would give them joy,
   'Twould give them liberty,
  To serve their former lord
  With wing and minstrelsy.

A sadder strain has mixed with their song,
  They've slowlier built their nests,
Since thou art gone
  Their lively labor rests.

Where is the finch—the thrush,
  I used to hear?
Ah! they could well abide
  The dying year.

Now they no more return,
  I hear them not;
They have remained to mourn,
  Or else forgot.

THIS IS MY CARNAC, WHOSE UNMEASURED DOME

This is my Carnac, whose unmeasured dome
Shelters the measuring art and measurer's home.
Behold these flowers, let us be up with time,
Not dreaming of three thousand years ago,
Erect ourselves and let those columns lie,
Not stoop to raise a foil against the sky.
Where is the spirit of that time but in
This present day, perchance the present line?
Three thousand years ago are not agone,
They are still lingering in this summer morn,
And Memnon's Mother sprightly greets us now,

Wearing her youthful radiance on her brow.
If Carnac's columns still stand on the plain,
To enjoy our opportunities they remain.

LOVE EQUALS SWIFT AND SLOW

Love equals swift and slow,
   And high and low,
Racer and lame,
   The hunter and his game.

THOUGH ALL THE FATES SHOULD PROVE UNKIND

Though all the fates should prove unkind,
Leave not your native land behind.
The ship, becalmed, at length stands still;
The steed must rest beneath the hill;
But swiftly still our fortunes pace
To find us out in every place.

The vessel, though her masts be firm,
Beneath her copper bears a worm;
Around the cape, across the line,
Till fields of ice her course confine;
It matters not how smooth the breeze,
How shallow or how deep the seas,
Whether she bears Manila twine,
Or in her hold Madeira wine,
Or China teas, or Spanish hides,
In port or quarantine she rides;
Far from New England's blustering shore,
New England's worm her hulk shall bore,
And sink her in the Indian seas,
Twine, wine, and hides, and China teas.

MANHOOD

I love to see the man, a long-lived child,
As yet uninjured by all worldly taint
As the fresh infant whose whole life is play.
'Tis a serene spectacle for a serene day;
But better still I love to contemplate
The mature soul of lesser innocence,
Who hath traveled far on life's dusty road
Far from the starting point of infancy
And proudly bears his small degen'racy
Blazon'd on his memorial standard high
Who from the sad experience of his fate
Since his bark struck on that unlucky rock
Has proudly steered his life with his own hands.
Though his face harbors less of innocence
Yet there do chiefly lurk within its depths
Furrowed by care, but yet all over spread
With the ripe bloom of a self-wrought content
Noble resolves which do reprove the gods
And it doth more assert man's eminence
Above the happy level of the brute
And more doth advertise me of the heights
To which no natural path doth ever lead
No natural light can ever light our steps,
—But the far-piercing ray that shines
From the recesses of a brave man's eye.

BETWEEN THE TRAVELER AND
THE SETTING SUN

Between the traveler and the setting sun,
Upon some drifting sand heap of the shore,
A hound stands o'er the carcass of a man.

NATURE

O nature I do not aspire
To be the highest in thy quire,
To be a meteor in the sky
Or comet that may range on high,
Only a zephyr that may blow
Among the reeds by the river low.
Give me thy most privy place
Where to run my airy race.
In some withdrawn unpublic mead
Let me sigh upon a reed,
Or in the woods with leafy din
Whisper the still evening in,
For I had rather be thy child
And pupil in the forest wild
Than be the king of men elsewhere
And most sovereign slave of care
To have one moment of thy dawn
Than share the city's year forlorn.
Some still work give me to do
Only be it near to you.

A Yankee in Canada

*Here is the opening episode in Thoreau's Canadian trav-
elogue. It records the first impact of a Catholic culture on
him. Thoreau stands much more aloof than he did during
his trip to Maine and he reacts with what Horace Greeley
termed a "defiant Pantheism." Since it takes more than guide-
books and history to prepare one for picturing a strange civilization, Thoreau does not make out too well. Nevertheless,
there is in this selection an intrinsic interest in a notable
American's view of Canada.*

C. B.

CONCORD TO MONTREAL

I FEAR that I have not got much to say about Canada, not having seen much; what I got by going to
Canada was a cold. I left Concord, Massachusetts,
Wednesday morning, September 25th, 1850, for Que-
bec. Fare, seven dollars there and back; distance from
Boston, five hundred and ten miles; being obliged to
leave Montreal on the return as soon as Friday, October
4th, or within ten days. I will not stop to tell the reader
the names of my fellow-travelers; there were said to be
fifteen hundred of them. I wished only to be set down
in Canada, and take one honest walk there as I might
in Concord woods of an afternoon.

The country was new to me beyond Fitchburg. In
Ashburnham and afterward, as we were whirled rapidly
along, I noticed the woodbine (*Ampelopsis quinque-
folia*), its leaves now changed, for the most part on dead
trees, draping them like a red scarf. It was a little exciting, suggesting bloodshed, or at least a military life,

like an epaulet or sash, as if it were dyed with the blood of the trees whose wounds it was inadequate to stanch. For now the bloody autumn was come, and an Indian warfare was waged through the forest. These military trees appeared very numerous, for our rapid progress connected those that were even some miles apart. Does the woodbine prefer the elm? The first view of Monadnock was obtained five or six miles this side of Fitzwilliam, but nearest and best at Troy and beyond. Then there were the Troy cuts and embankments. Keene Street strikes the traveler favorably, it is so wide, level, straight, and long. I have heard one of my relatives, who was born and bred there, say that you could see a chicken run across it a mile off. I have also been told that when this town was settled they laid out a street four rods wide, but at a subsequent meeting of the proprietors one rose and remarked, "We have plenty of land, why not make the street eight rods wide?" and so they voted that it should be eight rods wide, and the town is known far and near for its handsome street. It was a cheap way of securing comfort, as well as fame, and I wish that all new towns would take pattern from this. It is best to lay our plans widely in youth, for then land is cheap, and it is but too easy to contract our views afterward. Youths so laid out, with broad avenues and parks, that they may make handsome and liberal old men! Show me a youth whose mind is like some Washington city of magnificent distances, prepared for the most remotely successful and glorious life after all, when those spaces shall be built over and the idea of the founder be realized. I trust that every New England boy will begin by laying out a Keene Street through his head, eight rods wide. I know one such Washington city of a man, whose lots as yet are only surveyed and staked out, and, except a cluster of shanties here and there, only the Capitol stands there for all structures, and any day you may see from afar his princely idea borne coachwise along the spacious but yet empty avenues. Keene is built on a remarkably large and level interval, like the bed of a lake, and the surrounding hills, which are remote from its street, must afford some good walks. The scenery of mountain towns is commonly too much crowded. A town which is built on a plain of some extent, with an open horizon, and surrounded by hills at a distance, affords the best walks and views.

As we travel northwest up the country, sugar maples, beeches, birches, hemlocks, spruce, butternuts, and ash trees prevail more and more. To the rapid traveler the number of elms in a town is the measure of its civility. One man in the cars has a bottle full of some liquor. The whole company smile whenever it is exhibited. I find no difficulty in containing myself. The Westmoreland country looked attractive. I heard a passenger giving the very obvious derivation of this name, Westmoreland, as if it were purely American, and he had made a discovery; but I thought of "my cousin Westmoreland" in England. Every one will remember the approach to Bellows Falls, under a high cliff which rises from the Connecticut. I was disappointed in the size of the river here; it appeared shrunk to a mere mountain-stream. The water was evidently very low. The rivers which we had crossed this forenoon possessed more of the character of mountain-streams than those in the vicinity of Concord, and I was surprised to see everywhere traces of recent freshets, which had carried away bridges and injured the railroad, though I had heard nothing of it. In Ludlow, Mount Holly, and beyond, there is interesting mountain scenery, not rugged and stupendous, but such as you could easily ramble over—long, narrow, mountain vales through which to see the horizon. You

are in the midst of the Green Mountains. A few more
elevated blue peaks are seen from the neighborhood of
Mount Holly; perhaps Killington Peak is one. Sometimes, as on the Western Railroad, you are whirled over
mountainous embankments, from which the scared
horses in the valleys appear diminished to hounds. All
the hills blush; I think that autumn must be the best
season to journey over even the *Green* Mountains. You
frequently exclaim to yourself, What *red* maples! The
sugar maple is not so red. You see some of the latter
with rosy spots or cheeks only, blushing on one side like
fruit, while all the rest of the tree is green, proving
either some partiality in the light or frosts or some pre-
maturity in particular branches. Tall and slender ash
trees, whose foliage is turned to a dark mulberry color,
are frequent. The butternut, which is a remarkably
spreading tree, is turned completely yellow, thus proving its relation to the hickories. I was also struck by the
bright yellow tints of the yellow birch. The sugar maple
is remarkable for its clean ankle. The groves of these
trees looked like vast forest sheds, their branches stopping short at a uniform height, four or five feet from the
ground, like eaves, as if they had been trimmed by art,
so that you could look under and through the whole
grove with its leafy canopy, as under a tent whose curtain is raised.

As you approach Lake Champlain you begin to see
the New York mountains. The first view of the lake
at Vergennes is impressive, but rather from association
than from any peculiarity in the scenery. It lies there
so small (not appearing in that proportion to the width
of the State that it does on the map), but beautifully
quiet, like a picture of the Lake of Lucerne on a music-
box, where you trace the name of Lucerne among the
foliage; far more ideal than ever it looked on the map.

It does not say, "Here I am, Lake Champlain," as the conductor might for it, but having studied the geography thirty years, you crossed over a hill one afternoon and beheld it. But it is only a glimpse that you get here. At Burlington you rush to a wharf and go on board a steamboat, two hundred and thirty-two miles from Boston. We left Concord at twenty minutes before eight in the morning, and were in Burlington about six at night, but too late to see the lake. We got our first fair view of the lake at dawn, just before reaching Plattsburg, and saw blue ranges of mountains on either hand, in New York and in Vermont, the former especially grand. A few white schooners, like gulls, were seen in the distance, for it is not waste and solitary like a lake in Tartary; but it was such a view as leaves not much to be said; indeed, I have postponed Lake Champlain to another day.

The oldest reference to these waters that I have yet seen is in the account of Cartier's discovery and exploration of the St. Lawrence in 1535. Samuel Champlain actually discovered and paddled up the lake in July, 1609, eleven years before the settlement of Plymouth, accompanying a war-party of the Canadian Indians against the Iroquois. He describes the islands in it as not inhabited, although they are pleasant—on account of the continual wars of the Indians, in consequence of which they withdraw from the rivers and lakes into the depths of the land, that they may not be surprised. "Continuing our course," says he, "in this lake, on the western side, viewing the country, I saw on the eastern side very high mountains, where there was snow on the summit. I inquired of the savages if those places were inhabited. They replied that they were, and that they were Iroquois, and that in those places there were beautiful valleys and plains fertile in corn, such as

I have eaten in this country, with an infinity of other fruits." This is the earliest account of what is now Vermont.

The number of French-Canadian gentlemen and ladies among the passengers, and the sound of the French language, advertised us by this time that we were being whirled towards some foreign vortex. And now we have left Rouse's Point, and entered the Sorel River, and passed the invisible barrier between the States and Canada. The shores of the Sorel, Richelieu, or St. John's River are flat and reedy, where I had expected something more rough and mountainous for a natural boundary between two nations. Yet I saw a difference at once, in the few huts, in the pirogues on the shore, and as it were, in the shore itself. This was an interesting scenery to me, and the very reeds or rushes in the shallow water and the treetops in the swamps have left a pleasing impression. We had still a distant view behind us of two or three blue mountains in Vermont and New York. About nine o'clock in the forenoon we reached St. John's, an old frontier post three hundred and six miles from Boston, and twenty-four from Montreal. We now discovered that we were in a foreign country, in a stationhouse of another nation. This building was a barnlike structure, looking as if it were the work of the villagers combined, like a log house in a new settlement. My attention was caught by the double advertisements in French and English fastened to its posts, by the formality of the English, and the covert or open reference to their queen and the British lion. No gentlemanly conductor appeared, none whom you would know to be the conductor by his dress and demeanor; but ere long we began to see here and there a solid, red-faced, burly-looking Englishman, a little pursy perhaps, who made us ashamed of ourselves

and our thin and nervous countrymen—a grandfatherly
personage, at home in his greatcoat, who looked as if he
might be a stage proprietor, certainly a railroad director,
and knew, or had a right to know, when the cars did
start. Then there were two or three pale-faced, black-
eyed, loquacious Canadian-French gentlemen there,
shrugging their shoulders; pitted as if they had all had
the smallpox. In the meanwhile some soldiers, redcoats,
belonging to the barracks near by, were turned out to be
drilled. At every important point in our route the soldiers showed themselves ready for us; though they were
evidently rather raw recruits here, they maneuvered far
better than our soldiers; yet, as usual, I heard some
Yankees talk as if they were no great shakes, and they
had seen the Acton Blues maneuver as well. The officers
spoke sharply to them, and appeared to be doing their
part thoroughly. I heard one suddenly coming to the
rear, exclaim, "Michael Donouy, take his name!" though
I could not see what the latter did or omitted to do. It
was whispered that Michael Donouy would have to
suffer for that. I heard some of our party discussing the
possibility of their driving these troops off the field with
their umbrellas. I thought that the Yankee, though undis-
ciplined, had this advantage at least, that he especially
is a man who, everywhere and under all circumstances,
is fully resolved to better his condition essentially, and
therefore he could afford to be beaten at first; while the
virtue of the Irishman, and to a great extent the Englishman, consists in merely maintaining his ground or
condition. The Canadians here, a rather poor-looking
race, clad in gray homespun, which gave them the appearance of being covered with dust, were riding about
in caleches and small one-horse carts called charettes.
The Yankees assumed that all the riders were racing,
or at least exhibiting the paces of their horses, and sa-

luted them accordingly. We saw but little of the village
here, for nobody could tell us when the cars would start;
that was kept a profound secret, perhaps for political
reasons; and therefore we were tied to our seats. The
inhabitants of St. John's and vicinity are described by
an English traveler as "singularly unprepossessing,"
and before completing his period he adds, "besides, they
are generally very much disaffected to the British
crown." I suspect that that "besides" should have been
a because.

At length, about noon, the cars began to roll towards
La Prairie. The whole distance of fifteen miles was
over a remarkably level country, resembling a Western
prairie, with the mountains about Chambly visible in
the northeast. This novel but monotonous scenery was
exciting. At La Prairie we first took notice of the tinned
roofs, but above all of the St. Lawrence, which looked
like a lake; in fact it is considerably expanded here; it
was nine miles across diagonally to Montreal. Mount
Royal in the rear of the city, and the island of St. Helen's
opposite to it, were now conspicuous. We could also see
the Sault St. Louis about five miles up the river, and the
Sault Norman still farther eastward. The former are
described as the most considerable rapids in the St.
Lawrence; but we could see merely a gleam of light
there as from a cobweb in the sun. Soon the city of
Montreal was discovered with its tin roofs shining afar.
Their reflections fell on the eye like a clash of cymbals
on the ear. Above all the church of Notre Dame was
conspicuous, and anon the Bonsecours markethouse, occupying a commanding position on the quay, in the rear
of the shipping. This city makes the more favorable impression from being approached by water, and also being built of stone, a gray limestone found on the island.
Here, after traveling directly inland the whole breadth

of New England, we had struck upon a city's harbor—
it made on me the impression of a seaport—to which
ships of six hundred tons can ascend, and where vessels
drawing fifteen feet lie close to the wharf, five hundred
and forty miles from the Gulf, the St. Lawrence being
here two miles wide. There was a great crowd assembled on the ferryboat wharf and on the quay to receive
the Yankees, and flags of all colors were streaming from
the vessels to celebrate their arrival. When the gun was
fired, the gentry hurrahed again and again, and then the
Canadian caleche-drivers, who were most interested in
the matter, and who, I perceived, were separated from
the former by a fence, hurrahed their welcome; first the
broadcloth, then the homespun.

It was early in the afternoon when we stepped ashore.
With a single companion, I soon found my way to the
church of Notre Dame. I saw that it was of great size
and signified something. It is said to be the largest
ecclesiastical structure in North America, and can seat
ten thousand. It is two hundred and fifty-five and a half
feet long, and the groined ceiling is eighty feet above
your head. The Catholic are the only churches which
I have seen worth remembering, which are not almost
wholly profane. I do not speak only of the rich and
splendid like this, but of the humblest of them as well.
Coming from the hurrahing mob and the rattling carriages, we pushed aside the listed door of this church,
and found ourselves instantly in an atmosphere which
might be sacred to thought and religion, if one had any.
There sat one or two women who had stolen a moment
from the concerns of the day, as they were passing; but,
if there had been fifty people there, it would still have
been the most solitary place imaginable. They did not
look up at us, nor did one regard another. We walked
softly down the broad aisle with our hats in our hands.

Presently came in a troop of Canadians, in their home-spun, who had come to the city in the boat with us, and one and all kneeled down in the aisle before the high altar to their devotions, somewhat awkwardly, as cattle prepare to lie down, and there we left them. As if you were to catch some farmer's sons from Marlborough, come to cattle show, silently kneeling in Concord meetinghouse some Wednesday! Would there not soon be a mob peeping in at the windows? It is true, these Roman Catholics, priests and all, impress me as a people who have fallen far behind the significance of their symbols. It is as if an ox had strayed into a church and were trying to bethink himself. Nevertheless, they are capable of reverence; but we Yankees are a people in whom this sentiment has nearly died out, and in this respect we cannot bethink ourselves even as oxen. I did not mind the pictures nor the candles, whether tallow or tin. Those of the former which I looked at appeared tawdry. It matters little to me whether the pictures are by a neophyte of the Algonquin or the Italian tribe. But I was impressed by the quiet, religious atmosphere of the place. It was a great cave in the midst of a city; and what were the altars and the tinsel but the sparkling stalactites, into which you entered in a moment, and where the still atmosphere and the somber light disposed to serious and profitable thought? Such a cave at hand, which you can enter any day, is worth a thousand of our churches which are open only Sundays, hardly long enough for an airing, and then filled with a bustling congregation—a church where the priest is the least part, where you do your own preaching, where the universe preaches to you and can be heard. I am not sure but this Catholic religion would be an admirable one if the priest were quite omitted. I think that I might go to church myself some Monday, if I lived in a city where there was such a one to go to. In Concord, to be sure, we do not need such. Our forests are such a church, far grander and more sacred. We dare not leave *our* meeting-houses open for fear they would be profaned. Such a cave, such a shrine, in one of our groves, for instance, how long would it be respected? for what purposes would it be entered, by such baboons as we are? I think of its value not only to religion, but to philosophy and to poetry; besides a reading-room, to have a thinking-room in every city! Perchance the time will come when every house even will have not only its sleeping-rooms, and dining-room, and talking-room or parlor, but its thinking-room also, and the architects will put it into their plans. Let it be furnished and ornamented with whatever conduces to serious and creative thought. I should not object to the holy water, or any other simple symbol, if it were consecrated by the imagination of the worshipers.

I heard that some Yankees bet that the candles were not wax, but tin. A European assured them that they were wax; but, inquiring of the sexton, he was surprised to learn that they were tin filled with oil. The church was too poor to afford wax. As for the Protestant churches, here or elsewhere, they did not interest me, for it is only as caves that churches interest me at all, and in that respect they were inferior.

Montreal makes the impression of a larger city than you had expected to find, though you may have heard that it contains nearly sixty thousand inhabitants. In the newer parts, it appeared to be growing fast like a small New York, and to be considerably Americanized. The names of the squares reminded you of Paris—the Champ de Mars, the Place d'Armes, and others—and you felt as if a French revolution might break out any moment. Glimpses of Mount Royal rising behind the town, and the names of some streets in that direction, make one think of Edinburgh. That hill sets off this city wonderfully. I inquired at a principal bookstore for books published in Montreal. They said that there were none but schoolbooks and the like; they got their books from the States. From time to time we met a priest in the streets, for they are distinguished by their dress, like the *civil* police. Like clergymen generally, with or without the gown, they made on us the impression of effeminacy. We also met some Sisters of Charity, dressed in black, with Shaker-shaped black bonnets and crosses, and cadaverous faces, who looked as if they had almost cried their eyes out, their complexions parboiled with scalding tears; insulting the daylight by their presence, having taken an oath not to smile. By cadaverous I mean that their faces were like the faces of those who have been dead and buried for a year, and then untombed, with the life's grief upon them, and yet, for some unaccountable reason, the process of decay arrested.

> "Truth never fails her servant, sir, nor leaves him
> With the day's shame upon him."

They waited demurely on the sidewalk while a truck laden with raisins was driven in at the seminary of St. Sulpice, never once lifting their eyes from the ground.

The soldier here, as everywhere in Canada, appeared to be put forward, and by his best foot. They were in the proportion of the soldiers to the laborers in an African ant-hill. The inhabitants evidently rely on them in a great measure for music and entertainment. You would meet with them pacing back and forth before some guardhouse or passageway, guarding, regarding, and disregarding all kinds of law by turns, apparently for the sake of the discipline to themselves, and not because it was important to exclude anybody from entering that way. They reminded me of the men who are paid for piling up bricks and then throwing them down again. On every prominent ledge you could see England's hands holding the Canadas, and I judged by the redness of her knuckles that she would soon have to let go. In the rear of such a guardhouse, in a large graveled square or parade ground, called the Champ de Mars, we saw a large body of soldiers being drilled, we being as yet the only spectators. But they did not appear to notice us any more than the devotees in the church, but were seemingly as indifferent to fewness of spectators as the phenomena of nature are, whatever they might have been thinking under their helmets of the Yankees that were to come. Each man wore white kid gloves. It was one of the most interesting sights which I saw in Canada. The problem appeared to be how to smooth down all individual protuberances or idiosyncrasies, and make a thousand men move as one man, animated by one central will; and there was some approach to success. They obeyed the signals of a commander who stood at a great distance, wand in hand; and the precision, and promptness, and harmony of their movements could not easily have been matched. The harmony was far more remarkable than that of any choir or band, and obtained, no doubt, at a greater cost. They made on me the impression, not of many individuals, but of one vast centipede of a man, good for all sorts of pulling down; and why not then for some kinds of building up? If men could combine thus earnestly, and patiently, and harmoniously to some really worthy end, what might they not accomplish? They now put their hands, and partially perchance their heads together, and the result is that they are the imperfect tools of an imperfect and tyrannical government. But if they could put their hands and heads and hearts and all together, such a co-operation and harmony would be the very end and success for which government now exists in vain—a government, as it were, not only with tools, but stock to trade with.

I was obliged to frame some sentences that sounded like French in order to deal with the market-women, who, for the most part, cannot speak English. According to the guidebook the relative population of this city stands nearly thus: two fifths are French-Canadian; nearly one fifth British-Canadian; one and a half fifths English, Irish, and Scotch; somewhat less than one half fifth Germans, United States people, and others. I saw nothing like pie for sale, and no good cake to put in my bundle, such as you can easily find in our towns, but plenty of fair-looking apples, for which Montreal Island is celebrated, and also pears cheaper and I thought better than ours, and peaches, which, though they were probably brought from the South, were as cheap as they commonly are with us. So imperative is the law of demand and supply that, as I have been told, the market of Montreal is sometimes supplied with green apples from the State of New York some weeks even before they are ripe in the latter place. I saw here the spruce wax which the Canadians chew, done up in little silvered papers, a penny a roll; also a small and shriveled fruit which they called *cerises,* mixed with many little stems, somewhat like raisins, but I soon returned what I had bought, finding them rather insipid, only putting a sample in my pocket. Since my return, I find on comparison that it is the fruit of the sweet viburnum (*Viburnum Lentago*), which with us rarely holds on till it is ripe.

I stood on the deck of the steamer *John Munn,* late in the afternoon, when the second and third ferryboats arrived from La Prairie, bringing the remainder of the Yankees. I never saw so many caleches, cabs, charettes, and similar vehicles collected before, and doubt if New York could easily furnish more. The handsome and substantial stone quay which stretches a mile along the riverside and protects the street from the ice was thronged with the citizens who had turned out on foot and in carriages to welcome or to behold the Yankees. It was interesting to see the caleche-drivers dash up and down the slope of the quay with their active little horses. They drive much faster than in our cities. I have been told that some of them come nine miles into the city every morning and return every night, without changing their horses during the day. In the midst of the crowd of carts, I observed one deep one loaded with sheep with their legs tied together, and their bodies piled one upon another, as if the driver had forgotten that they were sheep and not yet mutton—a sight, I trust, peculiar to Canada, though I fear that it is not.

Walden

It was a long road to Walden, *but two men helped Thoreau
on his way, one with an action, the other with ideas. One
was Stearns Wheeler. He built a hut on a pondy shore near
Concord, and for six weeks, during their college days,
Thoreau stayed with him there as his guest. The other was
Emerson. When in 1836 he published his little book* Nature,
*it became almost at once the bible of Transcendentalism.
Clearly, Thoreau read it with closest attention; its ideas informed his early writing. But he went on to pen many hundreds of pages and to pass many years before finally sending
the manuscript of* Walden *to the printer. Thoreau reshaped
it seven times after leaving his hut; at the end the book was
uniquely his. Ticknor & Fields issued it in August 1854. By
then Transcendentalism was a dying movement, but its greatest document was at last in type.*

C. B.

ECONOMY

WHEN I wrote the following pages, or rather the
bulk of them, I lived alone, in the woods, a mile
from any neighbor, in a house which I had built myself,
on the shore of Walden Pond, in Concord, Massachusetts, and earned my living by the labor of my hands
only. I lived there two years and two months. At present
I am a sojourner in civilized life again.

I should not obtrude my affairs so much on the notice
of my readers if very particular inquiries had not been
made by my townsmen concerning my mode of life,
which some would call impertinent, though they do not

appear to me at all impertinent, but, considering the circumstances, very natural and pertinent. Some have asked what I got to eat; if I did not feel lonesome; if I was not afraid; and the like. Others have been curious to learn what portion of my income I devoted to charitable purposes; and some, who have large families, how many poor children I maintained. I will therefore ask those of my readers who feel no particular interest in me to pardon me if I undertake to answer some of these questions in this book. In most books, the I, or first person, is omitted; in this it will be retained; that, in respect to egotism, is the main difference. We commonly do not remember that it is, after all, always the first person that is speaking. I should not talk so much about myself if there were anybody else whom I knew as well. Unfortunately, I am confined to this theme by the narrowness of my experience. Moreover, I, on my side, require of every writer, first or last, a simple and sincere account of his own life, and not merely what he has heard of other men's lives; some such account as he would send to his kindred from a distant land; for if he has lived sincerely, it must have been in a distant land to me. Perhaps these pages are more particularly addressed to poor students. As for the rest of my readers, they will accept such portions as apply to them. I trust that none will stretch the seams in putting on the coat, for it may do good service to him whom it fits.

I would fain say something, not so much concerning the Chinese and Sandwich Islanders as you who read these pages, who are said to live in New England; something about your condition, especially your outward condition or circumstances in this world, in this town, what it is, whether it is necessary that it be as bad as it is, whether it cannot be improved as well as not. I have traveled a good deal in Concord; and everywhere, in shops, and offices, and fields, the inhabitants have appeared to me to be doing penance in a thousand remarkable ways. What I have heard of Bramins sitting exposed to four fires and looking in the face of the sun; or hanging suspended, with their heads downward, over flames; or looking at the heavens over their shoulders "until it becomes impossible for them to resume their natural position, while from the twist of the neck nothing but liquids can pass into the stomach"; or dwelling, chained for life, at the foot of a tree; or measuring with their bodies, like caterpillars, the breadth of vast empires; or standing on one leg on the tops of pillars—even these forms of conscious penance are hardly more incredible and astonishing than the scenes which I daily witness. The twelve labors of Hercules were trifling in comparison with those which my neighbors have undertaken; for they were only twelve, and had an end; but I could never see that these men slew or captured any monster or finished any labor. They have no friend Iolaus to burn with a hot iron the root of the hydra's head, but as soon as one head is crushed, two spring up.

I see young men, my townsmen, whose misfortune it is to have inherited farms, houses, barns, cattle, and farming tools; for these are more easily acquired than got rid of. Better if they had been born in the open pasture and suckled by a wolf, that they might have seen with clearer eyes what field they were called to labor in. Who made them serfs of the soil? Why should they eat their sixty acres, when man is condemned to eat only his peck of dirt? Why should they begin digging their graves as soon as they are born? They have got to live a man's life, pushing all these things before them, and get on as well as they can. How many a poor immortal soul have I met well nigh crushed and smothered under its load, creeping down the road of life, pushing before it a barn seventy-five feet by forty, its Augean stables never cleansed, and one hundred acres of land, tillage, mowing, pasture, and wood-lot! The portionless, who struggle with no such unnecessary inherited encumbrances, find it labor enough to subdue and cultivate a few cubic feet of flesh.

But men labor under a mistake. The better part of the man is soon ploughed into the soil for compost. By a seeming fate, commonly called necessity, they are employed, as it says in an old book, laying up treasures which moth and rust will corrupt and thieves break through and steal. It is a fool's life, as they will find when they get to the end of it, if not before. It is said that Deucalion and Pyrrha created men by throwing stones over their heads behind them:

> Inde genus durum sumus, experiensque laborum,
> Et documenta damus quâ simus origine nati.

Or, as Raleigh rhymes it in his sonorous way,

> "From thence our kind hard-hearted is, enduring pain and care,
> Approving that our bodies of a stony nature are."

So much for a blind obedience to a blundering oracle, throwing the stones over their heads behind them, and not seeing where they fell.

Most men, even in this comparatively free country, through mere ignorance and mistake, are so occupied with the factitious cares and superfluously coarse labors of life that its finer fruits cannot be plucked by them. Their fingers, from excessive toil, are too clumsy and tremble too much for that. Actually, the laboring man has not leisure for a true integrity day by day; he cannot afford to sustain the manliest relations to men; his labor would be depreciated in the market. He has no time to be anything but a machine. How can he remem-

ber well his ignorance—which his growth requires—
who has so often to use his knowledge? We should feed
and clothe him gratuitously sometimes, and recruit him
with our cordials, before we judge of him. The finest
qualities of our nature, like the bloom on fruits, can be
preserved only by the most delicate handling. Yet we do
not treat ourselves nor one another thus tenderly.

Some of you, we all know, are poor, find it hard to
live, are sometimes, as it were, gasping for breath. I
have no doubt that some of you who read this book are
unable to pay for all the dinners which you have actually eaten, or for the coats and shoes which are fast
wearing or are already worn out, and have come to this
page to spend borrowed or stolen time, robbing your
creditors of an hour. It is very evident what mean and
sneaking lives many of you live, for my sight has been
whetted by experience; always on the limits, trying to
get into business and trying to get out of debt, a very
ancient slough, called by the Latins *æs alienum*, another's brass, for some of their coins were made of brass;
still living, and dying, and buried by this other's brass;
always promising to pay, promising to pay, tomorrow,
and dying today, insolvent; seeking to curry favor, to get
custom, by how many modes, only not state-prison of-
fenses; lying, flattering, voting, contracting yourselves
into a nutshell of civility, or dilating into an atmosphere
of thin and vaporous generosity, that you may persuade
your neighbor to let you make his shoes, or his hat, or
his coat, or his carriage, or import his groceries for him;
making yourselves sick, that you may lay up something
against a sick day, something to be tucked away in an
old chest, or in a stocking behind the plastering, or,
more safely, in the brick bank; no matter where, no
matter how much or how little.

I sometimes wonder that we can be so frivolous, I

may almost say, as to attend to the gross but somewhat foreign form of servitude called Negro Slavery, there are so many keen and subtle masters that enslave both North and South. It is hard to have a Southern overseer; it is worse to have a Northern one; but worst of all when you are the slave-driver of yourself. Talk of a divinity in man! Look at the teamster on the highway, wending to market by day or night; does any divinity stir within him? His highest duty to fodder and water his horses! What is his destiny to him compared with the shipping interests? Does not he drive for Squire Make-a-stir? How godlike, how immortal, is he? See how he cowers and sneaks, how vaguely all the day he fears, not being immortal nor divine, but the slave and prisoner of his own opinion of himself, a fame won by his own deeds. Public opinion is a weak tyrant compared with our own private opinion. What a man thinks of himself, that it is which determines, or rather indicates, his fate. Self-emancipation even in the West Indian provinces of the fancy and imagination—what Wilberforce is there to bring that about? Think, also, of the ladies of the land weaving toilet cushions against the last day, not to betray too green an interest in their fates! As if you could kill time without injuring eternity.

The mass of men lead lives of quiet desperation. What is called resignation is confirmed desperation. From the desperate city you go into the desperate country, and have to console yourself with the bravery of minks and muskrats. A stereotyped but unconscious despair is concealed even under what are called the games and amusements of mankind. There is no play in them, for this comes after work. But it is a characteristic of wisdom not to do desperate things.

When we consider what, to use the words of the catechism, is the chief end of man, and what are the true necessaries and means of life, it appears as if men had deliberately chosen the common mode of living because they preferred it to any other. Yet they honestly think there is no choice left. But alert and healthy natures remember that the sun rose clear. It is never too late to give up our prejudices. No way of thinking or doing, however ancient, can be trusted without proof. What everybody echoes or in silence passes by as true today may turn out to be falsehood tomorrow, mere smoke of opinion, which some had trusted for a cloud that would sprinkle fertilizing rain on their fields. What old people say you cannot do you try and find that you can. Old deeds for old people, and new deeds for new. Old people did not know enough once, perchance, to fetch fresh fuel to keep the fire a-going; new people put a little dry wood under a pot, and are whirled round the globe with the speed of birds, in a way to kill old people, as the phrase is. Age is no better, hardly so well, qualified for an instructor as youth, for it has not profited so much as it has lost. One may almost doubt if the wisest man has learned anything of absolute value by living. Practically, the old have no very important advice to give the young, their own experience has been so partial, and their lives have been such miserable failures, for private reasons, as they must believe; and it may be that they have some faith left which belies that experience, and they are only less young than they were. I have lived some thirty years on this planet, and I have yet to hear the first syllable of valuable or even earnest advice from my seniors. They have told me nothing, and probably cannot tell me anything to the purpose. Here is life, an experiment to a great extent untried by me; but it does not avail me that they have tried it. If I have any experience which I think valuable, I am sure to reflect that this my Mentors said nothing about.

One farmer says to me, "You cannot live on vegetable food solely, for it furnishes nothing to make bones with"; and so he religiously devotes a part of his day to supplying his system with the raw material of bones; walking all the while he talks behind his oxen, which, with vegetable-made bones, jerk him and his lumbering plough along in spite of every obstacle. Some things are really necessaries of life in some circles, the most helpless and diseased, which in others are luxuries merely, and in others still are entirely unknown.

The whole ground of human life seems to some to have been gone over by their predecessors, both the heights and the valleys, and all things to have been cared for. According to Evelyn, "the wise Solomon prescribed ordinances for the very distances of trees; and the Roman prætors have decided how often you may go into your neighbor's land to gather the acorns which fall on it without trespass, and what share belongs to that neighbor." Hippocrates has even left directions how we should cut our nails; that is, even with the ends of the fingers, neither shorter nor longer. Undoubtedly the very tedium and ennui which presume to have exhausted the variety and the joys of life are as old as Adam. But man's capacities have never been measured; nor are we to judge of what he can do by any precedents, so little has been tried. Whatever have been thy failures hitherto, "be not afflicted, my child, for who shall assign to thee what thou hast left undone?"

We might try our lives by a thousand simple tests; as, for instance, that the same sun which ripens my beans illumines at once a system of earths like ours. If I had remembered this it would have prevented some mistakes. This was not the light in which I hoed them. The stars are the apexes of what wonderful triangles! What distant and different beings in the various mansions of the universe are contemplating the same one at the same moment! Nature and human life are as various as our several constitutions. Who shall say what prospect life offers to another? Could a greater miracle take place than for us to look through each other's eyes for an instant? We should live in all the ages of the world in an hour; ay, in all the worlds of the ages. History, Poetry, Mythology!—I know of no reading of another's experience so startling and informing as this would be.

The greater part of what my neighbors call good I believe in my soul to be bad, and if I repent of anything, it is very likely to be my good behavior. What demon possessed me that I behaved so well? You may say the wisest thing you can, old man—you who have lived seventy years, not without honor of a kind—I hear an irresistible voice which invites me away from all that. One generation abandons the enterprises of another like stranded vessels.

I think that we may safely trust a good deal more than we do. We may waive just so much care of ourselves as we honestly bestow elsewhere. Nature is as well adapted to our weakness as to our strength. The incessant anxiety and strain of some is a well-nigh incurable form of disease. We are made to exaggerate the importance of what work we do; and yet how much is not done by us! or, what if we had been taken sick? How vigilant we are! determined not to live by faith if we can avoid it; all the day long on the alert, at night we unwillingly say our prayers and commit ourselves to uncertainties. So thoroughly and sincerely are we compelled to live, reverencing our life, and denying the possibility of change. This is the only way, we say; but there are as many ways as there can be drawn radii from one center. All change is a miracle to contemplate; but it is a miracle which is taking place every instant. Confucius said, "To know that we know what we know, and that we do not know what we do not know, that is true knowledge." When one man has reduced a fact of the imagination to be a fact to his understanding, I foresee that all men will at length establish their lives on that basis.

Let us consider for a moment what most of the trouble and anxiety which I have referred to is about, and how much it is necessary that we be troubled, or at least careful. It would be some advantage to live a primitive and frontier life, though in the midst of an outward civilization, if only to learn what are the gross necessaries of life and what methods have been taken to obtain them; or even to look over the old daybooks of the merchants, to see what it was that men most commonly bought at the stores, what they stored, that is, what are the grossest groceries. For the improvements of ages have had but little influence on the essential laws of man's existence: as our skeletons, probably, are not to be distinguished from those of our ancestors.

By the words, *necessary of life,* I mean whatever, of all that man obtains by his own exertions, has been from the first, or from long use has become, so important to human life that few, if any, whether from savageness, or poverty, or philosophy, ever attempt to do without it. To many creatures there is in this sense but one necessary of life, Food. To the bison of the prairie it is a few inches of palatable grass, with water to drink; unless he seeks the Shelter of the forest or the mountain's shadow. None of the brute creation requires more than Food and Shelter. The necessaries of life for man in this climate may, accurately enough, be distributed under the several heads of Food, Shelter, Clothing, and Fuel; for not till we have secured these are we prepared to entertain the true problems of life with freedom and a prospect of

success. Man has invented not only houses but clothes
and cooked food; and possibly from the accidental discovery of the warmth of fire, and the consequent use of
it, at first a luxury, arose the present necessity to sit by
it. We observe cats and dogs acquiring the same second
nature. By proper Shelter and Clothing we legitimately
retain our own internal heat; but with an excess of these,
or of Fuel, that is, with an external heat greater than
our own internal, may not cookery properly be said to
begin? Darwin, the naturalist, says of the inhabitants of
Tierra del Fuego, that while his own party, who were
well clothed and sitting close to a fire, were far from too
warm, these naked savages, who were farther off, were
observed, to his great surprise, "to be streaming with
perspiration at undergoing such a roasting." So, we are
told, the New Hollander goes naked with impunity,
while the European shivers in his clothes. Is it impossible to combine the hardiness of these savages with the
intellectualness of the civilized man? According to Lie-
big, man's body is a stove, and food the fuel which
keeps up the internal combustion in the lungs. In cold
weather we eat more, in warm less. The animal heat is
the result of a slow combustion, and disease and death
take place when this is too rapid; or for want of fuel, or
from some defect in the draught, the fire goes out. Of
course the vital heat is not to be confounded with fire;
but so much for analogy. It appears, therefore, from the
above list, that the expression, *animal life,* is nearly synonymous with the expression, *animal heat;* for while
Food may be regarded as the Fuel which keeps up the
fire within us—and Fuel serves only to prepare that
Food or to increase the warmth of our bodies by addition from without—Shelter and Clothing also serve only
to retain the *heat* thus generated and absorbed.

The grand necessity, then, for our bodies, is to keep

warm, to keep the vital heat in us. What pains we accordingly take, not only with our Food, and Clothing, and Shelter, but with our beds, which are our night-clothes, robbing the nests and breasts of birds to prepare this shelter within a shelter, as the mole has its bed of grass and leaves at the end of its burrow! The poor man is wont to complain that this is a cold world; and to cold, no less physical than social, we refer directly a great part of our ails. The summer, in some climates, makes possible to man a sort of Elysian life. Fuel, except to cook his Food, is then unnecessary; the sun is his fire, and many of the fruits are sufficiently cooked by its rays; while Food generally is more various, and more easily obtained, and Clothing and Shelter are wholly or half unnecessary. At the present day, and in this country, as I find by my own experience, a few implements, a knife, an axe, a spade, a wheelbarrow, etc., and for the studious, lamplight, stationery, and access to a few books, rank next to necessaries, and can all be obtained at a trifling cost. Yet some, not wise, go to the other side of the globe, to barbarous and unhealthy regions, and devote themselves to trade for ten or twenty years, in order that they may live—that is, keep comfortably warm—and die in New England at last. The luxuriously rich are not simply kept comfortably warm, but unnaturally hot; as I implied before, they are cooked, of course à la mode.

Most of the luxuries, and many of the so-called comforts of life, are not only not indispensable, but positive hindrances to the elevation of mankind. With respect to luxuries and comforts, the wisest have ever lived a more simple and meager life than the poor. The ancient philosophers, Chinese, Hindu, Persian, and Greek, were a class than which none has been poorer in outward riches, none so rich in inward. We know not much about them.

It is remarkable that *we* know so much of them as we do. The same is true of the more modern reformers and benefactors of their race. None can be an impartial or wise observer of human life but from the vantage ground of what *we* should call voluntary poverty. Of a life of luxury the fruit is luxury, whether in agriculture, or commerce, or literature, or art. There are nowadays professors of philosophy, but not philosophers. Yet it is admirable to profess because it was once admirable to live. To be a philosopher is not merely to have subtle thoughts, nor even to found a school, but so to love wisdom as to live according to its dictates, a life of simplicity, independence, magnanimity, and trust. It is to solve some of the problems of life, not only theoretically, but practically. The success of great scholars and thinkers is commonly a courtier-like success, not kingly, not manly. They make shift to live merely by conformity, practically as their fathers did, and are in no sense the progenitors of a nobler race of men. But why do men degenerate ever? What makes families run out? What is the nature of the luxury which enervates and destroys nations? Are we sure that there is none of it in our own lives? The philosopher is in advance of his age even in the outward form of his life. He is not fed, sheltered, clothed, warmed, like his contemporaries. How can a man be a philosopher and not maintain his vital heat by better methods than other men?

When a man is warmed by the several modes which I have described, what does he want next? Surely not more warmth of the same kind, as more and richer food, larger and more splendid houses, finer and more abundant clothing, more numerous incessant and hotter fires, and the like. When he has obtained those things which are necessary to life, there is another alternative than to obtain the superfluities; and that is, to adventure on life now, his vacation from humbler toil having commenced. The soil, it appears, is suited to the seed, for it has sent its radicle downward, and it may now send its shoot upward also with confidence. Why has man rooted himself thus firmly in the earth, but that he may rise in the same proportion into the heavens above?—for the nobler plants are valued for the fruit they bear at last in the air and light, far from the ground, and are not treated like the humbler esculents, which, though they may be biennials, are cultivated only till they have perfected their root, and often cut down at top for this purpose, so that most would not know them in their flowering season.

I do not mean to prescribe rules to strong and valiant natures, who will mind their own affairs whether in heaven or hell, and perchance build more magnificently and spend more lavishly than the richest, without ever impoverishing themselves, not knowing how they live— if, indeed, there are any such, as has been dreamed; nor to those who find their encouragement and inspiration in precisely the present condition of things, and cherish it with the fondness and enthusiasm of lovers—and, to some extent, I reckon myself in this number; I do not speak to those who are well employed, in whatever circumstances, and they know whether they are well employed or not; but mainly to the mass of men who are discontented, and idly complaining of the hardness of their lot or of the times, when they might improve them. There are some who complain most energetically and inconsolably of any, because they are, as they say, doing their duty. I also have in my mind that seemingly wealthy, but most terribly impoverished class of all, who have accumulated dross, but know not how to use it, or get rid of it, and thus have forged their own golden or silver fetters.

If I should attempt to tell how I have desired to spend my life in years past, it would probably surprise those of my readers who are somewhat acquainted with its actual history; it would certainly astonish those who know nothing about it. I will only hint at some of the enterprises which I have cherished.

In any weather, at any hour of the day or night, I have been anxious to improve the nick of time, and notch it on my stick too; to stand on the meeting of two eternities, the past and future, which is precisely the present moment; to toe that line. You will pardon some obscurities, for there are more secrets in my trade than in most men's, and yet not voluntarily kept, but inseparable from its very nature. I would gladly tell all that I know about it, and never paint "No Admittance" on my gate.

I long ago lost a hound, a bay horse, and a turtle-dove, and am still on their trail. Many are the travelers I have spoken concerning them, describing their tracks and what calls they answered to. I have met one or two who had heard the hound, and the tramp of the horse, and even seen the dove disappear behind a cloud, and they seemed as anxious to recover them as if they had lost them themselves.

To anticipate, not the sunrise and the dawn merely, but, if possible, Nature herself! How many mornings, summer and winter, before yet any neighbor was stirring about his business, have I been about mine! No doubt, many of my townsmen have met me returning from this enterprise, farmers starting for Boston in the twilight, or woodchoppers going to their work. It is true, I never assisted the sun materially in his rising, but, doubt not, it was of the last importance only to be present at it.

So many autumn, ay, and winter days, spent outside

the town, trying to hear what was in the wind, to hear and carry it express! I well-nigh sunk all my capital in it, and lost my own breath into the bargain, running in the face of it. If it had concerned either of the political parties, depend upon it, it would have appeared in the Gazette with the earliest intelligence. At other times watching from the observatory of some cliff or tree, to telegraph any new arrival; or waiting at evening on the hilltops for the sky to fall, that I might catch something, though I never caught much, and that, manna-wise, would dissolve again in the sun.

For a long time I was reporter to a journal, of no very wide circulation, whose editor has never yet seen fit to print the bulk of my contributions, and, as is too common with writers, I got only my labor for my pains. However, in this case my pains were their own reward.

For many years I was self-appointed inspector of snowstorms and rainstorms, and did my duty faithfully; surveyor, if not of highways, then of forest paths and all across-lot routes, keeping them open, and ravines bridged and passable at all seasons, where the public heel had testified to their utility.

I have looked after the wild stock of the town, which give a faithful herdsman a good deal of trouble by leaping fences; and I have had an eye to the unfrequented nooks and corners of the farm; though I did not always know whether Jonas or Solomon worked in a particular field today; that was none of my business. I have watered the red huckleberry, the sand cherry and the nettle tree, the red pine and the black ash, the white grape and the yellow violet, which might have withered else in dry seasons.

In short, I went on thus for a long time (I may say it without boasting), faithfully minding my business, till it became more and more evident that my townsmen would not after all admit me into the list of town officers, nor make my place a sinecure with a moderate allowance. My accounts, which I can swear to have kept faithfully, I have, indeed, never got audited, still less accepted, still less paid and settled. However, I have not set my heart on that.

Not long since, a strolling Indian went to sell baskets at the house of a well-known lawyer in my neighborhood. "Do you wish to buy any baskets?" he asked. "No, we do not want any," was the reply. "What!" exclaimed the Indian as he went out the gate, "do you mean to starve us?" Having seen his industrious white neighbors so well off—that the lawyer had only to weave arguments, and by some magic wealth and standing followed—he had said to himself: I will go into business; I will weave baskets; it is a thing which I can do. Thinking that when he had made the baskets he would have done his part, and then it would be the white man's to buy them. He had not discovered that it was necessary for him to make it worth the other's while to buy them, or at least make him think that it was so, or to make something else which it would be worth his while to buy. I too had woven a kind of basket of a delicate texture, but I had not made it worth anyone's while to buy them. Yet not the less, in my case, did I think it worth my while to weave them, and instead of studying how to make it worth men's while to buy my baskets, I studied rather how to avoid the necessity of selling them. The life which men praise and regard as successful is but one kind. Why should we exaggerate any one kind at the expense of the others?

Finding that my fellow-citizens were not likely to offer me any room in the courthouse, or any curacy or living anywhere else, but I must shift for myself, I turned my face more exclusively than ever to the woods, where I was better known. I determined to go into business at once, and not wait to acquire the usual capital, using such slender means as I had already got. My purpose in going to Walden Pond was not to live cheaply nor to live dearly there, but to transact some private business with the fewest obstacles; to be hindered from accomplishing which for want of a little common sense, a little enterprise and business talent, appeared not so sad as foolish.

I have always endeavored to acquire strict business habits; they are indispensable to every man. If your trade is with the Celestial Empire, then some small counting-house on the coast, in some Salem harbor, will be fixture enough. You will export such articles as the country affords, purely native products, much ice and pine timber and a little granite, always in native bottoms. These will be good ventures. To oversee all the details yourself in person; to be at once pilot and captain, and owner and underwriter; to buy and sell and keep the accounts; to read every letter received, and write or read every letter sent; to superintend the discharge of imports night and day; to be upon many parts of the coast almost at the same time—often the richest freight will be discharged upon a Jersey shore; to be your own telegraph, unweariedly sweeping the horizon, speaking all passing vessels bound coastwise; to keep up a steady despatch of commodities, for the supply of such a distant and exorbitant market; to keep yourself informed of the state of the markets, prospects of war and peace everywhere, and anticipate the tendencies of trade and civilization—taking advantage of the results of all exploring expeditions, using new passages and all improvements in navigation; charts to be studied, the position of reefs and new lights and buoys to be ascertained, and ever, and ever, the logarithmic tables to be corrected, for by the error of some calculator the vessel often splits upon a rock that should have reached a friendly pier—there is the untold fate of La Perouse; universal science to be kept pace with, studying the lives of all great discoverers and navigators, great adventures and merchants, from Hanno and the Phoenicians down to our day; in fine, account of stock to be taken from time to time, to know how you stand. It is a labor to task the faculties of a man—such problems of profit and loss, of interest, of tare and tret, and gauging of all kinds in it, as demand a universal knowledge.

I have thought that Walden Pond would be a good place for business, not solely on account of the railroad and the ice trade; it offers advantages which it may not be good policy to divulge; it is a good post and a good foundation. No Neva marshes to be filled; though you must everywhere build on piles of your own driving. It is said that a flood-tide, with a westerly wind, and ice in the Neva, would sweep St. Petersburg from the face of the earth.

As this business was to be entered into without the usual capital, it may not be easy to conjecture where those means, that will still be indispensable to every such undertaking, were to be obtained. As for Clothing, to come at once to the practical part of the question, perhaps we are led oftener by the love of novelty and a regard for the opinions of men, in procuring it, than by a true utility. Let him who has work to do recollect that the object of clothing is, first, to retain the vital heat, and secondly, in this state of society, to cover nakedness, and he may judge how much of any necessary or important work may be accomplished without adding to his wardrobe. Kings and queens who wear a suit but once, though made by some tailor or dressmaker to their majesties, cannot know the comfort of wearing a suit that fits. They are no better than wooden horses to hang the clean clothes on. Every day our garments become more assimilated to ourselves, receiving the impress of the wearer's character, until we hesitate to lay them aside, without such delay and medical appliances and some such solemnity even as our bodies. No man ever stood the lower in my estimation for having a patch in his clothes; yet I am sure that there is greater anxiety, commonly, to have fashionable, or at least clean and unpatched clothes, than to have a sound conscience. But even if the rent is not mended, perhaps the worst vice betrayed is improvidence. I sometimes try my acquaintances by such tests as this: Who could wear a patch, or two extra seams only, over the knee? Most behave as if they believed that their prospects for life would be ruined if they should do it. It would be easier for them to hobble to town with a broken leg than with a broken pantaloon. Often if an accident happens to a gentleman's legs, they can be mended; but if a similar accident happens to the legs of his pantaloons, there is no help for it; for he considers, not what is truly respectable, but what is respected. We know but few men, a great many coats and breeches. Dress a scarecrow in your last shift, you standing shiftless by, who would not soonest salute the scarecrow? Passing a cornfield the other day, close by a hat and coat on a stake, I recognized the owner of the farm. He was only a little more weather-beaten than when I saw him last. I have heard of a dog that barked at every stranger who approached his master's premises with clothes on, but was easily quieted by a naked thief. It is an interesting question how far men would retain their relative rank if they were divested of their clothes. Could you, in such a case, tell surely of any company of civilized men which belonged to the most respected class? When Madam Pfeiffer, in her adventurous travels

round the world, from east to west, had got so near
home as Asiatic Russia, she says that she felt the necessity of wearing other than a traveling dress, when she
went to meet the authorities, for she "was now in a
civilized country, where . . . people are judged of by
their clothes." Even in our democratic New England
towns the accidental possession of wealth, and its mani-
festation in dress and equipage alone, obtain for the
possessor almost universal respect. But they who yield
such respect, numerous as they are, are so far heathen,
and need to have a missionary sent to them. Besides,
clothes introduced sewing, a kind of work which you
may call endless; a woman's dress, at least, is never
done.

A man who has at length found something to do will
not need to get a new suit to do it in; for him the old
will do, that has lain dusty in the garret for an indeter-
minate period. Old shoes will serve a hero longer than
they have served his valet—if a hero ever has a valet—
bare feet are older than shoes, and he can make them
do. Only they who go to soirées and legislative halls
must have new coats, coats to change as often as the
man changes in them. But if my jacket and trousers, my
hat and shoes, are fit to worship God in, they will do;
will they not? Who ever saw his old clothes—his old
coat, actually worn out, resolved into its primitive elements, so that it was not a deed of charity to bestow it
on some poor boy, by him perchance to be bestowed on
some poorer still, or shall we say richer, who could do
with less? I say, beware of all enterprises that require
new clothes, and not rather a new wearer of clothes. If
there is not a new man, how can the new clothes be
made to fit? If you have any enterprise before you, try
it in your old clothes. All men want, not something to
do with, but something to *do,* or rather something to *be.*

Perhaps we should never procure a new suit, however ragged or dirty the old, until we have so conducted, so enterprised or sailed in some way, that we feel like new men in the old, and that to retain it would be like keeping new wine in old bottles. Our moulting season, like that of the fowls, must be a crisis in our lives. The loon retires to solitary ponds to spend it. Thus also the snake casts its slough, and the caterpillar its wormy coat, by an internal industry and expansion; for clothes are but our outmost cuticle and mortal coil. Otherwise we shall be found sailing under false colors, and be inevitably cashiered at last by our own opinion, as well as that of mankind.

We don garment after garment, as if we grew like exogenous plants by addition without. Our outside and often thin and fanciful clothes are our epidermis, or false skin, which partakes not of our life, and may be stripped off here and there without fatal injury; our thicker garments, constantly worn, are our cellular integument, or cortex; but our shirts are our liber, or true bark, which cannot be removed without girdling and so destroying the man. I believe that all races at some seasons wear something equivalent to the shirt. It is desirable that a man be clad so simply that he can lay his hands on himself in the dark, and that he live in all respects so compactly and preparedly, that, if an enemy take the town, he can, like the old philosopher, walk out the gate empty-handed without anxiety. While one thick garment is, for most purposes, as good as three thin ones, and cheap clothing can be obtained at prices really to suit customers; while a thick coat can be bought for five dollars, which will last as many years, thick pantaloons for two dollars, cowhide boots for a dollar and a half a pair, a summer hat for a quarter of a dollar, and a winter cap for sixty-two and a half cents, or a better be made at home at a nominal cost, where is he so poor that, clad in such a suit, *of his own earning,* there will not be found wise men to do him reverence?

When I ask for a garment of a particular form, my tailoress tells me gravely, "They do not make them so now," not emphasizing the "They" at all, as if she quoted an authority as impersonal as the Fates, and I find it difficult to get made what I want, simply because she cannot believe that I mean what I say, that I am so rash. When I hear this oracular sentence, I am for a moment absorbed in thought, emphasizing to myself each word separately that I may come at the meaning of it, that I may find out by what degree of consanguinity *They* are related to *me,* and what authority they may have in an affair which affects me so nearly; and, finally, I am inclined to answer her with equal mystery, and without any more emphasis of the "they"—"It is true, they did not make them so recently, but they do now." Of what use this measuring of me if she does not measure my character, but only the breadth of my shoulders, as it were a peg to hang the coat on? We worship not the Graces, nor the Parcae, but Fashion. She spins and weaves and cuts with full authority. The head monkey at Paris puts on a traveler's cap, and all the monkeys in America do the same. I sometimes despair of getting anything quite simple and honest done in this world by the help of men. They would have to be passed through a powerful press first, to squeeze their old notions out of them, so that they would not soon get upon their legs again; and then there would be someone in the company with a maggot in his head, hatched from an egg deposited there nobody knows when, for not even fire kills these things, and you would have lost your labor. Nevertheless, we will not forget that some Egyptian wheat was handed down to us by a mummy.

On the whole, I think that it cannot be maintained that dressing has in this or any country risen to the dignity of an art. At present men make shift to wear what they can get. Like shipwrecked sailors, they put on what they can find on the beach, and at a little distance, whether of space or time, laugh at each other's masquerade. Every generation laughs at the old fashions, but follows religiously the new. We are amused at beholding the costume of Henry VIII, or Queen Elizabeth, as much as if it was that of the King and Queen of the Cannibal Islands. All costume off a man is pitiful or grotesque. It is only the serious eye peering from and the sincere life passed within it which restrain laughter and consecrate the costume of any people. Let Harlequin be taken with a fit of the colic and his trappings will have to serve that mood too. When the soldier is hit by a cannonball rags are as becoming as purple.

The childish and savage taste of men and women for new patterns keeps how many shaking and squinting through kaleidoscopes that they may discover the particular figure which this generation requires today. The manufacturers have learned that this taste is merely whimsical. Of two patterns which differ only by a few threads more or less of a particular color, the one will be sold readily, the other lie on the shelf, though it frequently happens that after the lapse of a season the latter becomes the most fashionable. Comparatively, tattooing is not the hideous custom which it is called. It is not barbarous merely because the printing is skin-deep and unalterable.

I cannot believe that our factory system is the best mode by which men may get clothing. The condition of the operatives is becoming every day more like that of the English; and it cannot be wondered at, since, as far as I have heard or observed, the principal object is not that mankind may be well and honestly clad but, unquestionably, that the corporations may be enriched. In the long run men hit only what they aim at. Therefore, though they should fail immediately, they had better aim at something high.

As for a Shelter, I will not deny that this is now a necessary of life, though there are instances of men having done without it for long periods in colder countries than this. Samuel Laing says that "the Laplander in his skin dress, and in a skin bag which he puts over his head and shoulders, will sleep night after night on the snow . . . in a degree of cold which would extinguish the life of one exposed to it in any woollen clothing." He had seen them asleep thus. Yet he adds, "They are not hardier than other people." But, probably, man did not live long on the earth without discovering the convenience which there is in a house, the domestic comforts, which phrase may have originally signified the satisfactions of the house more than of the family; though these must be extremely partial and occasional in those climates where the house is associated in our thoughts with winter or the rainy season chiefly, and two thirds of the year, except for a parasol, is unnecessary. In our climate, in the summer, it was formerly almost solely a covering at night. In the Indian gazettes a wigwam was the symbol of a day's march, and a row of them cut or painted on the bark of a tree signified that so many times they had camped. Man was not made so large limbed and robust but that he must seek to narrow his world, and wall in a space such as fitted him. He was at first bare and out of doors; but though this was pleasant enough in serene and warm weather, by daylight, the rainy season and the winter, to say nothing of the torrid sun, would perhaps have nipped his race in the bud if he had not made haste to clothe himself with the shelter of a house. Adam and Eve, according to the fable, wore the bower before other clothes. Man wanted a home, a place of warmth, or comfort, first of physical warmth, then the warmth of the affections.

We may imagine a time when, in the infancy of the human race, some enterprising mortal crept into a hollow in a rock for shelter. Every child begins the world again, to some extent, and loves to stay outdoors, even in wet and cold. It plays house, as well as horse, having an instinct for it. Who does not remember the interest with which, when young, he looked at shelving rocks, or any approach to a cave? It was the natural yearning of that portion of our most primitive ancestor which still survived in us. From the cave we have advanced to roofs of palm leaves, of bark and boughs, of linen woven and stretched, of grass and straw, of boards and shingles, of stones and tiles. At last, we know not what it is to live in the open air, and our lives are domestic in more senses than we think. From the hearth the field is a great distance. It would be well, perhaps, if we were to spend more of our days and nights without any obstruction between us and the celestial bodies, if the poet did not speak so much from under a roof, or the saint dwell there so long. Birds do not sing in caves, nor do doves cherish their innocence in dovecots.

However, if one designs to construct a dwelling house, it behooves him to exercise a little Yankee shrewdness, lest after all he find himself in a workhouse, a labyrinth without a clue, a museum, an almshouse, a prison, or a splendid mausoleum instead. Consider first how slight a shelter is absolutely necessary. I have seen Penobscot Indians, in this town, living in tents of thin cotton cloth, while the snow was nearly a foot deep around them, and I thought that they would be glad to

have it deeper to keep out the wind. Formerly, when
how to get my living honestly, with freedom left for my
proper pursuits, was a question which vexed me even
more than it does now, for unfortunately I am become
somewhat callous, I used to see a large box by the railroad, six feet long by three wide, in which the laborers
locked up their tools at night; and it suggested to me
that every man who was hard pushed might get such a
one for a dollar, and, having bored a few auger holes in
it, to admit the air at least, get into it when it rained and
at night, and hook down the lid, and so have freedom
in his love, and in his soul be free. This did not appear
the worst, nor by any means a despicable alternative.
You could sit up as late as you pleased, and, whenever
you got up, go abroad without any landlord or house-
lord dogging you for rent. Many a man is harassed to
death to pay the rent of a larger and more luxurious
box who would not have frozen to death in such a box
as this. I am far from jesting. Economy is a subject
which admits of being treated with levity, but it cannot
so be disposed of. A comfortable house for a rude and
hardy race, that lived mostly out of doors, was once
made here almost entirely of such materials as Nature
furnished ready to their hands. Gookin, who was superintendent of the Indians subject to the Massachusetts
Colony, writing in 1674, says, "The best of their houses
are covered very neatly, tight and warm, with barks of
trees, slipped from their bodies at those seasons when
the sap is up, and made into great flakes, with pressure of weighty timber, when they are green. . . . The
meaner sort are covered with mats which they make of
a kind of bulrush, and are also indifferently tight and
warm, but not so good as the former. . . . Some I
have seen, sixty or a hundred feet long and thirty feet
broad. . . . I have often lodged in their wigwams, and

found them as warm as the best English houses." He adds that they were commonly carpeted and lined within with well-wrought embroidered mats, and were furnished with various utensils. The Indians had advanced so far as to regulate the effect of the wind by a mat suspended over the hole in the roof and moved by a string. Such a lodge was in the first instance constructed in a day or two at most, and taken down and put up in a few hours; and every family owned one, or its apartment in one.

In the savage state every family owns a shelter as good as the best, and sufficient for its coarser and simpler wants; but I think that I speak within bounds when I say that, though the birds of the air have their nests, and the foxes their holes, and the savages their wigwams, in modern civilized society not more than one half the families own a shelter. In the large towns and cities, where civilization especially prevails, the number of those who own a shelter is a very small fraction of the whole. The rest pay an annual tax for this outside garment of all, become indispensable summer and winter, which would buy a village of Indian wigwams, but now helps to keep them poor as long as they live. I do not mean to insist here on the disadvantage of hiring compared with owning, but it is evident that the savage owns his shelter because it costs so little, while the civilized man hires his commonly because he cannot afford to own it; nor can he, in the long run, any better afford to hire. But, answers one, by merely paying this tax the poor civilized man secures an abode which is a palace compared with the savage's. An annual rent of from twenty-five to a hundred dollars (these are the country rates) entitles him to the benefit of the improvements of centuries, spacious apartments, clean paint and paper, Rumford fireplace, back plastering, Venetian blinds, copper pump, spring lock, a commodious cellar, and many other things. But how happens it that he who is said to enjoy these things is so commonly a *poor* civilized man, while the savage, who has them not, is rich as a savage? If it is asserted that civilization is a real advance in the condition of man—and I think that it is, though only the wise improve their advantages—it must be shown that it has produced better dwellings without making them more costly; and the cost of a thing is the amount of what I will call life which is required to be exchanged for it, immediately or in the long run. An average house in this neighborhood costs perhaps eight hundred dollars, and to lay up this sum will take from ten to fifteen years of the laborer's life, even if he is not encumbered with a family—estimating the pecuniary value of every man's labor at one dollar a day, for if some receive more, others receive less—so that he must have spent more than half his life commonly before *his* wigwam will be earned. If we suppose him to pay a rent instead, this is but a doubtful choice of evils. Would the savage have been wise to exchange his wigwam for a palace on these terms?

It may be guessed that I reduce almost the whole advantage of holding this superfluous property as a fund in store against the future, so far as the individual is concerned, mainly to the defraying of funeral expenses. But perhaps a man is not required to bury himself. Nevertheless this points to an important distinction between the civilized man and the savage; and, no doubt, they have designs on us for our benefit, in making the life of a civilized people an *institution,* in which the life of the individual is to a great extent absorbed, in order to preserve and perfect that of the race. But I wish to show at what a sacrifice this advantage is at present obtained, and to suggest that we may possibly so live as to secure all the advantage without suffering any of the disadvantage. What mean ye by saying that the poor ye have always with you, or that the fathers have eaten sour grapes, and the children's teeth are set on edge?

"As I live, saith the Lord God, ye shall not have occasion any more to use this proverb in Israel."

"Behold all souls are mine; as the soul of the father, so also the soul of the son is mine: the soul that sinneth it shall die."

When I consider my neighbors, the farmers of Concord, who are at least as well off as the other classes, I find that for the most part they have been toiling twenty, thirty, or forty years, that they may become the real owners of their farms, which commonly they have inherited with encumbrances, or else bought with hired money—and we may regard one third of that toil as the cost of their houses—but commonly they have not paid for them yet. It is true, the encumbrances sometimes outweigh the value of the farm, so that the farm itself becomes one great encumbrance, and still a man is found to inherit it, being well acquainted with it, as he says. On applying to the assessors, I am surprised to learn that they cannot at once name a dozen in the town who own their farms free and clear. If you would know the history of these homesteads, inquire at the bank where they are mortgaged. The man who has actually paid for his farm with labor on it is so rare that every neighbor can point to him. I doubt if there are three such men in Concord. What has been said of the merchants, that a very large majority, even ninety-seven in a hundred, are sure to fail, is equally true of the farmers. With regard to the merchants, however, one of them says pertinently that a great part of their failures are not genuine pecuniary failures, but merely failures to fulfill their engagements, because it is inconvenient; that is, it is the moral character that breaks down. But this puts an infinitely worse face on the matter, and suggests, besides, that probably not even the other three succeed in saving their souls, but are perchance bankrupt in a worse sense than they who fail honestly. Bankruptcy and repudiation are the springboards from which much of our civilization vaults and turns its somersets, but the savage stands on the unelastic plank of famine. Yet the Middlesex Cattle Show goes off here with éclat annually, as if all the joints of the agricultural machine were suent.

The farmer is endeavoring to solve the problem of a livelihood by a formula more complicated than the problem itself. To get his shoestrings he speculates in herds of cattle. With consummate skill he has set his trap with a hair springe to catch comfort and independence, and then, as he turned away, got his own leg into it. This is the reason he is poor; and for a similar reason we are all poor in respect to a thousand savage comforts, though surrounded by luxuries. As Chapman sings,

"The false society of men—
—for earthly greatness
All heavenly comforts rarefies to air."

And when the farmer has got his house, he may not be the richer but the poorer for it, and it be the house that has got him. As I understand it, that was a valid objection urged by Momus against the house which Minerva made, that she "had not made it movable, by which means a bad neighborhood might be avoided"; and it may still be urged, for our houses are such unwieldy property that we are often imprisoned rather than housed in them; and the bad neighborhood to be avoided is our own scurvy selves. I know one or two families; at least, in this town, who for nearly a generation have been wishing to sell their houses in the outskirts and move into the village, but have not been able to accomplish it, and only death will set them free.

Granted that the *majority* are able at last either to own or hire the modern house with all its improvements. While civilization has been improving our houses, it has not equally improved the men who are to inhabit them. It has created palaces, but it was not so easy to create noblemen and kings. And *if the civilized man's pursuits are no worthier than the savage's, if he is employed the greater part of his life in obtaining gross necessaries and comforts merely, why should he have a better dwelling than the former?*

But how do the poor *minority* fare? Perhaps it will be found that just in proportion as some have been placed in outward circumstances above the savage, others have been degraded below him. The luxury of one class is counterbalanced by the indigence of another. On the one side is the palace, on the other are the almshouse and "silent poor." The myriads who built the pyramids to be the tombs of the Pharaohs were fed on garlic, and it may be were not decently buried themselves. The mason who finishes the cornice of the palace returns at night perchance to a hut not so good as a wigwam. It is a mistake to suppose that, in a country where the usual evidences of civilization exist, the condition of a very large body of the inhabitants may not be as degraded as that of savages. I refer to the degraded poor, not now to the degraded rich. To know this I should not need to look farther than to the shanties which everywhere border our railroads, that last improvement in civilization; where I see in my daily walks human beings living in sties, and all winter with an open door, for the sake of light, without any visible, often imaginable, wood pile, and the forms of both old and young are permanently contracted by the long habit of shrinking from cold and misery, and the development of all their limbs and faculties is checked. It certainly is fair to look at that class by whose labor the works which distinguish this generation are accomplished. Such too, to a greater or less extent, is the condition of the operatives of every denomination in England, which is the great workhouse of the world. Or I could refer you to Ireland, which is marked as one of the white or enlightened spots on the map. Contrast the physical condition of the Irish with that of the North American Indian, or the South Sea Islander, or any other savage race before it was degraded by contact with the civilized man. Yet I have no doubt that that people's rulers are as wise as the average of civilized rulers. Their condition only proves what squalidness may consist with civilization. I hardly need refer now to the laborers in our Southern States who produce the staple exports of this country, and are themselves a staple production of the South. But to confine myself to those who are said to be in *moderate* circumstances.

Most men appear never to have considered what a house is, and are actually though needlessly poor all their lives because they think that they must have such a one as their neighbors have. As if one were to wear any sort of coat which the tailor might cut out for him, or, gradually leaving off palmleaf hat or cap of woodchuck skin, complain of hard times because he could not afford to buy him a crown! It is possible to invent a house still more convenient and luxurious than we have, which yet all would admit that man could not afford to pay for. Shall we always study to obtain more of these things, and not sometimes to be content with less? Shall the respectable citizen thus gravely teach, by precept and example, the necessity of the young man's providing a certain number of superfluous glow-shoes, and umbrellas, and empty guest chambers for empty guests, before he dies? Why should not our furniture be as simple as the Arab's or the Indian's? When I think of the benefactors of the race, whom we have apotheosized as messengers from heaven, bearers of divine gifts to man, I do not see in my mind any retinue at their heels, any carload of fashionable furniture. Or what if I were to allow—would it not be a singular allowance?—that our furniture should be more complex than the Arab's, in proportion as we are morally and intellectually his superiors! At present our houses are cluttered and defiled with it, and a good housewife would sweep out the greater part into the dust hole, and not leave her morning's work undone. Morning work! By the blushes of Aurora and the music of Memnon, what should be man's *morning work* in this world? I had three pieces of limestone on my desk, but I was terrified to find that they required to be dusted daily, when the furniture of my mind was all undusted still, and I threw them out the window in disgust. How, then, could I have a furnished house? I would rather sit in the open air, for no dust gathers on the grass, unless where man has broken ground.

It is the luxurious and dissipated who set the fashions which the herd so diligently follow. The traveler who stops at the best houses, so called, soon discovers this, for the publicans presume him to be a Sardanapalus, and if he resigned himself to their tender mercies he would soon be completely emasculated. I think that in the railroad car we are inclined to spend more on luxury than on safety and convenience, and it threatens without attaining these to become no better than a modern drawing-room, with its divans and ottomans and sunshades and a hundred other oriental things, which we are taking west with us, invented for the ladies of the harem and the effeminate natives of the Celestial Empire, which Jonathan should be ashamed to know the names of. I would rather sit on a pumpkin and have it all to myself than be crowded on a velvet cushion. I would rather ride on earth in an oxcart, with a free circulation, than go to heaven in the fancy car of an excursion train and breathe a *malaria* all the way.

The very simplicity and nakedness of man's life in the primitive ages imply this advantage, at least, that they left him still but a sojourner in nature. When he was refreshed with food and sleep he contemplated his journey again. He dwelt, as it were, in a tent in this world, and was either threading the valleys, or crossing the plains, or climbing the mountain tops. But lo! men have become the tools of their tools. The man who independently plucked the fruits when he was hungry is become a farmer; and he who stood under a tree for shelter, a housekeeper. We now no longer camp as for a night, but have settled down on earth and forgotten heaven. We have adopted Christianity merely as an improved method of *agri*-culture. We have built for this world a family mansion, and for the next a family tomb. The best works of art are the expression of man's struggle to free himself from this condition, but the effect of our art is merely to make this low state comfortable and that higher state to be forgotten. There is actually no place in this village for a work of *fine* art, if any had come down to us, to stand, for our lives, our houses, and streets furnish no proper pedestal for it. There is not a nail to hang a picture on, nor a shelf to receive the bust of a hero or a saint. When I consider how our houses are built and paid for, or not paid for, and their internal economy managed and sustained, I wonder that the floor does not give way under the visitor while he is admiring the gewgaws upon the mantelpiece, and let him through into the cellar, to some solid and honest though earthy foundation. I cannot but perceive that this so-called rich and refined life is a thing jumped at, and I do not get on in the enjoyment of the *fine* arts which adorn it, my attention being wholly occupied with the jump; for I remember that the greatest genuine leap due to human muscles alone, on record, is that of certain wandering Arabs, who are said to have cleared twenty-five feet on level ground. Without factitious support, man is sure to come to earth again beyond that distance. The first question which I am tempted to put to the proprietor of such great impropriety is, Who bolsters you? Are you one of the ninety-seven who fail, or the three who succeed? Answer me these questions, and then perhaps I may look at your baubles and find them ornamental. The cart before the horse is neither beautiful nor useful. Before we can adorn our houses with beautiful objects the walls must be stripped, and our lives must be stripped, and beautiful housekeeping and beautiful living be laid for a foundation: now, a taste for the beautiful is most cultivated out of doors, where there is no house and no housekeeper.

Old Johnson, in his "Wonder-Working Providence," speaking of the first settlers of this town, with whom he was contemporary, tells us that "they burrow themselves in the earth for their first shelter under some hillside, and, casting the soil aloft upon timber, they make a smoky fire against the earth, at the highest side." They did not "provide them houses," says he, "till the earth, by the Lord's blessing, brought forth bread to feed them," and the first year's crop was so light that "they were forced to cut their bread very thin for a long season." The secretary of the Province of New

Netherland, writing in Dutch, in 1650, for the information of those who wished to take up land there, states more particularly that "those in New Netherland, and especially in New England, who have no means to build farmhouses at first according to their wishes, dig a square pit in the ground, cellar fashion, six or seven feet deep, as long and as broad as they think proper, case the earth inside with wood all round the wall, and line the wood with the bark of trees or something else to prevent the caving in of the earth; floor this cellar with plank, and wainscot it overhead for a ceiling, raise a roof of spars clear up, and cover the spars with bark or green sods, so that they can live dry and warm in these houses with their entire families for two, three, and four years, it being understood that partitions are run through those cellars which are adapted to the size of the family. The wealthy and principal men in New England, in the beginning of the colonies, commenced their first dwelling houses in this fashion for two reasons: firstly, in order not to waste time in building, and not to want food the next season; secondly, in order not to discourage poor laboring people whom they brought over in numbers from Fatherland. In the course of three or four years, when the country became adapted to agriculture, they built themselves handsome houses, spending on them several thousands."

In this course which our ancestors took there was a show of prudence at least, as if their principle were to satisfy the more pressing wants first. But are the more pressing wants satisfied now? When I think of acquiring for myself one of our luxurious dwellings, I am deterred, for, so to speak, the country is not yet adapted to *human* culture, and we are still forced to cut our *spiritual* bread far thinner than our forefathers did their wheaten. Not that all architectural ornament is to be neglected even

in the rudest periods; but let our houses first be lined
with beauty, where they come in contact with our lives,
like the tenement of the shellfish, and not overlaid with
it. But, alas! I have been inside one or two of them, and
know what they are lined with.

Though we are not so degenerate but that we might
possibly live in a cave or a wigwam or wear skins today,
it certainly is better to accept the advantages, though
so dearly bought, which the invention and industry of
mankind offer. In such a neighborhood as this, boards
and shingles, lime and bricks, are cheaper and more
easily obtained than suitable caves, or whole logs, or
bark in sufficient quantities, or even well-tempered clay
or flat stones. I speak understandingly on this subject,
for I have made myself acquainted with it both theoretically and practically. With a little more wit we might
use these materials so as to become richer than the
richest now are, and make our civilization a blessing.
The civilized man is a more experienced and wiser savage. But to make haste to my own experiment.

Near the end of March, 1845, I borrowed an axe and
went down to the woods by Walden Pond, nearest to
where I intended to build my house, and began to cut
down some tall arrowy white pines, still in their youth,
for timber. It is difficult to begin without borrowing, but
perhaps it is the most generous course thus to permit
your fellow-men to have an interest in your enterprise.
The owner of the axe, as he released his hold on it, said
that it was the apple of his eye; but I returned it sharper
than I received it. It was a pleasant hillside where I
worked, covered with pine woods, through which I
looked out on the pond, and a small open field in the
woods where pines and hickories were springing up.
The ice in the pond was not yet dissolved, though there

were some open spaces, and it was all dark colored and saturated with water. There were some slight flurries of snow during the days that I worked there; but for the most part when I came out onto the railroad, on my way home, its yellow sand heap stretched away gleaming in the hazy atmosphere, and the rails shone in the spring sun, and I heard the lark and pewee and other birds already come to commence another year with us. They were pleasant spring days, in which the winter of man's discontent was thawing as well as the earth, and the life that had lain torpid began to stretch itself. One day, when my axe had come off and I had cut a green hickory for a wedge, driving it with a stone, and had placed the whole to soak in a pond hole in order to swell the wood, I saw a striped snake run into the water, and he lay on the bottom, apparently without inconvenience, as long as I stayed there, or more than a quarter of an hour; perhaps because he had not yet fairly come out of the torpid state. It appeared to me that for a like reason men remain in their present low and primitive condition; but if they should feel the influence of the spring of springs arousing them, they would of necessity rise to a higher and more ethereal life. I had previously seen the snakes in frosty mornings in my path with portions of their bodies still numb and inflexible, waiting for the sun to thaw them. On the 1st of April it rained and melted the ice, and in the early part of the day, which was very foggy, I heard a stray goose groping about over the pond and cackling as if lost, or like the spirit of the fog.

So I went on for some days cutting and hewing timber, and also studs and rafters, all with my narrow axe, not having many communicable or scholar-like thoughts, singing to myself,

Men say they know many things;
But lo! they have taken wings—
The arts and sciences,
And a thousand appliances;
The wind that blows
Is all that anybody knows.

I hewed the main timbers six inches square, most of the
studs on two sides only, and the rafters and floor timbers
on one side, leaving the rest of the bark on, so that they
were just as straight and much stronger than sawed
ones. Each stick was carefully mortised or tenoned by
its stump, for I had borrowed other tools by this time.
My days in the woods were not very long ones; yet I
usually carried my dinner of bread and butter, and read
the newspaper in which it was wrapped, at noon, sitting
amid the green pine boughs which I had cut off, and to
my bread was imparted some of their fragrance, for my
hands were covered with a thick coat of pitch. Before I
had done I was more the friend than the foe of the pine
tree, though I had cut down some of them, having become better acquainted with it. Sometimes a rambler in
the wood was attracted by the sound of my axe, and we
chatted pleasantly over the chips which I had made.

By the middle of April, for I made no haste in my
work, but rather made the most of it, my house was
framed and ready for the raising. I had already bought
the shanty of James Collins, an Irishman who worked
on the Fitchburg Railroad, for boards. James Collins'
shanty was considered an uncommonly fine one. When
I called to see it he was not at home. I walked about the
outside, at first unobserved from within, the window
was so deep and high. It was of small dimensions, with
a peaked cottage roof, and not much else to be seen, the
dirt being raised five feet all around as if it were a compost heap. The roof was the soundest part, though a

good deal warped and made brittle by the sun. Doorsill there was none, but a perennial passage for the hens under the door board. Mrs. C. came to the door and asked me to view it from the inside. The hens were driven in by my approach. It was dark, and had a dirt floor for the most part, dank, clammy, and aguish, only here a board and there a board which would not bear removal. She lighted a lamp to show me the inside of the roof and the walls, and also that the board floor extended under the bed, warning me not to step into the cellar, a sort of dust hole two feet deep. In her own words, they were "good boards overhead, good boards all around, and a good window"—of two whole squares originally, only the cat had passed out that way lately. There was a stove, a bed, and a place to sit, an infant in the house where it was born, a silk parasol, gilt-framed looking-glass, and a patent new coffee-mill nailed to an oak sapling, all told. The bargain was soon concluded, for James had in the meanwhile returned. I to pay four dollars and twenty-five cents tonight, he to vacate at five tomorrow morning, selling to nobody else meanwhile: I to take possession at six. It were well, he said, to be there early, and anticipate certain indistinct but wholly unjust claims on the score of ground rent and fuel. This he assured me was the only encumbrance. At six I passed him and his family on the road. One large bundle held their all—bed, coffee-mill, looking-glass, hens—all but the cat; she took to the woods and became a wild cat and, as I learned afterward, trod in a trap set for woodchucks, and so became a dead cat at last.

I took down this dwelling the same morning, drawing the nails, and removed it to the pond side by small cartloads, spreading the boards on the grass there to bleach and warp back again in the sun. One early thrush gave me a note or two as I drove along the woodland path. I was informed treacherously by a young Patrick that neighbor Seeley, an Irishman, in the intervals of the carting, transferred the still tolerable, straight, and drivable nails, staples, and spikes to his pocket, and then stood when I came back to pass the time of day, and look freshly up, unconcerned, with spring thoughts, at the devastation; there being a dearth of work, as he said. He was there to represent spectatordom, and help make this seemingly insignificant event one with the removal of the gods of Troy.

I dug my cellar in the side of a hill sloping to the south, where a woodchuck had formerly dug his burrow, down through sumach and blackberry roots, and the lowest stain of vegetation, six feet square by seven deep, to a fine sand where potatoes would not freeze in any winter. The sides were left shelving, and not stoned; but the sun having never shone on them, the sand still keeps its place. It was but two hours' work. I took particular pleasure in this breaking of ground, for in almost all latitudes men dig into the earth for an equable temperature. Under the most splendid house in the city is still to be found the cellar where they store their roots as of old, and long after the superstructure had disappeared posterity remark its dent in the earth. The house is still but a sort of porch at the entrance of a burrow.

At length, in the beginning of May, with the help of some of my acquaintances, rather to improve so good an occasion for neighborliness than from any necessity, I set up the frame of my house. No man was ever more honored in the character of his raisers than I. They are destined, I trust, to assist at the raising of loftier structures one day. I began to occupy my house on the 4th of July, as soon as it was boarded and roofed, for the boards were carefully feather-edged and lapped, so that it was perfectly impervious to rain, but before boarding I laid the foundation of a chimney at one end, bringing two cartloads of stones up the hill from the pond in my arms. I built the chimney after my hoeing in the fall, before a fire became necessary for warmth, doing my cooking in the meanwhile out of doors on the ground, early in the morning: which mode I still think is in some respects more convenient and agreeable than the usual one. When it stormed before my bread was baked, I fixed a few boards over the fire, and sat under them to watch my loaf, and passed some pleasant hours in that way. In those days, when my hands were much employed, I read but little, but the least scraps of paper which lay on the ground, my holder, or tablecloth, afforded me as much entertainment, in fact answered the same purpose as the Iliad.

It would be worth the while to build still more deliberately than I did, considering, for instance, what foundation a door, a window, a cellar, a garret, have in the nature of man, and perchance never raising any superstructure until we found a better reason for it than our temporal necessities even. There is some of the same fitness in a man's building his own house that there is in a bird's building its own nest. Who knows but if men constructed their dwellings with their own hands, and provided food for themselves and families simply and honestly enough, the poetic faculty would be universally developed, as birds universally sing when they are so engaged? But alas! we do like cowbirds and cuckoos, which lay their eggs in nests which other birds have built, and cheer no traveler with their chattering and unmusical notes. Shall we forever resign the pleasure of construction to the carpenter? What does architecture amount to in the experience of the mass of men? I never in all my walks came across a man engaged in so simple and natural an occupation as building his house. We belong to the community. It is not the tailor alone who is the ninth part of a man; it is as much the preacher, and the merchant, and the farmer. Where is this division of labor to end? and what object does it finally serve? No doubt another *may* also think for me; but it is not therefore desirable that he should do so to the exclusion of my thinking for myself.

True, there are architects so called in this country, and I have heard of one at least possessed with the idea of making architectural ornaments have a core of truth, a necessity, and hence a beauty, as if it were a revelation to him. All very well perhaps from his point of view, but only a little better than the common dilettantism. A sentimental reformer in architecture, he began at the cornice, not at the foundation. It was only now to put a core of truth within the ornaments, that every sugar plum in fact might have an almond or caraway seed in it—though I hold that almonds are most wholesome without the sugar—and not how the inhabitant, the indweller, might build truly within and without, and let the ornaments take care of themselves. What reasonable man ever supposed that ornaments were something outward and in the skin merely, that the tortoise got his spotted shell, or the shellfish its mother-o'-pearl tints, by such a contract as the inhabitants of Broadway their Trinity Church? But a man has no more to do with the style of architecture of his house than a tortoise with that of its shell: nor need the soldier be so idle as to try to paint the precise *color* of his virtue on his standard. The enemy will find it out. He may turn pale when the trial comes. This man seemed to me to lean over the cornice, and timidly whisper his half truth to the rude occupants who really knew it better than he. What of architectural beauty I now see, I know has gradually

grown from within outward, out of the necessities and
character of the indweller, who is the only builder—out
of some unconscious truthfulness, and nobleness, without ever a thought for the appearance; and whatever
additional beauty of this kind is destined to be produced
will be preceded by a like unconscious beauty of life.
The most interesting dwellings in this country, as the
painter knows, are the most unpretending, humble log
huts and cottages of the poor commonly; it is the life of
the inhabitants whose shells they are, and not any peculiarity in their surfaces merely, which makes them *picturesque;* and equally interesting will be the citizen's
suburban box, when his life shall be as simple and as
agreeable to the imagination, and there is as little straining after effect in the style of his dwelling. A great proportion of architectural ornaments are literally hollow,
and a September gale would strip them off, like borrowed plumes, without injury to the substantials. They
can do without *architecture* who have no olives nor
wines in the cellar. What if an equal ado were made
about the ornaments of style in literature, and the architects of our bibles spent as much time about their cor-
nices as the architects of our churches do? So are made
the belles-lettres and the beaux-arts and their professors.
Much it concerns a man, forsooth, how a few sticks are
slanted over him or under him, and what colors are
daubed upon his box. It would signify somewhat, if, in
any earnest sense, *he* slanted them and daubed it; but
the spirit having departed out of the tenant, it is of a
piece with constructing his own coffin—the architecture
of the grave, and "carpenter," is but another name for
"coffin-maker." One man says, in his despair or indifference to life, take up a handful of the earth at your
feet, and paint your house that color. Is he thinking of
his last and narrow house? Toss up a copper for it as
well. What an abundance of leisure he must have! Why

do you take up a handful of dirt? Better paint your house your own complexion; let it turn pale or blush for you. An enterprise to improve the style of cottage architecture! When you have got my ornaments ready I will wear them.

Before winter I built a chimney, and shingled the sides of my house, which were already impervious to rain, with imperfect and sappy shingles made of the first slice of the log, whose edges I was obliged to straighten with a plane.

I have thus a tight shingled and plastered house, ten feet wide by fifteen long, and eight-feet posts, with a garret and a closet, a large window on each side, two trap doors, one door at the end, and a brick fireplace opposite. The exact cost of my house, paying the usual price for such materials as I used, but not counting the work, all of which was done by myself, was as follows; and I give the details because very few are able to tell exactly what their houses cost, and fewer still, if any, the separate cost of the various materials which compose them:

Boards	$8.03½,	mostly shanty boards.
Refuse shingles for roof and sides	4.00	
Laths	1.25	
Two second-hand windows with glass	2.43	
One thousand old brick .	4.00	
Two casks of lime . .	2.40	That was high.
Hair	0.31	More than I needed.
Mantle-tree iron . . .	0.15	
Nails	3.90	
Hinges and screws . .	0.14	
Latch	0.10	
Chalk	0.01	
Transportation	1.40	} I carried a good part on my back.
In all	$28.12½	

These are all the materials excepting the timber, stones, and sand, which I claimed by squatter's right. I have also a small woodshed adjoining, made chiefly of the stuff which was left after building the house.

I intend to build me a house which will surpass any on the main street in Concord in grandeur and luxury, as soon as it pleases me as much and will cost me no more than my present one.

I thus found that the student who wishes for a shelter can obtain one for a lifetime at an expense not greater than the rent which he now pays annually. If I seem to boast more than is becoming, my excuse is that I brag for humanity rather than for myself; and my shortcomings and inconsistencies do not affect the truth of my statement. Notwithstanding much cant and hypocrisy—chaff which I find it difficult to separate from my wheat, but for which I am as sorry as any man—I will breathe freely and stretch myself in this respect, it is such a relief to both the moral and physical system; and I am resolved that I will not through humility become the devil's attorney. I will endeavor to speak a good word for the truth. At Cambridge College the mere rent of a student's room, which is only a little larger than my own, is thirty dollars each year, though the corporation had the advantage of building thirty-two side by side and under one roof, and the occupant suffers the inconvenience of many and noisy neighbors, and perhaps a residence in the fourth story. I cannot but think that if we had more true wisdom in these respects, not only less education would be needed, because, forsooth, more would already have been acquired, but the pecuniary expense of getting an education would in a great measure vanish. Those conveniences which the student requires at Cambridge or elsewhere cost him or somebody else ten times as great a sacrifice of life as they would with proper management on both sides. Those things for which the most money is demanded are never the things which the student most wants. Tuition, for instance, is an important item in the term bill, while for the far more valuable education which he gets by associating with the most cultivated of his contemporaries no charge is made. The mode of founding a college is, commonly, to get up a subscription of dollars and cents, and then following blindly the principles of a division of labor to its extreme, a principle which should never be followed but with circumspection, to call in a contractor who makes this a subject of speculation, and he employs Irishmen or other operatives actually to lay the foundations, while the students that are to be are said to be fitting themselves for it; and for these oversights successive generations have to pay. I think that it would be *better than this,* for the students, or those who desire to be benefited by it, even to lay the foundation themselves. The student who secures his coveted leisure and retirement by systematically shirking any labor necessary to man obtains but an ignoble and unprofitable leisure, defrauding himself of the experience which alone can make leisure fruitful. "But," says one, "you do not mean that the students should go to work with their hands instead of their heads?" I do not mean that exactly, but I mean something which he might think a good deal like that; I mean that they should not *play* life, or *study* it merely, while the community supports them at this expensive game, but earnestly *live* it from beginning to end. How could youths better learn to live than by at once trying the experiment of living? Methinks this would exercise their minds as much as mathematics. If I wished a boy to know something about the arts and sciences, for instance, I would not pursue the common course, which is merely to send him into the neighborhood of some professor, where anything is professed and practiced but the art of life; to survey the world through a telescope or a microscope, and never with his natural eye; to study chemistry, and not learn how his bread is made, or mechanics, and not learn how it is earned; to discover new satellites to Neptune, and not detect the motes in his eyes, or to what vagabond he is a satellite himself; or to be devoured by the monsters that swarm all around him, while contemplating the monsters in a drop of vinegar. Which would have advanced the most at the end of a month—the boy who had made his own jackknife from the ore which he had dug and smelted, reading as much as would be necessary for this—or the boy who had attended the lectures on metallurgy at the Institute in the meanwhile, and had received a Rogers' penknife from his father? Which would be most likely to cut his fingers? . . . To my astonishment I was informed on leaving college that I had studied navigation!—why, if I had taken one turn down the harbor I should have known more about it. Even the *poor* student studies and is taught only *political* economy, while that economy of living which is synonymous with philosophy is not even sincerely professed in our colleges. The consequence is, that while he is reading Adam Smith, Ricardo, and Say, he runs his father in debt irretrievably.

As with our colleges, so with a hundred "modern improvements"; there is an illusion about them; there is not always a positive advance. The devil goes on exacting compound interest to the last for his early share and numerous succeeding investments in them. Our inventions are wont to be pretty toys, which distract our attention from serious things. They are but improved means to an unimproved end, an end which it was already but too easy to arrive at; as railroads lead to Boston or New York. We are in great haste to construct a magnetic telegraph from Maine to Texas; but Maine and Texas, it may be, have nothing important to communicate. Either is in such a predicament as the man who was earnest to be introduced to a distinguished deaf woman, but when he was presented, and one end of her ear trumpet was put into his hand, had nothing to say. As if the main object were to talk fast and not to talk sensibly. We are eager to tunnel under the Atlantic and bring the old world some weeks nearer to the new; but perchance the first news that will leak through into the broad, flapping American ear will be that the Princess Adelaide has the whooping cough. After all, the man whose horse trots a mile in a minute does not carry the most important messages; he is not an evangelist, nor does he come round eating locusts and wild honey. I doubt if Flying Childers ever carried a peck of corn to mill.

One says to me, "I wonder that you do not lay up money; you love to travel; you might take the cars and go to Fitchburg today and see the country." But I am wiser than that. I have learned that the swiftest traveler is he that goes afoot. I say to my friend, Suppose we try who will get there first. The distance is thirty miles; the fare ninety cents. That is almost a day's wages. I remember when wages were sixty cents a day for laborers on this very road. Well, I start now on foot, and get there before night; I have traveled at that rate by the week together. You will in the meanwhile have earned your fare, and arrive there some time tomorrow, or possibly this evening, if you are lucky enough to get a job in season. Instead of going to Fitchburg, you will be working here the greater part of the day. And so, if the railroad reached round the world, I think that I should keep ahead of you; and as for seeing the country and getting experience of that kind, I should have to cut your acquaintance altogether.

Such is the universal law, which no man can ever outwit, and with regard to the railroad even we may say it is as broad as it is long. To make a railroad round the world available to all mankind is equivalent to grading the whole surface of the planet. Men have an indistinct notion that if they keep up this activity of joint stocks and spades long enough all will at length ride somewhere, in next to no time, and for nothing; but though a crowd rushes to the depot, and the conductor shouts "All aboard!" when the smoke is blown away and the vapor condensed, it will be perceived that a few are riding, but the rest are run over—and it will be called, and will be, "A melancholy accident." No doubt they can ride at last who shall have earned their fare, that is, if they survive so long, but they will probably have lost their elasticity and desire to travel by that time. This spending of the best part of one's life earning money in order to enjoy a questionable liberty during the least valuable part of it, reminds me of the Englishman who went to India to make a fortune first, in order that he might return to England and live the life of a poet. He should have gone up garret at once. "What!" exclaim a million Irishmen starting up from all the shanties in the land, "is not this railroad which we have built a good thing?" Yes, I answer, *comparatively* good, that is, you might have done worse; but I wish, as you are brothers of mine, that you could have spent your time better than digging in this dirt.

Before I finished my house, wishing to earn ten or twelve dollars by some honest and agreeable method, in order to meet my unusual expenses, I planted about two

acres and a half of light and sandy soil near it chiefly
with beans, but also a small part with potatoes, corn,
peas, and turnips. The whole lot contains eleven acres,
mostly growing up to pines and hickories, and was sold
the preceding season for eight dollars and eight cents
an acre. One farmer said that it was "good for nothing
but to raise cheeping squirrels on." I put no manure
whatever on this land, not being the owner, but merely
a squatter, and not expecting to cultivate so much again,
and I did not quite hoe it all once. I got out several cords
of stumps in ploughing, which supplied me with fuel for
a long time, and left small circles of virgin mould, easily
distinguishable through the summer by the greater luxuriance of the beans there. The dead and for the most part
unmerchantable wood behind my house, and the driftwood from the pond, have supplied the remainder of my
fuel. I was obliged to hire a team and a man for the
ploughing, though I held the plough myself. My farm
outgoes for the first season were, for implements, seed,
work, etc., $14.72½. The seed corn was given me. This
never costs anything to speak of, unless you plant more
than enough. I got twelve bushels of beans, and eighteen bushels of potatoes, besides some peas and sweet
corn. The yellow corn and turnips were too late to come
to anything. My whole income from the farm was

	$23.44
Deducting the outgoes . . .	14.72½
There are left	$ 8.71½,

beside produce consumed and on hand at the time this
estimate was made of the value of $4.50—the amount
on hand much more than balancing a little grass which
I did not raise. All things considered, that is, considering the importance of a man's soul and of today, notwithstanding the short time occupied by my experiment,

nay, partly even because of its transient character, I believe that that was doing better than any farmer in Concord did that year.

The next year I did better still, for I spaded up all the land which I required, about a third of an acre, and I learned from the experience of both years, not being in the least awed by many celebrated works on husbandry, Arthur Young among the rest, that if one would live simply and eat only the crop which he raised, and raise no more than he ate, and not exchange it for an insufficient quantity of more luxurious and expensive things, he would need to cultivate only a few rods of ground, and that it would be cheaper to spade up that than to use oxen to plough it, and to select a fresh spot from time to time than to manure the old, and he could do all his necessary farm work as it were with his left hand at odd hours in the summer; and thus he would not be tied to an ox, or horse, or cow, or pig, as at present. I desire to speak impartially on this point, and as one not interested in the success or failure of the present economical and social arrangements. I was more independent than any farmer in Concord, for I was not anchored to a house or farm, but could follow the bent of my genius, which is a very crooked one, every moment. Besides being better off than they already, if my house had been burned or my crops had failed, I should have been nearly as well off as before.

I am wont to think that men are not so much the keepers of herds as herds are the keepers of men, the former are so much the freer. Men and oxen exchange work; but if we consider necessary work only, the oxen will be seen to have greatly the advantage, their farm is so much the larger. Man does some of his part of the exchange work in his six weeks of haying, and it is no boy's play. Certainly no nation that lived simply in all respects, that is, no nation of philosophers, would commit so great a blunder as to use the labor of animals. True, there never was and is not likely soon to be a nation of philosophers, nor am I certain it is desirable that there should be. However, *I* should never have broken a horse or bull and taken him to board for any work he might do for me, for fear I should become a horse-man or a herds-man merely; and if society seems to be the gainer by so doing, are we certain that what is one man's gain is not another's loss, and that the stableboy has equal cause with his master to be satisfied? Granted that some public works would not have been constructed without this aid, and let man share the glory of such with the ox and horse; does it follow that he could not have accomplished works yet more worthy of himself in that case? When men begin to do, not merely unnecessary or artistic, but luxurious and idle work, with their assistance, it is inevitable that a few do all the exchange work with the oxen, or, in other words, become the slaves of the strongest. Man thus not only works for the animal within him but, for a symbol of this, he works for the animal without him. Though we have many substantial houses of brick or stone, the prosperity of the farmer is still measured by the degree to which the barn overshadows the house. This town is said to have the largest houses for oxen, cows, and horses hereabouts, and it is not behindhand in its public buildings; but there are very few halls for free worship or free speech in this county. It should not be by their architecture, but why not even by their power of abstract thought, that nations should seek to commemorate themselves? How much more admirable the Bhagvat-Geeta than all the ruins of the East! Towers and temples are the luxury of princes. A simple and independent mind does not toil at the bidding of any prince. Genius is not a retainer to any emperor, nor is its material silver, or gold, or marble, except to a trifling extent. To what end, pray, is so much stone hammered? In Arcadia, when I was there, I did not see any hammering stone. Nations are possessed with an insane ambition to perpetuate the memory of themselves by the amount of hammered stone they leave. What if equal pains were taken to smooth and polish their manners? One piece of good sense would be more memorable than a monument as high as the moon. I love better to see stones in place. The grandeur of Thebes was a vulgar grandeur. More sensible is a rod of stone wall that bounds an honest man's field than a hundred-gated Thebes that has wandered farther from the true end of life. The religion and civilization which are barbaric and heathenish build splendid temples; but what you might call Christianity does not. Most of the stone a nation hammers goes toward its tomb only. It buries itself alive. As for the Pyramids, there is nothing to wonder at in them so much as the fact that so many men could be found degraded enough to spend their lives constructing a tomb for some ambitious booby, whom it would have been wiser and manlier to have drowned in the Nile, and then given his body to the dogs. I might possibly invent some excuse for them and him, but I have no time for it. As for the religion and love of art of the builders, it is much the same all the world over, whether the building be an Egyptian temple or the United States Bank. It costs more than it comes to. The mainspring is vanity, assisted by the love of garlic and bread and butter. Mr. Balcom, a promising young architect, designs it on the back of his Vitruvius, with hard pencil and ruler, and the job is let out to Dobson & Sons, stone-cutters. When the thirty centuries begin to look down on it, mankind begin to look up at it.

As for your high towers and monuments, there was a crazy fellow once in this town who undertook to dig through to China, and he got so far that, as he said, he heard the Chinese pots and kettles rattle; but I think that I shall not go out of my way to admire the hole which he made. Many are concerned about the monuments of the West and the East, to know who built them. For my part, I should like to know who in those days did not build them, who were above such trifling. But to proceed with my statistics.

By surveying, carpentry, and day-labor of various other kinds in the village in the meanwhile, for I have as many trades as fingers, I had earned $13.34. The expense of food for eight months, namely, from July 4th to March 1st, the time when these estimates were made —though I lived there more than two years—not counting potatoes, a little green corn, and some peas, which I had raised, nor considering the value of what was on hand at the last date, was

Rice	$1.73½	
Molasses. . . .	1.73	Cheapest form of the saccharine.
Rye meal . . .	1.04¾	
Indian meal. . .	0.99¾	Cheaper than rye.
Pork	0.22	
Flour	0.88 }	Costs more than Indian meal, both money and trouble.
Sugar	0.80	
Lard	0.65	
Apples	0.25	
Dried apple. . .	0.22	
Sweet potatoes . .	0.10	
One pumpkin . .	0.06	
One watermelon .	0.02	
Salt	0.03	

All experiments which failed.

Yes, I did eat $8.74, all told; but I should not thus un-blushingly publish my guilt, if I did not know that most of my readers were equally guilty with myself, and that their deeds would look no better in print. The next year I sometimes caught a mess of fish for my dinner, and once I went so far as to slaughter a woodchuck which ravaged my beanfield—effect his transmigration, as a Tartar would say—and devour him, partly for experiment's sake; but though it afforded me a momentary enjoyment, notwithstanding a musky flavor, I saw that the longest use would not make that a good practice, however it might seem to have your woodchucks ready dressed by the village butcher.

Clothing and some incidental expenses within the same dates, though little can be inferred from this item, amounted to
$8.40¾
Oil and some household utensils . . 2.00

So that all the pecuniary outgoes, excepting for wash-ing and mending, which for the most part were done out of the house, and their bills have not yet been re-ceived—and these are all and more than all the ways by which money necessarily goes out in this part of the world—were

House	$28.12½
Farm one year	14.72½
Food eight months	8.74
Clothing, etc., eight months . . .	8.40¾
Oil, etc., eight months	2.00
In all	$61.99¾

I address myself now to those of my readers who have a living to get. And to meet this I have

For farm produce sold	$23.44
Earned by day-labor	13.34
In all	$36.78

which subtracted from the sum of the outgoes leaves a balance of $25.21¾ on the one side—this being very nearly the means with which I started, and the measure of expenses to be incurred—and on the other, besides the leisure and independence and health thus secured, a comfortable house for me as long as I choose to occupy it.

These statistics, however accidental and therefore uninstructive they may appear, as they have a certain completeness, have a certain value also. Nothing was given me of which I have not rendered some account. It appears from the above estimate, that my food alone cost me in money about twenty-seven cents a week. It was, for nearly two years after this, rye and Indian meal without yeast, potatoes, rice, a very little salt pork, molasses, and salt; and my drink, water. It was fit that I should live on rice, mainly, who loved so well the philosophy of India. To meet the objections of some inveterate cavilers, I may as well state, that if I dined out occasionally, as I always had done, and I trust shall have opportunities to do again, it was frequently to the detriment of my domestic arrangements. But the dining out, being, as I have stated, a constant element, does not in the least affect a comparative statement like this.

I learned from my two years' experience that it would cost incredibly little trouble to obtain one's necessary food, even in this latitude; that a man may use as simple a diet as the animals, and yet retain health and strength. I have made a satisfactory dinner, satisfactory on several accounts, simply off a dish of purslane (*Portulaca oleracea*) which I gathered in my cornfield, boiled and salted. I give the Latin on account of the savoriness of the trivial name. And pray what more can a reasonable man desire, in peaceful times, in ordinary noons, than a sufficient number of ears of green sweet-corn boiled, with the addition of salt? Even the little variety which I used was a yielding to the demands of appetite, and not of health. Yet men have come to such a pass that they frequently starve, not for want of necessaries, but for want of luxuries; and I know a good woman who thinks that her son lost his life because he took to drinking water only.

The reader will perceive that I am treating the subject rather from an economic than a dietetic point of view, and he will not venture to put my abstemiousness to the test unless he has a well-stocked larder.

Bread I at first made of pure Indian meal and salt, genuine hoecakes, which I baked before my fire out of doors on a shingle or the end of a stick of timber sawed off in building my house; but it was wont to get smoked and to have a piny flavor. I tried flour also; but have at last found a mixture of rye and Indian meal most convenient and agreeable. In cold weather it was no little amusement to bake several small loaves of this in succession, tending and turning them as carefully as an Egyptian his hatching eggs. They were a real cereal fruit which I ripened, and they had to my senses a fragrance like that of other noble fruits, which I kept in as long as possible by wrapping them in cloths. I made a study of the ancient and indispensable art of bread-making, consulting such authorities as offered, going back to the primitive days and first invention of the unleavened kind, when from the wildness of nuts and meats men first reached the mildness and refinement of this diet, and traveling gradually down in my studies through that accidental souring of the dough which, it is supposed, taught the leavening process, and through the various fermentations thereafter, till I came to "good, sweet, wholesome bread," the staff of life. Leaven, which some deem the soul of bread, the *spiritus* which fills its cellular tissue, which is religiously preserved like the vestal fire—some precious bottleful, I suppose, first brought over in the Mayflower, did the business for America, and its influence is still rising, swelling, spreading, in cerealian billows over the land—this seed I regularly and faithfully procured from the village, till at length one morning I forgot the rules, and scalded my yeast; by which accident I discovered that even this was not indispensable—for my discoveries were not by the synthetic but analytic process—and I have gladly omitted it since, though most housewives earnestly assured me that safe and wholesome bread without yeast might not be, and elderly people prophesied a speedy decay of the vital forces. Yet I find it not to be an essential ingredient, and after going without it for a year am still in the land of the living; and I am glad to escape the trivialness of carrying a bottleful in my pocket, which would sometimes pop and discharge its contents to my discomfiture. It is simpler and more respectable to omit it. Man is an animal who more than any other can adapt himself to all climates and circumstances. Neither did I put any sal-soda, or other acid or alkali, into my bread. It would seem that I made it according to the recipe which Marcus Porcius Cato gave about two centuries before Christ. "Panem depsticium sic facito. Manus mortariumque bene lavato. Farinam in mortarium indito, aquae paulatim addito, subigitoque pulchre. Ubi bene subegeris, defingito, coquitoque sub testu." Which I take to mean, "Make kneaded bread thus. Wash your hands and trough well. Put the meal into the trough, add water gradually, and knead it thoroughly. When you have kneaded it well, mould it, and bake it under a cover," that is, in a baking-kettle. Not a word about leaven. But I did not always use this staff of life. At one time, owing to the emptiness of my purse, I saw none of it for more than a month.

Every New Englander might easily raise all his own breadstuffs in this land of rye and Indian corn, and not depend on distant and fluctuating markets for them. Yet so far are we from simplicity and independence that, in Concord, fresh and sweet meal is rarely sold in the shops, and hominy and corn in a still coarser form are hardly used by any. For the most part the farmer gives to his cattle and hogs the grain of his own producing, and buys flour, which is at least no more wholesome, at a greater cost, at the store. I saw that I could easily raise my bushel or two of rye and Indian corn, for the former will grow on the poorest land, and the latter does not require the best, and grind them in a hand-mill, and so do without rice and pork; and if I must have some concentrated sweet, I found by experiment that I could make a very good molasses either of pumpkins or beets, and I knew that I needed only to set out a few maples to obtain it more easily still, and while these were growing I could use various substitutes beside those which I have named. "For," as the Forefathers sang,

> "we can make liquor to sweeten our lips
> Of pumpkins and parsnips and walnut-tree chips."

Finally, as for salt, that grossest of groceries, to obtain this might be a fit occasion for a visit to the seashore, or, if I did without it altogether, I should probably drink the less water. I do not learn that the Indians ever troubled themselves to go after it.

Thus I could avoid all trade and barter, so far as my food was concerned, and having a shelter already, it would only remain to get clothing and fuel. The pantaloons which I now wear were woven in a farmer's family—thank Heaven there is so much virtue still in man; for I think the fall from the farmer to the operative as great and memorable as that from the man to the farmer —and in a new country, fuel is an encumbrance. As for a habitat, if I were not permitted still to squat, I might purchase one acre at the same price for which the land I cultivated was sold—namely, eight dollars and eight cents. But as it was, I considered that I enhanced the value of the land by squatting on it.

There is a certain class of unbelievers who sometimes ask me such questions as, if I think that I can live on vegetable food alone; and to strike at the root of the matter at once—for the root is faith—I am accustomed to answer such, that I can live on board nails. If they cannot understand that, they cannot understand much that I have to say. For my part, I am glad to hear of experiments of this kind being tried; as that a young man tried for a fortnight to live on hard, raw corn on the ear, using his teeth for all mortar. The squirrel tribe tried the same and succeeded. The human race is interested in these experiments, though a few old women who are incapacitated for them, or who own their thirds in mills, may be alarmed.

My furniture, part of which I made myself, and the rest cost me nothing of which I have not rendered an account, consisted of a bed, a table, a desk, three chairs, a looking-glass three inches in diameter, a pair of tongs and andirons, a kettle, a skillet, and a frying-pan, a dipper, a wash-bowl, two knives and forks, three plates, one cup, one spoon, a jug for oil, a jug for molasses, and a japanned lamp. None is so poor that he need sit on a pumpkin. That is shiftlessness. There is a plenty of such chairs as I like best in the village garrets to be had for taking them away. Furniture! Thank God, I can sit and

I can stand without the aid of a furniture warehouse. What man but a philosopher would not be ashamed to see his furniture packed in a cart and going up country exposed to the light of heaven and the eyes of men, a beggarly account of empty boxes? That is Spaulding's furniture. I could never tell from inspecting such a load whether it belonged to a so-called rich man or a poor one; the owner always seemed poverty-stricken. Indeed, the more you have of such things the poorer you are. Each load looks as if it contained the contents of a dozen shanties; and if one shanty is poor, this is a dozen times as poor. Pray, for what do we *move* ever but to get rid of our furniture, our *exuviae;* at last to go from this world to another newly furnished, and leave this to be burned? It is the same as if all these traps were buckled to a man's belt, and he could not move over the rough country where our lines are cast without dragging them—dragging his trap. He was a lucky fox that left his tail in the trap. The muskrat will gnaw his third leg off to be free. No wonder man has lost his elasticity. How often he is at a dead set! "Sir, if I may be so bold, what do you mean by a dead set?" If you are a seer, whenever you meet a man you will see all that he owns, ay, and much that he pretends to disown, behind him, even to his kitchen furniture and all the trumpery which he saves and will not burn, and he will appear to be harnessed to it and making what headway he can. I think that the man is at a dead set who has got through a knot hole or gateway where his sledge load of furniture cannot follow him. I cannot but feel compassion when I hear some trig, compact-looking man, seemingly free, all girded and ready, speak of his "furniture," as whether it is insured or not. "But what shall I do with my furniture?" My gay butterfly is entangled in a spider's web then. Even those who seem for a long while not to have any, if you inquire more narrowly you will find have some stored in somebody's barn. I look upon England today as an old gentleman who is traveling with a great deal of baggage, trumpery which has accumulated from long housekeeping, which he has not the courage to burn; great trunk, little trunk, bandbox, and bundle. Throw away the first three at least. It would surpass the powers of a well man nowadays to take up his bed and walk, and I should certainly advise a sick one to lay down his bed and run. When I have met an immigrant tottering under a bundle which contained his all—looking like an enormous wen which had grown out of the nape of his neck—I have pitied him, not because that was his all, but because he had all *that* to carry. If I have got to drag my trap, I will take care that it be a light one and do not nip me in a vital part. But perchance it would be wisest never to put one's paw into it.

I would observe, by the way, that it costs me nothing for curtains, for I have no gazers to shut out but the sun and moon, and I am willing that they should look in. The moon will not sour milk nor taint meat of mine, nor will the sun injure my furniture or fade my carpet; and if he is sometimes too warm a friend, I find it still better economy to retreat behind some curtain which nature has provided, than to add a single item to the details of housekeeping. A lady once offered me a mat, but as I had no room to spare within the house, nor time to spare within or without to shake it, I declined it, preferring to wipe my feet on the sod before my door. It is best to avoid the beginnings of evil.

Not long since I was present at the auction of a deacon's effects, for his life had not been ineffectual:

"The evil that men do lives after them."

As usual, a great proportion was trumpery which had begun to accumulate in his father's day. Among the rest was a dried tapeworm. And now, after lying half a century in his garret and other dust holes, these things were not burned; instead of a *bonfire,* or purifying destruction of them, there was an *auction,* or increasing of them. The neighbors eagerly collected to view them, bought them all, and carefully transported them to their garrets and dust holes, to lie there till their estates are settled, when they will start again. When a man dies he kicks the dust.

The customs of some savage nations might, perchance, be profitably imitated by us, for they at least go through the semblance of casting their slough annually; they have the idea of the thing, whether they have the reality or not. Would it not be well if we were to celebrate such a "busk," or "feast of first fruits," as Bartram describes to have been the custom of the Mucclasse Indians? "When a town celebrates the busk," says he, "having previously provided themselves with new clothes, new pots, pans, and other household utensils and furniture, they collect all their worn-out clothes and other despicable things, sweep and cleanse their houses, squares, and the whole town, of their filth, which with all the remaining grain and other old provisions they cast together into one common heap, and consume it with fire. After having taken medicine, and fasted for three days, all the fire in the town is extinguished. During this fast they abstain from the gratification of every appetite and passion whatever. A general amnesty is proclaimed; all malefactors may return to their town."

"On the fourth morning, the high priest, by rubbing dry wood together, produces new fire in the public square, from whence every habitation in the town is supplied with the new and pure flame."

They then feast on the new corn and fruits, and dance and sing for three days, "and the four following days they receive visits and rejoice with their friends from neighboring towns who have in like manner purified and prepared themselves."

The Mexicans also practiced a similar purification at the end of every fifty-two years, in the belief that it was time for the world to come to an end.

I have scarcely heard of a truer sacrament, that is, as the dictionary defines it, "outward and visible sign of an inward and spiritual grace," than this, and I have no doubt that they were originally inspired directly from Heaven to do thus, though they have no biblical record of the revelation.

For more than five years I maintained myself thus solely by the labor of my hands, and I found, that by working about six weeks in a year, I could meet all the expenses of living. The whole of my winters, as well as most of my summers, I had free and clear for study. I have thoroughly tried school-keeping, and found that my expenses were in proportion, or rather out of proportion, to my income, for I was obliged to dress and train, not to say think and believe, accordingly, and I lost my time into the bargain. As I did not teach for the good of my fellow-men, but simply for a livelihood, this was a failure. I have tried trade; but I found that it would take ten years to get under way in that, and that then I should probably be on my way to the devil. I was actually afraid that I might by that time be doing what is called a good business. When formerly I was looking about to see what I could do for a living, some sad experience in conforming to the wishes of friends being fresh in my mind to tax my ingenuity, I thought often and seriously of picking huckleberries; that surely I could do, and its small profits might suffice—for my greatest skill has been to want but little—so little capital it required, so little distraction from my wonted moods, I foolishly thought. While my acquaintances went unhesitatingly into trade or the professions, I contemplated this occupation as most like theirs; ranging the hills all summer to pick the berries which came in my way, and thereafter carelessly dispose of them; so, to keep the flocks of Admetus. I also dreamed that I might gather the wild herbs, or carry evergreens to such villagers as loved to be reminded of the woods, even to the city, by hay-cart loads. But I have since learned that trade curses everything it handles; and though you trade in messages from heaven, the whole curse of trade attaches to the business.

As I preferred some things to others, and especially valued my freedom, as I could fare hard and yet succeed well, I did not wish to spend my time in earning rich carpets or other fine furniture, or delicate cookery, or a house in the Grecian or the Gothic style just yet. If there are any to whom it is no interruption to acquire these things, and who know how to use them when acquired, I relinquish to them the pursuit. Some are "industrious," and appear to love labor for its own sake, or perhaps because it keeps them out of worse mischief; to such I have at present nothing to say. Those who would not know what to do with more leisure than they now enjoy, I might advise to work twice as hard as they do—work till they pay for themselves, and get their free papers. For myself I found that the occupation of a day-laborer was the most independent of any, especially as it required only thirty or forty days in a year to support one. The laborer's day ends with the going down of the sun, and he is then free to devote himself to his chosen pursuit, independent of his labor; but his employer, who speculates from month to month, has no respite from one end of the year to the other.

In short, I am convinced, both by faith and experience, that to maintain one's self on this earth is not a hardship but a pastime, if we will live simply and wisely; as the pursuits of the simpler nations are still the sports of the more artificial. It is not necessary that a man should earn his living by the sweat of his brow, unless he sweats easier than I do.

One young man of my acquaintance, who has inherited some acres, told me that he thought he should live as I did, *if he had the means.* I would not have anyone adopt *my* mode of living on any account; for, besides that before he has fairly learned it I may have found out another for myself, I desire that there may be as many different persons in the world as possible; but I would have each one be very careful to find out and pursue *his own* way, and not his father's or his mother's or his neighbor's instead. The youth may build or plant or sail, only let him not be hindered from doing that which he tells me he would like to do. It is by a mathematical point only that we are wise, as the sailor or the fugitive slave keeps the polestar in his eye; but that is sufficient guidance for all our life. We may not arrive at our port within a calculable period, but we would preserve the true course.

Undoubtedly, in this case, what is true for one is truer still for a thousand, as a large house is not proportionally more expensive than a small one, since one roof may cover, one cellar underlie, and one wall separate several apartments. But for my part, I preferred the solitary dwelling. Moreover, it will commonly be cheaper to build the whole yourself than to convince another of the advantage of the common wall; and when you have done this, the common partition, to be much cheaper, must be a thin one, and that other may prove a bad neighbor, and also not keep his side in repair. The only co-operation which is commonly possible is exceedingly partial and superficial; and what little true co-operation there is, is as if it were not, being a harmony inaudible to men. If a man has faith, he will co-operate with equal faith everywhere; if he has not faith, he will continue to live like the rest of the world, whatever company he is joined to. To co-operate in the highest as well as the lowest sense, means *to get our living together.* I heard it proposed lately that two young men should travel together over the world, the one without money, earning his means as he went, before the mast and behind the plough, the other carrying a bill of exchange in his pocket. It was easy to see that they could not long be companions or co-operate, since one would not *operate* at all. They would part at the first interesting crisis in their adventures. Above all, as I have implied, the man who goes alone can start today; but he who travels with another must wait till that other is ready, and it may be a long time before they get off.

But all this is very selfish, I have heard some of my townsmen say. I confess that I have hitherto indulged very little in philanthropic enterprises. I have made some sacrifices to a sense of duty, and among others have sacrificed this pleasure also. There are those who have used all their arts to persuade me to undertake the support of some poor family in the town; and if I had nothing to do—for the devil finds employment for the idle—I might try my hand at some such pastime as that. However, when I have thought to indulge myself in this respect, and lay their Heaven under an obligation by maintaining certain poor persons in all respects as comfortably as I maintain myself, and have even ventured so far as to make them the offer, they have one and all unhesitatingly preferred to remain poor. While my townsmen and women are devoted in so many ways to the good of their fellows, I trust that one at least may be spared to other and less humane pursuits. You must have a genius for charity as well as for anything else. As for Doing-good, that is one of the professions which are full. Moreover, I have tried it fairly, and, strange as it may seem, am satisfied that it does not agree with my constitution. Probably I should not consciously and deliberately forsake my particular calling to do the good which society demands of me, to save the universe from annihilation; and I believe that a like but infinitely greater steadfastness elsewhere is all that now preserves it. But I would not stand between any man and his genius; and to him who does this work, which I decline, with his whole heart and soul and life, I would say, Persevere, even if the world call it doing evil, as it is most likely they will.

I am far from supposing that my case is a peculiar one; no doubt many of my readers would make a similar defense. At doing something—I will not engage that my neighbors shall pronounce it good—I do not hesitate to say that I should be a capital fellow to hire; but what that is, it is for my employer to find out. What *good* I do, in the common sense of that word, must be aside from my main path, and for the most part wholly unintended. Men say, practically, Begin where you are and such as you are, without aiming mainly to become of more worth, and with kindness aforethought go about doing good. If I were to preach at all in this strain, I should say rather, Set about being good. As if the sun should stop when he had kindled his fires up to the splendor of a moon or a star of the sixth magnitude, and go about like a Robin Goodfellow, peeping in at every cottage window, inspiring lunatics, and tainting meats, and making darkness visible, instead of steadily increasing his genial heat and beneficence till he is of such brightness that no mortal can look him in the face, and then, and in the meanwhile too, going about the world in his own orbit, doing it good, or rather, as a truer philosophy has discovered, the world going about him getting good. When Phaeton, wishing to prove his heavenly birth by his beneficence, had the sun's chariot but one day, and drove out of the beaten track, he burned several blocks of houses in the lower streets of heaven, and scorched the surface of the earth, and dried up every spring, and made the great desert of Sahara, till at length Jupiter hurled him headlong to the earth with a thunderbolt, and the sun, through grief at his death, did not shine for a year.

There is no odor so bad as that which arises from goodness tainted. It is human, it is divine, carrion. If I knew for a certainty that a man was coming to my house with the conscious design of doing me good, I should run for my life, as from that dry and parching wind of the African deserts called the simoom, which fills the mouth and nose and ears and eyes with dust till you are suffocated, for fear that I should get some of his good done to me, some of its virus mingled with my blood. No, in this case I would rather suffer evil the natural way. A man is not a good *man* to me because he will feed me if I should be starving, or warm me if I should be freezing, or pull me out of a ditch if I should ever fall into one. I can find you a Newfoundland dog that will do as much. Philanthropy is not love for one's fellow-man in the broadest sense. Howard was no doubt an exceedingly kind and worthy man in his way, and has his reward; but, comparatively speaking, what are a hundred Howards to *us,* if their philanthropy do not help *us* in our best estate, when we are most worthy to be helped? I never heard of a philanthropic meeting in which it was sincerely proposed to do any good to me or the like of me.

The Jesuits were quite balked by those Indians who, being burned at the stake, suggested new modes of torture to their tormentors. Being superior to physical suffering, it sometimes chanced that they were superior to any consolation which the missionaries could offer; and the law to do as you would be done by fell with less persuasiveness on the ears of those who, for their part, did not care how they were done by, who loved their enemies after a new fashion, and came very near freely forgiving them all they did.

Be sure that you give the poor the aid they most need, though it be your example which leaves them far behind. If you give money, spend yourself with it, and do not merely abandon it to them. We make curious mistakes sometimes. Often the poor man is not so cold and hungry as he is dirty and ragged and gross. It is partly his taste, and not merely his misfortune. If you give him money, he will perhaps buy more rags with it. I was wont to pity the clumsy Irish laborers who cut ice on the pond, in such mean and ragged clothes, while I shivered in my more tidy and somewhat more fashionable garments, till, one bitter cold day, one who had slipped into the water came to my house to warm him, and I saw him strip off three pairs of pants and two pairs of stockings ere he got down to the skin, though they were dirty and ragged enough, it is true, and that he could afford to refuse the *extra* garments which I offered him, he had so many *intra* ones. This ducking was the very thing he needed. Then I began to pity myself, and I saw that it would be a greater charity to bestow on me a flannel shirt than a whole slop-shop on him. There are a thousand hacking at the branches of evil to one who is striking at the root, and it may be that he who bestows the largest amount of time and money on the needy is doing the most by his mode of life to produce that misery which he strives in vain to relieve. It is the pious slave-breeder devoting the proceeds of every tenth slave to buy a Sunday's liberty for the rest. Some show their kindness to the poor by employing them in their kitchens. Would they not be kinder if they employed themselves there? You boast of spending a tenth part of your income in charity; maybe you should spend the nine tenths so, and have done with it. Society recovers only a tenth part of the property then. Is this owing to the generosity of him in whose possession it is found, or to the remissness of the officers of justice?

Philanthropy is almost the only virtue which is sufficiently appreciated by mankind. Nay, it is greatly overrated; and it is our selfishness which overrates it. A robust poor man, one sunny day here in Concord, praised a fellow-townsman to me, because, as he said, he was kind to the poor; meaning himself. The kind uncles and aunts of the race are more esteemed than its true spiritual fathers and mothers. I once heard a reverend lecturer on England, a man of learning and intelligence, after enumerating her scientific, literary, and political worthies, Shakespeare, Bacon, Cromwell, Milton, Newton, and others, speak next of her Christian heroes, whom, as if his profession required it of him, he elevated to a place far above all the rest, as the greatest of the great. They were Penn, Howard, and Mrs. Fry. Everyone must feel the falsehood and cant of this. The last were not England's best men and women; only, perhaps, her best philanthropists.

I would not subtract anything from the praise that is due to philanthropy, but merely demand justice for all who by their lives and works are a blessing to mankind. I do not value chiefly a man's uprightness and benevolence, which are, as it were, his stem and leaves. Those plants of whose greenness withered we make herb tea for the sick serve but a humble use, and are most employed by quacks. I want the flower and fruit of a man; that some fragrance be wafted over from him to me, and some ripeness flavor our intercourse. His goodness must not be a partial and transitory act, but a constant superfluity, which costs him nothing and of which he is unconscious. This is a charity that hides a multitude of sins. The philanthropist too often surrounds mankind with the remembrance of his own cast-off griefs as an atmosphere, and calls it sympathy. We should impart our courage, and not our despair, our health and ease, and not our disease, and take care that this does not spread by contagion. From what southern plains comes up the voice of wailing? Under what latitudes reside the heathen to whom we would send light? Who is that intemperate and brutal man whom we would redeem? If anything ail a man, so that he does not perform his functions, if he have a pain in his bowels even—for that is the seat of sympathy—he forthwith sets about reforming—the world. Being a microcosm himself, he discovers—and it is a true discovery, and he is the man to make it—that the world has been eating green apples; to his eyes, in fact, the globe itself is a great green apple, which there is danger awful to think of that the children of men will nibble before it is ripe; and straightway his drastic philanthropy seeks out the Esquimaux and the Patagonian, and embraces the populous Indian and Chinese villages; and thus, by a few years of philanthropic activity, the powers in the meanwhile using him for their own ends, no doubt, he cures himself of his dyspepsia, the globe acquires a faint blush on one or both of its cheeks, as if it were beginning to be ripe, and life loses its crudity and is once more sweet and wholesome to live. I never dreamed of any enormity greater than I have committed. I never knew, and never shall know, a worse man than myself.

I believe that what so saddens the reformer is not his sympathy with his fellows in distress, but, though he be the holiest son of God, is his private ail. Let this be righted, let the spring come to him, the morning rise over his couch, and he will forsake his generous companions without apology. My excuse for not lecturing against the use of tobacco is, that I never chewed it, that is a penalty which reformed tobacco-chewers have to pay; though there are things enough I have chewed which I could lecture against. If you should ever be betrayed into any of these philanthropies, do not let your left hand know what your right hand does, for it is not worth knowing. Rescue the drowning and tie your shoestrings. Take your time, and set about some free labor.

Our manners have been corrupted by communication with the saints. Our hymn books resound with a melodious cursing of God and enduring him forever. One would say that even the prophets and redeemers had rather consoled the fears than confirmed the hopes of man. There is nowhere recorded a simple and irrepressible satisfaction with the gift of life, any memorable praise of God. All health and success does me good, however far off and withdrawn it may appear; all disease and failure helps to make me sad and does me evil, however much sympathy it may have with me or I with it. If, then, we would indeed restore mankind by truly Indian, botanic, magnetic, or natural means, let us first be as simple and well as Nature ourselves, dispel the clouds which hang over our own brows, and take up a little life into our pores. Do not stay to be an overseer of the poor, but endeavor to become one of the worthies of the world.

I read in the Gulistan, or Flower Garden, of Sheik Sadi of Shiraz, that "They asked a wise man, saying: Of the many celebrated trees which the Most High God has created lofty and umbrageous, they call none azad, or free, excepting the cypress, which bears no fruit; what mystery is there in this? He replied: Each has its appropriate produce, and appointed season, during the continuance of which it is fresh and blooming, and during their absence dry and withered; to neither of which states is the cypress exposed, being always flourishing; and of this nature are the azads, or religious independents.—Fix not thy heart on that which is transitory; for the Dijlah, or Tigris, will continue to flow through Bagdad after the race of caliphs is extinct: if thy hand has plenty, be liberal as the date tree; but if it affords nothing to give away, be an azad, or free man, like the cypress."

COMPLEMENTAL VERSES

THE PRETENSIONS OF POVERTY

Thou dost presume too much, poor needy wretch,
To claim a station in the firmament
Because thy humble cottage, or thy tub,
Nurses some lazy or pedantic virtue
In the cheap sunshine or by shady springs,
With roots and pot-herbs; where thy right hand,
Tearing those humane passions from the mind,
Upon whose stocks fair blooming virtues flourish,
Degradeth nature, and benumbeth sense,
And, Gorgon-like, turns active men to stone.
We not require the dull society
Of your necessitated temperance,
Or that unnatural stupidity
That knows nor joy nor sorrow; nor your forc'd
Falsely exalted passive fortitude

Above the active. This low abject brood,
That fix their seats in mediocrity,
Become your servile minds; but we advance
Such virtues only as admit excess,
Brave, bounteous acts, regal magnificence,
All-seeing prudence, magnanimity
That knows no bound, and that heroic virtue
For which antiquity hath left no name,
But patterns only, such as Hercules,
Achilles, Theseus. Back to thy loath'd cell;
And when thou seest the new enlightened sphere,
Study to know but what those worthies were.

T. CAREW.

WHERE I LIVED, AND WHAT I LIVED FOR

At a certain season of our life we are accustomed to
consider every spot as the possible site of a house. I
have thus surveyed the country on every side within
a dozen miles of where I live. In imagination I have
bought all the farms in succession, for all were to be
bought, and I knew their price. I walked over each
farmer's premises, tasted his wild apples, discoursed on
husbandry with him, took his farm at his price, at any
price, mortgaging it to him in my mind; even put a
higher price on it—took everything but a deed of it—
took his word for his deed, for I dearly loved to talk—
cultivated it, and him too to some extent, I trust, and
withdrew when I had enjoyed it long enough, leaving
him to carry it on. This experience entitled me to be
regarded as a sort of real-estate broker by my friends.
Wherever I sat, there I might live, and the landscape
radiated from me accordingly. What is a house but a
sedes, a seat?—better if a country seat. I discovered
many a site for a house not likely to be soon improved,
which some might have thought too far from the village,
but to my eyes the village was too far from it. Well,

there I might live, I said; and there I did live, for an hour, a summer and a winter life; saw how I could let the years run off, buffet the winter through, and see the spring come in. The future inhabitants of this region, wherever they may place their houses, may be sure that they have been anticipated. An afternoon sufficed to lay out the land into orchard, woodlot, and pasture, and to decide what fine oaks or pines should be left to stand before the door, and whence each blasted tree could be seen to the best advantage; and then I let it lie, fallow perchance, for a man is rich in proportion to the number of things which he can afford to let alone.

My imagination carried me so far that I even had the refusal of several farms—the refusal was all I wanted— but I never got my fingers burned by actual possession. The nearest that I came to actual possession was when I bought the Hollowell place, and had begun to sort my seeds, and collected materials with which to make a wheelbarrow to carry it on or off with; but before the owner gave me a deed of it, his wife—every man has such a wife—changed her mind and wished to keep it, and he offered me ten dollars to release him. Now, to speak the truth, I had but ten cents in the world, and it surpassed my arithmetic to tell, if I was that man who had ten cents, or who had a farm, or ten dollars, or all together. However, I let him keep the ten dollars and the farm too, for I had carried it far enough; or rather, to be generous, I sold him the farm for just what I gave for it, and, as he was not a rich man, made him a present of ten dollars, and still had my ten cents, and seeds, and materials for a wheelbarrow left. I found thus that I had been a rich man without any damage to my poverty. But I retained the landscape, and I have since annually carried off what it yielded without a wheelbarrow. With respect to landscapes,

"I am monarch of all I *survey*,
My right there is none to dispute."

I have frequently seen a poet withdraw, having enjoyed the most valuable part of a farm, while the crusty farmer supposed that he had got a few wild apples only. Why, the owner does not know it for many years when a poet has put his farm in rhyme, the most admirable kind of invisible fence, has fairly impounded it, milked it, skimmed it, and got all the cream, and left the farmer only the skimmed milk.

The real attractions of the Hollowell farm, to me, were: its complete retirement, being about two miles from the village, half a mile from the nearest neighbor, and separated from the highway by a broad field; its bounding on the river, which the owner said protected it by its fogs from frosts in the spring, though that was nothing to me; the gray color and ruinous state of the house and barn, and the dilapidated fences, which put such an interval between me and the last occupant; the hollow and lichen-covered apple trees, gnawed by rabbits, showing what kind of neighbors I should have; but above all, the recollection I had of it from my earliest voyages up the river, when the house was concealed behind a dense grove of red maples, through which I heard the house-dog bark. I was in haste to buy it, before the proprietor finished getting out some rocks, cutting down the hollow apple trees, and grubbing up some young birches which had sprung up in the pasture, or, in short, had made any more of his improvements. To enjoy these advantages I was ready to carry it on; like Atlas, to take the world on my shoulders—I never heard what compensation he received for that—and do all those things which had no other motive or excuse but that I might pay for it and be unmolested in my possession of it; for I knew all the while that it

would yield the most abundant crop of the kind I
wanted if I could only afford to let it alone. But it turned
out as I have said.

All that I could say, then, with respect to farming on
a large scale (I have always cultivated a garden), was,
that I had had my seeds ready. Many think that seeds
improve with age. I have no doubt that time discrimi-
nates between the good and the bad; and when at last
I shall plant, I shall be less likely to be disappointed.
But I would say to my fellows, once for all, As long as
possible live free and uncommitted. It makes but little
difference whether you are committed to a farm or the
county jail.

Old Cato, whose *De Re Rustica* is my "Cultivator,"
says, and the only translation I have seen makes sheer
nonsense of the passage, "When you think of getting a
farm turn it thus in your mind, not to buy greedily; nor
spare your pains to look at it, and do not think it
enough to go round it once. The oftener you go there
the more it will please you, if it is good." I think I shall
not buy greedily, but go round and round it as long as
I live, and be buried in it first, that it may please me the
more at last.

The present was my next experiment of this kind,
which I purpose to describe more at length, for convenience, putting the experience of two years into one.
As I have said, I do not propose to write an ode to de-
jection, but to brag as lustily as chanticleer in the morning, standing on his roost, if only to wake my neighbors
up.

When first I took up my abode in the woods, that is,
began to spend my nights as well as days there, which,
by accident, was on Independence Day, or the Fourth
of July, 1845, my house was not finished for winter,

but was merely a defense against the rain, without plastering or chimney, the walls being of rough weatherstained boards, with wide chinks, which made it cool at night. The upright white hewn studs and freshly planed door and window casings gave it a clean and airy look, especially in the morning, when its timbers were saturated with dew, so that I fancied that by noon some sweet gum would exude from them. To my imagination it retained throughout the day more or less of this auroral character, reminding me of a certain house on a mountain which I had visited a year before. This was an airy and unplastered cabin, fit to entertain a traveling god, and where a goddess might trail her garments. The winds which passed over my dwelling were such as sweep over the ridges of mountains, bearing the broken strains, or celestial parts only, of terrestrial music. The morning wind forever blows, the poem of creation is uninterrupted; but few are the ears that hear it. Olympus is but the outside of the earth everywhere.

The only house I had been the owner of before, if I except a boat, was a tent, which I used occasionally when making excursions in the summer, and this is still rolled up in my garret; but the boat, after passing from hand to hand, has gone down the stream of time. With this more substantial shelter about me, I had made some progress toward settling in the world. This frame, so slightly clad, was a sort of crystallization around me, and reacted on the builder. It was suggestive somewhat as a picture in outlines. I did not need to go outdoors to take the air, for the atmosphere within had lost none of its freshness. It was not so much within doors as behind a door where I sat, even in the rainiest weather. The Harivansa says, "An abode without birds is like a meat without seasoning." Such was not my abode, for I found myself suddenly neighbor to the birds; not by having imprisoned one, but having caged myself near them. I was not only nearer to some of those which commonly frequent the garden and the orchard, but to those wilder and more thrilling songsters of the forest which never, or rarely, serenade a villager—the wood-thrush, the veery, the scarlet tanager, the field-sparrow, the whippoorwill, and many others.

I was seated by the shore of a small pond, about a mile and a half south of the village of Concord and somewhat higher than it, in the midst of an extensive wood between that town and Lincoln, and about two miles south of that our only field known to fame, Concord Battle Ground; but I was so low in the woods that the opposite shore, half a mile off, like the rest, covered with wood, was my most distant horizon. For the first week, whenever I looked out on the pond it impressed me like a tarn high up on the side of a mountain, its bottom far above the surface of other lakes, and, as the sun arose, I saw it throwing off its nightly clothing of mist, and here and there, by degrees, its soft ripples or its smooth reflecting surface was revealed, while the mists, like ghosts, were stealthily withdrawing in every direction into the woods, as at the breaking up of some nocturnal conventicle. The very dew seemed to hang upon the trees later into the day than usual, as on the sides of mountains.

This small lake was of most value as a neighbor in the intervals of a gentle rainstorm in August, when, both air and water being perfectly still, but the sky overcast, mid-afternoon had all the serenity of evening, and the wood-thrush sang around, and was heard from shore to shore. A lake like this is never smoother than at such a time; and the clear portion of the air above it being shallow and darkened by clouds, the water, full of light and reflections, becomes a lower heaven itself so much the more important. From a hilltop near by, where the wood had been recently cut off, there was a pleasing vista southward across the pond, through a wide indentation in the hills which form the shore there, where their opposite sides sloping toward each other suggested a stream flowing out in that direction through a wooded valley, but stream there was none. That way I looked between and over the near green hills to some distant and higher ones in the horizon, tinged with blue. Indeed, by standing on tiptoe I could catch a glimpse of some of the peaks of the still bluer and more distant mountain ranges in the northwest, those true-blue coins from heaven's own mint, and also of some portion of the village. But in other directions, even from this point, I could not see over or beyond the woods which surrounded me. It is well to have some water in your neighborhood, to give buoyancy to and float the earth. One value even of the smallest well is, that when you look into it you see that earth is not continent but insular. This is as important as that it keeps butter cool. When I looked across the pond from this peak toward the Sudbury meadows, which in time of flood I distinguished elevated perhaps by a mirage in their seething valley, like a coin in a basin, all the earth beyond the pond appeared like a thin crust insulated and floated even by this small sheet of intervening water, and I was reminded that this on which I dwelt was but *dry land*.

Though the view from my door was still more contracted, I did not feel crowded or confined in the least. There was pasture enough for my imagination. The low shrub-oak plateau to which the opposite shore arose, stretched away toward the prairies of the West and the steppes of Tartary, affording ample room for all the roving families of men. "There are none happy in the world but beings who enjoy freely a vast horizon," said Damodara, when his herds required new and larger pastures.

Both place and time were changed, and I dwelt nearer to those parts of the universe and to those eras in history which had most attracted me. Where I lived was as far off as many a region viewed nightly by astronomers. We are wont to imagine rare and delectable places in some remote and more celestial corner of the system, behind the constellation of Cassiopeia's Chair, far from noise and disturbance. I discovered that my house actually had its site in such a withdrawn, but forever new and unprofaned, part of the universe. If it were worth the while to settle in those parts near to the Pleiades or the Hyades, to Aldebaran or Altair, then I was really there, or at an equal remoteness from the life which I had left behind, dwindled and twinkling with as fine a ray to my nearest neighbor, and to be seen only in moonless nights by him. Such was that part of creation where I had squatted;

> "There was a shepherd that did live,
>   And held his thoughts as high
> As were the mounts whereon his flocks
>   Did hourly feed him by."

What should we think of the shepherd's life if his flocks always wandered to higher pastures than his thoughts?

Every morning was a cheerful invitation to make my life of equal simplicity, and I may say innocence, with Nature herself. I have been as sincere a worshiper of Aurora as the Greeks. I got up early and bathed in the pond; that was a religious exercise, and one of the best things which I did. They say that characters were engraven on the bathing tub of King Tching-thang to this effect: "Renew thyself completely each day; do it again, and again, and forever again." I can understand that. Morning brings back the heroic ages. I was as much affected by the faint hum of a mosquito making its invisible and unimaginable tour through my apartment at earliest dawn, when I was sitting with door and windows open, as I could be by any trumpet that ever sang of fame. It was Homer's requiem; itself an Iliad and Odyssey in the air, singing its own wrath and wanderings. There was something cosmical about it; a standing advertisement, till forbidden, of the everlasting vigor and fertility of the world. The morning, which is the most memorable season of the day, is the awakening hour. Then there is least somnolence in us; and for an hour, at least, some part of us awakes which slumbers all the rest of the day and night. Little is to be expected of that day, if it can be called a day, to which we are not awakened by our Genius, but by the mechanical nudgings of some servitor, are not awakened by our own newly acquired force and aspirations from within, accompanied by the undulations of celestial music, instead of factory bells, and a fragrance filling the air—to a higher life than we fell asleep from; and thus the darkness bear its fruit, and prove itself to be good, no less than the light. That man who does not believe that each day contains an earlier, more sacred and auroral hour than he has yet profaned, has despaired of life, and is pursuing a descending and darkening way. After a partial cessation of his sensuous life, the soul of man, or its organs rather, are reinvigorated each day, and his Genius tries again what noble life it can make. All memorable events, I should say, transpire in morning time and in a morning atmosphere. The Vedas say, "All intelligences awake with the morning." Poetry and art, and the fairest and most memorable of the actions of men, date from such an hour. All poets and heroes, like Memnon, are the children of Aurora, and emit their music at sunrise. To him whose elastic and vigorous thought keeps pace with the sun, the day is a perpetual morning. It matters not what the clocks say or the attitudes and labors of men. Morning is when I am awake and there is a dawn in me. Moral reform is the effort to throw off sleep. Why is it that men give so poor an account of their day if they have not been slumbering? They are not such poor calculators. If they had not been overcome with drowsiness they would have performed something. The millions are awake enough for physical labor; but only one in a million is awake enough for effective intellectual exertion, only one in a hundred millions to a poetic or divine life. To be awake is to be alive. I have never yet met a man who was quite awake. How could I have looked him in the face?

We must learn to reawaken and keep ourselves awake, not by mechanical aids, but by an infinite expectation of the dawn, which does not forsake us in our soundest sleep. I know of no more encouraging fact than the unquestionable ability of man to elevate his life by a conscious endeavor. It is something to be able to paint a particular picture, or to carve a statue, and so to make a few objects beautiful; but it is far more glorious to carve and paint the very atmosphere and medium through which we look, which morally we can do. To affect the quality of the day, that is the highest of arts. Every man is tasked to make his life, even in its details, worthy of the contemplation of his most elevated and critical hour. If we refused, or rather used up, such paltry information as we get, the oracles would distinctly inform us how this might be done.

I went to the woods because I wished to live deliberately, to front only the essential facts of life, and see if I could not learn what it had to teach, and not, when I came to die, discover that I had not lived. I did not wish to live what was not life, living is so dear; nor did I wish to practice resignation, unless it was quite necessary. I wanted to live deep and suck out all the marrow of life, to live so sturdily and Spartan-like as to put to rout all that was not life, to cut a broad swath and shave close, to drive life into a corner, and reduce it to its lowest terms, and, if it proved to be mean, why then to get the whole and genuine meanness of it, and publish its meanness to the world; or if it were sublime, to know it by experience, and be able to give a true account of it in my next excursion. For most men, it appears to me, are in a strange uncertainty about it, whether it is of the devil or of God, and have *somewhat hastily* concluded that it is the chief end of man here to "glorify God and enjoy him forever."

Still we live meanly, like ants; though the fable tells us that we were long ago changed into men; like pygmies we fight with cranes; it is error upon error, and clout upon clout, and our best virtue has for its occasion a superfluous and evitable wretchedness. Our life is frittered away by detail. An honest man has hardly need to count more than his ten fingers, or in extreme cases he may add his ten toes, and lump the rest. Simplicity, simplicity, simplicity! I say, let your affairs be as two or three, and not a hundred or a thousand; instead of a million count half a dozen, and keep your accounts on your thumb nail. In the midst of this chopping sea of civilized life, such are the clouds and storms and quicksands and thousand-and-one items to be allowed for, that a man has to live, if he would not founder and go to the bottom and not make his port at all, by dead reckoning, and he must be a great calculator indeed who succeeds. Simplify, simplify. Instead of three meals a day, if it be necessary eat but one; instead of a hundred dishes, five; and reduce other things in proportion. Our life is like a German Confederacy, made up of petty states, with its boundary forever fluctuating, so that even a German cannot tell you how it is bounded at any moment. The nation itself, with all its so-called internal improvements, which, by the way are all external and superficial, is just such an unwieldy and overgrown establishment, cluttered with furniture and tripped up by its own traps, ruined by luxury and heedless expense, by want of calculation and a worthy aim, as the million households in the land; and the only cure for it as for them is in a rigid economy, a stern and more than Spartan simplicity of life and elevation of purpose. It lives too fast. Men think that it is essential that the *Nation* have commerce, and export ice, and talk through a telegraph, and ride thirty miles an hour, without a doubt, whether *they* do or not; but whether we should live like baboons or like men, is a little uncertain. If we do not get out sleepers, and forge rails, and devote days and nights to the work, but go to tinkering upon our *lives* to improve *them,* who will build railroads? And if railroads are not built, how shall we get to heaven in season? But if we stay at home and mind our business, who will want railroads? We do not ride on the railroad; it rides upon us. Did you ever think what those sleepers are that underlie the railroad? Each one is a man, an Irishman, or a Yankee man. The rails are laid on them, and they are covered with sand, and the cars run smoothly over them. They are sound sleepers, I assure you. And every few years a new lot is laid down and run over; so that, if some have the pleasure of riding on a rail, others have the misfortune to be ridden upon. And when they run over a man that is walking in his sleep, a supernumerary sleeper in the wrong position, and wake him up, they suddenly stop the cars, and make a hue and cry about it, as if this were an exception. I am glad to know that it takes a gang of men for every five miles to keep the sleepers down and level in their beds as it is, for this is a sign that they may sometime get up again.

Why should we live with such hurry and waste of life? We are determined to be starved before we are hungry. Men say that a stitch in time saves nine, and so they take a thousand stitches today to save nine tomorrow. As for *work*, we haven't any of any consequence. We have the Saint Vitus' dance, and cannot possibly keep our heads still. If I should only give a few pulls at the parish bell-rope, as for a fire, that is, without setting the bell, there is hardly a man on his farm in the outskirts of Concord, notwithstanding that press of engagements which was his excuse so many times this morning, nor a boy, nor a woman, I might almost say, but would forsake all and follow that sound, not mainly to save property from the flames, but, if we will confess the truth, much more to see it burn, since burn it must, and we, be it known, did not set it on fire—or to see it put out, and have a hand in it, if that is done as handsomely; yes, even if it were the parish church itself. Hardly a man takes a half hour's nap after dinner, but when he wakes he holds up his head and asks, "What's the news?" as if the rest of mankind had stood his sentinels. Some give directions to be waked every half hour, doubtless for no other purpose; and then, to pay for it, they tell what they have dreamed. After a night's sleep the news is as indispensable as the breakfast. "Pray tell me anything new that has happened to a man anywhere on this globe"—and he reads it over his coffee and rolls, that a man has had his eyes gouged out this morning on the Wachito River; never dreaming the while that he lives in the dark unfathomed mammoth cave of this world, and has but the rudiment of an eye himself.

For my part, I could easily do without the post-office. I think that there are very few important communications made through it. To speak critically, I never received more than one or two letters in my life—I wrote this some years ago—that were worth the postage. The penny-post is, commonly, an institution through which you seriously offer a man that penny for his thoughts which is so often safely offered in jest. And I am sure that I never read any memorable news in a newspaper. If we read of one man robbed, or murdered, or killed by accident, or one house burned, or one vessel wrecked, or one steamboat blown up, or one cow run over on the Western Railroad, or one mad dog killed, or one lot of grasshoppers in the winter—we never need read of another. One is enough. If you are acquainted with the principle, what do you care for a myriad instances and applications? To a philosopher all *news*, as it is called, is gossip, and they who edit and read it are old women over their tea. Yet not a few are greedy after this gossip. There was such a rush, as I hear, the other day at one of the offices to learn the foreign news by the last arrival, that several large squares of plate glass belonging to the establishment were broken by the pressure—news which I seriously think a ready wit might write a twelvemonth or twelve years beforehand with sufficient accuracy. As for Spain, for instance, if you know how to throw in Don Carlos and the Infanta, and Don Pedro and Seville and Granada, from time to time in the right proportions—they may have changed the names a little since I saw the papers—and serve up a bull-fight when other entertainments fail, it will be true to the letter, and give us as good an idea of the exact state or ruin of things in Spain as the most succinct and lucid reports under this head in the newspapers: and as for England, almost the last significant scrap of news from that quarter was the revolution of 1649; and if you have learned the history of her crops for an average year, you never need attend to that thing again, unless your speculations are of a merely pecuniary character. If one may judge who rarely looks into the newspapers, nothing new does ever happen in foreign parts, a French revolution not excepted.

What news! how much more important to know what that is which was never old! "Kieou-he-yu (great dignitary of the state of Wei) sent a man to Khoung-tseu to know his news. Khoung-tseu caused the messenger to be seated near him, and questioned him in these terms: What is your master doing? The messenger answered with respect: My master desires to diminish the number of his faults, but he cannot come to the end of them. The messenger being gone, the philosopher remarked: What a worthy messenger! What a worthy messenger!" The preacher, instead of vexing the ears of drowsy farmers on their day of rest at the end of the week—for Sunday is the fit conclusion of an ill-spent week, and not the fresh and brave beginning of a new one—with this one other draggle-tail of a sermon, should shout with thundering voice—"Pause! Avast! Why so seeming fast, but deadly slow?"

Shams and delusions are esteemed for soundest truths, while reality is fabulous. If men would steadily observe realities only, and not allow themselves to be deluded, life, to compare it with such things as we know, would be like a fairy tale and the Arabian Nights' Entertainments. If we respected only what is inevitable and has a right to be, music and poetry would resound along the streets. When we are unhurried and wise, we perceive that only great and worthy things have any permanent and absolute existence—that petty fears and petty pleasures are but the shadow of the reality. This is always exhilarating and sublime. By closing the eyes and slumbering, and consenting to be deceived by shows, men establish and confirm their daily life of routine and habit everywhere, which still is built on purely illusory foundations. Children, who play life, discern its true law and relations more clearly than men, who fail to live it worthily, but who think that they are wiser by experience, that is, by failure. I have read in a Hindu book that "there was a king's son, who, being expelled in infancy from his native city, was brought up by a forester, and, growing up to maturity in that state, imagined himself to belong to the barbarous race with which he lived. One of his father's ministers, having discovered him, revealed to him what he was, and the misconception of his character was removed, and he knew himself to be a prince. So soul," continues the Hindu philosopher, "from the circumstances in which it is placed, mistakes its own character, until the truth is revealed to it by some holy teacher, and then it knows itself to be *Brahme.*" I perceive that we inhabitants of New England live this mean life that we do because our vision does not penetrate the surface of things. We think that that *is* which *appears* to be. If a man should walk through this town and see only the reality, where, think you, would the "Mill-dam" go to? If he should give us an account of the realities he beheld there, we should not recognize the place in his description. Look at a meeting-house, or a courthouse, or a jail, or a shop, or a dwelling-house, and say what that thing really is before a true gaze, and they would all go to pieces in your account of them. Men esteem truth remote, in the outskirts of the system, behind the farthest star, before Adam and after the last man. In eternity there is indeed something true and sublime. But all these times and places and occasions are now and here. God himself culminates in the present moment, and will never be more divine in the lapse of all the ages. And we are enabled to apprehend at all what is sublime and noble only by the perpetual instilling and drenching of the reality that surrounds us. The universe constantly and obediently answers to our conceptions; whether we travel fast or slow, the track is laid for us. Let us spend our lives in conceiving then. The poet or the artist never yet had so fair and noble a design but some of his posterity at least could accomplish it.

Let us spend one day as deliberately as Nature, and not be thrown off the track by every nutshell and mosquito's wing that falls on the rails. Let us rise early and fast, or break fast, gently and without perturbation; let company come and let company go, let the bells ring and the children cry—determined to make a day of it. Why should we knock under and go with the stream? Let us not be upset and overwhelmed in that terrible rapid and whirlpool called a dinner, situated in the meridian shallows. Weather this danger and you are safe, for the rest of the way is down hill. With unrelaxed nerves, with morning vigor, sail by it, looking another way, tied to the mast like Ulysses. If the engine whistles, let it whistle till it is hoarse for its pains. If the bell rings, why should we run? We will consider what kind of music they are like. Let us settle ourselves, and work and wedge our feet downward through the mud and slush of opinion, and prejudice, and tradition, and delusion, and appearance, that alluvion which covers the globe, through Paris and London, through New York and Boston and Concord, through church and state, through poetry and philosophy and religion, till we come to a hard bottom and rocks in place, which we can call *reality*, and say, This is, and no mistake; and then begin, having a *point d'appui*, below freshet and frost and fire, a place where you might found a wall or a state, or set a lamppost safely, or perhaps a gauge, not a Nilometer, but a Realometer, that future ages might know how deep a freshet of shams and appearances had gathered from time to time. If you stand right fronting and face to face to a fact, you will see the sun glimmer on both its surfaces, as if it were a cimeter, and feel its sweet edge dividing you through the heart and marrow, and so you will happily conclude your mortal career. Be it life or death, we crave only reality. If we are really dying, let us hear the rattle in our throats and feel cold in the extremities; if we are alive, let us go about our business.

Time is but the stream I go a-fishing in. I drink at it; but while I drink I see the sandy bottom and detect how shallow it is. Its thin current slides away, but eternity remains. I would drink deeper; fish in the sky, whose bottom is pebbly with stars. I cannot count one. I know not the first letter of the alphabet. I have always been regretting that I was not as wise as the day I was born. The intellect is a cleaver; it discerns and rifts its way into the secret of things. I do not wish to be any more busy with my hands than is necessary. My head is hands and feet. I feel all my best faculties concentrated in it. My instinct tells me that my head is an organ for burrowing, as some creatures use their snout and forepaws, and with it I would mine and burrow my way through these hills. I think that the richest vein is somewhere hereabouts; so by the divining rod and thin rising vapors I judge; and here I will begin to mine.

READING

With a little more deliberation in the choice of their pursuits, all men would perhaps become essentially students and observers, for certainly their nature and destiny are interesting to all alike. In accumulating property for ourselves or our posterity, in founding a family or a state, or acquiring fame even, we are mortal; but in dealing with truth we are immortal, and need fear no change nor accident. The oldest Egyptian or Hindu philosopher raised a corner of the veil from the statue of the divinity; and still the trembling robe remains raised, and I gaze upon as fresh a glory as he did, since it was I in him that was then so bold, and it is he in me that now reviews the vision. No dust has settled on that robe; no time has elapsed since that divinity was revealed. That time which we really improve, or which is improvable, is neither past, present, nor future.

My residence was more favorable, not only to thought, but to serious reading, than a university; and though I was beyond the range of the ordinary circulating library, I had more than ever come within the influence of those books which circulate round the world, whose sentences were first written on bark, and are now merely copied from time to time onto linen paper. Says the poet Mîr Camar Uddîn Mast, "Being seated to run through the region of the spiritual world, I have had this advantage in books. To be intoxicated by a single glass of wine; I have experienced this pleasure when I have drunk the liquor of the esoteric doctrines." I kept Homer's Iliad on my table through the summer, though I looked at his page only now and then. Incessant labor with my hands, at first, for I had my house to finish and my beans to hoe at the same time, made more study impossible. Yet I sustained myself by the prospect of such reading in future. I read one or two shallow books of travel in the intervals of my work, till that employment made me ashamed of myself, and I asked where it was then that I lived.

The student may read Homer or Aeschylus in the Greek without danger of dissipation or luxuriousness, for it implies that he in some measure emulate their heroes, and consecrate morning hours to their pages. The heroic books, even if printed in the character of our mother tongue, will always be in a language dead to degenerate times; and we must laboriously seek the meaning of each word and line, conjecturing a larger sense than common use permits out of what wisdom and valor and generosity we have. The modern cheap and fertile press, with all its translations, has done little to bring us nearer to the heroic writers of antiquity. They seem as solitary, and the letter in which they are printed as rare and curious, as ever. It is worth the expense of youthful days and costly hours, if you learn only some words of an ancient language, which are raised out of the trivialness of the street, to be perpetual suggestions and provocations. It is not in vain that the farmer remembers and repeats the few Latin words which he has heard. Men sometimes speak as if the study of the classics would at length make way for more modern and practical studies; but the adventurous student will always study classics, in whatever language they may be written and however ancient they may be. For what are the classics but the noblest recorded thoughts of man? They are the only oracles which are not decayed, and there are such answers to the most modern inquiry in them as Delphi and Dodona never gave. We might as well omit to study Nature because she is old. To read well, that is, to read true books in a true spirit, is a noble exercise, and one that will task the reader more than any exercise which the customs of the day esteem. It requires a training such as the athletes underwent, the steady intention almost of the whole life to this object. Books must be read as deliberately and reservedly as they were written. It is not enough even to be able to speak the language of that nation by which they are written, for there is a memorable interval between the spoken and the written language, the language heard and the language read. The one is commonly transitory, a sound, a tongue, a dialect merely, almost brutish, and we learn it unconsciously, like the brutes, of our mothers. The other is the maturity and experience of that; if that is our mother tongue, this is our father tongue, a reserved and select expression, too significant to be heard by the ear, which we must be born again in order to speak. The crowds of men who merely *spoke* the Greek and Latin tongues in the middle ages were not entitled by the accident of birth to *read* the works of genius written in those languages; for these were not written in that Greek or Latin which they knew, but in the select language of literature. They had not learned the nobler dialects of Greece and Rome, but the very materials on which they were written were waste paper to them, and they prized instead a cheap contemporary literature. But when the several nations of Europe had acquired distinct though rude written languages of their own, sufficient for the purposes of their rising literatures, then first learning revived, and scholars were enabled to discern from that remoteness the treasures of antiquity. What the Roman and Grecian multitude could not *hear,* after the lapse of ages a few scholars *read,* and a few scholars only are still reading it.

However much we may admire the orator's occasional bursts of eloquence, the noblest written words are commonly as far behind or above the fleeting spoken language as the firmament with its stars is behind the clouds. *There* are the stars, and they who can may read them. The astronomers forever comment on and observe them. They are not exhalations like our daily colloquies and vaporous breath. What is called eloquence in the forum is commonly found to be rhetoric in the study.

The orator yields to the inspiration of a transient occasion, and speaks to the mob before him, to those who can *hear* him; but the writer, whose more equable life is his occasion, and who would be distracted by the event and the crowd which inspire the orator, speaks to the intellect and heart of mankind, to all in any age who can *understand* him.

No wonder that Alexander carried the Iliad with him on his expeditions in a precious casket. A written word is the choicest of relics. It is something at once more intimate with us and more universal than any other work of art. It is the work of art nearest to life itself. It may be translated into every language, and not only be read but actually breathed from all human lips; not be represented on canvas or in marble only, but be carved out of the breath of life itself. The symbol of an ancient man's thought becomes a modern man's speech. Two thousand summers have imparted to the monuments of Grecian literature, as to her marbles, only a maturer golden and autumnal tint, for they have carried their own serene and celestial atmosphere into all lands to protect them against the corrosion of time. Books are the treasured wealth of the world and the fit inheritance of generations and nations. Books, the oldest and the best, stand naturally and rightfully on the shelves of every cottage. They have no cause of their own to plead, but while they enlighten and sustain the reader his common sense will not refuse them. Their authors are a natural and irresistible aristocracy in every society, and, more than kings or emperors, exert an influence on mankind. When the illiterate and perhaps scornful trader has earned by enterprise and industry his coveted leisure and independence, and is admitted to the circles of wealth and fashion, he turns inevitably at last to those still higher but yet inaccessible circles of intellect and genius, and is sensible only of the imperfection of his culture and the vanity and insufficiency of all his riches, and further proves his good sense by the pains which he takes to secure for his children that intellectual culture whose want he so keenly feels; and thus it is that he becomes the founder of a family.

Those who have not learned to read the ancient classics in the language in which they were written must have a very imperfect knowledge of the history of the human race; for it is remarkable that no transcript of them has ever been made into any modern tongue, unless our civilization itself may be regarded as such a transcript. Homer has never yet been printed in English, nor Aeschylus, nor Virgil even, works as refined, as solidly done, and as beautiful almost as the morning itself; for later writers, say what we will of their genius, have rarely, if ever, equaled the elaborate beauty and finish and the lifelong and heroic literary labors of the ancients. They only talk of forgetting them who never knew them. It will be soon enough to forget them when we have the learning and the genius which will enable us to attend to and appreciate them. That age will be rich indeed when those relics which we call Classics, and the still older and more than classic but even less known Scriptures of the nations, shall have still further accumulated, when the Vaticans shall be filled with Vedas and Zendavestas and Bibles, with Homers and Dantes and Shakespeares, and all the centuries to come shall have successively deposited their trophies in the forum of the world. By such a pile we may hope to scale heaven at last.

The works of the great poets have never yet been read by mankind, for only great poets can read them. They have only been read as the multitude read the stars, at most astrologically, not astronomically. Most men have learned to read to serve a paltry convenience, as they have learned to cipher in order to keep accounts and not be cheated in trade; but of reading as a noble intellectual exercise they know little or nothing; yet this only is reading, in a high sense, not that which lulls us as a luxury and suffers the nobler faculties to sleep the while, but what we have to stand on tiptoe to read and devote our most alert and wakeful hours to.

I think that having learned our letters we should read the best that is in literature, and not be forever repeating our a b abs, and words of one syllable, in the fourth or fifth classes, sitting on the lowest and foremost form all our lives. Most men are satisfied if they read or hear read, and perchance have been convicted by the wisdom of one good book, the Bible, and for the rest of their lives vegetate and dissipate their faculties in what is called easy reading. There is a work in several volumes in our Circulating Library entitled Little Reading, which I thought referred to a town of that name which I had not been to. There are those who, like cormorants and ostriches, can digest all sorts of this, even after the fullest dinner of meats and vegetables, for they suffer nothing to be wasted. If others are the machines to provide this provender, they are the machines to read it. They read the nine thousandth tale about Zebulon and Sephronia, and how they loved as none had ever loved before, and neither did the course of their true love run smooth—at any rate, how it did run and stumble, and get up again and go on! how some poor unfortunate got up onto a steeple, who had better never have gone up as far as the belfry; and then, having needlessly got him up there, the happy novelist rings the bell for all the world to come together and hear, O dear! how he did get down again! For my part, I think that they had better metamorphose all such aspiring heroes of universal noveldom into man weathercocks, as they used to put heroes among the constellations, and let them swing round there till they are rusty, and not come down at all to bother honest men with their pranks. The next time the novelist rings the bell I will not stir though the meeting-house burn down. "The Skip of the Tip-Toe-Hop, a Romance of the Middle Ages, by the celebrated author of 'Tittle-Tol-Tan,' to appear in monthly parts; a great rush; don't all come together." All this they read with saucer eyes, and erect and primitive curiosity, and with unwearied gizzard, whose corrugations even yet need no sharpening, just as some little four-year-old bencher his two-cent gilt-covered edition of Cinderella—without any improvement, that I can see, in the pronunciation, or accent, or emphasis, or any more skill in extracting or inserting the moral. The result is dullness of sight, a stagnation of the vital circulations, and a general deliquium and sloughing off of all the intellectual faculties. This sort of gingerbread is baked daily and more sedulously than pure wheat or rye-and-Indian in almost every oven, and finds a surer market.

The best books are not read even by those who are called good readers. What does our Concord culture amount to? There is in this town, with a very few exceptions, no taste for the best or for very good books even in English literature, whose words all can read and spell. Even the college-bred and so-called liberally educated men here and elsewhere have really little or no acquaintance with the English classics; and as for the recorded wisdom of mankind, the ancient classics and Bibles, which are accessible to all who will know of them, there are the feeblest efforts anywhere made to become acquainted with them. I know a woodchopper, of middle age, who takes a French paper, not for news as he says, for he is above that, but to "keep himself in practice," he being a Canadian by birth; and when I ask him what he considers the best thing he can do in this world, he says, beside this, to keep up and add to his English. This is about as much as the college-bred generally do or aspire to do, and they take an English paper for the purpose. One who has just come from reading perhaps one of the best English books will find how many with whom he can converse about it? Or suppose he comes from reading a Greek or Latin classic in the original, whose praises are familiar even to the so-called illiterate; he will find nobody at all to speak to, but must keep silence about it. Indeed, there is hardly the professor in our colleges, who, if he has mastered the difficulties of the language, has proportionally mastered the difficulties of the wit and poetry of a Greek poet, and has any sympathy to impart to the alert and heroic reader; and as for the sacred Scriptures, or Bibles of mankind, who in this town can tell me even their titles? Most men do not know that any nation but the Hebrews have had a scripture. A man, any man, will go considerably out of his way to pick up a silver dollar; but here are golden words, which the wisest men of antiquity have uttered, and whose worth the wise of every succeeding age have assured us of; and yet we learn to read only as far as Easy Reading, the primers and classbooks, and when we leave school, the "Little Reading," and storybooks, which are for boys and beginners; and our reading, our conversation and thinking, are all on a very low level, worthy only of pygmies and manikins.

I aspire to be acquainted with wiser men than this our Concord soil has produced, whose names are hardly known here. Or shall I hear the name of Plato and never read his book? As if Plato were my townsman and I never saw him—my next neighbor and I never heard him speak or attended to the wisdom of his words. But how actually is it? His Dialogues, which contain what was immortal in him, lie on the next shelf, and yet I never read them. We are underbred and low-lived and illiterate; and in this respect I confess I do not make any very broad distinction between the illiterateness of my townsman who cannot read at all and the illiterateness of him who has learned to read only what is for children and feeble intellects. We should be as good as the worthies of antiquity, but partly by first knowing how good they were. We are a race of tit-men, and soar but little higher in our intellectual flights than the columns of the daily paper.

It is not all books that are as dull as their readers. There are probably words addressed to our condition exactly, which, if we could really hear and understand, would be more salutary than the morning or the spring to our lives, and possibly put a new aspect on the face of things for us. How many a man has dated a new era in his life from the reading of a book! The book exists for us perchance which will explain our miracles and reveal new ones. The at present unutterable things we may find somewhere uttered. These same questions that disturb and puzzle and confound us have in their turn occurred to all the wise men; not one has been omitted; and each has answered them, according to his ability, by his words and his life. Moreover, with wisdom we shall learn liberality. The solitary hired man on a farm in the outskirts of Concord, who has had his second birth and peculiar religious experience, and is driven as he believes into silent gravity and exclusiveness by his faith, may think it is not true; but Zoroaster, thousands of years ago, traveled the same road and had the same experience; but he, being wise, knew it to be universal, and treated his neighbors accordingly, and is even said to have invented and established worship among men. Let him humbly commune with Zoroaster then, and through the liberalizing influence of all the worthies, with Jesus Christ himself, and let "our church" go by the board.

We boast that we belong to the nineteenth century and are making the most rapid strides of any nation. But consider how little this village does for its own culture. I do not wish to flatter my townsmen, nor to be flattered by them, for that will not advance either of us. We need to be provoked—goaded like oxen, as we are, into a trot. We have a comparatively decent system of common schools, schools for infants only; but excepting the half-starved Lyceum in the winter, and latterly the puny beginning of a library suggested by the state, no school for ourselves. We spend more on almost any article of bodily aliment or ailment than on our mental aliment. It is time that we had uncommon schools, that we did not leave off our education when we begin to be men and women. It is time that villages were universities, and their elder inhabitants the fellows of universities, with leisure—if they are indeed so well off—to pursue liberal studies the rest of their lives. Shall the world be confined to one Paris or one Oxford forever? Cannot students be boarded here and get a liberal education under the skies of Concord? Can we not hire some Abelard to lecture to us? Alas! what with foddering the cattle and tending the store, we are kept from school too long, and our education is sadly neglected. In this country, the village should in some respects take the place of the nobleman of Europe. It should be the patron of the fine arts. It is rich enough. It wants only the magnanimity and refinement. It can spend money enough on such things as farmers and traders value, but it is thought Utopian to propose spending money for things which more intelligent men know to be of far more worth. This town has spent seventeen thousand dollars on a town house, thank fortune or politics, but probably it will not spend so much on living wit, the true meat to put into that shell, in a hundred years. The one hundred and twenty-five dollars annually subscribed for a Lyceum in the winter is better spent than any other equal sum raised in the town. If we live in the nineteenth century, why should we not enjoy the advantages which the nineteenth century offers? Why should our life be in any respect provincial? If we will read newspapers, why not skip the gossip of Boston and take the best newspaper in the world at once?—not be sucking the pap of "neutral family" papers, or browsing "Olive-Branches" here in New England. Let the reports of all the learned societies come to us, and we will see if they know anything. Why should we leave it to Harper & Brothers and Redding & Co. to select our reading? As the nobleman of cultivated taste surrounds himself with whatever conduces to his culture: genius—learning—wit—books—paintings—statuary—music—philosophical instruments, and the like; so let the village do—not stop short at a pedagogue, a parson, a sexton, a parish library, and three selectmen, because our pilgrim forefathers got through a cold winter once on a bleak rock with these. To act collectively is according to the spirit of our institutions; and I am confident that, as our circumstances are more flourishing, our means are greater than the nobleman's. New England can hire all the wise men in the world to come and teach her, and board them round the while, and not be provincial at all. That is the *uncommon* school we want. Instead of noblemen, let us have noble villages of men. If it is necessary, omit one bridge over the river, go round a little there, and throw one arch at least over the darker gulf of ignorance which surrounds us.

SOUNDS

But while we are confined to books, though the most select and classic, and read only particular written languages, which are themselves but dialects and provincial, we are in danger of forgetting the language which all things and events speak without metaphor, which alone is copious and standard. Much is published, but little printed. The rays which stream through the shutter will be no longer remembered when the shutter is wholly removed. No method nor discipline can supersede the necessity of being forever on the alert. What is a course of history or philosophy, or poetry, no matter how well selected, or the best society, or the most admirable routine of life, compared with the discipline of looking always at what is to be seen? Will you be a reader, a student merely, or a seer? Read your fate, see what is before you, and walk on into futurity.

I did not read books the first summer; I hoed beans. Nay, I often did better than this. There were times when I could not afford to sacrifice the bloom of the present moment to any work, whether of the head or hands. I love a broad margin to my life. Sometimes, in a summer morning, having taken my accustomed bath, I sat in my sunny doorway from sunrise till noon, rapt in a revery, amidst the pines and hickories and sumachs, in undisturbed solitude and stillness, while the birds sang around or flitted noiseless through the house, until by the sun falling in at my west window, or the noise of some traveler's wagon on the distant highway, I was reminded of the lapse of time. I grew in those seasons like corn in the night, and they were far better than any work of the hands would have been. They were not time subtracted from my life, but so much over and above my usual allowance. I realized what the Orientals mean by contemplation and the forsaking of works. For the most part, I minded not how the hours went. The day advanced as if to light some work of mine; it was morning, and lo, now it is evening, and nothing memorable is accomplished. Instead of singing like the birds, I silently smiled at my incessant good fortune. As the sparrow had its trill, sitting on the hickory before my door, so had I my chuckle or suppressed warble which he might hear out of my nest. My days were not days of the week, bearing the stamp of any heathen deity, nor were they minced into hours and fretted by the ticking of a clock; for I lived like the Puri Indians, of whom it is said that "for yesterday, today, and tomorrow they have only one word, and they express the variety of meaning by pointing backward for yesterday, forward for tomorrow, and overhead for the passing day." This was sheer idleness to my fellow-townsmen, no doubt; but if the birds and flowers had tried me by their standard, I should not have been found wanting. A man must find his occasions in himself, it is true. The natural day is very calm, and will hardly reprove his indolence.

I had this advantage, at least, in my mode of life, over those who were obliged to look abroad for amusement, to society and the theater, that my life itself was become my amusement and never ceased to be novel. It was a drama of many scenes and without an end. If we were always indeed getting our living, and regulating our lives according to the last and best mode we had learned, we should never be troubled with ennui. Follow your genius closely enough, and it will not fail to show you a fresh prospect every hour. Housework was a pleasant pastime. When my floor was dirty, I rose early, and, setting all my furniture out of doors on the

grass, bed and bedstead making but one budget, dashed
water on the floor, and sprinkled white sand from the
pond on it, and then with a broom scrubbed it clean and
white; and by the time the villagers had broken their
fast the morning sun had dried my house sufficiently to
allow me to move in again, and my meditations were
almost uninterrupted. It was pleasant to see my whole
household effects out on the grass, making a little pile
like a gypsy's pack, and my three-legged table, from
which I did not remove the books and pen and ink,
standing amid the pines and hickories. They seemed
glad to get out themselves, and as if unwilling to be
brought in. I was sometimes tempted to stretch an awn-
ing over them and take my seat there. It was worth the
while to see the sun shine on these things, and hear the
free wind blow on them; so much more interesting most
familiar objects look out of doors than in the house. A
bird sits on the next bough, life-everlasting grows under
the table, and blackberry vines run round its legs; pine
cones, chestnut burs, and strawberry leaves are strewn
about. It looked as if this was the way these forms came
to be transferred to our furniture, to tables, chairs, and
bedsteads—because they once stood in their midst.

My house was on the side of a hill, immediately on
the edge of the larger wood, in the midst of a young
forest of pitch pines and hickories, and half a dozen rods
from the pond, to which a narrow footpath led down the
hill. In my front yard grew the strawberry, blackberry,
and life-everlasting, johnswort and goldenrod, shrub-
oaks and sand cherry, blueberry and groundnut. Near
the end of May, the sand cherry (*cerasus pumila*)
adorned the sides of the path with its delicate flowers
arranged in umbels cylindrically about its short stems,
which last, in the fall, weighed down with good-sized
and handsome cherries, fell over in wreaths like rays

on every side. I tasted them out of compliment to Nature, though they were scarcely palatable. The sumach (*rhus glabra*) grew luxuriantly about the house, pushing up through the embankment which I had made, and growing five or six feet the first season. Its broad pinnate tropical leaf was pleasant though strange to look on. The large buds, suddenly pushing out late in the spring from dry sticks which had seemed to be dead, developed themselves as by magic into graceful green and tender boughs, an inch in diameter; and sometimes, as I sat at my window, so heedlessly did they grow and tax their weak joints, I heard a fresh and tender bough suddenly fall like a fan to the ground, when there was not a breath of air stirring, broken off by its own weight. In August, the large masses of berries, which, when in flower, had attracted many wild bees, gradually assumed their bright velvety crimson hue, and by their weight again bent down and broke the tender limbs.

As I sit at my window this summer afternoon, hawks are circling about my clearing; the tantivy of wild pigeons, flying by twos and threes athwart my view, or perching restless on the white-pine boughs behind my house, gives a voice to the air; a fish hawk dimples the glassy surface of the pond and brings up a fish; a mink steals out of the marsh before my door and seizes a frog by the shore; the sedge is bending under the weight of the reed-birds flitting hither and thither; and for the last half hour I have heard the rattle of railroad cars, now dying away and then reviving like the beat of a partridge, conveying travelers from Boston to the country. For I did not live so out of the world as that boy, who, as I hear, was put out to a farmer in the east part of the town, but ere long ran away and came home again, quite down at the heel and homesick. He had never seen such a dull and out-of-the-way place; the folks were all gone off; why, you couldn't even hear the whistle! I doubt if there is such a place in Massachusetts now:

> "In truth, our village has become a butt
> For one of those fleet railroad shafts, and o'er
> Our peaceful plain its soothing sound is—Concord."

The Fitchburg Railroad touches the pond about a hundred rods south of where I dwell. I usually go to the village along its causeway, and am, as it were, related to society by this link. The men on the freight trains, who go over the whole length of the road, bow to me as to an old acquaintance, they pass me so often, and apparently they take me for an employee; and so I am. I too would fain be a track-repairer somewhere in the orbit of the earth.

The whistle of the locomotive penetrates my woods summer and winter, sounding like the scream of a hawk sailing over some farmer's yard, informing me that many restless city merchants are arriving within the circle of the town, or adventurous country traders from the other side. As they come under one horizon, they shout their warning to get off the track to the other, heard sometimes through the circles of two towns. Here come your groceries, country; your rations, countrymen! Nor is there any man so independent on his farm that he can say them nay. And here's your pay for them! screams the countryman's whistle; timber like long battering rams going twenty miles an hour against the city's walls, and chairs enough to seat all the weary and heavy laden that dwell within them. With such huge and lumbering civility the country hands a chair to the city. All the Indian huckleberry hills are stripped, all the cranberry meadows are raked into the city. Up comes the cotton, down goes the woven cloth; up comes the silk, down goes the woolen; up come the books, but down goes the wit that writes them.

When I meet the engine with its train of cars moving off with planetary motion—or, rather, like a comet, for the beholder knows not if with that velocity and with that direction it will ever revisit this system, since its orbit does not look like a returning curve—with its steam cloud like a banner streaming behind in golden and silver wreaths, like many a downy cloud which I have seen, high in the heavens, unfolding its masses to the light—as if this traveling demigod, this cloud-compeller, would ere long take the sunset sky for the livery of his train; when I hear the iron horse make the hills echo with his snort like thunder, shaking the earth with his feet, and breathing fire and smoke from his nostrils (what kind of winged horse or fiery dragon they will put into the new Mythology I don't know), it seems as if the earth had got a race now worthy to inhabit it. If all were as it seems, and men made the elements their servants for noble ends! If the cloud that hangs over the engine were the perspiration of heroic deeds, or as beneficent as that which floats over the farmer's fields, then the elements and Nature herself would cheerfully accompany men on their errands and be their escort.

I watch the passage of the morning cars with the same feeling that I do the rising of the sun, which is hardly more regular. Their train of clouds stretching far behind and rising higher and higher, going to heaven while the cars are going to Boston, conceals the sun for a minute and casts my distant field into the shade, a celestial train beside which the petty train of cars which hugs the earth is but the barb of the spear. The stabler of the iron horse was up early this winter morning by the light of the stars amid the mountains, to fodder and harness his steed. Fire, too, was awakened thus early to put the vital heat in him and get him off. If the enterprise were as innocent as it is early! If the snow lies deep, they strap on his snowshoes, and with the giant plough plough a furrow from the mountains to the seaboard, in which the cars, like a following drill-barrow, sprinkle all the restless men and floating merchandise in the country for seed. All day the fire-steed flies over the country, stopping only that his master may rest, and I am awakened by his tramp and defiant snort at midnight, when in some remote glen in the woods he fronts the elements incased in ice and snow; and he will reach his stall only with the morning star, to start once more on his travels without rest or slumber. Or perchance, at evening, I hear him in his stable blowing off the superfluous energy of the day, that he may calm his nerves and cool his liver and brain for a few hours of iron slumber. If the enterprise were as heroic and commanding as it is protracted and unwearied!

Far through unfrequented woods on the confines of towns, where once only the hunter penetrated by day, in the darkest night dart these bright saloons without the knowledge of their inhabitants; this moment stopping at some brilliant station-house in town or city, where a social crowd is gathered, the next in the Dismal Swamp, scaring the owl and fox. The startings and arrivals of the cars are now the epochs in the village day. They go and come with such regularity and precision, and their whistle can be heard so far, that the farmers set their clocks by them, and thus one well conducted institution regulates a whole country. Have not men improved somewhat in punctuality since the railroad was invented? Do they not talk and think faster in the depot than they did in the stage-office? There is something electrifying in the atmosphere of the former place. I have been astonished at the miracles it has wrought;

that some of my neighbors, who, I should have prophesied, once for all, would never get to Boston by so prompt a conveyance, are on hand when the bell rings. To do things "railroad fashion" is now the byword; and it is worth the while to be warned so often and so sincerely by any power to get off its track. There is no stopping to read the riot act, no firing over the heads of the mob, in this case. We have constructed a fate, an *Atropos*, that never turns aside. (Let that be the name of your engine.) Men are advertised that at a certain hour and minute these bolts will be shot toward particular points of the compass; yet it interferes with no man's business, and the children go to school on the other track. We live the steadier for it. We are all educated thus to be sons of Tell. The air is full of invisible bolts. Every path but your own is the path of fate. Keep on your own track, then.

What recommends commerce to me is its enterprise and bravery. It does not clasp its hands and pray to Jupiter. I see these men every day go about their business with more or less courage and content, doing more even than they suspect, and perchance better employed than they could have consciously devised. I am less affected by their heroism who stood up for half an hour in the front line at Buena Vista, than by the steady and cheerful valor of the men who inhabit the snowplough for their winter quarters; who have not merely the three-o'-clock in the morning courage, which Bonaparte thought was the rarest, but whose courage does not go to rest so early, who go to sleep only when the storm sleeps or the sinews of their iron steed are frozen. On this morning of the Great Snow, perchance, which is still raging and chilling men's blood, I hear the muffled tone of their engine bell from out the fog bank of their chilled breath, which announces that the cars *are com-*

ing, without long delay, notwithstanding the veto of a New England northeast snowstorm, and I behold the ploughmen covered with snow and rime, their heads peering above the mould-board which is turning down other than daisies and the nests of field mice, like boulders of the Sierra Nevada, that occupy an outside place in the universe.

Commerce is unexpectedly confident and serene, alert, adventurous, and unwearied. It is very natural in its methods withal, far more so than many fantastic enterprises and sentimental experiments, and hence its singular success. I am refreshed and expanded when the freight train rattles past me, and I smell the stores which go dispensing their odors all the way from Long Wharf to Lake Champlain, reminding me of foreign parts, of coral reefs, and Indian oceans, and tropical climes, and the extent of the globe. I feel more like a citizen of the world at the sight of the palm-leaf which will cover so many flaxen New England heads the next summer, the Manila hemp and coconut husks, the old junk, gunny bags, scrap iron, and rusty nails. This carload of torn sails is more legible and interesting now than if they should be wrought into paper and printed books. Who can write so graphically the history of the storms they have weathered as these rents have done? They are proofsheets which need no correction. Here goes lumber from the Maine woods, which did not go out to sea in the last freshet, risen four dollars on the thousand because of what did go out or was split up; pine, spruce, cedar—first, second, third and fourth qualities, so lately all of one quality, to wave over the bear, and moose, and caribou. Next rolls Thomaston lime, a prime lot, which will get far among the hills before it gets slacked. These rags in bales, of all hues and qualities, the lowest condition to which cotton and linen descend, the final

result of dress—of patterns which are now no longer
cried up, unless it be in Milwaukee, as those splendid
articles, English, French, or American prints, ginghams,
muslins, etc., gathered from all quarters both of fashion
and poverty, going to become paper of one color or a
few shades only, on which forsooth will be written tales
of real life, high and low, and founded on fact! This
closed car smells of salt fish, the strong New England
and commercial scent, reminding me of the Grand
Banks and the fisheries. Who has not seen a salt fish,
thoroughly cured for this world, so that nothing can
spoil it, and putting the perseverance of the saints to
the blush? with which you may sweep or pave the
streets, and split your kindlings, and the teamster shelter
himself and his lading against sun, wind, and rain behind it—and the trader, as a Concord trader once did,
hang it up by his door for a sign when he commences
business, until at last his oldest customer cannot tell
surely whether it be animal, vegetable, or mineral, and
yet it shall be as pure as a snowflake, and if it be put
into a pot and boiled, will come out an excellent dun
fish for a Saturday's dinner. Next Spanish hides, with
the tails still preserving their twist and the angle of
elevation they had when the oxen that wore them were
careering over the pampas of the Spanish main—a type
of all obstinacy, and evincing how almost hopeless and
incurable are all constitutional vices. I confess, that
practically speaking, when I have learned a man's real
disposition, I have no hopes of changing it for the better
or worse in this state of existence. As the Orientals say,
"A cur's tail may be warmed, and pressed, and bound
round with ligatures, and after a twelve years' labor
bestowed upon it, still it will retain its natural form."
The only effectual cure for such inveteracies as these
tails exhibit is to make glue of them, which I believe is

what is usually done with them, and then they will stay put and stick. Here is a hogshead of molasses or of brandy directed to John Smith, Cuttingsville, Vermont, some trader among the Green Mountains, who imports for the farmers near his clearing, and now perchance stands over his bulkhead and thinks of the last arrivals on the coast, how they may affect the price for him, telling his customers this moment, as he has told them twenty times before this morning, that he expects some by the next train of prime quality. It is advertised in the Cuttingsville Times.

While these things go up, other things come down. Warned by the whizzing sound, I look up from my book and see some tall pine, hewn on far northern hills, which has winged its way over the Green Mountains and the Connecticut, shot like an arrow through the township within ten minutes, and scarce another eye beholds it; going

> "to be the mast
> Of some great ammiral."

And hark! here comes the cattle-train bearing the cattle of a thousand hills, sheepcots, stables, and cowyards in the air, drovers with their sticks, and shepherd boys in the midst of their flocks, all but the mountain pastures, whirled along like leaves blown from the mountains by the September gales. The air is filled with the bleating of calves and sheep, and the hustling of oxen, as if a pastoral valley were going by. When the old bell-wether at the head rattles his bell, the mountains do indeed skip like rams and the little hills like lambs. A carload of drovers, too, in the midst, on a level with their droves now, their vocation gone, but still clinging to their useless sticks as their badge of office. But their dogs, where are they? It is a stampede to them; they are quite thrown out; they have lost the scent. Methinks

I hear them barking behind the Peterboro' Hills, or panting up the western slope of the Green Mountains. They will not be in at the death. Their vocation, too, is gone. Their fidelity and sagacity are below par now. They will slink back to their kennels in disgrace, or perchance run wild and strike a league with the wolf and the fox. So is your pastoral life whirled past and away. But the bell rings, and I must get off the track and let the cars go by—

> What's the railroad to me?
> I never go to see
> Where it ends.
> It fills a few hollows,
> And makes banks for the swallows,
> It sets the sand a-blowing,
> And the blackberries a-growing,

but I cross it like a cart-path in the woods. I will not have my eyes put out and my ears spoiled by its smoke and steam and hissing.

Now that the cars are gone by and all the restless world with them, and the fishes in the pond no longer feel their rumbling, I am more alone than ever. For the rest of the long afternoon, perhaps, my meditations are interrupted only by the faint rattle of a carriage or team along the distant highway.

Sometimes, on Sundays, I heard the bells, the Lincoln, Acton, Bedford, or Concord bell, when the wind was favorable, a faint, sweet, and, as it were, natural melody, worth importing into the wilderness. At a sufficient distance over the woods this sound acquires a certain vibratory hum, as if the pine needles in the horizon were the strings of a harp which it swept. All sound heard at the greatest possible distance produces one and the same effect, a vibration of the universal lyre, just as the intervening atmosphere makes a distant ridge of earth interesting to our eyes by the azure tint it imparts to it. There came to me in this case a melody which the air had strained, and which had conversed with every leaf and needle of the wood, that portion of the sound which the elements had taken up and modulated and echoed from vale to vale. The echo is, to some extent, an original sound, and therein is the magic and charm of it. It is not merely a repetition of what was worth repeating in the bell, but partly the voice of the wood, the same trivial words and notes sung by a wood-nymph.

At evening, the distant lowing of some cow in the horizon beyond the woods sounded sweet and melodious, and at first I would mistake it for the voices of certain minstrels by whom I was sometimes serenaded, who might be straying over hill and dale; but soon I was not unpleasantly disappointed when it was prolonged into the cheap and natural music of the cow. I do not mean to be satirical, but to express my appreciation of those youths' singing, when I state that I perceived clearly that it was akin to the music of the cow, and they were at length one articulation of Nature.

Regularly at half past seven, in one part of the summer, after the evening train had gone by, the whippoorwills chanted their vespers for half an hour, sitting on a stump by my door, or upon the ridgepole of the house. They would begin to sing almost with as much precision as a clock, within five minutes of a particular time, referred to the setting of the sun, every evening. I had a rare opportunity to become acquainted with their habits. Sometimes I heard four or five at once in different parts of the wood, by accident one a bar behind another, and so near me that I distinguished not only the cluck after each note, but often that singular buzzing sound like a fly in a spider's web, only proportionally louder. Sometimes one would circle round and round me in the woods a few feet distant as if tethered by a string, when probably I was near its eggs. They sang at intervals throughout the night, and were again as musical as ever just before and about dawn.

When other birds are still the screech owls take up the strain, like mourning women their ancient u-lu-lu. Their dismal scream is truly Ben Jonsonian. Wise midnight hags! It is no honest and blunt tu-whit tu-who of the poets, but, without jesting, a most solemn graveyard ditty, the mutual consolations of suicide lovers remembering the pangs and the delights of supernal love in the infernal groves. Yet I love to hear their wailing, their doleful responses, trilled along the woodside; reminding me sometimes of music and singing birds; as if it were the dark and tearful side of music, the regrets and sighs that would fain be sung. They are the spirits, the low spirits and melancholy forebodings, of fallen souls that once in human shape night-walked the earth and did the deeds of darkness, now expiating their sins with their wailing hymns or threnodies in the scenery of their transgressions. They give me a new sense of the variety and capacity of that nature which is our common dwelling. *Oh-o-o-o-o that I never had been bor-r-r-r-n!* sighs one on this side of the pond, and circles with the restlessness of despair to some new perch on the gray oaks. Then—*that I never had been bor-r-r-r-n!* echoes another on the farther side with tremulous sincerity, and—*bor-r-r-r-n!* comes faintly from far in the Lincoln woods.

I was also serenaded by a hooting owl. Near at hand you could fancy it the most melancholy sound in Nature, as if she meant by this to stereotype and make permanent in her choir the dying moans of a human being, some poor weak relic of mortality who has left

hope behind, and howls like an animal, yet with human
sobs, on entering the dark valley, made more awful by
a certain gurgling melodiousness—I find myself beginning with the letters gl when I try to imitate it—expressive of a mind which has reached the gelatinous
mildewy stage in the mortification of all healthy and
courageous thought. It reminded me of ghouls and
idiots and insane howlings. But now one answers from
far woods in a strain made really melodious by distance,
Hoo hoo hoo, hoorer hoo; and indeed for the most part
it suggested only pleasing associations, whether heard
by day or night, summer or winter.

I rejoice that there are owls. Let them do the idiotic
and maniacal hooting for men. It is a sound admirably
suited to swamps and twilight woods which no day
illustrates, suggesting a vast and undeveloped nature
which men have not recognized. They represent the
stark twilight and unsatisfied thoughts which all have.
All day the sun has shone on the surface of some savage
swamp, where the single spruce stands hung with usnea
lichens, and small hawks circulate above, and the chickadee lisps amid the evergreens, and the partridge and
rabbit skulk beneath; but now a more dismal and fitting
day dawns, and a different race of creatures awakes to
express the meaning of Nature there.

Late in the evening I heard the distant rumbling of
wagons over bridges, a sound heard farther than almost any other at night, the baying of dogs, and sometimes again the lowing of some disconsolate cow in a
distant barnyard. In the meanwhile all the shore rang
with the trump of bullfrogs, the sturdy spirits of ancient
wine-bibbers and wassailers, still unrepentant, trying to
sing a catch in their Stygian lake—if the Walden nymphs
will pardon the comparison, for though there are almost no weeds, there are frogs there—who would fain

keep up the hilarious rules of their old festal tables, though their voices have waxed hoarse and solemnly grave, mocking at mirth, and the wine has lost its flavor, and become only liquor to distend their paunches, and sweet intoxication never comes to drown the memory of the past, but mere saturation and waterloggedness and distention. The most aldermanic, with his chin upon a heartleaf, which serves for a napkin to his drooling chaps, under this northern shore quaffs a deep draught of the once scorned water, and passes round the cup with the ejaculation *tr-r-r-oonk, tr-r-r-oonk, tr-r-r-oonk!* and straightway comes over the water from some distant cove the same password repeated, where the next in seniority and girth has gulped down to his mark; and when this observance has made the circuit of the shores, then ejaculates the master of ceremonies, with satisfaction, *tr-r-r-oonk!* and each in his turn repeats the same down to the least distended, leakiest, and flabbiest paunched, that there be no mistake; and then the bowl goes round again and again, until the sun disperses the morning mist, and only the patriarch is not under the pond, but vainly bellowing *troonk* from time to time, and pausing for a reply.

I am not sure that I ever heard the sound of cockcrowing from my clearing, and I thought that it might be worth the while to keep a cockerel for his music merely, as a singing bird. The note of this once wild Indian pheasant is certainly the most remarkable of any bird's, and if they could be naturalized without being domesticated, it would soon become the most famous sound in our woods, surpassing the clangor of the goose and the hooting of the owl; and then imagine the cackling of the hens to fill the pauses when their lords' clarions rested! No wonder that man added this bird to his tame stock—to say nothing of the eggs and drumsticks. To walk in a winter morning in a wood where these birds abounded, their native woods, and hear the wild cockerels crow on the trees, clear and shrill for miles over the resounding earth, drowning the feebler notes of other birds—think of it! It would put nations on the alert. Who would not be early to rise, and rise earlier and earlier every successive day of his life, till he became unspeakably healthy, wealthy, and wise? This foreign bird's note is celebrated by the poets of all countries along with the notes of their native songsters. All climates agree with brave Chanticleer. He is more indigenous even than the natives. His health is ever good, his lungs are sound, his spirits never flag. Even the sailor on the Atlantic and Pacific is awakened by his voice; but its shrill sound never roused me from my slumbers. I kept neither dog, cat, cow, pig, nor hens, so that you would have said there was a deficiency of domestic sounds; neither the churn, nor the spinning-wheel, nor even the singing of the kettle, nor the hissing of the urn, nor children crying, to comfort one. An old-fashioned man would have lost his senses or died of ennui before this. Not even rats in the wall, for they were starved out, or rather were never baited in—only squirrels on the roof and under the floor, a whippoorwill on the ridgepole, a bluejay screaming beneath the window, a hare or woodchuck under the house, a screech-owl or a cat-owl behind it, a flock of wild geese or a laughing loon on the pond, and a fox to bark in the night. Not even a lark or an oriole, those mild planta-tion birds, ever visited my clearing. No cockerels to crow nor hens to cackle in the yard. No yard! but un-fenced Nature reaching up to your very sills. A young forest growing up under your windows, and wild su-machs and blackberry vines breaking through into your cellar; sturdy pitch-pines rubbing and creaking against the shingles for want of room, their roots reaching quite under the house. Instead of a scuttle or a blind blown off in the gale, a pine tree snapped off or torn up by the roots behind your house for fuel. Instead of no path to the front-yard gate in the Great Snow, no gate—no front yard—and no path to the civilized world.

SOLITUDE

This is a delicious evening, when the whole body is one sense, and imbibes delight through every pore. I go and come with a strange liberty in Nature, a part of herself. As I walk along the stony shore of the pond in my shirt sleeves, though it is cool as well as cloudy and windy, and I see nothing special to attract me, all the elements are unusually congenial to me. The bullfrogs trump to usher in the night, and the note of the whippoorwill is borne on the rippling wind from over the water. Sympathy with the fluttering alder and poplar leaves almost takes away my breath; yet, like the lake, my serenity is rippled but not ruffled. These small waves raised by the evening wind are as remote from storm as the smooth reflecting surface. Though it is now dark, the wind still blows and roars in the wood, the waves still dash, and some creatures lull the rest with their notes. The repose is never complete. The wildest animals do not repose, but seek their prey now; the fox, and skunk, and rabbit, now roam the fields and woods without fear. They are Nature's watchmen—links which connect the days of animated life.

When I return to my house I find that visitors have been there and left their cards, either a bunch of flowers, or a wreath of evergreen, or a name in pencil on a yellow walnut leaf or a chip. They who come rarely to the woods take some little piece of the forest into their hands to play with by the way, which they leave, either intentionally or accidentally. One has peeled a willow wand, woven it into a ring, and dropped it on my table. I could always tell if visitors had called in my absence, either by the bended twigs or grass, or the print of their shoes, and generally of what sex or age or quality they were by some slight trace left, as a flower dropped, or a bunch of grass plucked and thrown away, even as far off as the railroad, half a mile distant, or by the lingering odor of a cigar or pipe. Nay, I was frequently notified of the passage of a traveler along the highway sixty rods off by the scent of his pipe.

There is commonly sufficient space about us. Our horizon is never quite at our elbows. The thick wood is not just at our door, nor the pond, but somewhat is always clearing, familiar and worn by us, appropriated and fenced in some way, and reclaimed from Nature. For what reason have I this vast range and circuit, some square miles of unfrequented forest, for my privacy, abandoned to me by men? My nearest neighbor is a mile distant, and no house is visible from any place but the hilltops within half a mile of my own. I have my horizon bounded by woods all to myself; a distant view of the railroad where it touches the pond on the one hand, and of the fence which skirts the woodland road on the other. But for the most part it is as solitary where I live as on the prairies. It is as much Asia or Africa as New England. I have, as it were, my own sun and moon and stars, and a little world all to myself. At night there was never a traveler passed my house, or knocked at my door, more than if I were the first or last man; unless it were in the spring, when at long intervals some came from the village to fish for pouts—they plainly fished much more in the Walden Pond of their own natures, and baited their hooks with darkness—but they soon retreated, usually with light baskets, and left "the world to darkness and to me," and the black kernel of the night was never profaned by any human neighborhood. I believe that men are generally still a little afraid of the dark, though the witches are all hung, and Christianity and candles have been introduced.

Yet I experienced sometimes that the most sweet and tender, the most innocent and encouraging society may be found in any natural object, even for the poor misanthrope and most melancholy man. There can be no very black melancholy to him who lives in the midst of Nature and has his senses still. There was never yet such a storm but it was Aeolian music to a healthy and innocent ear. Nothing can rightly compel a simple and brave man to a vulgar sadness. While I enjoy the friendship of the seasons I trust that nothing can make life a burden to me. The gentle rain which waters my beans and keeps me in the house today is not drear and melancholy, but good for me too. Though it prevents my hoeing them, it is of far more worth than my hoeing. If it should continue so long as to cause the seeds to rot in the ground and destroy the potatoes in the lowlands, it would still be good for the grass on the uplands, and, being good for the grass, it would be good for me. Sometimes, when I compare myself with other men, it seems as if I were more favored by the gods than they, beyond any deserts that I am conscious of; as if I had a warrant and surety at their hands which my fellows have not, and were especially guided and guarded. I do not flatter myself, but if it be possible they flatter me. I have never felt lonesome, or in the least oppressed by a sense of solitude, but once, and that was a few weeks after I came to the woods, when, for an hour, I doubted if the near neighborhood of man was not essential to a serene and healthy life. To be alone was something unpleasant. But I was at the same time conscious of a slight insanity in my mood, and seemed to foresee my recovery. In the midst of a gentle rain while these thoughts prevailed, I was suddenly sensible of such sweet and beneficent society in Nature, in the very pattering of the drops, and in every sound and sight around my house, an infinite and unaccountable friendliness all at once like an atmosphere sustaining me, as made the fancied advantages of human neighborhood insignificant, and I have never thought of them since. Every little pine needle expanded and swelled with sympathy and befriended me. I was so distinctly made aware of the presence of something kindred to me, even in scenes which we are accustomed to call wild and dreary, and also that the nearest of blood to me and humanest was not a person nor a villager, that I thought no place could ever be strange to me again.

> "Mourning untimely consumes the sad;
> Few are their days in the land of the living,
> Beautiful daughter of Toscar."

Some of my pleasantest hours were during the long rainstorms in the spring or fall, which confined me to the house for the afternoon as well as the forenoon, soothed by their ceaseless roar and pelting; when an early twilight ushered in a long evening in which many thoughts had time to take root and unfold themselves. In those driving northeast rains which tried the village houses so, when the maids stood ready with mop and pail in front entries to keep the deluge out, I sat behind my door in my little house, which was all entry, and thoroughly enjoyed its protection. In one heavy thunder-shower the lightning struck a large pitch pine across the pond, making a very conspicuous and perfectly regular spiral groove from top to bottom, an inch or more deep, and four or five inches wide, as you would groove a walking-stick. I passed it again the other day, and was struck with awe on looking up and beholding that mark, now more distinct than ever, where a terrific and resistless bolt came down out of the harmless sky eight years ago. Men frequently say to me, "I should think you would feel lonesome down there, and want to be nearer to folks, rainy and snowy days and nights especially." I am tempted to reply to such, This whole earth which we inhabit is but a point in space. How far apart, think you, dwell the two most distant inhabitants of yonder star, the breadth of whose disk cannot be appreciated by our instruments? Why should I feel lonely? is not our planet in the Milky Way? This which you put seems to me not to be the most important question. What sort of space is that which separates a man from his fellows and makes him solitary? I have found that no exertion of the legs can bring two minds much nearer to one another. What do we want most to dwell near to? Not to many men surely, the depot, the post-office, the barroom, the meeting-house, the school-house, the grocery, Beacon Hill, or the Five Points, where men most congregate, but to the perennial source of our life, whence in all our experience we have found that to issue, as the willow stands near the water and sends out its roots in that direction. This will vary with different natures, but this is the place where a wise man will dig his cellar. . . . I one evening overtook one of my townsmen, who has accumulated what is called "a handsome property"—though I never got a *fair* view of it—on the Walden road, driving a pair of cattle to market, who inquired of me how I could bring my mind to give up so many of the comforts of life. I answered that I was very sure I liked it passably well; I was not joking. And so I went home to my bed, and left him to pick his way through the darkness and the mud to Brighton—or Brighttown—which place he would reach some time in the morning.

Any prospect of awakening or coming to life to a dead man makes indifferent all times and places. The place where that may occur is always the same, and indescribably pleasant to all our senses. For the most part we allow only outlying and transient circumstances to make our occasions. They are, in fact, the cause of our distraction. Nearest to all things is that power which fashions their being. *Next* to us the grandest laws are continually being executed. *Next* to us is not the workman whom we have hired, with whom we love so well to talk, but the workman whose work we are.

"How vast and profound is the influence of the subtile powers of Heaven and of Earth!

"We seek to perceive them, and we do not see them; we seek to hear them, and we do not hear them; identified with the substance of things, they cannot be separated from them.

"They cause that in all the universe men purify and sanctify their hearts, and clothe themselves in their holiday garments to offer sacrifices and oblations to their ancestors. It is an ocean of subtile intelligences. They are everywhere, above us, on our left, on our right; they environ us on all sides."

We are the subjects of an experiment which is not a little interesting to me. Can we not do without the society of our gossips a little while under these circumstances, have our own thoughts to cheer us? Confucius says truly, "Virtue does not remain as an abandoned orphan; it must of necessity have neighbors."

With thinking we may be beside ourselves in a same sense. By a conscious effort of the mind we can stand aloof from actions and their consequences; and all things, good and bad, go by us like a torrent. We are not wholly involved in Nature. I may be either the driftwood in the stream, or Indra in the sky looking down on it. I *may* be affected by a theatrical exhibition; on the other hand, I *may not* be affected by an actual event which appears to concern me much more. I only know myself as a human entity; the scene, so to speak, of thoughts and affections; and am sensible of a certain doubleness by which I can stand as remote from myself as from another. However intense my experience, I am conscious of the presence and criticism of a part of me, which, as it were, is not a part of me, but spectator, sharing no experience, but taking note of it; and that is no more I than it is you. When the play, it may be the tragedy, of life is over, the spectator goes his way. It was a kind of fiction, a work of the imagination only, so far as he was concerned. This doubleness may easily make us poor neighbors and friends sometimes.

I find it wholesome to be alone the greater part of the time. To be in company, even with the best, is soon wearisome and dissipating. I love to be alone. I never found the companion that was so companionable as solitude. We are for the most part more lonely when we go abroad among men than when we stay in our chambers. A man thinking or working is always alone, let him be where he will. Solitude is not measured by the miles of space that intervene between a man and his fellows. The really diligent student in one of the crowded hives of Cambridge College is as solitary as a dervish in the desert. The farmer can work alone in the field or the woods all day, hoeing or chopping, and not feel lonesome, because he is employed; but when he comes home at night he cannot sit down in a room alone, at the mercy of his thoughts, but must be where he can "see the folks," and recreate, and as he thinks remunerate, himself for his day's solitude; and hence he wonders how the student can sit alone in the house all night and most of the day without ennui and "the blues"; but he does not realize that the student, though in the house, is still at work in *his* field, and chopping in *his* woods, as the farmer in his, and in turn seeks the same recreation and society that the latter does, though it may be a more condensed form of it.

Society is commonly too cheap. We meet at very short intervals, not having had time to acquire any new value for each other. We meet at meals three times a day, and give each other a new taste of that old musty cheese that we are. We have had to agree on a certain set of rules, called etiquette and politeness, to make this frequent meeting tolerable and that we need not come to open war. We meet at the post-office, and at the sociable, and about the fireside every night; we live thick and are in each other's way, and stumble over one another, and I think that we thus lose some respect for one another. Certainly less frequency would suffice for all important and hearty communications. Consider the girls in a factory—never alone, hardly in their dreams. It would be better if there were but one inhabitant to a square mile, as where I live. The value of a man is not in his skin, that we should touch him.

I have heard of a man lost in the woods and dying of famine and exhaustion at the foot of a tree, whose loneliness was relieved by the grotesque visions with which, owing to bodily weakness, his diseased imagination surrounded him, and which he believed to be real. So also, owing to bodily and mental health and strength, we may be continually cheered by a like but more normal and natural society, and come to know that we are never alone.

I have a great deal of company in my house; especially in the morning, when nobody calls. Let me suggest a few comparisons, that someone may convey an idea of my situation. I am no more lonely than the loon in the pond that laughs so loud, or than Walden Pond itself. What company has that lonely lake, I pray? And yet it has not the blue devils, but the blue angels in it, in the azure tint of its waters. The sun is alone, except in thick weather, when there sometimes appear to be two, but one is a mock sun. God is alone—but the devil, he is far from being alone; he sees a great deal of company; he is legion. I am no more lonely than a single mullein or dandelion in a pasture, or a bean leaf, or sorrel, or a horsefly, or a humblebee. I am no more lonely than the Mill Brook, or a weathercock, or the North Star, or the south wind, or an April shower, or a January thaw, or the first spider in a new house.

I have occasional visits in the long winter evenings, when the snow falls fast and the wind howls in the wood, from an old settler and original proprietor, who is reported to have dug Walden Pond, and stoned it, and fringed it with pine woods; who tells me stories of old time and of new eternity; and between us we manage to pass a cheerful evening with social mirth and pleasant views of things, even without apples or cider —a most wise and humorous friend, whom I love much, who keeps himself more secret than ever did Goffe or Whalley; and though he is thought to be dead, none can show where he is buried. An elderly dame, too, dwells in my neighborhood, invisible to most persons, in whose odorous herb garden I love to stroll sometimes, gathering simples and listening to her fables; for she has a genius of unequaled fertility, and her memory runs back farther than mythology, and she can tell me the original of every fable, and on what fact every one is founded, for the incidents occurred when she was young. A ruddy and lusty old dame, who delights in all weathers and seasons, and is likely to outlive all her children yet.

The indescribable innocence and beneficence of Nature—of sun and wind and rain, of summer and winter—such health, such cheer, they afford forever! and such sympathy have they ever with our race, that all Nature would be affected, and the sun's brightness fade, and the winds would sigh humanely, and the clouds rain tears, and the woods shed their leaves and put on mourning in midsummer, if any man should ever for a just cause grieve. Shall I not have intelligence with the earth? Am I not partly leaves and vegetable mould myself?

What is the pill which will keep us well, serene, contented? Not my or thy great-grandfather's, but our great-grandmother Nature's universal, vegetable, botanic medicines, by which she has kept herself young always, outlived so many old Parrs in her day, and fed her health with their decaying fatness. For my panacea, instead of one of those quack vials of a mixture dipped from Acheron and the Dead Sea, which come out of those long shallow black-schooner-looking wagons which we sometimes see made to carry bottles, let me have a draught of undiluted morning air. Morning air! If men will not drink of this at the fountainhead of the day, why, then, we must even bottle up some and sell it in the shops, for the benefit of those who have lost their subscription ticket to morning time in this world. But remember, it will not keep quite till noonday even in the coolest cellar, but drive out the stopples long ere that and follow westward the steps of Aurora. I am no worshiper of Hygeia, who was the daughter of that old herb-doctor Aesculapius, and who is represented on monuments holding a serpent in one hand, and in the other a cup out of which the serpent sometimes drinks; but rather of Hebe, cupbearer to Jupiter, who was the daughter of Juno and wild lettuce, and who had the power of restoring gods and men to the vigor of youth. She was probably the only thoroughly sound-conditioned, healthy, and robust young lady that ever walked the globe, and wherever she came it was spring.

VISITORS

I think that I love society as much as most, and am ready enough to fasten myself like a bloodsucker for the time to any full-blooded man that comes in my way. I am naturally no hermit, but might possibly sit out the sturdiest frequenter of the barroom, if my business called me thither.

I had three chairs in my house; one for solitude, two for friendship, three for society. When visitors came in larger and unexpected numbers there was but the third chair for them all, but they generally economized the room by standing up. It is surprising how many great men and women a small house will contain. I have had twenty-five or thirty souls, with their bodies, at once under my roof, and yet we often parted without being aware that we had come very near to one another. Many of our houses, both public and private, with their almost innumerable apartments, their huge halls and their cellars for the storage of wines and other munitions of peace, appear to me extravagantly large for their inhabitants. They are so vast and magnificent that the latter seem to be only vermin which infest them. I am surprised when the herald blows his summons before some Tremont or Astor or Middlesex House, to see come creeping out over the piazza for all inhabitants a ridiculous mouse, which soon again slinks into some hole in the pavement.

One inconvenience I sometimes experienced in so small a house, the difficulty of getting to a sufficient distance from my guest when we began to utter the big thoughts in big words. You want room for your thoughts to get into sailing trim and run a course or two before they make their port. The bullet of your thought must have overcome its lateral and ricochet motion and fallen into its last and steady course before it reaches the ear of the hearer, else it may plough out again through the side of his head. Also, our sentences wanted room to unfold and form their columns in the interval. Individuals, like nations, must have suitable broad and natural boundaries, even a considerable neutral ground, between them. I have found it a singular luxury to talk across the pond to a companion on the opposite side. In my house we were so near that we could not begin to hear—we could not speak low enough to be heard; as when you throw two stones into calm water so near that they break each other's undulations. If we are merely loquacious and loud talkers, then we can afford to stand very near together, cheek by jowl, and feel each other's breath; but if we speak reservedly and thoughtfully, we want to be farther apart, that all animal heat and moisture may have a chance to evaporate. If we would enjoy the most intimate society with that in each of us which is without, or above, being spoken to, we must not only be silent, but commonly so far apart bodily that we cannot possibly hear each other's voice in any case. Referred to this standard, speech is for the convenience of those who are hard of hearing; but there are many fine things which we cannot say if we have to shout. As the conversation began to assume a loftier and grander tone, we gradually shoved our chairs farther apart till they touched the wall in opposite corners, and then commonly there was not room enough.

My "best" room, however, my withdrawing room, always ready for company, on whose carpet the sun rarely fell, was the pine wood behind my house. Thither in summer days, when distinguished guests came, I took them, and a priceless domestic swept the floor and dusted the furniture and kept the things in order.

If one guest came he sometimes partook of my frugal meal, and it was no interruption to conversation to be stirring a hasty-pudding, or watching the rising and maturing of a loaf of bread in the ashes, in the meanwhile. But if twenty came and sat in my house there was nothing said about dinner, though there might be bread enough for two, more than if eating were a forsaken habit; but we naturally practiced abstinence; and this was never felt to be an offense against hospitality, but the most proper and considerate course. The waste and decay of physical life, which so often needs repair, seemed miraculously retarded in such a case, and the vital vigor stood its ground. I could entertain thus a thousand as well as twenty; and if any ever went away disappointed or hungry from my house when they found me at home, they may depend upon it that I sympathized with them at least. So easy is it, though many housekeepers doubt it, to establish new and better customs in the place of the old. You need not rest your reputation on the dinners you give. For my own part, I was never so effectually deterred from frequenting a man's house, by any kind of Cerberus whatever, as by the parade one made about dining me, which I took to be a very polite and roundabout hint never to trouble him so again. I think I shall never revisit those scenes.

I should be proud to have for the motto of my cabin those lines of Spenser which one of my visitors inscribed on a yellow walnut leaf for a card:

"Arrivéd there, the little house they fill,
    Ne looke for entertainment where none was;
Rest is their feast, and all things at their will:
    The noblest mind the best contentment has."

When Winslow, afterward governor of the Plymouth Colony, went with a companion on a visit of ceremony to Massasoit on foot through the woods, and arrived tired and hungry at his lodge, they were well received by the king, but nothing was said about eating that day. When the night arrived, to quote their own words, "He laid us on the bed with himself and his wife, they at the one end and we at the other, it being only plank, laid a foot from the ground, and a thin mat upon them. Two more of his chief men, for want of room, pressed by and upon us; so that we were worse weary of our lodging than of our journey." At one o'clock the next day Massasoit "brought two fishes that he had shot," about thrice as big as a bream; "these being boiled, there were at least forty looked for a share in them. The most ate of them. This meal only we had in two nights and a day; and had not one of us bought a partridge, we had taken our journey fasting." Fearing that they would be lightheaded for want of food and also sleep, owing to "the savages' barbarous singing (for they used to sing themselves asleep)" and that they might get home while they had strength to travel, they departed. As for lodging, it is true they were but poorly entertained, though what they found an inconvenience was no doubt intended for an honor; but as far as eating was concerned, I do not see how the Indians could have done better. They had nothing to eat themselves, and they were wiser than to think that apologies could supply the place of food to their guests; so they drew their belts tighter and said nothing about it. Another time when Winslow visited them, it being a season of plenty with them, there was no deficiency in this respect.

As for men, they will hardly fail one anywhere. I had more visitors while I lived in the woods than at any other period of my life; I mean that I had some. I met several there under more favorable circumstances than I could anywhere else. But fewer came to see me on trivial business. In this respect, my company was winnowed by my mere distance from town. I had withdrawn so far within the great ocean of solitude, into which the rivers of society empty, that for the most part, so far as my needs were concerned, only the finest sediment was deposited around me. Besides, there were wafted to me evidences of unexplored and uncultivated continents on the other side.

Who should come to my lodge this morning but a true Homeric or Paphlagonian man—he had so suitable and poetic a name that I am sorry I cannot print it here—a Canadian, a woodchopper and postmaker, who can hole fifty posts in a day, who made his last supper on a woodchuck which his dog caught. He, too, has heard of Homer, and, "if it were not for books," would "not know what to do rainy days," though perhaps he has not read one wholly through for many rainy seasons. Some priest who could pronounce the Greek itself taught him to read his verse in the testament in his native parish far away; and now I must translate to him, while he holds the book, Achilles' reproof to Patroclus for his sad countenance.—"Why are you in tears, Patroclus, like a young girl?"—

"Or have you alone heard some news from Phthia?
They say that Menoetius lives yet, son of Actor,

And Peleus lives, son of Aeacus, among the Myrmidons,
Either of whom having died, we should greatly grieve."

He says, "That's good." He has a great bundle of white-
oak bark under his arm for a sick man, gathered this
Sunday morning. "I suppose there's no harm in going
after such a thing today," says he. To him Homer was
a great writer, though what his writing was about he
did not know. A more simple and natural man it would
be hard to find. Vice and disease, which cast such
a somber moral hue over the world, seemed to have
hardly any existence for him. He was about twenty-
eight years old, and had left Canada and his father's
house a dozen years before to work in the States, and
earn money to buy a farm with at last, perhaps in his
native country. He was cast in the coarsest mould; a
stout but sluggish body, yet gracefully carried, with a
thick sunburned neck, dark bushy hair, and dull sleepy
blue eyes, which were occasionally lit up with expression. He wore a flat gray cloth cap, a dingy wool-colored
greatcoat, and cowhide boots. He was a great consumer
of meat, usually carrying his dinner to his work a couple
of miles past my house—for he chopped all summer—in
a tin pail; cold meats, often cold woodchucks, and coffee in a stone bottle which dangled by a string from his
belt; and sometimes he offered me a drink. He came
along early, crossing my beanfield, though without anxiety or haste to get to his work, such as Yankees exhibit.
He wasn't a-going to hurt himself. He didn't care if he
only earned his board. Frequently he would leave his
dinner in the bushes, when his dog had caught a woodchuck by the way, and go back a mile and a half to
dress it and leave it in the cellar of the house where he
boarded, after deliberating first for half an hour whether
he could not sink it in the pond safely till nightfall,
loving to dwell long upon these themes. He would say,

as he went by in the morning, "How thick the pigeons are! If working every day were not my trade, I could get all the meat I should want by hunting—pigeons, woodchucks, rabbits, partridges—by gosh! I could get all I should want for a week in one day."

He was a skillful chopper, and indulged in some flourishes and ornaments in his art. He cut his trees level and close to the ground, that the sprouts which came up afterward might be more vigorous and a sled might slide over the stumps; and instead of leaving a whole tree to support his corded wood, he would pare it away to a slender stake or splinter which you could break off with your hand at last.

He interested me because he was so quiet and solitary and so happy withal; a well of good humor and contentment which overflowed at his eyes. His mirth was without alloy. Sometimes I saw him at his work in the woods, felling trees, and he would greet me with a laugh of inexpressible satisfaction, and a salutation in Canadian French, though he spoke English as well. When I approached him he would suspend his work, and with half-suppressed mirth lie along the trunk of a pine which he had felled, and, peeling off the inner bark, roll it up into a ball and chew it while he laughed and talked. Such an exuberance of animal spirits had he that he sometimes tumbled down and rolled on the ground with laughter at anything which made him think and tickled him. Looking round upon the trees he would exclaim, "By George! I can enjoy myself well enough here chopping; I want no better sport." Sometimes, when at leisure, he amused himself all day in the woods with a pocket pistol, firing salutes to himself at regular intervals as he walked. In the winter he had a fire by which at noon he warmed his coffee in a kettle; and as he sat on a log to eat his dinner the chickadees would sometimes come round and alight on his arm and peck at the potato in his fingers; and he said that he "liked to have the little *fellers* about him."

In him the animal man chiefly was developed. In physical endurance and contentment he was cousin to the pine and the rock. I asked him once if he was not sometimes tired at night, after working all day; and he answered, with a sincere and serious look, "Gorrappit, I never was tired in my life." But the intellectual and what is called spiritual man in him were slumbering as in an infant. He had been instructed only in that innocent and ineffectual way in which the Catholic priests teach the aborigines, by which the pupil is never educated to the degree of consciousness, but only to the degree of trust and reverence, and a child is not made a man, but kept a child. When Nature made him, she gave him a strong body and contentment for his portion, and propped him on every side with reverence and reliance, that he might live out his threescore years and ten a child. He was so genuine and unsophisticated that no introduction would serve to introduce him, more than if you introduced a woodchuck to your neighbor. He had got to find him out as you did. He would not play any part. Men paid him wages for work, and so helped to feed and clothe him; but he never exchanged opinions with them. He was so simply and naturally humble—if he can be called humble who never aspires —that humility was no distinct quality in him, nor could he conceive of it. Wiser men were demigods to him. If you told him that such a one was coming, he did as if he thought that anything so grand would expect nothing of himself, but take all the responsibility on itself, and let him be forgotten still. He never heard the sound of praise. He particularly reverenced the writer and the preacher. Their performances were miracles. When I told him that I wrote considerably, he thought for a long time that it was merely the handwriting which I meant, for he could write a remarkably good hand himself. I sometimes found the name of his native parish handsomely written in the snow by the highway, with the proper French accent, and knew that he had passed. I asked him if he ever wished to write his thoughts. He said that he had read and written letters for those who could not, but he never tried to write thoughts—no, he could not, he could not tell what to put first, it would kill him, and then there was spelling to be attended to at the same time!

I heard that a distinguished wise man and reformer asked him if he did not want the world to be changed; but he answered with a chuckle of surprise in his Canadian accent, not knowing that the question had ever been entertained before, "No, I like it well enough." It would have suggested many things to a philosopher to have dealings with him. To a stranger he appeared to know nothing of things in general; yet I sometimes saw in him a man whom I had not seen before, and I did not know whether he was as wise as Shakespeare or as simply ignorant as a child, whether to suspect him of a fine poetic consciousness or of stupidity. A townsman told me that when he met him sauntering through the village in his small close-fitting cap, and whistling to himself, he reminded him of a prince in disguise.

His only books were an almanac and an arithmetic, in which last he was considerably expert. The former was a sort of cyclopedia to him, which he supposed to contain an abstract of human knowledge, as indeed it does to a considerable extent. I loved to sound him on the various reforms of the day, and he never failed to look at them in the most simple and practical light. He had never heard of such things before. Could he do

without factories? I asked. He had worn the homemade
Vermont gray, he said, and that was good. Could he
dispense with tea and coffee? Did this country afford
any beverage beside water? He had soaked hemlock
leaves in water and drank it, and thought that was
better than water in warm weather. When I asked him
if he could do without money, he showed the convenience of money in such a way as to suggest and coincide
with the most philosophical accounts of the origin of
this institution, and the very derivation of the word
pecunia. If an ox were his property, and he wished
to get needles and thread at the store, he thought it
would be inconvenient and impossible soon to go on
mortgaging some portion of the creature each time to
that amount. He could defend many institutions better
than any philosopher, because, in describing them as
they concerned him, he gave the true reason for their
prevalence, and speculation had not suggested to him
any other. At another time, hearing Plato's definition
of a man—a biped without feathers—and that one exhibited a cock plucked and called it Plato's man, he
thought it an important difference that the *knees* bent
the wrong way. He would sometimes exclaim, "How I
love to talk! By George, I could talk all day!" I asked
him once, when I had not seen him for many months,
if he had got a new idea this summer. "Good Lord,"
said he, "a man that has to work as I do, if he does not
forget the ideas he has had, he will do well. Maybe
the man you hoe with is inclined to race; then, by
gorry, your mind must be there; you think of weeds."
He would sometimes ask me first on such occasions, if
I had made any improvement. One winter day I asked
him if he was always satisfied with himself, wishing to
suggest a substitute within him for the priest without,
and some higher motive for living. "Satisfied!" said he;

"some men are satisfied with one thing, and some with another. One man, perhaps, if he has got enough, will be satisfied to sit all day with his back to the fire and his belly to the table, by George!" Yet I never, by any maneuvering, could get him to take the spiritual view of things; the highest that he appeared to conceive of was a simple expediency, such as you might expect an animal to appreciate; and this, practically, is true of most men. If I suggested any improvement in his mode of life, he merely answered, without expressing any regret, that it was too late. Yet he thoroughly believed in honesty and the like virtues.

There was a certain positive originality, however slight, to be detected in him, and I occasionally observed that he was thinking for himself and expressing his own opinion, a phenomenon so rare that I would any day walk ten miles to observe it, and it amounted to the re-origination of many of the institutions of society. Though he hesitated, and perhaps failed to express himself distinctly, he always had a presentable thought behind. Yet his thinking was so primitive and immersed in his animal life, that, though more promising than a merely learned man's, it rarely ripened to anything which can be reported. He suggested that there might be men of genius in the lowest grades of life, however permanently humble and illiterate, who take their own view always, or do not pretend to see at all; who are as bottomless even as Walden Pond was thought to be, though they may be dark and muddy.

Many a traveler came out of his way to see me and the inside of my house, and, as an excuse for calling, asked for a glass of water. I told them that I drank at the pond, and pointed thither, offering to lend them a dipper. Far off as I lived, I was not exempted from that annual visitation which occurs, methinks, about the first of April, when everybody is on the move; and I had my share of good luck, though there were some curious specimens among my visitors. Half-witted men from the almshouse and elsewhere came to see me; but I endeavored to make them exercise all the wit they had, and make their confessions to me; in such cases making wit the theme of our conversation; and so was compensated. Indeed, I found some of them to be wiser than the so-called *overseers* of the poor and selectmen of the town, and thought it was time that the tables were turned. With respect to wit, I learned that there was not much difference between the half and the whole. One day, in particular, an inoffensive, simple-minded pauper, whom with others I had often seen used as fencing stuff, standing or sitting on a bushel in the fields to keep cattle and himself from straying, visited me, and expressed a wish to live as I did. He told me, with the utmost simplicity and truth, quite superior, or rather *inferior*, to anything that is called humility, that he was "deficient in intellect." These were his words. The Lord had made him so, yet he supposed the Lord cared as much for him as for another. "I have always been so," said he, "from my childhood; I never had much mind; I was not like other children; I am weak in the head. It was the Lord's will, I suppose." And there he was to prove the truth of his words. He was a metaphysical puzzle to me. I have rarely met a fellow-man on such promising ground—it was so simple and sincere and so true, all that he said. And, true enough, in proportion as he appeared to humble himself was he exalted. I did not know at first but it was the result of a wise policy. It seemed that from such a basis

of truth and frankness as the poor weakheaded pauper
had laid, our intercourse might go forward to something
better than the intercourse of sages.

I had some guests from those not reckoned commonly
among the town's poor, but who should be; who are
among the world's poor, at any rate; guests who appeal,
not to your hospitality, but to your *hospitalality;* who
earnestly wish to be helped, and preface their appeal
with the information that they are resolved, for one
thing, never to help themselves. I require of a visitor
that he be not actually starving, though he may have
the very best appetite in the world, however he got it.
Objects of charity are not guests. Men who did not
know when their visit had terminated, though I went
about my business again, answering them from greater
and greater remoteness. Men of almost every degree of
wit called on me in the migrating season. Some who
had more wits than they knew what to do with; runaway slaves with plantation manners, who listened from
time to time, like the fox in the fable, as if they heard
the hounds a-baying on their track, and looked at me
beseechingly, as much as to say,

"O Christian, will you send me back?"

One real runaway slave, among the rest, whom I helped
to forward toward the North Star. Men of one idea, like
a hen with one chicken, and that a duckling; men of a
thousand ideas, and unkempt heads, like those hens
which are made to take charge of a hundred chickens,
all in pursuit of one bug, a score of them lost in every
morning's dew—and become frizzled and mangy in
consequence—men of ideas instead of legs, a sort of
intellectual centipede that made you crawl all over. One
man proposed a book in which visitors should write

their names, as at the White Mountains; but, alas! I have too good a memory to make that necessary.

I could not but notice some of the peculiarities of my visitors. Girls and boys and young women generally seemed glad to be in the woods. They looked in the pond and at the flowers, and improved their time. Men of business, even farmers, thought only of solitude and employment, and of the great distance at which I dwelt from something or other; and though they said that they loved a ramble in the woods occasionally, it was obvious that they did not. Restless committed men, whose time was all taken up in getting a living or keeping it; ministers who spoke of God as if they enjoyed a monopoly of the subject, who could not bear all kinds of opinions; doctors, lawyers, uneasy housekeepers who pried into my cupboard and bed when I was out—how came Mrs. —— to know that my sheets were not as clean as hers?—young men who had ceased to be young, and had concluded that it was safest to follow the beaten track of the professions—all these generally said that it was not possible to do so much good in my position. Ay! there was the rub. The old and infirm and the timid, of whatever age or sex, thought most of sickness, and sudden accident and death; to them life seemed full of danger—what danger is there if you don't think of any?—and they thought that a prudent man would carefully select the safest position, where Dr. B. might be on hand at a moment's warning. To them the village was literally a *com-munity*, a league for mutual defense, and you would suppose that they would not go a-huckleberrying without a medicine chest. The amount of it is, if a man is alive, there is always *danger* that he may die, though the danger must be allowed to be less in proportion as he is dead-and-alive to begin with. A man sits as many risks as he runs. Finally, there were the self-styled reformers, the greatest bores of all, who thought that I was forever singing,

> This is the house that I built;
> This is the man that lives in the house that I built;

but they did not know that the third line was,

> These are the folks that worry the man
> That lives in the house that I built.

I did not fear the hen-harriers, for I kept no chickens; but I feared the men-harriers rather.

I had more cheering visitors than the last. Children come a-berrying, railroad men taking a Sunday morning walk in clean shirts, fishermen and hunters, poets and philosophers; in short, all honest pilgrims, who came out to the woods for freedom's sake, and really left the village behind, I was ready to greet with, "Welcome, Englishmen! Welcome, Englishmen!" for I had had communication with that race.

THE BEAN FIELD

Meanwhile my beans, the length of whose rows, added together, was seven miles already planted, were impatient to be hoed, for the earliest had grown considerably before the latest were in the ground; indeed they were not easily to be put off. What was the meaning of this so steady and self-respecting, this small Herculean labor, I knew not. I came to love my rows, my beans, though so many more than I wanted. They attached me to the earth, and so I got strength like Antaeus. But why should I raise them? Only Heaven knows. This was my curious labor all summer—to make this portion of the earth's surface, which had yielded only cinquefoil, blackberries, johnswort, and the like, before, sweet wild fruits and pleasant flowers, produce instead this pulse. What shall I learn of beans or beans of me? I cherish them, I hoe them, early and late I have an eye to them; and this is my day's work. It is a fine broad leaf to look on. My auxiliaries are the dews and rains which water this dry soil, and what fertility is in the soil itself, which for the most part is lean and effete. My enemies are worms, cool days, and most of all woodchucks. The last have nibbled for me a quarter of an acre clean. But what right had I to oust johnswort and the rest, and break up their ancient herb garden? Soon, however, the remaining beans will be too tough for them, and go forward to meet new foes.

When I was four years old, as I well remember, I was brought from Boston to this my native town, through these very woods and this field, to the pond. It is one of the oldest scenes stamped on my memory. And now tonight my flute has waked the echoes over that very water. The pines still stand here older than I; or, if some have fallen, I have cooked my supper with their stumps, and a new growth is rising all around, preparing another aspect for new infant eyes. Almost the same johnswort springs from the same perennial root in this pasture, and even I have at length helped to clothe that fabulous landscape of my infant dreams, and one of the results of my presence and influence is seen in these bean leaves, corn blades, and potato vines.

I planted about two acres and a half of upland; and as it was only about fifteen years since the land was cleared, and I myself had got out two or three cords of stumps, I did not give it any manure; but in the course of the summer it appeared by the arrowheads which I turned up in hoeing, that an extinct nation had anciently dwelt here and planted corn and beans ere white men came to clear the land, and so, to some extent, had exhausted the soil for this very crop.

Before yet any woodchuck or squirrel had run across the road, or the sun had got above the shrub-oaks, while all the dew was on, though the farmers warned me against it—I would advise you to do all your work if possible while the dew is on—I began to level the ranks of haughty weeds in my bean field and throw dust upon their heads. Early in the morning I worked barefooted, dabbling like a plastic artist in the dewy and crumbling sand, but later in the day the sun blistered my feet. There the sun lighted me to hoe beans, pacing slowly backward and forward over that yellow gravelly upland, between the long green rows, fifteen rods, the one end terminating in a shrub oak copse where I could rest in the shade, the other in a blackberry field where the green berries deepened their tints by the time I had made another bout. Removing the weeds, putting fresh soil about the bean stems, and encouraging this weed which I had sown, making the yellow soil express its summer thought in bean leaves and blossoms rather than in wormwood and piper and millet grass, making the earth say beans instead of grass—this was my daily work. As I had little aid from horses or cattle, or hired men or boys, or improved implements of husbandry, I was much slower, and became much more intimate with my beans than usual. But labor of the hands, even when pursued to the verge of drudgery, is perhaps never the worst form of idleness. It has a constant and imperishable moral, and to the scholar it yields a classic result. A very *agricola laboriosus* was I to travelers bound westward through Lincoln and Wayland to nobody knows where; they sitting at their ease in gigs, with elbows on knees, and reins loosely hanging in festoons; I the home-staying, laborious native of the soil. But soon my homestead was out of their sight and thought. It was the only open and cultivated field for a great distance on either side of the road, so they made the most of it; and sometimes the man in the field heard more of travelers' gossip and comment than was meant for his ear: "Beans so late! peas so late!"——for I continued to plant when others had begun to hoe——the ministerial husbandman had not suspected it. "Corn, my boy, for fodder; corn for fodder." "Does he *live* there?" asks the black bonnet of the gray coat; and the hard-featured farmer reins up his grateful dobbin to inquire what you are doing where he sees no manure in the furrow, and recommends a little chip dirt, or any little waste stuff, or it may be ashes or plaster. But here were two acres and a half of furrows, and only a hoe for cart and two hands to draw it——there being an aversion to other carts and horses—— and chip dirt far away. Fellow-travelers as they rattled by compared it aloud with the fields which they had passed, so that I came to know how I stood in the agricultural world. This was one field not in Mr. Coleman's report. And, by the way, who estimates the value of the crop which Nature yields in the still wilder fields unimproved by man? The crop of *English* hay is carefully weighed, the moisture calculated, the silicates and the potash; but in all dells and pond holes in the woods and pastures and swamps grows a rich and various crop only unreaped by man. Mine was, as it were, the connecting link between wild and cultivated fields; as some states are civilized, and others half-civilized, and others savage or barbarous, so my field was, though not in a bad sense, a half-cultivated field. They were beans cheerfully returning to their wild and primitive state that I cultivated, and my hoe played the *Ranz des Vaches* for them.

Near at hand, upon the topmost spray of a birch,

sings the brown-thrasher—or red mavis, as some love to call him—all the morning, glad of your society, that would find out another farmer's field if yours were not here. While you are planting the seed, he cries, "Drop it, drop it—cover it up, cover it up—pull it up, pull it up, pull it up." But this was not corn, and so it was safe from such enemies as he. You may wonder what his rigmarole, his amateur Paganini performances on one string or on twenty, have to do with your planting, and yet prefer it to leached ashes or plaster. It was a cheap sort of top dressing in which I had entire faith.

As I drew a still fresher soil about the rows with my hoe, I disturbed the ashes of unchronicled nations who in primeval years lived under these heavens, and their small implements of war and hunting were brought to the light of this modern day. They lay mingled with other natural stones, some of which bore the marks of having been burned by Indian fires, and some by the sun, and also bits of pottery and glass brought hither by the recent cultivators of the soil. When my hoe tinkled against the stones, that music echoed to the woods and the sky, and was an accompaniment to my labor which yielded an instant and immeasurable crop. It was no longer beans that I hoed, nor I that hoed beans; and I remembered with as much pity as pride, if I remembered at all, my acquaintances who had gone to the city to attend the oratorios. The night-hawk circled overhead in the sunny afternoon—for I sometimes made a day of it—like a mote in the eye, or in heaven's eye, falling from time to time with a swoop and a sound as if the heavens were rent, torn at last to very rags and tatters, and yet a seamless cope remained; small imps that fill the air and lay their eggs on the ground on bare sand or rocks on the tops of hills, where few have found them; graceful and slender like ripples caught up from the pond, as leaves are raised by the wind to float in the heavens; such kindredship is in Nature. The hawk is aerial brother of the wave which he sails over and surveys, those his perfect air-inflated wings answering to the elemental unfledged pinions of the sea. Or sometimes I watched a pair of hen-hawks circling high in the sky, alternately soaring and descending, approaching and leaving one another, as if they were the embodiment of my own thoughts. Or I was attracted by the passage of wild pigeons from this wood to that, with a slight quivering winnowing sound and carrier haste; or from under a rotten stump my hoe turned up a sluggish, portentous, and outlandish spotted salamander, a trace of Egypt and the Nile, yet our contemporary. When I paused to lean on my hoe, these sounds and sights I heard and saw anywhere in the row, a part of the inexhaustible entertainment which the country offers.

On gala days the town fires its great guns, which echo like popguns to these woods, and some waifs of martial music occasionally penetrate thus far. To me, away there in my bean field at the other end of the town, the big guns sounded as if a puff ball had burst; and when there was a military turnout of which I was ignorant, I have sometimes had a vague sense all the day of some sort of itching and disease in the horizon, as if some eruption would break out there soon, either scarlatina or canker-rash, until at length some more favorable puff of wind, making haste over the fields and up the Wayland road, brought me information of the "trainers." It seemed by the distant hum as if somebody's bees had swarmed, and that the neighbors, according to Virgil's advice, by a faint *tintinnabulum* upon the most sonorous of their domestic utensils, were endeavoring to call them down into the hive again. And when the sound died quite away, and the hum had ceased, and the most favorable breezes told no tale, I knew that they had got the last drone of them all safely into the Middlesex hive, and that now their minds were bent on the honey with which it was smeared.

I felt proud to know that the liberties of Massachusetts and of our fatherland were in such safe keeping; and as I turned to my hoeing again I was filled with an inexpressible confidence, and pursued my labor cheerfully with a calm trust in the future.

When there were several bands of musicians, it sounded as if all the village was a vast bellows, and all the buildings expanded and collapsed alternately with a din. But sometimes it was a really noble and inspiring strain that reached these woods, and the trumpet that sings of fame, and I felt as if I could spit a Mexican with a good relish—for why should we always stand for trifles?—and looked round for a woodchuck or a skunk to exercise my chivalry upon. These martial strains seemed as far away as Palestine, and reminded me of a march of crusaders in the horizon, with a slight tantivy and tremulous motion of the elm-tree tops which overhang the village. This was one of the *great* days; though the sky had from my clearing only the same everlastingly great look that it wears daily, and I saw no difference in it.

It was a singular experience that long acquaintance which I cultivated with beans, what with planting, and hoeing, and harvesting, and threshing, and picking over and selling them—the last was the hardest of all—I might add eating, for I did taste. I was determined to know beans. When they were growing, I used to hoe from five o'clock in the morning till noon, and commonly spent the rest of the day about other affairs. Consider the intimate and curious acquaintance one makes with various kinds of weeds—it will bear some iteration in the account, for there was no little iteration in the labor—disturbing their delicate organizations so ruthlessly, and making such invidious distinctions with his hoe, leveling whole ranks of one species, and sedulously cultivating another. That's Roman wormwood, that's pigweed, that's sorrel, that's piper-grass—have at him, chop him up, turn his roots upward to the sun, don't let him have a fiber in the shade, if you do he'll turn himself t'other side up and be as green as a leek in two days. A long war, not with cranes, but with weeds, those Trojans who had sun and rain and dews on their side. Daily the beans saw me come to their rescue armed with a hoe, and thin the ranks of their enemies, filling up the trenches with weedy dead. Many a lusty crest-waving Hector, that towered a whole foot above his crowding comrades, fell before my weapon and rolled in the dust.

Those summer days which some of my contemporaries devoted to the fine arts in Boston or Rome, and others to contemplation in India, and others to trade in London or New York, I thus, with the other farmers of New England, devoted to husbandry. Not that I wanted beans to eat, for I am by nature a Pythagorean, so far as beans are concerned, whether they mean porridge or voting, and exchanged them for rice; but, perchance, as some must work in fields if only for the sake of tropes and expression, to serve a parable-maker one day. It was on the whole a rare amusement, which, continued too long, might have become a dissipation. Though I gave them no manure, and did not hoe them all once, I hoed them unusually well as far as I went, and was paid for it in the end, "there being in truth," as Evelyn says, "no compost or laetation whatsoever comparable to this continual motion, repastination, and turning of the mould with the spade." "The earth," he adds elsewhere, "especially if fresh, has a certain magnetism in it, by which it attracts the salt, power, or virtue (call it either) which gives it life, and is the logic of all the labor and stir we keep about it, to sustain us; all dungings and other sordid temperings being but the vicars succedaneous to this improvement." Moreover, this being one of those "worn-out and exhausted lay fields which enjoy their sabbath," had perchance, as Sir Kenelm Digby thinks likely, attracted "vital spirits" from the air. I harvested twelve bushels of beans.

But to be more particular, for it is complained that Mr. Coleman has reported chiefly the expensive experiments of gentlemen farmers, my outgoes were—

For a hoe	$0.54
Ploughing, harrowing, and furrowing .	7.50 Too much.
Beans for seed	3.12½
Potatoes "	1.33
Peas "	0.40
Turnip seed	0.06
White line for crow fence	0.02
Horse cultivator and boy three hours .	1.00
Horse and cart to get crop	0.75
In all	$14.72½

My income was (*patrem familias vendacem, non emacem esse oportet*) from

Nine bushels and twelve quarts of beans sold .	$16.94
Five " large potatoes	2.50
Nine " small	2.25
Grass	1.00
Stalks	0.75
In all	$23.44
Leaving a pecuniary profit, as I have elsewhere said, of	$ 8.71½

This is the result of my experience in raising beans. Plant the common small white bush bean about the first of June, in rows three feet by eighteen inches apart,

being careful to select fresh round and unmixed seed.
First look out for worms, and supply vacancies by planting anew. Then look out for woodchucks, if it is an exposed place, for they will nibble off the earliest tender
leaves almost clean as they go; and again, when the
young tendrils make their appearance, they have notice
of it, and will shear them off with both buds and young
pods, sitting erect like a squirrel. But above all harvest
as early as possible, if you would escape frosts and have
a fair and salable crop; you may save much loss by this
means.

This further experience also I gained. I said to myself,
I will not plant beans and corn with so much industry
another summer, but such seeds, if the seed is not lost,
as sincerity, truth, simplicity, faith, innocence, and the
like, and see if they will not grow in this soil, even with
less toil and manurance, and sustain me, for surely it has
not been exhausted for these crops. Alas! I said this to
myself; but now another summer is gone, and another,
and another, and I am obliged to say to you, Reader,
that the seeds which I planted, if indeed they *were* the
seeds of those virtues, were wormeaten or had lost their
vitality, and so did not come up. Commonly men will
only be brave as their fathers were brave, or timid. This
generation is very sure to plant corn and beans each
new year precisely as the Indians did centuries ago and
taught the first settlers to do, as if there were a fate in it.
I saw an old man the other day, to my astonishment,
making the holes with a hoe for the seventieth time at
least, and not for himself to lie down in! But why should
not the New Englander try new adventures, and not lay
so much stress on his grain, his potato and grass crop,
and his orchards—raise other crops than these? Why
concern ourselves so much about our beans for seed,
and not be concerned at all about a new generation of

men? We should really be fed and cheered if when we met a man we were sure to see that some of the qualities which I have named, which we all prize more than those other productions, but which are for the most part broadcast and floating in the air, had taken root and grown in him. Here comes such a subtle and ineffable quality, for instance, as truth or justice, though the slightest amount or new variety of it, along the road. Our ambassadors should be instructed to send home such seeds as these, and Congress help to distribute them over all the land. We should never stand upon ceremony with sincerity. We should never cheat and insult and banish one another by our meanness, if there were present the kernel of worth and friendliness. We should not meet thus in haste. Most men I do not meet at all, for they seem not to have time; they are busy about their beans. We would not deal with a man thus plodding ever, leaning on a hoe or a spade as a staff between his work, not as a mushroom, but partially risen out of the earth, something more than erect, like swallows alighted and walking on the ground:

> "And as he spake, his wings would now and then
> Spread, as he meant to fly, then close again—"

so that we should suspect that we might be conversing with an angel. Bread may not always nourish us; but it always does us good, it even takes stiffness out of our joints, and makes us supple and buoyant, when we knew not what ailed us, to recognize any generosity in man or Nature, to share any unmixed and heroic joy.

Ancient poetry and mythology suggest, at least, that husbandry was once a sacred art; but it is pursued with irreverent haste and heedlessness by us, our object being to have large farms and large crops merely. We have no festival, nor procession, nor ceremony, not excepting our cattle-shows and so called Thanksgiving, by which the farmer expresses a sense of the sacredness of his calling, or is reminded of its sacred origin. It is the premium and the feast which tempt him. He sacrifices not to Ceres and the Terrestrial Jove, but to the infernal Plutus rather. By avarice and selfishness, and a groveling habit, from which none of us is free, of regarding the soil as property, or the means of acquiring property chiefly, the landscape is deformed, husbandry is degraded with us, and the farmer leads the meanest of lives. He knows Nature but as a robber. Cato says that the profits of agriculture are particularly pious or just (*maximeque pius quoestus*), and according to Varro the old Romans "called the same earth Mother and Ceres, and thought that they who cultivated it led a pious and useful life, and that they alone were left of the race of King Saturn."

We are wont to forget that the sun looks on our cultivated fields and on the prairies and forests without distinction. They all reflect and absorb his rays alike, and the former make but a small part of the glorious picture which he beholds in his daily course. In his view the earth is all equally cultivated like a garden. Therefore we should receive the benefit of his light and heat with a corresponding trust and magnanimity. What though I value the seed of these beans, and harvest that in the fall of the year? This broad field which I have looked at so long looks not to me as the principal cultivator, but away from me to influences more genial to it, which water and make it green. These beans have results which are not harvested by me. Do they not grow for woodchucks partly? The ear of wheat (in Latin *spica*, obsoletely *speca*, from *spe*, hope) should not be the only hope of the husbandman; its kernel or grain (*granum*, from *gerendo*, bearing) is not all that its bears. How,

then, can our harvest fail? Shall I not rejoice also at the
abundance of the weeds whose seeds are the granary of
the birds? It matters little comparatively whether the
fields fill the farmer's barns. The true husbandman will
cease from anxiety, as the squirrels manifest no concern
whether the woods will bear chestnuts this year or not,
and finish his labor with every day, relinquishing all
claim to the produce of his fields, and sacrificing in his
mind not only his first but his last fruits also.

THE VILLAGE

After hoeing, or perhaps reading and writing, in the
forenoon, I usually bathed again in the pond, swimming
across one of its coves for a stint, and washed the dust of
labor from my person, or smoothed out the last wrinkle
which study had made, and for the afternoon was absolutely free. Every day or two I strolled to the village to
hear some of the gossip which is incessantly going on
there, circulating either from mouth to mouth, or from
newspaper to newspaper, and which, taken in homeo-
pathic doses, was really as refreshing in its way as the
rustle of leaves and the peeping of frogs. As I walked in
the woods to see the birds and squirrels, so I walked in
the village to see the men and boys; instead of the wind
among the pines I heard the carts rattle. In one direction from my house there was a colony of muskrats in
the river meadows; under the grove of elms and buttonwoods in the other horizon was a village of busy men,
as curious to me as if they had been prairie dogs, each
sitting at the mouth of its burrow, or running over to a
neighbor's to gossip. I went there frequently to observe
their habits. The village appeared to me a great news
room; and on one side, to support it, as once at Redding
& Company's on State Street, they kept nuts and raisins,

or salt and meal and other groceries. Some have such a vast appetite for the former commodity, that is, the news, and such sound digestive organs, that they can sit forever in public avenues without stirring, and let it simmer and whisper through them like the Etesian winds, or as if inhaling ether, it only producing numbness and insensibility to pain—otherwise it would often be painful to hear—without affecting the consciousness. I hardly ever failed, when I rambled through the village, to see a row of such worthies, either sitting on a ladder sunning themselves, with their bodies inclined forward and their eyes glancing along the line this way and that, from time to time, with a voluptuous expression, or else leaning against a barn with their hands in their pockets, like caryatids, as if to prop it up. They, being commonly out of doors, heard whatever was in the wind. These are the coarsest mills, in which all gossip is first rudely digested or cracked up before it is emptied into finer and more delicate hoppers within doors. I observed that the vitals of the village were the grocery, the barroom, the post-office, and the bank; and, as a necessary part of the machinery, they kept a bell, a big gun, and a fire engine, at convenient places; and the houses were so arranged as to make the most of mankind, in lanes and fronting one another, so that every traveler had to run the gauntlet, and every man, woman, and child might get a lick at him. Of course, those who were stationed nearest to the head of the line, where they could most see and be seen, and have the first blow at him, paid the highest prices for their places; and the few straggling inhabitants in the outskirts, where long gaps in the line began to occur, and the traveler could get over walls or turn aside into cowpaths, and so escape, paid a very slight ground or window tax. Signs were hung out on all sides to allure him; some to catch him by the appetite, as the

tavern and victualing cellar; some by the fancy, as the
dry goods store and the jeweler's; and others by the hair
or the feet or the skirts, as the barber, the shoemaker, or
the tailor. Besides, there was a still more terrible standing invitation to call at every one of these houses, and
company expected about these times. For the most part
I escaped wonderfully from these dangers, either by
proceeding at once boldly and without deliberation to
the goal, as is recommended to those who run the gauntlet, or by keeping my thoughts on high things, like Orpheus, who, "loudly singing the praises of the gods to
his lyre, drowned the voices of the Sirens, and kept out
of danger." Sometimes I bolted suddenly, and nobody
could tell my whereabouts, for I did not stand much
about gracefulness, and never hesitated at a gap in a
fence. I was even accustomed to make an irruption into
some houses, where I was well entertained, and after
learning the kernels and very last sieveful of news,
what had subsided, the prospects of war and peace, and
whether the world was likely to hold together much
longer, I was let out through the rear avenues, and so
escaped to the woods again.

It was very pleasant, when I stayed late in town, to
launch myself into the night, especially if it was dark
and tempestuous, and set sail from some bright village
parlor or lecture room, with a bag of rye or Indian meal
upon my shoulder, for my snug harbor in the woods,
having made all tight without and withdrawn under
hatches with a merry crew of thoughts, leaving only my
outer man at the helm, or even tying up the helm when
it was plain sailing. I had many a genial thought by the
cabin fire "as I sailed." I was never cast away nor dis-
tressed in any weather, though I encountered some severe storms. It is darker in the woods, even in common
nights, than most suppose. I frequently had to look up

at the opening between the trees above the path in order to learn my route, and, where there was no cart-path, to feel with my feet the faint track which I had worn, or steer by the known relation of particular trees which I felt with my hands, passing between two pines for instance, not more than eighteen inches apart, in the midst of the woods, invariably in the darkest night. Sometimes, after coming home thus late in a dark and muggy night, when my feet felt the path which my eyes could not see, dreaming and absent-minded all the way, until I was aroused by having to raise my hand to lift the latch, I have not been able to recall a single step of my walk, and I have thought that perhaps my body would find its way home if its master should forsake it, as the hand finds its way to the mouth without assistance. Several times, when a visitor chanced to stay into evening, and it proved a dark night, I was obliged to conduct him to the cart-path in the rear of the house, and then point out to him the direction he was to pursue, and in keeping which he was to be guided rather by his feet than his eyes. One very dark night I directed thus on their way two young men who had been fishing in the pond. They lived about a mile off through the woods, and were quite used to the route. A day or two after one of them told me that they wandered about the greater part of the night, close by their own premises, and did not get home till toward morning, by which time, as there had been several heavy showers in the meanwhile, and the leaves were very wet, they were drenched to their skins. I have heard of many going astray even in the village streets, when the darkness was so thick that you could cut it with a knife, as the saying is. Some who live in the outskirts, having come to town a-shopping in their wagons, have been obliged to put up for the night; and gentlemen and ladies making a call have gone half a mile out of their way, feeling the sidewalk only with their feet, and not knowing when they turned. It is a surprising and memorable, as well as valuable experience, to be lost in the woods any time. Often in a snowstorm, even by day, one will come out upon a well-known road and yet find it impossible to tell which way leads to the village. Though he knows that he has traveled it a thousand times, he cannot recognize a feature in it, but it is as strange to him as if it were a road in Siberia. By night, of course, the perplexity is infinitely greater. In our most trivial walks, we are constantly, though unconsciously, steering like pilots by certain well-known beacons and headlands, and if we go beyond our usual course we still carry in our minds the bearing of some neighboring cape; and not till we are completely lost, or turned round—for a man needs only to be turned round once with his eyes shut in this world to be lost—do we appreciate the vastness and strangeness of Nature. Every man has to learn the points of compass again as often as he awakes, whether from sleep or any abstraction. Not till we are lost, in other words, not till we have lost the world, do we begin to find ourselves, and realize where we are and the infinite extent of our relations.

One afternoon, near the end of the first summer, when I went to the village to get a shoe from the cobbler's, I was seized and put into jail, because, as I have elsewhere related, I did not pay a tax to, or recognize the authority of, the state which buys and sells men, women, and children, like cattle at the door of its senate-house. I had gone down to the woods for other purposes. But, wherever a man goes, men will pursue and paw him with their dirty institutions, and, if they can, constrain him to belong to their desperate odd-fellow society. It is true, I might have resisted forcibly with more or less

effect, might have run "amok" against society; but I
preferred that society should run "amok" against me, it
being the desperate party. However, I was released the
next day, obtained my mended shoe, and returned to
the woods in season to get my dinner of huckleberries
on Fair Haven Hill. I was never molested by any person
but those who represented the state. I had no lock nor
bolt but for the desk which held my papers, not even a
nail to put over my latch or windows. I never fastened
my door night or day, though I was to be absent several
days; not even when the next fall I spent a fortnight in
the woods of Maine. And yet my house was more respected than if it had been surrounded by a file of soldiers. The tired rambler could rest and warm himself
by my fire, the literary amuse himself with the few books
on my table, or the curious, by opening my closet door,
see what was left of my dinner, and what prospect I had
of a supper. Yet, though many people of every class
came this way to the pond, I suffered no serious inconvenience from these sources, and I never missed anything but one small book, a volume of Homer, which
perhaps was improperly gilded, and this I trust a soldier
of our camp has found by this time. I am convinced,
that if all men were to live as simply as I then did, thiev-
ing and robbery would be unknown. These take place
only in communities where some have got more than
is sufficient while others have not enough. The Pope's
Homers would soon get properly distributed—

> "Nec bella fuerunt,
> Faginus astabat dum scyphus ante dapes."
> "Nor wars did men molest,
> When only beechen bowls were in request."

"You who govern public affairs, what need have you to
employ punishments? Love virtue, and the people will

be virtuous. The virtues of a superior man are like the wind; the virtues of a common man are like the grass; the grass, when the wind passes over it, bends."

THE PONDS

Sometimes, having had a surfeit of human society and gossip, and worn out all my village friends, I rambled still farther westward than I habitually dwell, into yet more unfrequented parts of the town, "to fresh woods and pastures new," or, while the sun was setting, made my supper of huckleberries and blueberries on Fair Haven Hill, and laid up a store for several days. The fruits do not yield their true flavor to the purchaser of them, nor to him who raises them for the market. There is but one way to obtain it, yet few take that way. If you would know the flavor of huckleberries, ask the cowboy or the partridge. It is a vulgar error to suppose that you have tasted huckleberries who never plucked them. A huckleberry never reaches Boston; they have not been known there since they grew on her three hills. The ambrosial and essential part of the fruit is lost with the bloom which is rubbed off in the market cart, and they become mere provender. As long as Eternal Justice reigns, not one innocent huckleberry can be transported thither from the country's hills.

Occasionally, after my hoeing was done for the day, I joined some impatient companion who had been fishing on the pond since morning, as silent and motionless as a duck or a floating leaf, and, after practicing various kinds of philosophy, had concluded commonly, by the time I arrived, that he belonged to the ancient sect of Cenobites. There was one older man, an excellent fisher and skilled in all kinds of woodcraft, who was pleased to look upon my house as a building erected for the convenience of fishermen; and I was equally pleased when he sat in my doorway to arrange his lines. Once in a while we sat together on the pond, he at one end of the boat, and I at the other; but not many words passed between us, for he had grown deaf in his later years, but he occasionally hummed a psalm, which harmonized well enough with my philosophy. Our intercourse was thus altogether one of unbroken harmony, far more pleasing to remember than if it had been carried on by speech. When, as was commonly the case, I had none to commune with, I used to raise the echoes by striking with a paddle on the side of my boat, filling the surrounding woods with circling and dilating sound, stirring them up as the keeper of a menagerie his wild beasts, until I elicited a growl from every wooded vale and hillside.

In warm evenings I frequently sat in the boat playing the flute, and saw the perch, which I seem to have charmed, hovering around me, and the moon traveling over the ribbed bottom, which was strewed with the wrecks of the forest. Formerly I had come to this pond adventurously, from time to time, in dark summer nights, with a companion, and making a fire close to the water's edge, which we thought attracted the fishes, we caught pouts with a bunch of worms strung on a thread, and when we had done, far in the night, threw the burning brands high into the air like skyrockets, which, coming down into the pond, were quenched with a loud hissing, and we were suddenly groping in total darkness. Through this, whistling a tune, we took our way to the haunts of men again. But now I had made my home by the shore.

Sometimes, after staying in a village parlor till the family had all retired, I have returned to the woods, and, partly with a view to the next day's dinner, spent the hours of midnight fishing from a boat by moonlight, serenaded by owls and foxes, and hearing, from time to time, the creaking note of some unknown bird close at hand. These experiences were very memorable and valuable to me, anchored in forty feet of water, and twenty or thirty rods from the shore, surrounded sometimes by thousands of small perch and shiners, dimpling the surface with their tails in the moonlight, and communicating by a long flaxen line with mysterious nocturnal fishes which had their dwelling forty feet below, or sometimes dragging sixty feet of line about the pond as I drifted in the gentle night breeze, now and then feeling a slight vibration along it, indicative of some life prowling about its extremity, of dull uncertain blundering purpose there, and slow to make up its mind. At length you slowly raise, pulling hand over hand, some horned pout squeaking and squirming to the upper air. It was very queer, especially in dark nights, when your thoughts had wandered to vast and cosmogonal themes in other spheres, to feel this faint jerk, which came to interrupt your dreams and link you to Nature again. It seemed as if I might next cast my line upward into the air, as well as downward into this element, which was scarcely more dense. Thus I caught two fishes as it were with one hook.

The scenery of Walden is on a humble scale, and, though very beautiful, does not approach to grandeur, nor can it much concern one who has not long frequented it or lived by its shore; yet this pond is so remarkable for its depth and purity as to merit a particular description. It is a clear and deep green well, half a mile long and a mile and three quarters in circumference, and contains about sixty-one and a half acres; a perennial spring in the midst of pine and oak woods, without

any visible inlet or outlet except by the clouds and
evaporation. The surrounding hills rise abruptly from
the water to the height of forty to eighty feet, though on
the southeast and east they attain to about one hundred
and one hundred and fifty feet respectively, within a
quarter and a third of a mile. They are exclusively woodland. All our Concord waters have two colors at least; one
when viewed at a distance, and another, more proper,
close at hand. The first depends more on the light, and
follows the sky. In clear weather, in summer, they appear blue at a little distance, especially if agitated, and at
a great distance all appear alike. In stormy weather they
are sometimes of a dark slate color. The sea, however,
is said to be blue one day and green another without
any perceptible change in the atmosphere. I have seen
our river, when, the landscape being covered with snow,
both water and ice were almost as green as grass. Some
consider blue "to be the color of pure water, whether
liquid or solid." But, looking directly down into our
waters from a boat, they are seen to be of very different
colors. Walden is blue at one time and green at another,
even from the same point of view. Lying between the
earth and the heavens, it partakes of the color of both.
Viewed from a hilltop it reflects the color of the sky; but
near at hand it is of a yellowish tint next the shore
where you can see the sand, then a light green, which
gradually deepens to a uniform dark green in the body
of the pond. In some lights, viewed even from a hilltop,
it is of a vivid green next the shore. Some have referred
this to the reflection of the verdure; but it is equally
green there against the railroad sand-bank, and in the
spring, before the leaves are expanded, and it may be
simply the result of the prevailing blue mixed with the
yellow of the sand. Such is the color of its iris. This is
that portion, also, where in the spring, the ice being

warmed by the heat of the sun reflected from the bottom, and also transmitted through the earth, melts first and forms a narrow canal about the still frozen middle. Like the rest of our waters, when much agitated, in clear weather, so that the surface of the waves may reflect the sky at the right angle, or because there is more light mixed with it, it appears at a little distance of a darker blue than the sky itself; and at such a time, being on its surface, and looking with divided vision, so as to see the reflection, I have discerned a matchless and indescribable light blue, such as watered or changeable silks and sword blades suggest, more cerulean than the sky itself, alternating with the original dark green on the opposite sides of the waves, which last appeared but muddy in comparison. It is a vitreous greenish blue, as I remember it, like those patches of the winter sky seen through cloud vistas in the west before sundown. Yet a single glass of its water held up to the light is as colorless as an equal quantity of air. It is well known that a large plate of glass will have a green tint, owing, as the makers say, to its "body," but a small piece of the same will be colorless. How large a body of Walden water would be required to reflect a green tint, I have never proved. The water of our river is black or a very dark brown to one looking directly down on it, and, like that of most ponds, imparts to the body of one bathing in it a yellowish tinge; but this water is of such crystalline purity that the body of the bather appears of an alabaster whiteness, still more unnatural, which, as the limbs are magnified and distorted withal, produces a monstrous effect, making fit studies for a Michaelangelo.

The water is so transparent that the bottom can easily be discerned at the depth of twenty-five or thirty feet. Paddling over it, you may see many feet beneath the surface the schools of perch and shiners, perhaps only an inch long, yet the former easily distinguished by their transverse bars, and you think that they must be ascetic fish that find a subsistence there. Once, in the winter, many years ago, when I had been cutting holes through the ice in order to catch pickerel, as I stepped ashore I tossed my axe back onto the ice, but, as if some evil genius had directed it, it slid four or five rods directly into one of the holes, where the water was twenty-five feet deep. Out of curiosity, I lay down on the ice and looked through the hole, until I saw the axe a little on one side, standing on its head, with its helve erect and gently swaying to and fro with the pulse of the pond; and there it might have stood erect and swaying till in the course of time the handle rotted off, if I had not disturbed it. Making another hole directly over it with an ice chisel which I had, and cutting down the longest birch which I could find in the neighborhood with my knife, I made a slip noose, which I attached to its end, and, letting it down carefully, passed it over the knob of the handle, and drew it by a line along the birch, and so pulled the axe out again.

The shore is composed of a belt of smooth rounded white stones like paving-stones, excepting one or two short sand beaches, and is so steep that in many places a single leap will carry you into water over your head; and were it not for its remarkable transparency, that would be the last to be seen of its bottom till it rose on the opposite side. Some think it is bottomless. It is nowhere muddy, and a casual observer would say that there were no weeds at all in it; and of noticeable plants, except in the little meadows recently overflowed, which do not properly belong to it, a closer scrutiny does not detect a flag nor a bulrush, nor even a lily, yellow or white, but only a few small heartleaves and potamogetons, and perhaps a water target or two; all which however a bather might not perceive; and these plants are clean and bright like the element they grow in. The stones extend a rod or two into the water, and then the bottom is pure sand, except in the deepest parts, where there is usually a little sediment, probably from the decay of the leaves which have been wafted onto it so many successive falls, and a bright green weed is brought up on anchors even in midwinter.

We have one other pond just like this, White Pond, in Nine Acre Corner, about two and a half miles westerly; but, though I am acquainted with most of the ponds within a dozen miles of this center, I do not know a third of this pure and well-like character. Successive nations perchance have drank at, admired, and fathomed it, and passed away, and still its water is green and pellucid as ever. Not an intermitting spring! Perhaps on that spring morning when Adam and Eve were driven out of Eden Walden Pond was already in existence, and even then breaking up in a gentle spring rain accompanied with mist and a southerly wind, and covered with myriads of ducks and geese, which had not heard of the fall, when still such pure lakes sufficed them. Even then it had commenced to rise and fall, and had clarified its waters and colored them of the hue they now wear, and obtained a patent of Heaven to be the only Walden Pond in the world and distiller of celestial dews. Who knows in how many unremembered nations' literatures this has been the Castalian Fountain? or what nymphs presided over it in the Golden Age? It is a gem of the first water which Concord wears in her coronet.

Yet perchance the first who came to this well have left some trace of their footsteps. I have been surprised to detect encircling the pond, even where a thick wood has just been cut down on the shore, a narrow shelflike path in the steep hillside, alternately rising and falling, approaching and receding from the water's edge, as old probably as the race of man here, worn by the feet of aboriginal hunters, and still from time to time unwittingly trodden by the present occupants of the land. This is particularly distinct to one standing on the middle of the pond in winter, just after a light snow has fallen, appearing as a clear undulating white line, unobscured by weeds and twigs, and very obvious a quarter of a mile off in many places where in summer it is hardly distinguishable close at hand. The snow reprints it, as it were, in clear white type alto-relievo. The ornamented grounds of villas which will one day be built here may still preserve some trace of this.

The pond rises and falls, but whether regularly or not, and within what period, nobody knows, though, as usual, many pretend to know. It is commonly higher in the winter and lower in the summer, though not corresponding to the general wet and dryness. I can remember when it was a foot or two lower, and also when it was at least five feet higher, than when I lived by it. There is a narrow sandbar running into it, with very deep water on one side, on which I helped boil a kettle of chowder, some six rods from the main shore, about the year 1824, which it has not been possible to do for twenty-five years; and, on the other hand, my friends used to listen with incredulity when I told them, that a few years later I was accustomed to fish from a boat in a secluded cove in the woods, fifteen rods from the only shore they knew, which place was long since converted into a meadow. But the pond has risen steadily for two years, and now, in the summer of '52, is just five feet higher than when I lived there, or as high as it was thirty years ago, and fishing goes on again in the meadow. This makes a difference of level, at the outside, of six or seven feet; and yet the water shed by the surrounding hills is insignificant in amount, and this overflow must be referred to causes which affect the deep springs. This same summer the pond has begun to fall again. It is remarkable that this fluctuation, whether periodical or not, appears thus to require many years for its accomplishment. I have observed one rise and a part of two falls, and I expect that a dozen or fifteen years hence the water will again be as low as I have ever known it. Flints' Pond, a mile eastward, allowing for the disturbance occasioned by its inlets and outlets, and the smaller intermediate ponds also, sympathize with Walden, and recently attained their greatest height at the same time with the latter. The same is true, as far as my observation goes, of White Pond.

This rise and fall of Walden at long intervals serves this use at least: the water standing at this great height for a year or more, though it makes it difficult to walk round it, kills the shrubs and trees which have sprung up about its edge since the last rise—pitch pines, birches, alders, aspens, and others—and, falling again, leaves an unobstructed shore; for, unlike many ponds and all waters which are subject to a daily tide, its shore is cleanest when the water is lowest. On the side of the pond next my house a row of pitch pines, fifteen feet high, has been killed and tipped over as if by a lever, and thus a stop put to their encroachments; and their size indicates how many years have elapsed since the last rise to this height. By this fluctuation the pond asserts its title to a shore, and thus the *shore* is *shorn,* and the trees cannot hold it by right of possession. These are the lips of the lake on which no beard grows. It licks its chaps from time to time. When the water is at its height, the alders, willows, and maples send forth a mass of fibrous red roots several feet long from all sides of their

stems in the water, and to the height of three or four
feet from the ground, in the effort to maintain themselves; and I have known the high-blueberry bushes
about the shore, which commonly produce no fruit, bear
an abundant crop under these circumstances.

Some have been puzzled to tell how the shore became so regularly paved. My townsmen have all heard
the tradition, the oldest people tell me that they heard it
in their youth, that anciently the Indians were holding
a powwow upon a hill here, which rose as high into the
heavens as the pond now sinks deep into the earth, and
they used much profanity, as the story goes, though this
vice is one of which the Indians were never guilty, and
while they were thus engaged the hill shook and suddenly sank, and only one old squaw, named Walden,
escaped, and from her the pond was named. It has been
conjectured that when the hill shook these stones rolled
down its side and became the present shore. It is very
certain, at any rate, that once there was no pond here,
and now there is one; and this Indian fable does not
in any respect conflict with the account of that ancient
settler whom I have mentioned, who remembers so well
when he first came here with his divining rod, saw a
thin vapor rising from the sward, and the hazel pointed
steadily downward, and he concluded to dig a well
here. As for the stones, many still think that they are
hardly to be accounted for by the action of the waves
on these hills; but I observe that the surrounding hills
are remarkably full of the same kind of stones, so that
they have been obliged to pile them up in walls on both
sides of the railroad cut nearest the pond; and, moreover, there are most stones where the shore is most
abrupt; so that, unfortunately, it is no longer a mystery
to me. I detect the paver. If the name was not derived

from that of some English locality—Saffron Walden, for instance—one might suppose that it was called originally *Walled-in* Pond.

The pond was my well ready dug. For four months in the year its water is as cold as it is pure at all times; and I think that it is then as good as any, if not the best, in the town. In the winter, all water which is exposed to the air is colder than springs and wells which are protected from it. The temperature of the pond water which had stood in the room where I sat from five o'clock in the afternoon till noon the next day, the sixth of March, 1846, the thermometer having been up to 65° or 70° some of the time, owing partly to the sun on the roof, was 42°, or one degree colder than the water of one of the coldest wells in the village just drawn. The temperature of the Boiling Spring the same day was 45°, or the warmest of any water tried, though it is the coldest that I know of in summer, when, besides, shallow and stagnant surface water is not mingled with it. Moreover, in summer, Walden never becomes so warm as most water which is exposed to the sun, on account of its depth. In the warmest weather I usually placed a pailful in my cellar, where it became cool in the night, and remained so during the day; though I also resorted to a spring in the neighborhood. It was as good when a week old as the day it was dipped, and had no taste of the pump. Whoever camps for a week in summer by the shore of a pond, needs only bury a pail of water a few feet deep in the shade of his camp to be independent of the luxury of ice.

There have been caught in Walden pickerel, one weighing seven pounds—to say nothing of another which carried off a reel with great velocity, which the fisherman safely set down at eight pounds because he did not see him—perch and pouts, some of each weighing over two pounds, shiners, chivins or roach (*Leuciscus pulchellus*), a very few breams, and a couple of eels, one weighing four pounds—I am thus particular because the weight of a fish is commonly its only title to fame, and these are the only eels I have heard of here—also, I have a faint recollection of a little fish some five inches long, with silvery sides and a greenish back, somewhat dace-like in its character, which I mention here chiefly to link my facts to fable. Nevertheless, this pond is not very fertile in fish. Its pickerel, though not abundant, are its chief boast. I have seen at one time lying on the ice pickerel of at least three different kinds: a long and shallow one, steel-colored, most like those caught in the river; a bright golden kind, with greenish reflections and remarkably deep, which is the most common here; and another, golden-colored, and shaped like the last, but peppered on the sides with small dark brown or black spots, intermixed with a few faint blood-red ones, very much like a trout. The specific name *reticulatus* would not apply to this; it should be *guttatus* rather. These are all very firm fish, and weigh more than their size promises. The shiners, pouts, and perch also, and indeed all the fishes which inhabit this pond, are much cleaner, handsomer, and firmer fleshed than those in the river and most other ponds, as the water is purer, and they can easily be distinguished from them. Probably many ichthyologists would make new varieties of some of them. There are also a clean race of frogs and tortoises, and a few muscles in it; muskrats and minks leave their traces about it, and occasionally a traveling mud-turtle visits it. Sometimes, when I pushed off my boat in the morning, I disturbed a great mud-turtle which had secreted himself under the boat in the night. Ducks and geese frequent it in the spring and fall, the white-bellied swallows (*Hirundo bi-*

color) skim over it, and the peetweets (*Totanus macularius*) "teter" along its stony shores all summer. I have sometimes disturbed a fish hawk sitting on a white pine over the water; but I doubt if it is ever profaned by the wing of a gull, like Fair Haven. At most, it tolerates one annual loon. These are all the animals of consequence which frequent it now.

You may see from a boat, in calm weather, near the sandy eastern shore, where the water is eight or ten feet deep, and also in some other parts of the pond, some circular heaps half a dozen feet in diameter by a foot in height, consisting of small stones less than a hen's egg in size, where all around is bare sand. At first you wonder if the Indians could have formed them on the ice for any purpose, and so, when the ice melted, they sank to the bottom; but they are too regular and some of them plainly too fresh for that. They are similar to those found in rivers; but as there are no suckers nor lampreys here, I know not by what fish they could be made. Perhaps they are the nests of the chivin. These lend a pleasing mystery to the bottom.

The shore is irregular enough not to be monotonous. I have in my mind's eye the western indented with deep bays, the bolder northern, and the beautifully scolloped southern shore, where successive capes overlap each other and suggest unexplored coves between. The forest has never so good a setting, nor is so distinctly beautiful, as when seen from the middle of a small lake amid hills which rise from the water's edge; for the water in which it is reflected not only makes the best foreground in such a case, but, with its winding shore, the most natural and agreeable boundary to it. There is no rawness nor imperfection in its edge there, as where the axe has cleared a part, or a cultivated field abuts on it. The trees have ample room to expand on the water side, and each sends forth its most vigorous branch in that direction. There Nature has woven a natural selvage, and the eye rises by just gradations from the low shrubs of the shore to the highest trees. There are few traces of man's hand to be seen. The water laves the shore as it did a thousand years ago.

A lake is the landscape's most beautiful and expressive feature. It is earth's eye; looking into which the beholder measures the depth of his own nature. The fluviatile trees next the shore are the slender eyelashes which fringe it, and the wooded hills and cliffs around are its overhanging brows.

Standing on the smooth sandy beach at the east end of the pond, in a calm September afternoon, when a slight haze makes the opposite shore line indistinct, I have seen whence came the expression, "the glassy surface of a lake." When you invert your head, it looks like a thread of finest gossamer stretched across the valley, and gleaming against the distant pine woods, separating one stratum of the atmosphere from another. You would think that you could walk dry under it to the opposite hills, and that the swallows which skim over might perch on it. Indeed, they sometimes dive below the line, as it were by mistake, and are undeceived. As you look over the pond westward you are obliged to employ both your hands to defend your eyes against the reflected as well as the true sun, for they are equally bright; and if, between the two, you survey its surface critically, it is literally as smooth as glass, except where the skater insects, at equal intervals scattered over its whole extent, by their motions in the sun produce the finest imaginable sparkle on it, or, perchance, a duck plumes itself, or, as I have said, a swallow skims so low as to touch it. It may be that in the distance a fish describes an arc of three or four feet in the air, and there is one bright flash where it emerges, and another where it strikes the water; sometimes the whole silvery arc is revealed; or here and there, perhaps, is a thistledown floating on its surface, which the fishes dart at and so dimple it again. It is like molten glass cooled but not congealed, and the few motes in it are pure and beautiful like the imperfections in glass. You may often detect a yet smoother and darker water, separated from the rest as if by an invisible cobweb, boon of the water nymphs, resting on it. From a hilltop you can see a fish leap in almost any part; for not a pickerel or shiner picks an insect from this smooth surface but it manifestly disturbs the equilibrium of the whole lake. It is wonderful with what elaborateness this simple fact is advertised—this piscine murder will out—and from my distant perch I distinguish the circling undulations when they are half a dozen rods in diameter. You can even detect a water-bug (*Gyrinus*) ceaselessly progressing over the smooth surface a quarter of a mile off; for they furrow the water slightly, making a conspicuous ripple bounded by two diverging lines, but the skaters glide over it without rippling it perceptibly. When the surface is considerably agitated there are no skaters nor waterbugs on it, but apparently, in calm days, they leave their havens and adventurously glide forth from the shore by short impulses till they completely cover it. It is a soothing employment, on one of those fine days in the fall when all the warmth of the sun is fully appreciated, to sit on a stump on such a height as this, overlooking the pond, and study the dimpling circles which are incessantly inscribed on its otherwise invisible surface amid the reflected skies and trees. Over this great expanse there is no disturbance but it is thus at once gently smoothed away and assuaged, as, when a vase of water is jarred, the trembling circles seek the shore and all is smooth

again. Not a fish can leap or an insect fall on the pond
but it is thus reported in circling dimples, in lines of
beauty, as it were the constant welling up of its fountain, the gentle pulsing of its life, the heaving of its
breast. The thrills of joy and thrills of pain are undistinguishable. How peaceful the phenomena of the lake!
Again the works of man shine as in the spring. Ay,
every leaf and twig and stone and cobweb sparkles now
at mid-afternoon as when covered with dew in a spring
morning. Every motion of an oar or an insect produces
a flash of light; and if an oar falls, how sweet the echo!

In such a day, in September or October, Walden is
a perfect forest mirror, set round with stones as precious
to my eye as if fewer or rarer. Nothing so fair, so pure,
and at the same time so large, as a lake, perchance, lies
on the surface of the earth. Sky water. It needs no fence.
Nations come and go without defiling it. It is a mirror
which no stone can crack, whose quicksilver will never
wear off, whose gilding Nature continually repairs; no
storms, no dust, can dim its surface ever fresh; a mirror
in which all impurity presented to it sinks, swept and
dusted by the sun's hazy brush—this the light dustcloth
—which retains no breath that is breathed on it, but
sends its own to float as clouds high above its surface,
and be reflected in its bosom still.

A field of water betrays the spirit that is in the air.
It is continually receiving new life and motion from
above. It is intermediate in its nature between land and
sky. On land only the grass and trees wave, but the
water itself is rippled by the wind. I see where the
breeze dashes across it by the streaks or flakes of light.
It is remarkable that we can look down on its surface.
We shall, perhaps, look down thus on the surface of air
at length, and mark where a still subtler spirit sweeps
over it.

The skaters and waterbugs finally disappear in the latter part of October, when the severe frosts have come; and then and in November, usually, in a calm day, there is absolutely nothing to ripple the surface. One November afternoon, in the calm at the end of a rainstorm of several days' duration, when the sky was still completely overcast and the air was full of mist, I observed that the pond was remarkably smooth, so that it was difficult to distinguish its surface; though it no longer reflected the bright tints of October, but the somber November colors of the surrounding hills. Though I passed over it as gently as possible, the slight undulations produced by my boat extended almost as far as I could see, and gave a ribbed appearance to the reflections. But, as I was looking over the surface, I saw here and there at a distance a faint glimmer, as if some skater insects which had escaped the frosts might be collected there, or, perchance, the surface, being so smooth, betrayed where a spring welled up from the bottom. Paddling gently to one of these places, I was surprised to find myself surrounded by myriads of small perch, about five inches long, of a rich bronze color in the green water, sporting there, and constantly rising to the surface and dimpling it, sometimes leaving bubbles on it. In such transparent and seemingly bottomless water, reflecting the clouds, I seemed to be floating through the air as in a balloon, and their swimming impressed me as a kind of flight or hovering, as if they were a compact flock of birds passing just beneath my level on the right or left, their fins, like sails, set all around them. There were many such schools in the pond, apparently improving the short season before winter would draw an icy shutter over their broad skylight, sometimes giving to the surface an appearance as if a slight breeze struck it, or a few raindrops fell there.

When I approached carelessly and alarmed them, they made a sudden plash and rippling with their tails, as if one had struck the water with a brushy bough, and instantly took refuge in the depths. At length the wind rose, the mist increased, and the waves began to run, and the perch leaped much higher than before, half out of water, a hundred black points, three inches long, at once above the surface. Even as late as the fifth of December, one year, I saw some dimples on the surface, and thinking it was going to rain hard immediately, the air being full of mist, I made haste to take my place at the oars and row homeward; already the rain seemed rapidly increasing, though I felt none on my cheek, and I anticipated a thorough soaking. But suddenly the dimples ceased, for they were produced by the perch, which the noise of my oars had scared into the depths, and I saw their schools dimly disappearing; so I spent a dry afternoon after all.

An old man who used to frequent this pond nearly sixty years ago, when it was dark with surrounding forests, tells me that in those days he sometimes saw it all alive with ducks and other water fowl, and that there were many eagles about it. He came here a-fishing, and used an old log canoe which he found on the shore. It was made of two white-pine logs dug out and pinned together, and was cut off square at the ends. It was very clumsy, but lasted a great many years before it became waterlogged and perhaps sank to the bottom. He did not know whose it was; it belonged to the pond. He used to make a cable for his anchor of strips of hickory bark tied together. An old man, a potter, who lived by the pond before the Revolution, told him once that there was an iron chest at the bottom, and that he had seen it. Sometimes it would come floating up to the shore; but when you went toward it, it would go back into deep water and disappear. I was pleased to hear of the old log canoe, which took the place of an Indian one of the same material but more graceful construction, which perchance had first been a tree on the bank, and then, as it were, fell into the water, to float there for a generation, the most proper vessel for the lake. I remember that when I first looked into these depths there were many large trunks to be seen indistinctly lying on the bottom, which had either been blown over formerly, or left on the ice at the last cutting, when wood was cheaper; but now they have mostly disappeared.

When I first paddled a boat on Walden, it was completely surrounded by thick and lofty pine and oak woods, and in some of its coves grape vines had run over the trees next the water and formed bowers under which a boat could pass. The hills which form its shores are so steep, and the woods on them were then so high, that, as you looked down from the west end, it had the appearance of an amphitheater for some kind of sylvan spectacle. I have spent many an hour, when I was younger, floating over its surface as the zephyr willed, having paddled my boat to the middle, and lying on my back across the seats, in a summer forenoon, dreaming awake, until I was aroused by the boat touching the sand, and I arose to see what shore my fates had impelled me to; days when idleness was the most attractive and productive industry. Many a forenoon have I stolen away, preferring to spend thus the most valued part of the day; for I was rich, if not in money, in sunny hours and summer days, and spent them lavishly; nor do I regret that I did not waste more of them in the workshop or the teacher's desk. But since I left those shores the woodchoppers have still further laid them waste, and now for many a year there will be no more rambling through the aisles of the wood, with occasional vistas through which you see the water. My Muse may be excused if she is silent henceforth. How can you expect the birds to sing when their groves are cut down?

Now the trunks of trees on the bottom, and the old log canoe, and the dark surrounding woods, are gone, and the villagers, who scarcely know where it lies, instead of going to the pond to bathe or drink, are thinking to bring its water, which should be as sacred as the Ganges at least, to the village in a pipe, to wash their dishes with!—to earn their Walden by the turning of a cock or drawing of a plug! That devilish Iron Horse, whose ear-rending neigh is heard throughout the town, has muddied the Boiling Spring with his foot, and he it is that has browsed off all the woods on Walden shore, that Trojan horse, with a thousand men in his belly, introduced by mercenary Greeks! Where is the country's champion, the Moore of Moore Hall, to meet him at the Deep Cut and thrust an avenging lance between the ribs of the bloated pest?

Nevertheless, of all the characters I have known, perhaps Walden wears best, and best preserves its purity. Many men have been likened to it, but few deserve that honor. Though the woodchoppers have laid bare first this shore and then that, and the Irish have built their sties by it, and the railroad has infringed on its border, and the icemen have skimmed it once, it is itself unchanged, the same water which my youthful eyes fell on; all the change is in me. It has not acquired one permanent wrinkle after all its ripples. It is perennially young, and I may stand and see a swallow dip apparently to pick an insect from its surface as of yore. It struck me again tonight, as if I had not seen it almost daily for more than twenty years—Why, here is Walden, the same woodland lake that I discovered so many years ago; where a forest was cut down last winter another is springing up by its shore as lustily as ever; the same thought is welling up to its surface that was then; it is the same liquid joy and happiness to itself and its Maker, ay, and it *may* be to me. It is the work of a brave man surely, in whom there was no guile! He rounded this water with his hand, deepened and clarified it in his thought, and in his will bequeathed it to Concord. I see by its face that it is visited by the same reflection; and I can almost say, Walden, is it you?

> It is no dream of mine,
> To ornament a line;
> I cannot come nearer to God and Heaven
> Than I live to Walden even.
> I am its stony shore,
> And the breeze that passes o'er;
> In the hollow of my hand
> Are its water and its sand,
> And its deepest resort
> Lies high in my thought.

The cars never pause to look at it; yet I fancy that the engineers and firemen and brakemen, and those passengers who have a season ticket and see it often, are better men for the sight. The engineer does not forget at night, or his nature does not, that he has beheld this vision of serenity and purity once at least during the day. Though seen but once, it helps to wash out State Street and the engine's soot. One proposes that it be called "God's Drop."

I have said that Walden has no visible inlet nor outlet, but it is on the one hand distantly and indirectly related to Flints' Pond, which is more elevated, by a chain of small ponds coming from that quarter, and on the other directly and manifestly to Concord River, which is lower, by a similar chain of ponds through which in some other geological period it may have flowed, and by a little digging, which God forbid, it can be made to flow thither again. If by living thus reserved and austere, like a hermit in the woods, so long, it has acquired such wonderful purity, who would not regret that the comparatively impure waters of Flints' Pond should be mingled with it, or itself should ever go to waste its sweetness in the ocean wave?

Flints', or Sandy Pond, in Lincoln, our greatest lake and inland sea, lies about a mile east of Walden. It is much larger, being said to contain one hundred and ninety-seven acres, and is more fertile in fish; but it is comparatively shallow, and not remarkably pure. A walk through the woods thither was often my recreation. It was worth the while, if only to feel the wind blow on your cheek freely, and see the waves run, and remember the life of mariners. I went a-chestnutting there in the fall, on windy days, when the nuts were dropping into the water and were washed to my feet; and one day, as I crept along its sedgy shore, the fresh spray blowing in my face, I came upon the mouldering wreck of a boat, the sides gone, and hardly more than the impression of its flat bottom left amid the rushes; yet its model was sharply defined, as if it were a large decayed pad, with its veins. It was as impressive a wreck as one could imagine on the seashore, and had as good a moral. It is by this time mere vegetable mould and undistinguishable pond shore, through which rushes and flags have pushed up. I used to admire the ripple marks on the sandy bottom, at the north end of this pond, made firm and hard to the feet of the wader by the pressure of the water, and the rushes which grew in Indian file, in waving lines, corresponding to these marks, rank behind rank, as if the waves had planted them. There also I have found, in considerable quantities, curious balls, composed apparently of fine grass or roots, of pipewort perhaps, from half an inch to four inches in diameter, and perfectly spherical. These wash back and forth in shallow water on a sandy bottom, and are sometimes cast on the shore. They are either solid grass, or have a little sand in the middle. At first you would say that they were formed by the action of the waves, like a pebble; yet the smallest are made of equally coarse materials, half an inch long, and they are produced only at one season of the year. Moreover, the waves, I suspect, do not so much construct as wear down a material which has already acquired consistency. They preserve their form when dry for an indefinite period.

Flints' Pond! Such is the poverty of our nomenclature. What right had the unclean and stupid farmer, whose farm abutted on this sky water, whose shores he has ruthlessly laid bare, to give his name to it? Some skinflint, who loved better the reflecting surface of a dollar, or a bright cent, in which he could see his own brazen face; who regarded even the wild ducks which settled in it as trespassers; his fingers grown into crooked and horny talons from the long habit of grasping harpy-like; so it is not named for me. I go not there to see him nor to hear of him; who never *saw* it, who never bathed in it, who never loved it, who never protected it, who never spoke a good word for it, nor thanked God that He had made it. Rather let it be named from the fishes that swim in it, the wild fowl or quadrupeds which frequent it, the wild flowers which grow by its shores, or some wild man or child the thread of whose history is interwoven with its own; not from him who could show no title to it but the deed which a like-minded neighbor or legislature gave him—him who thought only of its money value; whose presence perchance cursed all the shore; who exhausted the land around it, and would fain have exhausted the waters within it; who regretted only that it was not English hay or cranberry meadow —there was nothing to redeem it, forsooth, in his eyes —and would have drained and sold it for the mud at its bottom. It did not turn his mill, and it was no *privilege* to him to behold it. I respect not his labors, his farm where everything has its price, who would carry the landscape, who would carry his God, to market, if he could get anything for him; who goes to market *for* his god as it is; on whose farm nothing grows free, whose fields bear no crops, whose meadows no flowers, whose trees no fruits, but dollars; who loves not the beauty of his fruits, whose fruits are not ripe for him till they are turned to dollars. Give me the poverty that enjoys true wealth. Farmers are respectable and interesting to me in proportion as they are poor—poor farmers. A model farm! where the house stands like a fungus in a muck-heap, chambers for men, horses, oxen, and swine, cleansed and uncleansed, all contiguous to one another! Stocked with men! A great grease-spot, redolent of manures and buttermilk! Under a high state of cultivation, being manured with the hearts and brains of men! As if you were to raise your potatoes in the churchyard! Such is a model farm.

No, no; if the fairest features of the landscape are to be named after men, let them be the noblest and worthiest men alone. Let our lakes receive as true names at least as the Icarian Sea, where "still the shore" a "brave attempt resounds."

Goose Pond, of small extent, is on my way to Flints'; Fair Haven, an expansion of Concord River, said to contain some seventy acres, is a mile southwest; and White Pond, of about forty acres, is a mile and a half beyond Fair Haven. This is my lake country. These, with Concord River, are my water privileges; and night and day, year in year out, they grind such grist as I carry to them.

Since the woodcutters, and the railroad, and I myself have profaned Walden, perhaps the most attractive, if not the most beautiful, of all our lakes, the gem of the woods, is White Pond—a poor name from its commonness, whether derived from the remarkable purity of its waters or the color of its sands. In these as in other respects, however, it is a lesser twin of Walden. They are so much alike that you would say they must be connected under ground. It has the same stony shore, and its waters are of the same hue. As at Walden, in sultry dog-day weather, looking down through the woods on some of its bays which are not so deep but that the reflection from the bottom tinges them, its waters are of a misty bluish-green or glaucous color. Many years since I used to go there to collect the sand by cartloads, to make sandpaper with, and I have continued to visit it ever since. One who frequents it proposes to call it Virid Lake. Perhaps it might be called Yellow-Pine Lake, from the following circumstance. About fifteen years ago you could see the top of a pitch pine, of the kind called yellow pine hereabouts, though it is not a distinct species, projecting above the surface in deep water, many rods from the shore. It was even supposed by some that the pond had sunk, and this was one of the primitive forest that formerly stood there. I find that even so long ago as 1792, in a "Topographical Description of the Town of Concord," by one of its citizens, in the Collections of the Massachusetts Historical Society, the author, after speaking of Walden and White Ponds, adds: "In the middle of the latter may be seen, when the water is very low, a tree which appears as if it grew in the place where it now stands, although the roots are fifty feet below the surface of the water; the top of this tree is broken off, and at that place measures fourteen inches in diameter." In the spring of '49 I talked with the man who lives nearest the pond in Sudbury, who told me that it was he who got out this tree ten or fifteen years before. As near as he could remember, it stood twelve or fifteen rods from the shore, where the water was thirty or forty feet deep. It was in the winter, and he had been getting out ice in the forenoon, and had resolved that in the afternoon, with the aid of his neighbors, he would take out the old yellow pine. He sawed a channel in the ice toward the shore, and hauled it over and along and out onto the ice with oxen; but, before he had gone far in his work, he was surprised to find that it was wrong end upward, with the stumps of the branches pointing down, and the small end firmly fastened in the sandy bottom. It was about a foot in diameter at the big end, and he had expected to get a good saw log, but it was so rotten as to be fit only for fuel, if for that. He had some of it in his shed then. There were marks of an axe and of woodpeckers on the butt. He thought that it might have been a dead tree on the shore, but was finally blown over into the pond, and after the top had become waterlogged, while the butt-end was still dry and light, had drifted out and sunk wrong end up. His father, eighty years old, could not remember when it was not there. Several pretty large logs may still be seen lying on the bottom, where, owing to the undulation of the surface, they look like huge water snakes in motion.

This pond has rarely been profaned by a boat, for there is little in it to tempt a fisherman. Instead of the white lily, which requires mud, or the common sweet flag, the blue flag (*Iris versicolor*) grows thinly in the pure water, rising from the stony bottom all around the shore, where it is visited by hummingbirds in June; and the color both of its bluish blades and its flowers and especially their reflections, are in singular harmony with the glaucous water.

White Pond and Walden are great crystals on the surface of the earth, Lakes of Light. If they were permanently congealed, and small enough to be clutched, they would, perchance, be carried off by slaves, like precious stones, to adorn the heads of emperors; but being liquid, and ample, and secured to us and our successors forever, we disregard them, and run after the diamond of Kohinoor. They are too pure to have a market value; they contain no muck. How much more beautiful than our lives, how much more transparent than our characters, are they! We never learned meanness of them. How much fairer than the pool before the farmer's door, in which his ducks swim! Hither the clean wild ducks come. Nature has no human inhabitant who appreciates her. The birds with their plumage and their notes are in harmony with the flowers, but what youth or maiden conspires with the wild luxuriant beauty of Nature? She flourishes most alone, far from the towns where they reside. Talk of heaven! ye disgrace earth.

BAKER FARM

Sometimes I rambled to pine groves, standing like temples, or like fleets at sea, full-rigged, with wavy boughs, and rippling with light, so soft and green and shady that the Druids would have foresaken their oaks to worship in them; or to the cedar wood beyond Flints' Pond, where the trees, covered with hoary blue berries, spiring higher and higher, are fit to stand before Valhalla, and the creeping juniper covers the ground with wreaths full of fruit; or to swamps where the usnea lichen hangs in festoons from the white-spruce trees, and toadstools, round tables of the swamp gods, cover the ground, and more beautiful fungi adorn the stumps, like butterflies or shells, vegetable winkles; where the swamp-pink and dogwood grow, the red alderberry glows like eyes of imps, the waxwork grooves and crushes the hardest woods in its folds, and the wild-holly berries make the beholder forget his home with their beauty, and he is dazzled and tempted by nameless other wild forbidden fruits, too fair for mortal taste. Instead of calling on some scholar, I paid many a visit to particular trees, of kinds which are rare in this neighborhood, standing far away in the middle of some pasture, or in the depths of a wood or swamp, or on a hilltop; such as the black birch, of which we have some handsome specimens two feet in diameter; its cousin, the yellow birch, with its loose golden vest, perfumed like the first; the beech, which has so neat a bole and beautifully lichen-painted, perfect in all its details, of which, excepting scattered specimens, I know but one small grove of sizable trees left in the township, supposed by some to have been planted by the pigeons that were once baited with beech nuts near by; it is worth the while to see the silver grain sparkle when you split this wood; the bass; the hornbeam; the *celtis occidentalis*, or false elm, of which we have but one well-grown; some taller mast of a pine, a shingle tree, or a more perfect hemlock than usual, standing like a pagoda in the midst of the woods; and many others I could mention. These were the shrines I visited both summer and winter.

Once it chanced that I stood in the very abutment of a rainbow's arch, which filled the lower stratum of the atmosphere, tinging the grass and leaves around, and dazzling me as if I looked through colored crystal. It was a lake of rainbow light, in which, for a short while, I lived like a dolphin. If it had lasted longer it might have tinged my employments and life. As I walked on the railroad causeway, I used to wonder at the halo of light around my shadow, and would fain fancy myself one of the elect. One who visited me declared that the shadows of some Irishmen before him had no halo about them, that it was only natives that were so distinguished. Benvenuto Cellini tells us in his memoirs, that, after a certain terrible dream or vision which he had during his confinement in the castle of St. Angelo, a resplendent light appeared over the shadow of his head at morning and evening, whether he was in Italy or France, and it was particularly conspicuous when the grass was moist with dew. This was probably the same phenomenon to which I have referred, which is especially observed in the morning, but also at other times, and even by moonlight. Though a constant one, it is not commonly noticed, and, in the case of an excitable imagination like Cellini's, it would be basis enough for superstition. Beside, he tells us that he showed it to very few. But are they not indeed distinguished who are conscious that they are regarded at all?

I set out one afternoon to go a-fishing to Fair Haven, through the woods, to eke out my scanty fare of vegetables. My way led through Pleasant Meadow, an adjunct of the Baker Farm, that retreat of which a poet has since sung, beginning,

> "Thy entry is a pleasant field,
> Which some mossy fruit trees yield
> Partly to a ruddy brook,
> By gliding musquash undertook,

> And mercurial trout,
> Darting about."

I thought of living there before I went to Walden. I
"hooked" the apples, leaped the brook, and scared the
musquash and the trout. It was one of those afternoons
which seem indefinitely long before one, in which many
events may happen, a large portion of our natural life,
though it was already half spent when I started. By
the way there came up a shower, which compelled me
to stand half an hour under a pine, piling boughs over
my head, and wearing my handkerchief for a shed; and
when at length I had made one cast over the pickerel-
weed, standing up to my middle in water, I found myself suddenly in the shadow of a cloud, and the thunder
began to rumble with such emphasis that I could do
no more than listen to it. The gods must be proud,
thought I, with such forked flashes to rout a poor un-
armed fisherman. So I made haste for shelter to the
nearest hut, which stood half a mile from any road, but
so much the nearer to the pond, and had long been uninhabited:

> "And here a poet builded,
> In the completed years,
> For behold a trivial cabin
> That to destruction steers."

So the Muse fables. But therein, as I found, dwelt now
John Field, an Irishman, and his wife, and several children, from the broad-faced boy who assisted his father
at his work, and now came running by his side from the
bog to escape the rain, to the wrinkled, sibyl-like, cone-
headed infant that sat upon its father's knee as in the
palaces of nobles, and looked out from its home in the
midst of wet and hunger inquisitively upon the stranger,
with the privilege of infancy, not knowing but it was
the last of a noble line, and the hope and cynosure of

the world, instead of John Field's poor starveling brat. There we sat together under that part of the roof which leaked the least, while it showered and thundered without. I had sat there many times of old before the ship was built that floated this family to America. An honest, hard-working, but shiftless man plainly was John Field; and his wife, she too was brave to cook so many successive dinners in the recesses of that lofty stove; with round greasy face and bare breast, still thinking to improve her condition one day; with the never absent mop in one hand, and yet no effects of it visible anywhere. The chickens, which had also taken shelter here from the rain, stalked about the room like members of the family, too humanized methought to roast well. They stood and looked in my eye or pecked at my shoe significantly. Meanwhile my host told me his story, how hard he worked "bogging" for a neighboring farmer, turning up a meadow with a spade or bog hoe at the rate of ten dollars an acre and the use of the land with manure for one year, and his little broad-faced son worked cheerfully at his father's side the while, not knowing how poor a bargain the latter had made. I tried to help him with my experience, telling him that he was one of my nearest neighbors, and that I too, who came a-fishing here, and looked like a loafer, was getting my living like himself; that I lived in a tight, light, and clean house, which hardly cost more than the annual rent of such a ruin as his commonly amounts to; and how, if he chose, he might in a month or two build himself a palace of his own; that I did not use tea, nor coffee, nor butter, nor milk, nor fresh meat, and so did not have to work to get them; again, as I did not work hard, I did not have to eat hard, and it cost me but a trifle for my food; but as he began with tea, and coffee, and butter, and milk, and beef, he had to work hard to pay for them, and when he had worked hard he had to eat hard again to repair the waste of his system—and so it was as broad as it was long, indeed it was broader than it was long, for he was discontented and wasted his life into the bargain; and yet he had rated it as a gain in coming to America, that here you could get tea, and coffee, and meat every day. But the only true America is that country where you are at liberty to pursue such a mode of life as may enable you to do without these, and where the state does not endeavor to compel you to sustain the slavery and war and other superfluous expenses which directly or indirectly result from the use of such things. For I purposely talked to him as if he were a philosopher, or desired to be one. I should be glad if all the meadows on the earth were left in a wild state, if that were the consequence of men's beginning to redeem themselves. A man will not need to study history to find out what is best for his own culture. But alas! the culture of an Irishman is an enterprise to be undertaken with a sort of moral bog hoe. I told him, that as he worked so hard at bogging, he required thick boots and stout clothing, which yet were soon soiled and worn out, but I wore light shoes and thin clothing, which cost not half so much, though he might think that I was dressed like a gentleman, which, however, was not the case, and in an hour or two, without labor, but as a recreation, I could, if I wished, catch as many fish as I should want for two days, or earn enough money to support me a week. If he and his family would live simply, they might all go a-huckleberrying in the summer for their amusement. John heaved a sigh at this, and his wife stared with arms akimbo, and both appeared to be wondering if they had capital enough to begin such a course with, or arithmetic enough to carry it through. It was sailing by dead reckoning to them, and they saw not clearly how to make their port so; therefore I suppose they still take life bravely, after their fashion, face to face, giving it tooth and nail, not having skill to split its massive columns with any fine entering wedge, and rout it in detail; thinking to deal with it roughly, as one should handle a thistle. But they fight at an overwhelming disadvantage—living, John Field, alas! without arithmetic, and failing so.

"Do you ever fish?" I asked. "Oh, yes, I catch a mess now and then when I am lying by; good perch I catch." "What's your bait?" "I catch shiners with fishworms, and bait the perch with them." "You'd better go now, John," said his wife, with glistening and hopeful face; but John demurred.

The shower was now over, and a rainbow above the eastern woods promised a fair evening; so I took my departure. When I had got without I asked for a dish, hoping to get a sight of the well bottom, to complete my survey of the premises; but there, alas! are shallows and quicksands, and rope broken withal, and bucket irrecoverable. Meanwhile the right culinary vessel was selected, water was seemingly distilled, and after consultation and long delay passed out to the thirsty one— not yet suffered to cool, not yet to settle. Such gruel sustains life here, I thought; so, shutting my eyes, and excluding the motes by a skillfully directed undercurrent, I drank to genuine hospitality the heartiest draught I could. I am not squeamish in such cases when manners are concerned.

As I was leaving the Irishman's roof after the rain, bending my steps again to the pond, my haste to catch pickerel, wading in retired meadows, in sloughs and bogholes, in forlorn and savage places, appeared for an instant trivial to me who had been sent to school and college; but as I ran down the hill toward the reddening west, with the rainbow over my shoulder, and some faint tinkling sounds borne to my ear through the cleansed air, from I know not what quarter, my Good Genius seemed to say, Go fish and hunt far and wide day by day—farther and wider—and rest thee by many brooks and hearthsides without misgiving. Remember thy Creator in the days of thy youth. Rise free from care before the dawn, and seek adventures. Let the noon find thee by other lakes, and the night overtake thee everywhere at home. There are no larger fields than these, no worthier games than may here be played. Grow wild according to thy nature, like these sedges and brakes, which will never become English hay. Let the thunder rumble; what if it threaten ruin to farmers' crops? that is not its errand to thee. Take shelter under the cloud, while they flee to carts and sheds. Let not to get a living be thy trade, but thy sport. Enjoy the land, but own it not. Through want of enterprise and faith men are where they are, buying and selling, and spending their lives like serfs.

O Baker Farm!

> "Landscape where the richest element
> Is a little sunshine innocent."

> "No one runs to revel
> On thy rail-fenced lea."

> "Debate with no man hast thou,
> With questions art never perplexed,
> As tame at the first sight as now,
> In thy plain russet gabardine dressed."

> "Come ye who love,
> And ye who hate,
> Children of the Holy Dove,
> And Guy Faux of the state,
> And hang conspiracies
> From the tough rafters of the trees!"

Men come tamely home at night only from the next field or street, where their household echoes haunt, and their life pines because it breathes its own breath over again; their shadows morning and evening reach farther than their daily steps. We should come home from far, from adventures, and perils, and discoveries every day, with new experience and character.

Before I had reached the pond some fresh impulse had brought out John Field, with altered mind, letting go "bogging" ere this sunset. But he, poor man, disturbed only a couple of fins while I was catching a fair string, and he said it was his luck; but when we changed seats in the boat luck changed seats too. Poor John Field! I trust he does not read this, unless he will improve by it —thinking to live by some derivative old country mode in this primitive new country—to catch perch with shiners. It is good bait sometimes, I allow. With his horizon all his own, yet he a poor man, born to be poor, with his inherited Irish poverty or poor life, his Adam's grandmother and boggy ways, not to rise in this world, he nor his posterity, till their wading webbed bog-trotting feet get *talaria* to their heels.

HIGHER LAWS

As I came home through the woods with my string of fish, trailing my pole, it being now quite dark, I caught a glimpse of a woodchuck stealing across my path, and felt a strange thrill of savage delight, and was strongly tempted to seize and devour him raw; not that I was hungry then, except for that wildness which he represented. Once or twice, however, while I lived at the pond, I found myself ranging the woods, like a half-starved hound, with a strange abandonment, seeking some kind of venison which I might devour, and no morsel could have been too savage for me. The wildest scenes had become unaccountably familiar. I found in myself, and still find, an instinct toward a higher, or, as it is named, spiritual life, as do most men, and another toward a primitive rank and savage one, and I reverence them both. I love the wild not less than the good. The wildness and adventure that are in fishing still recommended it to me. I like sometimes to take rank hold on life and spend my day more as the animals do. Perhaps I have owed to this employment and to hunting, when quite young, my closest acquaintance with Nature. They early introduce us to and detain us in scenery with which otherwise, at that age, we should have little acquaintance. Fishermen, hunters, woodchoppers, and others, spending their lives in the fields and woods, in a peculiar sense a part of Nature themselves, are often in a more favorable mood for observing her, in the intervals of their pursuits, than philosophers or poets even, who approach her with expectation. She is not afraid to exhibit herself to them. The traveler on the prairie is naturally a hunter, on the headwaters of the Missouri and Columbia a trapper, and at the Falls of St. Mary a fisherman. He who is only a traveler learns things at second-hand and by the halves, and is poor authority. We are most interested when science reports what those men already know practically or instinctively, for that alone is a true *humanity,* or account of human experience.

They mistake who assert that the Yankee has few amusements, because he has not so many public holidays, and men and boys do not play so many games as they do in England, for here the more primitive but solitary amusements of hunting, fishing, and the like have not yet given place to the former. Almost every New England boy among my contemporaries shouldered a fowling piece between the ages of ten and fourteen; and his hunting and fishing grounds were not limited, like the preserves of an English nobleman, but were more boundless even than those of a savage. No wonder, then, that he did not oftener stay to play on the common. But already a change is taking place, owing not to an increased humanity but to an increased scarcity of game, for perhaps the hunter is the greatest friend of the animals hunted, not excepting the Humane Society.

Moreover, when at the pond, I wished sometimes to add fish to my fare for variety, I have actually fished from the same kind of necessity that the first fishers did. Whatever humanity I might conjure up against it was all factitious, and concerned my philosophy more than my feelings. I speak of fishing only now, for I had long felt differently about fowling, and sold my gun before I went to the woods. Not that I am less humane than others, but I did not perceive that my feelings were much affected. I did not pity the fishes nor the worms. This was habit. As for fowling, during the last years that I carried a gun my excuse was that I was studying ornithology, and sought only new or rare birds. But I confess that I am now inclined to think that there is a finer way of studying ornithology than this. It requires so much closer attention to the habits of the birds, that, if for that reason only, I have been willing to omit the gun. Yet notwithstanding the objection on the score of humanity, I am compelled to doubt if equally valuable sports are ever substituted for these; and when some of my friends have asked me anxiously about their boys, whether they should let them hunt, I have answered, yes—remembering that it was one of the best parts of my education—*make* them hunters, though sportsmen only at first, if possible, mighty hunters at last, so that they shall not find game large enough for them in this or any vegetable wilderness—hunters as well as fishers of men. Thus far I am of the opinion of Chaucer's nun, who

"yave not of the text a pulled hen
That saith that hunters ben not holy men."

There is a period in the history of the individual, as of the race, when the hunters are the "best men," as the Algonquins called them. We cannot but pity the boy who has never fired a gun; he is no more humane, while his education has been sadly neglected. This was my answer with respect to those youths who were bent on this pursuit, trusting that they would soon outgrow it. No humane being, past the thoughtless age of boyhood, will wantonly murder any creature, which holds its life by the same tenure that he does. The hare in its extremity cries like a child. I warn you, mothers, that my sympathies do not always make the usual phil-*anthropic* distinctions.

Such is oftenest the young man's introduction to the forest, and the most original part of himself. He goes thither at first as a hunter and fisher, until at last, if he has the seeds of a better life in him, he distinguishes his proper objects, as a poet or naturalist it may be, and leaves the gun and fish-pole behind. The mass of men are still and always young in this respect. In some countries a hunting parson is no uncommon sight. Such a one might make a good shepherd's dog, but is far from being the Good Shepherd. I have been surprised to consider that the only obvious employment, except wood-chopping, ice-cutting, or the like business, which ever to my knowledge detained at Walden Pond for a whole half day any of my fellow citizens, whether fathers or children of the town, with just one exception, was fishing. Commonly they did not think that they were lucky, or well paid for their time, unless they got a long string of fish, though they had the opportunity of seeing the pond all the while. They might go there a thousand times before the sediment of fishing would sink to the bottom and leave their purpose pure; but no doubt such a clarifying process would be going on all the while. The governor and his council faintly remember the pond, for they went a-fishing there when they were boys; but now they are too old and dignified to go a-fishing, and so they know it no more forever. Yet even they expect to go to heaven at last. If the legislature regards it, it is chiefly to regulate the number of hooks to be used there; but they know nothing about the hook of hooks with which to angle for the pond itself, impaling the legislature for a bait. Thus, even in civilized communities, the embryo man passes through the hunter stage of development.

I have found repeatedly, of late years, that I cannot fish without falling a little in self-respect. I have tried it again and again. I have skill at it, and, like many of my fellows, a certain instinct for it, which revives from time to time, but always when I have done I feel that it would have been better if I had not fished. I think that I do not mistake. It is a faint intimation, yet so are the first streaks of morning. There is unquestionably this instinct in me which belongs to the lower orders of creation; yet with every year I am less a fisherman, though without more humanity or even wisdom; at present I am no fisherman at all. But I see that if I were to live in a wilderness I should again be tempted to become a fisher and hunter in earnest. Beside, there is something essentially unclean about this diet and all flesh, and I began to see where housework commences, and whence the endeavor, which costs so much, to wear

a tidy and respectable appearance each day, to keep the
house sweet and free from all ill odors and sights. Having been my own butcher and scullion and cook, as well
as the gentleman for whom the dishes were served up,
I can speak from an unusually complete experience.
The practical objection to animal food in my case was
its uncleanness; and besides, when I had caught and
cleaned and cooked and eaten my fish, they seemed
not to have fed me essentially. It was insignificant and
unnecessary, and cost more than it came to. A little
bread or a few potatoes would have done as well, with
less trouble and filth. Like many of my contemporaries,
I had rarely for many years used animal food, or tea,
or coffee, etc.; not so much because of any ill effects
which I had traced to them, as because they were not
agreeable to my imagination. The repugnance to animal
food is not the effect of experience, but is an instinct.
It appeared more beautiful to live low and fare hard in
many respects; and though I never did so, I went far
enough to please my imagination. I believe that every
man who has ever been earnest to preserve his higher
or poetic faculties in the best condition has been particularly inclined to abstain from animal food, and from
much food of any kind. It is a significant fact, stated by
entomologists, I find it in Kirby and Spence, that "some
insects in their perfect state, though furnished with
organs of feeding, make no use of them"; and they lay
it down as "a general rule, that almost all insects in this
state eat much less than in that of larvae. The voracious
caterpillar when transformed into a butterfly . . . and
the gluttonous maggot when become a fly," content
themselves with a drop or two of honey or some other
sweet liquid. The abdomen under the wings of the butterfly still represents the larva. This is the tidbit which
tempts his insectivorous fate. The gross feeder is a man

in the larva state; and there are whole nations in that condition, nations without fancy or imagination, whose vast abdomens betray them.

It is hard to provide and cook so simple and clean a diet as will not offend the imagination; but this, I think, is to be fed when we feed the body; they should both sit down at the same table. Yet perhaps this may be done. The fruits eaten temperately need not make us ashamed of our appetites, nor interrupt the worthiest pursuits. But put an extra condiment into your dish, and it will poison you. It is not worth the while to live by rich cookery. Most men would feel shame if caught preparing with their own hands precisely such a dinner, whether of animal or vegetable food, as is every day prepared for them by others. Yet till this is otherwise we are not civilized, and, if gentlemen and ladies, are not true men and women. This certainly suggests what change is to be made. It may be vain to ask why the imagination will not be reconciled to flesh and fat. I am satisfied that it is not. Is it not a reproach that man is a carnivorous animal? True, he can and does live, in a great measure, by preying on other animals; but this is a miserable way—as anyone who will go to snaring rabbits, or slaughtering lambs, may learn—and he will be regarded as a benefactor of his race who shall teach man to confine himself to a more innocent and wholesome diet. Whatever my own practice may be, I have no doubt that it is a part of the destiny of the human race, in its gradual improvement, to leave off eating animals, as surely as the savage tribes have left off eating each other when they came in contact with the more civilized.

If one listens to the faintest but constant suggestions of his genius, which are certainly true, he sees not to what extremes, or even insanity, it may lead him; and yet that way, as he grows more resolute and faithful, his road lies. The faintest assured objection which one healthy man feels will at length prevail over the arguments and customs of mankind. No man ever followed his genius till it misled him. Though the result were bodily weakness, yet perhaps no one can say that the consequences were to be regretted, for these were a life in conformity to higher principles. If the day and the night are such that you greet them with joy, and life emits a fragrance like flowers and sweet-scented herbs, is more elastic, more starry, more immortal—that is your success. All nature is your congratulation, and you have cause momentarily to bless yourself. The greatest gains and values are farthest from being appreciated. We easily come to doubt if they exist. We soon forget them. They are the highest reality. Perhaps the facts most astounding and most real are never communicated by man to man. The true harvest of my daily life is somewhat as intangible and indescribable as the tints of morning or evening. It is a little stardust caught, a segment of the rainbow which I have clutched.

Yet, for my part, I was never unusually squeamish; I could sometimes eat a fried rat with a good relish, if it were necessary. I am glad to have drunk water so long, for the same reason that I prefer the natural sky to an opium-eater's heaven. I would fain keep sober always; and there are infinite degrees of drunkenness. I believe that water is the only drink for a wise man; wine is not so noble a liquor; and think of dashing the hopes of a morning with a cup of warm coffee, or of an evening with a dish of tea! Ah, how low I fall when I am tempted by them! Even music may be intoxicating. Such apparently slight causes destroyed Greece and Rome, and will destroy England and America. Of all ebriosity, who does not prefer to be intoxicated by the air he breathes? I have found it to be the most serious objection to coarse labors long continued, that they compelled me to eat and drink coarsely also. But to tell the truth, I find myself at present somewhat less particular in these respects. I carry less religion to the table, ask no blessing; not because I am wiser than I was, but, I am obliged to confess, because, however much it is to be regretted, with years I have grown more coarse and indifferent. Perhaps these questions are entertained only in youth, as most believe of poetry. My practice is "nowhere," my opinion is here. Nevertheless I am far from regarding myself as one of those privileged ones to whom the Ved refers when it says, that "he who has true faith in the Omnipresent Supreme Being may eat all that exists," that is, is not bound to inquire what is his food, or who prepares it; and even in their case it is to be observed, as a Hindu commentator has remarked, that the Vedant limits this privilege to "the time of distress."

Who has not sometimes derived an inexpressible satisfaction from his food in which appetite had no share? I have been thrilled to think that I owed a mental perception to the commonly gross sense of taste, that I have been inspired through the palate, that some berries which I had eaten on a hillside had fed my genius. "The soul not being mistress of herself," says Thseng-tseu, "one looks, and one does not see; one listens, and one does not hear; one eats, and one does not know the savor of food." He who distinguishes the true savor of his food can never be a glutton; he who does not cannot be otherwise. A puritan may go to his brown-bread crust with as gross an appetite as ever an alderman to his turtle. Not that food which entereth into the mouth defileth a man, but the appetite with which it is eaten. It is neither the quality nor the quantity, but the devotion to sensual savors; when that which is eaten is not a viand to sustain our animal, or inspire our spiritual life, but food for the worms that possess us. If the hunter has a taste for mud-turtles, muskrats, and other such savage tidbits, the fine lady indulges a taste for jelly made of a calf's foot, or for sardines from over the sea, and they are even. He goes to the mill-pond, she to her preserve-pot. The wonder is how they, how you and I, can live this slimy beastly life, eating and drinking.

Our whole life is startlingly moral. There is never an instant's truce between virtue and vice. Goodness is the only investment that never fails. In the music of the harp which trembles round the world it is the insisting on this which thrills us. The harp is the traveling patterer for the Universe's Insurance Company, recommending its laws, and our little goodness is all the assessment that we pay. Though the youth at last grows indifferent, the laws of the universe are not indifferent, but are forever on the side of the most sensitive. Listen to every zephyr for some reproof, for it is surely there, and he is unfortunate who does not hear it. We cannot touch a string or move a stop but the charming moral transfixes us. Many an irksome noise, go a long way off, is heard as music, a proud sweet satire on the meanness of our lives.

We are conscious of an animal in us, which awakens in proportion as our higher nature slumbers. It is reptile and sensual, and perhaps cannot be wholly expelled; like the worms which, even in life and health, occupy our bodies. Possibly we may withdraw from it, but never change its nature. I fear that it may enjoy a certain health of its own; that we may be well, yet not pure. The other day I picked up the lower jaw of a hog, with white and sound teeth and tusks, which suggested that there was an animal health and vigor distinct from the spiritual. This creature succeeded by other means than temperance and purity. "That in which men differ from brute beasts," says Mencius, "is a thing very inconsiderable; the common herd lose it very soon; superior men preserve it carefully." Who knows what sort of life would result if we had attained to purity? If I knew so wise a man as could teach me purity I would go to seek him forthwith. "A command over our passions, and over the external senses of the body, and good acts, are declared by the Ved to be indispensable in the mind's approximation to God." Yet the spirit can for the time pervade and control every member and function of the body, and transmute what in form is the grossest sensuality into purity and devotion. The generative energy, which, when we are loose, dissipates and makes us unclean, when we are continent invigorates and inspires us. Chastity is the flowering of man; and what are called Genius, Heroism, Holiness, and the like, are but various fruits which succeed it. Man flows at once to God when the channel of purity is open. By turns our purity inspires and our impurity casts us down. He is blessed who is assured that the animal is dying out in him day by day, and the divine being established. Perhaps there is none but has cause for shame on account of the inferior and brutish nature to which he is allied. I fear that we are such gods or demigods only as fauns and satyrs, the divine allied to beasts, the creatures of appetite, and that, to some extent, our very life is our disgrace.—

"How happy 's he who hath due place assigned
To his beasts and disafforested his mind!
.   .   .   .   .   .
Can use his horse, goat, wolf, and ev'ry beast,
And is not ass himself to all the rest!
Else man not only is the herd of swine,
But he 's those devils too which did incline
Them to a headlong rage, and made them worse."

All sensuality is one, though it takes many forms; all purity is one. It is the same whether a man eat, or drink, or cohabit, or sleep sensually. They are but one appetite, and we only need to see a person do any one of these things to know how great a sensualist he is. The impure can neither stand nor sit with purity. When the reptile is attacked at one mouth of his burrow, he shows himself at another. If you would be chaste, you must be temperate. What is chastity? How shall a man know if he is chaste? He shall not know it. We have heard of this virtue, but we know not what it is. We speak conformably to the rumor which we have heard. From exertion come wisdom and purity; from sloth ignorance and sensuality. In the student sensuality is a sluggish habit of mind. An unclean person is universally a slothful one, one who sits by a stove, whom the sun shines on prostrate, who reposes without being fatigued. If you would avoid uncleanness, and all the sins, work earnestly, though it be at cleaning a stable. Nature is hard to be overcome, but she must be overcome. What avails it that you are Christian, if you are not purer than the heathen, if you deny yourself no more, if you are not more religious? I know of many systems of religion esteemed heathenish whose precepts fill the reader with shame, and provoke him to new endeavors, though it be to the performance of rites merely.

I hesitate to say these things, but it is not because of the subject—I care not how obscene my *words* are—but because I cannot speak of them without betraying my impurity. We discourse freely without shame of one form of sensuality, and are silent about another. We are so degraded that we cannot speak simply of the necessary functions of human nature. In earlier ages, in some countries, every function was reverently spoken of and regulated by law. Nothing was too trivial for the Hindu lawgiver, however offensive it may be to modern taste. He teaches how to eat, drink, cohabit, void excrement and urine, and the like, elevating what is mean, and does not falsely excuse himself by calling these things trifles.

Every man is the builder of a temple, called his body, to the god he worships, after a style purely his own, nor can he get off by hammering marble instead. We are all sculptors and painters, and our material is our own flesh and blood and bones. Any nobleness begins at once to refine a man's features, any meanness or sensuality to imbrute them.

John Farmer sat at his door one September evening, after a hard day's work, his mind still running on his labor more or less. Having bathed he sat down to re-create his intellectual man. It was a rather cool evening, and some of his neighbors were apprehending a frost. He had not attended to the train of his thoughts long when he heard someone playing on a flute, and that sound harmonized with his mood. Still he thought of his work; but the burden of his thought was, that though this kept running in his head, and he found himself planning and contriving it against his will, yet it con-cerned him very little. It was no more than the scurf of his skin, which was constantly shuffled off. But the notes of the flute came home to his ears out of a different sphere from that he worked in, and suggested work for certain faculties which slumbered in him. They gently did away with the street, and the village, and the state in which he lived. A voice said to him, Why do you stay here and live this mean moiling life, when a glorious existence is possible for you? Those same stars twinkle over other fields than these. But how to come out of this condition and actually migrate thither? All that he could think of was to practice some new austerity, to let his mind descend into his body and redeem it, and treat himself with ever increasing respect.

BRUTE NEIGHBORS

Sometimes I had a companion in my fishing, who came through the village to my house from the other side of town, and the catching of the dinner was as much a social exercise as the eating of it.

Hermit. I wonder what the world is doing now. I have not heard so much as a locust over the sweet fern these three hours. The pigeons are all asleep upon their roosts—no flutter from them. Was that a farmer's noon horn which sounded from beyond the woods just now? The hands are coming in to boiled salt beef and cider and Indian bread. Why will men worry themselves so? He that does not eat need not work. I wonder how much they have reaped. Who would live there where a body can never think for the barking of Bose? And O, the housekeeping! to keep bright the devil's doorknobs, and scour his tubs this bright day! Better not keep a house. Say, some hollow tree; and then for morning calls and dinner-parties! Only a woodpecker tapping. Oh, they swarm; the sun is too warm there; they are born too far into life for me. I have water from the spring, and a loaf of brown bread on the shelf. Hark! I hear a rustling of the leaves. Is it some ill-fed village hound yielding to the instinct of the chase? or the lost pig which is said to be in these woods, whose tracks I saw after the rain? It comes on apace; my sumachs and sweetbriers tremble.—Eh, Mr. Poet, is it you? How do you like the world today?

Poet. See those clouds; how they hang! That's the greatest thing I have seen today. There's nothing like it in old paintings, nothing like it in foreign lands—unless when we were off the coast of Spain. That's a true Mediterranean sky. I thought, as I have my living to get, and have not eaten today, that I might go a-fishing. That's the true industry for poets. It is the only trade I have learned. Come, let's along.

Hermit. I cannot resist. My brown bread will soon be gone. I will go with you gladly soon, but I am just concluding a serious meditation. I think that I am near the end of it. Leave me alone, then, for a while. But that we may not be delayed, you shall be digging the bait meanwhile. Angleworms are rarely to be met with in these parts, where the soil was never fattened with manure; the race is nearly extinct. The sport of digging the bait is nearly equal to that of catching the fish, when one's appetite is not too keen; and this you may have all to yourself today. I would advise you to set in the spade down yonder among the groundnuts, where you see the johnswort waving. I think that I may warrant you one worm to every three sods you turn up, if you look well in among the roots of the grass, as if you were weeding. Or, if you choose to go farther, it will not be unwise, for I have found the increase of fair bait to be very nearly as the squares of the distances.

Hermit alone. Let me see; where was I? Methinks I was nearly in this frame of mind; the world lay about at this angle. Shall I go to heaven or a-fishing? If I should soon bring this meditation to an end, would another so sweet occasion be likely to offer? I was as near being resolved into the essence of things as ever I was in my life. I fear my thoughts will not come back to me. If it would do any good, I would whistle for them. When they make us an offer, is it wise to say, We will think of it? My thoughts have left no track, and I cannot find the path again. What was it that I was thinking of? It was a very hazy day. I will just try these three sentences of Con-fut-see; they may fetch that state about again. I know not whether it was the dumps or a budding ecstasy. Mem. There never is but one opportunity of a kind.

Poet. How now, Hermit, is it too soon? I have got just thirteen whole ones, besides several which are imperfect or undersized; but they will do for the smaller fry; they do not cover up the hook so much. Those village worms are quite too large; a shiner may make a meal off one without finding the skewer.

Hermit. Well, then, let's be off. Shall we to the Concord? There's good sport there if the water be not too high.

Why do precisely these objects which we behold make a world? Why has man just these species of animals for his neighbors; as if nothing but a mouse could have filled this crevice? I suspect that Pilpay & Co. have put animals to their best use, for they are all beasts of burden, in a sense, made to carry some portion of our thoughts.

The mice which haunted my house were not the common ones, which are said to have been introduced into the country, but a wild native kind not found in the village. I sent one to a distinguished naturalist, and it interested him much. When I was building, one of these had its nest underneath the house, and before I had laid the second floor, and swept out the shavings, would come out regularly at lunch time and pick up the crumbs at my feet. It probably had never seen a man before; and it soon became quite familiar, and would run over my shoes and up my clothes. It could readily ascend the sides of the room by short impulses, like a squirrel, which it resembled in its motions. At length, as I leaned with my elbow on the bench one day, it ran up my clothes, and along my sleeve, and round and round the paper which held my dinner, while I kept the latter close, and dodged and played at bo-peep with it; and when at last I held still a piece of cheese between my thumb and finger, it came and nibbled it, sitting in my hand, and afterward cleaned its face and paws, like a fly, and walked away.

A phoebe soon built in my shed, and a robin for protection in a pine which grew against the house. In June the partridge (*Tetrao umbellus*) which is so shy a bird, led her brood past my windows, from the woods in the rear to the front of my house, clucking and calling to them like a hen, and in all her behavior proving herself the hen of the woods. The young suddenly disperse on your approach, at a signal from the mother, as if a whirl-wind had swept them away, and they so exactly resemble the dried leaves and twigs that many a traveler has placed his foot in the midst of a brood, and heard the whir of the old bird as she flew off, and her anxious calls and mewing, or seen her trail her wings to attract his attention, without suspecting their neighborhood. The parent will sometimes roll and spin round before you in such a dishabille, that you cannot for a few moments detect what kind of creature it is. The young squat still and flat, often running their heads under a leaf, and mind only their mother's directions given from a distance, nor will your approach make them run again and betray themselves. You may even tread on them, or have your eyes on them for a minute, without discovering them. I have held them in my open hand at such a time, and still their only care, obedient to their mother and their instinct, was to squat there without fear or trembling. So perfect is this instinct, that once, when I had laid them on the leaves again, and one accidentally fell on its side, it was found with the rest in exactly the same position ten minutes afterward. They are not callow like the young of most birds, but more perfectly developed and precocious even than chickens. The remarkably adult yet innocent expression of their open and serene eyes is very memorable. All intelligence seems reflected in them. They suggest not merely the purity of infancy, but a wisdom clarified by experience. Such an eye was not born when the bird was, but is coeval with the sky it reflects. The woods do not yield another such a gem. The traveler does not often look into such a limpid well. The ignorant or reckless sportsman often shoots the parent at such a time, and leaves these innocents to fall a prey to some prowling beast or bird, or gradually mingle with the decaying leaves which they so much resemble. It is said that when hatched by a hen they will directly disperse on some alarm, and so are lost, for they never hear the mother's call which gathers them again. These were my hens and chickens.

It is remarkable how many creatures live wild and free though secret in the woods, and still sustain themselves in the neighborhood of towns, suspected by hunters only. How retired the otter manages to live here! He grows to be four feet long, as big as a small boy, perhaps without any human being getting a glimpse of him. I formerly saw the raccoon in the woods behind where my house is built, and probably still heard their whinnering at night. Commonly I rested an hour or two in the shade at noon, after planting, and ate my lunch, and read a little by a spring which was the source of a swamp and of a brook, oozing from under Brister's Hill, half a mile from my field. The approach to this was through a succession of descending grassy hollows, full of young pitch pines, into a larger wood about the swamp. There, in a very secluded and shaded spot, under a spreading white pine, there was yet a clean firm sward to sit on. I had dug out the spring and made a well of clear gray water, where I could dip up a pailful without roiling it, and thither I went for this purpose almost every day in mid-summer, when the pond was warmest. Thither too the woodcock led her brood, to probe the mud for worms, flying but a foot above them down the bank, while they ran in a troop beneath; but at last, spying me, she would leave her young and circle round and round me, nearer and nearer till within four or five feet, pretending broken wings and legs, to attract my attention, and get off her young, who would already have taken up their march, with faint wiry peep, single file through the swamp, as she directed. Or I heard the peep of the young when I could not see the parent bird. There too the turtle-doves sat over the spring, or fluttered from bough to bough of the soft white pines over my head; or the red squirrel, coursing down the nearest bough, was particularly familiar and inquisitive. You only need sit still long enough in some attractive spot in the woods that all its inhabitants may exhibit themselves to you by turns.

I was witness to events of a less peaceful character. One day when I went out to my wood pile, or rather my pile of stumps, I observed two large ants, the one red, the other much larger, nearly half an inch long, and black, fiercely contending with one another. Having once got hold they never let go, but struggled and wrestled and rolled on the chips incessantly. Looking farther, I was surprised to find that the chips were covered with such combatants, that it was not a *duellum,* but a *bellum,* a war between two races of ants, the red always pitted against the black, and frequently two red ones to one black. The legions of these Myrmidons covered all the hills and vales in my wood-yard, and the ground was already strewn with the dead and dying, both red and

black. It was the only battle which I have ever witnessed, the only battlefield I ever trod while the battle
was raging; internecine war; the red republicans on the
one hand, and the black imperialists on the other. On
every side they were engaged in deadly combat, yet
without any noise that I could hear, and human soldiers
never fought so resolutely. I watched a couple that were
fast locked in each other's embraces, in a little sunny
valley amid the chips, now at noonday prepared to fight
till the sun went down, or life went out. The smaller red
champion had fastened himself like a vice to his adversary's front, and through all the tumblings on that field
never for an instant ceased to gnaw at one of his feelers
near the root, having already caused the other to go by
the board; while the stronger black one dashed him
from side to side, and, as I saw on looking nearer, had
already divested him of several of his members. They
fought with more pertinacity than bulldogs. Neither
manifested the least disposition to retreat. It was evident
that their battle-cry was Conquer or die. In the meanwhile there came along a single red ant on the hillside of
this valley, evidently full of excitement, who either had
despatched his foe, or had not yet taken part in the battle; probably the latter, for he had lost none of his limbs;
whose mother had charged him to return with his shield
or upon it. Or perchance he was some Achilles, who had
nourished his wrath apart, and had now come to avenge
or rescue his Patroclus. He saw this unequal combat from
afar—for the blacks were nearly twice the size of the
red—he drew near with rapid pace till he stood on
his guard within half an inch of the combatants; then,
watching his opportunity, he sprang upon the black
warrior, and commenced his operations near the root of
his right foreleg, leaving the foe to select among his
own members; and so there were three united for life,

as if a new kind of attraction had been invented which put all other locks and cements to shame. I should not have wondered by this time to find that they had their respective musical bands stationed on some eminent chip, and playing their national airs the while, to excite the slow and cheer the dying combatants. I was myself excited somewhat even as if they had been men. The more you think of it, the less the difference. And certainly there is not the fight recorded in Concord history, at least, if in the history of America, that will bear a moment's comparison with this, whether for the numbers engaged in it, or for the patriotism and heroism displayed. For numbers and for carnage it was an Austerlitz or Dresden. Concord Fight! Two killed on the patriots' side, and Luther Blanchard wounded! Why here every ant was a Buttrick—"Fire! for God's sake fire!"—and thousands shared the fate of Davis and Hosmer. There was not one hireling there. I have no doubt that it was a principle they fought for, as much as our ancestors, and not to avoid a three-penny tax on their tea; and the results of this battle will be as important and memorable to those whom it concerns as those of the battle of Bunker Hill, at least.

I took up the chip on which the three I have particularly described were struggling, carried it into my house, and placed it under a tumbler on my window sill, in order to see the issue. Holding a microscope to the first-mentioned. red ant, I saw that, though he was assiduously gnawing at the near foreleg of his enemy, having severed his remaining feeler, his own breast was all torn away, exposing what vitals he had there to the jaws of the black warrior, whose breastplate was apparently too thick for him to pierce; and the dark carbuncles of the sufferer's eyes shone with ferocity such as war only could excite. They struggled half an hour longer under

the tumbler, and when I looked again the black soldier
had severed the heads of his foes from their bodies, and
the still living heads were hanging on either side of him
like ghastly trophies at his saddle-bow, still apparently
as firmly fastened as ever, and he was endeavoring with
feeble struggles, being without feelers and with only the
remnant of a leg, and I know not how many other
wounds, to divest himself of them; which at length,
after half an hour more, he accomplished. I raised the
glass, and he went off over the window sill in that crip-
pled state. Whether he finally survived that combat,
and spent the remainder of his days in some Hotel des
Invalides, I do not know; but I thought that his industry
would not be worth much thereafter. I never learned
which party was victorious, nor the cause of the war;
but I felt for the rest of that day as if I had had my feelings excited and harrowed by witnessing the struggle,
the ferocity and carnage, of a human battle before my
door.

Kirby and Spence tell us that the battles of ants have
long been celebrated and the date of them recorded,
though they say that Huber is the only modern author
who appears to have witnessed them. "Aeneas Sylvius,"
say they, "after giving a very circumstantial account of
one contested with great obstinacy by a great and small
species on the trunk of a pear tree," adds that "'This
action was fought in the pontificate of Eugenius the
Fourth, in the presence of Nicholas Pistoriensis, an eminent lawyer, who related the whole history of the battle
with the greatest fidelity.' A similar engagement between great and small ants is recorded by Olaus Mag-
nus, in which the small ones, being victorious, are said
to have buried the bodies of their own soldiers, but left
those of their giant enemies a prey to the birds. This
event happened previous to the expulsion of the tyrant

Christiern the Second from Sweden." The battle which
I witnessed took place in the Presidency of Polk, five
years before the passage of Webster's Fugitive-Slave
Bill.

Many a village Bose, fit only to course a mud-turtle
in a victualing cellar, sported his heavy quarters in the
woods, without the knowledge of his master, and ineffectually smelled at old fox burrows and woodchucks'
holes; led perchance by some slight cur which nimbly
threaded the wood, and might still inspire a natural
terror in its denizens; now far behind his guide, barking like a canine bull toward some small squirrel which
had treed itself for scrutiny, then, cantering off, blend-
ing the bushes with his weight, imagining that he is on
the track of some stray member of the jerbilla family.
Once I was surprised to see a cat walking along the
stony shore of the pond, for they rarely wander so far
from home. The surprise was mutual. Nevertheless the
most domestic cat, which has lain on a rug all her days,
appears quite at home in the woods, and, by her sly and
stealthy behavior, proves herself more native there than
the regular inhabitants. Once, when berrying, I met
with a cat with young kittens in the woods, quite wild,
and they all, like their mother, had their backs up and
were fiercely spitting at me. A few years before I lived
in the woods there was what was called a "winged cat"
in one of the farmhouses in Lincoln nearest the pond,
Mr. Gilian Baker's. When I called to see her in June,
1842, she was gone a-hunting in the woods, as was her
wont (I am not sure whether it was a male or female,
and so use the more common pronoun), but her mistress
told me that she came into the neighborhood a little
more than a year before, in April, and was finally taken
into their house; that she was of a dark brownish-gray
color, with a white spot on her throat, and white feet,

and had a large bushy tail like a fox; that in the winter the fur grew thick and flatted out along her sides, forming strips ten or twelve inches long by two and a half wide, and under her chin like a muff, the upper side loose, the under matted like felt, and in the spring these appendages dropped off. They gave me a pair of her "wings," which I keep still. There is no appearance of a membrane about them. Some thought it was part flying-squirrel or some other wild animal, which is not impossible, for, according to naturalists, prolific hybrids have been produced by the union of the marten and domestic cat. This would have been the right kind of cat for me to keep, if I had kept any; for why should not a poet's cat be winged as well as his horse?

In the fall the loon (*Colymbus glacialis*) came, as usual, to moult and bathe in the pond, making the woods ring with his wild laughter before I had risen. At rumor of his arrival all the Mill-dam sportsmen are on the alert, in gigs and on foot, two by two and three by three, with patent rifles and conical balls and spyglasses. They come rustling through the woods like autumn leaves, at least ten men to one loon. Some station themselves on this side of the pond, some on that, for the poor bird cannot be omnipresent; if he dive here he must come up there. But now the kind October wind rises, rustling the leaves and rippling the surface of the water, so that no loon can be heard or seen, though his foes sweep the pond with spyglasses, and make the woods resound with their discharges. The waves generously rise and dash angrily, taking sides with all water-fowl, and our sportsmen must beat a retreat to town and shop and unfinished jobs. But they were too often successful. When I went to get a pail of water early in the morning I frequently saw this stately bird sailing out of my cove within a few rods. If I endeavored to overtake

him in a boat, in order to see how he would maneuver,
he would dive and be completely lost, so that I did not
discover him again, sometimes, till the latter part of the
day. But I was more than a match for him on the surface.
He commonly went off in a rain.

As I was paddling along the north shore one very
calm October afternoon, for such days especially they
settle onto the lakes, like the milkweed down, having
looked in vain over the pond for a loon, suddenly one,
sailing out from the shore toward the middle a few rods
in front of me, set up his wild laugh and betrayed himself. I pursued with a paddle and he dived, but when he
came up I was nearer than before. He dived again, but
I miscalculated the direction he would take, and we
were fifty rods apart when he came to the surface this
time, for I had helped to widen the interval; and again
he laughed long and loud, and with more reason than
before. He maneuvered so cunningly that I could not
get within half a dozen rods of him. Each time, when
he came to the surface, turning his head this way and
that, he coolly surveyed the water and the land, and apparently chose his course so that he might come up
where there was the widest expense of water and at the
greatest distance from the boat. It was surprising how
quickly he made up his mind and put his resolve into
execution. He led me at once to the widest part of the
pond, and could not be driven from it. While he was
thinking one thing in his brain, I was endeavoring to
divine his thought in mine. It was a pretty game, played
on the smooth surface of the pond, a man against a loon.
Suddenly your adversary's checker disappears beneath
the board, and the problem is to place yours nearest to
where his will appear again. Sometimes he would come
up unexpectedly on the opposite side of me, having
apparently passed directly under the boat. So long-

winded was he and so unweariable, that when he had
swum farthest he would immediately plunge again,
nevertheless; and then no wit could divine where in the
deep pond, beneath the smooth surface, he might be
speeding his way like a fish, for he had time and ability
to visit the bottom of the pond in its deepest part. It is
said that loons have been caught in the New York lakes
eighty feet beneath the surface, with hooks set for trout
—though Walden is deeper than that. How surprised
must the fishes be to see this ungainly visitor from another sphere speeding his way amid their schools! Yet
he appeared to know his course as surely under water
as on the surface, and swam much faster there. Once or
twice I saw a ripple where he approached the surface,
just put his head out to reconnoiter, and instantly dived
again. I found that it was as well for me to rest on my
oars and wait his reappearing as to endeavor to calculate
where he would rise; for again and again, when I was
straining my eyes over the surface one way, I would
suddenly be startled by his unearthly laugh behind me.
But why, after displaying so much cunning, did he invariably betray himself the moment he came up by that
loud laugh? Did not his white breast enough betray
him? He was indeed a silly loon, I thought. I could commonly hear the plash of the water when he came up,
and so also detected him. But after an hour he seemed
as fresh as ever, dived as willingly, and swam yet farther than at first. It was surprising to see how serenely
he sailed off with unruffled breast when he came to
the surface, doing all the work with his webbed feet
beneath. His usual note was this demoniac laughter,
yet somewhat like that of a waterfowl; but occasionally,
when he had balked me most successfully and come up
a long way off, he uttered a long-drawn unearthly howl,
probably more like that of a wolf than any bird; as when

a beast puts his muzzle to the ground and deliberately howls. This was his looning, perhaps the wildest sound that is ever heard here, making the woods ring far and wide. I concluded that he laughed in derision of my efforts, confident of his own resources. Though the sky was by this time overcast, the pond was so smooth that I could see where he broke the surface when I did not hear him. His white breast, the stillness of the air, and the smoothness of the water were all against him. At length, having come up fifty rods off, he uttered one of those prolonged howls, as if calling on the god of loons to aid him, and immediately there came a wind from the east and rippled the surface, and filled the whole air with misty rain, and I was impressed as if it were the prayer of the loon answered, and his god was angry with me; and so I left him disappearing far away on the tumultuous surface.

For hours, in fall days, I watched the ducks cunningly tack and veer and hold the middle of the pond, far from the sportsman; tricks which they will have less need to practice in Louisiana bayous. When compelled to rise they would sometimes circle round and round and over the pond at a considerable height, from which they could easily see to other ponds and the river, like black motes in the sky; and, when I thought they had gone off thither long since, they would settle down by a slanting flight of a quarter of a mile onto a distant part which was left free; but what beside safety they got by sailing in the middle of Walden I do not know, unless they love its water for the same reason that I do.

HOUSEWARMING

In October I went a-graping to the river meadows, and loaded myself with clusters more precious for their

beauty and fragrance than for food. There too I admired,
though I did not gather, the cranberries, small waxen
gems, pendants of the meadow grass, pearly and red,
which the farmer plucks with an ugly rake, leaving the
smooth meadow in a snarl, heedlessly measuring them
by the bushel and the dollar only, and sells the spoils of
the meads to Boston and New York; destined to be
jammed, to satisfy the tastes of lovers of Nature there.
So butchers rake the tongues of bison out of the prairie
grass, regardless of the torn and drooping plant. The
barberry's brilliant fruit was likewise food for my eyes
merely; but I collected a small store of wild apples for
coddling, which the proprietor and travelers had overlooked. When chestnuts were ripe I laid up half a bushel
for winter. It was very exciting at that season to roam
the then boundless chestnut woods of Lincoln—they
now sleep their long sleep under the railroad—with a
bag on my shoulder, and a stick to open burrs with in
my hand, for I did not always wait for the frost, amid
the rustling of leaves and the loud reproofs of the red-
squirrels and the jays, whose half-consumed nuts I
sometimes stole, for the burrs which they had selected
were sure to contain sound ones. Occasionally I climbed
and shook the trees. They grew also behind my house,
and one large tree, which almost overshadowed it, was,
when in flower, a bouquet which scented the whole
neighborhood, but the squirrels and the jays got most
of its fruit; the last coming in flocks early in the morning
and picking the nuts out of the burrs before they fell. I
relinquished these trees to them and visited the more
distant woods composed wholly of chestnut. These nuts,
as far as they went, were a good substitute for bread.
Many other substitutes might, perhaps, be found. Digging one day for fish-worms I discovered the groundnut
(*Apios tuberosa*) on its string, the potato of the aborig-

ines, a sort of fabulous fruit, which I had begun to doubt
if I had ever dug and eaten in childhood, as I had told,
and had not dreamed it. I had often since seen its crim-
pled red velvety blossom supported by the stems of
other plants without knowing it to be the same. Cultivation has well-nigh exterminated it. It has a sweetish
taste, much like that of a frostbitten potato, and I found
it better boiled than roasted. This tuber seemed like
a faint promise of Nature to rear her own children and
feed them simply here at some future period. In these
days of fatted cattle and waving grainfields this humble
root, which was once the *totem* of an Indian tribe, is
quite forgotten, or known only by its flowering vine; but
let wild Nature reign here once more, and the tender
and luxurious English grains will probably disappear
before a myriad of foes, and without the care of man the
crow may carry back even the last seed of corn to the
great cornfield of the Indian's God in the southwest,
whence he is said to have brought it; but the now almost
exterminated groundnut will perhaps revive and flourish
in spite of frosts and wildness, prove itself indigenous,
and resume its ancient importance and dignity as the
diet of the hunter tribe. Some Indian Ceres or Minerva
must have been the inventor and bestower of it; and
when the reign of poetry commences here, its leaves
and string of nuts may be represented on our works of
art.

Already, by the first of September, I had seen two or
three small maples turned scarlet across the pond, beneath where the white stems of three aspens diverged,
at the point of a promontory, next the water. Ah, many
a tale their color told! And gradually from week to week
the character of each tree came out, and it admired itself
reflected in the smooth mirror of the lake. Each morning the manager of this gallery substituted some new

picture, distinguished by more brilliant or harmonious coloring, for the old upon the walls.

The wasps came by thousands to my lodge in October, as to winter quarters, and settled on my windows within and on the walls overhead, sometimes deterring visitors from entering. Each morning, when they were numbed with cold, I swept some of them out, but I did not trouble myself much to get rid of them; I even felt complimented by their regarding my house as a desirable shelter. They never molested me seriously, though they bedded with me; and they gradually disappeared, into what crevices I do not know, avoiding winter and unspeakable cold.

Like the wasps, before I finally went into winter quarters in November, I used to resort to the northeast side of Walden, which the sun, reflected from the pitch-pine woods and the stony shore, made the fireside of the pond; it is so much pleasanter and wholesomer to be warmed by the sun while you can be, than by an artificial fire. I thus warmed myself by the still-glowing embers which the summer, like a departed hunter, had left.

When I came to build my chimney I studied masonry. My bricks being second-hand ones required to be cleaned with a trowel, so that I learned more than usual of the qualities of bricks and trowels. The mortar on them was fifty years old, and was said to be still growing harder; but this is one of those sayings which men love to repeat whether they are true or not. Such sayings themselves grow harder and adhere more firmly with age, and it would take many blows with a trowel to clean an old wiseacre of them. Many of the villages of Mesopotamia are built of second-hand bricks of a very good quality, obtained from the ruins of Babylon, and the cement on them is older and probably harder still. However that may be, I was struck by the peculiar toughness of the steel which bore so many violent blows without being worn out. As my bricks had been in a chimney before, though I did not read the name of Nebuchadnezzar on them, I picked out as many fireplace bricks as I could find, to save work and waste, and I filled the spaces between the bricks about the fireplace with stones from the pond shore, and also made my mortar with the white sand from the same place. I lingered most about the fireplace, as the most vital part of the house. Indeed, I worked so deliberately, that though I commenced at the ground in the morning, a course of bricks raised a few inches above the floor served for my pillow at night; yet I did not get a stiff neck for it that I remember; my stiff neck is of older date. I took a poet to board for a fortnight about those times, which caused me to be put to it for room. He brought his own knife, though I had two, and we used to scour them by thrusting them into the earth. He shared with me the labors of cooking. I was pleased to see my work rising so square and solid by degrees, and reflected, that, if it proceeded slowly, it was calculated to endure a long time. The chimney is to some extent an independent structure, standing on the ground, and rising through the house to the heavens; even after the house is burned it still stands sometimes, and its importance and independence are apparent. This was toward the end of summer. It was now November.

The north wind had already begun to cool the pond, though it took many weeks of steady blowing to accomplish it, it is so deep. When I began to have a fire at evening, before I plastered my house, the chimney carried smoke particularly well, because of the numerous chinks between the boards. Yet I passed some cheerful evenings in that cool and airy apartment, surrounded by the rough brown boards full of knots, and rafters with the bark on high overhead. My house never pleased my eye so much after it was plastered, though I was obliged to confess that it was more comfortable. Should not every apartment in which man dwells be lofty enough to create some obscurity overhead, where flickering shadows may play at evening about the rafters? These forms are more agreeable to the fancy and imagination than fresco paintings or other the most expensive furniture. I now first began to inhabit my house, I may say, when I began to use it for warmth as well as shelter. I had got a couple of old firedogs to keep the wood from the hearth, and it did me good to see the soot form on the back of the chimney which I had built, and I poked the fire with more right and more satisfaction than usual. My dwelling was small, and I could hardly entertain an echo in it; but it seemed larger for being a single apartment and remote from neighbors. All the attractions of a house were concentrated in one room; it was kitchen, chamber, parlor, and keeping-room; and whatever satisfaction parent or child, master or servant, derive from living in a house, I enjoyed it all. Cato says, the master of a family (*patremfamilias*) must have in his rustic villa *"cellam oleariam, vinariam, dolia multa, uti lubeat caritatem expectare, et rei, et virtuti, et gloriae erit,"* that is, "an oil and wine cellar, many casks, so that it may be pleasant to expect hard times; it will be for his advantage, and virtue, and glory." I had in my cellar a firkin of potatoes, about two quarts of peas with the weevil in them, and on my shelf a little rice, a jug of molasses, and of rye and Indian meal a peck each.

I sometimes dream of a larger and more populous house, standing in a golden age, of enduring materials, and without gingerbread work, which shall still consist

of only one room, a vast, rude, substantial, primitive
hall, without ceiling or plastering, with bare rafters and
purlins supporting a sort of lower heaven over one's
head—useful to keep off rain and snow, where the king
and queen posts stand out to receive your homage,
when you have done reverence to the prostrate Saturn
of an older dynasty on stepping over the sill; a cavernous house, wherein you must reach up a torch upon a
pole to see the roof; where some may live in the fireplace, some in the recess of a window, and some on
settles, some at one end of the hall, some at another, and
some aloft on rafters with the spiders, if they choose; a
house which you have got into when you have opened the
outside door, and the ceremony is over; where the weary
traveler may wash, and eat, and converse, and sleep,
without further journey; such a shelter as you would be
glad to reach in a tempestuous night, containing all the
essentials of a house, and nothing for housekeeping;
where you can see all the treasures of the house at one
view, and everything hangs upon its peg that a man
should use; at once kitchen, pantry, parlor, chamber,
storehouse, and garret; where you can see so necessary
a thing as a barrel or a ladder, so convenient a thing as
a cupboard, and hear the pot boil, and pay your respects
to the fire that cooks your dinner, and the oven that
bakes your bread, and the necessary furniture and utensils are the chief ornaments; where the washing is not
put out, nor the fire, nor the mistress, and perhaps you
are sometimes requested to move from off the trap-door,
when the cook would descend into the cellar, and so
learn whether the ground is solid or hollow beneath
you without stamping. A house whose inside is as open
and manifest as a bird's nest, and you cannot go in at
the front door and out at the back without seeing some
of its inhabitants; where to be a guest is to be presented

with the freedom of the house, and not to be carefully excluded from seven eighths of it, shut up in a particular cell, and told to make yourself at home there—in solitary confinement. Nowadays the host does not admit you to *his* hearth, but has got the mason to build one for yourself somewhere in his alley, and hospitality is the art of *keeping* you at the greatest distance. There is as much secrecy about the cooking as if he had a design to poison you. I am aware that I have been on many a man's premises, and might have been legally ordered off, but I am not aware that I have been in many men's houses. I might visit in my old clothes a king and queen who lived simply in such a house as I have described, if I were going their way; but backing out of a modern palace will be all that I shall desire to learn, if ever I am caught in one.

It would seem as if the very language of our parlors would lose all its nerve and degenerate into *parlaver* wholly, our lives pass at such remoteness from its symbols, and its metaphors and tropes are necessarily so far fetched, through slides and dumbwaiters, as it were; in other words, the parlor is so far from the kitchen and workshop. The dinner even is only the parable of a dinner, commonly. As if only the savage dwelt near enough to Nature and Truth to borrow a trope from them. How can the scholar, who dwells away in the Northwest Territory or the Isle of Man, tell what is parliamentary in the kitchen?

However, only one or two of my guests were ever bold enough to stay and eat a hasty-pudding with me; but when they saw that crisis approaching they beat a hasty retreat rather, as if it would shake the house to its foundations. Nevertheless, it stood through a great many hasty-puddings.

I did not plaster till it was freezing weather. I brought

over some whiter and cleaner sand for this purpose from the opposite shore of the pond in a boat, a sort of conveyance which would have tempted me to go much farther if necessary. My house had in the meanwhile been shingled down to the ground on every side. In lathing I was pleased to be able to send home each nail with a single blow of the hammer, and it was my ambition to transfer the plaster from the board to the wall neatly and rapidly. I remembered the story of a conceited fellow, who, in fine clothes, was wont to lounge about the village once, giving advice to workmen. Venturing one day to substitute deeds for words, he turned up his cuffs, seized a plasterer's board, and having loaded his trowel without mishap, with a complacent look toward the lathing overhead, made a bold gesture thitherward; and straightway, to his complete discomfiture, received the whole contents in his ruffled bosom. I admired anew the economy and convenience of plastering, which so effectually shuts out the cold and takes a handsome finish, and I learned the various casualties to which the plasterer is liable. I was surprised to see how thirsty the bricks were which drank up all the moisture in my plaster before I had smoothed it, and how many pailfuls of water it takes to christen a new hearth. I had the previous winter made a small quantity of lime by burning the shells of the *Unio fluviatilis*, which our river affords, for the sake of the experiment; so that I knew where my materials came from. I might have got good limestone within a mile or two and burned it myself, if I had cared to do so.

The pond had in the meanwhile skimmed over in the shadiest and shallowest coves, some days or even weeks before the general freezing. The first ice is especially interesting and perfect, being hard, dark, and transparent,

and affords the best opportunity that ever offers for ex-
amining the bottom where it is shallow; for you can lie
at your length on ice only an inch thick, like a skater insect on the surface of the water, and study the bottom at
your leisure, only two or three inches distant, like a picture behind a glass, and the water is necessarily always
smooth then. There are many furrows in the sand where
some creature has traveled about and doubled on its
tracks; and, for wrecks, it is strewn with the cases of
caddis worms made of minute grains of white quartz.
Perhaps these have creased it, for you find some of their
cases in the furrows, though they are deep and broad for
them to make. But the ice itself is the object of most interest, though you must improve the earliest opportunity to study it. If you examine it closely the morning
after it freezes, you find that the greater part of the
bubbles, which at first appeared to be within it, are
against its under surface, and that more are continually
rising from the bottom; while the ice is as yet comparatively solid and dark, that is, you see the water through
it. These bubbles are from an eightieth to an eighth of
an inch in diameter, very clear and beautiful, and you
see your face reflected in them through the ice. There
may be thirty or forty of them to a square inch. There
are also already within the ice narrow oblong perpendicular bubbles about half an inch long, sharp cones with
the apex upward; or oftener, if the ice is quite fresh,
minute spherical bubbles one directly above another,
like a string of beads. But these within the ice are not so
numerous nor obvious as those beneath. I sometimes
used to cast on stones to try the strength of the ice, and
those which broke through carried in air with them,
which formed very large and conspicuous white bubbles
beneath. One day when I came to the same place forty-
eight hours afterward, I found that those large bubbles

were still perfect, though an inch more of ice had
formed, as I could see distinctly by the seam in the edge
of a cake. But as the last two days had been very warm,
like an Indian summer, the ice was not now transparent,
showing the dark green color of the water, and the bottom, but opaque and whitish or gray, and though twice
as thick was hardly stronger than before, for the air bubbles had greatly expanded under this heat and run together, and lost their regularity; they were no longer
one directly over another, but often like silvery coins
poured from a bag, one overlapping another, or in thin
flakes, as if occupying slight cleavages. The beauty of
the ice was gone, and it was too late to study the bottom. Being curious to know what position my great
bubbles occupied with regard to the new ice, I broke
out a cake containing a middling sized one, and turned
it bottom upward. The new ice had formed around and
under the bubble, so that it was included between the
two ices. It was wholly in the lower ice, but close against
the upper, and was flattish, or perhaps slightly lenticu-
lar, with a rounded edge, a quarter of an inch deep by
four inches in diameter; and I was surprised to find that
directly under the bubble the ice was melted with great
regularity in the form of a saucer reversed, to the height
of five eighths of an inch in the middle, leaving a thin
partition there between the water and the bubble,
hardly an eighth of an inch thick; and in many places
the small bubbles in this partition had burst out downward, and probably there was no ice at all under the
largest bubbles, which were a foot in diameter. I inferred that the infinite number of minute bubbles which
I had first seen against the under surface of the ice were
now frozen in likewise, and that each, in its degree, had
operated like a burning-glass on the ice beneath to melt

and rot it. These are the little air-guns which contribute to make the ice crack and whoop.

At length the winter set in in good earnest, just as I had finished plastering, and the wind began to howl around the house as if it had not had permission to do so till then. Night after night the geese came lumbering in in the dark with a clangor and a whistling of wings, even after the ground was covered with snow, some to alight in Walden, and some flying low over the woods toward Fair Haven, bound for Mexico. Several times, when returning from the village at ten or eleven o'clock at night, I heard the tread of a flock of geese, or else ducks, on the dry leaves in the woods by a pond-hole behind my dwelling, where they had come up to feed, and the faint honk or quack of their leader as they hurried off. In 1845 Walden froze entirely over for the first time on the night of the 22d of December, Flints' and other shallower ponds and the river having been frozen ten days or more; in '46, the 16th; in '49, about the 31st; and in '50, about the 27th of December; in '52, the 5th of January; in '53, the 31st of December. The snow had already covered the ground since the 25th of November, and surrounded me suddenly with the scenery of winter. I withdrew yet farther into my shell, and endeavored to keep a bright fire both within my house and within my breast. My employment out of doors now was to collect the dead wood in the forest, bringing it in my hands or on my shoulders, or sometimes trailing a dead pine tree under each arm to my shed. An old forest fence which had seen its best days was a great haul for me. I sacrificed it to Vulcan, for it was past serving the god Terminus. How much more interesting an event is that man's supper who has just been forth in the snow to

hunt, nay, you might say, steal, the fuel to cook it with!
His bread and meat are sweet. There are enough fagots
and waste wood of all kinds in the forests of most of our
towns to support many fires, but which at present warm
none, and, some think, hinder the growth of the young
wood. There was also the driftwood of the pond. In the
course of the summer I had discovered a raft of pitch-
pine logs with the bark on, pinned together by the Irish
when the railroad was built. This I hauled up partly on
the shore. After soaking two years and then lying high
six months it was perfectly sound, though waterlogged
past drying. I amused myself one winter day with slid-
ing this piecemeal across the pond, nearly half a mile,
skating behind with one end of a log fifteen feet long on
my shoulder, and the other on the ice; or I tied several
logs together with a birch withe, and then, with a longer
birch or alder which had a hook at the end, dragged
them across. Though completely waterlogged and almost as heavy as lead, they not only burned long, but
made a very hot fire; nay, I thought that they burned
better for the soaking, as if the pitch, being confined by
the water, burned longer as in a lamp.

Gilpin, in his account of the forest borderers of England, says that "the encroachments of trespassers, and
the houses and fences thus raised on the borders of the
forest," were "considered as great nuisances by the old
forest law, and were severely punished under the name
of *purprestures,* as tending *ad terrorem ferarum—ad
nocumentum forestae,* etc.," to the frightening of the
game and the detriment of the forest. But I was interested in the preservation of the venison and the vert
more than the hunters or woodchoppers, and as much as
though I had been the Lord Warden himself; and if any
part was burned, though I burned it myself by accident,
I grieved with a grief that lasted longer and was more

inconsolable than that of the proprietors; nay, I grieved when it was cut down by the proprietors themselves. I would that our farmers when they cut down a forest felt some of that awe which the old Romans did when they came to thin, or let in the light to, a consecrated grove (*lucum conlucare*), that is, would believe that it is sacred to some god. The Roman made an expiatory offering, and prayed, Whatever god or goddess thou art to whom this grove is sacred, be propitious to me, my family, and children, etc.

It is remarkable what a value is still put on upon wood even in this age and in this new country, a value more permanent and universal than that of gold. After all our discoveries and inventions no man will go by a pile of wood. It is as precious to us as it was to our Saxon and Norman ancestors. If they made their bows of it, we make our gun stocks of it. Michaux, more than thirty years ago, says that the price of wood for fuel in New York and Philadelphia "nearly equals, and sometimes exceeds, that of the best wood in Paris, though this immense capital annually requires more than three hundred thousand cords, and is surrounded to the distance of three hundred miles by cultivated plains." In this town the price of wood rises almost steadily, and the only question is, how much higher it is to be this year than it was the last. Mechanics and tradesmen who come in person to the forest on no other errand, are sure to attend the wood auction, and even pay a high price for the privilege of gleaning after the woodchopper. It is now many years that men have resorted to the forest for fuel and the materials of the arts: the New Englander and the New Hollander, the Parisian and the Celt, the farmer and Robinhood, Goody Blake and Harry Gill; in most parts of the world the prince and the peasant, the scholar and the savage, equally require still a few sticks from the forest to warm them and cook their food. Neither could I do without them.

Every man looks at his wood pile with a kind of affection. I loved to have mine before my window, and the more chips the better to remind me of my pleasing work. I had an old axe which nobody claimed, with which by spells in winter days, on the sunny side of the house, I played about the stumps which I had got out of my beanfield. As my driver prophesied when I was ploughing, they warmed me twice—once while I was splitting them, and again when they were on the fire, so that no fuel could give out more heat. As for the axe, I was advised to get the village blacksmith to "jump" it; but I jumped him, and, putting a hickory helve from the woods into it, made it do. If it was dull, it was at least hung true.

A few pieces of fat pine were a great treasure. It is interesting to remember how much of this food for fire is still concealed in the bowels of the earth. In previous years I had often gone "prospecting" over some bare hill side, where a pitch-pine wood had formerly stood, and got out the fat pine roots. They are almost indestructible. Stumps thirty or forty years old, at least, will still be sound at the core, though the sapwood has all become vegetable mould, as appears by the scales of the thick bark forming a ring level with the earth four or five inches distant from the heart. With axe and shovel you explore this mine, and follow the marrowy store, yellow as beef tallow, or as if you had struck on a vein of gold, deep into the earth. But commonly I kindled my fire with the dry leaves of the forest, which I had stored up in my shed before the snow came. Green hickory finely split makes the woodchopper's kindlings, when he has a camp in the woods. Once in a while I got a little of this. When the villagers were light-

ing their fires beyond the horizon, I too gave notice to
the various wild inhabitants of Walden vale, by a smoky
streamer from my chimney, that I was awake.

> Light-winged Smoke, Icarian bird,
> Melting thy pinions in thy upward flight,
> Lark without song, and messenger of dawn,
> Circling above the hamlets as thy nest;
> Or else, departing dream, and shadowy form
> Of midnight vision, gathering up thy skirts;
> By night star-veiling, and by day
> Darkening the light and blotting out the sun;
> Go thou my incense upward from this hearth,
> And ask the gods to pardon this clear flame.

Hard green wood just cut, though I used but little of
that, answered my purpose better than any other. I
sometimes left a good fire when I went to take a walk in
a winter afternoon; and when I returned, three or four
hours afterward, it would be still alive and glowing. My
house was not empty though I was gone. It was as if I
had left a cheerful housekeeper behind. It was I and
Fire that lived there; and commonly my housekeeper
proved trustworthy. One day, however, as I was splitting wood, I thought that I would just look in at the
window and see if the house was not on fire; it was the
only time I remember to have been particularly anxious
on this score; so I looked and saw that a spark had
caught my bed, and I went in and extinguished it when
it had burned a place as big as my hand. But my house
occupied so sunny and sheltered a position, and its roof
was so low, that I could afford to let the fire go out in
the middle of almost any winter day.

The moles nested in my cellar, nibbling every third
potato, and making a snug bed even there of some hair
left after plastering and of brown paper; for even the
wildest animals love comfort and warmth as well as
man, and they survive the winter only because they are

so careful to secure them. Some of my friends spoke as
if I was coming to the woods on purpose to freeze myself. The animal merely makes a bed, which he warms
with his body, in a sheltered place; but man, having
discovered fire, boxes up some air in a spacious apartment, and warms that, instead of robbing himself,
makes that his bed, in which he can move about divested of more cumbrous clothing, maintain a kind of
summer in the midst of winter, and by means of windows even admit the light, and with a lamp lengthen
out the day. Thus he goes a step or two beyond instinct,
and saves a little time for the fine arts. Though, when
I had been exposed to the rudest blasts a long time, my
whole body began to grow torpid, when I reached the
genial atmosphere of my house I soon recovered my
faculties and prolonged my life. But the most luxuriously housed has little to boast of in this respect, nor
need we trouble ourselves to speculate how the human
race may be at last destroyed. It would be easy to cut
their threads any time with a little sharper blast from
the north. We go on dating from Cold Fridays and
Great Snows; but a little colder Friday, or greater snow,
would put a period to man's existence on the globe.

The next winter I used a small cooking stove for economy, since I did not own the forest; but it did not keep
fire so well as the open fireplace. Cooking was then, for
the most part, no longer a poetic, but merely a chemic
process. It will soon be forgotten, in these days of
stoves, that we used to roast potatoes in the ashes, after
the Indian fashion. The stove not only took up room
and scented the house, but it concealed the fire, and I
felt as if I had lost a companion. You can always see a
face in the fire. The laborer, looking into it at evening,
purifies his thoughts of the dross and earthiness which
they have accumulated during the day. But I could no

longer sit and look into the fire, and the pertinent words
of a poet recurred to me with new force.

"Never, bright flame, may be denied to me
 Thy dear, life imaging, close sympathy.
What but my hopes shot upward e'er so bright?
What but my fortunes sunk so low in night?
Why art thou banished from our hearth and hall,
Thou who art welcomed and beloved by all?
Was thy existence then too fanciful
For our life's common light, who are so dull?
Did thy bright gleam mysterious converse hold
With our congenial souls? secrets too bold?

Well, we are safe and strong, for now we sit
Beside a hearth where no dim shadows flit,
Where nothing cheers nor saddens, but a fire
Warms feet and hands—nor does to more aspire;
By whose compact utilitarian heap
The present may sit down and go to sleep,
Nor fear the ghosts who from the dim past walked,
And with us by the unequal light of the old wood fire
 talked."

FORMER INHABITANTS; AND WINTER VISITORS

I weathered some merry snowstorms, and spent some
cheerful winter evenings by my fireside, while the snow
whirled wildly without, and even the hooting of the
owl was hushed. For many weeks I met no one in my
walks but those who came occasionally to cut wood and
sled it to the village. The elements, however, abetted
me in making a path through the deepest snow in the
woods, for when I had once gone through, the wind
blew the oak leaves into my tracks, where they lodged,
and by absorbing the rays of the sun melted the snow,
and so not only made a dry bed for my feet, but in the
night their dark line was my guide. For human society
I was obliged to conjure up the former occupants of

these woods. Within the memory of many of my townsmen the road near which my house stands resounded
with the laugh and gossip of inhabitants, and the
woods which border it were notched and dotted here
and there with their little gardens and dwellings, though
it was then much more shut in by the forest than now.
In some places, within my own remembrance, the pines
would scrape both sides of a chaise at once, and women
and children who were compelled to go this way to
Lincoln alone and on foot did it with fear, and often
ran a good part of the distance. Though mainly but a
humble route to neighboring villages, or for the woodman's team, it once amused the traveler more than now
by its variety, and lingered longer in his memory.
Where now firm open fields stretch from the village to
the woods, it then ran through a maple swamp on a
foundation of logs, the remnants of which, doubtless,
still underlie the present dusty highway, from the Stratten, now the Alms House, Farm, to Brister's Hill.

East of my bean field, across the road, lived Cato Ingraham, slave of Duncan Ingraham, Esquire, gentleman, of Concord village, who built his slave a house,
and gave him permission to live in Walden Woods—
Cato, not Uticensis, but Concordiensis. Some say that
he was a Guinea Negro. There are a few who remember
his little patch among the walnuts, which he let grow
up till he should be old and need them; but a younger
and whiter speculator got them at last. He too, however,
occupies an equally narrow house at present. Cato's
half-obliterated cellar hole still remains, though known
to few, being concealed from the traveler by a fringe
of pines. It is now filled with the smooth sumach (*Rhus
glabra*), and one of the earliest species of goldenrod
(*Solidago stricta*) grows there luxuriantly.

Here, by the very corner of my field, still nearer to

town, Zilpha, a colored woman, had her little house, where she spun linen for the townsfolk, making the Walden Woods ring with her shrill singing, for she had a loud and notable voice. At length, in the war of 1812, her dwelling was set on fire by English soldiers, prisoners on parole, when she was away, and her cat and dog and hens were all burned up together. She led a hard life, and somewhat inhumane. One old frequenter of these woods remembers, that as he passed her house one noon he heard her muttering to herself over her gurgling pot, "Ye are all bones, bones!" I have seen bricks amid the oak copse there.

Down the road, on the right hand, on Brister's Hill, lived Brister Freeman, "a handy Negro," slave of Squire Cummings once—there where grow still the apple trees which Brister planted and tended; large old trees now, but their fruit still wild and ciderish to my taste. Not long since I read his epitaph in the old Lincoln burying-ground, a little on one side, near the unmarked graves of some British grenadiers who fell in the retreat from Concord—where he is styled "Sippio Brister"—Scipio Africanus he had some title to be called—"a man of color," as if he were discolored. It also told me, with staring emphasis, when he died; which was but an indirect way of informing me that he ever lived. With him dwelt Fenda, his hospitable wife, who told fortunes, yet pleasantly—large, round, and black, blacker than any of the children of night, such a dusky orb as never rose on Concord before or since.

Farther down the hill, on the left, on the old road in the woods, are marks of some homestead of the Stratten family; whose orchard once covered all the slope of Brister's Hill, but was long since killed out by pitch pines, excepting a few stumps, whose old roots furnish still the wild stocks of many a thrifty village tree.

Nearer yet to town, you come to Breed's location, on the other side of the way, just on the edge of the wood; ground famous for the pranks of a demon not distinctly named in old mythology, who has acted a prominent and astounding part in our New England life, and deserves, as much as any mythological character, to have his biography written one day; who first comes in the guise of a friend or hired man, and then robs and murders the whole family—New England Rum. But history must not yet tell the tragedies enacted here; let time intervene in some measure to assuage and lend an azure tint to them. Here the most indistinct and dubious tradition says that once a tavern stood; the well the same, which tempered the traveler's beverage and refreshed his steed. Here then men saluted one another, and heard and told the news, and went their ways again.

Breed's hut was standing only a dozen years ago, though it had long been unoccupied. It was about the size of mine. It was set on fire by mischievous boys, one Election night, if I do not mistake. I lived on the edge of the village then, and had just lost myself over Davenant's Gondibert, that winter that I labored with a lethargy, which, by the way, I never knew whether to regard as a family complaint, having an uncle who goes to sleep shaving himself, and is obliged to sprout potatoes in a cellar Sundays, in order to keep awake and keep the Sabbath, or as the consequence of my attempt to read Chalmers' collection of English poetry without skipping. It fairly overcame my Nervii. I had just sunk my head on this when the bells rung fire, and in hot haste the engines rolled that way, led by a straggling troop of men and boys, and I among the foremost, for I had leaped the brook. We thought it was far south over the woods—we who had run to fires before—barn, shop, or dwelling-house, or all together. "It's Baker's barn," cried one. "It is the Codman place," affirmed another. And then fresh sparks went up above the wood, as if the roof fell in, and we all shouted "Concord to the rescue!" Wagons shot past with furious speed and crushing loads, bearing, perchance, among the rest, the agent of the Insurance Company, who was bound to go however far; and ever and anon the engine bell tinkled behind, more slow and sure; and rearmost of all, as it was afterward whispered, came they who set the fire and gave the alarm. Thus we kept on like true idealists, rejecting the evidence of our senses, until at a turn in the road we heard the crackling and actually felt the heat of the fire from over the wall, and realized, alas! that we were there. The very nearness of the fire but cooled our ardor. At first we thought to throw a frog-pond on to it; but concluded to let it burn, it was so far gone and so worthless. So we stood round our engine, jostled one another, expressed our sentiments through speaking-trumpets, or in lower tone referred to the great conflagrations which the world has witnessed, including Bascom's shop, and, between ourselves, we thought that, were we there in season with our "tub," and a full frog-pond by, we could turn that threatened last and universal one into another flood. We finally retreated without doing any mischief—returned to sleep and Gondibert. But as for Gondibert, I would except that passage in the preface about wit being the soul's powder, "but most of mankind are strangers to wit, as Indians are to powder."

It chanced that I walked that way across the fields the following night, about the same hour, and hearing a low moaning at this spot, I drew near in the dark, and discovered the only survivor of the family that I know, the heir of both its virtues and its vices, who alone was interested in this burning, lying on his stomach and looking over the cellar wall at the still smouldering cinders beneath, muttering to himself, as is his wont. He had been working far off in the river meadows all day, and had improved the first moments that he could call his own to visit the home of his fathers and his youth. He gazed into the cellar from all sides and points of view by turns, always lying down to it, as if there was some treasure, which he remembered, concealed between the stones, where there was absolutely nothing but a heap of bricks and ashes. The house being gone, he looked at what there was left. He was soothed by the sympathy which my mere presence implied, and showed me, as well as the darkness permitted, where the well was covered up; which, thank Heaven, could never be burned; and he groped long about the wall to find the well-sweep which his father had cut and mounted, feeling for the iron hook or staple by which a burden had been fastened to the heavy end—all that he could now cling to—to convince me that it was no common "rider." I felt it, and still remark it almost daily in my walks, for by it hangs the history of a family.

Once more, on the left, where are seen the well and lilac bushes by the wall, in the now open field, lived Nutting and LeGrosse. But to return toward Lincoln.

Farther in the woods than any of these, where the road approaches nearest to the pond, Wyman the potter squatted, and furnished his townsmen with earthenware, and left descendants to succeed him. Neither were they rich in worldly goods, holding the land by sufferance while they lived; and there often the sheriff came in vain to collect the taxes, and "attached a chip," for form's sake, as I have read in his accounts, there being nothing else that he could lay his hands on. One day in midsummer, when I was hoeing, a man who was carrying a load of pottery to market stopped his horse against my field and inquired concerning Wyman the younger. He had long ago bought a potter's wheel of him, and wished to know what had become of him. I had read of the potter's clay and wheel in Scripture, but it had never occurred to me that the pots we use were not such as had come down unbroken from those days, or grown on trees like gourds somewhere, and I was pleased to hear that so fictile an art was ever practiced in my neighborhood.

The last inhabitant of these woods before me was an Irishman, Hugh Quoil (if I have spelt his name with coil enough) who occupied Wyman's tenement—Col. Quoil, he was called. Rumor said that he had been a soldier at Waterloo. If he had lived I should have made him fight his battles over again. His trade here was that of a ditcher. Napoleon went to St. Helena; Quoil came to Walden Woods. All I know of him is tragic. He was a man of manners, like one who had seen the world, and was capable of more civil speech than you could well attend to. He wore a greatcoat in midsummer, being affected with the trembling delirium, and his face was the color of carmine. He died in the road at the foot of Brister's Hill shortly after I came to the woods, so that I have not remembered him as a neighbor. Before his house was pulled down, when his comrades avoided it as "an unlucky castle," I visited it. There lay his old clothes curled up by use, as if they were himself, upon his raised plank bed. His pipe lay broken on the hearth, instead of a bowl broken at the fountain. The last could never have been the symbol of his death, for he confessed to me that, though he had heard of Brister's Spring, he had never seen it; and soiled cards, kings of diamonds, spades, and hearts, were scattered over the floor. One black chicken which the administrator could not catch, black as night and as silent, not even croaking, awaiting Reynard, still went to roost in the next apartment. In the rear there was the dim outline of a garden, which had been planted but had never received its first hoeing, owing to those terrible shaking fits, though it was now harvest time. It was overrun with Roman wormwood and beggarticks, which last stuck to my clothes for all fruit. The skin of a woodchuck was freshly stretched upon the back of the house, a trophy of his last Waterloo; but no warm cap or mittens would he want more.

Now only a dent in the earth marks the site of these dwellings, with buried cellar stones, and strawberries, raspberries, thimble-berries, hazel-bushes, and sumachs growing in the sunny sward there; some pitch pine or gnarled oak occupies what was the chimney nook, and a sweet-scented black-birch, perhaps, waves where the doorstone was. Sometimes the well dent is visible, where once a spring oozed; now dry and tearless grass; or it was covered deep—not to be discovered till some late day—with a flat stone under the sod, when the last of the race departed. What a sorrowful act must that be —the covering up of wells! coincident with the opening of wells of tears. These cellar dents, like deserted fox burrows, old holes, are all that is left where once were the stir and bustle of human life, and "fate, free-will, foreknowledge absolute," in some form and dialect or other were by turns discussed. But all I can learn of their conclusions amounts to just this, that "Cato and Brister pulled wool;" which is about as edifying as the history of more famous schools of philosophy.

Still grows the vivacious lilac a generation after the door and lintel and the sill are gone, unfolding its sweet-scented flowers each spring, to be plucked by the amusing traveler; planted and tended once by children's hands, in front yard plots—now standing by wall-sides in retired pastures, and giving place to new-rising forests—the last of that strip, sole survivor of that family. Little did the dusky children think that the puny slip with its two eyes only, which they stuck in the ground in the shadow of the house and daily watered, would root itself so, and outlive them, and house itself in the rear that shaded it, and grown man's garden and orchard, and tell their story faintly to the lone wanderer a half century after they had grown up and died—blossoming as fair, and smelling as sweet, as in that first spring. I mark its still tender, civil, cheerful, lilac colors.

But this small village, germ of something more, why did it fail while Concord keeps its ground? Were there no natural advantages, no water privileges, forsooth? Ay, the deep Walden Pond and cool Brister's Spring— privilege to drink long and healthy draughts at these, all unimproved by these men but to dilute their glass. They were universally a thirsty race. Might not the basket, stable-broom, mat-making, corn-parching, linen-spinning, and pottery business have thrived here, making the wilderness to blossom like the rose, and a numerous posterity have inherited the land of their fathers? The sterile soil would at least have been proof against a lowland degeneracy. Alas! how little does the memory of these human inhabitants enhance the beauty of the landscape! Again, perhaps, Nature will try, with me for a first settler, and my house raised last spring to be the oldest in the hamlet.

I am not aware that any man has ever built on the spot which I occupy. Deliver me from a city built on the site of a more ancient city, whose materials are ruins, whose gardens cemeteries. The soil is blanched and accursed there, and before that becomes necessary the earth itself will be destroyed. With such reminiscences I repeopled the woods and lulled myself asleep.

At this season I seldom had a visitor. When the snow lay deepest no wanderer ventured near my house for a week or fortnight at a time, but there I lived as snug as a meadow mouse, or as cattle and poultry which are said to have survived for a long time buried in drifts, even without food; or like that early settler's family in the town of Sutton, in this state, whose cottage was completely covered by the great snow of 1717 when he was absent, and an Indian found it only by the hole which the chimney's breath made in the drift, and so relieved the family. But no friendly Indian concerned himself about me; nor needed he, for the master of the house was at home. The Great Snow! How cheerful it is to hear of! When the farmers could not get to the woods and swamps with their teams, and were obliged to cut down the shade trees before their houses, and when the crust was harder cut off the trees in the swamps ten feet from the ground, as it appeared the next spring.

In the deepest snows, the path which I used from the highway to my house, about half a mile long, might have been represented by a meandering dotted line, with wide intervals between the dots. For a week of even weather I took exactly the same number of steps, and of the same length, coming and going, stepping deliberately and with the precision of a pair of dividers in my own deep tracks—to such routine the winter reduces us—yet often they were filled with heaven's own blue. But no weather interfered fatally with my walks, or rather my going abroad, for I frequently tramped eight or ten miles through the deepest snow to keep an appointment with a beech tree, or a yellow birch, or an old acquaintance among the pines; when the ice and snow causing their limbs to droop, and so sharpening their tops, had changed the pines into fir trees; wading to the tops of the highest hills when the snow was nearly two feet deep on a level, and shaking down another snowstorm on my head at every step; or sometimes creeping and floundering thither on my hands and knees, when the hunters had gone into winter quarters. One afternoon I amused myself by watching a barred owl (*Strix nebulosa*) sitting on one of the lower dead limbs of a white pine, close to the trunk, in broad daylight, I standing within a rod of him. He could hear me when I moved and cronched the snow with my feet, but could not plainly see me. When I made most noise he would stretch out his neck, and erect his neck feathers, and open his eyes wide; but their lids soon fell again, and he began to nod. I too felt a slumberous influence after watching him half an hour, as he sat thus with his eyes half open, like a cat, winged brother of the cat. There was only a narrow slit left between their lids, by which he preserved a peninsular relation to me; thus, with half-shut eyes, looking out from the land of dreams, and endeavoring to realize me, vague object or mote that interrupted his visions. At length, on some louder noise or my nearer approach, he would grow uneasy and sluggishly turn about on his perch, as if impatient at having his dreams disturbed; and when he launched himself off and flapped through the pines, spreading his wings to unexpected breadth, I could not hear the slightest sound from them. Thus, guided amid the pine boughs rather by a delicate sense of their neighborhood than by sight, feeling his twilight way as it were with his sensitive pinions, he found a new perch, where he might in peace await the dawning of his day.

As I walked over the long causeway made for the railroad through the meadows, I encountered many a blustering and nipping wind, for nowhere has it freer play; and when the frost had smitten me on one cheek, heathen as I was, I turned to it the other also. Nor was it much better by the carriage road from Brister's Hill. For I came to town still, like a friendly Indian, when the contents of the broad open fields were all piled up between the walls of the Walden road, and half an hour sufficed to obliterate the tracks of the last traveler. And when I returned new drifts would have formed, through which I floundered, where the busy northwest wind had been depositing the powdery snow round a sharp angle in the road, and not a rabbit's track, nor even the fine print, the small type, of a meadow mouse was to be seen. Yet I rarely failed to find, even in midwinter, some warm and springy swamp where the grass and the skunk-cabbage still put forth with perennial verdure, and some hardier bird occasionally awaited the return of spring.

Sometimes, notwithstanding the snow, when I returned from my walk at evening I crossed the deep tracks of a woodchopper leading from my door, and found his pile of whittlings on the hearth, and my house filled with the odor of his pipe. Or on a Sunday afternoon, if I chanced to be at home, I heard the cronching of the snow made by the step of a longheaded farmer, who from far through the woods sought my house, to have a social "crack"; one of the few of his vocation who are "men on their farms"; who donned a frock instead of a professor's gown, and is as ready to extract the moral out of church or state as to haul a load of manure from his barnyard. We talked of rude and simple times, when men sat about large fires in cold bracing weather, with clear heads; and when other dessert failed, we tried our teeth on many a nut which wise squirrels have long since abandoned, for those which have the thickest shells are commonly empty.

The one who came from farthest to my lodge, through deepest snows and most dismal tempests, was a poet.

A farmer, a hunter, a soldier, a reporter, even a philosopher, may be daunted; but nothing can deter a poet, for he is actuated by pure love. Who can predict his comings and goings? His business calls him out at all hours, even when doctors sleep. We made that small house ring with boisterous mirth and resound with the murmur of much sober talk, making amends then to Walden vale for the long silences. Broadway was still and deserted in comparison. At suitable intervals there were regular salutes of laughter, which might have been referred indifferently to the last uttered or the forthcoming jest. We made many a "bran new" theory of life over a thin dish of gruel, which combined the advantages of conviviality with the clearheadedness which philosophy requires.

I should not forget that during my last winter at the pond there was another welcome visitor, who at one time came through the village, through snow and rain and darkness, till he saw my lamp through the trees, and shared with me some long winter evenings. One of the last of the philosophers—Connecticut gave him to the world—he peddled first her wares, afterwards, as he declares, his brains. These he peddles still, prompting God and disgracing man, bearing for fruit his brain only, like the nut its kernel. I think that he must be the man of the most faith of any alive. His words and attitude always suppose a better state of things than other men are acquainted with, and he will be the last man to be disappointed as the ages revolve. He has no venture in the present. But though comparatively disregarded now, when his day comes, laws unsuspected by most will take effect, and masters of families and rulers will come to him for advice.

"How blind that cannot see serenity!"

A true friend of man; almost the only friend of human progress. An Old Mortality, say rather an Immortality, with unwearied patience and faith making plain the image engraven in men's bodies, the God of whom they are but defaced and leaning monuments. With his hospitable intellect he embraces children, beggars, insane, and scholars, and entertains the thought of all, adding to it commonly some breadth and elegance. I think that he should keep a caravansary on the world's highway, where philosophers of all nations might put up, and on his sign should be printed, "Entertainment for man, but not for his beast. Enter ye that have leisure and a quiet mind, who earnestly seek the right road." He is perhaps the sanest man and has the fewest crotchets of any I chance to know; the same yesterday and tomorrow. Of yore we had sauntered and talked, and effectually put the world behind us; for he was pledged to no institution in it, freeborn, *ingenuus*. Whichever way we turned, it seemed that the heavens and the earth had met together, since he enhanced the beauty of the landscape. A blue-robed man, whose fittest roof is the overarching sky which reflects his serenity. I do not see how he can ever die; Nature cannot spare him.

Having each some shingles of thought well dried, we sat and whittled them, trying our knives, and admiring the clear yellowish grain of the pumpkin pine. We waded so gently and reverently, or we pulled together so smoothly, that the fishes of thought were not scared from the stream, nor feared any angler on the bank, but came and went grandly, like the clouds which float through the western sky, and the mother-o'-pearl flocks which sometimes form and dissolve there. There we worked, revising mythology, rounding a fable here and there, and building castles in the air for which earth offered no worthy foundation. Great Looker! Great Expecter! to converse with whom was a New England Night's Entertainment. Ah! such discourse we had, hermit and philosopher, and the old settler I have spoken of—we three—it expanded and racked my little house; I should not dare to say how many pounds' weight there was above the atmospheric pressure on every circular inch; it opened its seams so that they had to be calked with much dullness thereafter to stop the consequent leak; but I had enough of that kind of oakum already picked.

There was one other with whom I had "solid seasons," long to be remembered, at his house in the village, and who looked in upon me from time to time; but I had no more for society there.

There too, as everywhere, I sometimes expected the Visitor who never comes. The Vishnu Purana says, "The house-holder is to remain at eventide in his courtyard as long as it takes to milk a cow, or longer if he pleases, to await the arrival of a guest." I often performed this duty of hospitality, waited long enough to milk a whole herd of cows, but did not see the man approaching from the town.

WINTER ANIMALS

When the ponds were firmly frozen, they afforded not only new and shorter routes to many points, but new views from their surfaces of the familiar landscape around them. When I crossed Flints' Pond, after it was covered with snow, though I had often paddled about and skated over it, it was so unexpectedly wide and so strange that I could think of nothing but Baffin's Bay. The Lincoln hills rose up around me at the extremity of a snowy plain, in which I did not remember to have stood before; and the fishermen, at an indeterminable distance over the ice, moving slowly about with their wolfish dogs, passed for sealers or Esquimaux, or in misty weather loomed like fabulous creatures, and I did not know whether they were giants or pygmies. I took this course when I went to lecture in Lincoln in the evening, traveling in no road and passing no house between my own hut and the lecture room. In Goose Pond, which lay in my way, a colony of muskrats dwelt, and raised their cabins high above the ice, though none could be seen abroad when I crossed it. Walden, being like the rest usually bare of snow, or with only shallow and interrupted drifts on it, was my yard where I could walk freely when the snow was nearly two feet deep on a level elsewhere and the villagers were confined to their streets. There, far from the village street, and except at very long intervals, from the jingle of sleighbells, I slid and skated, as in a vast moose-yard well trodden, overhung by oak woods and solemn pines bent down with snow or bristling with icicles.

For sounds in winter nights, and often in winter days, I heard the forlorn but melodious note of a hooting owl indefinitely far; such a sound as the frozen earth would yield if struck with a suitable plectrum, the very *lingua vernacula* of Walden Wood, and quite familiar to me at last, though I never saw the bird while it was making it. I seldom opened my door in a winter evening without hearing it; *Hoo hoo hoo, hooret hoo,* sounded sonorously, and the first three syllables accented somewhat like *how der do;* or sometimes *hoo hoo* only. One night in the beginning of winter, before the pond froze over, about nine o'clock, I was startled by the loud honking of a goose, and, stepping to the door, heard the sound of their wings like a tempest in the woods as they flew low over my house. They passed over the pond toward Fair

Haven, seemingly deterred from settling by my light, their commodore honking all the while with a regular beat. Suddenly an unmistakable cat-owl from very near me, with the most harsh and tremendous voice I ever heard from any inhabitant of the woods, responded at regular intervals to the goose, as if determined to expose and disgrace this intruder from Hudson's Bay by exhibiting a greater compass and volume of voice in a native, and *boo-hoo* him out of Concord horizon. What do you mean by alarming the citadel at this time of night consecrated to me? Do you think I am ever caught napping at such an hour, and that I have not got lungs and a larynx as well as yourself? *Boo-hoo, boo-hoo, boo-hoo!* It was one of the most thrilling discords I ever heard. And yet, if you had a discriminating ear, there were in it the elements of a concord such as these plains never saw nor heard.

I also heard the whooping of the ice in the pond, my great bedfellow in that part of Concord, as if it were restless in its bed and would fain turn over, were troubled with flatulency and bad dreams; or I was waked by the cracking of the ground by the frost, as if some one had driven a team against my door, and in the morning would find a crack in the earth a quarter of a mile long and a third of an inch wide.

Sometimes I heard the foxes as they ranged over the snow crust, in moonlight nights, in search of a partridge or other game, barking raggedly and demoniacally like forest dogs, as if laboring with some anxiety, or seeking expression, struggling for light and to be dogs outright and run freely in the streets; for if we take the ages into our account, may there not be a civilization going on among brutes as well as men? They seemed to me to be rudimental, burrowing men, still standing on their defence, awaiting their transformation. Sometimes one came near to my window, attracted by my light, barked a vulpine curse at me, and then retreated.

Usually the red squirrel (*Sciurus Hudsonius*) waked me in the dawn, coursing over the roof and up and down the sides of the house, as if sent out of the woods for this purpose. In the course of the winter I threw out half a bushel of ears of sweet corn, which had not got ripe, onto the snow crust by my door, and was amused by watching the motions of the various animals which were baited by it. In the twilight and the night the rabbits came regularly and made a hearty meal. All day long the red squirrels came and went, and afforded me much entertainment by their maneuvers. One would approach at first warily through the shrub-oaks, running over the snow crust by fits and starts like a leaf blown by the wind, now a few paces this way, with wonderful speed and waste of energy, making inconceivable haste with his "trotters," as if it were for a wager, and now as many paces that way, but never getting on more than half a rod at a time; and then suddenly pausing with a ludicrous expression and a gratuitous somerset, as if all the eyes in the universe were fixed on him—for all the motions of a squirrel, even in the most solitary recesses of the forest, imply spectators as much as those of a dancing girl—wasting more time in delay and circumspection than would have sufficed to walk the whole distance—I never saw one walk—and then suddenly, before you could say Jack Robinson, he would be in the top of a young pitch pine, winding up his clock and chiding all imaginary spectators, soliloquizing and talking to all the universe at the same time—for no reason that I could ever detect, or he himself was aware of, I suspect. At length he would reach the corn, and selecting a suitable ear, frisk about in the same uncertain trigo-

nometrical way to the topmost stick of my woodpile,
before my window, where he looked me in the face, and
there sit for hours, supplying himself with a new ear
from time to time, nibbling at first voraciously and
throwing the half-naked cobs about; till at length he
grew more dainty still and played with his food, tasting
only the inside of the kernel, and the ear, which was
held balanced over the stick by one paw, slipped from
his careless grasp and fell to the ground, when he would
look over at it with a ludicrous expression of uncertainty,
as if suspecting that it had life, with a mind not made
up whether to get it again, or a new one, or be off; now
thinking of corn, then listening to hear what was in the
wind. So the little impudent fellow would waste many
an ear in a forenoon; till at last, seizing some longer and
plumper one, considerably bigger than himself, and
skillfully balancing it, he would set out with it to the
woods, like a tiger with a buffalo, by the same zigzag
course and frequent pauses, scratching along with it as
if it were too heavy for him and falling all the while,
making its fall a diagonal between a perpendicular and
horizontal, being determined to put it through at any
rate—a singularly frivolous and whimsical fellow—and
so he would get off with it to where he lived, perhaps
carry it to the top of a pine tree forty or fifty rods distant,
and I would afterwards find the cobs strewn about the
woods in various directions.

At length the jays arrive, whose discordant screams
were heard long before, as they were warily making
their approach an eighth of a mile off, and in a stealthy
and sneaking manner they flit from tree to tree, nearer
and nearer, and pick up the kernels which the squirrels
have dropped. Then, sitting on a pitch-pine bough, they
attempt to swallow in their haste a kernel which is too
big for their throats and chokes them; and after great

labor they disgorge it, and spend an hour in the endeavor to crack it by repeated blows with their bills.
They were manifestly thieves, and I had not much respect for them; but the squirrels, though at first shy,
went to work as if they were taking what was their own.

Meanwhile also came the chickadees in flocks, which,
picking up the crumbs the squirrels had dropped, flew
to the nearest twig, and, placing them under their claws,
hammered away at them with their little bills, as if it
were an insect in the bark, till they were sufficiently reduced for their slender throats. A little flock of these
titmice came daily to pick a dinner out of my woodpile,
or the crumbs at my door, with faint flitting lisping
notes, like the tinkling of icicles in the grass, or else with
sprightly *day day day*, or more rarely, in springlike days,
a wiry summery *phe-be* from the woodside. They were
so familiar that at length one alighted on an armful of
wood which I was carrying in, and pecked at the sticks
without fear. I once had a sparrow alight upon my
shoulder for a moment while I was hoeing in a village
garden, and I felt that I was more distinguished by that
circumstance than I should have been by any epaulet I
could have worn. The squirrels also grew at last to be
quite familiar, and occasionally stepped upon my shoe,
when that was the nearest way.

When the ground was not yet quite covered, and
again near the end of winter, when the snow was melted
on my south hillside and about my woodpile, the partridges came out of the woods morning and evening to
feed there. Whichever side you walk in the woods the
partridge bursts away on whirring wings, jarring the
snow from the dry leaves and twigs on high, which
comes sifting down in the sunbeams like golden dust,
for this brave bird is not to be scared by winter. It is
frequently covered up by drifts, and, it is said, "some-

times plunges from on wing into the soft snow, where it remains concealed for a day or two." I used to start them in the open land also, where they had come out of the woods at sunset to "bud" the wild apple trees. They will come regularly every evening to particular trees, where the cunning sportsman lies in wait for them, and the distant orchards next the woods suffer thus not a little. I am glad that the partridge gets fed, at any rate. It is Nature's own bird which lives on buds and diet-drink.

In dark winter mornings, or in short winter afternoons, I sometimes heard a pack of hounds threading all the woods with hounding cry and yelp, unable to resist the instinct of the chase, and the note of the hunting horn at intervals, proving that man was in the rear. The woods ring again, and yet no fox bursts forth onto the open level of the pond, nor following pack pursuing their Actaeon. And perhaps at evening I see the hunters returning with a single brush trailing from their sleigh for a trophy, seeking their inn. They tell me that if the fox would remain in the bosom of the frozen earth he would be safe, or if he would run in a straight line away no foxhound could overtake him; but, having left his pursuers far behind, he stops to rest and listen till they come up, and when he runs he circles round to his old haunts, where the hunters await him. Sometimes, however, he will run upon a wall many rods, and then leap off far to one side, and he appears to know that water will not retain his scent. A hunter told me that he once saw a fox pursued by hounds burst out onto Walden when the ice was covered with shallow puddles, run part way across, and then return to the same shore. Ere long the hounds arrived, but here they lost the scent. Sometimes a pack hunting by themselves would pass my door, and circle round my house, and yelp and hound without regarding me, as if afflicted by a species of madness, so that nothing could divert them from the pursuit. Thus they circle until they fall upon the recent trail of a fox, for a wise hound will forsake everything else for this. One day a man came to my hut from Lexington to inquire after his hound that made a large track, and had been hunting for a week by himself. But I fear that he was not the wiser for all I told him, for every time I attempted to answer his questions he interrupted me by asking, "What do you do here?" He had lost a dog, but found a man.

One old hunter who has a dry tongue, who used to come to bathe in Walden once every year when the water was warmest, and at such times looked in upon me, told me that many years ago he took his gun one afternoon and went out for a cruise in Walden Wood; and as he walked the Wayland road he heard the cry of hounds approaching, and ere long a fox leaped the wall into the road, and as quick as thought leaped the other wall out of the road, and his swift bullet had not touched him. Some way behind came an old hound and her three pups in full pursuit, hunting on their own account, and disappeared again in the woods. Late in the afternoon, as he was resting in the thick woods south of Walden, he heard the voice of the hounds far over toward Fair Haven still pursuing the fox; and on they came, their hounding cry which made all the woods ring sounding nearer and nearer, now from Well-Meadow, now from the Baker Farm. For a long time he stood still and listened to their music, so sweet to a hunter's ear, when suddenly the fox appeared, threading the solemn aisles with an easy coursing pace, whose sound was concealed by a sympathetic rustle of the leaves, swift and still, keeping the ground, leaving his pursuers far behind; and, leaping upon a rock amid the woods, he sat erect and listening, with his back to the hunter. For a moment compassion restrained the latter's arm; but that was a short-lived mood, and as quick as thought can follow thought his piece was leveled, and *whang!*—the fox rolling over the rock lay dead on the ground. The hunter still kept his place and listened to the hounds. Still on they came, and now the near woods resounded through all their aisles with their demoniac cry. At length the old hound burst into view with muzzle to the ground, and snapping the air as if possessed, and ran directly to the rock; but spying the dead fox she suddenly ceased her hounding, as if struck dumb with amazement, and walked round and round him in silence; and one by one her pups arrived, and, like their mother, were sobered into silence by the mystery. Then the hunter came forward and stood in their midst, and the mystery was solved. They waited in silence while he skinned the fox, then followed the brush a while, and at length turned off into the woods again. That evening a Weston Squire came to the Concord hunter's cottage to inquire for his hounds, and told how for a week they had been hunting on their own account from Weston woods. The Concord hunter told him what he knew and offered him the skin; but the other declined it and departed. He did not find his hounds that night, but the next day learned that they had crossed the river and put up at a farmhouse for the night, whence, having been well fed, they took their departure early in the morning.

The hunter who told me this could remember one Sam Nutting, who used to hunt bears on Fair Haven Ledges, and exchange their skins for rum in Concord village; who told him, even, that he had seen a moose there. Nutting had a famous foxhound named Burgoyne —he pronounced it Bugine—which my informant used to borrow. In the "Wast Book" of an old trader of this town, who was also a captain, town-clerk, and representative, I find the following entry. Jan. 18th, 1742-43, "John Melven Cr. by 1 Grey Fox 0—2—3"; they are not now found here; and in his ledger, Feb. 7th, 1743, Hezekiah Stratton has credit "by ½ a Catt skin 0—1—4½"; of course, a wildcat, for Stratton was a sergeant in the old French war, and would not have got credit for hunting less noble game. Credit is given for deer skins also, and they were daily sold. One man still preserves the horns of the last deer that was killed in this vicinity, and another has told me the particulars of the hunt in which his uncle was engaged. The hunters were formerly a numerous and merry crew here. I remember well one gaunt Nimrod who would catch up a leaf by the roadside and play a strain on it wilder and more melodious, if my memory serves me, than any hunting horn.

At midnight, when there was a moon, I sometimes met with hounds in my path prowling about the woods, which would skulk out of my way, as if afraid, and stand silent amid the bushes till I had passed.

Squirrels and wild mice disputed for my store of nuts. There were scores of pitch pines around my house, from one to four inches in diameter, which had been gnawed by mice the previous winter—a Norwegian winter for them, for the snow lay long and deep, and they were obliged to mix a large proportion of pine bark with their other diet. These trees were alive and apparently flourishing at midsummer, and many of them had grown a foot, though completely girdled; but after another winter such were without exception dead. It is remarkable that a single mouse should thus be allowed a whole pine tree for its dinner, gnawing round instead of up and down it; but perhaps it is necessary in order to thin these trees, which are wont to grow up densely.

The hares (*Lepus Americanus*) were very familiar. One had her form under my house all winter, separated from me only by the flooring, and she startled me each morning by her hasty departure when I began to stir—thump, thump, thump, striking her head against the floor timbers in her hurry. They used to come round my door at dusk to nibble the potato parings which I had thrown out, and were so nearly the color of the ground that they could hardly be distinguished when still. Sometimes in the twilight I alternately lost and recovered sight of one sitting motionless under my window. When I opened my door in the evening, off they would go with a squeak and a bounce. Near at hand they only excited my pity. One evening one sat by my door two paces from me, at first trembling with fear, yet unwilling to move; a poor wee thing, lean and bony, with ragged ears and sharp nose, scant tail and slender paws. It looked as if Nature no longer contained the breed of nobler bloods, but stood on her last toes. Its large eyes appeared young and unhealthy, almost dropsical. I took a step, and lo, away it scud with an elastic spring over the snow crust, straightening its body and its limbs into graceful length, and soon put the forest between me and itself—the wild free venison, asserting its vigor and the dignity of Nature. Not without reason was its slenderness. Such then was its nature. (*Lepus, levipes,* lightfoot some think.)

What is a country without rabbits and partridges? They are among the most simple and indigenous animal products; ancient and venerable families known to antiquity as to modern times; of the very hue and substance of Nature, nearest allied to leaves and to the ground—and to one another; it is either winged or it is legged. It is hardly as if you had seen a wild creature when a rabbit or a partridge bursts away, only a natural one, as much to be expected as rustling leaves. The partridge and the rabbit are still sure to thrive, like true natives of the soil, whatever revolutions occur. If the forest is cut off, the sprouts and bushes which spring up afford them concealment, and they become more numerous than ever. That must be a poor country indeed that does not support a hare. Our woods teem with them both, and around every swamp may be seen the partridge or rabbit walk, beset with twiggy fences and horsehair snares, which some cowboy tends.

THE POND IN WINTER

After a still winter night I awoke with the impression that some question had been put to me, which I had been endeavoring in vain to answer in my sleep, as what —how—when—where? But there was dawning Nature, in whom all creatures live, looking in my broad windows with serene and satisfied face, and no question on *her* lips. I awoke to an answered question, to Nature and daylight. The snow lying deep on the earth dotted with young pines, and the very slope of the hill on which my house is placed, seemed to say, Forward! Nature puts no question and answers none which we mortals ask. She has long ago taken her resolution. "O Prince, our eyes contemplate with admiration and transmit to the soul the wonderful and varied spectacle of this universe. The night veils without doubt a part of this glorious creation; but day comes to reveal to us this great work, which extends from earth even into the plains of the ether."

Then to my morning work. First I take an axe and pail and go in search of water, if that be not a dream. After a cold and snowy night it needed a divining rod to find it. Every winter the liquid and trembling surface of the pond, which was so sensitive to every breath, and reflected every light and shadow, becomes solid to the depth of a foot or a foot and a half, so that it will support the heaviest teams, and perchance the snow covers it to an equal depth, and it is not to be distinguished from any level field. Like the marmots in the surrounding hills, it closes its eyelids and becomes dormant for three months or more. Standing on the snow-covered plain, as if in a pasture amid the hills, I cut my way first through a foot of snow, and then a foot of ice, and open a window under my feet, where, kneeling to drink, I look down into the quiet parlor of the fishes, pervaded by a softened light as through a window of ground glass, with its bright sanded floor the same as in summer; there a perennial waveless serenity reigns as in the amber twilight sky, corresponding to the cool and even temperament of the inhabitants. Heaven is under our feet as well as over our heads.

Early in the morning, while all things are crisp with frost, men come with fishing reels and slender lunch, and let down their fine lines through the snowy field to take pickerel and perch; wild men, who instinctively follow other fashions and trust other authorities than their townsmen, and by their goings and comings stitch towns together in parts where else they would be ripped. They sit and eat their luncheon in stout fear-naughts on the dry oak leaves on the shore, as wise in natural lore as the citizen is in artificial. They never consulted with books, and know and can tell much less than they have done. The things which they practice are said not yet to be known. Here is one fishing for pickerel with grown perch for bait. You look into his pail with wonder as into a summer pond, as if he kept summer locked up at home, or knew where she had retreated. How, pray, did he get these in midwinter? O, he got worms out of rotten logs since the ground froze, and so he caught them. His life itself passes deeper in Nature than the studies of the naturalist penetrate; himself a subject for the naturalist.

The latter raises the moss and bark gently with his knife
in search of insects; the former lays open logs to their
core with his axe, and moss and bark fly far and wide.
He gets his living by barking trees. Such a man has
some right to fish, and I love to see Nature carried out
in him. The perch swallows the grub-worm, the pickerel
swallows the perch, and the fisherman swallows the
pickerel; and so all the chinks in the scale of being are
filled.

When I strolled around the pond in misty weather I
was sometimes amused by the primitive mode which some
ruder fisherman had adopted. He would perhaps have
placed alder branches over the narrow holes in the ice,
which were four or five rods apart and an equal distance
from the shore, and having fastened the end of the line
to a stick to prevent its being pulled through, have
passed the slack line over a twig of the alder, a foot or
more above the ice, and tied a dry oak leaf to it, which,
being pulled down, would show when he had a bite.
These alders loomed through the mist at regular intervals as you walked half way round the pond.

Ah, the pickerel of Walden! when I see them lying
on the ice, or in the well which the fisherman cuts in the
ice, making a little hole to admit the water, I am always
surprised by their rare beauty, as if they were fabulous fishes, they are so foreign to the streets, even to the
woods, foreign as Arabia to our Concord life. They possess a quite dazzling and transcendent beauty which
separates them by a wide interval from the cadaverous
cod and haddock whose fame is trumpeted in our streets.
They are not green like the pines, nor gray like the
stones, nor blue like the sky; but they have, to my eyes,
if possible, yet rarer colors, like flowers and precious
stones, as if they were the pearls, the animalized *nuclei*
or crystals of the Walden water. They, of course, are

Walden all over and all through; are themselves small Waldens in the animal kingdom, Waldenses. It is surprising that they are caught here, that in this deep and capacious spring, far beneath the rattling teams and chaises and tinkling sleighs that travel the Walden road, this great gold and emerald fish swims. I never chanced to see its kind in any market; it would be the cynosure of all eyes there. Easily, with a few convulsive quirks, they give up their watery ghosts, like a mortal translated before his time to the thin air of heaven.

As I was desirous to recover the long lost bottom of Walden Pond, I surveyed it carefully, before the ice broke up, early in '46, with compass and chain and sounding line. There have been many stories told about the bottom, or rather no bottom, of this pond, which certainly had no foundation for themselves. It is remarkable how long men will believe in the bottomlessness of a pond without taking the trouble to sound it. I have visited two such Bottomless Ponds in one walk in this neighborhood. Many have believed that Walden reached quite through to the other side of the globe. Some who have lain flat on the ice for a long time, looking down through the illusive medium, perchance with watery eyes into the bargain, and driven to hasty conclusions by the fear of catching cold in their breasts, have seen vast holes "into which a load of hay might be driven," if there were anybody to drive it, the undoubted source of the Styx and entrance to the Infernal Regions from these parts. Others have gone down from the village with a "fifty-six" and a wagon-load of inch rope, but yet have failed to find any bottom; for while the "fifty-six" was resting by the way, they were paying out the rope in the vain attempt to fathom their truly immeasurable capacity for marvelousness. But I can assure my readers that

Walden has a reasonably tight bottom at a not unreasonable, though at an unusual, depth. I fathomed it easily with a cod-line and a stone weighing about a pound and a half, and could tell accurately when the stone left the bottom, by having to pull so much harder before the water got underneath to help me. The greatest depth was exactly one hundred and two feet; to which may be added the five feet which it has risen since, making one hundred and seven. This is a remarkable depth for so small an area; yet not an inch of it can be spared by the imagination. What if all ponds were shallow? Would it not react on the minds of men? I am thankful that this pond was made deep and pure for a symbol. While men believe in the infinite some ponds will be thought to be bottomless.

A factory owner, hearing what depth I had found, thought that it could not be true, for, judging from his acquaintance with dams, sand would not lie at so steep an angle. But the deepest ponds are not so deep in proportion to their area as most suppose, and, if drained, would not leave very remarkable valleys. They are not like cups between the hills; for this one, which is so unusually deep for its area, appears in a vertical section through its center not deeper than a shallow plate. Most ponds, emptied, would leave a meadow no more hollow than we frequently see. William Gilpin, who is so admirable in all that relates to landscapes, and usually so correct, standing at the head of Loch Fyne, in Scotland, which he describes as "a bay of salt water, sixty or seventy fathoms deep, four miles in breadth," and about fifty miles long, surrounded by mountains, observes, "If we could have seen it immediately after the diluvian crash, or whatever convulsion of Nature occasioned it, before the waters gushed in, what a horrid chasm it must have appeared!

"So high as heaved the tumid hills, so low
   Down sunk a hollow bottom, broad, and deep,
   Capacious bed of waters———."

But if, using the shortest diameter of Loch Fyne, we
apply these proportions to Walden, which, as we have
seen, appears already in a vertical section only like a
shallow plate, it will appear four times as shallow. So
much for the *increased* horrors of the chasm of Loch
Fyne when emptied. No doubt many a smiling valley
with its stretching cornfields occupies exactly such a
"horrid chasm," from which the waters have receded,
though it requires the insight and the far sight of the
geologist to convince the unsuspecting inhabitants of
this fact. Often an inquisitive eye may detect the shores
of a primitive lake in the low horizon hills, and no subsequent elevation of the plain have been necessary to
conceal their history. But it is easiest, as they who work
on the highways know, to find the hollows by the puddles after a shower. The amount of it is, the imagination,
give it the least license, dives deeper and soars higher
than Nature goes. So, probably, the depth of the ocean
will be found to be very inconsiderable compared with
its breadth.

As I sounded through the ice I could determine the
shape of the bottom with greater accuracy than is possible in surveying harbors which do not freeze over, and
I was surprised at its general regularity. In the deepest
part there are several acres more level than almost any
field which is exposed to the sun, wind, and plough. In
one instance, on a line arbitrarily chosen, the depth did
not vary more than one foot in thirty rods; and generally,
near the middle, I could calculate the variation for each
one hundred feet in any direction beforehand within
three or four inches. Some are accustomed to speak of
deep and dangerous holes even in quiet sandy ponds

like this, but the effect of water under these circumstances is to level all inequalities. The regularity of the bottom and its conformity to the shores and the range of the neighboring hills were so perfect that a distant promontory betrayed itself in the soundings quite across the pond, and its direction could be determined by observing the opposite shore. Cape becomes bar, and plain shoal, and valley and gorge deep water and channel.

When I had mapped the pond by the scale of ten rods to an inch, and put down the soundings, more than a hundred in all, I observed this remarkable coincidence. Having noticed that the number indicating the greatest depth was apparently in the center of the map, I laid a rule on the map lengthwise, and then breadthwise, and found, to my surprise, that the line of greatest length intersected the line of greatest breadth *exactly* at the point of greatest depth, notwithstanding that the middle is so nearly level, the outline of the pond far from regular, and the extreme length and breadth were got by measuring into the coves; and I said to myself, Who knows but this hint would conduct to the deepest part of the ocean as well as of a pond or puddle? Is not this the rule also for the height of mountains, regarded as the opposite of valleys? We know that a hill is not highest at its narrowest part.

Of five coves, three, or all which had been sounded, were observed to have a bar quite across their mouths and deeper water within, so that the bay tended to be an expansion of water within the land not only horizontally but vertically, and to form a basin or independent pond, the direction of the two capes showing the course of the bar. Every harbor on the seacoast, also, has its bar at its entrance. In proportion as the mouth of the cove was wider compared with its length, the water over the bar was deeper compared with that in the basin. Given, then, the length and breadth of the cove, and the character of the surrounding shore, and you have almost elements enough to make out a formula for all cases.

In order to see how nearly I could guess, with this experience, at the deepest point in a pond, by observing the outlines of its surface and the character of its shores alone, I made a plan of White Pond, which contains about forty-one acres, and, like this, has no island in it, nor any visible inlet or outlet; and as the line of greatest breadth fell very near the line of least breadth, where two opposite capes approached each other and two opposite bays receded, I ventured to mark a point a short distance from the latter line, but still on the line of greatest length, as the deepest. The deepest part was found to be within one hundred feet of this, still farther in the direction to which I had inclined, and was only one foot deeper, namely, sixty feet. Of course, a stream running through, or an island in the pond, would make the problem much more complicated.

If we knew all the laws of Nature, we should need only one fact, or the description of one actual phenomenon, to infer all the particular results at that point. Now we know only a few laws, and our result is vitiated, not, of course, by any confusion or irregularity in Nature, but by our ignorance of essential elements in the calculation. Our notions of law and harmony are commonly confined to those instances which we detect; but the harmony which results from a far greater number of seemingly conflicting, but really concurring, laws, which we have not detected, is still more wonderful. The particular laws are as our points of view, as, to the traveler, a mountain outline varies with every step, and it has an infinite number of profiles, though absolutely but one form. Even when cleft or bored through it is not comprehended in its entirety.

What I have observed of the pond is no less true in ethics. It is the law of average. Such a rule of the two diameters not only guides us toward the sun in the system and the heart in man, but draw lines through the length and breadth of the aggregate of a man's particular daily behaviors and waves of life into his coves and inlets, and where they intersect will be the height or depth of his character. Perhaps we need only to know how his shores trend and his adjacent country or circumstances, to infer his depth and concealed bottom. If he is surrounded by mountainous circumstances, an Achillean shore, whose peaks overshadow and are reflected in his bosom, they suggest a corresponding depth in him. But a low and smooth shore proves him shallow on that side. In our bodies, a bold projecting brow falls off to and indicates a corresponding depth of thought. Also there is a bar across the entrance of our every cove, or particular inclination; each is our harbor for a season, in which we are detained and partially land-locked. These inclinations are not whimsical usually, but their form, size, and direction are determined by the promontories of the shore, the ancient axes of elevation. When this bar is gradually increased by storms, tides, or currents, or there is a subsidence of the waters, so that it reaches to the surface, that which was at first but an inclination in the shore in which a thought was harbored becomes an individual lake, cut off from the ocean, wherein the thought secures its own conditions—changes, perhaps, from salt to fresh, becomes a sweet sea, dead sea, or a marsh. At the advent of each individual into this life, may we not suppose that such a bar has risen to the surface somewhere? It is true, we are such poor navigators that our thoughts, for the most part, stand off and on upon a harborless coast, are conversant only with the bights of the bays of poesy, or steer for the public ports of entry, and go into the dry docks of science, where they merely refit for this world, and no natural currents concur to individualize them.

As for the inlet or outlet of Walden, I have not discovered any but rain and snow and evaporation, though perhaps, with a thermometer and a line, such places may be found, for where the water flows into the pond it will probably be coldest in summer and warmest in winter. When the icemen were at work here in '46-'47, the cakes sent to the shore were one day rejected by those who were stacking them up there, not being thick enough to lie side by side with the rest; and the cutters thus discovered that the ice over a small space was two or three inches thinner than elsewhere, which made them think that there was an inlet there. They also showed me in another place what they thought was a "leach hole," through which the pond leaked out under a hill into a neighboring meadow, pushing me out on a cake of ice to see it. It was a small cavity under ten feet of water; but I think that I can warrant the pond not to need soldering till they find a worse leak than that. One has suggested, that if such a "leach hole" should be found, its connection with the meadow, if any existed, might be proved by conveying some colored powder or sawdust to the mouth of the hole, and then putting a strainer over the spring in the meadow, which would catch some of the particles carried through by the current.

While I was surveying, the ice, which was sixteen inches thick, undulated under a slight wind like water. It is well known that a level cannot be used on ice. At one rod from the shore its greatest fluctuation, when observed by means of a level on land directed toward a graduated staff on the ice, was three quarters of an inch, though the ice appeared firmly attached to the shore. It was probably greater in the middle. Who knows but if our instruments were delicate enough we might detect an undulation in the crust of the earth? When two legs of my level were on the shore and the third on the ice, and the sights were directed over the latter, a rise or fall of the ice of an almost infinitesimal amount made a difference of several feet on a tree across the pond. When I began to cut holes for sounding there were three or four inches of water on the ice under a deep snow which had sunk it thus far; but the water began immediately to run into these holes, and continued to run for two days in deep streams, which wore away the ice on every side, and contributed essentially, if not mainly, to dry the surface of the pond; for, as the water ran in, it raised and floated the ice. This was somewhat like cutting a hole in the bottom of a ship to let the water out. When such holes freeze, and a rain succeeds, and finally a new freezing forms a fresh smooth ice over all, it is beautifully mottled internally by dark figures, shaped somewhat like a spider's web, what you may call ice rosettes, produced by the channels worn by the water flowing from all sides to a center. Sometimes, also, when the ice was covered with shallow puddles, I saw a double shadow of myself, one standing on the head of the other, one on the ice, the other on the trees or hillside.

While yet it is cold January, and snow and ice are thick and solid, the prudent landlord comes from the village to get ice to cool his summer drink; impressively, even pathetically, wise, to foresee the heat and thirst of July now in January—wearing a thick coat and mittens! when so many things are not provided for. It may be that he lays up no treasures in this world which will cool his summer drink in the next. He cuts and saws the solid pond, unroofs the house of fishes, and carts off their very element and air, held fast by chains and stakes like corded wood, through the favoring winter air, to wintry cellars, to underlie the summer there. It looks like solidified azure, as, far off, it is drawn through the streets. These ice-cutters are a merry race, full of jest and sport, and when I went among them they were wont to invite me to saw pit-fashion with them, I standing underneath.

In the winter of '46-'47 there came a hundred men of Hyperborean extraction swoop down onto our pond one morning, with many carloads of ungainly-looking farming tools—sleds, ploughs, drill-barrows, turf-knives, spades, saws, rakes, and each man was armed with a double-pointed pike-staff, such as is not described in the New England Farmer or the Cultivator. I did not know whether they had come to sow a crop of winter rye, or some other kind of grain recently introduced from Iceland. As I saw no manure, I judged that they meant to skim the land, as I had done, thinking the soil was deep and had lain fallow long enough. They said that a gentleman farmer, who was behind the scenes, wanted to double his money, which, as I understood, amounted to half a million already; but in order to cover each one of his dollars with another, he took off the only coat, ay, the skin itself, of Walden Pond in the midst of a hard winter. They went to work at once, ploughing, harrowing, rolling, furrowing, in admirable order, as if they were bent on making this a model farm; but when I was looking sharp to see what kind of seed they dropped into the furrow, a gang of fellows by my side suddenly began to hook up the virgin mould itself, with a peculiar jerk, clean down to the sand, or rather the water—for it was a very springy soil—indeed all the *terra firma* there was—and haul it away on sleds, and then I guessed that they must be cutting peat in a bog. So they came and went every day, with a peculiar shriek from the locomotive, from and to some point of the polar regions, as it seemed to me, like a flock of arctic snow-birds. But sometimes Squaw Walden had her revenge, and a hired man, walking behind his team, slipped through a crack in the ground down toward Tartarus, and he who was so brave before suddenly became but the ninth part of a man, almost gave up his animal heat, and was glad to take refuge in my house, and acknowl-edged that there was some virtue in a stove; or some-times the frozen soil took a piece of steel out of a ploughshare, or a plough got set in the furrow and had to be cut out.

To speak literally, a hundred Irishmen, with Yankee overseers, came from Cambridge every day to get out the ice. They divided it into cakes by methods too well known to require description, and these, being sledded to the shore, were rapidly hauled off onto an ice plat-form, and raised by grappling irons and block and tackle, worked by horses, on to a stack, as surely as so many barrels of flour, and there placed evenly side by side, and row upon row, as if they formed the solid base of an obelisk designed to pierce the clouds. They told me that in a good day they could get out a thousand tons, which was the yield of about one acre. Deep ruts and "cradle holes" were worn in the ice, as on *terra firma,* by the passage of the sleds over the same track, and the horses invariably ate their oats out of cakes of ice hollowed out like buckets. They stacked up the cakes thus in the open air in a pile thirty-five feet high on one side and six or seven rods square, putting hay between the outside layers to exclude the air; for when the wind, though never so cold, finds a passage through, it will wear large cavities, leaving slight supports or studs only

here and there, and finally topple it down. At first it
looked like a vast blue fort or Valhalla; but when they
began to tuck the coarse meadow hay into the crevices,
and this became covered with rime and icicles, it looked
like a venerable moss-grown and hoary ruin, built of
azure-tinted marble, the abode of Winter, that old man
we see in the almanac—his shanty, as if he had a design
to estivate with us. They calculated that not twenty-five
per cent of this would reach its destination, and that two
or three per cent would be wasted in the cars. However,
a still greater part of this heap had a different destiny
from what was intended; for, either because the ice was
found not to keep so well as was expected, containing
more air than usual, or for some other reason, it never
got to market. This heap, made in the winter of '46-'47
and estimated to contain ten thousand tons, was finally
covered with hay and boards; and though it was un-
roofed the following July, and a part of it carried off, the
rest remaining exposed to the sun, it stood over that
summer and the next winter, and was not quite melted
till September, 1848. Thus the pond recovered the
greater part.

Like the water, the Walden ice, seen near at hand,
has a green tint, but at a distance is beautifully blue,
and you can easily tell it from the white ice of the river,
or the merely greenish ice of some ponds, a quarter of a
mile off. Sometimes one of those great cakes slips from
the iceman's sled into the village street, and lies there
for a week like a great emerald, an object of interest to
all passers. I have noticed that a portion of Walden
which in the state of water was green will often, when
frozen, appear from the same point of view blue. So the
hollows about this pond will, sometimes, in the winter,
be filled with a greenish water somewhat like its own,
but the next day will have frozen blue. Perhaps the blue

color of water and ice is due to the light and air they contain, and the most transparent is the bluest. Ice is an interesting subject for contemplation. They told me that they had some in the icehouses at Fresh Pond five years old which was as good as ever. Why is it that a bucket of water soon becomes putrid, but frozen remains sweet forever? It is commonly said that this is the difference between the affections and the intellect.

Thus for sixteen days I saw from my window a hundred men at work like busy husbandmen, with teams and horses and apparently all the implements of farming, such a picture as we see on the first page of the almanac; and as often as I looked out I was reminded of the fable of the lark and the reapers, or the parable of the sower, and the like; and now they are all gone, and in thirty days more, probably, I shall look from the same window on the pure sea-green Walden water there, reflecting the clouds and the trees, and sending up its evaporations in solitude, and no traces will appear that a man has ever stood there. Perhaps I shall hear a solitary loon laugh as he dives and plumes himself, or shall see a lonely fisher in his boat, like a floating leaf, beholding his form reflected in the waves, where lately a hundred men securely labored.

Thus it appears that the sweltering inhabitants of Charleston and New Orleans, of Madras and Bombay and Calcutta, drink at my well. In the morning I bathe my intellect in the stupendous and cosmogonal philosophy of the Bhagvat Geeta, since whose composition years of the gods have elapsed, and in comparison with which our modern world and its literature seem puny and trivial; and I doubt if that philosophy is not to be referred to a previous state of existence, so remote is its sublimity from our conceptions. I lay down the book and go to my well for water, and lo! there I meet the servant of the Bramin, priest of Brahma and Vishnu and Indra, who still sits in his temple on the Ganges reading the Vedas, or dwells at the root of a tree with his crust and water jug. I meet his servant come to draw water for his master, and our buckets as it were grate together in the same well. The pure Walden water is mingled with the sacred water of the Ganges. With favoring winds it is wafted past the site of the fabulous islands of Atlantis and the Hesperides, makes the periplus of Hanno, and, floating by Ternate and Tidore and the mouth of the Persian Gulf, melts in the tropic gales of the Indian seas, and is landed in ports of which Alexander only heard the names.

SPRING

The opening of large tracts by the ice-cutters commonly causes a pond to break up earlier; for the water, agitated by the wind, even in cold weather, wears away the surrounding ice. But such was not the effect on Walden that year, for she had soon got a thick new garment to take the place of the old. This pond never breaks up so soon as the others in this neighborhood, on account both of its greater depth and its having no stream passing through it to melt or wear away the ice. I never knew it to open in the course of a winter, not excepting that of '52-'53, which gave the ponds so severe a trial. It commonly opens about the first of April, a week or ten days later than Flints' Pond and Fair Haven, beginning to melt on the north side and in the shallower parts where it began to freeze. It indicates better than any water hereabouts the absolute progress of the season, being least affected by transient changes of temperature. A severe cold of a few days' duration in March may very much retard the opening of the former ponds, while the temperature of Walden increases almost uninterruptedly. A thermometer thrust into the middle of Walden on the 6th of March, 1847, stood at 32°, or freezing point; near the shore at 33°; in the middle of Flints' Pond, the same day, at 32½°; at a dozen rods from the shore, in shallow water, under ice a foot thick, at 36°. This difference of three and a half degrees between the temperature of the deep water and the shallow in the latter pond, and the fact that a great proportion of it is comparatively shallow, show why it should break up so much sooner than Walden. The ice in the shallowest part was at this time several inches thinner than in the middle. In midwinter the middle had been the warmest and the ice thinnest there. So, also, everyone who has waded about the shores of a pond in summer must have perceived how much warmer the water is close to the shore, where only three or four inches deep, than a little distance out, and on the surface where it is deep, than near the bottom. In spring the sun not only exerts an influence through the increased temperature of the air and earth, but its heat passes through ice a foot or more thick, and is reflected from the bottom in shallow water, and so also warms the water and melts the under side of the ice, at the same time that it is melting it more directly above, making it uneven, and causing the air bubbles which it contains to extend themselves upward and downward until it is completely honeycombed, and at last disappears suddenly in a single spring rain. Ice has its grain as well as wood, and when a cake begins to rot or "comb," that is, assume the appearance of honeycomb, whatever may be its position, the air cells are at right angles with what was the water surface. Where there is a rock or a log rising near to the surface the ice over it is much thinner, and is frequently quite dissolved by this reflected heat;

and I have been told that in the experiment at Cambridge to freeze water in a shallow wooden pond, though the cold air circulated underneath, and so had access to both sides, the reflection of the sun from the bottom more than counterbalanced this advantage. When a warm rain in the middle of the winter melts off the snow-ice from Walden, and leaves a hard dark or transparent ice on the middle, there will be a strip of rotten though thicker white ice, a rod or more wide, about the shores, created by this reflected heat. Also, as I have said, the bubbles themselves within the ice operate as burning-glasses to melt the ice beneath.

The phenomena of the year take place every day in a pond on a small scale. Every morning, generally speaking, the shallow water is being warmed more rapidly than the deep, though it may not be made so warm after all, and every evening it is being cooled more rapidly until the morning. The day is an epitome of the year. The night is the winter, the morning and evening are the spring and fall, and the noon is the summer. The cracking and booming of the ice indicate a change of temperature. One pleasant morning after a cold night, February 24th, 1850, having gone to Flints' Pond to spend the day, I noticed with surprise, that when I struck the ice with the head of my axe, it resounded like a gong for many rods around, or as if I had struck on a tight drumhead. The pond began to boom about an hour after sunrise, when it felt the influence of the sun's rays slanted upon it from over the hills; it stretched itself and yawned like a waking man with a gradually increasing tumult, which was kept up three or four hours. It took a short siesta at noon, and boomed once more toward night, as the sun was withdrawing his influence. In the right stage of the weather a pond fires its evening gun with great regularity. But in the middle of the day, being full of cracks, and the air also being less elastic, it had completely lost its resonance, and probably fishes and muskrats could not then have been stunned by a blow on it. The fishermen say that the "thundering of the pond" scares the fishes and prevents their biting. The pond does not thunder every evening, and I cannot tell surely when to expect its thundering; but though I may perceive no difference in the weather, it does. Who would have suspected so large and cold and thick-skinned a thing to be so sensitive? Yet it has its law to which it thunders obedience when it should as surely as the buds expand in the spring. The earth is all alive and covered with papillae. The largest pond is as sensitive to atmospheric changes as the globule of mercury in its tube.

One attraction in coming to the woods to live was that I should have leisure and opportunity to see the Spring come in. The ice in the pond at length begins to be honeycombed, and I can set my heel in it as I walk. Fogs and rains and warmer suns are gradually melting the snow; the days have grown sensibly longer; and I see how I shall get through the winter without adding to my woodpile, for large fires are no longer necessary. I am on the alert for the first signs of spring, to hear the chance note of some arriving bird, or the striped squirrel's chirp, for his stores must be now nearly exhausted, or see the woodchuck venture out of his winter quarters. On the 13th of March, after I had heard the bluebird, song-sparrow, and red-wing, the ice was still nearly a foot thick. As the weather grew warmer it was not sensibly worn away by the water, nor broken up and floated off as in rivers, but, though it was completely melted for half a rod in width about the shore, the middle was merely honeycombed and saturated with water, so that you could put your foot through it when six inches thick; but by the next day evening, perhaps, after a warm rain followed by fog, it would have wholly disappeared, all gone off with the fog, spirited away. One year I went across the middle only five days before it disappeared entirely. In 1845 Walden was first completely open on the 1st of April; in '46, the 25th of March; in '47, the 8th of April; in '51, the 28th of March; in '52, the 18th of April; in '53, the 23d of March; in '54, about the 7th of April.

Every incident connected with the breaking up of the rivers and ponds and the settling of the weather is particularly interesting to us who live in a climate of so great extremes. When the warmer days come, they who dwell near the river hear the ice crack at night with a startling whoop as loud as artillery, as if its icy fetters were rent from end to end, and within a few days see it rapidly going out. So the alligator comes out of the mud with quakings of the earth. One old man, who has been a close observer of Nature, and seems as thoroughly wise in regard to all her operations as if she had been put upon the stocks when he was a boy, and he had helped to lay her keel—who has come to his growth, and can hardly acquire more of natural lore if he should live to the age of Methuselah—told me, and I was surprised to hear him express wonder at any of Nature's operations, for I thought that there were no secrets between them, that one spring day he took his gun and boat, and thought that he would have a little sport with the ducks. There was ice still on the meadows, but it was all gone out of the river, and he dropped down without obstruction from Sudbury, where he lived, to Fair Haven Pond, which he found, unexpectedly, covered for the most part with a firm field of ice. It was a warm day, and he was surprised to see so great a body of ice remaining. Not seeing any ducks, he hid his boat on the north or back side of an island in the pond, and then concealed himself in the bushes on the south side, to await them. The ice was melted for three or four rods from the shore, and there was a smooth and warm sheet of water, with a muddy bottom, such as the ducks love, within, and he thought it likely that some would be along pretty soon. After he had lain still there about an hour he heard a low and seemingly very distant sound, but singularly grand and impressive, unlike anything he had ever heard, gradually swelling and increasing as if it would have a universal and memorable ending, a sullen rush and roar, which seemed to him all at once like the sound of a vast body of fowl coming in to settle there, and, seizing his gun, he started up in haste and excited; but he found, to his surprise, that the whole body of the ice had started while he lay there, and drifted in to the shore, and the sound he had heard was made by its edge grating on the shore—at first gently nibbled and crumbled off, but at length heaving up and scattering its wrecks along the island to a considerable height before it came to a stand still.

At length the sun's rays have attained the right angle, and warm winds blow up mist and rain and melt the snow banks, and the sun dispersing the mist smiles on a checkered landscape of russet and white smoking with incense, through which the traveler picks his way from islet to islet, cheered by the music of a thousand tinkling rills and rivulets whose veins are filled with the blood of winter which they are bearing off.

Few phenomena gave me more delight than to observe the forms which thawing sand and clay assume in flowing down the sides of a deep cut on the railroad through which I passed on my way to the village, a phenomenon not very common on so large a scale, though the number of freshly exposed banks of the right material must have been greatly multiplied since railroads were invented. The material was sand of every degree of fineness and of various rich colors, commonly mixed with a little clay. When the frost comes out in the spring, and even in a thawing day in the winter, the sand begins to flow down the slopes like lava, sometimes bursting out through the snow and overflowing it where no sand was to be seen before. Innumerable little streams overlap and interlace one with another, exhibiting a sort of hybrid product, which obeys half way the law of currents, and half way that of vegetation. As it flows it takes the forms of sappy leaves or vines, making heaps of pulpy sprays a foot or more in depth, and resembling, as you look down on them, the laciniated, lobed, and imbricated thalluses of some lichens; or you are reminded of coral, of leopards' paws or birds' feet, of brains or lungs or bowels, and excrements of all kinds. It is a truly *grotesque* vegetation, whose forms and color we see imitated in bronze, a sort of architectural foliage more ancient and typical than acanthus, chicory, ivy, vine, or any vegetable leaves; destined perhaps, under some circumstances, to become a puzzle to future geologists. The whole cut impressed me as if it were a cave with its stalactites laid open to the light. The various shades of the sand are singularly rich and agreeable, embracing the different iron colors, brown, gray, yellowish, and reddish. When the flowing mass reaches the drain at the foot of the bank it spreads out flatter into *strands*, the separate streams losing their semi-cylindrical form and gradually becoming more flat and broad, running together as they are more moist, till they form an almost flat *sand*, still variously and beautifully shaded, but in which you can trace the original forms of vegetation; till at length, in the water itself, they are converted into *banks,* like those formed off the mouths of rivers, and the forms of vegetation are lost in the ripple marks on the bottom.

The whole bank, which is from twenty to forty feet high, is sometimes overlaid with a mass of this kind of foliage, or sandy rupture, for a quarter of a mile on one or both sides, the produce of one spring day. What makes this sand foliage remarkable is its springing into existence thus suddenly. When I see on the one side the inert bank—for the sun acts on one side first—and on the other this luxuriant foliage, the creation of an hour, I am affected as if in a peculiar sense I stood in the laboratory of the Artist who made the world and me— had come to where he was still at work, sporting on this bank, and with excess of energy strewing his fresh designs about. I feel as if I were nearer to the vitals of the globe, for this sandy overflow is something such a foliaceous mass as the vitals of the animal body. You find thus in the very sands an anticipation of the vegetable leaf. No wonder that the earth expresses itself outwardly in leaves, it so labors with the idea inwardly. The atoms have already learned this law, and are pregnant by it. The overhanging leaf sees here its prototype. *Internally,* whether in the globe or animal body, it is a moist thick *lobe,* a word especially applicable to the liver and lungs and the *leaves* of fat (λείβω, *labor, lapsus,* to flow or slip downward, a lapsing; λοβός, *globus,* lobe, globe; also lap, flap, and many other words); *externally,* a dry thin *leaf,* even as the *f* and *v* are a pressed and dried *b.* The radicals of lobe are *lb,* the soft mass of the *b* (single lobed, or B, doubled lobed) with the liquid *l* behind it pressing it forward. In globe, *glb,* the guttural *g* adds to the meaning the capacity of the throat. The feathers and wings of birds are still drier and thinner leaves. Thus, also, you pass from the lumpish grub in the earth to the airy and fluttering butterfly. The very globe continually transcends and translates itself, and becomes winged in its orbit. Even ice begins with delicate crystal leaves, as if it had flowed into moulds which the fronds of water plants have impressed on the watery mirror. The whole tree itself is but one leaf, and rivers are still vaster leaves whose pulp is intervening earth, and towns and cities are the ova of insects in their axils.

When the sun withdraws the sand ceases to flow, but in the morning the streams will start once more and branch and branch again into a myriad of others. You here see perchance how blood vessels are formed. If you look closely you observe that first there pushes forward from the thawing mass a stream of softened sand with a droplike point, like the ball of the finger, feeling its way slowly and blindly downward, until at last with more heat and moisture, as the sun gets higher, the most fluid portion, in its effort to obey the law to which the most inert also yields, separates from the latter and forms for itself a meandering channel or artery within that, in which is seen a little silvery stream glancing like lightning from one stage of pulpy leaves or branches to another, and ever and anon swallowed up in the sand. It is wonderful how rapidly yet perfectly the sand organizes itself as it flows, using the best material its mass affords to form the sharp edges of its channel. Such are the sources of rivers. In the silicious matter which the water deposits is perhaps the bony system, and in the still finer soil and organic matter the fleshy fiber or cellular tissue. What is man but a mass of thawing clay? The ball of the human finger is but a drop congealed. The fingers and toes flow to their extent from the thawing mass of the body. Who knows what the human body would expand and flow out to under a more genial heaven? Is not the hand a spreading *palm* leaf with its lobes and veins? The ear may be regarded, fancifully, as a lichen, *umbilicaria,* on the side of the head, with its lobe or drop. The lip—*labium,* from *labor* (?)—laps or lapses from the sides of the cavernous mouth. The nose is a manifest congealed drop or stalactite. The chin is a still larger drop, the confluent dripping of the face. The cheeks are a slide from the brows into the valley of the face, opposed and diffused by the cheek bones. Each rounded lobe of the vegetable leaf, too, is a thick and now loitering drop, larger or smaller; the lobes are the fingers of the leaf; and as many lobes as it has, in so many directions it tends to flow, and more heat or other genial influences would have caused it to flow yet farther.

Thus it seemed that this one hillside illustrated the principle of all the operations of Nature. The Maker of this earth but patented a leaf. What Champollion will decipher this hieroglyphic for us, that we may turn over a new leaf at last? This phenomenon is more exhilarating to me than the luxuriance and fertility of vineyards. True, it is somewhat excrementitious in its character, and there is no end to the heaps of liver, lights, and bowels, as if the globe were turned wrong side outward; but this suggests at least that Nature has some bowels, and there again is mother of humanity. This is the frost coming out of the ground; this is Spring. It precedes the green and flowery spring, as mythology precedes regular poetry. I know of nothing more purgative of winter fumes and indigestions. It convinces me that Earth is still in her swaddling clothes, and stretches forth baby fingers on every side. Fresh curls spring from the baldest brow. There is nothing inorganic. These foliaceous heaps lie along the bank like the slag of a furnace, showing that Nature is "in full blast" within.

The earth is not a mere fragment of dead history, stratum upon stratum like the leaves of a book, to be studied by geologists and antiquaries chiefly, but living poetry like the leaves of a tree, which precede flowers and fruit—not a fossil earth, but a living earth; compared with whose great central life all animal and vegetable life is merely parasitic. Its throes will heave our exuviae from their graves. You may melt your metals and cast them into the most beautiful moulds you can; they will never excite me like the forms which this molten earth flows out into. And not only it, but the institutions upon it are plastic like clay in the hands of the potter.

Ere long, not only on these banks, but on every hill and plain and in every hollow, the frost comes out of the ground like a dormant quadruped from its burrow, and seeks the sea with music, or migrates to other climes in clouds. Thaw with his gentle persuasion is more powerful than Thor with his hammer. The one melts, the other but breaks in pieces.

When the ground was partially bare of snow, and a few warm days had dried its surface somewhat, it was pleasant to compare the first tender signs of the infant year just peeping forth with the stately beauty of the withered vegetation which had withstood the winter —life-everlasting, goldenrods, pinweeds, and graceful wild grasses, more obvious and interesting frequently than in summer even, as if their beauty was not ripe till then; even cotton-grass, cat-tails, mulleins, johns-wort, hard-hack, meadow-sweet, and other strong-stemmed plants, those unexhausted granaries which entertain the earliest birds—decent weeds, at least, which widowed Nature wears. I am particularly attracted by the arching and sheaflike top of the wool-grass; it brings back the summer to our winter memories, and is among the forms which art loves to copy, and which, in the vegetable kingdom, have the same relation to types already in the mind of man that astronomy has. It is an antique style, older than Greek or Egyptian. Many of the phenomena of Winter are suggestive of an inexpressible tenderness and fragile delicacy. We are accustomed to hear this king described as a rude and boisterous tyrant; but with the gentleness of a lover he adorns the tresses of Summer.

At the approach of spring the red-squirrels got under my house, two at a time, directly under my feet as I sat reading or writing, and kept up the queerest chuckling and chirruping and vocal pirouetting and gurgling sounds that ever were heard; and when I stamped they only chirruped the louder, as if past all fear and respect in their mad pranks, defying humanity to stop them. No you don't—chickaree—chickaree. They were wholly deaf to my arguments, or failed to perceive their force, and fell into a strain of invective that was irresistible.

The first sparrow of spring! The year beginning with younger hope than ever! The faint silvery warblings heard over the partially bare and moist fields from the bluebird, the song-sparrow, and the redwing, as if the last flakes of winter tinkled as they fell! What at such a time are histories, chronologies, traditions, and all written revelations? The brooks sing carols and glees to the spring. The marsh-hawk sailing low over the meadow is already seeking the first slimy life that awakes. The sinking sound of melting snow is heard in all dells, and the ice dissolves apace in the ponds. The grass flames up on the hillsides like a spring fire— "et primitus oritur herba imbribus primoribus evocata" —as if the earth sent forth an inward heat to greet the returning sun; not yellow but green is the color of its flame; the symbol of perpetual youth, the grass-blade, like a long green ribbon, streams from the sod into the

summer, checked indeed by the frost, but anon pushing on again, lifting its spear of last year's hay with the
fresh life below. It grows as steadily as the rill oozes
out of the ground. It is almost identical with that, for
in the growing days of June, when the rills are dry, the
grass blades are their channels, and from year to year
the herds drink at this perennial green stream, and the
mower draws from it betimes their winter supply. So
our human life but dies down to its root, and still puts
forth its green blade to eternity.

Walden is melting apace. There is a canal two rods
wide along the northerly and westerly sides, and wider
still at the east end. A great field of ice has cracked off
from the main body. I hear a song-sparrow singing from
the bushes on the shore—*olit, olit, olit*—*chip, chip,
chip, che char*—*che wiss, wiss, wiss.* He too is helping
to crack it. How handsome the great sweeping curves
in the edge of the ice, answering somewhat to those of
the shore, but more regular! It is unusually hard, owing
to the recent severe but transient cold, and all watered
or waved like a palace floor. But the wind slides eastward over its opaque surface in vain, till it reaches the
living surface beyond. It is glorious to behold this ribbon of water sparkling in the sun, the bare face of the
pond full of glee and youth, as if it spoke the joy of the
fishes within it, and of the sands on its shore—a silvery
sheen as from the scales of a *leuciscus,* as it were all
one active fish. Such is the contrast between winter and
spring. Walden was dead and is alive again. But this
spring it broke up more steadily, as I have said.

The change from storm and winter to serene and mild
weather, from dark and sluggish hours to bright and
elastic ones, is a memorable crisis which all things pro-
claim. It is seemingly instantaneous at last. Suddenly an
influx of light filled my house, though the evening was

at hand, and the clouds of winter still overhung it, and the eaves were dripping with sleety rain. I looked out the window, and lo! where yesterday was cold gray ice there lay the transparent pond already calm and full of hope as in a summer evening, reflecting a summer evening sky in its bosom, though none was visible overhead, as if it had intelligence with some remote horizon. I heard a robin in the distance, the first I had heard for many a thousand years, methought, whose note I shall not forget for many a thousand more—the same sweet and powerful song as of yore. O the evening robin, at the end of a New England summer day! If I could ever find the twig he sits upon! I mean *he;* I mean *the twig.* This at least is not the *Turdus migratorius.* The pitch pines and shrub-oaks about my house, which had so long drooped, suddenly resumed their several characters, looked brighter, greener, and more erect and alive, as if effectually cleansed and restored by the rain. I knew that it would not rain any more. You may tell by looking at any twig of the forest, ay, at your very woodpile, whether its winter is past or not. As it grew darker, I was startled by the *honking* of geese flying low over the woods, like weary travelers getting in late from southern lakes, and indulging at last in unrestrained complaint and mutual consolation. Standing at my door, I could hear the rush of their wings; when, driving toward my house, they suddenly spied my light, and with hushed clamor wheeled and settled in the pond. So I came in, and shut the door, and passed my first spring night in the woods.

In the morning I watched the geese from the door through the mist, sailing in the middle of the pond, fifty rods off, so large and tumultuous that Walden appeared like an artificial pond for their amusement. But when I stood on the shore they at once rose up with a great flapping of wings at the signal of their commander, and when they had got into rank circled about over my head, twenty-nine of them, and then steered straight to Canada, with a regular *honk* from the leader at intervals, trusting to break their fast in muddier pools. A "plump" of ducks rose at the same time and took the route to the north in the wake of their noisier cousins.

For a week I heard the circling groping clangor of some solitary goose in the foggy mornings, seeking its companion, and still peopling the woods with the sound of a larger life than they could sustain. In April the pigeons were seen again flying ·express in small flocks, and in due time I heard the martins twittering over my clearing, though it had not seemed that the township contained so many that it could afford me any, and I fancied that they were peculiarly of the ancient race that dwelt in hollow trees ere white men came. In almost all climes the tortoise and the frog are among the precursors and heralds of this season, and birds fly with song and glancing plumage, and plants spring and bloom, and winds blow, to correct this slight oscillation of the poles and preserve the equilibrium of Nature.

As every season seems best to us in its turn, so the coming in of spring is like the creation of Cosmos out of Chaos and the realization of the Golden Age.

> "Eurus ad Auroram, Nabathacaque regna recessit,
> Persidaque, et radiis juga subdita matutinis."

"The East-Wind withdrew to Aurora and the Nabathaean
  kingdom,
And the Persian, and the ridges placed under the morning
  rays.

. . . .

Man was born. Whether that Artificer of things,
The origin of a better world, made him from the divine
  seed;

> Or the earth being recent and lately sundered from the
>   high
> Ether, retained some seeds of cognate heaven."

A single gentle rain makes the grass many shades greener. So our prospects brighten on the influx of better thoughts. We should be blessed if we lived in the present always, and took advantage of every accident that befell us, like the grass which confesses the influence of the slightest dew that falls on it; and did not spend our time in atoning for the neglect of past opportunities, which we call doing our duty. We loiter in winter while it is already spring. In a pleasant spring morning all men's sins are forgiven. Such a day is a truce to vice. While such a sun holds out to burn, the vilest sinner may return. Through our own recovered innocence we discern the innocence of our neighbors. You may have known your neighbor yesterday for a thief, a drunkard, or a sensualist, and merely pitied or despised him, and despaired of the world; but the sun shines bright and warm this first spring morning, re-creating the world, and you meet him at some serene work, and see how his exhausted and debauched veins expand with still joy and bless the new day, feel the spring influence with the innocence of infancy, and all his faults are forgotten. There is not only an atmosphere of good will about him, but even a savor of holiness groping for expression, blindly and ineffectually perhaps, like a new-born instinct; and for a short hour the south hillside echoes to no vulgar jest. You see some innocent fair shoots preparing to burst from his gnarled rind and try another year's life, tender and fresh as the youngest plant. Even he has entered into the joy of his Lord. Why the jailer does not leave open his prison doors—why the judge does not dismiss his case—why the preacher does not dismiss his congregation! It is because they do not obey the hint which God gives them, nor accept the pardon which he freely offers to all.

"A return to goodness produced each day in the tranquil and beneficent breath of the morning, causes that in respect to the love of virtue and the hatred of vice, one approaches a little the primitive nature of man, as the sprouts of the forest which has been felled. In like manner the evil which one does in the interval of a day prevents the germs of virtues which began to spring up again from developing themselves and destroys them.

"After the germs of virtue have thus been prevented many times from developing themselves, then the beneficent breath of evening does not suffice to preserve them. As soon as the breath of evening does not suffice longer to preserve them, then the nature of man does not differ much from that of the brute. Men seeing the nature of this man like that of the brute, think that he has never possessed the innate faculty of reason. Are those the true and natural sentiments of man?"

"The Golden Age was first created, which without any
   avenger
Spontaneously without law cherished fidelity and rectitude.
Punishment and fear were not; nor were threatening words
   read
On suspended brass; nor did the suppliant crowd fear
The words of their judge; but were safe without an
   avenger.
Not yet the pine felled on its mountains had descended
To the liquid waves that it might see a foreign world,
And mortals knew no shores but their own.
    .   .   .   .
There was eternal spring, and placid zephyrs with warm
Blasts soothed the flowers born without seed."

On the 29th of April, as I was fishing from the bank of the river near the Nine-Acre-Corner bridge, standing on the quaking grass and willow roots, where the muskrats lurk, I heard a singular rattling sound, somewhat like that of the sticks which boys play with their fingers, when, looking up, I observed a very slight and graceful hawk, like a night-hawk, alternately soaring like a ripple and tumbling a rod or two over and over, showing the underside of its wings, which gleamed like a satin ribbon in the sun, or like the pearly inside of a shell. This sight reminded me of falconry and what nobleness and poetry are associated with that sport. The Merlin it seemed to me it might be called: but I care not for its name. It was the most ethereal flight I had ever witnessed. It did not simply flutter like a butterfly, nor soar like the larger hawks, but it sported with proud reliance in the fields of air; mounting again and again with its strange chuckle, it repeated its free and beautiful fall, turning over and over like a kite, and then recovering from its lofty tumbling, as if it had never set its foot on *terra firma*. It appeared to have no companion in the universe—sporting there alone—and to need none but the morning and the ether with which it played. It was not lonely, but made all the earth lonely beneath it. Where was the parent which hatched it, its kindred, and its father in the heavens? The tenant of the air, it seemed related to the earth but by an egg hatched some time in the crevice of a crag; or was its native nest made in the angle of a cloud, woven of the rainbow's trimmings and the sunset sky, and lined with some soft midsummer haze caught up from earth? Its eyry now some cliffy cloud.

Beside this I got a rare mess of golden and silver and bright cupreous fishes, which looked like a string of jewels. Ah! I have penetrated to those meadows on the morning of many a first spring day, jumping from hummock to hummock, from willow root to willow root, when the wild river valley and the woods were bathed

in so pure and bright a light as would have waked the
dead, if they had been slumbering in their graves, as
some suppose. There needs no stronger proof of immortality. All things must live in such a light. O Death,
where was thy sting? O Grave, where was thy victory,
then?

Our village life would stagnate if it were not for the
unexplored forests and meadows which surround it.
We need the tonic of wildness—to wade sometimes in
marshes where the bittern and the meadow-hen lurk,
and hear the booming of the snipe; to smell the whispering sedge where only some wilder and more solitary
fowl builds her nest, and the mink crawls with its belly
close to the ground. At the same time that we are earnest to explore and learn all things, we require that all
things be mysterious and unexplorable, that land and
sea be infinitely wild, unsurveyed and unfathomed by
us because unfathomable. We can never have enough
of Nature. We must be refreshed by the sight of inexhaustible vigor, vast and Titanic features, the seacoast
with its wrecks, the wilderness with its living and its decaying trees, the thundercloud, and the rain which lasts
three weeks and produces freshets. We need to witness
our own limits transgressed, and some life pasturing
freely where we never wander. We are cheered when
we observe the vulture feeding on the carrion, which
disgusts and disheartens us, and deriving health and
strength from the repast. There was a dead horse in the
hollow by the path to my house, which compelled me
sometimes to go out of my way, especially in the night
when the air was heavy, but the assurance it gave me of
the strong appetite and inviolable health of Nature was
my compensation for this. I love to see that Nature is
so rife with life that myriads can be afforded to be
sacrificed and suffered to prey on one another; that ten-

der organizations can be so serenely squashed out of existence like pulp—tadpoles which herons gobble up, and tortoises and toads run over in the road; and that sometimes it has rained flesh and blood! With the liability to accident, we must see how little account is to be made of it. The impression made on a wise man is that of universal innocence. Poison is not poisonous after all, nor are any wounds fatal. Compassion is a very untenable ground. It must be expeditious. Its pleadings will not bear to be stereotyped.

Early in May, the oaks, hickories, maples, and other trees, just putting out amidst the pine woods around the pond, imparted a brightness like sunshine to the landscape, especially in cloudy days, as if the sun were breaking through mists and shining faintly on the hillsides here and there. On the third or fourth of May I saw a loon in the pond, and during the first week of the month I heard the whippoorwill, the brown-thrasher, the veery, the wood-pewee, the chewink, and other birds. I had heard the wood-thrush long before. The phoebe had already come once more and looked in at my door and window, to see if my house was cavern-like enough for her, sustaining herself on humming wings with clinched talons, as if she held by the air, while she surveyed the premises. The sulphur-like pollen of the pitch pine soon covered the pond and the stones and rotten wood along the shore, so that you could have collected a barrelful. This is the "sulphur showers" we hear of. Even in Calidas' drama of Sacontala, we read of "rills dyed yellow with the golden dust of the lotus." And so the seasons went rolling on into summer, as one rambles into higher and higher grass.

Thus was my first year's life in the woods completed; and the second year was similar to it. I finally left Walden September 6th, 1847.

CONCLUSION

To the sick the doctors wisely recommend a change of air and scenery. Thank Heaven, here is not all the world. The buckeye does not grow in New England, and the mocking-bird is rarely heard here. The wild goose is more of a cosmopolite than we; he breaks his fast in Canada, takes a luncheon in the Ohio, and plumes himself for the night in a southern bayou. Even the bison, to some extent, keeps pace with the seasons, cropping the pastures of the Colorado only till a greener and sweeter grass awaits him by the Yellowstone. Yet we think that if rail fences are pulled down, and stone walls piled up on our farms, bounds are henceforth set to our lives and our fates decided. If you are chosen town clerk, forsooth, you cannot go to Tierra del Fuego this summer: but you may go to the land of infernal fire nevertheless. The universe is wider than our views of it.

Yet we should oftener look over the tafferel of our craft, like curious passengers, and not make the voyage like stupid sailors picking oakum. The other side of the globe is but the home of our correspondent. Our voyaging is only great-circle sailing, and the doctors prescribe for diseases of the skin merely. One hastens to Southern Africa to chase the giraffe; but surely that is not the game he would be after. How long, pray, would a man hunt giraffes if he could? Snipes and woodcocks also may afford rare sport; but I trust it would be nobler game to shoot one's self.

> "Direct your eye right inward, and you'll find
> A thousand regions in your mind
> Yet undiscovered. Travel them, and be
> Expert in home-cosmography."

What does Africa, what does the West, stand for? Is not our own interior white on the chart? black though it may prove, like the coast, when discovered. Is it the source of the Nile, or the Niger, or the Mississippi, or a Northwest Passage around this continent, that we would find? Are these the problems which most concern mankind? Is Franklin the only man who is lost, that his wife should be so earnest to find him? Does Mr. Grinnell know where he himself is? Be rather the Mungo Park, the Lewis and Clarke and Frobisher, of your own streams and oceans; explore your own higher latitudes—with shiploads of preserved meats to support you, if they be necessary; and pile the empty cans sky-high for a sign. Were preserved meats invented to preserve meat merely? Nay, be a Columbus to whole new continents and worlds within you, opening new channels, not of trade, but of thought. Every man is the lord of a realm beside which the earthly empire of the Czar is but a petty state, a hummock left by the ice. Yet some can be patriotic who have no *self*-respect, and sacrifice the greater to the less. They love the soil which makes their graves, but have no sympathy with the spirit which may still animate their clay. Patriotism is a maggot in their heads. What was the meaning of that South-Sea Exploring Expedition, with all its parade and expense, but an indirect recognition of the fact, that there are continents and seas in the moral world, to which every man is an isthmus or an inlet, yet unexplored by him, but that it is easier to sail many thousand miles through cold and storm and cannibals, in a government ship, with five hundred men and boys to assist one, than it is to explore the private sea, the Atlantic and Pacific Ocean of one's being alone.

> "Erret, et extremos alter scrutetur Iberos.
> Plus habet hic vitae, plus habet ille viae."

Let them wander and scrutinize the outlandish Australians.
I have more of God, they more of the road.

It is not worth the while to go round the world to count
the cats in Zanzibar. Yet do this even till you can do
better, and you may perhaps find some "Symmes' Hole"
by which to get at the inside at last. England and
France, Spain and Portugal, Gold Coast and Slave
Coast, all front on this private sea; but no bark from
them has ventured out of sight of land, though it is without doubt the direct way to India. If you would learn
to speak all tongues and conform to the customs of all
nations, if you would travel farther than all travelers, be
naturalized in all climes, and cause the Sphinx to dash
her head against a stone, even obey the precept of the
old philosopher, and Explore thyself. Herein are demanded the eye and the nerve. Only the defeated and
deserters go to the wars, cowards that run away and en-
list. Start now on that farthest western way, which does
not pause at the Mississippi or the Pacific, nor conduct
toward a worn-out China or Japan, but leads on direct a
tangent to this sphere, summer and winter, day and
night, sundown, moondown, and at last earth down too.

It is said that Mirabeau took to highway robbery "to
ascertain what degree of resolution was necessary in
order to place one's self in formal opposition to the most
sacred laws of society." He declared that "a soldier who
fights in the ranks does not require half so much courage
as a foot-pad"—"that honor and religion have never
stood in the way of a well-considered and a firm resolve." This was manly, as the world goes; and yet it
was idle, if not desperate. A saner man would have
found himself often enough "in formal opposition" to
what are deemed "the most sacred laws of society,"
through obedience to yet more sacred laws, and to have

tested his resolution without going out of his way. It is not for a man to put himself in such an attitude to society, but to maintain himself in whatever attitude he find himself through obedience to the laws of his being which will never be one of opposition to a just government, if he should chance to meet with such.

I left the woods for as good a reason as I went there. Perhaps it seemed to me that I had several more lives to live, and could not spare any more time for that one. It is remarkable how easily and insensibly we fall into a particular route, and make a beaten track for ourselves. I had not lived there a week before my feet wore a path from my door to the pond-side; and though it is five or six years since I trod it, it is still quite distinct. It is true, I fear that others may have fallen into it, and so helped to keep it open. The surface of the earth is soft and impressible by the feet of men; and so with the paths which the mind travels. How worn and dusty, then, must be the highways of the world, how deep the ruts of tradition and conformity! I did not wish to take a cabin passage, but rather to go before the mast and on the deck of the world, for there I could best see the moonlight amid the mountains. I do not wish to go below now.

I learned this, at least, by my experiment; that if one advances confidently in the direction of his dreams, and endeavors to live the life which he has imagined, he will meet with a success unexpected in common hours. He will put some things behind, will pass an invisible boundary; new, universal, and more liberal laws will begin to establish themselves around and within him; or the old laws be expanded, and interpreted in his favor in a more liberal sense, and he will live with the license of a higher order of beings. In proportion as he simplifies his life, the laws of the universe will appear less complex, and solitude will not be solitude, nor poverty poverty, nor weakness weakness. If you have built castles in the air, your work need not be lost; that is where they should be. Now put the foundations under them.

It is a ridiculous demand which England and America make, that you shall speak so that they can understand you. Neither men nor toadstools grow so. As if that were important, and there were not enough to understand you without them. As if Nature could support but one order of understandings, could not sustain birds as well as quadrupeds, flying as well as creeping things, and *hush* and *who*, which Bright can understand, were the best English. As if there were safety in stupidity alone. I fear chiefly lest my expression may not be *extra-vagant* enough, may not wander far enough beyond the narrow limits of my daily experience, so as to be adequate to the truth of which I have been convinced. *Extra vagance!* it depends on how you are yarded. The migrating buffalo, which seeks new pastures in another latitude, is not extravagant like the cow which kicks over the pail, leaps the cowyard fence, and runs after her calf, in milking time. I desire to speak somewhere *without* bounds; like a man in a waking moment, to men in their waking moments; for I am convinced that I cannot exaggerate enough even to lay the foundation of a true expression. Who that has heard a strain of music feared then lest he should speak extravagantly any more forever? In view of the future or possible, we should live quite laxly and undefined in front, our outlines dim and misty on that side; as our shadows reveal an insensible perspiration toward the sun. The volatile truth of our words should continually betray the inadequacy of the residual statement. Their truth is instantly *translated;* its literal monument alone remains. The words which express our faith and piety are not definite; yet they are significant and fragrant like frankincense to superior natures.

Why level downward to our dullest perception always, and praise that as common sense? The commonest sense is the sense of men asleep, which they express by snoring. Sometimes we are inclined to class those who are once-and-a-half witted with the half-witted, because we appreciate only a third part of their wit. Some would find fault with the morning-red, if they ever got up early enough. "They pretend," as I hear, "that the verses of Kabir have four different senses; illusion, spirit, intellect, and the exoteric doctrine of the Vedas"; but in this part of the world it is considered a ground for complaint if a man's writings admit of more than one interpretation. While England endeavors to cure the potato-rot, will not any endeavor to cure the brain-rot, which prevails so much more widely and fatally?

I do not suppose that I have attained to obscurity, but I should be proud if no more fatal fault were found with my pages on this score than was found with the Walden ice. Southern customers objected to its blue color, which is the evidence of its purity, as if it were muddy, and preferred the Cambridge ice, which is white, but tastes of weeds. The purity men love is like the mists which envelop the earth, and not like the azure ether beyond.

Some are dinning in our ears that we Americans, and moderns generally, are intellectual dwarfs compared with the ancients, or even the Elizabethan men. But what is that to the purpose? A living dog is better than a dead lion. Shall a man go and hang himself because he belongs to the race of pygmies, and not be the biggest pygmy that he can? Let everyone mind his own business, and endeavor to be what he was made.

Why should we be in such desperate haste to succeed and in such desperate enterprises? If a man does not keep pace with his companions, perhaps it is because he hears a different drummer. Let him step to the music which he hears, however measured or far away. It is not important that he should mature as soon as an apple tree or an oak. Shall he turn his spring into summer? If the condition of things which we were made for is not yet, what were any reality which we can substitute? We will not be shipwrecked on a vain reality. Shall we with pains erect a heaven of blue glass over ourselves, though when it is done we shall be sure to gaze still at the true ethereal heaven far above, as if the former were not?

There was an artist in the city of Kouroo who was disposed to strive after perfection. One day it came into his mind to make a staff. Having considered that in an imperfect work time is an ingredient, but into a perfect work time does not enter, he said to himself, It shall be perfect in all respects, though I should do nothing else in my life. He proceeded instantly to the forest for wood, being resolved that it should not be made of unsuitable material; and as he searched for and rejected stick after stick, his friends gradually deserted him, for they grew old in their works and died, but he grew not older by a moment. His singleness of purpose and resolution, and his elevated piety, endowed him, without his knowledge, with perennial youth. As he made no compromise with Time, Time kept out of his way, and only sighed at a distance because he could not overcome him. Before he had found a stock in all respects suitable the city of Kouroo was a hoary ruin, and he sat on one of its mounds to peel the stick. Before he had given it the proper shape the dynasty of the Candahars was at an end, and with the point of the stick he wrote the name of the last of that race in the sand, and then resumed his work. By the time he had smoothed and polished the staff Kalpa was no longer the pole-star; and ere he had put on the ferule and the head adorned with precious stones, Brahma had awoke and slumbered many times. But why do I stay to mention these things? When the finishing stroke was put to his work, it suddenly expanded before the eyes of the astonished artist into the fairest of all the creations of Brahma. He had made a new system in making a staff, a world with full and fair proportions; in which, though the old cities and dynasties had passed away, fairer and more glorious ones had taken their places. And now he saw by the heap of shavings still fresh at his feet, that, for him and his work, the former lapse of time had been an illusion, and that no more time had elapsed than is required for a single scintillation from the brain of Brahma to fall on and inflame the tinder of a mortal brain. The material was pure, and his art was pure; how could the result be other than wonderful?

No face which we can give to a matter will stead us so well at last as the truth. This alone wears well. For the most part, we are not where we are, but in a false position. Through an infirmity of our natures, we suppose a case, and put ourselves into it, and hence are in two cases at the same time, and it is doubly difficult to get out. In sane moments we regard only the facts, the case that is. Say what you have to say, not what you ought. Any truth is better than make-believe. Tom Hyde, the tinker, standing on the gallows, was asked if he had anything to say. "Tell the tailors," said he, "to remember to make a knot in their thread before they take the first stitch." His companion's prayer is forgotten.

However mean your life is, meet it and live it; do not shun it and call it hard names. It is not so bad as you are. It looks poorest when you are richest. The fault-finder will find faults even in paradise. Love your life, poor as it is. You may perhaps have some pleasant, thrilling, glorious hours, even in a poorhouse. The setting sun is reflected from the windows of the almshouse as brightly as from the rich man's abode; the snow melts before its door as early in the spring. I do not see but a quiet mind may live as contentedly there, and have as cheering thoughts, as in a palace. The town's poor seem to me often to live the most independent lives of any. Maybe they are simply great enough to receive without misgiving. Most think that they are above being supported by the town; but it oftener happens that they are not above supporting themselves by dishonest means, which should be more disreputable. Cultivate poverty like a garden herb, like sage. Do not trouble yourself much to get new things, whether clothes or friends. Turn the old; return to them. Things do not change; we change. Sell your clothes and keep your thoughts. God will see that you do not want society. If I were confined to a corner of a garret all my days, like a spider, the world would be just as large to me while I had my thoughts about me. The philosopher said: "From an army of three divisions one can take away its general, and put it in disorder; from the man the most abject and vulgar one cannot take away his thought." Do not seek so anxiously to be developed, to subject yourself to many influences to be played on; it is all dissipation. Humility like darkness reveals the heavenly lights. The shadows of poverty and meanness gather around us, "and lo! creation widens to our view." We are often reminded that if there were bestowed on us the wealth of Croesus, our aims must still be the same, and our means essentially the same. Moreover, if you are restricted in your range by poverty, if you cannot buy books and newspapers, for instance, you are but confined to the most significant and vital experiences; you are compelled to deal with the material which yields the most sugar and the most starch. It is life near the bone where it is sweetest. You are defended from being a trifler. No man loses ever on a lower level by magnanimity on a higher. Superfluous wealth can buy superfluities only. Money is not required to buy one necessary of the soul.

I live in the angle of a leaden wall, into whose composition was poured a little alloy of bell metal. Often, in the repose of my midday, there reaches my ears a confused *tintinnabulum* from without. It is the noise of my contemporaries. My neighbors tell me of their adventures with famous gentlemen and ladies, what notabilities they met at the dinner-table; but I am no more interested in such things than in the contents of the Daily Times. The interest and the conversation are about costume and manners. chiefly; but a goose is a goose still, dress it as you will. They tell me of California and Texas, of England and the Indies, of the Hon. Mr.. —— of Georgia or of Massachusetts, all transient and fleeting phenomena, till I am ready to leap from their courtyard like the Mameluke bey. I delight to come to my bearings—not walk in procession with pomp and parade, in a conspicuous place, but to walk even with the Builder of the universe, if I may—not to live in this restless, nervous, bustling, trivial nineteenth century, but stand or sit thoughtfully while it goes by. What are men celebrating? They are all on a committee of arrangements, and hourly expect a speech from somebody. God is only the president of the day, and Webster is his orator. I love to weigh, to settle, to gravitate toward that which most strongly and rightfully attracts me; not hang by the beam of the scale and try to weigh less, not suppose a case, but take the case that is; to travel the only path I can, and that on which no power can resist me. It affords me no satisfaction to commence to spring an arch before I have got a solid foundation. Let us not play at kittlybenders. There is a solid bottom everywhere. We read that the traveler asked the boy if the swamp before him had a hard bottom. The boy replied that it had. But presently the traveler's horse sank in up to the girths, and he observed to the boy, "I thought you said that this bog had a hard bottom." "So it has," answered the latter, "but you have not got half way to it yet." So it is with the bogs and quicksands of society; but he is an old boy that knows it. Only what is thought, said, or done at a certain rare coincidence is good. I would not be one of those who will foolishly drive a nail into mere lath and plastering; such a deed would keep me awake nights. Give me a hammer, and let me feel for the furrowing. Do not depend on the putty. Drive a nail home and clinch it so faithfully that you can wake up in the night and think of your work with satisfaction—a work at which you would not be ashamed to invoke the Muse. So will help you God, and so only. Every nail driven should be as another rivet in the machine of the universe, you carrying on the work.

Rather than love, than money, than fame, give me truth. I sat at a table where were rich food and wine in abundance, and obsequious attendance, but sincerity and truth were not; and I went away hungry from the inhospitable board. The hospitality was as cold as the ices. I thought that there was no need of ice to freeze them. They talked to me of the age of the wine and the fame of the vintage; but I thought of an older, a newer, and purer wine, of a more glorious vintage, which they had not got, and could not buy. The style, the house and grounds and "entertainment" pass for nothing with me. I called on the king, but he made me wait in his hall, and conducted like a man incapacitated for hospitality. There was a man in my neighborhood who lived in a hollow tree. His manners were truly regal. I should have done better had I called on him.

How long shall we sit in our porticoes practicing idle

and musty virtues, which any work would make impertinent? As if one were to begin the day with long-suffering, and hire a man to hoe his potatoes, and in the afternoon go forth to practice Christian meekness and charity with goodness aforethought! Consider the China pride and stagnant self-complacency of mankind. This generation inclines a little to congratulate itself on being the last of an illustrious line; and in Boston and London and Paris and Rome, thinking of its long descent, it speaks of its progress in art and science and literature with satisfaction. There are the Records of the Philosophical Societies, and the public Eulogies of *Great Men!* It is the good Adam contemplating his own virtue. "Yes, we have done great deeds, and sung divine songs, which shall never die"—that is, as long as *we* can remember them. The learned societies and great men of Assyria— where are they? What youthful philosophers and experimentalists we are! There is not one of my readers who has yet lived a whole human life. These may be but the spring months in the life of the race. If we have had the seven-years' itch, we have not seen the seventeen-year locust yet in Concord. We are acquainted with a mere pellicle of the globe on which we live. Most have not delved six feet beneath the surface, nor leaped as many above it. We know not where we are. Besides, we are sound asleep nearly half our time. Yet we esteem ourselves wise, and have an established order on the surface. Truly, we are deep thinkers, we are ambitious spirits! As I stand over the insect crawling amid the pine needles on the forest floor, and endeavoring to conceal itself from my sight, and ask myself why it will cherish those humble thoughts, and hide its head from me who might, perhaps, be its benefactor, and impart to its race some cheering information, I am reminded of the greater

Benefactor and Intelligence that stands over me the human insect.

. There is an incessant influx of novelty into the world, and yet we tolerate incredible dullness. I need only suggest what kind of sermons are still listened to in the most enlightened countries. There are such words as joy and sorrow, but they are only the burden of a psalm, sung with a nasal twang, while we believe in the ordinary and mean. We think that we can change our clothes only. It is said that the British Empire is very large and respectable, and that the United States are a first-rate power. We do not believe that a tide rises and falls behind every man which can float the British Empire like a chip, if he should ever harbor it in his mind. Who knows what sort of seventeen-year locust will next come out of the ground? The government of the world I live in was not framed, like that of Britain, in after-dinner conversations over the wine.

The life in us is like the water in the river. It may rise this year higher than man has ever known it, and flood the parched uplands; even this may be the eventful year, which will drown out all our muskrats. It was not always dry land where we dwell. I see far inland the banks which the stream anciently washed, before science began to record its freshets. Every one has heard the story which has gone the rounds of New England, of a strong and beautiful bug which came out of the dry leaf of an old table of apple-tree wood, which had stood in a farmer's kitchen for sixty years, first in Connecticut, and afterward in Massachusetts—from an egg deposited in the living tree many years earlier still, as appeared by counting the annual layers beyond it; which was heard gnawing out for several weeks, hatched perchance by the heat of an urn. Who does not feel his faith in a resurrection and immortality strengthened by hearing of this? Who knows what beautiful and winged life, whose egg has been buried for ages under many concentric layers of woodenness in the dead dry life of society, deposited at first in the alburnum of the green and living tree, which has been gradually converted into the semblance of its well-seasoned tomb—heard perchance gnawing out now for years by the astonished family of man, as they sat round the festive board—may unexpectedly come forth from amidst society's most trivial and hand-selled furniture, to enjoy its perfect summer life at last!

I do not say that John or Jonathan will realize all this; but such is the character of that morrow which mere lapse of time can never make to dawn. The light which puts out our eyes is darkness to us. Only that day dawns to which we are awake. There is more day to dawn. The sun is but a morning-star.

Journal

In the basement of the J. Pierpont Morgan Library in New York City there is a sturdy wooden box. Thoreau built it himself and it houses the thirty-odd ledgers that compose his famous Journal. The first volumes are written in a round, almost schoolboyish hand, and the last are filled with the swift scrawls of a surveyor who sat down at night to recall practically every natural detail of the day. Thoreau's Journal became his mine of raw material. First drafts of everything from letters to lectures can be seen there. The most important aspect of the Journal, however, is that it furnishes a daily account of the growth, change, and observations of an essential American writer. The selection for 1858 given below shows Thoreau in transition. The great writing and the Transcendentalism have pretty well gone, but the final obsession with natural detail has not yet become complete. This portion starts with New Year's Day, but for all of Thoreau one would never know it.

C. B.

JANUARY, 1858

(Age 40)

Jan. 1. There are many words which are genuine and indigenous and have their root in our natures, not made by scholars, and as well understood by the illiterate as others. There are also a great many words which are spurious and artificial, and can only be used in a bad sense, since the thing they signify is not fair and substantial—such as the *church,* the *judiciary,* to *impeach,* etc., etc. They who use them do not stand on solid ground. It is in vain to try to preserve them by attaching other words to them as the *true* church, etc. It is like towing a sinking ship with a canoe.

I have lately been surveying the Walden woods so extensively and minutely that I now see it mapped in my mind's eye—as, indeed, on paper—as so many men's woodlots, and am aware when I walk there that I am at a given moment passing from such a one's wood-lot to such another's. I fear this particular dry knowl-edge may affect my imagination and fancy, that it will not be easy to see so much wildness and native vigor there as formerly. No thicket will seem so unexplored now that I know that a stake and stones may be found in it. In these respects those Maine woods differed essen-tially from ours. There you are never reminded that the wilderness which you are threading is, after all, some villager's familiar woodlot from which his ancestors have sledded their fuel for generations, or some widow's thirds, minutely described in some old deed, which is recorded, of which the owner has got a plan, too, and old bound marks may be found every forty rods if you will search. What a history this Concord wilderness which I affect so much may have had! How many old deeds describe it—some particular wild spot—how it passed from Cole to Robinson, and Robinson to Jones, and Jones finally to Smith, in course of years! Some have cut it over three times during their lives, and some burned it and sowed it with rye, and built walls and made a pasture of it, perchance. All have renewed the bounds and reblazed the trees many times. Here you are not reminded of these things. 'Tis true the map informs you that you stand on land granted by the State to such an academy, or on Bingham's Purchase, but these names do not impose on you, for you see nothing to remind you of the academy or of Bingham.

Jan. 3. Sunday. I see a flock of *F. hyemalis* this afternoon, the weather is hitherto so warm.

About, in his lively "Greece and the Greeks," says, "These are the most exquisite delights to be found in Greece, next to, or perhaps before, the pleasure of admiring the masterpieces of art—a little cool water under a genial sun." I have no doubt that this is true. Why, then, travel so far when the same pleasures may be found near home?

The slosh on Walden had so much water in it that it has now frozen perfectly smooth and looks like a semi-transparent marble. Being, however, opaque, it reminds one the more of some vast hall or corridor's floor, yet probably not a human foot has trodden it yet. Only the track-repairers and stokers have cast stones and billets of wood onto it to prove it.

Going to the Andromeda Ponds, I was greeted by the warm brown-red glow of the *Andromeda calyculata* toward the sun. I see where I have been through, the more reddish under sides apparently being turned up. It is long since a human friend has met me with such a glow.

Jan. 4. P.M.—The weather still remarkably warm; the ice too soft for skating. I go through by the Andromeda Ponds and down river from Fair Haven. I am encouraged by the sight of men fishing in Fair Haven Pond, for it reminds me that they have animal spirits for such adventures. I am glad to be reminded that any go a-fishing. When I get down near to Cardinal Shore, the sun near setting, its light is wonderfully reflected from a narrow edging of yellowish stubble at the edge of the meadow ice and foot of the hill, an edging only two or three feet wide, and the stubble but a few inches high.

(I am looking east.) It is remarkable because the ice is but a dull lead-color (it is so soft and sodden), reflecting no light, and the hill beyond is a dark russet, here and there patched with snow, but this narrow intermediate line of stubble is all aglow. I get its true color and brightness best when I do not look directly at it, but a little above it toward the hill, seeing it with the lower part of my eye more truly and abstractly. It is as if all the rays slid over the ice and lodged against and were reflected by the stubble. It is surprising how much sunny light a little straw that survives the winter will reflect.

The channel of the river is open part of the way. The *Cornus sericea* and some quite young willow shoots are the red-barked twigs so conspicuous now along the riversides.

That bright and warm reflection of sunlight from the insignificant edging of stubble was remarkable. I was coming downstream over the meadows, on the ice, within four or five rods of the eastern shore. The sun on my left was about a quarter of an hour above the horizon. The ice was soft and sodden, of a dull lead-color, quite dark and reflecting no light as I looked eastward, but my eyes caught by accident a singular sunny brightness reflected from the narrow border of stubble only three or four inches high (and as many feet wide perhaps) which rose along the edge of the ice at the foot of the hill. It was not a mere brightening of the bleached stubble, but the warm and yellow light of the sun, which, it appeared, it was peculiarly fitted to reflect. It was that amber light from the west which we sometimes witness after a storm, concentrated on this stubble, for the hill beyond was merely a dark russet spotted with snow. All the yellow rays seemed to be reflected by this insignificant stubble alone, and when I looked more generally a little above it, seeing it with the under part of my eye, it appeared yet more truly and more bright; the reflected light made its due impression on my eye, separated from the proper color of the stubble, and it glowed almost like a low, steady, and serene fire. It was precisely as if the sunlight had mechanically slid over the ice, and lodged against the stubble. It will be enough to say of something warmly and sunnily bright that it glowed like lit stubble. It was remarkable that, looking eastward, this was the only evidence of the light in the west.

Here and there in the meadow, etc., near springy places, you see where the thinner ice has been pushed up tentwise (∧ or ⌒) and cracked,

either for want of room, two fields crowding together, or expanding with heat from below.

Jan. 5. P.M.—I see one of those fuzzy winter caterpillars, black at the two ends and brown-red in middle, crawling on a rock by the Hunt's Bridge causeway.

Mr. Hosmer is loading hay in his barn. It is meadow-hay, and I am interested in it chiefly as a botanist. If meadow-hay is of less worth in the market, it is more interesting to the poet. In this there is a large proportion of *Osmunda regalis*. But I fear that in the long run it is not so interesting to the cattle to contemplate and chew this as English hay and clover. How completely a load of hay in the winter revives the memory of past summers! Summer in us is only a little dried like it. The rowen in Hosmer's barn has a finer and greener look than the first crop. And so the ferns in coal remind us of summer still longer past.

Jan. 6. The first snowstorm of much importance. By noon it *may be* six inches deep.

P.M.—Up railroad to North River.

The main stream, barely skimmed over with snow, which has sunk the thin ice and is saturated with water, is of a dull-brown color between the white fields.

I detect a very tall and slender tupelo by its thorny-looking twigs. It is close by a white oak, at the yellow gerardia up railroad. It is nearly fifty feet high and only one foot through at the ground. I derive a certain excitement, not to be refused, even from going through Dennis's Swamp on the opposite side of the railroad, where the poison-dogwood abounds. This simple-stemmed bush is very full of fruit, hanging in loose, dry, pale-green drooping panicles. Some of them are a foot long. It impresses me as the most fruitful shrub thereabouts. I cannot refrain from plucking it and bringing home some pretty sprigs. Other fruits there are there which belong to the hard season, the enduring panicled andromeda and a few partly decayed prinos berries. I walk amid the bare midribs of cinnamon ferns, with at most a terminal leafet, and here and there I see a little dark water at the bottom of a dimple in the snow, over which the snow has not yet been able to prevail.

I was feeling very cheap, nevertheless, reduced to make the most of dry dogwood berries. Very little evidence of God or man did I see just then, and life not as rich and inviting an enterprise as it should be, when my attention was caught by a snowflake on my coatsleeve. It was one of those perfect, crystalline, star-shaped ones, six-rayed, like a flat wheel with six spokes, only the spokes were perfect little pine trees in shape, arranged around a central spangle. This little object, which, with many of its fellows, rested unmelting on my coat, so perfect and beautiful, reminded me that Nature had not lost her pristine vigor yet, and why should man lose heart? Sometimes the pines were worn and had lost their branches, and again it appeared as if several stars had impinged on one another at various angles, making a somewhat spherical mass. These little wheels came down like the wrecks of chariots from a battle waged in the sky. There were mingled with these starry flakes small downy pellets also. This was at mid-afternoon, and it has not quite ceased snowing yet (at 10 P.M.). We are rained and snowed on with gems. I confess that I was a little encouraged, for I was beginning to believe that Nature was poor and mean, and I was now convinced that she turned off as good work as ever. What a world we live in! Where are the jewelers' shops? There is nothing handsomer than a snowflake and a dewdrop. I may say that the maker of the world exhausts his skill with each snowflake and dewdrop that he sends down. We think that the one mechanically coheres and that the other simply flows together and falls, but in truth they are the product of *enthusiasm,* the children of an ecstasy, finished with the artist's utmost skill.

The North River is not frozen over. I see tree sparrows twittering and moving with a low creeping and jerking motion amid the chenopodium in a field, upon the snow, so chubby or puffed out on account of the cold that at first I took them for the arctic birds, but soon I see their bright-chestnut crowns and clear white bars; as the poet says, "a thousand feeding like one,"— though there are not more than a dozen here.

Jan. 7. The storm is over, and it is one of those beautiful winter mornings when a vapor is seen hanging in the air between the village and the woods. Though the snow is only some six inches deep, the yards appear full of those beautiful crystals (star or wheel shaped flakes), lying light, as a measure is full of grain.

9 A.M.—To Hill.

It snowed so late last night, and so much has fallen from the trees, that I notice only one squirrel, and a fox, and perhaps partridge track, into which the snow has blown. The fox has been beating the bush along walls and fences. The surface of the snow in the woods is thickly marked by the snow which has fallen from the trees onto it. The mice have not been forth since the snow, or perhaps in some places where they have, their tracks are obliterated.

By 10:30 A.M. it begins to blow hard, the snow comes down from the trees in fine showers, finer far than ever falls direct from the sky, completely obscuring the view through the aisles of the wood, and in open fields it is rapidly drifting. It is too light to make good sleighing.

By 10 o'clock I notice a very long level stratum of cloud not very high in the southeastern sky—all the rest being clear—which I suspect to be the vapor from the sea. This lasts for several hours.

These are true mornings of creation, original and poetic days, not mere repetitions of the past. There is no lingering of yesterday's fogs, only such a mist as might have adorned the first morning.

P.M.—I see some tree sparrows feeding on the fine grass seed above the snow, near the road on the hillside below the Dutch house. They are flitting along one at a time, their feet commonly sunk in the snow, uttering occasionally a low sweet warble and seemingly as happy there, and with this wintry prospect before them for the night and several months to come, as any man by his fireside. One occasionally hops or flies toward another, and the latter suddenly jerks away from him. They are reaching or hopping up to the fine grass, or oftener picking the seeds from the snow. At length the whole ten have collected within a space a dozen feet square, but soon after, being alarmed, they utter a different and less musical chirp and flit away into an apple tree.

Jan. 8. P.M.—To that small meadow just above the Boaz Brown meadow.

Going through the swamp, the snow balled so as to raise me three inches higher than usual.

Jan. 9. Snows again.

P.M.—To Deep Cut.

The wind is southwest, and the snow is very moist, with large flakes. Looking toward Trillium Wood, the nearer flakes appear to move quite swiftly, often making the impression of a continuous white line. They are also seen to move directly and nearly horizontally, but the more distant flakes appear to loiter in the air, as if uncertain how they will approach the earth, or even to cross the course of the former, and are always seen as simple and distinct flakes. I think that this difference is simply owing to the fact that the former pass quickly over the field of view, while the latter are much longer in it.

This moist snow has affected the yellow sulphur parmelias and others. They have all got a green hue, and the fruit of the smallest lichen looks fresh and fair. And the wet willow bark is a brighter yellow.

Some chickadees come flitting close to me, and one utters its spring note, *phe-be,* for which I feel under obligations to him.

Jan. 10. Sunday. P.M.—To Goose Pond across Walden.

The north side of Walden is a warm walk in sunny weather. If you are sick and despairing, go forth in winter and see the red alder catkins dangling at the extremities of the twigs, all in the wintry air, like long, hard mulberries, promising a new spring and the fulfillment of all our hopes. We prize any tenderness, any softening, in the winter—catkins, birds' nests, insect life, etc., etc. The most I get, perchance, is the sight of a mulberry-like red catkin which I know has a dormant life in it, seemingly greater than my own.

Jan. 11. Monday. Rain, rain—washes off almost every vestige of snow.

Jan. 13. Wednesday. Go to Lynn to lecture, *via* Cambridge.

4:30 P.M.—At Jonathan Buffum's, Lynn. Lecture in John B. Alley's parlor. Mr. J. Buffum describes to me ancient wolf-traps, made probably by the early settlers in Lynn, perhaps after an Indian model; one some two miles from the shore near Saugus, another more northerly; holes say seven feet deep, about as long, and some three feet wide, stoned up very smoothly, and perhaps converging a little, so that the wolf could not get out. Tradition says that a wolf and a squaw were one morning found in the same hole, staring at each other.

Jan. 14. Mr. Buffum says that in 1817 or 1819 he saw the sea-serpent at Swampscott, and so did several hundred others. He was to be seen off and on for some time. There were many people on the beach the first time, in carriages partly in the water, and the serpent came so near that they, thinking that he might come ashore, involuntarily turned their horses to the shore as with a general consent, and this movement caused him to shear off also. The road from Boston was lined with people directly, coming to see the monster. Prince came with his spyglass, saw, and printed his account of him. Buffum says he has seen him twenty times, once alone, from the rocks at Little Nahant, when he passed along close to the shore just beneath the surface, and within fifty or sixty feet of him, so that he could have touched him with a very long pole, if he had dared to. Buffum is about sixty, and it should be said, as affecting the value of his evidence, that he is a firm believer in Spiritualism.

This forenoon I rode to Nahant with Mr. Buffum. All the country bare. A fine warm day; neither snow nor ice, unless you search narrowly for them. On the way we pass Mr. Alonzo Lewis's cottage. On the top of each of his stone posts is fastened a very perfectly egg-shaped pebble of sienite from Kettle Cove, fifteen to eighteen inches long and of proportionate diameter. I never saw any of that size so perfect. There are some fifteen of them about his house, and on one flatter, circular one he has made a dial, by which I learned the hour (9:30 A.M.). Says he was surveying once at Kettle Cove, where they form a beach a third of a mile long and two to ten feet deep, and he brought home as many as his horse could draw. His house is clapboarded with hemlock bark; now some twenty years old. He says that he built it himself.

Called at the shop where lately Samuel Jillson, now of Feltonville, set up birds—for he is a taxidermist and very skillful; kills his own birds and with blowguns, which he makes and sells, some seven feet long, of glass, using a clay ball. Is said to be a dead shot at six rods!

Warm and fall-like as it is, saw many snow buntings at the entrance to the beach. Saw many black ducks (so Lewis said; may they not have been velvet ducks, i. e. coot?) on the sea. Heard of a flock of geese (!) (may they not have been brant, or some other species?), etc.; ice [?] divers. On the south side of Little Nahant a large mass of *fine* pudding-stone. Nahant is said to have been

well-wooded, and furnished timber for the wharves of
Boston, i.e. to build them. Now a few willows and
balm-of-Gileads are the only trees, if you except two or
three small cedars. They say others will not grow on account of wind. The rocks are porphyry, with dykes of
dark greenstone in it, and, at the extremity of Nahant,
argillaceous slate, very distinctly stratified, with fossil
corallines in *it* (?), looking like shells. Egg Rock, it
seems, has a fertile garden on the top.

P.M.—Rode with J. Buffum, Parker Pillsbury, and
Mr. Mudge, a lawyer and geologist of Lynn, into the
northwest part of Lynn, to the Danvers line. After a
mile or two, we passed beyond the line of the porphyry
into the sienite. The sienite is more rounded. Saw some
furrows in sienite. On a ledge of sienite in the woods,
the rocky woods near Danvers line, saw many boulders
of sienite, part of the same flock of which Ship Rock (so
called) in Danvers is one. One fifteen feet long, ten
wide, and five or six deep rested on four somewhat
rounded (at least water-worn) stones, eighteen inches
in diameter or more, so that you could crawl under it,
on the top of a cliff, and projected about eight feet over
it—just as it was dropped by an iceberg. A fine broad-
backed ledge of sienite just beyond, north or northwest,
from which we saw Wachusett, Watatic, Monadnock,
and the Peterboro Hills.

Also saw where one Boyse (if that is the spelling), a
miller in old times, got out millstones in a primitive way,
so said an old man who was chopping there. He pried
or cracked off a piece of the crust of the ledge, lying
horizontal, some sixteen or eighteen inches thick, then
made a fire on it about its edges, and, pouring on water,
cracked or softened it, so that he could break off the

edges and make it round with his sledge. Then he picked a hole through the middle and hammered it as smooth as he could, and it was done. But this old man said that he had heard old folks say that the stones were so rough in old times that they made a noise like thunder as they revolved, and much grit was mixed with the meal.

Returning down a gully, I thought I would look for a new plant and found at once what I suppose to be *Genista tinctoria*, dyers'-green-weed—the stem is quite green, with a few pods and leaves left. It is said to have become naturalized on the hills of Essex County. Close by was a mass of sienite some seven or eight feet high, with a cedar some two inches thick springing from a mere crack in its top.

Visited Jordan's or the Lynn Quarry (of sienite) on our return, more southerly. The stone cracks very squarely and into very large masses. In one place was a dyke of dark greenstone, of which, joined to the sienite, I brought off two specimens, *q. v.* The more yellowish and rotten surface stone, lying above the hard and grayer, is called the sap by the quarrymen.

From these rocks and wooded hills three or four miles inland in the northwest edge of Lynn, we had an extensive view of the ocean from Cape Ann to Scituate, and realized how the aborigines, when hunting, berrying, might perchance have looked out thus on the early navigators sailing along the coast—thousands of them —when they little suspected it—how patent to the inhabitants their visit must have been. A vessel could hardly have passed within half a dozen miles of the shore, even—at one place only, in pleasant weather— without being seen by hundreds of savages.

Mudge gave me Saugus jasper, graywacke, amygdaloid (greenstone with nodules of feldspar), asbestos, hornstone (?); Buffum some porphyry, epidote, argillaceous slate from end of Nahant.

Mr. Buffum tells me that they never eat the sea-clams without first taking out "the worm," as it is called, about as large as the small end of a pipe-stem. He supposes it is the penis.

Jan. 15. At Natural History Rooms, Boston.

Looked at the little grebe. Its feet are not webbed with lobes on the side like the coot, and it is quite white beneath. Saw the good-sized duck—velvet duck, with white spot on wing—which is commonly called "coot" on salt water. They have a living young bald eagle in the cellar. Talked with Dr. Kneeland. They have a golden eagle from Lexington, which K. obtained two or three years since, the first Dr. Cabot has heard of in Massachusetts. Speaking to him of my night-warbler, he asked if it uttered such a note, making the note of the myrtle-bird, *ah, te-te-te te-ta-te te-te-te,* exactly, and said that that was the note of the white-throated sparrow, which he heard at Lake Superior, at night as well as by day. *Vide* his report, July 15, 1857.

Same afternoon, saw Dr. Durkee in Howard Street. He has not seen the common glowworm, and called his a variety of *Lampyris noctiluca.* Showed to Agassiz, Gould, and Jackson, and it was new to them. They thought it a variety of the above. His were luminous throughout, mine only in part of each segment.

Saw some beautiful painted leaves in a shop window, —maple and oak.

Jan. 17. Sunday. P.M.—To Conantum.

The common birch fungus, which is horizontal and

turned downwards, splits the bark as it pushes out very simply, thus: ⬍ I see a large downy owl's feather adhering to a sweet-fern twig, looking like the down of a plant blowing in the wind. This is near where I have found them before, on Conantum, above first Cliff. They would be very ornamental to a bonnet, so soft and fine with their reflections that the eye hardly rests on the down.

Jan. 18. At the Dugan Desert, I notice, under the overhanging or nearly horizontal small white oaks and shrub oaks about the edge, singular little hollows in the sand, evidently made by drops of rain or melting snow falling from the same part of the twig, a foot or two, on the same spot a long time. They are very numerous under every such low horizontal bough, on an average about three quarters of an inch apart or more. They are a third of an inch wide and a quarter to even three quarters of an inch deep; made some days ago evidently.

The *F. hyemalis* about. I hear that the Emerson children found ladies'-delights out yesterday.

Jan. 19. F. *hyemalis.*

Jan. 23. Saturday. The wonderfully mild and pleasant weather continues. The ground has been bare since the 11th. This morning was colder than before. I have not been able to walk up the North Branch this winter, nor along the channel of the South Branch at any time.

P.M.—To Saw Mill Brook.

A fine afternoon. There has been but little use for gloves this winter, though I have been surveying a great deal for three months. The sun, and cockcrowing, bare ground, etc., etc., remind me of March.

Standing on the bridge over the Mill Brook on the Turnpike, there being but little ice on the south side, I see several small waterbugs (*Gyrinus*) swimming about, as in the spring.

I see the terminal shield fern very fresh, as an evergreen, at Saw Mill Brook, and (I think it is) the marginal fern and *Lycopodium lucidulum*.

I go up the brook, walking on it most of the way, surprised to find that it will bear me. How it falls from rock to rock, as down a flight of stairs, all through that rocky wood, from the swamp which is its source to the Everett farm! The bays or more stagnant parts are thickest frozen, the channel oftenest open, and here and there the water has overflowed the ice and covered it with a thickening mass of glistening spiculae. The white markings on the under side are very rich and varied— the currency of the brook, the impression of its fleeting bubbles even. It comes out of a meadow of about an acre.

I go near enough to Flints' Pond, about 4 P.M., to hear it thundering. In summer I should not have suspected its presence an eighth of a mile off through the woods, but in such a winter day as this it speaks and betrays itself.

Returning through Britton's field, I notice the stumps of chestnuts cut a dozen years ago. This tree grows rapidly, and one layer seems not to adhere very firmly to another. I can easily count the concentric circles of growth on these old stumps as I stand over them, for they are worn into conspicuous furrows along the lines of the pores of the wood. One or more rings often gape an eighth of an inch or more, at about their twenty-fourth or twenty-fifth year, when the growth, in three or four cases that I examined, was most rapid.

Looking toward the woods in the horizon, it is seen to be very hazy.

At Ditch Pond I hear what I suppose to be a fox barking, an exceedingly husky, hoarse, and ragged note, prolonged perhaps by the echo, like a feeble puppy, or even a child endeavoring to scream, but choked with fear, yet it is on a high key. It sounds so through the wood, while I am in the hollow, that I cannot tell from which side it comes. I hear it bark forty or fifty times at least. It is a peculiar sound, quite unlike any other woodland sound that I know.

Walden, I think, begins to crack and boom first on the south side, which is first in the shade, for I hear it cracking there, though it is still in the sun around me. It is not so sonorous and like the dumping of frogs as I have heard it, but more like the cracking of crockery. It suggests the very brittlest material, as if the globe you stood on were a hollow sphere of glass and might fall to pieces on the slightest touch. Most shivering, splintery, screeching cracks these are, as if the ice were no thicker than a tumbler, though it is probably nine or ten inches. Methinks my weight sinks it and helps to crack sometimes.

Who can doubt that men are by a certain fate what they are, contending with unseen and unimagined difficulties, or encouraged and aided by equally mysterious auspicious circumstances? Who can doubt this essential and innate difference between man and man, when he considers a whole race, like the Indian, inevitably and resignedly passing away in spite of our efforts to Christianize and educate them? Individuals accept their fate and live according to it, as the Indian does. Everybody notices that the Indian retains his habits wonderfully —is still the same man that the discoverers found. The fact is, the history of the white man is a history of improvement, that of the red man a history of fixed habits of stagnation.

To insure health, a man's relation to Nature must come very near to a personal one; he must be conscious of a friendliness in her; when human friends fail or die, she must stand in the gap to him. I cannot conceive of any life which deserves the name, unless there is a certain tender relation to Nature. This it is which makes winter warm, and supplies society in the desert and wilderness. Unless Nature sympathizes with and speaks to us, as it were, the most fertile and blooming regions are barren and dreary.

Mrs. William Monroe told Sophia last evening that she remembered her (Sophia's) grandfather very well, that he was taller than Father, and used to ride out to their house—she was a Stone and lived where she and her husband did afterward, now Darius Merriam's— when they made cheeses, to drink the whey, being in consumption. She said that she remembered Grandmother too, Jennie Burns, how she came to the schoolroom (in Middle Street (?), Boston) once, leading her little daughter Elizabeth, the latter so small that she could not tell her name distinctly, but spoke thick and lispingly—"Elizabeth Orrock Thoreau."

The dog is to the fox as the white man to the red. The former has attained to more clearness in his bark; it is more ringing and musical, more developed; he explodes the vowels of his alphabet better; and beside he has made his place so good in the world that he can run without skulking in the open field. What a smothered, ragged, feeble, and unmusical sound is the bark of the fox! It seems as if he scarcely dared raise his voice lest it should catch the ear of his tame cousin and inveterate foe.

I observe that the ice of Walden is heaved up more than a foot over that bar between the pond and Cyrus Hubbard's basin. The gravelly bank or bar itself is also heaved up considerably where exposed. So that I am inclined to think that such a tilting is simply the result of a thawing beneath and not merely of a crowding or pressure on the two sides.

I do not see that I can live tolerably without affection for Nature. If I feel no softening toward the rocks, what do they signify?

I do not think much of that chemistry that can extract corn and potatoes out of a barren [soil], but rather of that chemistry that can extract thoughts and sentiments out of the life of a man on any soil. It is in vain to write on the seasons unless you have the seasons in you.

Walking

Thoreau was almost too ill to care by the time practical recognition began to come his way. The Atlantic Monthly applied for articles and he drew from his Journal and lectures as well as he could to supply them. By the time the articles were in proof he himself was unable to write and had to dictate his correspondence about them to his sister Sophia. And when "Walking," the first one of the group, was published in the Atlantic's pages, he had been dead for a month. There is no sign in the essay itself, though, that its author had been moribund; its tone is vigorous and vital.

C. B.

I WISH to speak a word for Nature, for absolute freedom and wildness, as contrasted with a freedom and culture merely civil—to regard man as an inhabitant, or a part and parcel of Nature, rather than a member of society. I wish to make an extreme statement, if so I may make an emphatic one, for there are enough champions of civilization: the minister and the school committee and every one of you will take care of that.

I have met with but one or two persons in the course of my life who understood the art of Walking, that is, of taking walks—who had a genius, so to speak, for *sauntering*, which word is beautifully derived "from idle people who roved about the country, in the Middle Ages, and asked charity, under pretense of going *à la Sainte Terre*," to the Holy Land, till the children exclaimed, "There goes a *Sainte-Terrer*," a Saunterer, a Holy-Lander. They who never go to the Holy Land in their walks, as they pretend, are indeed mere idlers and vagabonds; but they who do go there are saunterers in the good sense, such as I mean. Some, however, would derive the word from *sans terre,* without land or a home, which, therefore, in the good sense, will mean, having no particular home, but equally at home everywhere. For this is the secret of successful sauntering. He who sits still in a house all the time may be the greatest vagrant of all; but the saunterer, in the good sense, is no more vagrant than the meandering river, which is all the while sedulously seeking the shortest course to the sea. But I prefer the first, which, indeed, is the most probable derivation. For every walk is a sort of crusade, preached by some Peter the Hermit in us, to go forth and reconquer this Holy Land from the hands of the Infidels.

It is true, we are but faint-hearted crusaders, even the walkers, nowadays, who undertake no persevering, never-ending enterprises. Our expeditions are but tours, and come round again at evening to the old hearthside from which we set out. Half the walk is but retracing our steps. We should go forth on the shortest walk, perchance, in the spirit of undying adventure, never to return, prepared to send back our embalmed hearts only as relics to our desolate kingdoms. If you are ready to leave father and mother, and brother and sister, and wife and child and friends, and never see them again— if you have paid your debts, and made your will, and settled all your affairs, and are a free man—then you are ready for a walk.

To come down to my own experience, my companion and I, for I sometimes have a companion, take pleasure in fancying ourselves knights of a new, or rather an old, order—not Equestrians or Chevaliers, not Ritters or Riders, but Walkers, a still more ancient and honorable class, I trust. The chivalric and heroic spirit which once belonged to the Rider seems now to reside in, or perchance to have subsided into, the Walker—not the Knight, but Walker, Errant. He is a sort of fourth estate, outside of Church and State and People.

We have felt that we almost alone hereabouts practiced this noble art; though, to tell the truth, at least if their own assertions are to be received, most of my townsmen would fain walk sometimes, as I do, but they cannot. No wealth can buy the requisite leisure, freedom, and independence which are the capital in this profession. It comes only by the grace of God. It requires a direct dispensation from Heaven to become a walker. You must be born into the family of the Walkers. *Ambulator nascitur, non fit.* Some of my townsmen, it is true, can remember and have described to me some walks which they took ten years ago, in which they were so blessed as to lose themselves for half an hour in the woods; but I know very well that they have confined themselves to the highway ever since, whatever pretensions they may make to belong to this select class. No doubt they were elevated for a moment as by the reminiscence of a previous state of existence, when even they were foresters and outlaws.

> "When he came to grene wode,
>   In a mery mornynge,
> There he herde the notes small
>   Of byrdes mery syngynge.
>
> "It is ferre gone, sayd Robyn,
>   That I was last here;
> Me lyste a lytell for to shote
>   At the donne dere."

I think that I cannot preserve my health and spirits, unless I spend four hours a day at least—and it is commonly more than that—sauntering through the woods and over the hills and fields, absolutely free from all worldly engagements. You may safely say, A penny for your thoughts, or a thousand pounds. When sometimes I am reminded that the mechanics and shopkeepers stay in their shops not only all the forenoon, but all the afternoon too, sitting with crossed legs, so many of them —as if the legs were made to sit upon, and not to stand or walk upon—I think that they deserve some credit for not having all committed suicide long ago.

I, who cannot stay in my chamber for a single day without acquiring some rust, and when sometimes I have stolen forth for a walk at the eleventh hour, or four o'clock in the afternoon, too late to redeem the day, when the shades of night were already beginning to be mingled with the daylight, have felt as if I had committed some sin to be atoned for—I confess that I am astonished at the power of endurance, to say nothing of the moral insensibility, of my neighbors who confine themselves to shops and offices the whole day for weeks and months, aye, and years almost together. I know not what manner of stuff they are of, sitting there now at three o'clock in the afternoon, as if it were three o'clock in the morning. Bonaparte may talk of the three-o'clock-in-the-morning courage, but it is nothing to the courage which can sit down cheerfully at this hour in the afternoon over against one's self whom you have known all the morning, to starve out a garrison to whom you are bound by such strong ties of sympathy. I wonder that about this time, or say between four and five o'clock in the afternoon, too late for the morning papers and too early for the evening ones, there is not a general explosion heard up and down the street, scattering a legion of antiquated and house-bred notions and whims to the four winds for an airing—and so the evil cure itself.

How womankind, who are confined to the house still more than men, stand it I do not know; but I have ground to suspect that most of them do not *stand* it at all. When, early in a summer afternoon, we have been shaking the dust of the village from the skirts of our garments, making haste past those houses with purely Doric or Gothic fronts, which have such an air of repose about them, my companion whispers that probably about these times their occupants are all gone to bed. Then it is that I appreciate the beauty and the glory of architecture, which itself never turns in, but forever stands out and erect, keeping watch over the slumberers.

No doubt temperament, and, above all, age, have a good deal to do with it. As a man grows older, his ability to sit still and follow indoor occupations increases. He grows vespertinal in his habits as the evening of life approaches, till at last he comes forth only just before sundown, and gets all the walk that he requires in half an hour.

But the walking of which I speak has nothing in it akin to taking exercise, as it is called, as the sick take medicine at stated hours—as the swinging of dumbbells or chairs; but is itself the enterprise and adventure of the day. If you would get exercise, go in search of the springs of life. Think of a man's swinging dumbbells for his health, when those springs are bubbling up in far-off pastures unsought by him!

Moreover, you must walk like a camel, which is said to be the only beast which ruminates when walking. When a traveler asked Wordsworth's servant to show him her master's study, she answered, "Here is his library, but his study is out of doors."

Living much out of doors, in the sun and wind, will no doubt produce a certain roughness of character—

will cause a thicker cuticle to grow over some of the finer qualities of our nature, as on the face and hands, or as severe manual labor robs the hands of some of their delicacy of touch. So staying in the house, on the other hand, may produce a softness and smoothness, not to say thinness of skin, accompanied by an increased sensibility to certain impressions. Perhaps we should be more susceptible to some influences important to our intellectual and moral growth, if the sun had shone and the wind blown on us a little less; and no doubt it is a nice matter to proportion rightly the thick and thin skin. But methinks that is a scurf that will fall off fast enough—that the natural remedy is to be found in the proportion which the night bears to the day, the winter to the summer, thought to experience. There will be so much the more air and sunshine in our thoughts. The callous palms of the laborer are conversant with finer tissues of self-respect and heroism, whose touch thrills the heart, than the languid fingers of idleness. That is mere sentimentality that lies abed by day and thinks itself white, far from the tan and callus of experience.

When we walk, we naturally go to the fields and woods: what would become of us, if we walked only in a garden or a mall? Even some sects of philosophers have felt the necessity of importing the woods to themselves, since they did not go to the woods. "They planted groves and walks of Platanes," where they took *subdiales ambulationes* in porticos open to the air. Of course it is of no use to direct our steps to the woods, if they do not carry us thither. I am alarmed when it happens that I have walked a mile into the woods bodily, without getting there in spirit. In my afternoon walk I would fain forget all my morning occupations and my obligations to society. But it sometimes happens that I cannot easily shake off the village. The thought of some work will run in my head and I am not where my body is—I am out of my senses. In my walks I would fain return to my senses. What business have I in the woods, if I am thinking of something out of the woods? I suspect myself, and cannot help a shudder, when I find myself so implicated even in what are called good works—for this may sometimes happen.

My vicinity affords many good walks; and though for so many years I have walked almost every day, and sometimes for several days together, I have not yet exhausted them. An absolutely new prospect is a great happiness, and I can still get this any afternoon. Two or three hours' walking will carry me to as strange a country as I expect ever to see. A single farmhouse which I had not seen before is sometimes as good as the dominions of the King of Dahomey. There is in fact a sort of harmony discoverable between the capabilities of the landscape within a circle of ten miles' radius, or the limits of an afternoon walk, and the threescore years and ten of human life. It will never become quite familiar to you.

Nowadays almost all man's improvements, so called, as the building of houses and the cutting down of the forest and of all large trees, simply deform the landscape, and make it more and more tame and cheap. A people who would begin by burning the fences and let the forest stand! I saw the fences half consumed, their ends lost in the middle of the prairie, and some worldly miser with a surveyor looking after his bounds, while heaven had taken place around him, and he did not see the angels going to and fro, but was looking for an old post-hole in the midst of paradise. I looked again, and saw him standing in the middle of a boggy Stygian fen, surrounded by devils, and he had found his bounds without a doubt, three little stones, where a stake had been driven, and looking nearer, I saw that the Prince of Darkness was his surveyor.

I can easily walk ten, fifteen, twenty, any number of miles, commencing at my own door, without going by any house, without crossing a road except where the fox and the mink do: first along by the river, and then the brook, and then the meadow and the woodside. There are square miles in my vicinity which have no inhabitant. From many a hill I can see civilization and the abodes of man afar. The farmers and their works are scarcely more obvious than woodchucks and their burrows. Man and his affairs, church and state and school, trade and commerce, and manufactures and agriculture, even politics, the most alarming of them all—I am pleased to see how little space they occupy in the landscape. Politics is but a narrow field, and that still narrower highway yonder leads to it. I sometimes direct the traveler thither. If you would go to the political world, follow the great road, follow that market-man, keep his dust in your eyes, and it will lead you straight to it; for it, too, has its place merely, and does not occupy all space. I pass from it as from a bean field into the forest, and it is forgotten. In one half-hour I can walk off to some portion of the earth's surface where a man does not stand from one year's end to another, and there, consequently, politics are not, for they are but as the cigar-smoke of a man.

The village is the place to which the roads tend, a sort of expansion of the highway, as a lake of a river. It is the body of which roads are the arms and legs— a trivial or quadrivial place, the thoroughfare and ordinary of travelers. The word is from the Latin *villa*, which together with *via*, a way, or more anciently *ved* and *vella*, Varro derives from veho, to carry, because the villa is the place to and from which things are car-

ried. They who got their living by teaming were said
vellaturam facere. Hence, too, the Latin word *vilis* and
our vile, also *villain.* This suggests what kind of degeneracy villagers are liable to. They are wayworn by the
travel that goes by and over them, without traveling
themselves.

Some do not walk at all; others walk in the highways;
a few walk across lots. Roads are made for horses and
men of business. I do not travel in them much, comparatively, because I am not in a hurry to get to any
tavern or grocery or livery-stable or depot to which they
lead. I am a good horse to travel, but not from choice
a roadster. The landscape-painter uses the figures of
men to mark a road. He would not make that use of my
figure. I walk out into a nature such as the old prophets
and poets, Menu, Moses, Homer, Chaucer, walked in.
You may name it America, but it is not America; neither Americus Vespucius, nor Columbus, nor the rest
were the discoverers of it. There is a truer account of it
in mythology than in any history of America, so called,
that I have seen.

However, there are a few old roads that may be trodden with profit, as if they led somewhere now that they
are nearly discontinued. There is the Old Marlborough
Road, which does not go to Marlborough now, methinks, unless that is Marlborough where it carries me.
I am the bolder to speak of it here, because I presume
that there are one or two such roads in every town.

THE OLD MARLBOROUGH ROAD

Where they once dug for money,
But never found any;
Where sometimes Martial Miles
Singly files,
And Elijah Wood,
I fear for no good:

No other man,
Save Elisha Dugan—
O man of wild habits,
Partridges and rabbits,
Who hast no cares
Only to set snares,
Who liv'st all alone,
Close to the bone,
And where life is sweetest
Constantly eatest.
When the spring stirs my blood
With the instinct to travel,
I can get enough gravel
On the Old Marlborough Road.
Nobody repairs it,
For nobody wears it;
It is a living way,
As the Christians say.
Not many there be
Who enter therein,
Only the guests of the
Irishman Quin.
What is it, what is it,
But a direction out there,
And the bare possibility
Of going somewhere?
Great guide-boards of stone,
But travelers none;
Cenotaphs of the towns
Named on their crowns.
It is worth going to see
Where you *might* be.
What king
Did the thing,
I am still wondering;
Set up how or when,
By what selectmen,
Gourgas or Lee,
Clark or Darby?
They're a great endeavor
To be something forever;
Blank tablets of stone,
Where a traveler might groan,

> And in one sentence
> Grave all that is known;
> Which another might read,
> In his extreme need.
> I know one or two
> Lines that would do,
> Literature that might stand
> All over the land,
> Which a man could remember
> Till next December,
> And read again in the spring,
> After the thawing.
> If with fancy unfurled
> You leave your abode,
> You may go round the world
> By the Old Marlborough Road.

At present, in this vicinity, the best part of the land is not private property; the landscape is not owned, and the walker enjoys comparative freedom. But possibly the day will come when it will be partitioned off into so-called pleasure-grounds, in which a few will take a narrow and exclusive pleasure only—when fences shall be multiplied, and man-traps and other engines invented to confine men to the *public* road, and walking over the surface of God's earth shall be construed to mean trespassing on some gentleman's grounds. To enjoy a thing exclusively is commonly to exclude yourself from the true enjoyment of it. Let us improve our opportunities, then, before the evil days come.

What is it that makes it so hard sometimes to determine whither we will walk? I believe that there is a subtle magnetism in Nature, which, if we unconsciously yield to it, will direct us aright. It is not indifferent to us which way we walk. There is a right way; but we are very liable from heedlessness and stupidity to take the wrong one. We would fain take that walk, never yet taken by us through this actual world, which is perfectly symbolical of the path which we love to travel in the interior and ideal world; and sometimes, no doubt, we find it difficult to choose our direction, because it does not yet exist distinctly in our idea.

When I go out of the house for a walk, uncertain as yet whither I will bend my steps, and submit myself to my instinct to decide for me, I find, strange and whimsical as it may seem, that I finally and inevitably settle southwest, toward some particular wood or meadow or deserted pasture or hill in that direction. My needle is slow to settle, varies a few degrees, and does not always point due southwest, it is true, and it has good authority for this variation, but it always settles between west and south-southwest. The future lies that way to me, and the earth seems more unexhausted and richer on that side. The outline which would bound my walks would be, not a circle, but a parabola, or rather like one of those cometary orbits which have been thought to be non-returning curves, in this case opening westward, in which my house occupies the place of the sun. I turn round and round irresolute sometimes for a quarter of an hour, until I decide, for a thousandth time, that I will walk into the southwest or west. Eastward I go only by force; but westward I go free. Thither no business leads me. It is hard for me to believe that I shall find fair landscapes or sufficient wildness and freedom behind the eastern horizon. I am not excited by the prospect of a walk thither; but I believe that the forest which I see in the western horizon stretches uninterruptedly toward the setting sun, and there are no towns nor cities in it of enough consequence to disturb me. Let me live where I will, on this side is the city, on that the wilderness, and ever I am leaving the city more and more, and withdrawing into the wilderness. I should not lay so much stress on this fact, if I did not believe that something like this is the prevailing tendency of my countrymen. I must walk toward Oregon, and not toward Europe. And that way the nation is moving, and I may say that mankind progress from east to west. Within a few years we have witnessed the phenomenon of a southeastward migration, in the settlement of Australia; but this affects us as a retrograde movement, and, judging from the moral and physical character of the first generation of Australians, has not yet proved a successful experiment. The eastern Tartars think that there is nothing west beyond Thibet. "The world ends there," say they; "beyond there is nothing but a shoreless sea." It is unmitigated East where they live.

We go eastward to realize history and study the works of art and literature, retracing the steps of the race; we go westward as into the future, with a spirit of enterprise and adventure. The Atlantic is a Lethean stream, in our passage over which we have had an opportunity to forget the Old World and its institutions. If we do not succeed this time, there is perhaps one more chance for the race left before it arrives on the banks of the Styx; and that is in the Lethe of the Pacific, which is three times as wide.

I know not how significant it is, or how far it is an evidence of singularity, that an individual should thus consent in his pettiest walk with the general movement of the race; but I know that something akin to the migratory instinct in birds and quadrupeds—which, in some instances, is known to have affected the squirrel tribe, impelling them to a general and mysterious movement, in which they were seen, say some, crossing the broadest rivers, each on its particular chip, with its tail raised for a sail, and bridging narrower streams with their dead—that something like the *furor* which affects

the domestic cattle in the spring, and which is referred
to a worm in their tails, affects both nations and individuals, either perennially or from time to time. Not a
flock of wild geese cackles over our town, but it to some
extent unsettles the value of real estate here, and, if I
were a broker, I should probably take that disturbance
into account.

> "Than longen folk to gon on pilgrimages,
> And palmeres for to seken strange strondes."

Every sunset which I witness inspires me with the
desire to go to a West as distant and as fair as that into
which the sun goes down. He appears to migrate westward daily, and tempt us to follow him. He is the Great
Western Pioneer whom the nations follow. We dream
all night of those mountain-ridges in the horizon, though
they may be of vapor only, which were last gilded by
his rays. The island of Atlantis, and the islands and gardens of the Hesperides, a sort of terrestrial paradise,
appear to have been the Great West of the ancients,
enveloped in mystery and poetry. Who has not seen in
imagination, when looking into the sunset sky, the gardens of the Hesperides, and the foundation of all those
fables?

Columbus felt the westward tendency more strongly
than any before. He obeyed it, and found a New World
for Castile and Leon. The herd of men in those days
scented fresh pastures from afar.

> "And now the sun had stretched out all the hills,
> And now was dropped into the western bay;
> At last *he* rose, and twitched his mantle blue;
> Tomorrow to fresh woods and pastures new."

Where on the globe can there be found an area of
equal extent with that occupied by the bulk of our
States, so fertile and so rich and varied in its produc-

tions, and at the same time so habitable by the European, as this is? Michaux, who knew but part of them, says that "the species of large trees are much more numerous in North America than in Europe; in the United States there are more than one hundred and forty species that exceed thirty feet in height; in France there are but thirty that attain this size." Later botanists more than confirm his observations. Humboldt came to America to realize his youthful dreams of a tropical vegetation, and he beheld it in its greatest perfection in the primitive forests of the Amazon, the most gigantic wilderness on the earth, which he has so eloquently described. The geographer Guyot, himself a European, goes farther—farther than I am ready to follow him; yet not when he says: "As the plant is made for the animal, as the vegetable world is made for the animal world, America is made for the man of the Old World. . . . The man of the Old World sets out upon his way. Leaving the highlands of Asia, he descends from station to station towards Europe. Each of his steps is marked by a new civilization superior to the preceding, by a greater power of development. Arrived at the Atlantic, he pauses on the shore of this unknown ocean, the bounds of which he knows not, and turns upon his footprints for an instant." When he has exhausted the rich soil of Europe, and reinvigorated himself, "then recommences his adventurous career westward as in the earliest ages." So far Guyot.

From this western impulse coming in contact with the barrier of the Atlantic sprang the commerce and enterprise of modern times. The younger Michaux, in his *Travels West of the Alleghanies in 1802*, says that the common inquiry in the newly settled West was, "'From what part of the world have you come?' As if these vast and fertile regions would naturally be the place of meeting and common country of all the inhabitants of the globe."

To use an obsolete Latin word, I might say, *Ex Oriente lux; ex Occidente* FRUX. From the East light; from the West fruit.

Sir Francis Head, an English traveler and a Governor-General of Canada, tells us that "in both the northern and southern hemispheres of the New World, Nature has not only outlined her works on a larger scale, but has painted the whole picture with brighter and more costly colors than she used in delineating and in beautifying the Old World. . . . The heavens of America appear infinitely higher, the sky is bluer, the air is fresher, the cold is intenser, the moon looks larger, the stars are brighter, the thunder is louder, the lightning is vivider, the wind is stronger, the rain is heavier, the mountains are higher, the rivers longer, the forests bigger, the plains broader." This statement will do at least to set against Buffon's account of this part of the world and its productions.

Linnaeus said long ago, *"Nescio quae facies* laeta, glabra *plantis Americanis"* (I know not what there is of joyous and smooth in the aspect of American plants); and I think that in this country there are no, or at most very few, *Africanae bestiae,* African beasts, as the Romans called them, and that in this respect also it is peculiarly fitted for the habitation of man. We are told that within three miles of the center of the East-Indian city of Singapore, some of the inhabitants are annually carried off by tigers; but the traveler can lie down in the woods at night almost anywhere in North America without fear of wild beasts.

These are encouraging testimonies. If the moon looks larger here than in Europe, probably the sun looks larger also. If the heavens of America appear infinitely higher, and the stars brighter, I trust that these facts are symbolical of the height to which the philosophy and poetry and religion of her inhabitants may one day soar. At length, perchance, the immaterial heaven will appear as much higher to the American mind, and the intimations that star it as much brighter. For I believe that climate does thus react on man—as there is something in the mountain air that feeds the spirit and inspires. Will not man grow to greater perfection intellectually as well as physically under these influences? Or is it unimportant how many foggy days there are in his life? I trust that we shall be more imaginative, that our thoughts will be clearer, fresher, and more ethereal, as our sky—our understanding more comprehensive and broader, like our plains—our intellect generally on a grander scale, like our thunder and lightning, our rivers and mountains and forests—and our hearts shall even correspond in breadth and depth and grandeur to our inland seas. Perchance there will appear to the traveler something, he knows not what, of *laeta* and *glabra*, of joyous and serene, in our very faces. Else to what end does the world go on, and why was America discovered?

To Americans I hardly need to say,

"Westward the star of empire takes its way."

As a true patriot, I should be ashamed to think that Adam in paradise was more favorably situated on the whole than the backwoodsman in this country.

Our sympathies in Massachusetts are not confined to New England; though we may be estranged from the South, we sympathize with the West. There is the home of the younger sons, as among the Scandinavians they took to the sea for their inheritance. It is too late to be studying Hebrew; it is more important to understand even the slang of today.

Some months ago I went to see a panorama of the Rhine. It was like a dream of the Middle Ages. I floated down its historic stream in something more than imagination, under bridges built by the Romans, and repaired by later heroes, past cities and castles whose very names were music to my ears, and each of which was the subject of a legend. There were Eh. enbreitstein and Rolandseck and Coblentz, which I knew only in history. They were ruins that interested me chiefly. There seemed to come up from its waters and its vine-clad hills and valleys a hushed music as of Crusaders departing for the Holy Land. I floated along under the spell of enchantment, as if I had been transported to an heroic age, and breathed an atmosphere of chivalry.

Soon after, I went to see a panorama of the Mississippi, and as I worked my way up the river in the light of today, and saw the steamboats wooding up, counted the rising cities, gazed on the fresh ruins of Nauvoo, beheld the Indians moving west across the stream, and, as before I had looked up the Moselle, now looked up the Ohio and the Missouri and heard the legends of Dubuque and of Wenona's Cliff—still thinking more of the future than of the past or present—I saw that this was a Rhine stream of a different kind; that the foundations of castles were yet to be laid, and the famous bridges were yet to be thrown over the river; and I felt that *this was the heroic age itself*, though we know it not, for the hero is commonly the simplest and obscurest of men.

The West of which I speak is but another name for the Wild; and what I have been preparing to say is, that in Wildness is the preservation of the World. Every tree sends its fibers forth in search of the Wild. The cities import it at any price. Men plow and sail for it.

From the forest and wilderness come the tonics and barks which brace mankind. Our ancestors were savages. The story of Romulus and Remus being suckled by a wolf is not a meaningless fable. The founders of every state which has risen to eminence have drawn their nourishment and vigor from a similar wild source. It was because the children of the Empire were not suckled by the wolf that they were conquered and displaced by the children of the northern forests who were.

I believe in the forest, and in the meadow, and in the night in which the corn grows. We require an infusion of hemlock, spruce or arbor vitae in our tea. There is a difference between eating and drinking for strength and from mere gluttony. The Hottentots eagerly devour the marrow of the koodoo and other antelopes raw, as a matter of course. Some of our northern Indians eat raw the marrow of the Arctic reindeer, as well as various other parts, including the summits of the antlers, as long as they are soft. And herein, perchance, they have stolen a march on the cooks of Paris. They get what usually goes to feed the fire. This is probably better than stall-fed beef and slaughterhouse pork to make a man of. Give me a wildness whose glance no civilization can endure—as if we lived on the marrow of koodoos devoured raw.

There are some intervals which border the strain of the wood thrush, to which I would migrate—wild lands where no settler has squatted; to which, methinks, I am already acclimated.

The African hunter Cumming tells us that the skin of the eland, as well as that of most other antelopes just killed, emits the most delicious perfume of trees and grass. I would have every man so much like a wild antelope, so much a part and parcel of nature, that his very person should thus sweetly advertise our senses of his presence, and remind us of those parts of nature which he most haunts. I feel no disposition to be satirical, when the trapper's coat emits the odor of musquash even; it is a sweeter scent to me than that which commonly exhales from the merchant's or the scholar's garments. When I go into their wardrobes and handle their vestments, I am reminded of no grassy plains and flowery meads which they have frequented, but of dusty merchants' exchanges and libraries rather.

A tanned skin is something more than respectable, and perhaps olive is a fitter color than white for a man —a denizen of the woods. "The pale white man!" I do not wonder that the African pitied him. Darwin the naturalist says, "A white man bathing by the side of a Tahitian was like a plant bleached by the gardener's art, compared with a fine, dark green one, growing vigorously in the open fields."

Ben Jonson exclaims,

"How near to good is what is fair!"

So I would say,

How near to good is what is *wild!*

Life consists with wildness. The most alive is the wildest. Not yet subdued to man, its presence refreshes him. One who pressed forward incessantly and never rested from his labors, who grew fast and made infinite demands on life, would always find himself in a new country or wilderness, and surrounded by the raw material of life. He would be climbing over the prostrate stems of primitive forest-trees.

Hope and the future for me are not in lawns and cultivated fields, not in towns and cities, but in the impervious and quaking swamps. When, formerly, I have analyzed my partiality for some farm which I had con-

templated purchasing, I have frequently found that I
was attracted solely by a few square rods of impermea-
ble and unfathomable bog—a natural sink in one corner
of it. That was the jewel which dazzled me. I derive
more of my subsistence from the swamps which surround my native town than from the cultivated gardens
in the village. There are no richer parterres to my eyes
than the dense beds of dwarf andromeda (*Cassandra
calyculata*) which cover these tender places on the
earth's surface. Botany cannot go farther than tell me
the names of the shrubs which grow there—the high
blueberry, panicled andromeda, lambkill, azalea, and
rhodora—all standing in the quaking sphagnum. I often
think that I should like to have my house front on this
mass of dull red bushes, omitting other flower plots and
borders, transplanted spruce and trim box, even graveled
walks—to have this fertile spot under my windows, not
a few imported barrowfuls of soil only to cover the sand
which was thrown out in digging the cellar. Why not
put my house, my parlor, behind this plot, instead of
behind that meager assemblage of curiosities, that poor
apology for a Nature and Art, which I call my front
yard? It is an effort to clear up and make a decent appearance when the carpenter and mason have departed,
though done as much for the passer-by as the dweller
within. The most tasteful front-yard fence was never
an agreeable object of study to me; the most elaborate
ornaments, acorn tops, or what not, soon wearied and
disgusted me. Bring your sills up to the very edge of
the swamp, then (though it may not be the best place
for a dry cellar), so that there be no access on that side
to citizens. Front yards are not made to walk in, but,
at most, through, and you could go in the back way.

Yes, though you may think me perverse, if it were
proposed to me to dwell in the neighborhood of the

most beautiful garden that ever human art contrived, or else of a Dismal Swamp, I should certainly decide for the swamp. How vain, then, have been all your labors, citizens, for me!

My spirits infallibly rise in proportion to the outward dreariness. Give me the ocean, the desert, or the wilderness! In the desert, pure air and solitude compensate for want of moisture and fertility. The traveler Burton says of it: "Your *morale* improves; you become frank and cordial, hospitable and single-minded. . . . In the desert, spirituous liquors excite only disgust. There is a keen enjoyment in a mere animal existence." They who have been traveling long on the steppes of Tartary say, "On re-entering cultivated lands, the agitation, perplexity, and turmoil of civilization oppressed and suffocated us; the air seemed to fail us, and we felt every moment as if about to die of asphyxia." When I would recreate myself, I seek the darkest wood, the thickest and most interminable and, to the citizen, most dismal, swamp. I enter a swamp as a sacred place, a *sanctum sanctorum*. There is the strength, the marrow, of Nature. The wildwood covers the virgin mould, and the same soil is good for men and for trees. A man's health requires as many acres of meadow to his prospect as his farm does loads of muck. There are the strong meats on which he feeds. A town is saved, not more by the righteous men in it than by the woods and swamps that surround it. A township where one primitive forest waves above while another primitive forest rots below—such a town is fitted to raise not only corn and potatoes, but poets and philosophers for the coming ages. In such a soil grew Homer and Confucius and the rest, and out of such a wilderness comes the Reformer eating locusts and wild honey.

To preserve wild animals implies generally the creation of a forest for them to dwell in or resort to. So it is with man. A hundred years ago they sold bark in our streets peeled from our own woods. In the very aspect of those primitive and rugged trees there was, methinks, a tanning principle which hardened and consolidated the fibers of men's thoughts. Ah! already I shudder for these comparatively degenerate days of my native village, when you cannot collect a load of bark of good thickness, and we no longer produce tar and turpentine.

The civilized nations—Greece, Rome, England— have been sustained by the primitive forests which anciently rotted where they stand. They survive as long as the soil is not exhausted. Alas for human culture! little is to be expected of a nation, when the vegetable mould is exhausted, and it is compelled to make manure of the bones of its fathers. There the poet sustains himself merely by his own superfluous fat, and the philosopher comes down on his marrow-bones.

It is said to be the task of the American "to work the virgin soil," and that "agriculture here already assumes proportions unknown everywhere else." I think that the farmer displaces the Indian even because he redeems the meadow, and so makes himself stronger and in some respects more natural. I was surveying for a man the other day a single straight line one hundred and thirty-two rods long, through a swamp at whose entrance might have been written the words which Dante read over the entrance to the infernal regions, "Leave all hope, ye that enter"—that is, of ever getting out again; where at one time I saw my employer actually up to his neck and swimming for his life in his property, though it was still winter. He had another similar swamp which I could not survey at all, because it was completely under water, and nevertheless, with regard to a third swamp, which I did *survey* from a distance, he remarked to me, true to his instincts, that he would not part with it for any consideration, on account of the mud which it contained. And that man intends to put a girdling ditch round the whole in the course of forty months, and so redeem it by the magic of his spade. I refer to him only as the type of a class.

The weapons with which we have gained our most important victories, which should be handed down as heirlooms from father to son, are not the sword and the lance, but the bushwhack, the turf-cutter, the spade, and the bog hoe, rusted with the blood of many a meadow, and begrimed with the dust of many a hard-fought field. The very winds blew the Indian's cornfield into the meadow, and pointed out the way which he had not the skill to follow. He had no better implement with which to intrench himself in the land than a clam-shell. But the farmer is armed with plow and spade.

In literature it is only the wild that attracts us. Dullness is but another name for tameness. It is the uncivilized free and wild thinking in Hamlet and the Iliad, in all the scriptures and mythologies, not learned in the schools, that delights us. As the wild duck is more swift and beautiful than the tame, so is the wild—the mallard—thought, which 'mid falling dews wings its way above the fens. A truly good book is something as natural, and as unexpectedly and unaccountably fair and perfect, as a wild-flower discovered on the prairies of the West or in the jungles of the East. Genius is a light which makes the darkness visible, like the lightning's flash, which perchance shatters the temple of knowledge itself—and not a taper lighted at the hearthstone of the race, which pales before the light of common day.

English literature, from the days of the minstrels to the Lake Poets—Chaucer and Spenser and Milton, and even Shakespeare, included—breathes no quite fresh

and, in this sense, wild strain. It is an essentially tame
and civilized literature, reflecting Greece and Rome.
Her wilderness is a greenwood, her wild man a Robin
Hood. There is plenty of genial love of Nature, but not
so much of Nature herself. Her chronicles inform us
when her wild animals, but not when the wild man in
her, became extinct.

The science of Humboldt is one thing, poetry is another thing. The poet today, notwithstanding all the discoveries of science, and the accumulated learning of
mankind, enjoys no advantage over Homer.

Where is the literature which gives expression to Nature? He would be a poet who could impress the winds
and streams into his service, to speak for him; who
nailed words to their primitive senses, as farmers drive
down stakes in the spring, which the frost has heaved;
who derived his words as often as he used them—transplanted them to his page with earth adhering to their
roots; whose words were so true and fresh and natural
that they would appear to expand like the buds at the
approach of spring, though they lay half smothered between two musty leaves in a library—aye, to bloom and
bear fruit there, after their kind, annually, for the faithful reader, in sympathy with surrounding Nature.

I do not know of any poetry to quote which adequately expresses this yearning for the Wild. Approached from this side, the best poetry is tame. I do
not know where to find in any literature, ancient or
modern, any account which contents me of that Nature
with which even I am acquainted. You will perceive
that I demand something which no Augustan nor Elizabethan age, which no *culture*, in short, can give. Mythology comes nearer to it than anything. How much
more fertile a Nature, at least, has Grecian mythology
its root in than English literature! Mythology is the crop

which the Old World bore before its soil was exhausted, before the fancy and imagination were affected with blight; and which it still bears, wherever its pristine vigor is unabated. All other literatures endure only as the elms which overshadow our houses; but this is like the great dragon-tree of the Western Isles, as old as mankind, and, whether that does or not, will endure as long; for the decay of other literatures makes the soil in which it thrives.

The West is preparing to add its fables to those of the East. The valleys of the Ganges, the Nile, and the Rhine having yielded their crop, it remains to be seen what the valleys of the Amazon, the Plate, the Orinoco, the St. Lawrence, and the Mississippi will produce. Perchance, when, in the course of ages, American liberty has become a fiction of the past—as it is to some extent a fiction of the present—the poets of the world will be inspired by American mythology.

The wildest dreams of wild men, even, are not the less true, though they may not recommend themselves to the sense which is most common among Englishmen and Americans today. It is not every truth that recommends itself to the common sense. Nature has a place for the wild clematis as well as for the cabbage. Some expressions of truth are reminiscent, others merely *sensible,* as the phrase is, others prophetic. Some forms of disease, even, may prophesy forms of health. The geologist has discovered that the figures of serpents, griffins, flying dragons, and other fanciful embellishments of heraldry, have their prototypes in the forms of fossil species which were extinct before man was created, and hence "indicate a faint and shadowy knowledge of a previous state of organic existence." The Hindus dreamed that the earth rested on an elephant, and the elephant on a tortoise, and the tortoise on a serpent;

and though it may be an unimportant coincidence, it will not be out of place here to state, that a fossil tortoise has lately been discovered in Asia large enough to support an elephant. I confess that I am partial to these wild fancies, which transcend the order of time and development. They are the sublimest recreation of the intellect. The partridge loves peas, but not those that go with her into the pot.

In short, all good things are wild and free. There is something in a strain of music, whether produced by an instrument or by the human voice—take the sound of a bugle in a summer night, for instance—which by its wildness, to speak without satire, reminds me of the cries emitted by wild beasts in their native forests. It is so much of their wildness as I can understand. Give me for my friends and neighbors wild men, not tame ones. The wildness of the savage is but a faint symbol of the awful ferity with which good men and lovers meet.

I love even to see the domestic animals reassert their native rights—any evidence that they have not wholly lost their original wild habits and vigor; as when my neighbor's cow breaks out of her pasture early in the spring and boldly swims the river, a cold, gray tide, twenty-five or thirty rods wide, swollen by the melted snow. It is the buffalo crossing the Mississippi. This exploit confers some dignity on the herd in my eyes—already dignified. The seeds of instinct are preserved under the thick hides of cattle and horses, like seeds in the bowels of the earth, an indefinite period.

Any sportiveness in cattle is unexpected. I saw one day a herd of a dozen bullocks and cows running about and frisking in unwieldy sport, like huge rats, even like kittens. They shook their heads, raised their tails, and rushed up and down a hill, and I perceived by their horns, as well as by their activity, their relation to the deer tribe. But, alas! a sudden loud *Whoa!* would have damped their ardor at once, reduced them from venison to beef, and stiffened their sides and sinews like the locomotive. Who but the Evil One has cried "Whoa!" to mankind? Indeed, the life of cattle, like that of many men, is but a sort of locomotiveness; they move a side at a time, and man, by his machinery, is meeting the horse and the ox halfway. Whatever part the whip has touched is thenceforth palsied. Who would ever think of a *side* of any of the supple cat tribe, as we speak of a *side* of beef?

I rejoice that horses and steers have to be broken before they can be made the slaves of men, and that men themselves have some wild oats still left to sow before they become submissive members of society. Undoubtedly, all men are not equally fit subjects for civilization; and because the majority, like dogs and sheep, are tame by inherited disposition, this is no reason why the others should have their natures broken that they may be reduced to the same level. Men are in the main alike, but they were made several in order that they might be various. If a low use is to be served, one man will do nearly or quite as well as another; if a high one, individual excellence is to be regarded. Any man can stop a hole to keep the wind away, but no other man could serve so rare a use as the author of this illustration did. Confucius says, "The skins of the tiger and the leopard, when they are tanned, are as the skins of the dog and the sheep tanned." But it is not the part of a true culture to tame tigers, any more than it is to make sheep ferocious; and tanning their skins for shoes is not the best use to which they can be put.

When looking over a list of men's names in a foreign language, as of military officers, or of authors who have written on a particular subject, I am reminded once more that there is nothing in a name. The name Menschikoff, for instance, has nothing in it to my ears more human than a whisker, and it may belong to a rat. As the names of the Poles and Russians are to us, so are ours to them. It is as if they had been named by the child's rigmarole, *Iery wiery ichery van, tittle-tol-tan.* I see in my mind a herd of wild creatures swarming over the earth, and to each the herdsman has affixed some barbarous sound in his own dialect. The names of men are, of course, as cheap and meaningless as *Bose* and *Tray,* the names of dogs.

Methinks it would be some advantage to philosophy if men were named merely in the gross, as they are known. It would be necessary only to know the genus and perhaps the race or variety, to know the individual. We are not prepared to believe that every private soldier in a Roman army had a name of his own—because we have not supposed that he had a character of his own.

At present our only true names are nicknames. I knew a boy who, from his peculiar energy, was called "Buster" by his playmates, and this rightly supplanted his Christian name. Some travelers tell us that an Indian had no name given him at first, but earned it, and his name was his fame; and among some tribes he acquired a new name with every new exploit. It is pitiful when a man bears a name for convenience merely, who has earned neither name nor fame.

I will not allow mere names to make distinctions for me, but still see men in herds for all them. A familiar name cannot make a man less strange to me. It may be given to a savage who retains in secret his own wild title earned in the woods. We have a wild savage in us, and a savage name is perchance somewhere recorded as ours. I see that my neighbor, who bears the familiar epithet

William or Edwin, takes it off with his jacket. It does not adhere to him when asleep or in anger, or aroused by any passion or inspiration. I seem to hear pronounced by some of his kin at such a time his original wild name in some jaw-breaking or else melodious tongue.

Here is this vast, savage, howling mother of ours, Nature, lying all around, with such beauty, and such affection for her children, as the leopard; and yet we are so early weaned from her breast to society, to that culture which is exclusively an interaction of man on man —a sort of breeding in and in, which produces at most a merely English nobility, a civilization destined to have a speedy limit.

In society, in the best institutions of men, it is easy to detect a certain precocity. When we should still be growing children, we are already little men. Give me a culture which imports much muck from the meadows, and deepens the soil—not that which trusts to heating manures, and improved implements and modes of culture only!

Many a poor sore-eyed student that I have heard of would grow faster, both intellectually and physically, if, instead of sitting up so very late, he honestly slumbered a fool's allowance.

There may be an excess even of informing light. Niepce, a Frenchman, discovered "actinism," that power in the sun's rays which produces a chemical effect; that granite rocks, and stone structures, and statues of metal "are all alike destructively acted upon during the hours of sunshine, and, but for provisions of Nature no less wonderful, would soon perish under the delicate touch of the most subtile of the agencies of the universe." But he observed that "those bodies which underwent this change during the daylight possessed the power of restoring themselves to their original conditions during the hours of night, when this excitement was no longer influencing them." Hence it has been inferred that "the hours of darkness are as necessary to the inorganic creation as we know night and sleep are to the organic kingdom." Not even does the moon shine every night, but gives place to darkness.

I would not have every man nor every part of a man cultivated, any more than I would have every acre of earth cultivated: part will be tillage, but the greater part will be meadow and forest, not only serving an immediate use, but preparing a mould against a distant future, by the annual decay of the vegetation which it supports.

There are other letters for the child to learn than those which Cadmus invented. The Spaniards have a good term to express this wild and dusky knowledge, *Gramática parda,* tawny grammar, a kind of mother-wit derived from that same leopard to which I have referred.

We have heard of a Society for the Diffusion of Useful Knowledge. It is said that knowledge is power, and the like. Methinks there is equal need of a Society for the Diffusion of Useful Ignorance, what we will call Beautiful Knowledge, a knowledge useful in a higher sense: for what is most of our boasted so-called knowledge but a conceit that we know something, which robs us of the advantage of our actual ignorance? What we call knowledge is often our positive ignorance; ignorance our negative knowledge. By long years of patient industry and reading of the newspapers—for what are the libraries of science but files of newspapers?—a man accumulates a myriad facts, lays them up in his memory, and then when in some spring of his life he saunters abroad into the Great Fields of thought, he, as it were, goes to grass like a horse and leaves all his harness behind in the stable. I would say to the Society for the Diffusion of Useful Knowledge, sometimes, Go to grass. You have eaten hay long enough. The spring has come with its green crop. The very cows are driven to their country pastures before the end of May; though I have heard of one unnatural farmer who kept his cow in the barn and fed her on hay all the year round. So, frequently, the Society for the Diffusion of Useful Knowledge treats its cattle.

A man's ignorance sometimes is not only useful, but beautiful—while his knowledge, so called, is oftentimes worse than useless, besides being ugly. Which is the best man to deal with—he who knows nothing about a subject, and, what is extremely rare, knows that he knows nothing, or he who really knows something about it, but thinks that he knows all?

My desire for knowledge is intermittent, but my desire to bathe my head in atmospheres unknown to my feet is perennial and constant. The highest that we can attain to is not Knowledge, but Sympathy with Intelligence. I do not know that this higher knowledge amounts to anything more definite than a novel and grand surprise on a sudden revelation of the insufficiency of all that we called Knowledge before—a discovery that there are more things in heaven and earth than are dreamed of in our philosophy. It is the lighting up of the mist by the sun. Man cannot *know* in any higher sense than this, any more than he can look serenely and with impunity in the face of the sun: Ὡς τὶ νοῶν, οὐ κεῖνον νοήσεις, "You will not perceive that, as perceiving a particular thing," say the Chaldean Oracles.

There is something servile in the habit of seeking after a law which we may obey. We may study the laws of matter at and for our convenience, but a successful life knows no law. It is an unfortunate discovery certainly, that of a law which binds us where we did not know before that we were bound. Live free, child of the mist—and with respect to knowledge we are all children of the mist. The man who takes the liberty to live is superior to all the laws, by virtue of his relation to the lawmaker. "That is active duty," says the Vishnu Purana, "which is not for our bondage; that is knowledge which is for our liberation: all other duty is good only unto weariness; all other knowledge is only the cleverness of an artist."

It is remarkable how few events or crises there are in our histories, how little exercised we have been in our minds, how few experiences we have had. I would fain be assured that I am growing apace and rankly, though my very growth disturb this dull equanimity—though it be with struggle through long, dark, muggy nights or seasons of gloom. It would be well if all our lives were a divine tragedy even, instead of this trivial comedy or farce. Dante, Bunyan, and others appear to have been exercised in their minds more than we: they were subjected to a kind of culture such as our district schools and colleges do not contemplate. Even Mahomet, though many may scream at his name, had a good deal more to to live for, aye, and to die for, than they have commonly.

When, at rare intervals, some thought visits one, as perchance he is walking on a railroad, then, indeed, the cars go by without his hearing them. But soon, by some inexorable law, our life goes by and the cars return.

> "Gentle breeze, that wanderest unseen,
> And bendest the thistles round Loira of storms,
> Traveler of the windy glens,
> Why hast thou left my ear so soon?"

While almost all men feel an attraction drawing them to society, few are attracted strongly to Nature. In their reaction to Nature men appear to me for the most part, notwithstanding their arts, lower than the animals. It is not often a beautiful relation, as in the case of the animals. How little appreciation of the beauty of the landscape there is among us! We have to be told that the Greeks called the world Κόσμος, Beauty, or Order, but we do not see clearly why they did so, and we esteem it at best only a curious philological fact.

For my part, I feel that with regard to Nature I live a sort of border life, on the confines of a world into which I make occasional and transient forays only, and my patriotism and allegiance to the state into whose territories I seem to retreat are those of a moss-trooper. Unto a life which I call natural I would gladly follow even a will-o'-the-wisp through bogs and sloughs unimaginable, but no moon nor firefly has shown me the causeway to it. Nature is a personality so vast and universal that we have never seen one of her features. The walker in the familiar fields which stretch around my native town sometimes finds himself in another land than is described in their owners' deeds, as it were in some faraway field on the confines of the actual Concord, where her jurisdiction ceases, and the idea which the word Concord suggests ceases to be suggested. These farms which I have myself surveyed, these bounds which I have set up, appear dimly still as through a mist; but they have no chemistry to fix them; they fade from the surface of the glass, and the picture which the painter painted stands out dimly from beneath. The world with which we are commonly acquainted leaves no trace, and it will have no anniversary.

I took a walk on Spaulding's Farm the other afternoon. I saw the setting sun lighting up the opposite side of a stately pine wood. Its golden rays straggled into the aisles of the wood as into some noble hall. I was im-

pressed as if some ancient and altogether admirable and
shining family had settled there in that part of the land
called Concord, unknown to me—to whom the sun was
servant—who had not gone into society in the village—
who had not been called on. I saw their park, their
pleasure-ground, beyond through the wood, in Spaulding's cranberry-meadow. The pines furnished them with
gables as they grew. Their house was not obvious to
vision; the trees grew through it. I do not know whether
I heard the sounds of a suppressed hilarity or not. They
seemed to recline on the sunbeams. They have sons and
daughters. They are quite well. The farmer's cart-path,
which leads directly through their hall, does not in the
least put them out, as the muddy bottom of a pool is
sometimes seen through the reflected skies. They never
heard of Spaulding, and do not know that he is their
neighbor—notwithstanding I heard him whistle as he
drove his team through the house. Nothing can equal
the serenity of their lives. Their coat-of-arms is simply a
lichen. I saw it painted on the pines and oaks. Their
attics were in the tops of the trees. They are of no politics. There was no noise of labor. I did not perceive that
they were weaving or spinning. Yet I did detect, when
the wind lulled and hearing was done away, the finest
imaginable sweet musical hum—as of a distant hive in
May—which perchance was the sound of their thinking.
They had no idle thoughts, and no one without could
see their work, for their industry was not as in knots and
excrescences embayed.

But I find it difficult to remember them. They fade
irrevocably out of my mind even now while I speak,
and endeavor to recall them and recollect myself. It is
only after a long and serious effort to recollect my best
thoughts that I become again aware of their cohab-

itancy. If it were not for such families as this, I think I should move out of Concord.

We are accustomed to say in New England that few and fewer pigeons visit us every year. Our forests furnish no mast for them. So, it would seem, few and fewer thoughts visit each growing man from year to year, for the grove in our minds is laid waste—sold to feed unnecessary fires of ambition, or sent to mill—and there is scarcely a twig left for them to perch on. They no longer build nor breed with us. In some more genial season, perchance, a faint shadow flits across the landscape of the mind, cast by the *wings* of some thought in its vernal or autumnal migration, but, looking up, we are unable to detect the substance of the thought itself. Our winged thoughts are turned to poultry. They no longer soar, and they attain only to a Shanghai and Cochin-China grandeur. Those *gra-a-ate thoughts,* those *gra-a-ate men* you hear of!

We hug the earth—how rarely we mount! Methinks we might elevate ourselves a little more. We might climb a tree, at least. I found my account in climbing a tree once. It was a tall white pine, on the top of a hill; and though I got well pitched, I was well paid for it, for I discovered new mountains in the horizon which I had never seen before—so much more of the earth and the heavens. I might have walked about the foot of the tree for threescore years and ten, and yet I certainly should never have seen them. But, above all, I discovered around me—it was near the end of June—on the ends of the topmost branches only, a few minute and delicate red conelike blossoms, the fertile flower of the white pine looking heavenward. I carried straightway to the

village the topmost spire, and showed it to stranger jury-
men who walked the streets—for it was court week—
and to farmers and lumber-dealers and woodchoppers
and hunters, and not one had ever seen the like before,
but they wondered as at a star dropped down. Tell of
ancient architects finishing their works on the tops of
columns as perfectly as on the lower and more visible
parts! Nature has from the first expanded the minute
blossoms of the forest only toward the heavens, above
men's heads and unobserved by them. We see only the
flowers that are under our feet in the meadows. The
pines have developed their delicate blossoms on the
highest twigs of the wood every summer for ages, as well
over the heads of Nature's red children as of her white
ones; yet scarcely a farmer or hunter in the land has
ever seen them.

Above all, we cannot afford not to live in the present.
He is blessed over all mortals who loses no moment of
the passing life in remembering the past. Unless our
philosophy hears the cock crow in every barnyard
within our horizon, it is belated. That sound commonly
reminds us that we are growing rusty and antique in our
employments and habits of thought. His philosophy
comes down to a more recent time than ours. There is
something suggested by it that is a newer testament—
the gospel according to this moment. He has not fallen
astern; he has got up early and kept up early, and to be
where he is is to be in season, in the foremost rank of
time. It is an expression of the health and soundness of
Nature, a brag for all the world—healthiness as of a
spring burst forth, a new fountain of the Muses, to celebrate this last instant of time. Where he lives no fugitive
slave laws are passed. Who has not betrayed his master
many times since last he heard that note?

The merit of this bird's strain is in its freedom from all plaintiveness. The singer can easily move us to tears or to laughter, but where is he who can excite in us a pure morning joy? When, in doleful dumps, breaking the awful stillness of our wooden sidewalk on a Sunday, or, perchance, a watcher in the house of mourning, I hear a cockerel crow far or near, I think to myself, "There is one of us well, at any rate," and with a sudden gush return to my senses.

We had a remarkable sunset one day last November. I was walking in a meadow, the source of a small brook, when the sun at last, just before setting, after a cold, gray day, reached a clear stratum in the horizon, and the softest, brightest morning sunlight fell on the dry grass and on the stems of the trees in the opposite horizon and on the leaves of the shrub oaks on the hillside, while our shadows stretched long over the meadow eastward, as if we were the only motes in its beams. It was such a light as we could not have imagined a moment before, and the air also was so warm and serene that nothing was wanting to make a paradise of that meadow. When we reflected that this was not a solitary phenomenon, never to happen again, but that it would happen forever and ever, an infinite number of evenings, and cheer and reassure the latest child that walked there, it was more glorious still.

The sun sets on some retired meadow, where no house is visible, with all the glory and splendor that it lavishes on cities, and perchance as it has never set before—where there is but a solitary marsh hawk to have his wings gilded by it, or only a musquash looks out from his cabin, and there is some little black-veined brook in the midst of the marsh, just beginning to meander, winding slowly round a decaying stump. We

walked in so pure and bright a light, gilding the withered grass and leaves, so softly and serenely bright, I
thought I had never bathed in such a golden flood,
without a ripple or a murmur to it. The west side of
every wood and rising ground gleamed like the boundary of Elysium, and the sun on our backs seemed like a
gentle herdsman driving us home at evening.

So we saunter toward the Holy Land, till one day
the sun shall shine more brightly than ever he has done,
shall perchance shine into our minds and hearts, and
light up our whole lives with a great awakening light,
as warm and serene and golden as on a bankside in
autumn.

Life Without Principle

In our culture the businessman is supposedly ruthless, while the poet is ineffectual. "Life Without Principle" gives the lie to that. This essay is as hard and harder than any State Street merchant. In it Thoreau depicts the way most people live as a matter for contempt. He had his reasons—to live in terms of his own ideals he had to be intransigent. He paid the penalty of the individualist and paid it readily; yet he was still human enough to fling a Transcendental stone at the deacons and tradesmen who derided him.

C. B.

AT A LYCEUM, not long since, I felt that the lecturer had chosen a theme too foreign to himself, and so failed to interest me as much as he might have done. He described things not in or near to his heart, but toward his extremities and superficies. There was, in this sense, no truly central or centralizing thought in the lecture. I would have had him deal with privatest experience, as the poet does. The greatest compliment that was ever paid me was when one asked me what I *thought*, and attended to my answer. I am surprised, as well as delighted, when this happens, it is such a rare use he would make of me, as if he were acquainted with the tool. Commonly, if men want anything of me, it is only to know how many acres I make of their land—since I am a surveyor—or, at most, what trivial news I have burdened myself with. They never will go to law for my meat; they prefer the shell. A man once came a considerable distance to ask me to lecture on Slavery; but on conversing with him, I found that he and his clique

expected seven eighths of the lecture to be theirs, and
only one eighth mine; so I declined. I take it for granted,
when I am invited to lecture anywhere—for I have had
a little experience in that business—that there is a desire to hear what *I think* on some subject, though I may
be the greatest fool in the country, and not that I should
say pleasant things merely, or such as the audience will
assent to; and I resolve, accordingly, that I will give
them a strong dose of myself. They have sent for me,
and engaged to pay for me, and I am determined that
they shall have me, though I bore them beyond all precedent.

So now I would say something similar to you, my
readers. Since *you* are my readers, and I have not been
much of a traveler, I will not talk about people a thousand miles off, but come as near home as I can. As the
time is short, I will leave out all the flattery, and retain
all the criticism.

Let us consider the way in which we spend our lives.

This world is a place of business. What an infinite
bustle! I am awaked almost every night by the panting
of the locomotive. It interrupts my dreams. There is no
sabbath. It would be glorious to see mankind at leisure
for once. It is nothing but work, work, work. I cannot
easily buy a blankbook to write thoughts in; they are
commonly ruled for dollars and cents. An Irishman, seeing me making a minute in the fields, took it for granted
that I was calculating my wages. If a man was tossed
out of a window when an infant, and so made a cripple
for life, or scared out of his wits by the Indians, it is
regretted chiefly because he was thus incapacitated for
—business! I think that there is nothing, not even crime,
more opposed to poetry, to philosophy, ay, to life itself,
than this incessant business.

There is a coarse and boisterous money-making fellow

in the outskirts of our town, who is going to build a bank-wall under the hill along the edge of his meadow. The powers have put this into his head to keep him out of mischief, and he wishes me to spend three weeks digging there with him. The result will be that he will perhaps get some more money to hoard, and leave for his heirs to spend foolishly. If I do this, most will commend me as an industrious and hard-working man; but if I choose to devote myself to certain labors which yield more real profit, though but little money, they may be inclined to look on me as an idler. Nevertheless, as I do not need the police of meaningless labor to regulate me, and do not see anything absolutely praiseworthy in this fellow's undertaking any more than in many an enterprise of our own or foreign governments, however amusing it may be to him or them, I prefer to finish my education at a different school.

If a man walk in the woods for love of them half of each day, he is in danger of being regarded as a loafer; but if he spends his whole day as a speculator, shearing off those woods and making earth bald before her time, he is esteemed an industrious and enterprising citizen. As if a town had no interest in its forests but to cut them down!

Most men would feel insulted if it were proposed to employ them in throwing stones over a wall, and then in throwing them back, merely that they might earn their wages. But many are no more worthily employed now. For instance: just after sunrise, one summer morning, I noticed one of my neighbors walking beside his team, which was slowly drawing a heavy hewn stone swung under the axle, surrounded by an atmosphere of industry—his day's work begun, his brow commenced to sweat—a reproach to all sluggards and idlers—pausing abreast the shoulders of his oxen, and half turning round with a flourish of his merciful whip, while they gained their length on him. And I thought, Such is the labor which the American Congress exists to protect— honest, manly toil—honest as the day is long—that makes his bread taste sweet, and keeps society sweet— which all men respect and have consecrated; one of the sacred band, doing the needful but irksome drudgery. Indeed, I felt a slight reproach, because I observed this from a window, and was not abroad and stirring about a similar business. The day went by, and at evening I passed the yard of another neighbor, who keeps many servants, and spends much money foolishly, while he adds nothing to the common stock, and there I saw the stone of the morning lying beside a whimsical structure intended to adorn this Lord Timothy Dexter's premises, and the dignity forthwith departed from the teamster's labor, in my eyes. In my opinion, the sun was made to light worthier toil than this. I may add that his employer has since run off, in debt to a good part of the town, and, after passing through Chancery, has settled somewhere else, there to become once more a patron of the arts.

The ways by which you may get money almost without exception lead downward. To have done anything by which you earned money *merely* is to have been truly idle or worse. If the laborer gets no more than the wages which his employer pays him, he is cheated, he cheats himself. If you would get money as a writer or lecturer, you must be popular, which is to go down perpendicularly. Those services which the community will most readily pay for, it is most disagreeable to render. You are paid for being something less than a man. The state does not commonly reward a genius any more wisely. Even the poet laureate would rather not have to celebrate the accidents of royalty. He must be bribed with a pipe of wine; and perhaps another poet is called away from his muse to gauge that very pipe. As for my own business, even that kind of surveying which I could do with most satisfaction my employers do not want. They would prefer that I should do my work coarsely and not too well, ay, not well enough. When I observe that there are different ways of surveying, my employer commonly asks which will give him the most land, not which is most correct. I once invented a rule for measuring cordwood, and tried to introduce it in Boston; but the measurer there told me that the sellers did not wish to have their wood measured correctly—that he was already too accurate for them, and therefore they commonly got their wood measured in Charlestown before crossing the bridge.

The aim of the laborer should be, not to get his living, to get "a good job," but to perform well a certain work; and, even in a pecuniary sense, it would be economy for a town to pay its laborers so well that they would not feel that they were working for low ends, as for a livelihood merely, but for scientific, or even moral ends. Do not hire a man who does your work for money, but him who does it for love of it.

It is remarkable that there are few men so well employed, so much to their minds, but that a little money or fame would commonly buy them off from their present pursuit. I see advertisements for *active* young men, as if activity were the whole of a young man's capital. Yet I have been surprised when one has with confidence proposed to me, a grown man, to embark in some enterprise of his, as if I had absolutely nothing to do, my life having been a complete failure hitherto. What a doubtful compliment this to pay me! As if he had met me halfway across the ocean beating up against the wind, but bound nowhere, and proposed to me to go along with him! If I did, what do you think the underwriters would say? No, no! I am not without employment at this stage of the voyage. To tell the truth, I saw an advertisement for able-bodied seamen, when I was a boy, sauntering in my native port, and as soon as I came of age I embarked.

The community has no bribe that will tempt a wise man. You may raise money enough to tunnel a mountain, but you cannot raise money enough to hire a man who is minding *his own* business. An efficient and valuable man does what he can, whether the community pay him for it or not. The inefficient offer their inefficiency to the highest bidder, and are forever expecting to be put into office. One would suppose that they were rarely disappointed.

Perhaps I am more than usually jealous with respect to my freedom. I feel that my connection with and obligation to society are still very slight and transient. Those slight labors which afford me a livelihood, and by which it is allowed that I am to some extent serviceable to my contemporaries, are as yet commonly a pleasure to me, and I am not often reminded that they are a necessity. So far I am successful. But I foresee that if my wants should be much increased, the labor required to supply them would become a drudgery. If I should sell both my forenoons and afternoons to society, as most appear to do, I am sure that for me there would be nothing left worth living for. I trust that I shall never thus sell my birthright for a mess of pottage. I wish to suggest that a man may be very industrious, and yet not spend his time well. There is no more fatal blunderer than he who consumes the greater part of his life getting his living. All great enterprises are self-supporting. The poet, for instance, must sustain his body by his poetry, as a steam planing-mill feeds its boilers with the shavings it makes. You must get your living by loving. But as it is said of the merchants that ninety-seven in a hundred fail, so the life of men generally, tried by this standard, is a failure, and bankruptcy may be surely prophesied.

Merely to come into the world the heir of a fortune is not to be born; but to be stillborn, rather. To be supported by the charity of friends, or a government pension—provided you continue to breathe—by whatever fine synonyms you describe these relations, is to go into the almshouse. On Sundays the poor debtor goes to church to take an account of stock, and finds, of course, that his outgoes have been greater than his income. In the Catholic Church, especially, they go into chancery, make a clean confession, give up all, and think to start again. Thus men will lie on their backs, talking about the fall of man, and never make an effort to get up.

As for the comparative demand which men make on life, it is an important difference between two, that the one is satisfied with a level success, that his marks can all be hit by point-blank shots, but the other, however low and unsuccessful his life may be, constantly elevates his aim, though at a very slight angle to the horizon. I should much rather be the last man, though, as the Orientals say, "Greatness doth not approach him who is forever looking down; and all those who are looking high are growing poor."

It is remarkable that there is little or nothing to be remembered written on the subject of getting a living; how to make getting a living not merely honest and honorable, but altogether inviting and glorious; for if *getting* a living is not so, then living is not. One would think, from looking at literature, that this question had never disturbed a solitary individual's musings. Is it that men are too much disgusted with their experience to speak of it? The lesson of value which money teaches, which the Author of the Universe has taken so much pains to teach us, we are inclined to skip altogether. As for the means of living, it is wonderful how indifferent men of all classes are about it, even reformers, so called —whether they inherit, or earn, or steal it. I think that Society has done nothing for us in this respect, or at least has undone what she has done. Cold and hunger seem more friendly to my nature than those methods which men have adopted and advise to ward them off.

The title *wise* is, for the most part, falsely applied. How can one be a wise man, if he does not know any better how to live than other men?—if he is only more cunning and intellectually subtle? Does Wisdom work in a treadmill? or does she teach how to succeed *by her example?* Is there any such thing as wisdom not applied to life? Is she merely the miller who grinds the finest logic? It is pertinent to ask if Plato got his *living* in a better way or more successfully than his contemporaries —or did he succumb to the difficulties of life like other men? Did he seem to prevail over some of them merely by indifference, or by assuming grand airs? or find it easier to live, because his aunt remembered him in her will? The ways in which most men get their living, that is, live, are mere makeshifts, and a shirking of the real business of life—chiefly because they do not know, but partly because they do not mean, any better.

The rush to California, for instance, and the attitude, not merely of merchants, but of philosophers and prophets, so called, in relation to it, reflect the greatest disgrace on mankind. That so many are ready to live by luck, and so get the means of commanding the labor of others less lucky, without contributing any value to society! And that is called enterprise! I know of no more startling development of the immorality of trade, and all the common modes of getting a living. The philosophy and poetry and religion of such a mankind are not worth the dust of a puffball. The hog that gets his living by rooting, stirring up the soil so, would be ashamed of such company. If I could command the wealth of all the worlds by lifting my finger, I would not pay *such* a price for it. Even Mahomet knew that God did not make this world in jest. It makes God to be a moneyed gentleman who scatters a handful of pennies in order to see mankind scramble for them. The world's raffle! A subsistence in the domains of Nature a thing to be raffled for! What a comment, what a satire, on our institutions! The conclusion will be, that mankind will hang itself upon a tree. And have all the precepts in all the Bibles taught men only this? and is the last and most admirable invention of the human race only an improved muck-rake? Is this the ground on which Orientals and Occidentals meet? Did God direct us so to get our living, digging where we never planted—and He would, perchance, reward us with lumps of gold?

God gave the righteous man a certificate entitling him to food and raiment, but the unrighteous man found a facsimile of the same in God's coffers, and appropriated it, and obtained food and raiment like the former. It is one of the most extensive systems of counterfeiting that the world has seen. I did not know that mankind was suffering for want of gold. I have seen a little of it. I know that it is very malleable, but not so malleable as wit. A grain of gold will gild a great surface, but not so much as a grain of wisdom.

The gold digger in the ravines of the mountains is as much a gambler as his fellow in the saloons of San Francisco. What difference does it make whether you shake dirt or shake dice? If you win, society is the loser. The gold digger is the enemy of the honest laborer, whatever checks and compensations there may be. It is not enough to tell me that you worked hard to get your gold. So does the Devil work hard. The way of transgressors may be hard in many respects. The humblest observer who goes to the mines sees and says that gold digging is of the character of a lottery; the gold thus obtained is not the same thing with the wages of honest toil. But, practically, he forgets what he has seen, for he has seen only the fact, not the principle, and goes into trade there, that is, buys a ticket in what commonly proves another lottery, where the fact is not so obvious.

After reading Howitt's account of the Australian gold diggings one evening, I had in my mind's eye, all night, the numerous valleys, with their streams, all cut up with foul pits, from ten to one hundred feet deep, and half a dozen feet across, as close as they can be dug, and partly filled with water—the locality to which men furiously rush to probe for their fortunes—uncertain where they shall break ground—not knowing but the gold is under their camp itself—sometimes digging one hundred and sixty feet before they strike the vein, or then missing it by a foot—turned into demons, and regardless of each others' rights, in their thirst for riches—whole valleys, for thirty miles, suddenly honeycombed by the pits of the miners, so that even hundreds are drowned in them—standing in water, and covered with mud and clay, they work night and day, dying of exposure and disease. Having read this, and partly forgotten it, I was thinking, accidentally, of my own unsatisfactory life, doing as others do; and with that vision of the diggings still before me, I asked myself why I might not be washing some gold daily, though it were only the finest particles—why I might not sink a shaft down to the gold within me, and work that mine. There is a Ballarat, a Bendigo for you—what though it were a sulky-gully? At any rate, I might pursue some path, however solitary and narrow and crooked, in which I could walk with love and reverence. Wherever a man separates from the multitude, and goes his own way in this mood, there indeed is a fork in the road, though ordinary travelers may see only a gap in the paling. His solitary path across lots will turn out the *higher way* of the two.

Men rush to California and Australia as if the true gold were to be found in that direction; but that is to go to the very opposite extreme to where it lies. They go prospecting farther and farther away from the true lead, and are most unfortunate when they think themselves most successful. Is not our *native* soil auriferous? Does not a stream from the golden mountains flow through our native valley? and has not this for more than geologic ages been bringing down the shining particles and forming the nuggets for us? Yet, strange to tell, if a digger steal away, prospecting for this true gold, into the unexplored solitudes around us, there is no danger that any will dog his steps, and endeavor to supplant him. He may claim and undermine the whole valley even, both the cultivated and the uncultivated portions, his whole life long in peace, for no one will ever dispute his claim. They will not mind his cradles or his toms. He is not confined to a claim twelve feet square, as at Ballarat, but may mine anywhere, and wash the whole wide world in his tom.

Howitt says of the man who found the great nugget which weighed twenty-eight pounds, at the Bendigo diggings in Australia: "He soon began to drink; got a horse, and rode all about, generally at full gallop, and, when he met people, called out to inquire if they knew who he was, and then kindly informed them that he was 'the bloody wretch that had found the nugget.' At last he rode full speed against a tree, and nearly knocked his brains out." I think, however, there was no danger of that, for he had already knocked his brains out against the nugget. Howitt adds, "He is a hopelessly ruined man." But he is a type of the class. They are all fast men. Hear some of the names of the places where they dig: "Jackass Flat"—"Sheep's-Head Gully"—"Murderer's Bar," etc. Is there no satire in these names? Let them carry their ill-gotten wealth where they will, I am thinking it will still be "Jackass Flat," if not "Murderer's Bar," where they live.

The last resource of our energy has been the robbing of graveyards on the Isthmus of Darien, an enterprise which appears to be but in its infancy; for, according to late accounts, an act has passed its second reading in the legislature of New Granada, regulating this kind of mining; and a correspondent of the *Tribune* writes: "In the dry season, when the weather will permit of the country being properly prospected, no doubt other rich *guacas* [that is, graveyards] will be found." To emigrants he says: "Do not come before December; take the Isthmus route in preference to the Boca del Toro one; bring no useless baggage, and do not cumber yourself with a tent; but a good pair of blankets will be necessary; a pick, shovel, and axe of good material will be almost all that is required": advice which might have been taken from the "Burker's Guide." And he concludes with this line in italics and small capitals: "*If you are doing well at home,* STAY THERE," which may fairly be interpreted to mean, "If you are getting a good living by robbing graveyards at home, stay there."

But why go to California for a text? She is the child of New England, bred at her own school and church.

It is remarkable that among all the preachers there are so few moral teachers. The prophets are employed in excusing the ways of men. Most reverend seniors, the *illuminati* of the age, tell me, with a gracious, reminiscent smile, betwixt an aspiration and a shudder, not to be too tender about these things—to lump all that, that is, make a lump of gold of it. The highest advice I have heard on these subjects was groveling. The burden of it was—It is not worth your while to undertake to reform the world in this particular. Do not ask how your bread is buttered; it will make you sick, if you do—and the like. A man had better starve at once than lose his innocence in the process of getting his bread. If within the sophisticated man there is not an unsophisticated one, then he is but one of the devil's angels. As we grow old, we live more coarsely, we relax a little in our disciplines, and, to some extent, cease to obey our finest instincts. But we should be fastidious to the extreme of sanity, disregarding the gibes of those who are more unfortunate than ourselves.

In our science and philosophy, even, there is commonly no true and absolute account of things. The spirit of sect and bigotry has planted its hoof amid the stars. You have only to discuss the problem, whether the stars are inhabited or not, in order to discover it. Why must we daub the heavens as well as the earth? It was an unfortunate discovery that Dr. Kane was a Mason, and that Sir John Franklin was another. But it was a more cruel suggestion that possibly that was the reason why the former went in search of the latter. There is not a popular magazine in this country that would dare to print a child's thought on important subjects without comment. It must be submitted to the D.D.'s I would it were the chickadee-dees.

You come from attending the funeral of mankind to attend to a natural phenomenon. A little thought is sexton to all the world.

I hardly know an *intellectual* man, even, who is so broad and truly liberal that you can think aloud in his society. Most with whom you endeavor to talk soon come to a stand against some institution in which they appear to hold stock, that is, some particular, not universal, way of viewing things. They will continually thrust their own low roof, with its narrow skylight, between you and the sky, when it is the unobstructed heavens you would view. Get out of the way with your cobwebs; wash your windows, I say! In some lyceums they tell me that they have voted to exclude the subject of religion. But how do I know what their religion is, and when I am near to or far from it? I have walked into such an arena and done my best to make a clean breast of what religion I have experienced, and the audience never suspected what I was about. The lecture was as harmless as moonshine to them. Whereas, if I had read to them the biography of the greatest scamps in history, they might have thought that I had written the lives of the deacons of their church. Ordinarily, the inquiry is, Where did you come from? or, Where are you going? That was a more pertinent question which I overheard one of my auditors put to another once— "What does he lecture for?" It made me quake in my shoes.

To speak impartially, the best men that I know are not serene, a world in themselves. For the most part, they dwell in forms, and flatter and study effect only more finely than the rest. We select granite for the underpinning of our houses and barns; we build fences of stone; but we do not ourselves rest on an underpinning of granitic truth, the lowest primitive rock. Our sills are rotten. What stuff is the man made of who is not coexistent in our thought with the purest and subtilest truth? I often accuse my finest acquaintances of an immense frivolity; for, while there are manners and compliments we do not meet, we do not teach one another the lessons of honesty and sincerity that the brutes do, or of steadiness and solidity that the rocks do. The fault is commonly mutual, however; for we do not habitually demand any more of each other.

That excitement about Kossuth, consider how characteristic, but superficial, it was!—only another kind of politics or dancing. Men were making speeches to him all over the country, but each expressed only the thought, or the want of thought, of the multitude. No man stood on truth. They were merely banded together, as usual one leaning on another, and all together on nothing; as the Hindus made the world rest on an elephant, the elephant on a tortoise, and the tortoise on a serpent, and had nothing to put under the serpent. For all fruit of that stir we have the Kossuth hat.

Just so hollow and ineffectual, for the most part, is our ordinary conversation. Surface meets surface. When our life ceases to be inward and private, conversation degenerates into mere gossip. We rarely meet a man who can tell us any news which he has not read in a newspaper, or been told by his neighbor; and, for the most part, the only difference between us and our fellow is that he has seen the newspaper, or been out to tea, and we have not. In proportion as our inward life fails, we go more constantly and desperately to the post office. You may depend on it, that the poor fellow who walks away with the greatest number of letters, proud of his extensive correspondence, has not heard from himself this long while.

I do not know but it is too much to read one newspaper a week. I have tried it recently, and for so long it seems to me that I have not dwelt in my native region. The sun, the clouds, the snow, the trees say not so much to me. You cannot serve two masters. It requires more than a day's devotion to know and to possess the wealth of a day.

We may well be ashamed to tell what things we have read or heard in our day. I do not know why my news should be so trivial—considering what one's dreams and expectations are, why the developments should be so paltry. The news we hear, for the most part, is not news to our genius. It is the stalest repetition. You are often tempted to ask why such stress is laid on a particular experience which you have had—that, after twenty-five years, you should meet Hobbins, Registrar of Deeds, again on the sidewalk. Have you not budged an inch, then? Such is the daily news. Its facts appear to float in the atmosphere, insignificant as the sporules of fungi, and impinge on some neglected *thallus*, or surface of our minds, which affords a basis for them, and hence a parasitic growth. We should wash ourselves clean of such news. Of what consequence, though our planet explode, if there is no character involved in the explosion? In health we have not the least curiosity about such events. We do not live for idle amusement. I would not run round a corner to see the world blow up.

All summer, and far into the autumn, perchance, you unconsciously went by the newspapers and the news, and now you find it was because the morning and the evening were full of news to you. Your walks were full of incidents. You attended, not to the affairs of Europe, but to your own affairs in Massachusetts fields. If you chance to live and move and have your being in that thin stratum in which the events that make the news transpire—thinner than the paper on which it is printed —then these things will fill the world for you; but if you soar above or dive below that plane, you cannot remember nor be reminded of them. Really to see the sun rise or go down every day, so to relate ourselves to a universal fact, would preserve us sane forever. Nations! What are nations? Tartars, and Huns, and China-

men! Like insects, they swarm. The historian strives in
vain to make them memorable. It is for want of a man
that there are so many men. It is individuals that popu-
late the world. Any man thinking may say with the
Spirit of Lodin,

> "I look down from my height on nations,
> And they become ashes before me;—
> Calm is my dwelling in the clouds;
> Pleasant are the great fields of my rest."

Pray, let us live without being drawn by dogs, Es-
quimaux-fashion, tearing over hill and dale, and biting
each other's ears.

Not without a slight shudder at the danger, I often
perceive how near I had come to admitting into my
mind the details of some trivial affair—the news of the
street; and I am astonished to observe how willing men
are to lumber their minds with such rubbish—to permit
idle rumors and incidents of the most insignificant kind
to intrude on ground which should be sacred to thought.
Shall the mind be a public arena, where the affairs of
the street and the gossip of the tea-table chiefly are discussed? Or shall it be a quarter of heaven itself—an hy-
pethral temple, consecrated to the service of the gods?
I find it so difficult to dispose of the few facts which to
me are significant, that I hesitate to burden my attention with those which are insignificant, which only a
divine mind could illustrate. Such is, for the most part,
the news in newspapers and conversation. It is important to preserve the mind's chastity in this respect. Think
of admitting the details of a single case of the criminal court into our thoughts, to stalk profanely through
their very *sanctum sanctorum* for an hour, ay, for many
hours! to make a very barroom of the mind's inmost
apartment, as if for so long the dust of the street had
occupied us—the very street itself, with all its travel,

its bustle, and filth, had passed through our thoughts' shrine! Would it not be an intellectual and moral suicide? When I have been compelled to sit spectator and auditor in a courtroom for some hours, and have seen my neighbors, who were not compelled, stealing in from time to time, and tiptoeing about with washed hands and faces, it has appeared to my mind's eye, that, when they took off their hats, their ears suddenly expanded into vast hoppers for sound, between which even their narrow heads were crowded. Like the vanes of windmills, they caught the broad but shallow stream of sound, which, after a few titillating gyrations in their coggy brains, passed out the other side. I wondered if, when they got home, they were as careful to wash their ears as before their hands and faces. It has seemed to me, at such a time, that the auditors and the witnesses, the jury and the counsel, the judge and the criminal at the bar—if I may presume him guilty before he is convicted—were all equally criminal, and a thunderbolt might be expected to descend and consume them all together.

By all kinds of traps and signboards, threatening the extreme penalty of the divine law, exclude such trespassers from the only ground which can be sacred to you. It is so hard to forget what it is worse than useless to remember! If I am to be a thoroughfare, I prefer that it be of the mountain brooks, the Parnassian streams, and not the town sewers. There is inspiration, that gossip which comes to the ear of the attentive mind from the courts of heaven. There is the profane and stale revelation of the barroom and the police court. The same ear is fitted to receive both communications. Only the character of the hearer determines to which it shall be open, and to which closed. I believe that the mind can be permanently profaned by the habit of attending to trivial things, so that all our thoughts shall be tinged with triviality. Our very intellect shall be macadamized, as it were, its foundation broken into fragments for the wheels of travel to roll over; and if you would know what will make the most durable pavement, surpassing rolled stones, spruce blocks, and asphaltum, you have only to look into some of our minds which have been subjected to this treatment so long.

If we have thus desecrated ourselves—as who has not?—the remedy will be by wariness and devotion to reconsecrate ourselves, and make once more a fane of the mind. We should treat our minds, that is, ourselves, as innocent and ingenuous children, whose guardians we are, and be careful what objects and what subjects we thrust on their attention. Read not the Times. Read the Eternities. Conventionalities are at length as bad as impurities. Even the facts of science may dust the mind by their dryness, unless they are in a sense effaced each morning, or rather rendered fertile by the dews of fresh and living truth. Knowledge does not come to us by details, but in flashes of light from heaven. Yes, every thought that passes through the mind helps to wear and tear it, and to deepen the ruts, which, as in the streets of Pompeii, evince how much it has been used. How many things there are concerning which we might well deliberate whether we had better know them—had better let their peddling-carts be driven, even at the slowest trot or walk, over that bridge of glorious span by which we trust to pass at last from the farthest brink of time to the nearest shore of eternity! Have we no culture, no refinement—but skill only to live coarsely and serve the Devil?—to acquire a little worldly wealth, or fame, or liberty, and make a false show with it, as if we were all husk and shell, with no tender and living kernel to us? Shall our institutions be like those chestnut burs which contain abortive nuts, perfect only to prick the fingers?

America is said to be the arena on which the battle of freedom is to be fought; but surely it cannot be freedom in a merely political sense that is meant. Even if we grant that the American has freed himself from a political tyrant, he is still the slave of an economical and moral tyrant. Now that the republic—the *res-publica*—has been settled, it is time to look after the *res-privata*—the private state—to see, as the Roman senate charged its consuls, *"ne quid res-PRIVATA detrimenti caperet,"* that the *private* state receive no detriment.

Do we call this the land of the free? What is it to be free from King George and continue the slaves of King Prejudice? What is it to be born free and not to live free? What is the value of any political freedom, but as a means to moral freedom? Is it a freedom to be slaves, or a freedom to be free, of which we boast? We are a nation of politicians, concerned about the outmost defenses only of freedom. It is our children's children who may perchance be really free. We tax ourselves unjustly. There is a part of us which is not represented. It is taxation without representation. We quarter troops, we quarter fools and cattle of all sorts upon ourselves. We quarter our gross bodies on our poor souls, till the former eat up all the latter's substance.

With respect to a true culture and manhood, we are essentially provincial still, not metropolitan—mere Jonathans. We are provincial, because we do not find at home our standards; because we do not worship truth, but the reflection of truth; because we are warped and narrowed by an exclusive devotion to trade and commerce and manufactures and agriculture and the like, which are but means, and not the end.

So is the English Parliament provincial. Mere country bumpkins, they betray themselves, when any more important question arises for them to settle, the Irish question, for instance—the English question why did I not say? Their natures are subdued to what they work in. Their "good breeding" respects only secondary objects. The finest manners in the world are awkwardness and fatuity when contrasted with a finer intelligence. They appear but as the fashions of past days—mere courtliness, knee-buckles and smallclothes, out of date. It is the vice, but not the excellence of manners, that they are continually being deserted by the character; they are cast-off clothes or shells, claiming the respect which belonged to the living creature. You are presented with the shells instead of the meat, and it is no excuse generally, that, in the case of some fishes, the shells are of more worth than the meat. The man who thrusts his manners upon me does as if he were to insist on introducing me to his cabinet of curiosities, when I wished to see himself. It was not in this sense that the poet Decker called Christ "the first true gentleman that ever breathed." I repeat that in this sense the most splendid court in Christendom is provincial, having authority to consult about Transalpine interests only, and not the affairs of Rome. A praetor or proconsul would suffice to settle the questions which absorb the attention of the English Parliament and the American Congress.

Government and legislation! these I thought were respectable professions. We have heard of heaven-born Numas, Lycurguses, and Solons, in the history of the world, whose *names* at least may stand for ideal legislators; but think of legislating to *regulate* the breeding of slaves, or the exportation of tobacco! What have divine legislators to do with the exportation or the importation of tobacco? what humane ones with the breeding of slaves? Suppose you were to submit the question to any son of God—and has He no children in the Nineteenth Century? is it a family which is extinct?—in what condition would you get it again? What shall a State like Virginia say for itself at the last day, in which these have been the principal, the staple productions? What ground is there for patriotism in such a State? I derive my facts from statistical tables which the States themselves have published.

A commerce that whitens every sea in quest of nuts and raisins, and makes slaves of its sailors for this purpose! I saw, the other day, a vessel which had been wrecked, and many lives lost, and her cargo of rags, juniper berries, and bitter almonds were strewn along the shore. It seemed hardly worth the while to tempt the dangers of the sea between Leghorn and New York for the sake of a cargo of juniper berries and bitter almonds. America sending to the Old World for her bitters! Is not the sea-brine, is not shipwreck, bitter enough to make the cup of life go down here? Yet such, to a great extent, is our boasted commerce; and there are those who style themselves statesmen and philosophers who are so blind as to think that progress and civilization depend on precisely this kind of interchange and activity—the activity of flies about a molasses-hogshead. Very well, observes one, if men were oysters. And very well, answer I, if men were mosquitoes.

Lieutenant Herndon, whom our government sent to explore the Amazon, and, it is said, to extend the area of slavery, observed that there was wanting there "an industrious and active population, who know what the comforts of life are, and who have artificial wants to draw out the great resources of the country." But what are the "artificial wants" to be encouraged? Not the love of luxuries, like the tobacco and slaves of, I believe, his native Virginia, nor the ice and granite and other material wealth of our native New England; nor are "the great resources of a country" that fertility or barrenness of soil which produces these. The chief want, in every State that I have been into, was a high and earnest purpose in its inhabitants. This alone draws out "the great resources" of Nature, and at last taxes her beyond her resources; for man naturally dies out of her. When we want culture more than potatoes, and illumination more than sugar-plums, then the great resources of a world are taxed and drawn out, and the result, or staple production, is, not slaves, nor operatives, but men— those rare fruits called heroes, saints, poets, philosophers, and redeemers.

In short, as a snowdrift is formed where there is a lull in the wind, so, one would say, where there is a lull of truth, an institution springs up. But the truth blows right on over it, nevertheless, and at length blows it down.

What is called politics is comparatively something so superficial and inhuman, that practically I have never fairly recognized that it concerns me at all. The newspapers, I perceive, devote some of their columns specially to politics or government without charge; and this, one would say, is all that saves it; but as I love literature and to some extent the truth also, I never read those columns at any rate. I do not wish to blunt my sense of right so much. I have not got to answer for having read a single President's Message. A strange age of the world this, when empires, kingdoms, and republics come a-begging to a private man's door, and utter their complaints at his elbow! I cannot take up a newspaper but I find that some wretched government or other, hard pushed and on its last legs, is interceding with me, the reader, to vote for it—more importunate than an Italian beggar; and if I have a mind to look at its certificate, made, perchance, by some benevolent merchant's clerk, or the skipper that brought it over, for it cannot speak a word of English itself, I shall probably read of the eruption of some Vesuvius, or the overflowing of some Po, true or forged, which brought it into this condition. I do not hesitate, in such a case, to suggest work, or the almshouse; or why not keep its castle in silence, as I do commonly? The poor President, what with preserving his popularity and doing his duty, is completely bewildered. The newspapers are the ruling power. Any other government is reduced to a few marines at Fort Independence. If a man neglects to read the Daily Times, government will go down on its knees to him, for this is the only treason in these days.

Those things which now most engage the attention of men, as politics and the daily routine, are, it is true, vital functions of human society, but should be unconsciously performed, like the corresponding functions of the physical body. They are *infra*-human, a kind of vegetation. I sometimes awake to a half-consciousness of them going on about me, as a man may become conscious of some of the processes of digestion in a morbid state, and so have the dyspepsia, as it is called. It is as if a thinker submitted himself to be rasped by the great gizzard of creation. Politics is, as it were, the gizzard of society, full of grit and gravel, and the two political parties are its two opposite halves—sometimes split into quarters, it may be, which grind on each other. Not only individuals, but states, have thus a confirmed dyspepsia, which expresses itself, you can imagine by what sort of eloquence. Thus our life is not altogether a forgetting, but also, alas! to a great extent, a remembering, of that which we should never have been conscious of, certainly not in our waking hours. Why should we not meet, not always as dyspeptics, to tell our bad dreams, but sometimes as *eu*peptics, to congratulate each other on the ever-glorious morning? I do not make an exorbitant demand, surely.

Cape Cod

That "bared and bended arm of Massachusetts" was what Thoreau called Cape Cod. He enjoyed his rambles over Cape Cod thoroughly. This essay about it is another in the group which The Atlantic Monthly *printed shortly after his death. The account of Thoreau's meeting with the Wellfleet oysterman preserves the best and saltiest of his observation of men. Here Thoreau is seasoned and at ease.*

C. B.

THE WELLFLEET OYSTERMAN

HAVING walked about eight miles since we struck the beach, and passed the boundary between Wellfleet and Truro, a stone post in the sand—for even this sand comes under the jurisdiction of one town or another —we turned inland over barren hills and valleys, whither the sea, for some reason, did not follow us, and, tracing up a Hollow, discovered two or three sober-looking houses within half a mile, uncommonly near the eastern coast. Their garrets were apparently so full of chambers, that their roofs could hardly lie down straight, and we did not doubt that there was room for us there. Houses near the sea are generally low and broad. These were a story and a half high; but if you merely counted the windows in their gable ends, you would think that there were many stories more, or, at any rate, that the half-story was the only one thought worthy of being illustrated. The great number of windows in the ends of the houses, and their irregularity in size and position, here and elsewhere on the Cape, struck us agreeably—as if each of the various occupants who had their *cunabula* behind had punched a hole where his necessities required it, and according to his size and stature, without regard to outside effect. There were windows for the grown folks, and windows for the children—three or four apiece; as a certain man had a large hole cut in his barn door for the cat, and another smaller one for the kitten. Sometimes they were so low under the eaves that I thought they must have perforated the plate beam for another apartment, and I noticed some which were triangular, to fit that part more exactly. The ends of the houses had thus as many muzzles as a revolver, and, if the inhabitants have the same habit of staring out the windows that some of our neighbors have, a traveler must stand a small chance with them.

Generally, the old-fashioned and unpainted houses on the Cape looked more comfortable, as well as picturesque, than the modern and more pretending ones, which were less in harmony with the scenery, and less firmly planted.

These houses were on the shores of a chain of ponds, seven in number, the source of a small stream called Herring River, which empties into the Bay. There are many Herring Rivers on the Cape; they will, perhaps, be more numerous than herrings soon. We knocked at the door of the first house, but its inhabitants were all gone away. In the meanwhile, we saw the occupants of the next one looking out the window at us, and before we reached it an old woman came out and fastened the door of her bulkhead, and went in again. Nevertheless, we did not hesitate to knock at her door, when a grizzly-looking man appeared, whom we took to be sixty or seventy years old. He asked us, at first, suspiciously, where we were from, and what our business was; to which we returned plain answers.

"How far is Concord from Boston?" he inquired.

"Twenty miles by railroad."

"Twenty miles by railroad," he repeated.

"Didn't you ever hear of Concord of Revolutionary fame?"

"Didn't I ever hear of Concord? Why, I heard guns fire at the battle of Bunker Hill. [They hear the sound of heavy cannon across the Bay.] I am almost ninety; I am eighty-eight year old. I was fourteen year old at the time of Concord Fight—and where were you then?"

We were obliged to confess that we were not in the fight.

"Well, walk in, we'll leave it to the women," said he.

So we walked in, surprised, and sat down, an old woman taking our hats and bundles, and the old man continued, drawing up to the large, old-fashioned fireplace:

"I am a poor, good-for-nothing crittur, as Isaiah says; I am all broken down this year. I am under petticoat government here."

The family consisted of the old man, his wife, and his daughter, who appeared nearly as old as her mother, a fool, her son (a brutish-looking, middle-aged man, with a prominent lower face, who was standing by the hearth when we entered, but immediately went out), and a little boy of ten.

While my companion talked with the women, I talked with the old man. They said that he was old and foolish, but he was evidently too knowing for them.

"These women," said he to me, "are both of them poor good-for-nothing critturs. This one is my wife. I married her sixty-four years ago. She is eighty-four years old, and as deaf as an adder, and the other is not much better."

He thought well of the Bible, or at least he *spoke*

well, and did not *think* ill, of it, for that would not have
been prudent for a man of his age. He said that he had
read it attentively for many years, and he had much of
it at his tongue's end. He seemed deeply impressed
with a sense of his own nothingness, and would repeatedly exclaim:

"I am a nothing. What I gather from my Bible is
just this; that man is a poor good-for-nothing crittur,
and everything is just as God sees fit and disposes."

"May I ask your name?" I said.

"Yes," he answered, "I am not ashamed to tell my
name. My name is ——. My great-grandfather came
over from England and settled here."

He was an old Wellfleet oysterman, who had acquired a competency in that business, and had sons
still engaged in it.

Nearly all the oyster shops and stands in Massachusetts, I am told, are supplied and kept by natives of
Wellfleet, and a part of this town is still called Billingsgate from the oysters having been formerly planted
there; but the native oysters are said to have died in
1770. Various causes are assigned for this, such as a
ground frost, the carcasses of blackfish, kept to rot in
the harbor, and the like, but the most common account
of the matter is—and I find that a similar superstition
with regard to the disappearance of fishes exists almost
everywhere—that when Wellfleet began to quarrel with
the neighboring towns about the right to gather them,
yellow specks appeared in them, and Providence caused
them to disappear. A few years ago sixty thousand
bushels were annually brought from the South and
planted in the harbor of Wellfleet till they attained "the
proper relish of Billingsgate"; but now they are imported commonly full-grown, and laid down near their
markets, at Boston and elsewhere, where the water,

being a mixture of salt and fresh, suits them better. The business was said to be still good and improving.

The old man said that the oysters were liable to freeze in the winter, if planted too high; but if it were not "so cold as to strain their eyes" they were not injured. The inhabitants of New Brunswick have noticed that "ice will not form over an oyster-bed, unless the cold is very intense indeed, and when the bays are frozen over the oyster-beds are easily discovered by the water above them remaining unfrozen, or as the French residents say, *dégelée*." Our host said that they kept them in cellars all winter.

"Without anything to eat or drink?" I asked.

"Without anything to eat or drink," he answered.

"Can the oysters move?"

"Just as much as my shoe."

But when I caught him saying that they "bedded themselves down in the sand, flat side up, round side down," I told him that my shoe could not do that, without the aid of my foot in it; at which he said that they merely settled down as they grew; if put down in a square they would be found so; but the clam could move quite fast. I have since been told by oystermen of Long Island, where the oyster is still indigenous and abundant, that they are found in large masses attached to the parent in their midst, and are so taken up with their tongs; in which case, they say, the age of the young proves that there could have been no motion for five or six years at least. And Buckland in his *Curiosities of Natural History* (page 50) says: "An oyster, who has once taken up his position and fixed himself when quite young, can never make a change. Oysters, nevertheless, that have not fixed themselves, but remain loose at the bottom of the sea, have the power of locomotion; they open their shells to their fullest extent,

and then suddenly contracting them, the expulsion of
the water forwards gives a motion backwards. A fisherman at Guernsey told me that he had frequently seen
oysters moving in this way."

Some still entertain the question "whether the oyster
was indigenous in Massachusetts Bay," and whether
Wellfleet Harbor was a "natural habitat" of this fish;
but, to say nothing of the testimony of old oystermen,
which, I think, is quite conclusive, though the native
oyster may now be extinct there, I saw that their shells,
opened by the Indians, were strewn all over the Cape.
Indeed, the Cape was at first thickly settled by Indians
on account of the abundance of these and other fish.
We saw many traces of their occupancy after this, in
Truro, near Great Hollow, and at High Head, near East
Harbor River—oysters, clams, cockles, and other shells,
mingled with ashes and the bones of deer and other
quadrupeds. I picked up half a dozen arrow-heads, and
in an hour or two could have filled my pockets with
them. The Indians lived about the edges of the swamps,
then probably in some instances ponds, for shelter and
water. Moreover, Champlain, in the edition of his "Voyages" printed in 1613, says that in the year 1606 he and
Poitrincourt explored a harbor (Barnstable Harbor?) in
the southerly part of what is now called Massachusetts
Bay, in latitude 42°, about five leagues south, one point
west of *Cap Blanc* (Cape Cod), and there they found
many good oysters, and they named it *"le Port aux
Huistres"* [sic] (Oyster Harbor). In one edition of his
map (1632), the *"R. aux Escailles"* is drawn emptying
into the same part of the bay, and on the map *"Novi
Belgii,"* in Ogilby's America (1670), the words *"Port
aux Huistres"* are placed against the same place. Also
William Wood, who left New England in 1633, speaks,
in his *New England's Prospect*, published in 1634, of "a

great oyster-bank" in Charles River, and of another in the Mistick, each of which obstructed the navigation of its river. "The oysters," says he, "be great ones in form of a shoe-horn; some be a foot long; these breed on certain banks that are bare every spring tide. This fish without the shell is so big, that it must admit of a division before you can well get it into your mouth." Oysters are still found there.[1]

Our host told us that the sea-clam, or hen, was not easily obtained; it was raked up, but never on the Atlantic side, only cast ashore there in small quantities in storms. The fisherman sometimes wades in water several feet deep, and thrusts a pointed stick into the sand before him. When this enters between the valves of a clam, he closes them on it, and is drawn out. It has been known to catch and hold coot and teal which were preying on it. I chanced to be on the bank of the Acushnet at New Bedford one day since this, watching some ducks, when a man informed me that, having let out his young ducks to seek their food amid the samphire (*Salicornia*) and other weeds along the riverside at low tide that morning, at length he noticed that one remained stationary, amid the weeds, something preventing it from following the others, and going to it he found its foot tightly shut in a quahog's shell. He took up both together, carried them to his home, and his wife opening the shell with a knife released the duck and cooked the quahog. The old man said that the great clams were good to eat, but that they always took out a certain part which was poisonous, before they cooked them. "People said it would kill a cat." I did not tell him that I had eaten a large one entire that afternoon, but began to think that I was tougher than a cat. He stated that peddlers came round

---

[1] Also, see Thomas Morton's New English Canaan, p. 90.

there, and sometimes tried to sell the women folks a skimmer, but he told them that their women had got a better skimmer than *they* could make, in the shell of their clams; it was shaper just right for this purpose. They call them "skim-alls" in some places. He also said that the sun-squall was poisonous to handle, and when the sailors came across it, they did not meddle with it, but heaved it out of their way. I told him that I had handled it that afternoon, and had felt no ill effects as yet. But he said it made the hands itch, especially if they had previously been scratched, or if I put it into my bosom, I should find out what it was.

He informed us that no ice ever formed on the back side of the Cape, or not more than once in a century, and but little snow lay there, it being either absorbed or blown or washed away. Sometimes in winter, when the tide was down, the beach was frozen, and afforded a hard road up the back side for some thirty miles, as smooth as a floor. One winter when he was a boy, he and his father "took right out into the Back Side before daylight, and walked to Provincetown and back to dinner."

When I asked what they did with all that barren-looking land, where I saw so few cultivated fields— "Nothing," he said.

"Then why fence your fields?"

"To keep the sand from blowing and covering up the whole."

"The yellow sand," said he, "has some life in it, but the white little or none."

When, in answer to his questions, I told him that I was a surveyor, he said that they who surveyed his farm were accustomed, where the ground was uneven, to loop up each chain as high as their elbows; that was the allowance they made, and he wished to know if I could tell him why they did not come out according to his deed, or twice alike. He seemed to have more respect for surveyors of the old school, which I did not wonder at. "King George the Third," said he, "laid out a road four rods wide and straight, the whole length of the Cape," but where it was now he could not tell.

This story of the surveyors reminded me of a Long Islander, who once, when I had made ready to jump from the bow of his boat to the shore, and he thought that I underrated the distance and would fall short— though I found afterward that he judged of the elasticity of my joints by his own—told me that when he came to a brook which he wanted to get over, he held up one leg, and then, if his foot appeared to cover any part of the opposite bank, he knew that he could jump it. "Why," I told him, "to say nothing of the Mississippi, and other small watery streams, I could blot out a star with my foot, but I would not engage to jump that distance," and asked how he knew when he had got his leg at the right elevation. But he regarded his legs as no less accurate than a pair of screw dividers or an ordinary quadrant, and appeared to have a painful recollection of every degree and minute in the arc which they described; and he would have had me believe that there was a kind of hitch in his hip-joint which answered the purpose. I suggested that he should connect his two ankles by a string of the proper length, which should be the chord of an arc, measuring his jumping ability on horizontal surfaces—assuming one leg to be a perpendicular to the plane of the horizon, which, however, may have been too bold an assumption in this case. Nevertheless, this was a kind of geometry in the legs which it interested me to hear of.

Our host took pleasure in telling us the names of the ponds, most of which we could see from his windows, and making us repeat them after him, to see if we had got them right. They were Gull Pond, the largest and a very handsome one, clear and deep, and more than a mile in circumference, Newcomb's, Swett's, Slough, Horse-Leech, Round, and Herring Ponds, all connected at high water, if I do not mistake. The coast-surveyors had come to him for their names, and he told them of one which they had not detected. He said that they were not so high as formerly. There was an earthquake about four years before he was born, which cracked the pans of the ponds, which were of iron, and caused them to settle. I did not remember to have read of this. Innumerable gulls used to resort to them; but the large gulls were now very scarce, for, as he said, the English robbed their nests far in the north, where they breed. He remembered well when gulls were taken in the gull . house, and when small birds were killed by means of a frying-pan and fire at night. His father once lost a valuable horse from this cause. A party from Wellfleet having lighted their fire for this purpose, one dark night, on Billingsgate Island, twenty horses which were pastured there, and this colt among them, being frightened by it, and endeavoring in the dark to cross the passage which separated them from the neighboring beach, and which was then fordable at low tide, were all swept out to sea and drowned. I observed that many horses were still turned out to pasture all summer on the islands and beaches in Wellfleet, Eastham, and Orleans, as a kind of common. He also described the killing of what he called "wild hens," here, after they had gone to roost in the woods, when he was a boy. Perhaps they were "prairie hens" (pinnated grouse).

He liked the beach pea (*Lathyrus maritimus*), cooked green, as well as the cultivated. He had seen it growing very abundantly in Newfoundland, where also the inhabitants ate them, but he had never been able to obtain any ripe for seed. We read, under the head of Chatham, that "in 1555, during a time of great scarcity, the people about Orford, in Sussex [England] were preserved from perishing by eating the seeds of this plant, which grew there in great abundance upon the sea coast. Cows, horses, sheep, and goats eat it." But the writer who quoted this could not learn that they had been used in Barnstable County.

He had been a voyager, then? Oh, he had been about the world in his day. He once considered himself a pilot for all our coast; but now they had changed the names so he might be bothered.

He gave us to taste what he called the Summer Sweeting, a pleasant apple which he raised, and frequently grafted from, but had never seen growing elsewhere, except once—three trees on Newfoundland, or at the bay of Chaleur, I forget which, as he was sailing by. He was sure that he could tell the tree at a distance.

At length the fool, whom my companion called the wizard, came in, muttering between his teeth, "Damn book-peddlers—all the time talking about books. Better do something. Damn 'em. I'll shoot 'em. Got a doctor down here. Damn him, I'll get a gun and shoot him"; never once holding up his head. Whereat the old man stood up and said in a loud voice, as if he was accustomed to command, and this was not the first time he had been obliged to exert his authority there: "John, go sit down, mind your business—we've heard you talk before—precious little you'll do—your bark is worse than your bite." But, without minding, John muttered the same gibberish over again, and then sat down at the table which the old folks had left. He ate all there was on it, and then turned to the apples, which his aged mother was paring, that she might give her guests some applesauce for breakfast, but she drew them away and sent him off.

When I approached this house the next summer, over the desolate hills between it and the shore, which are worthy to have been the birthplace of Ossian, I saw the wizard in the midst of a corn field on the hillside, but, as usual, he loomed so strangely, that I mistook him for a scarecrow.

This was the merriest old man that we had ever seen, and one of the best preserved. His style of conversation was coarse and plain enough to have suited Rabelais. He would have made a good Panurge. Or rather he was a sober Silenus, and we were the boys Chromis and Mnasilus, who listened to his story.

"Not by Haemonian hills the Thracian bard,
Nor awful Phoebus was on Pindus heard
With deeper silence or with more regard."

There was a strange mingling of past and present in his conversation, for he had lived under King George, and might have remembered when Napoleon and the moderns generally were born. He said that one day, when the troubles between the Colonies and the mother country first broke out, as he, a boy of fifteen, was pitching hay out of a cart, one Donne, an old Tory, who was talking with his father, a good Whig, said to him, "Why, Uncle Bill, you might as well undertake to pitch that pond into the ocean with a pitchfork, as for the Colonies to undertake to gain their independence." He remembered well General Washington, and how he rode his horse along the streets of Boston, and he stood up to show us how he looked.

"He was a r—a—ther large and portly-looking man, a manly and resolute-looking officer, with a pretty good leg as he sat on his horse."—"There, I'll tell you, this was the way with Washington." Then he jumped up again, and bowed gracefully to right and left, making show as if he were waving his hat. Said he, "*That* was Washington."

He told us many anecdotes of the Revolution, and was much pleased when we told him that we had read the same in history, and that his account agreed with the written.

"Oh," he said, "I know, I know! I was a young fellow of sixteen, with my ears wide open; and a fellow of that age, you know, is pretty wide awake, and likes to know everything that's going on. Oh, I know!"

He told us the story of the wreck of the Franklin, which took place there the previous spring; how a boy came to his house early in the morning to know whose boat that was by the shore, for there was a vessel in distress, and he, being an old man, first ate his breakfast, and then walked over to the top of the hill by the shore, and sat down there, having found a comfortable seat, to see the ship wrecked. She was on the bar, only a quarter of a mile from him, and still nearer to the men on the beach, who had got a boat ready, but could render no assistance on account of the breakers, for there was a pretty high sea running. There were the passengers all crowded together in the forward part of the ship, and some were getting out of the cabin windows and were drawn on deck by the others.

"I saw the captain get out his boat," said he; "he had one little one; and then they jumped into it one after another, down as straight as an arrow. I counted them. There were nine. One was a woman, and she jumped as straight as any of them. Then they shoved off. The sea took them back, one wave went over them, and when they came up there were six still clinging to the boat; I counted them. The next wave turned the boat bottom upward, and emptied them all out. None of them ever came ashore alive. There were the rest of them all crowded together on the forecastle, the other parts of the ship being under water. They had seen all that happened to the boat. At length a heavy sea separated the forecastle from the rest of the wreck, and set it inside of the worst breaker, and the boat was able to reach them, and it saved all that were left, but one woman."

He also told us of the steamer Cambria's getting aground on this shore a few months before we were there, and of her English passengers who roamed over his grounds, and who, he said, thought the prospect from the high hill by the shore, "the most delightsome they had ever seen," and also of the pranks which the ladies played with his scoop-net in the ponds. He spoke of these travelers with their purses full of guineas, just as our provincial fathers used to speak of British bloods in the time of King George the Third.

Quid loquar? Why repeat what he told us?

> "Aut Scyllam Nisi, quam fama secuta est,
> Candida succinctam latrantibus inguina monstris,
> Dulichias vexâsse rates, et gurgite in alto
> Ah! timidos nautas canibus lacerâsse marinis?"

In the course of the evening I began to feel the potency of the clam which I had eaten, and I was obliged to confess to our host that I was no tougher than the cat he told of; but he answered, that he was a plain-spoken man, and he could tell me that it was all imagination. At any rate, it proved an emetic in my case, and I was made quite sick by it for a short time, while he laughed at my expense. I was pleased to read afterward, in Mourt's Relation of the landing of the Pilgrims in Provincetown Harbor, these words: "We found great muscles [the old editor says that they were undoubtedly sea-clams] and very fat and full of sea-pearl; but we could not eat them, for they made us all sick that did eat, as well sailors as passengers, . . . but they were soon well again." It brought me nearer to the Pilgrims to be thus reminded by a similar experience that I was so like them. Moreover, it was a valuable confirmation of their story, and I am prepared now to believe every word of Mourt's Relation. I was also pleased to find that man and the clam lay still at the same angle to one another. But I did not notice sea-pearl. Like Cleopatra, I must have swallowed it. I have since dug these clams on a flat in the Bay and observed them. They could squirt full ten feet before the wind, as appeared by the marks of the drops on the sand.

"Now I am going to ask you a question," said the old man, "and I don't know as you can tell me; but you are a learned man, and I never had any learning, only what I got by natur."—It was in vain that we reminded him that he could quote Josephus to our confusion.—"I've thought, if I ever met a learned man I should like to ask him this question. Can you tell me how *Axy* is spelt, and what it means? *Axy*," says he; "there's a girl over here is named *Axy*. Now what is it? What does it mean? Is it Scripture? I've read my Bible twenty-five years over and over, and I never came across it."

"Did you read it twenty-five years for this object?" I asked.

"Well, *how* is it spelt? Wife, how is it spelt?"

She said, "It is in the Bible; I've seen it."

"Well, how do you spell it?"

"I don't know. A c h, ach, s e h, seh,—Achseh."

"Does that spell Axy? Well, do *you* know what it means?" asked he, turning to me.

"No," I replied, "I never heard the sound before."

"There was a schoolmaster down here once, and they

asked him what it meant, and he said it had no more meaning than a bean-pole."

I told him that I held the same opinion with the schoolmaster. I had been a schoolmaster myself, and had had strange names to deal with. I also heard of such names as Zoheth, Beriah, Amaziah, Bethuel, and Shearjashub, hereabouts.

At length the little boy, who had a seat quite in the chimney-corner, took off his stockings and shoes, warmed his feet, and having had his sore leg freshly salved, went off to bed; then the fool made bare his knotty-looking feet and legs, and followed him; and finally the old man exposed his calves also to our gaze. We had never had the good fortune to see an old man's legs before, and were surprised to find them fair and plump as an infant's, and we thought that he took a pride in exhibiting them. He then proceeded to make preparations for retiring, discoursing meanwhile with Panurgic plainness of speech on the ills to which old humanity is subject. We were a rare haul for him. He could commonly get none but ministers to talk to, though sometimes ten of them at once, and he was glad to meet some of the laity at leisure. The evening was not long enough for him. As I had been sick, the old lady asked if I would not go to bed—it was getting late for old people; but the old man, who had not yet done his stories, said, "You ain't particular, are you?"

"Oh, no," said I, "I am in no hurry. I believe I have weathered the Clam cape."

"They are good," said he; "I wish I had some of them now."

"They never hurt me," said the old lady.

"But then you took out the part that killed a cat," said I.

At last we cut him short in the midst of his stories,

which he promised to resume in the morning. Yet, after all, one of the old ladies who came into our room in the night to fasten the fire-board, which rattled, as she went out took the precaution to fasten us in. Old women are by nature more suspicious than old men. However, the winds howled around the house, and made the fire-boards as well as the casements rattle well that night. It was probably a windy night for any locality, but we could not distinguish the roar which was proper to the ocean from that which was due to the wind alone.

The sounds which the ocean makes must be very significant and interesting to those who live near it. When I was leaving the shore at this place the next summer, and had got a quarter of a mile distant, ascending a hill, I was startled by a sudden, loud sound from the sea, as if a large steamer were letting off steam by the shore, so that I caught my breath and felt my blood run cold for an instant, and I turned about, expecting to see one of the Atlantic steamers thus far out of her course, but there was nothing unusual to be seen. There was a low bank at the entrance of the Hollow, between me and the ocean, and suspecting that I might have risen into another stratum of air in ascending the hill—which had wafted to me only the ordinary roar of the sea—I immediately descended again, to see if I lost hearing of it; but, without regard to my ascending or descending, it died away in a minute or two, and yet there was scarcely any wind all the while. The old man said that this was what they called the "rut," a peculiar roar of the sea before the wind changes, which, however, he could not account for. He thought that he could tell all about the weather from the sounds which the sea made.

Old Josselyn, who came to New England in 1638, has it among his weather-signs, that "the resounding of the sea from the shore, and murmuring of the winds in the woods, without apparent wind, sheweth wind to follow."

Being on another part of the coast one night since this, I heard the roar of the surf a mile distant, and the inhabitants said it was a sign that the wind would work round east, and we should have rainy weather. The ocean was heaped up somewhere at the eastward, and this roar was occasioned by its effort to preserve its equilibrium, the wave reaching the shore before the wind. Also the captain of a packet between this country and England told me that he sometimes met with a wave on the Atlantic coming against the wind, perhaps in a calm sea, which indicated that at a distance the wind was blowing from an opposite quarter, but the undulation had traveled faster than it. Sailors tell of "tide-rips" and "ground-swells," which they suppose to have been occasioned by hurricanes and earthquakes, and to have traveled many hundred, and sometimes even two or three thousand miles.

Before sunrise the next morning they let us out again, and I ran over to the beach to see the sun come out of the ocean. The old woman of eighty-four winters was already out in the cold morning wind, bareheaded, tripping about like a young girl, and driving up the cow to milk. She got the breakfast with dispatch, and without noise or bustle; and meanwhile the old man resumed his stories, standing before us, who were sitting, with his back to the chimney, and ejecting his tobacco-juice right and left into the fire behind him, without regard to the various dishes which were there preparing. At breakfast we had eels, buttermilk cake, cold bread, green beans, doughnuts, and tea. The old man talked a steady stream; and when his wife told him he had better eat his breakfast, he said, "Don't hurry me; I have lived too long to be hurried." I ate of the applesauce and the doughnuts,

which I thought had sustained the least detriment from
the old man's shots, but my companion refused the
applesauce, and ate of the hot cake and green beans,
which had appeared to him to occupy the safest part of
the hearth. But on comparing notes afterward, I told
him that the buttermilk cake was particularly exposed,
and I saw how it suffered repeatedly, and therefore I
avoided it; but he declared that, however that might be,
he witnessed that the applesauce was seriously injured,
and had therefore declined that. After breakfast we
looked at his clock, which was out of order, and oiled it
with some "hen's grease," for want of sweet oil, for he
scarcely could believe that we were not tinkers or peddlers; meanwhile, he told a story about visions, which
had reference to a crack in the clock-case made by frost
one night. He was curious to know to what religious sect
we belonged. He said that he had been to hear thirteen
kinds of preaching in one month, when he was young,
but he did not join any of them—he stuck to his Bible.
There was nothing like any of them in his Bible. While
I was shaving in the next room, I heard him ask my
companion to what sect he belonged, to which he answered,—

"Oh, I belong to the Universal Brotherhood."

"What's that?" he asked, "Sons o' Temperance?"

Finally, filling our pockets with doughnuts, which he
was pleased to find that we called by the same name
that he did, and paying for our entertainment, we took
our departure; but he followed us out of doors, and
made us tell him the names of the vegetables which he
had raised from seeds that came out of the Franklin.
They were cabbage, broccoli, and parsley. As I had
asked him the names of so many things, he tried me in
turn with all the plants which grew in his garden, both
wild and cultivated. It was about half an acre, which he

cultivated wholly himself. Besides the common garden vegetables, there were yellow dock, lemon balm, hyssop, gill-go-over-the-ground, mouse-ear, chick-weed, Roman wormwood, elecampane, and other plants. As we stood there, I saw a fish hawk stoop to pick a fish out of his pond.

"There," said I, "he has got a fish."

"Well," said the old man, who was looking all the while, but could see nothing, "he didn't dive, he just wet his claws."

And, sure enough, he did not this time, though it is said that they often do, but he merely stooped low enough to pick him out with his talons; but as he bore his shining prey over the bushes, it fell to the ground, and we did not see that he recovered it. That is not their practice.

Thus, having had another crack with the old man, he standing bareheaded under the eaves, he directed us "athwart the fields," and we took to the beach again for another day, it being now late in the morning.

It was but a day or two after this that the safe of the Provincetown Bank was broken open and robbed by two men from the interior, and we learned that our hospitable entertainers did at least transiently harbor the suspicion that we were the men.

The Last Days of John Brown

In the stern accents of "The Last Days of John Brown" we hear the voice of a man profoundly moved. Thoreau had been invited to attend a memorial service for Brown on July 4, 1860, at the upstate New York village of North Elba. He declined but sent some thoughts about Brown which he had originally penned in his Journal. They were read for Thoreau at the service and were printed later in July in the abolitionists Liberator. They are reprinted below, the last of the selections in this anthology of Thoreau's work, in the belief that they make a natural bridge to the Epilogue.

C. B.

JOHN BROWN'S career for the last six weeks of his life was meteor-like, flashing through the darkness in which we live. I know of nothing so miraculous in our history.

If any person, in a lecture or conversation at that time, cited any ancient example of heroism, such as Cato or Tell or Winkelried, passing over the recent deeds and words of Brown, it was felt by any intelligent audience of Northern men to be tame and inexcusably far-fetched.

For my own part, I commonly attend more to nature than to man, but any affecting human event may blind our eyes to natural objects. I was so absorbed in him as to be surprised whenever I detected the routine of the natural world surviving still, or met persons going about their affairs indifferent. It appeared strange to me that the "little dipper" should be still diving quietly in the river, as of yore; and it suggested that this bird might continue to dive here when Concord should be no more.

I felt that he, a prisoner in the midst of his enemies and under sentence of death, if consulted as to his next step or resource, could answer more wisely than all his countrymen beside. He best understood his position; he contemplated it most calmly. Comparatively, all other men, North and South, were beside themselves. Our thoughts could not revert to any greater or wiser or better man with whom to contrast him, for he, then and there, was above them all. The man this country was about to hang appeared the greatest and best in it.

Years were not required for a revolution of public opinion; days, nay hours, produced marked changes in this case. Fifty who were ready to say, on going into our meeting in honor of him in Concord, that he ought to be hung, would not say it when they came out. They heard his words read; they saw the earnest faces of the congregation; and perhaps they joined at last in singing the hymn in his praise.

The order of instructors was reversed. I heard that one preacher, who at first was shocked and stood aloof, felt obliged at last, after he was hung, to make him the subject of a sermon, in which, to some extent, he eulogized the man, but said that his act was a failure. An influential class-teacher thought it necessary, after the services, to tell his grown-up pupils that at first he thought as the preacher did then, but now he thought that John Brown was right. But it was understood that his pupils were as much ahead of the teacher as he was ahead of the priest; and I know for a certainty that very little boys at home had already asked their parents, in a tone of surprise, why God did not interfere to save him. In each case, the constituted teachers were only half conscious that they were not *leading*, but being *dragged*, with some loss of time and power.

The more conscientious preachers, the Bible men, they who talk about principle, and doing to others as you would that they should do unto you,—how could they fail to recognize him, by far the greatest preacher of them all, with the Bible in his life and in his acts, the embodiment of principle, who actually carried out the golden rule? All whose moral sense had been aroused, who had a calling from on high to preach, sided with him. What confessions he extracted from the cold and conservative! It is remarkable, but on the whole it is well, that it did not prove the occasion for a new sect of *Brownites* being formed in our midst.

They, whether within the Church or out of it, who adhere to the spirit and let go the letter, and are accordingly called infidel, were as usual foremost to recognize him. Men have been hung in the South before for attempting to rescue slaves, and the North was not much stirred by it. Whence, then, this wonderful difference? We were not so sure of *their* devotion to principle. We made a subtle distinction, forgot human laws, and did homage to an idea. The North, I mean the *living* North, was suddenly all transcendental. It went behind the human law, it went behind the apparent failure, and recognized eternal justice and glory. Commonly, men live according to a formula, and are satisfied if the order of law is observed, but in this instance they, to some extent, returned to original perceptions, and there was a slight revival of old religion. They saw that what was called order was confusion, what was called justice, injustice, and that the best was deemed the worst. This attitude suggested a more intelligent and generous spirit than that which actuated our forefathers, and the possibility, in the course of ages, of a revolution in behalf of another and an oppressed people.

Most Northern men, and a few Southern ones, were wonderfully stirred by Brown's behavior and words. They saw and felt that they were heroic and noble, and that there had been nothing quite equal to them in their kind in this country, or in the recent history of the world. But the minority were unmoved by them. They were only surprised and provoked by the attitude of their neighbors. They saw that Brown was brave, and that he believed that he had done right, but they did not detect any further peculiarity in him. Not being accustomed to make fine distinctions, or to appreciate magnanimity, they read his letters and speeches as if they read them not. They were not aware when they approached a heroic statement,—they did not know when they *burned*. They did not feel that he spoke with authority, and hence they only remembered that the *law* must be executed. They remembered the old formula, but did not hear the new revelation. The man who does not recognize in Brown's words a wisdom and nobleness, and therefore an authority, superior to our laws, is a modern Democrat. This is the test by which to discover him. He is not willfully but constitutionally blind on this side, and he is consistent with himself. Such has been his past life; no doubt of it. In like manner he has read history and his Bible, and he accepts, or seems to accept, the last only as an established formula, and not because he has been convicted by it. You will not find kindred sentiments in his commonplace-book, if he has one.

When a noble deed is done, who is likely to appreciate it? They who are noble themselves. I was not surprised that certain of my neighbors spoke of John Brown as an ordinary felon, for who are they? They have either much flesh, or much office, or much coarseness of some kind. They are not ethereal natures in any sense. The dark qualities predominate in them. Several of them are decidedly pachydermatous. I say it in sorrow, not in anger. How can a man behold the light who has no answering inward light? They are true to their *sight*, but when they look this way they *see* nothing, they are blind. For the children of the light to contend with them is as if there should be a contest between eagles and owls. Show me a man who feels bitterly toward John Brown, and let me hear what noble verse he can repeat. He'll be as dumb as if his lips were stone.

It is not every man who can be a Christian, even in a very moderate sense, whatever education you give him. It is a matter of constitution and temperament, after all. He may have to be born again many times. I have known many a man who pretended to be a Christian, in whom it was ridiculous, for he had no genius for it. It is not every man who can be a free man, even.

Editors persevered for a good while in saying that Brown was crazy; but at last they said only that it was "a crazy scheme," and the only evidence brought to prove it was that it cost him his life. I have no doubt that if he had gone with five thousand men, liberated a thousand slaves, killed a hundred or two slaveholders, and had as many more killed on his own side, but not lost his own life, these same editors would have called it by a more respectable name. Yet he has been far more successful than that. He has liberated many thousands of slaves, both North and South. They seem to have known nothing about living or dying for a principle. They all called him crazy then; who calls him crazy now?

All through the excitement occasioned by his remarkable attempt and subsequent behavior the Massachusetts legislature, not taking any steps for the defense of her citizens who were likely to be carried to Virginia as witnesses and exposed to the violence of a slave-holding mob, was wholly absorbed in a liquor-agency question, and indulging in poor jokes on the word "extension." Bad spirits occupied their thoughts. I am sure that no statesman up to the occasion could have attended to that question at all at that time,—a very vulgar question to attend to at any time! . . .

Nothing could his enemies do but it redounded to his infinite advantage,—that is, to the advantage of his cause. They did not hang him at once, but reserved him to preach to them. And then there was another great blunder. They did not hang his four followers with him; that scene was still postponed; and so his victory was prolonged and completed. No theatrical manager could have arranged things so wisely to give effect to his behavior and words. And who, think you, *was* the manager? *Who* placed the slave-woman and her child, whom he stooped to kiss for a symbol, between his prison and the gallows?

We soon saw, as he saw, that he was not to be pardoned or rescued by men. That would have been to disarm him, to restore to him a material weapon, a Sharp's rifle, when he had taken up the sword of the spirit,—the sword with which he has really won his greatest and most memorable victories Now he has not laid aside the sword of the spirit, for he is pure spirit himself, and his sword is pure spirit also.

> He nothing common did or mean
> Upon that memorable scene, . . .
> Nor called the gods with vulgar spite,
> To vindicate his helpless right;
> But bowed his comely head
> Down, as upon a bed.

What a transit was that of his horizontal body alone, but just cut down from the gallows-tree! We read that at such a time it passed through Philadelphia, and by Saturday night had reached New York. Thus like a meteor it shot through the Union from the Southern regions toward the North! No such freight had the cars borne since they carried him southward alive.

On the day of his translation, I heard, to be sure, that he was *hung,* but I did not know what that meant; I felt no sorrow on that account; but not for a day or two did I even *hear* that he was *dead,* and not after any number of days shall I believe it. Of all the men who were said to be my contemporaries, it seemed to me that John Brown was the only one who *had not died.* I never hear of a man named Brown now,—and I hear of them pretty often,—I never hear of any particularly brave and earnest man, but my first thought is of John Brown, and what relation he may be to him. I meet him at every turn. He is more alive than ever he was. He has earned immortality. He is not confined to North Elba nor to Kansas. He is no longer working in secret. He works in public, and in the clearest light that shines on this land.

Epilogue by the Editor

Emerson, the man who knew Thoreau best, once spoke of his "simple and hidden life." Simple it was, in the sense of being Spartan, and hidden too in ways no biographer has published. This is not to say that there was scandal in Thoreau's life; it is that his subconscious side has largely gone unstudied. The insights and valuable hypotheses of Freudian psychology have been ignored in the various biographies. Time has modified some of Sigmund Freud's constructions; fresh research has upset some of his analogies. But there is little doubt that we can comprehend Thoreau better if we take his unconscious into account. The finicky critic is put off, even today, by the Freudian emphasis on sexuality. The Freudian stress on childhood experience may seem unwarranted. And the very fact that there is a Freudian jargon can prejudice the reader. Yet the life of Thoreau remains full of riddles and the writing of Thoreau abounds in nuances that still need to be understood. The only Freudian study of any length is an unpublished doctoral dissertation done in 1957 by Raymond Gozzi. Most of its deductions come from an analysis of the imagery in Thoreau's writing, the rest from an interpretation of certain biographical data. After taking account of Gozzi's remarkable findings we can put Thoreau into another perspective, look at him from one more point of view.

It is not at all impossible that we shall see things we may not wish to see. For our conclusion will be that Thoreau was not a normal man—though his writing was the richer for it.

To the Freudian, abnormality is mainly a matter of degree. Other children suffer the shocks that Thoreau doubtless did; other youths and men endure the same frustrations. Yet few others react as vehemently. It is normal for a boy to replay the Oedipus myth, to wish to marry his mother and obliterate his father, and then to be maimed by his unconscious feeling of guilt. It is not normal to have the effects linger throughout manhood and maturity. Much can be explained in Thoreau by assuming that they did, however.

A highly aware observer of his own psyche, he sensed what had happened to him and projected it on others. "How many men," he once exclaimed, "meet with some blast in the moist growing days of their youth, and what should have been a sweet and palatable fruit in them becomes a mere puff and excrescence!" He realized that he had been warped. Under the rubric of "Chastity and Sensuality" he collected many of his thoughts and enclosed them in a letter to his disciple H. G. O. Blake. "I send you the thoughts," Thoreau wrote, "with diffidence and shame, not knowing how far . . . I betray my peculiar defects." The salient defect, to the Freudian, was that Thoreau never outgrew his mother-fixation. It was ambivalent, with some hate supporting the love, in the typical way of the unconscious. Cynthia Thoreau dominated her husband and children, outliving them all, incidentally, except for one daughter. When Henry before leaving college asked her what profession he should choose, she answered him pleasantly, "You can buckle on your knapsack, and roam abroad to seek your fortune"; and

tears came to his eyes. With the imputed exception of
a girl named Ellen Sewall, young women failed to
interest him even when he was a young man. He could
see the reason for looking at pretty girls but not for
trying to talk with them. That was his point of view.
From their point of view, the matter was summed up
when Elizabeth Hoar remarked that, as for taking
Henry's arm she would as soon think of taking the arm
of an elm tree.

With an older woman Thoreau could be more re-
sponsive. There was above all Lidian, Ralph Waldo
Emerson's severely beautiful wife; and she was nearly
fifteen years his senior. He once wrote to her, "You
must know that you represent to me woman." She
remained, if by default, the principal love of his life.
Yet it is worth remembering that another older woman
preceded her. She was Lidian's own sister. To Mrs.
Lucy Jackson Brown, three years older than Lidian, he
sent his best youthful effort, the poem "Sic Vita," along
with a bunch of violets. Mrs. Brown joined the Thoreau
family at intervals over a period of several years. She
and Henry found no dearth of things to say when they
met, and when distance separated them they corre-
sponded. The correspondence included a good deal
of platonizing though not quite enough for Henry's
taste. "Dear Friend," he suggested in one letter, "We
always seem to be living just on the brink of a pure and
lofty intercourse." He meant not only himself and
Lucy Brown but the world. With Lidian the brink was
passed more than once. Thoreau continued to be attracted to older women rather than younger ones; and
up to the end he kept his devotion to his mother.

Because nothing in his culture could countenance a
mother-fixation, Thoreau sought to shift its psychic
energies to other ends. One was this attachment to

older women. The other, with bountiful creative results, was his writing. There he adapted and extended the idea of Mother Nature until it became one of his chief conceptions. Kind, lovely, she let him immerse his loneliness and tension in her. Yet in her kindness and love she could be strict as a mother is strict. "In her most genial moment her laws are . . . steadfastly and relentlessly fulfilled." In Freudian terms this is nature as the superego, the conscience. This is Cynthia Thoreau demanding obedience. Out of a loving, strict Nature Henry's needs were met, or so he maintained. The attitude he took is exemplified in a telling image: "I make it my business to extract from Nature whatever nutriment she can furnish me. . . . I milk the sky and the earth."

Alma Natura appeared both in his ideas and in their expression. The amount of female matter in his nature writing is remarkable. Perhaps the most illuminating thing is his love for swamps. He enjoys being in them, enjoys writing about them. His friend Ellery Channing, who walked with him as often as anyone, noted the interest in swamps and bogs. It proved to be long-lived. As early as 1840 Thoreau could rhapsodize, "Would it not be a luxury to stand up to one's chin in some retired swamp for a whole summer's day?" And as late as 1857 he could still write with relish, "Methinks every swamp tends to have or suggests . . . an interior tender spot. The sphagnous crust that surrounds the pool is pliant and quaking, like the skin or muscles of the abdomen." Sometimes the subject or the imagery was masculine. The male too could find analogue and metaphor in Thoreau's writing. Throughout the pages on nature there are many references, masculine and feminine, overt and covert, which have a Freudian significance. The towering pine, the shrub oak, the snake in the stream, the unclimbable mountain: these are among them. At its apex Thoreau's sexual energy emerges as a desire for mystic union with nature. This is clearest perhaps in his poem "The Thaw":

> Fain would I stretch me by the highway-side,
> To thaw and trickle with the melting snow,
> That mingled soul and body with the tide,
> I too may through the pores of nature flow.

Beyond the domain of nature and nature's sexual images, Thoreau's energy was channeled into ideas about friendship and into their figurative expression. The ideas at the conscious level were austere, for Thoreau set a superhumanly high standard. At the unconscious level it can be guessed that they were marked by an incipient homosexuality. The same mother-fixation that barred a normal sexual partnership with a woman also prejudiced a normal friendship with a man by charging it with undue emphasis and tension. Such a friendship Thoreau never had. We can recall the judgment Emerson pronounced: "No equal companion stood in affectionate relations with one so pure and guileless."

To make up for his deficiency Thoreau consistently showed far more than the usual amount of aggressiveness and independence. It is indeed in a combination of the two that the world has come to recognize the stance typical of him. The literary results have been brilliant, *Walden* and "Civil Disobedience" most notably; but there are four or five other essays, such as "Life without Principle" and "Slavery in Massachusetts," which also radiate those qualities. The act of writing as well as what was written stems from his aggressiveness and independence. He had to prove himself. He made a point of doing so by word and deed.

The roots of this attitude can be traced back to his earliest years. We may remember that he was a grave, withdrawn child. As a boy he was called "The Judge." Some friends of his family thought he resembled an Indian in his iron demeanor. Before college he belonged to a debating society where he often showed himself cross-grained. In his college days he was known to unbend at times but he customarily kept to himself. And so he did during the rest of his life. One reason for the attitude lies, in all probability, in the Oedipal conflict; his reserved demeanor, I believe, resulted mostly from the strength of his repressions. From the outset his unconscious urge to displace his father and enjoy his mother must have been unusually keen. And yet his developing superego, his implanted conscience, certainly asserted that this was sinful. Here we see the typical Freudian ambivalence, which would flourish in Thoreau. Here is hate for the father, but also love for him and shame for wanting to displace him. Here is the ancestor of the more general love-hate which became a staple of Thoreau's life and works. The two emotions are aspects of one, as Thoreau himself testified.

Because of inadequacies in his father and himself which we can guess at, he felt compelled to search for a father-substitute. His father, John Thoreau, Sr., was a mechanic and a bumbling businessman. He relished the crowded company of his fellows. No introverted scholar, he was still not quite strong enough to make Henry want to identify with him through fear. The search for the father took several forms during Thoreau's life but was always tinged—except at the end when John Brown satisfied Thoreau's deepest requirements—with hostility and even hate. No satisfactory God as Father could be found in Thoreau's religion.

No satisfactory father could be found among his relatives or teachers. There was not even one among Thoreau's older friends and this in spite of the fact that the number included Emerson. But Emerson clearly came the closest.

When Thoreau at twenty returned to Concord to live, Emerson was thirty-four. The enormous influence he had on Thoreau was not only mental but physical. Understandably, the first impact was the greatest. James Russell Lowell, for instance, a classmate of Thoreau's at Harvard, wrote dryly in 1838: "I met Thoreau last night, and it is exquisitely amusing to see how he imitates Emerson's tone and manner. With my eyes shut, I shouldn't know them apart." Yet when he was nearly forty Thoreau could still wear his collar turned over like Emerson's. Although Emerson's influence would diminish and Thoreau would certainly become his own man, it is easy to see why he was originally impressed. Emerson was by all accounts an American saint. Bronson Alcott, most captious of the Transcendentalists, testified that his friendship with Emerson was "the greatest prize and privilege" he enjoyed aside from his family life. That was praise from somebody who knew him intimately, but even his lecture audiences recognized that they were listening to a most impressive man. In view of the widespread admiration Emerson commanded, it is the more revealing to see Thoreau gradually reject him. The love for him as father in Thoreau's heart is more and more offset by hate. Or if hate is too strong a word, then by a growing and carping hostility; or, to put it at its mildest as Thoreau tried to, by a "certain bitter-sweet sentiment." However, I think we could stand by the word "hate," for with the passing of time Thoreau added the classic Freudian incentive to hate when he fell in love with

Lidian, with the wife of his father-substitute. The Oedipal drama played itself out, leaving him to fight a painful sense of shame.

So far in our examination of Thoreau's unconscious we have been saying that its main characteristic was a marked Oedipus complex which aborted his emotional life but richly informed his writing. It made him look for a mother in older women instead of a mate and look for a father in Emerson (and later John Brown). It allowed him to compensate, however, by developing an extraordinary aggressiveness and independence; and it allowed him to sublimate through literary creation.

Now we have three more propositions to advance. One is that Thoreau's hatred for the state was an extension of his Oedipal hatred for his father and of his occasional dislike (the other side of the coin of love) of his dominating mother. Another is that he finally found his father-substitute in John Brown, as the fanatical leader who detested the state and defied it to the death. The last is that Thoreau, with a history of conversion maladies, found his burden of guilt so great when his father and Brown died, both within the same year, that he became convinced he too must die in expiation. Each of these three can be supported from Freudian psychology, although certain evidence is lacking and the likelihood of the propositions must be based partly on the previous constructions.

We can safely conclude that Thoreau resented parental authority. To understand his resentment of his father we need to look again at the character of John Thoreau, Sr. There is ground for stressing that he was not merely the mild man married to Cynthia Thoreau. Professor Gozzi suggests in his dissertation that the older Thoreau was capable of violent speech if not

violent action, that he had an air of some firmness and
determination, and that he was well respected outside
his house. Though he was more of a man outside his
house than inside, even there he gradually proved able
to get his son to play Apollo to his King Admetus.
He managed, that is, to involve the reluctant Henry
in the family business from time to time and when his
father died Henry was forced to succeed him in charge
of it. Accordingly, he had qualities that could increase
his son's unconscious resentment. He stood, in essence,
for the talky, noisy world of trade which Thoreau despised. Much as Thoreau loved his mother he could
also be irked by her authority on occasion. More than
one passage in his Journal suggests his animosity. And
he had hard things as well as kind ones to say about
parents in general. It is probable that he suppressed
many of the criticisms of his father and mother. Yet
there are at least a few times when he could not restrain
his bitterness. Surely he was looking at his own household as well as others when he cried, "The fathers and
the mothers of the town . . . don't want to have any
prophets born into their families—damn them!"

For Thoreau it was only a step from resentment of
the authority of the parent to resentment of the authority of the state. The first recorded conflict came
when the state, according to Thoreau, "commanded
me to pay a certain sum toward the support of a clergyman." He declined, although another man saw fit to
pay it for him. He had made his point, however, and
was never dunned for the church tax again. At the
request of the state's nearest representatives, the selectmen of Concord, Thoreau prepared a declaration for
their files: "Know all men by these presents, that I,
Henry Thoreau, do not wish to be regarded as a member of any incorporated society which I have not

joined." This sweeping affirmation represented another victory but not a permanent one. For Thoreau after declining for six years to pay a second tax, his poll tax, was put in jail on this account. A little of the edge was taken off that battle too, it must be admitted, because someone else, once again, paid the tax. But not before Thoreau had the opportunity to pass his memorable night in jail. When he wrote about it later he tinged his words with amusement and contempt for authority. However, his jailer reported that Thoreau was "mad as the devil" when released. Fighting audaciously against the state, he had been punished like a stubborn child, by being shut up. His imprisonment helped to embitter and harden Thoreau to such an extent that in the next decade he could approve of armed rebellion, of war itself. And that was what John Brown determined to wage against the United States of America.

He waged it on rocklike principle, to Thoreau's absolute satisfaction. He had already met Brown, we know, and been impressed by him two years before the attack on Harper's Ferry. But the chain of events beginning with the assault and ending with Brown's being hanged on December 2, 1859, stirred Thoreau almost incredibly. Ellery Channing reported that Thoreau's "hands involuntarily clenched together at the mention of Captain Brown." There can be little doubt that the strongest aggressions in him found an outlet through Brown. He identified himself with Brown and fought by empathy at his side. So strong did the empathy prove that, after briefly considering that Brown was dead before his trial, Thoreau refused to accept the idea that Brown was dead at all. He was not speaking metaphorically when he said, "I heard, to be sure, that he was hung, but I did not know what that meant." When he wrote and spoke passionately for Brown he was also justifying himself. And justification was needed, it may be assumed, for Thoreau could realize that Brown's hanging was the greatest punishment the state could inflict. In his stormy ambivalence Thoreau no doubt felt that Brown was completely right but also that the punishment he suffered was a judgment. It was a mistaken one to Thoreau but a judgment nonetheless. In one sense as Brown had failed so had he. In a feverish resolution of the problem he likened Brown to a Christ crucified by the state for the slaveholder.

We come now to the last and most controversial of the three propositions: that Thoreau died because he felt he should—and died content. I agree with the past biographers that on the conscious level he died of tuberculosis; and so I have said elsewhere. But I agree with Professor Gozzi that at the unconscious level Thoreau ended his life of his own accord. He was convinced that he had to die chiefly because John Brown and his father had died. He had to expiate his intolerably increasing load of guilt. Christian contrition was not for him but leaving life represented ample expiation.

If this seems unbelievable to admirers of Thoreau, we can look back into his life to find out if anything there has a bearing on the matter. By first noting that his family had a history of lingering illness—typically the Thoreaus were said to die from consumption—we can isolate a physical factor which would make it easier for the psychic ones to operate. On the psychic side we can start, ordinarily enough, with the child who became sick at thunderstorms. About Thoreau's health during his boyhood we cannot be sure but we know that he was sick in college. When he was nineteen he wrote to a Harvard classmate that his health was so much improved that he would return next term; the letter was written in August 1836. In February 1841 he had another siege of illness, probably having to do with his lungs. During the next year he experienced a case of illness through empathy which is a classic. For when his brother John died in January 1842 after bitter suffering, Henry suffered too. Shortly after John's death Emerson wrote that Thoreau "was ill and threatened with *lockjaw!* his brother's disease. It is strange—unaccountable—yet the symptoms seem precise and on the increase." Though the disease left after a while, its marks on Thoreau's psyche remained for a long time. According to one source it was years before he could speak of John's death without perceptible pain. In 1843 he became ill at least twice. Once it was apparently pulmonary weakness but in the other case it was probably because he had abandoned his beloved Concord for a term on Staten Island as a tutor. He himself called that illness unaccountable. Then came some years of better health. However, by the spring of 1855 he had contracted a lingering disorder from which he failed to recover until the summer of 1857. This siege too looks psychosomatic. Sometime after it started he wrote to H. G. O. Blake saying that he had been on his back for two or three months. He added, "I should feel a little less ashamed if I could give any name to my disorder, but I cannot, and our doctor cannot help me to it."

By the late 1850s he was alternating periods of health with growing periods of sickness. The most damaging blow to him before Brown's death was the death of John Thoreau, Sr., in February 1859. With his father dead Henry's Oedipal foe was gone. The son had triumphed, the mother was his. He had become head of the house and was responsible for conducting the family business as well. His feeling of guilt, though, at replacing his father must have been severe. His psyche now had suffered serious damage. His state of mind grew more and more depressed. He found some surcease in his writing and in the abolitionist movement but drew none from the family business and little from his friends. Brown's crusade jolted him out of himself for a time, giving him a cause to which he could dedicate his diminishing energies. There is an important if oblique statement to that effect in the Journal for October 22, 1859: "How many a man who was lately contemplating suicide has now something to live for!" But then came the crushing end to the crusade, Brown's execution. As Ellery Channing recalled, "At the time of the John Brown tragedy, Thoreau was driven sick." Actually, it must have been the final blow to his spirit.

His end would not, however, come swiftly nor would his decline be steady. He would live for two years and some months more. Though I think that he soon realized he had no other recourse but death, I am sure that the will to die was not consistent. It waxed and waned. Thoreau could still write and talk even if the writing grew sluggish and the talk torpid. He could still show himself capable of indignation especially about the South and slavery. Yet gradually his fists unclenched. Returning to Concord in July 1861 after a futile trip to Minnesota for his health, he tried to go on his accustomed rounds. It was no use. By November he had written the last of the manifold pages of his Journal; by December he had taken to his bed. Nearing death he told Ellery Channing that he had no wish to live except for his mother and sister. "Some things must end," he observed significantly to Channing. But perhaps the most significant comment was made by a visitor to his bedside, Sam Staples. Sam, who was Thoreau's friend as well as his onetime jailer, spoke to Emerson about the visit. "Never spent an hour with more satisfaction," he said. "Never saw a man dying with so much pleasure and peace."

By the time he died he had already published his two best books, *A Week* and *Walden*. His most provocative essay, "Civil Disobedience," had reached print and so had the passionate polemics for John Brown. So had most of his poetry. After his death the finest of his nature essays appeared, essays better than anyone else could write, then or now. "Walking," "Autumnal Tints," "Wild Apples": each is an artist's and a naturalist's delight. Last came the travel books, edited for the most part by his surviving sister and Ellery Channing, *The Maine Woods, Cape Cod, A Yankee in Canada*. As public interest in Thoreau grew, much of his private writing was published, particularly the extensive Journal. In the past decades bits and pieces have been appearing: a little more of the Journal for instance, some college essays, and a few other fugitive pages of prose. The *Collected Poems* have also appeared, as well the collected *Correspondence*. Now a genuinely definitive edition of the complete works is under way, led by *Walden*. There are many more volumes to come, but the best both of the old and new have been in print long enough to establish Thoreau as a writer whom the world would ignore only to its loss. And it is to understand Thoreau as a writer that we have speculated about his unconscious, theorized about his psychological problems. If our speculation seems forced, perhaps we can go back to the gentle, moderate way he himself once put it: "The poet cherishes his chagrins and sets his sighs to music."

Bibliography

The Writings of Henry David Thoreau, Walden edition. Twenty volumes. Boston: Houghton Mifflin Company; 1906. (Only edition of the complete works. Journal reprinted 1949.)

The Writings of Henry D. Thoreau. In process, starting with *Walden*, 1971. Princeton: Princeton University Press. (Will be the definitive edition.)

Henry David Thoreau: Representative Selections, by B. V. Crawford. New York: American Book Co.; 1934. (Portions of Thoreau's writing presented with critical apparatus.)

The Best of Thoreau's Journals, edited by Carl Bode. Carbondale: Southern Illinois University Press, 1971. (Drawn from the fourteen volumes of Thoreau's printed Journal.)

Collected Poems of Henry Thoreau, edited by Carl Bode. Chicago: Packard & Co.; 1943.. Revised edition, Baltimore: Johns Hopkins Press; 1964. (Useful for the understanding of Thoreau's early career and production.)

The Correspondence of Henry David Thoreau, edited by Walter Harding and Carl Bode. New York: New York University Press; 1957. (Contains all available letters to Thoreau as well as those from him.)

Consciousness in Concord, with notes and commentary by Perry Miller. Boston: Houghton Mifflin Company; 1958. (The text of Thoreau's "lost" Journal for portions of 1840 and 1841.)

The Making of Walden, by James Lyndon Shanley. Chicago: University of Chicago Press; 1957. (The text of the first version of *Walden*, with a comprehensive explanation of how it was determined.)

CANBY, H. S., *Thoreau*. Boston: Houghton Mifflin Company; 1939. (A biography with many insights, if sometimes unsettling ones.)

HARDING, WALTER, *The Days of Henry Thoreau*. New York: Alfred A. Knopf, Inc.; 1965. (The definitive biography.)

LEBEAUX, RICHARD, *Young Man Thoreau*. Amherst: University of Massachusetts Press; 1977. (Depth psychology used to describe Thoreau's maturing.)

SANBORN, F. B., *The Life of Henry David Thoreau*. Boston: Houghton Mifflin Company; 1917. (Valuable because written by someone who knew Thoreau, but uneven and poorly organized.)

ANDERSON, CHARLES R., *The Magic Circle of Walden*. New York: Holt, Rinehart and Winston; 1968. (First-rate study of *Walden* purely as literature.)

CAVELL, STANLEY. *The Senses of Walden*. New York: The Viking Press, 1972. (Penetrating essay on Thoreau's techniques.)

MATTHIESSEN, F. O., *American Renaissance*. New York: Oxford University Press; 1941. (Devoted in part to penetrating analysis of Thoreau's ideas as interwoven with those of other leading Transcendentalists.)

PAUL, SHERMAN, *The Shores of America: Thoreau's Inward Exploration*. Urbana: University of Illinois Press; 1958.

SEYBOLD, ETHEL, *Thoreau: The Quest and the Classics*. New Haven: Yale University Press; 1951. (Examines Thoreau as a devoted student of the classics of Greece and Rome.)

MCINTOSH, JAMES. *Thoreau as Romantic Naturalist: His Shifting Stance toward Nature*. Ithaca: Cornell University Press; 1974.

HARDING, WALTER, *The Thoreau Handbook*. New York: New York University Press; 1959. (Since issued in paperback. Best single guide to Thoreau.)

LEARY, LEWIS, "Thoreau," in *Eight American Authors: A Review of Research and Criticism*, edited by James Woodress. New York: W. W. Norton, 1971.

A Bibliography of Henry David Thoreau, compiled by F. H. Allen. Boston: Houghton Mifflin Company; 1908. (Careful listing of items by and about Thoreau from the beginning of his career to 1908.)

A Henry David Thoreau Bibliography, 1908-1937, by William White. Boston: F. W. Faxon Co.; 1939. (Continues Allen's bibliography.)

"Contribution to a Bibliography of Thoreau, 1938-1945," by Philip Burnham and Carvel Collins, *Bulletin of Bibliography*, XIX (1946-47), pp. 16-18, 37-39. (Continues White).

Thoreau Society Bulletin, 1941—, edited by Walter Harding. (Current bibliography in each issue of this quarterly.)